FOURTH EDITION

WRITING ABOUT WRITING

ELIZABETH WARDLE
Miami University

DOUG DOWNS
Montana State University

 bedford/st.martin's
Macmillan Learning
Boston | New York

FOR BEDFORD/ST. MARTIN'S

Vice President, Editorial, Macmillan Learning Humanities: Edwin Hill
Executive Program Director for English: Leasa Burton
Senior Program Manager: John E. Sullivan III
Executive Marketing Manager: Joy Fisher Williams
Director of Content Development, Humanities: Jane Knetzger
Senior Development Editor: Cynthia Ward
Editorial Assistants: Alex Markle and William Hwang
Content Project Manager: Pamela Lawson
Senior Workflow Project Manager: Lisa McDowell
Production Supervisor: Robin Besofsky
Advanced Media Project Manager: Sarah O'Connor
Executive Media Editor: Adam Whitehurst
Senior Manager of Publishing Services: Andrea Cava
Composition: Lumina Datamatics, Inc.
Text Permissions Manager: Kalina Ingham
Text Permissions Researchers: Kristen Janssen/Mark Schaefer, Lumina Datamatics, Inc.
Photo Permissions Editor: Angela Boehler
Photo Researcher: Richard Fox, Lumina Datamatics, Inc.
Director of Design, Content Management: Diana Blume
Text Design: Laura Shaw Design, Inc./Diana Blume
Cover Design: William Boardman
Printing and Binding: LSC Communications

Manufactured in the United States of America.

1 2 3 4 5 6   24 23 22 21 20 19

For information, write: Bedford/St. Martin's, 75 Arlington Street, Boston, MA 02116

ISBN 978-1-319-19586-1 (Student Edition)
ISBN 978-1-319-24337-1 (Instructor's Edition)
ISBN 978-1-319-28155-7 (Loose-leaf Edition)

ACKNOWLEDGMENTS

CONTENTS

PART ONE
Exploring Threshold Concepts of Writing through Inquiry   1

PART TWO
Joining Conversations about Writing 81

4 Composing 83
Threshold Concept: Writing Is a Process, and All Writers Have More to Learn

Famous essay on the nature of drafting and revision, emphasizing the frequent need to let early drafts be bad drafts.

Classic observational study of inexperienced writers' composing, emphasizing patterns emerging from carefully coded texts and notes.

Methodological exploration of early process-research protocols, comparing lab-based process observations against naturalistic observation of professional writer Donald Murray.

5 Literacies   240

Threshold Concept: Writing Is Impacted by Identities and Prior Experiences

6   Rhetoric   366

Threshold Concept: "Good" Writing Is Contextual

7   Communities   504

Threshold Concept: People Collaborate to Get Things Done with Writing

PREFACE FOR INSTRUCTORS

Writing about Writing is part of a movement that continues to grow. As composition instructors, we have always focused on teaching students how writing works and on helping them develop ways of thinking that would enable them to succeed as writers in college. We found ourselves increasingly frustrated, however, teaching traditional composition courses based on topics that had nothing to do with writing. It made far more sense to us to have students really engage with writing in the writing course; the best way to do this, we decided, was to adopt a "writing about writing" approach, introducing students directly to what writing researchers have learned about writing and challenging them to respond by writing and doing research of their own. After years of experimenting with readings and assignments, and watching our colleagues do the same, we developed *Writing about Writing*, a textbook for first-year composition students that presents the subjects of composition, discourse, and literacy as its content. Here's why we think *Writing about Writing* is a smart choice for composition courses.

Writing about Writing **engages students in a relevant subject.** One of the major goals of the writing course, as we see it, is to move students' ideas about language and writing from the realm of the automatic and unconscious to the forefront of their thinking. In conventional composition courses, students are too often asked to write about an arbitrary topic unrelated to writing. In our experience, when students are asked to read and interact with academic scholarly conversations about writing and test their opinions through their own research, they become more engaged with the goals of the writing course and — most important — they learn more about writing.

Writing about Writing **engages students' own areas of expertise.** By the time they reach college, students are expert language users with multiple literacies: They are experienced student writers, and they're engaged in many other discourses as well — blogging, texting, instant messaging, posting to social networking sites like

Facebook and Snapchat, and otherwise using language and writing on a daily basis. *Writing about Writing* asks students to work from their own experience to consider how writing works, who they are as writers, and how they use (and don't use) writing. Students might wonder, for example, why they did so poorly on the SAT writing section or why some groups of people use writing that is so specialized it seems intended to leave others out. This book encourages students to discover how others — including Sondra Perl, Deborah Brandt, James Paul Gee, their instructors, and their classmates — have answered these questions and then to find out more by doing meaningful research of their own.

***Writing about Writing* helps students transfer what they learn.** Teachers often assume that students can automatically and easily "apply" what they learn in a writing course to all their other writing — or at the very least, to other college writing. This assumption sees writing and reading as "basic" universal skills that work the same regardless of situation. Yet research on transfer of learning suggests that there is nothing automatic about it: Learning transfer researchers David Perkins and Gavriel Salomon found that in order to transfer knowledge, students need to explicitly create general principles based on their own experience and learning; to be self-reflective, so that they keep track of what they are thinking and learning as they do it; and to be mindful — that is, alert to their surroundings and to what they are doing rather than just doing things automatically and unconsciously. A writing course that takes language, writing, reading, and literacy as its subjects can help students achieve these goals by teaching them to articulate general principles such as "Carefully consider what your audience needs and wants this document to do." In addition, it teaches them to reflect on their own reading, writing, and research processes.

***Writing about Writing* has been extensively class tested — and it works.** The principles of this writing-about-writing approach have been well tested and supported by the experience of hundreds of writing instructors and tens of thousands of students across the country. *Writing about Writing* was formally class tested in a pilot at the University of Central Florida, an experiment that yielded impressive outcomes in comparative portfolio assessment with more traditional composition courses. Assessment results suggest, among other things, that the writing-about-writing approach had a statistically significant impact on higher-order thinking skills — rhetorical analysis, critical thinking about ideas, and using and integrating the ideas of others. The writing-about-writing approach also had a significant impact on how students and teachers engaged in writing as a process. The first three editions of *Writing about Writing* were adopted across a variety of composition programs nationwide, and based on positive feedback from those users, we have even greater confidence that this approach — and this fourth edition — will create good learning experiences for your students.

Features of *Writing about Writing*

FRAMED AROUND THRESHOLD CONCEPTS ABOUT WRITING

"Threshold concepts" are concepts that learners must become acquainted with in order to progress in a particular field or area of study — they are gateways to learning. Because they are often assumed and unstated, threshold concepts when explicitly identified can better help students come to understand ideas that are central to that field or phenomenon. The approach of naming and using threshold concepts to improve teaching and learning has been used in a variety of disciplines, in the United Kingdom and now increasingly in the United States and other countries. It is well-suited to the field of Writing Studies, with its rich body of research (for example, see the 2015 publication *Naming What We Know: Threshold Concepts of Writing Studies*). We have chosen a set of threshold concepts and principles about writing that we think are especially useful for first-year writing students, and these are central to our approach.

Researchers Ray Land and Jan (Erik) Meyer have argued that threshold concepts are often troublesome and can conflict with common knowledge about a phenomenon. We think that this is particularly true when it comes to writing. Much of what we have learned as a field conflicts with commonly held assumptions about writing. For example, many people believe that "good writers" are people for whom writing is easy, while research about writing suggests that "good writers" are people who persist, revise, and are willing to learn from their failures. In *Writing about Writing*, we encourage students to see the limitations of commonly held assumptions by engaging with Writing Studies research. In Part One, "Exploring Threshold Concepts of Writing through Inquiry," we introduce ideas that will be central to their investigations, while in Part Two, "Joining Conversations about Writing," we focus each chapter on a threshold concept and bring in a variety of perspectives on that concept. In this way, students grapple with ideas that are central to their lives as writers.

SUPPORT FOR EXPLORING WRITING THROUGH INQUIRY

This fourth edition includes a new accessible guide to help students use primary inquiry to join researchers' conversations on writing and threshold concepts related to it. Here's what we cover in this new Part One, "Exploring Threshold Concepts of Writing through Conversational Inquiry":

- **Chapter 1, "Investigating Writing: Threshold Concepts and Transfer,"** introduces and defines threshold concepts and describes some central concepts about writing that conflict with common ideas of writing in popular culture. The chapter also helps students consider learning transfer and the value of studying writing about writing.

- **Chapter 2, "Readers, Writers, and Texts: Understanding Genre and Rhetorical Reading,"** gives students an accessible introduction to genre theory and links genre to rhetorical reading practices; these concepts will help students as they encounter readings throughout the book. Students will also understand the role that reading plays in participating in the ongoing conversations that characterize scholarly inquiry.

- **Chapter 3, "Participating in Conversational Inquiry about Writing,"** shows students how to join scholarly conversations by offering an extended walk-through of primary research processes, from developing research questions to choosing methods and attending to research ethics. Built around an example of one undergraduate's published study of writing students, the chapter also provides a series of easily reviewable information boxes on various aspects of the research process, from forming research questions to researching existing conversations to developing students' own research methods in ethical ways.

- Along with "Write Reflectively" and "Try Thinking Differently" activities that get students writing and thinking actively about each threshold concept, each chapter in Part One includes short reference lists of "Sources That Informed This Chapter," reflection activities including "Questions for Discussion and Journaling" and "Applying and Exploring Ideas" to allow students to reflect on the entire chapter and their conceptions of writing from the beginning of the course, and "Major Writing Assignments" linked to the material and activities each chapter focuses on.

CHALLENGING AND ENGAGING READINGS ABOUT WRITING

Because our intention in putting this book together was to invite students directly into scholarly conversations about writing, most readings in Part Two of the book are articles by rhetoric and composition scholars. We've chosen work that is readable by undergraduates, relevant to student experience, effective in modeling how to research and write about writing, and useful for helping students frame and analyze writing-related issues. We've drawn not only on our own experience with students but also on feedback from a nationwide network of faculty using writing-about-writing approaches to composition and on the feedback of teachers who used the first three editions of the book. The articles in this edition expose students to some of the longest-standing questions and some of the most interesting work in our field, encouraging them to wrestle with concepts we're all trying to figure out.

Of course, we don't expect first-year students to read these texts as graduate students or scholars would — that is, with a central focus on the content of the readings, for the purposes of critiquing them and extending their ideas. Instead, we intend for them to be used as springboards to exploration of students' own writing and reading experiences. The readings — and thus this book — are not the center of the course; instead, they help students develop language and ideas for thinking through the threshold concepts identified above, and begin exploring them by considering their own experiences with writing, discourse, and literacy, and their (and the field's) open questions.

While most readings are scholarly, we include a number of other sorts of texts throughout this edition. Chapters 1 through 3 are written directly by us for the student readers of this book, as is an introduction to rhetoric by **Doug Downs** (in Chapter 6). We also include short pieces by fiction and nonfiction writers (including **Anne Lamott**, **Sandra Cisneros**, **Perri Klass**, and **Barbara Mellix**). These readings, combined with the others in the book, help students approach the threshold concepts about writing from a variety of perspectives.

REAL STUDENT WRITING

Writing about Writing also includes student voices, with six pieces of student writing in Part Two. We have continued to draw from *Young Scholars in Writing*, the national peer-reviewed journal of undergraduate research in Writing Studies and rhetoric, and from *Stylus*, the University of Central Florida Writing Program's peer-reviewed first-year student publication. Given their nature as reprinted scholarly articles, we have treated the student essays the same way we have treated the professional essays: They are framed and introduced and accompanied by questions and activities. We want the students who use this book to see other students as participants in the ongoing conversations about writing; we hope this will enable them to see themselves as potential contributors to these conversations. Student readings are integrated throughout Chapters 4 through 7 where they best fit the conversation.

SCAFFOLDED SUPPORT FOR READING

The material presented in this book is challenging. We've found that students need guidance in order to engage with it constructively, and many instructors appreciate support in teaching it. Therefore, we've scaffolded the material in ways that help make individual readings more accessible to students and that help them build toward mastery of often complex rhetorical concepts.

- We've expanded discussion of **reading strategies** based on genre theory and John Swales's CARS model of scholarly article introductions, which helps students analyze and understand the moves made in the introductions of most readings in Chapters 4–7. In Chapter 2, students will find discussions of genre and rhetorical reading, including an outline of reading strategies based on these theories, which help them engage in the readings of this book (and those in the rest of their college experience). Swales's CARS model is newly designed as a compact guide to analysis in Chapter 3 (see page 62). For further guidance on how to approach texts, we include Richard Straub's article addressed to students on how to read other writer's work in progress, "Responding — Really Responding — to Other Students' Writing," in Chapter 4.

- Chapters 4–7 begin with a **chapter introduction** that explains the chapter's threshold concepts, summarizes the chapter's content and goals, and describes the role of each reading within the larger conversation at play within the chapter. These introductions provide background knowledge and principles to prepare students for the work of the chapter.

- Each reading begins with a **Framing the Reading** section offering background on the author and the text as well as **Getting Ready to Read** suggestions for activities to do *before* reading and questions to ask *during* reading.

- Each reading is followed by two sets of questions: **Questions for Discussion and Journaling**, which can be used in class or for homework, and **Applying and Exploring Ideas**, which recommends medium-scale reading-related writing activities (both individual and group). A **Meta Moment** concludes the post-reading question set and asks students to reflect on the selection's ideas in the context of the chapter's threshold concept and of their own writing experiences. These questions and activities are designed to make teachers' jobs easier by providing a variety of prompts that have been class tested by others.

- Each chapter ends with the **Major Writing Assignments** section. Building on one or more of the readings from the chapter, assignments are designed to help students achieve the goals outlined in the chapter introduction. Though these assignments hardly scratch the surface of what's possible, they have proven to be favorites with us, our students, and other teachers.

- The book includes a **glossary** of technical terms in composition that students will encounter in their readings. Terms in the glossary, such as *rhetorical situation* and *discourse*, are noted in the chapter and reading introductions via bold print.

A note on citation styles. While the selection introductions reflect current MLA style from the eighth edition of the *MLA Handbook* (2016) in citation and documentation, other material in the book, all previously published, remains written in the citation styles used by the journals and books in which they were originally published, current at those times. This means you should expect to see a great deal of variation from current MLA, APA, CMS, or journal-specific style guidelines — a decision that we hope will provide instructors with an excellent starting point for conversation about how citation actually works in the "real world" of academic publication over time.

SUPPORT FOR TEACHERS IN THE INSTRUCTOR'S MANUAL

Some teachers won't need any supplements at all, including the discussion questions and major assignment options. But we have designed the book to be as accessible and supportive as possible to composition instructors with a wide range of experience, including new graduate students and very busy adjuncts. Toward that end, we provide a revised instructor's manual written by Matt Bryan, which builds on his work with Deborah Weaver in the previous edition. Matt is a teacher-trainer at the University of Central Florida who has used multiple versions of this book and taught the material in it to many other composition teachers there. This material, bound together with the student text in a special Instructor's Edition, includes the following:

- four sample semester-length syllabi keyed to different themes
- frequently asked questions
- chapter overviews
- lists of key vocabulary for each chapter
- key student goals for each chapter
- summaries and take-home points for each reading
- supplemental activities that help teach to each goal

The manual is also available for download on the instructor's resources tab on the catalog page for *Writing about Writing* at **macmillanlearning.com**.

New to the Fourth Edition

A NEW TWO-PART ORGANIZATION HELPS STUDENTS ENTER THE CONVERSATION ABOUT WRITING

For **Part One: Exploring Threshold Concepts of Writing through Inquiry** (Chapters 1–3) we wrote an accessible guide for students that introduces ideas and methods they need to know in order to explore threshold concepts through conversational inquiry. In **Part Two: Joining Conversations about Writing** (Chapters 4–7), which will be familiar to current users, we bring together readings and scaffolded support around four key threshold concepts. Together, these two parts will support students as they join researchers' conversations on writing and threshold concepts related to it.

NEW CHAPTERS 1–3 PROVIDE A FRAMEWORK FOR INQUIRY

The new **Chapter 1, Investigating Writing: Threshold Concepts and Transfer**, now frames threshold concepts not simply as necessary conceptions of writing to understand, but as a framework for doing one's own inquiry into writing. **Chapter 2, Readers, Writers, and Texts: Understanding Genre and Rhetorical Reading**, explains genre theory and rhetorical reading as threshold concepts that not only assist academic reading and writing but that are also integral to participating in scholarly conversation first-hand. **Chapter 3, Participating in Conversational Inquiry about Writing**, closes that conversation by offering a completely new focused guide for conducting primary research on writing.

NEW READINGS IN CHAPTERS 4–7 REFLECT THE CURRENT STATE OF WRITING STUDIES

As in the previous edition, we have organized professional and student writing about writing in four chapters, each focused on a threshold concept. For this fourth edition, we have changed the sequence of chapters to better align with how teachers are using the book, and we moved some readings into different chapters. We also streamlined the number of readings so that students can better navigate the chapters. Note that **Richard Straub**'s popular essay on peer review is now in Chapter 4.

We have brought seven new readings into Chapters 4–7, with an eye to topics and perspectives that will challenge students' commonly held conceptions about writing. The new professional essays are **Michael-John DePalma**'s and **Kara Poe Alexander**'s "A Bag Full of Snakes: Negotiating the Challenges of Multimodal Composition," **Vershawn Ashanti Young**'s "Should Writers Use They Own English," and **John Swales**'s "Reflections on the Concept of Discourse Community." New student voices include **Jaydelle Celestine** on writing process, **Julie Wan** on multilingualism and racism, **Julia Arbutus** on uses of rhetoric in popular culture, and **Arielle Feldman** on writing strategies used by *Star Wars* bloggers.

NEW MAJOR WRITING ASSIGNMENTS OFFER MORE OPTIONS FOR INQUIRY

Among the six new projects are multimodal options and projects that respond to new concepts in Part One and new readings in Part Two. These include a collage and artist's statement on what writing is and how it works in the world, a genre analysis, an analysis of a Burkean Parlor, an assignment for developing a research question, an illustration of writers' processes, and a project on navigating sources that disagree.

Acknowledgments

We came to writing-about-writing independently of one another, in different ways, and became better at it as a result of working together. David Russell was a mentor for us both. Elizabeth came to writing-about-writing as a result of her dissertation research, which Russell chaired and supported. Doug came to it as a result of questions about building better research pedagogy, directly fueled by Russell's work on the history of college research-writing instruction and his chapter in Joseph Petraglia's *Reconceiving Writing*. Initially, Elizabeth's interest was theoretical ("this might be an interesting idea") while Doug's was quite practical (he designed and studied a writing-about-writing class for his dissertation). We discovered each other's common interest through dialog on the WPA-L listserv, and a long-term collaboration was born. It is fair to say that neither of us would have written this book without the other, as we both seem to get a lot more done when working collaboratively. (We remember vividly two hours in the sunshine at the University of Delaware, at the 2004 WPA conference, when we took our first steps at figuring out collaboration.) In the years since the first edition, we have continued this collaboration both through continually developing the book and through other scholarly writing projects that have advanced the field's learning on writing-about-writing pedagogy, threshold concepts and transfer, and the discipline of Writing Studies. So we would like to acknowledge collaboration in general, our collaboration in particular, and tenure and promotion systems at our institutions that have recognized collaborative work for the valid, challenging, and rewarding process it is.

To many, many people — colleagues, mentors, and friends — we owe a deep debt of gratitude for putting the ideas grounding *Writing about Writing* "in the air." In addition, over the five years that it took to build the first edition of this book, and the three years we planned and wrote the second edition, the year and a half it took to write the third edition, and the year we've spent on the fourth edition, we met many wonderful teacher-scholars who inspired us to keep going. Over many dinners, SIGs, conference panels, e-mail discussions, and drinks, we learned and are still learning a lot from them. A partial list of people who helped us start on this path or rethink it and make it better includes Linda Adler-Kassner, Anis Bawarshi, Barbara Bird, Jessie Blackburn, Shannon Carter, Jackie Cason, Colin Charlton, Jonikka Charlton, Dana Driscoll, Heidi Estrem, Sarah Kloewer, Michelle LaFrance, Moriah McCracken, Susan McLeod, Laurie McMillan, Michael Michaud, Ben Miller, Michael Murphy, Andrea Olinger, Laurie Pinkert, Sarah Read, Jan Rieman, David Russell, Betsy Sargent, Jody Shipka, David Slomp, Susan Thomas, Lisa Tremain, Scott Warnock, Jennifer Wells, Kathi Yancey, and Leah Zuidema.

Each of us is also deeply indebted to the wonderful teachers, scholars, and students at the institutions where we piloted these ideas and pushed our thinking on what is possible in a writing-about-writing classroom. At UCF, some of these people included Matt Bryan, Mark Hall, Dan Martin, Matt McBride, Lindee Owens, Adele

Richardson, Angela Rounsaville, Nichole Stack, Mary Tripp, Debbie Weaver, and Thomas Wright. At Montana State, some of these people included Jean Arthur, Julie Christen, ZuZu Feder, Jake Henan, Kimberly Hoover, Katie Jo LaRiviere, Miles Nolte, Ashley Rives, Mark Schlenz, and Aaron Yost.

Many of these people are now on the FYC as Writing Studies listserv; members of the Writing about Writing Network founded by Betsy Sargent; participants in or leaders of the CCCC standing group, the Writing about Writing Development Group; or contributors to the 2019 research collection *Next Steps: New Directions In / For Writing about Writing*, edited by Barbara Bird, Doug Downs, Moriah McCracken, and Jan Rieman. Through such interaction, they continue to develop research projects, create conference presentations and workshops, and inspire us — and one another — with their curricular creativity. Writing-about-writing students have also been given a national platform to publish their work, thanks to the editorial board of the national, peer-reviewed undergraduate journal of Writing Studies, *Young Scholars in Writing*. Editor Laurie Grobman created a First-year Writing Feature (continued as the Spotlight on First-year Writing under the editorship of Jane Greer) co-edited over time by Shannon Carter, Doug Downs, David Elder, Heidi Estrem, Patti Hanlon-Baker, Holly Ryan, Heather Bastian, and Angela Glotfelter.

We are grateful to those instructors who gave us valuable feedback as we worked on this edition: Jean Arthur, Montana State University; Rebecca Babcock, University of Texas, Permian Basin; Elias Dominguez Barajas, University of Arkansas; Mark Blaauw-Hara, North Central Michigan College; Dominic Borowiak, North Central Michigan College; Jennifer Bray, Texas A&M University, Corpus Christi; Matthew Bryan, University of Central Florida; Jacqueline Cason, University of Alaska Anchorage; Rebecca Chatham, University of Arkansas; Ryan Dippre, University of Maine; Violet Dutcher, Eastern Mennonite University; Heidi Estrem, Boise State University; Katherine Fredlund, University of Memphis; Sonya Green, Lipscomb University; Elif Guler, Longwood University; Tekla Hawkins, University of Texas Rio Grande Valley; Andrew Hollinger, University of Texas Rio Grande Valley; Dennis Jerz, Seton Hill University; Erik Juergensmeyer, Fort Lewis College; Sarah Kloewer, Miles Community College; Jennifer Maher, University of Maryland Baltimore County; Sarah Marshall, Thomas Jefferson University, East Falls Campus; Holly McSpadden, Missouri Southern State University; Michael Michaud, Rhode Island College; Susan Mills, University of Texas Rio Grande Valley; Randall Monty, University of Texas Rio Grande Valley; Allison Morrow, University of South Alabama; Juli Parrish, University of Denver; Maria Rankin-Brown, Pacific Union College; Jan Rieman, University of North Carolina, Charlotte; Danielle Roach, Wright State University; Loren Roberson, University of Memphis; Jennifer Wells, New College of Florida; Christy Wenger, Shepherd University; John Whicker, Fontbonne University; Emily Wierszewski, Seton Hill University; Lydia Wilkes, Idaho State University; and Bret Zawilski, Appalachian State University.

We owe a massive thank you to Bedford/St. Martin's, and to Leasa Burton and Joan Feinberg in particular, who had the vision to believe that this book might really find an audience if they published it. To all the Bedford crew who made it real the first time and improved it the second and third times, we are deeply grateful. We are grateful to John Sullivan, our second edition editor and current Senior Program Manager at Bedford, who unfailingly believed and continues to believe in our ideas and vision, and who encourages others to trust us when our ideas might not immediately seem possible; his mentorship and advocacy on the second edition helped make what's come since then possible to begin with. Leah Rang showed us new possibilities for the book's design as editor of our third edition, and in her current role as Development Editor has continued to offer insightful input on the book. The award for *best process ever* goes to Cynthia Ward, Development Editor of this fourth edition. Cynthia immediately understood the *Writing about Writing* ethos (both as a pedagogy and a textbook), flexed with our desire to implement a two-part structure with brief-rhetoric elements, graciously edited us with her scrupulous work on our prose, and provided the snappiest and timeliest creative process yet for this book. Cynthia's trains run on time, and we are all better for it. Working with her has left us excited and rejuvenated. We owe this book to Cynthia.

Ultimately, our students deserve the most acknowledgment. They have inspired us to keep teaching writing about writing. They have demonstrated that the focus is one that continues to excite and motivate, and their ideas continue to inspire and teach us.

ELIZABETH WARDLE

DOUG DOWNS

Bedford/St. Martin's puts writers first

From day one, our goal has been simple: to provide inspiring resources that are grounded in best practices for teaching reading and writing. For more than thirty-five years, Bedford/St. Martin's has partnered with the field, listening to teachers, scholars, and students about the support writers need. We are committed to helping every writing instructor make the most of our resources.

HOW CAN WE HELP *YOU*?

- Our editors can align our resources to your outcomes through correlation and transition guides for your syllabus. Just ask us.

- Our sales representatives specialize in helping you find the right materials to support your course goals.

- Our *Bits* blog on the Bedford/St. Martin's English Community (**community .macmillan.com**) publishes fresh teaching ideas weekly. You'll also find easily downloadable professional resources and links to author webinars on our community site.

Contact your Bedford/St. Martin's sales representative or visit **macmillanlearning.com** to learn more.

PRINT AND DIGITAL OPTIONS FOR *WRITING ABOUT WRITING*

Choose the format that works best for your course, and ask about our packaging options that offer savings for students.

Print

- *Paperback.* To order the fourth edition, use ISBN 978-1-319-19586-1.
- *Loose-leaf edition.* This format does not have a traditional binding; its pages are loose and hole punched to provide flexibility and a lower price to students (ISBN: 978-1-319-28155-7). It can be packaged with our digital space for additional savings.
- To order the loose-leaf packaged with Achieve, use ISBN 978-1-319-33021-9.

Digital

- *Innovative digital learning space.* Bedford/St. Martin's suite of digital tools makes it easy to get everyone on the same page by putting student writers at the center. For details, visit **macmillanlearning.com/college/us/englishdigital**.
- *Popular e-book formats.* For details about our e-book partners, visit **macmillanlearning.com/ebooks**.
- *Inclusive Access.* Enable every student to receive their course materials through your LMS on the first day of class. Macmillan Learning's Inclusive Access program is the easiest, most affordable way to ensure all students have access to quality educational resources. Find out more at **macmillanlearning.com/inclusiveaccess**.

YOUR COURSE, YOUR WAY

No two writing programs or classrooms are exactly alike. Our Curriculum Solutions team works with you to design custom options that provide the resources your students need. (Options below require enrollment minimums.)

- *ForeWords for English.* Customize any print resource to fit the focus of your course or program by choosing from a range of prepared topics, such as Sentence Guides for Academic Writers.

- *Macmillan Author Program (MAP).* Add excerpts or package acclaimed works from Macmillan's trade imprints to connect students with prominent authors and public conversations. A list of popular examples or academic themes is available upon request.

- *Bedford Select.* Build your own print handbook or anthology from a database of more than 900 selections, and add your own materials to create your ideal text. Package with any Bedford/St. Martin's text for additional savings. Visit **macmillanlearning.com/bedfordselect**.

INSTRUCTOR RESOURCES

You have a lot to do in your course. We want to make it easy for you to find the support you need—and to get it quickly.

The *Instructor's Manual for Writing about Writing* is available as a PDF that can be downloaded from **macmillanlearning.com**. In addition to chapter overviews, reading summaries, and additional activities, the Instructor's Manual includes advice for implementing a writing about writing approach as well as four sample syllabi. This instructor's manual is also bound into evaluation copies of the book (Instructor's Edition ISBN: 978-1-319-24337-1).

How *Writing about Writing* Supports WPA Outcomes for First-Year Composition

WPA OUTCOMES	RELEVANT FEATURES FROM *WRITING ABOUT WRITING*, FOURTH EDITION
Rhetorical Knowledge	
Learn and use key rhetorical concepts through analyzing and composing a variety of texts.	• Chapters 1–3 (Part One), written by the authors for a student audience, introduce threshold concepts of writing and rhetoric. • Chapters 4–7 (Part Two), which combine readings and scaffolded instruction, engage students in analyzing and composing a variety of texts that explore threshold concepts of writing and rhetoric. • Chapter 6 is fully devoted to rhetoric, including an overview of rhetorical theory geared to first-year students and six other readings that take up rhetorical concepts. • Assignments such as "Genre Analysis" (Chapter 2), "Rhetorical Analysis of a Previous Writing Experience" (Chapter 6), and "Rhetorical Reading Analysis" (Chapter 6) ask students to apply key rhetorical concepts.
Gain experience reading and composing in several genres to understand how genre conventions shape and are shaped by readers' and writers' practices and purposes.	• Chapter 2 discusses explicitly how genres work and how to read rhetorically. It also includes a Genre Analysis assignment. • Assignments throughout the text cover a broad range of genres, such as a collage and artist's statement (Chapter 1), a reflective writer's portrait (Chapter 4), and a social sciences ethnography (Chapter 7). • The readings in Part Two include a variety of genres, from peer-reviewed research articles to personal essays on the writing process by writers like Anne Lamott.

WPA OUTCOMES	RELEVANT FEATURES FROM *WRITING ABOUT WRITING*, FOURTH EDITION
Rhetorical Knowledge	
Develop facility in responding to a variety of situations and contexts calling for purposeful shifts in voice, tone, level of formality, design, medium, and / or structure.	• The sixteen assignment options in the book call for varied genres; many are multimodal, as indicated by the multimodal icon next to the assignment title. • The idea that different rhetorical situations call for different responses is explored throughout the book, especially in Chapters 2 ("Readers, Writers, and Texts"), 4 ("Composing"), 6 ("Rhetoric"), and 7 ("Communities").
Understand and use a variety of technologies to address a range of audiences.	• A number of assignments, marked with a multimodal icon, ask students to use a variety of technologies. For example, Chapter 1 includes a collage and artist's statement, and Chapter 4 includes a social sciences autoethnography, a reflective writer's portrait, and a multimodal representation of the processes of different writers. • Readings such as DePalma's and Poe Alexander's "A Bag Full of Snakes: Negotiating the Challenges of Multimodal Composition" (Chapter 4) explore the use of new technologies.
Match the capacities of different environments (e.g., print and electronic) to varying rhetorical situations.	• This outcome is supported through readings that consider scenes and genres of multimodal writing, such as Feldman's "Galaxy-Wide Writing Strategies Used by Official *Star Wars* Bloggers" (Chapter 7). • Students can practice this skill through assignments with both traditional print and multimodal options and pathways, such as "Portrait of a Writer" and "Illustrating Writers' Processes" in Chapter 4.
Critical Thinking, Reading, and Composing	
Use composing and reading for inquiry, learning, critical thinking, and communicating in various rhetorical contexts.	• Chapters 2 and 3 are designed around the idea of conversational inquiry and how to engage in it. • Throughout the text, students are asked to reflect on and respond to ideas through "Meta Moment" boxes.

WPA OUTCOMES	RELEVANT FEATURES FROM *WRITING ABOUT WRITING,* FOURTH EDITION
Read a diverse range of texts, attending especially to relationships between assertion and evidence, to patterns of organization, to the interplay between verbal and nonverbal elements, and to how these features function for different audiences and situations.	• Part Two offers thirty-two readings that represent a diverse range of texts on the subject of writing. • "Questions for Discussion and Journaling" and "Applying and Exploring Ideas" after each reading engage students in thinking about rhetorical contexts and strategies. • Chapter 2 explicitly addresses the features of genres and how to read rhetorically.
Locate and evaluate (for credibility, sufficiency, accuracy, timeliness, bias, and so on) primary and secondary research materials, including journal articles and essays, books, scholarly and professionally established and maintained databases or archives, and informal electronic networks and Internet sources.	• Chapter 3 explains how to engage in the inquiry process, including formulating a question, searching databases, evaluating sources, and analyzing data. • The assignment, "Developing a Research Question," guides students through the process of locating and evaluating research materials.
Use strategies—such as interpretation, synthesis, response, critique, and design/redesign—to compose texts that integrate the writer's ideas with those from appropriate sources.	• Both end-of-reading reflection exercises (such as "Questions for Discussion and Journaling" and "Applying and Exploring Ideas") and major assignment options are designed with an explicit eye toward these cognitive and metacognitive strategies and activities.
Processes	
Develop a writing project through multiple drafts.	Every major assignment in the book is designed to be completed as part of a process and includes instructions about planning, drafting, and revising.
Develop flexible strategies for reading, drafting, reviewing, collaborating, revising, rewriting, rereading, and editing.	• Every major assignment in the book includes instructions about planning, drafting, and revising. • One of the primary threshold concepts of the book is about composing and how it works (see Chapters 1 and 4).
Use composing processes and tools as a means to discover and reconsider ideas.	Chapters 2 and 3 are devoted to ideas about inquiry and how to ask questions that can be answered through writing, reading, and conversation.

WPA OUTCOMES	RELEVANT FEATURES FROM *WRITING ABOUT WRITING*, FOURTH EDITION
Processes	
Experience the collaborative and social aspects of writing processes.	• This outcome is reflected in several of the book's threshold concepts: writing is a process; "good" writing is contextual; and people collaborate to get things done with writing. • Chapter 5's critical study of literacy is grounded in the notion that identities which are central to writing are socially formed through shared language and culture. • All the major writing assignments in the book emphasize the need to plan and draft with others.
Learn to give and to act on productive feedback to works in progress.	• Responding to peer review is a topic in Chapter 3. • In Chapter 4, Straub's "Responding—Really Responding—to Other Students' Writing" offers extensive advice and examples for giving productive feedback.
Adapt composing processes for a variety of technologies and modalities.	Many assignments call on students to use a variety of technologies and modalities; multimodal assignments are indicated with an icon. Most assignments can be easily adapted to include whatever modalities a teacher wishes to emphasize.
Reflect on the development of composing practices and how those practices influence their work.	• The book is designed to incorporate self-reflection and metacognition at every turn. This is explained in Chapter 1 and emphasized through features such as "Meta Moment" prompts and the "Questions for Discussion and Journaling." • This concept is directly discussed in Chapters 1 and 4. • This idea is taken up in multiple assignments, including all the major assignments in Chapter 4.
Knowledge of Conventions	
Develop knowledge of linguistic structures, including grammar, punctuation, and spelling, through practice in composing and revising.	• Specific readings throughout the book critically examine both cultural expectations for linguistic structures in specific genres and discourse communities, and writers' development of facility with such conventions. See, for example, Perl's "The Composing Processes of Unskilled College Writers" (Chapter 4), Williams's "The Phenomenology of Error" (Chapter 5), Young's "Should Writers Use They Own English?" (Chapter 5), and Mirabelli's "Learning to Serve" (Chapter 7).

WPA OUTCOMES	RELEVANT FEATURES FROM *WRITING ABOUT WRITING*, FOURTH EDITION
	• A central theme of Chapter 5 (Literacies) is placing linguistic structures in the context of language acquisition and the cultural roles of language more broadly, and emphasizing the conventional nature of these structures by calling into question uses of orthographic conventions to mark and marginalize non-privileged versions of languages and discourses.
Understand why genre conventions for structure, paragraphing, tone, and mechanics vary.	The variability of genre conventions is discussed directly in Chapter 2 (Readers, Writers, and Texts: Understanding Genre and Rhetorical Reading), where students are also asked to engage in genre analysis of conventions themselves.
Gain experience negotiating variations in genre conventions.	• The major assignments in the book ask students to explore various genres and practice using their conventions. • The entire concept of the book is to help students build fluency with various genre conventions of a new form of discourse to them, scholarly inquiry.
Learn common formats and/or design features for different kinds of texts.	• The readings in Part Two represent a range of genres and illustrate common formats for those genres. • Chapter 2 invites students to engage in genre analysis of conventions themselves. • The major assignments in the book ask students to explore various genres and practice using their conventions.
Explore the concepts of intellectual property (such as fair use and copyright) that motivate documentation conventions.	Chapter 3 considers source material from a conversational perspective that explains documentation conventions as ways of participating in a communal, shared activity of open circulation.
Practice applying citation conventions systematically in their own work.	• Chapter 3 discusses inquiry, which is a prerequisite for understanding how citation works. • A number of the major assignments in the book require outside research that must be cited. • All of the writing in the text models the use of citation conventions for students.

ABOUT THE AUTHORS

Elizabeth Wardle is the Roger and Joyce Howe Distinguished Professor of Written Communication and Director of the Roger and Joyce Howe Center for Writing Excellence at Miami University (OH). She was Chair of the Department of Writing and Rhetoric at the University of Central Florida (UCF), and Director of Writing Programs at UCF and University of Dayton. These experiences fed her interest in how students learn and repurpose what they know in new settings. With Linda Adler-Kassner, she is co-editor of *Naming What We Know: Threshold Concepts of Writing Studies* (2015), winner of the WPA Award for Outstanding Contribution to the Discipline (2016), and of the forthcoming book *(Re)Considering What We Know: Learning Thresholds in Writing, Composition, Rhetoric, and Literacy*; with Rita Malenczyk, Susan Miller-Cochran, and Kathleen Blake Yancey, she is co-editor of *Composition, Rhetoric, and Disciplinarity* (2018). Her current research focuses on how to enact grassroots change via writing across the curriculum programs.

Doug Downs is Associate Professor of Writing Studies and former Director of the Core Writing Program in the Department of English at Montana State University (Bozeman). His interests are in college-level writing, research, and reading pedagogy, especially as these intersect in first-year composition courses and in undergraduate research. He served as editor of *Young Scholars in Writing*, the national peer-reviewed journal of undergraduate research on writing and rhetoric, from 2015 through 2019. His current research projects examine students' reading practices in our present screen-literacy paradigm, undergraduate research mentoring, and the eventual paths of English majors into non-humanities and non-teaching professional positions.

PART 1

Exploring Threshold Concepts of Writing through Inquiry

INVESTIGATING WRITING
Threshold Concepts and Transfer

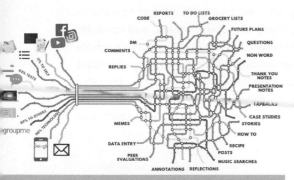

Colette Frommeyer

This untitled collage was created by Miami University student Colette Frommeyer. It illustrates the results of her research findings in response to the second assignment at the end of this chapter. She uses a tree, whose roots are a collection of the genres in which she writes. Each genre, she says, "funnels into a strong writing foundation which develops stems and leaves. . . . The genres intersect and interact with other genres, channels, and audiences to create a culmination of new, culturally-relevant sub-genres. Like a tree, these genres are affected by outside forces like weather, which represent the social forces that shape and determine its longevity." Frommeyer's collage was created using Canva.

Have you ever wondered why every teacher seems to have a different set of rules for writing? Or why writing seems to be more difficult for some people than for others? Or why some people use big words or special jargon when it seems like they don't have to? This book invites you to explore questions such as these by reading research about writing, comparing your own writing experiences with those of others, and finding your own answers by conducting research and writing.

This book invites you to engage with research about writing conducted in the field of **Writing Studies**,[1] much as your textbooks in biology or psychology introduce you to and invite you to engage with the research of those fields. Writing Studies researchers study how writing works, how people write, and how best to learn writing. From this book, then, you'll learn about the subject — writing — just as you would learn about biology from a biology textbook or about psychology from a psychology textbook. You will be introduced to **threshold concepts** in writing — ideas based on Writing Studies research that can transform the way you approach writing.

---

[1]**Boldface** terms are further defined in the end-of-book Glossary.

Writing about Writing asks you to think about writing as something we know about, not just something we do. It offers you these kinds of learning:

- Deeper understanding of what's going on with your own writing and how writing works
- Knowledge about writing that you can take with you to help you navigate other writing situations
- Experience engaging with scholarly articles and other research
- An invitation to engage in inquiry-driven research on unanswered questions (this is a type of research we will refer to as "conversational inquiry")

In the process of learning about writing, you will also have a lot of opportunities to engage in writing — to draft, revise, share ideas with others, and consider how to hone these skills in writing for other classes and in situations outside school settings. Both of these together — learning *about* the threshold concepts of writing and engaging in extensive *writing practice* — are necessary to help you **transfer** ideas and practices about writing to other situations. This chapter will introduce the threshold concepts of writing that you'll be exploring in this book and help you understand how transfer works.

Why Study Writing?

Why is it helpful to learn about writing rather than simply be told how to write? What good will this do you as a writer? Changing what you know about writing can change the way you write. Much of the research in this book questions everyday assumptions about writing — such as the idea that you can't use your own **voice** in writing for school, or that writing is just easy for some people and hard for others, or that literacy is only about how well you can read. If you change your ideas about what writing is supposed to be, you're likely to do things differently — more effectively — when you write.

There are additional advantages to studying writing in a writing course:

- Writing is relevant to all of us. Most of us do it every day, and all of us live in a world in which writing, reading, and other related uses of language are primary means of communication.
- What you learn about writing now will be directly useful to you long after the class ends. In college, at work, and in everyday life, writing well can have a measurable impact on your current and future success.
- You already have a great deal of experience with writing and reading, so you are a more knowledgeable investigator of these subjects than you might be of a lot of others.
- Doing research on writing will give you the opportunity to contribute new knowledge about your subject, not simply gather and repeat what many other people have already said.

[Handwritten annotation: "Unnecessary prepositional phrase" with circle around "of a lot"]

ACTIVITY 1.1 | Write Reflectively

What are your own assumptions about writing? Before continuing in this chapter, jot down your ideas about the following:

- Writing is . . .
- Good writing is . . .
- Good writers do or are . . .
- Writers are influenced by . . .
- Learning to write involves . . .

At the end of the chapter (in Writing Assignment Option 1) we will ask you to revisit your ideas to see if they have changed. In fact, throughout the book, we will ask you to note how and what you think about writing so that you can return to your ideas, track how they change, and, most importantly, see whether they impact what you do as a writer.

TWO STORIES ABOUT WRITING

You might be thinking that we're making writing harder than it has to be: Can't people just tell you how to write for any new situation or task? Even if studying about writing can help you write differently and better, wouldn't it be more direct to simply tell you the rules and let you practice and memorize them?

Actually, no. Writing doesn't work like that. It might be possible to just tell you the rules if the traditional story about writing that most of us learn in school were accurate. The traditional story about writing tells us that "writing" is a basic grammatical skill of transcribing speech to print, a skill that can transfer (be used again) unaltered from the situation in which you learn it (high school and college English classes, usually) to any other writing situation. Because, according to this story, the rules of English writing don't change. English is English, whether you're in a chemistry class or the boardroom of a bank. And, according to this story, what makes writing "good" is following all the rules and avoiding errors: Just don't do anything wrong and your writing will be okay.

According to this view of writing, people who are good at writing are people who break the fewest rules and write with the greatest ease; writing is hard because following the rules is hard; so if you can learn the rules, you can write more easily and thus be a good writer. That's the story that the majority of high school graduates seem to have learned. It's likely that no one stood in front of you and told you this story directly; but instead, it is a story that you learned by watching how people around you modeled this behavior.

For example, when teachers read your papers and ignored your ideas but corrected your grammatical mistakes, they were telling you this story: Writing is nothing but error-avoidance.

When you took standardized tests (like the SAT) and were given a prompt you had never seen before and told to write about it in thirty minutes, and then a stranger read it and ignored your ideas and facts and instead rated you on correctness and organization, they were telling you this story: Writing is not about content; it is about correctness.

If you think about the views of writing that you see on the news ("Kids today can't write! Texting is ruining their spelling!") or what you saw teachers and test-makers model, you will start to recognize how widespread this story of writing is.

But there's another story about writing that is research-based. "Research-based" ideas are ones that have been studied and tested, and they have been demonstrated to work for experienced writers. In this research-based story, "writing" is much fuller and richer. Writing is about what you say (content, material), how you say something (form, arrangement), how you come up with your ideas (invention), how you go through the act of thinking and writing (process), and whether what you've said and how you've said it successfully meet the current situation (rhetoric).

In this research-based story, avoiding errors that get in the way of the readers' understanding is only one small part of writing. Writing is about communicating in ways that work, that do something in the world. Writing is much more than grammar, and it's also much more than the final text you create; writing is the whole process of creating that text. In this story, there is not one universal set of rules for writing correctly, but rather many sets of habits adopted by groups of people using particular texts to accomplish particular ends or activities. For example, the habits and conventions of engineers' writing are vastly different than the habits and conventions of lawyers' writing or your writing for your history class. That means there is no easily transferable set of rules from one writing situation to another. What transfers is not *how to write*, but *what to ask and observe* about writing.

This second, alternative story about writing is one you have also been exposed to, but maybe not in school. When you text your friends, for example, you already know that what you say and how you say it matter, and that the text will be successful if your friend reads it and understands it and responds somehow. If your friend ignores it or finds it insulting or can't quite decipher the new shorthand you devised, then it's not "good writing." You also know that when you write an essay in your history class, you can't write the same way you do when you are texting your friends. You know these things even if no one has ever told them to you directly.

As a writer you have likely been experiencing the two competing stories about, or **conceptions** of, writing throughout much of your life. This might have led to confusing and frustrating experiences with writing. Teachers might have said they want to hear your personal voice and heartfelt opinion on something and then respond only to spelling and comma splices in your papers. School might have turned into a place where writing is simply an opportunity for you to be told that you've made mistakes. But at the same time, you might have a rich writing life through texting and Facebooking, writing fanfiction, writing on gaming chatboards, writing songs or poetry. In those worlds, writing is used to communicate, to share ideas, to get things done. These competing experiences with writing are enacting different conceptions of what writing is, and those conceptions of writing lead you to do different things. If you think that writing is avoiding error, it is unlikely you will spend much time developing ideas. If you think that a reader is going to respond and react to your ideas, you are quite likely to spend a lot of time developing them and thinking about your reader's possible reactions.

CONCEPTIONS: WITH OUR THOUGHTS WE MAKE THE WORLD

Our conceptions of writing — the stories we tell ourselves about it, what we assume about it — really matter. What you believe about writing directly impacts what you do or are willing to do. If you think you are a bad writer because you struggle with timed writing tests, you might not be willing to try other kinds of writing, or you might not recognize how good you are at coming up with smart ideas when you have a lot of time to think them over. If you think that good writing is writing with no errors, you might struggle to put words on paper (or on the screen) as you attempt to avoid errors. And in the process, you might forget what you wanted to say, or get so frustrated that you give up, or write much less than you would have otherwise. Your conceptions about writing shape what you do and what you are able to create. As Buddha said, "With our thoughts we make the world."

Much of the research described in this book suggests that some of our cultural beliefs about reading and writing aren't exactly right, and our lives as readers and writers would make a lot more sense if we could see these beliefs as *misconceptions* — that is, as ideas and stories about writing that don't really hold up to interrogation and research. The ideas, readings, research (inquiry) projects, and writing assignments in this book are intended to challenge your everyday ideas about writing; as you engage with them, you will recognize that writing is much more complicated (and interesting) when we actually pay close attention to how texts work and what readers and writers are doing when they engage them. You'll find that you are less controlled by universal, mysterious rules than you might have been taught. You can construct different ideas about writing, and you can construct meaning for yourself in ways that can empower you as a writer. But construct is not only a verb (conSTRUCT); it is also a noun (CONstruct). **Constructs** (noun) are mental frameworks that people build in order to make sense of the world around them. And you can choose to operate using different constructs of writing.

So in large part this book intends to help you become aware of your ideas about writing — your conceptions about writing that construct your world — and to give you the language to explore those ideas. It will put you in touch with other people's ideas and research about writing and help you engage in your own research about ideas that concern or interest you. Our goal is to help you have robust, healthy, research-based conceptions about writing that will make you a more successful writer.

Threshold Concepts of Writing

Some conceptions of writing matter more than others. Recently, Jan Meyer and Ray Land, researchers from the United Kingdom, identified what they call threshold concepts — ideas that are so central to understanding a particular subject that a learner can't move forward in that area without grasping them. Threshold concepts emerge from research, from inquiry, across time. However, grasping threshold concepts can be difficult because they are based in the research of particular fields or areas of study, and that research is often in conflict with popular, commonsense ideas about topics that haven't been tested or thought through carefully.

For example, one of us conducted a research project with some historians and was surprised to learn that professional historians don't think that there is a single authoritative story of the past that their job is to relay, but rather that their work involves analyzing evidence from the past, and this evidence can yield different interpretations or narratives. Historians debate these interpretations in their pursuit of a better understanding of why and how past events happened and how events were experienced by people at the time. These historians were frustrated that the History Channel and common conversations about history lead people to misunderstand what history is and how to study it. When students engage in their history classes, the historians have to spend a lot of time (years, sometimes) helping students understand what narratives are, what it means to see narratives as someone's interpretation of past events, and how to research the context of the narratives. Until students can do these things, they can't engage deeply with historical questions and problems.

As the history example illustrates, when learners are introduced to threshold concepts in different disciplines, they can find them troublesome, and it can take a long time to grasp them. While learners are struggling with the ideas, they find themselves in a *"liminal" space* — a space where they move back and forth, start to get a handle on the ideas, then realize they don't really have a handle on them. This liminal space can be uncomfortable because learners see that what they used to know no longer works, but they don't have anything new to replace it with. Thus they can feel unsteady, off balance, anxious, uncertain.

Threshold concepts of writing are no different than other threshold concepts in their troublesomeness. In some ways, threshold concepts about writing may be even more troublesome to learn than threshold concepts in many other disciplines. Because everyone writes, and writing is so common in our schools, lives, and daily experiences, by the time we get to a place where we are actually studying writing (usually in college writing classes) we've had a long time to solidify our non-research-based views about writing. As you grapple with the threshold concepts that are previewed in this chapter and covered at length in Part 2, you are likely to experience the liminal space. Don't expect to fully "get" the threshold concepts after reading this chapter, and know that as you engage with them throughout the course, you may struggle to grasp their meaning.

But when you finally do grasp these threshold concepts, the way you see things will be changed — transformed, likely for good. Different ideas and experiences will make sense and seem related in ways they hadn't before — in other words, learning threshold concepts is what Meyer and Land call an integrative experience.

META-CONCEPT: WRITING IS NOT JUST SOMETHING PEOPLE DO, BUT SOMETHING PEOPLE STUDY THROUGH INQUIRY

In order to really engage with threshold concepts about writing, there is one basic underlying concept — a meta-concept — that you'll need to grapple with first: Writing is not just something that you *do*, but also something that people *study*. Writing can be studied because it is a complex activity about which little is actually known. It is not, as you may have been taught, simply a basic skill involving rules of grammar, style, and form. As you'll learn in the class for which you're using this book, there is nothing "basic" about writing, which is one reason there are scholars who study how writing works and don't have all the answers yet.

Writing scholars want to know things like how we learn to write, how we can teach writing well, how technologies affect our writing processes, why some styles of writing are seen as more valuable than others, how we use writing to accomplish our goals, communicate, and persuade one another. The study of persuasion goes back a long way, to Aristotle (c. 350 BCE) and before. The formal study of how writing works, though, is more recent, beginning sometime in the 1950s. The activity of writing is difficult to study because people use it for so many different things and go about it in so many different ways. And compared with many other academic fields, the field of Writing Studies has had only a short time to get started on that research. At first, most study of writing concentrated on student writers, but it gradually became apparent that writing assignments didn't look a lot like writing outside of school, so writing research expanded to more sites and scenes. Throughout this time, some of the main research questions have been fairly stable, and you will find them discussed in various chapters in this book:

- How do writers actually get writing done? (Chapters 4 and 7)
- What keeps writers from accomplishing what they hope to accomplish? (Chapter 4)
- How do ideas about error, rules, and "teacher voices" impact how people write? (Chapters 4 and 5)
- How do our prior experiences, identities, and home and community languages influence who we are as writers and what we feel we can accomplish? (Chapter 5)
- What do we believe to be true about writing, and where do these beliefs come from? (Chapter 5)
- Why doesn't a piece of writing mean the same thing to all readers? How does meaning depend on context, including readers? (Chapter 6)

- How do people make meaning together through writing, especially when they disagree? (Chapters 2 and 6)
- How do writers get things done in new situations and when writing with and for others? (Chapter 7)

While all these are still open questions (requiring more research), there is also much we do know now about writing, and this research can help us better understand what we do as writers, what we need to do, what works, and what doesn't. In other words, if we can recognize that writing isn't just something we *do*, but something we can also *learn more about*, we can be empowered to change our ideas about writing and, in turn, change our writing practices.

We have used the questions of Writing Studies to guide the content in this book; the answers are, in effect, some of the threshold concepts resulting from these many decades of study about writing. In other words, research and inquiry are how we learn about writing. Threshold concepts are some of what we know as a result of that extended inquiry and conversation.

Next we invite you to engage with a few of these threshold concepts. Again, *no one expects you to thoroughly understand these threshold concepts here in Chapter 1*. It is likely that you'll still be working to understand how they work in your life long after this class is over; threshold concepts often take a long time to enact and understand — or learners come to understand them more deeply at different times in their lives. But we want you to start to think about these concepts here in Chapter 1, to begin to question the conceptions you are bringing with you to this class, and to have some basis for beginning your inquiry into the ideas about writing that are not only discussed in the rest of this book but are also enacted in your everyday life.

THRESHOLD CONCEPT: WRITING IS A PROCESS, AND ALL WRITERS HAVE MORE TO LEARN (CHAPTER 4: COMPOSING)

Writing is a process of composing. It generally takes time and practice to compose an effective piece of writing. And when you write texts that are new to you, or longer texts, or write with new kinds of technology, you are likely to need even more time and practice. No matter how much you practice, what you write will never be perfect. This is because readers make meaning out of what you write, and the situation in which your writing is read makes a difference in how effective the writing is (this is a threshold concept we will discuss later); in other words, you can't know for sure that whoever reads what you write will understand it or be persuaded by it. Thus, there is no such thing as perfect writing; writing is not in the category of things that are perfectible. Rather, you can compose, revise, develop a piece of your writing that may work more or less effectively for the purposes you are trying to use it. Because the texts you compose can be more or less effective (though never perfect), there are strategies and habits that can help you write more easily, more quickly, more effectively — and asking for feedback is, of course, always a good way to improve.

ACTIVITY 1.2 | Write Reflectively

Think of something difficult that you had to write recently. Difficult doesn't necessarily mean long. It might have been difficult to think of the right words to ask for money or to quit your summer job. Now think about the process that you engaged in to get that piece of writing done. Don't think about just the time you spent putting words on a page. How did you go about coming up with ideas? How did you figure out how to organize those ideas? Did you write and then revise, either in your mind or on paper or on the computer? How did you know when you were "finished"? Now think of a very different kind of writing task you completed recently. What was your writing process for that piece of writing? What helped you get these two writing tasks done? How did you know what to do? Were the processes similar or different? Why?

You likely already recognize that some kinds of writing come easier to you than others. You might have a pretty easy time writing lab reports and texts to your friends, but a much harder time writing a paper about *Moby-Dick* or writing a poem. One reason for this is that what you do and who you are as a writer is informed by your prior experiences (which is the next threshold concept we will discuss). You might have had more practice with certain kinds of writing, you might be fact-oriented, you might have read a lot of nonfiction books but not many novels. There are many reasons why some kinds of writing come more easily to you than other kinds. But you can improve at all kinds of writing with practice, feedback, and revision.

The good news is that this threshold concept is true for everyone: Writing requires practice for everyone, and *all writers* have more to learn. This concept will remain true for each writer's entire life: Writers *always* have more to learn. Learning is the key — and writers can always learn to be a little better at writing something that is not their strong suit. You should feel a kind of freedom in this realization: If you feel like you have a lot more to learn about writing or some kinds of writing, you're not "behind" or lacking; you're like everyone else. This understanding of writing should be very liberating because it helps you recognize that good writers aren't born that way; they're made through practice and circumstance. How you feel about yourself as a writer, and what you do as a writer, can change for the better if you realize that no writers are perfect, good writing depends on the situation, all writers have more to learn, and you can learn things about writing and how to write that can help you write more effectively. If you can stop thinking of yourself as a "bad writer" or a person "who just can't write," you can be freed up to try new things with writing.

ACTIVITY 1.3 | Try Thinking Differently

If writing is not perfectible, then writing is not about "getting it right" (either the first time or in later tries). If writing is not about "getting it right," then what is it about? If you're not prioritizing perfection in your writing, what are you prioritizing instead? In other words, if you know there is no "perfect" piece of writing, what are you going to aim for and keep in mind when you start writing something that is difficult for you? Try to keep this in mind when you write from now on. How will this change in focus impact how you write and how you feel about yourself as a writer?

THRESHOLD CONCEPT: WRITING IS IMPACTED BY IDENTITIES AND PRIOR EXPERIENCES (CHAPTER 5: LITERACIES)

How and why you write, what you think about writing, and how you make sense of texts when you read are impacted by all that you've done and experienced. Your experiences with literacy (reading and writing) are part of who you are, part of your identity. As Kathleen Blake Yancey explains it, "each writer is a combination of the collective set of different dimensions and traits and features that make us human" (52).

ACTIVITY 1.4 | Write Reflectively

Spend about ten minutes writing freely about your most important memories of reading, writing, and speaking. What were your experiences at home and outside school? What were your experiences in school? How do these impact what you believe, feel, and do with writing and reading today? How do these make you feel about writing and yourself as a writer?

Our experiences with writing and language start very early — in our homes, with our families — and then are impacted by activities, events, and groups — from clubs, library visits, and religious organizations to online interactions, hobbies, and schooling. We bring this rich, varied, and extensive history of reading and writing practices with us whenever we read, write, or receive feedback on our writing, or give feedback to someone else. When we encounter a new and challenging writing situation or task, we bring all of our previous experiences to bear. Who we are, where we've been, what we've done, the technologies we've used or been exposed to (or not) are all involved in our writing practices, attitudes, strengths, and weaknesses.

Andrea Lunsford, writing researcher and former director of Stanford University's writing program, conducted a study of people's early writing memories, and found that many people "reported something painful associated with writing: being made to sit on their left hands so they had to write right-handed" or "being made to write 'I will not X' a hundred times in punishment for some mistake" (54). Our prior experiences with writing can create negative or positive feelings about writing, and those attitudes and feelings remain with people throughout their lives.

Feelings and ideas can change, of course, but we are all always an accumulation of everything we have experienced and done. If our experiences happen to be those that are valued by the dominant (school) culture, we tend to have easier and more positive literacy experiences. But if our experiences do not mirror those of the dominant culture, we can often have very negative feelings about reading, writing, school, and/or ourselves. For example, if we come from a white, English-speaking, middle-class, Midwestern family that had a variety of books at home, we likely started school in the United States with a leg up on reading and speaking the dominant version of English. But if we come from an immigrant family, and our parents speak, for example, Spanish or Portuguese, and we had no books written in English at home, we likely started school without the literacy experiences that teachers expect, speaking and writing with an accent that set us apart.

Remember the earlier claim of this chapter, that thoughts make the world? We might modify that here to say that our thoughts and experiences make our own *literate* worlds. (*Literate* here means reading and writing, not traditional "literature.") Thus the accumulation of our experiences with reading and writing affects what we think about writing, what we do as readers and writers, and how we feel about ourselves as writers. We may never have stopped to think why reading and writing in school has been easy or hard for us, why teachers singled us out for praise or criticism, why we loved writing online with friends in Wattpad but dreaded writing for our teachers. But if we stop to think through our experiences with literacy, our feelings and experiences can begin to make more sense. We can be empowered to own and explain them, and to take control of them. For example, instead of feeling like a victim if a teacher criticizes your accent, you might learn to take pride in the fact that you speak several languages, and that you can choose just the right word in any of those languages to express how you feel.

ACTIVITY 1.5 | Try Thinking Differently

Think of a reading or writing situation when your usual habits didn't work to complete the task or communicate effectively, or when your writing made you feel like an outsider. Instead of denigrating yourself, ask where your ideas and feelings and practices came from, and how they compared with those of the people around you at the time. Was there something others could have learned to do or understand differently from you and your experiences? If so, what was it? Can the practice of trying to value your unique language experiences help you feel more confident in the future, when you are singled out as being different, or not writing or speaking in ways that others do?

THRESHOLD CONCEPT: "GOOD" WRITING IS CONTEXTUAL (CHAPTER 6: RHETORIC)

Whether or not writing is "good" depends on whether it gets things done, and whether it accomplishes what the writer (and readers) need it to. In other words, writing is rhetorical — it is always **situated** in a particular context and part of a communicative act. This threshold concept of writing likely conflicts with a lot of what school writing situations may have led you to believe. In school, it's easy to believe that good writing is writing that doesn't have grammatical errors or that follows the directions. But just by looking at examples from your own life, you can start to test and prove that such school-based ideas about writing are not accurate. Rather, the writing you do in your daily life "works" if it is appropriate for the task at hand, the readers, the technologies being used, and the purpose.

Consider what makes writing work when you are texting your friends. Do they think your texts are good if you use full sentences, correct grammar, and spell all words correctly? Probably not — and quite likely, the opposite. If you did those things, texting would take a long time, and your friends might tease you. Why? Because good writing is writing that is appropriate to the situation, your purpose as a writer, and the technology you use to write, and in this case, typing on a phone might make it inefficient to spell out all the words and write in complete sentences.

Of course, you can't use the rules of good texting when you write job application letters, your history exam, fanfiction, or poetry in your journal. Sometimes, the rules about writing you learned in school do hold true; when you apply for a job, for example, you want to show that you have a good grasp of formal language, that you can punctuate sentences and write clearly, and that you pay attention to details and go back and edit what you've written before sharing it with someone who could choose whether or not to hire you.

But even in cases where more formal and "correct" writing is appropriate, what counts as formal and correct can differ widely across contexts. For example, scientists often write using the passive voice. (In other words, their sentences don't necessarily tell readers who did the action; for example, they may write "Tests were conducted.") One major reason is that scientists value objectivity and group discovery, so the passive voice helps focus on what was done or learned, rather than individuals who did it. But in the humanities, writers are usually discouraged from using the passive voice and told to write to emphasize the action and the person doing the acting. For example, you might hear, "Shakespeare plays with the meaning of words" in a literature class. This is because in fields such as literature and history and philosophy and art, the person performing the action (the painting, the novel, the play) really does matter. So even though both passive and active sentences are grammatically correct, they may be appropriate or inappropriate depending on the situation and readers for whom you are writing.

ACTIVITY 1.6 | Write Reflectively

Try to remember a time when a rule or rules you were taught about didn't work when you used it in another situation. What was the rule? Where did you learn it? Where does that rule seem to work? Where does the rule not work?

As you might have guessed by now, the writer isn't the only person making meaning from writing. Readers make meaning, too, based on their own prior experiences, the purpose of the writing, the situation in which they are reading it, and their values and those of the group(s) they belong to. Your history teacher might find the language you use to write a lab report so unappealing that he or she can't really make a lot of sense of it, and your great-grandmother might find your text messages offensive or incoherent. So when you write, it's important to remember not just what you want to say, but who you want to make meaning for and with.

And, of course, today your writing might circulate among many different groups of people whom you may never have thought about. This is a result of social media and other online platforms. Something you wrote for one purpose and audience might circulate far beyond intended audience and initial context. Many a politician or business executive, for example, makes one statement privately to a narrow set of constituents, such as close staff or shareholders or family members, and then finds that statement shared to a wider audience they had not anticipated. Think of Donald Sterling, the owner of the Los Angeles Clippers basketball team: He made racist comments privately to his mistress. She secretly recorded them, and they were shared widely on the Internet and TV. As a result, his private comments cost him $2.5 million and he received a lifetime ban from the National Basketball Association. When private statements become public or circulate to unintended audiences, writers and speakers find they must explain themselves to those audiences. Of course in this case, his original comments and actions were deeply problematic, and this was exacerbated by the fact the he did not consider the impact on audience or the consequences of his comments on multiple audiences beyond the one to whom he originally made the comments.

So, writing is **contingent** — it depends upon the context. This can be a hard threshold concept to learn because you've been in school for so long, being taught rules that were treated as universal even though they were actually only specific to that time and place, that audience and purpose. However, if you test this threshold concept against your daily experiences writing across different contexts and technologies, you can quickly start to see how accurate it is. And if you can understand this threshold concept, it can help you start to make sense of things that may otherwise really frustrate you. Instead of being upset that your history teacher and your biology teacher want you to write differently, and being confused about "who's right," you can recognize that the differences stem from different ideas about what good writing is — and these ideas are related to what historians and biologists do with writing. They aren't trying to frustrate you; they are trying to help you write like historians or biologists, and sound credible when you do. In other words, understanding this threshold concept can really empower you to see that many kinds of writing can be good, and that you may be better at some kinds than others.

ACTIVITY 1.7 | Try Thinking Differently

Writing researchers frequently hear students say that they dislike writing for school because it seems to be mostly about following rules and structures, and being judged as a failure if they don't or can't use all the rules correctly. In contrast, students often report preferring "self-sponsored" writing outside of school (sometimes they call it "creative" writing, sometimes "personal" writing) because they are free to write whatever they like without being constrained by rule structures. Try this thought experiment: What would your school writing look like if you could approach it as you do "home" or personal writing, and if you could expect the same kind of responses that you receive to your home and school writing? What if all your school readers thought about your work as an attempt to communicate with them and get something done in a particular context, rather than focusing on correctness? What would you do differently in your school writing? Would you spend more time on it or treat it differently? How would your writing itself change?

THRESHOLD CONCEPT: PEOPLE COLLABORATE TO GET THINGS DONE WITH WRITING (CHAPTER 7: COMMUNITIES)

People use writing to get things done, and they use writing and language to make meaning together. This might seem obvious, but when we have spent the majority of our lives writing for school tasks, as has been the case for most students, we can forget the power that writing has to actually accomplish something within a community. School writing can sometimes be what writing researcher Joseph Petraglia calls "pseudotransactional" — in other words, school writing tasks often pretend (that's the *pseudo* part) to be the kind of writing that communicates with other people (that's the *transactional* part), but really it is often just that: pretend. Quite a lot of the time in non-school settings, writing is about communicating with, for, and to others — to plan a party or write a report or figure out how to solve a problem. Frequently, this happens in collaboration — not, perhaps, official collaboration (what you might recognize as "group projects" in school) but collaboratively in a looser sense: People give feedback, share ideas, make changes, respond to pieces of writing in ways that are, in essence, collaborative and social.

ACTIVITY 1.8 | Write Reflectively

Make a list of all of the reasons that you use writing in a given week (for example, to remember things, to argue, etc.). Be sure to remember all the reasons you write, not just the formal reasons you write for school. For each reason on the list, consider audience (who you are writing for) and others who are involved either directly or indirectly (for example, you might be talking on the phone with someone and working together on your fantasy football league list), as well as purpose. How does the presence of others impact what you do, what you write, and how you write?

In the rest of our lives outside of school — at work, online, at church, and so on — we know that writing helps us communicate and make meaning with others, and get things done. We know this without being told because we use writing like this all the time. If you are feeling lonely, you might text three friends and see if they want to meet you at the gym later. They text you back and negotiate the activity (maybe they need to study instead, so suggest meeting at the library) and the time (they have a sorority meeting at 6, but could meet you at 8). Even in this simple example, you've made meaning and gotten things done with others — a plan with a purpose has been created. Through the writing you are doing together, you've created a world where friends support one another.

This same principle holds true for all kinds of writing that takes place within and between groups of people. At work, three or four people might be on a deadline to finish a report, and they negotiate how to write that report together; when they turn it in, they may find that their working group gets more funding next year than they had last year. In our sororities, we have written guidelines and rituals that help us know who we are and what we stand for. When we make lists for our fanfiction league, we confer widely to make the best decisions, and if we are new, we depend on others to show us how it is done. If we write fanfiction online in Wattpad, hundreds or thousands of people might read and comment on what we write, and we know how to write fanfiction because we have read the examples others have written on Wattpad and have seen how readers there commented on those examples.

Writing helps people get things done, which makes writing powerful. But how and why particular writing does (or does not) work depends on who the people are, where they come from, what their goals are, what technologies they have available to them, and the kinds of texts (**genres**) they are writing (genres are discussed more in Chapter 2).

There are "rules" or at least unspoken but known conventions for how groups of people use writing together, and these rules constrain what writers and readers can do. If people are going to use writing successfully, they have to learn these rules (of course, rules can change — and writers themselves are the ones to change them). Think about the example above, of texting your friends to see if they want to join you at the gym later. No one taught you and your friends the rules of texting. You learned abbreviations and emojis by texting with more experienced writers. You likely found that it can be easy to misinterpret some things in text messages, so you probably learned to be more careful with your word choice. You may have discovered that some people don't respond well to texting (like your great-grandmother). And you may have developed in-jokes and special shorthand with your friends that could puzzle outsiders. All kinds of communities have these unspoken rules for how to say things, established by usage. For example, when surgeons write or talk about their work, they have a very specialized vocabulary that helps them be extremely precise and accurate. There is a hierarchy regarding who can say, do, and write when in the hospital, and that hierarchy helps ensure that everyone knows what their job is, and patients are protected.

The same is true in college. As you move to different subjects, you'll find the rules are different for how and what you write, and what you can do with writing. These rules might seem arbitrary, but they aren't. The writing that historians do looks and sounds a certain way in order to help them accomplish their goals as part of an academic discipline. Their writing looks very different from the writing of biologists, whose goals and purposes for writing are quite different. So writing helps people get things done and make meaning together. But as groups of people spend more and more time together, how and why they use writing in particular ways can be increasingly difficult for outsiders to comprehend. If you know this, and you understand what is happening, you can have an easier time as a newcomer to a situation or a particular form of writing. You'll understand that there are certain questions you need to ask, and you'll need to watch what other people do — and try to discover who does what and when.

ACTIVITY 1.9 | Try Thinking Differently

In Activity 1.8, you listed all of the reasons that you write in a given week. Go back to that list and think about kinds of writing (genres) that you might produce for two or three of those purposes — for example, "to remember" might entail lists, notes from class, etc. Pick one of those (for example, notes from class) and ask yourself how you learned to write that kind of text for that purpose. Who else writes like that? Who reads that writing when you produce it? How do you know when that kind of text has been effective, or succeeded? The next time you are asked to write in a new way or for a new purpose, consider how you learned to write in other new situations and what might help you here. Who else writes like this? Who are you writing for and with? What will make writing effective in this situation?

Transfer: Applying Learning to New Writing Situations

We said earlier in this chapter that with your thoughts you make the world, and we have emphasized this idea repeatedly: Your ideas matter, and when you write in new situations, your ideas about writing impact what you do (or don't do). So you may be wondering now how that happens. How is it that we take ideas, knowledge, and skills about writing and use them (or not) in new situations (effectively or not)? That is a very good question, one that researchers have been trying to answer now for more than a century. This is really a question about what researchers sometimes call "transfer": applying learning in one situation to later situations in new places. Below we draw on a variety of research about transfer; to learn more, consult "Sources That Informed This Chapter."

"NEAR" AND "FAR" TRANSFER

We know that transfer of some kinds of knowledge happens all the time, without even thinking about it. For example, every time you see an acquaintance on campus you don't have to wonder what to do; American conventions and experiences lead you to expect to say "Hi, how are you?" and then say "Fine" and probably keep walking. You have transferred prior knowledge into this situation. It's a situation that resembles thousands of others, and your prior experience helps you know what to do. This is a kind of transfer called "near transfer," where the new situation is very similar to all the situations you have faced before. You can quite often use prior knowledge without thinking, just because you have used it so many times before. This degree of near transfer is called "low road transfer," where you don't have to contemplate or reflect, you can just act.

But there are situations that require further — but still pretty near — transfer. If the person you say hi to stops and starts giving you a long response about what a terrible week they have had, you have to readjust a bit. But, again, this has likely happened before, so with a little bit of reflection and common sense you can figure out what to do. Another example of this near-but-slightly-further transfer is driving: If you learn to drive a car and now need to drive a small pickup truck, for example, you can figure out what to do with a little reflection and adjustment.

Writing something for our own purposes that is not evaluated in any high-stakes way and something that we write frequently can entail this sort of near or pretty near transfer. If you go to the grocery you need a list to help you remember what to get. You likely don't have to think too hard about what a list is or how a list should look. You just do what you have done before, with whatever tools are at hand. If you forget something because you can't read your handwriting or your phone ran out of battery and the list is lost to you, then you will likely remember this and "transfer" that experience to the next list-making experience, all without too much trouble or without a lot of careful reflection.

ACTIVITY 1.10 | Write Reflectively

Think of some activity in which you engage regularly where you typically do things automatically — you know what to do and what works, and you don't have to think very much about how to remember what you know.

However, writing in new situations or classes, in new genres, for new purposes and audiences, and for high-stakes events like tests or entrance exams or major course grades is never near transfer of prior writing knowledge. There are so many things to know, figure out, and bring to bear, so everything becomes potentially difficult. Sentences and paragraphs, word choice, format, appearance of text on the page, what counts as evidence, what readers will find persuasive — all of these require us to draw on and use what we know from previous experience. This is generally understood as "far transfer."

But quite often these situations do not require *only* that we simply draw on what we already know: We have to *adapt* it to the new situation, genre, purpose, audience, technology in ways that will work there. This requires us to actually "repurpose" some of what we know for the current situation. For example, if we learned to write a five-paragraph essay in high school with a main claim and at least three points of evidence to support it, that won't work "as is" for most college classrooms. We have to repurpose what we know: We know how to make a claim and support it, but we have to expand beyond five paragraphs in order to do this effectively.

ACTIVITY 1.11 | Write Reflectively

Think of a time when you had to accomplish something (written or otherwise) and you realized that you probably did know how to do this, but it was different enough from what you did before that you had to switch things up, make some changes, in order to accomplish the task.

In many of our most difficult writing and learning tasks, we are required to go beyond repurposing what we know to also *learn new things*, and then combine those new things with our existing and repurposed knowledge about writing. This kind of transfer happens with non-writing tasks all the time. If you learned to drive a car that shifts automatically, and then had to learn to drive a stick shift, you have to repurpose what you knew about driving but also learn some new skills related to shifting gears. When it comes to writing, we may know, for example, that the five-paragraph essay won't work in our history class and that we need more evidence and more pages to explain that evidence. But we don't know what it is that our history teacher thinks counts as evidence: textbooks, personal experience, lecture notes, primary source material, scholarly books, Wikipedia, TV shows? We have to read examples and listen to our teacher's instruction about this. And while we probably did learn how to cite our sources in high school, we probably did *not* learn how historians credit their sources — often through the Chicago-style "notes and bibliography" system. So we have to learn that and adapt what we already know about citation to work in this new situation.

ACTIVITY 1.12 | Write Reflectively

Think of a time when you had to do something (whether related to writing or something else) when you knew some of what you needed to know in order to accomplish it, but also had to learn new information and skills in order to fully complete the task. What was it and how did you go about doing this?

Whenever we have to transfer and repurpose prior knowledge to new and challenging situations, we can only engage in the new task successfully if we engage in what scholars David Perkins and Gavriel Salomon call "high-road transfer"; this requires not just mindlessly doing what we always do but instead reflecting on what we know and don't know, finding and analyzing examples of what is expected, asking questions, drafting and getting feedback — in other words, writing in "far" situations using high-road techniques requires a lot more time and effort on our part to be successful. And we can't expect success on the first try in a complicated and new situation. Transferring and repurposing what we know about writing, and learning new things about writing, require reflection, effort, and practice. And we already know, as we discussed above, that writing is not perfectible anyway — even if it is a kind of writing we have done many times before — *and* all writers always have more to learn. So: We can do our best to learn in new situations, but our expectations should be realistic, and in this way we can find the resources we need *and* learn not to be discouraged if our first try doesn't earn an A or convince someone of our opinion.

What can you do to become the kind of learner who effectively draws on your prior knowledge, no matter how "near" or "far" the new situation is to what you've already done? Writing researchers know a few things about this, and we share some of what they know below in order to help you become a reflective writer and thinker across varied contexts.

PRACTICING REFLECTION TO AID TRANSFER

You may have noticed that *reflection* has come up a lot in this chapter. We have suggested that understanding your ideas and reflecting on them can impact how you act. We have argued that learning to complete a new task for which you only have partially adequate prior knowledge requires some reflection and repurposing. We have also asked you to frequently stop and write reflectively about the ideas in this chapter.

Reflection and meta-awareness or metacognition are important parts of being able to write effectively across situations and time, especially when those situations are different from what you have encountered before. What is meta-awareness? It is the ability at any given time to step back, step outside yourself, and consciously think about the situation in which you find yourself. Metacognition involves thinking about your own thinking. So, instead of just doing something, meta-awareness and metacognition help you step back and assess and reflect on what is happening.

Doing this is very helpful in situations of far transfer, where you have to repurpose what you know and/or learn new things in order be able to write effectively. In these cases, just doing what you do without thinking about it can lead to frustration, failure, and generally finding that your writing strategies and knowledge have not been effective.

When you are in an unfamiliar situation or are asked to write a kind of text you don't remember writing before, there are some questions you can ask yourself in order to be reflective and meta-aware in helpful ways. For example,

What is this like and not like that I have done before? Research shows that people who can identify differences in what they are writing now and what they have written before are more likely to be able to do new writing tasks effectively.

- *What needs to be different? What examples can help me identify differences and similarities to what I have written previously?* If you recognize that the new writing task is unlike what you have written before, what do you need to do differently? Can you find some successful examples of the new kind of writing that you could examine in order to see what you need to do differently from what you have done before?

- *What else do I need to learn?* If you recognize that the new type of writing is quite different than what you have written before, what do you need to learn to complete it successfully? For example, if the citation format is completely different, what citation guide do you need? If the task requires evidence, how can you learn what kinds of evidence are credible and appropriate?

- *Am I flexible about what the writing should be like, or I am "guarding" something that I know how to do and feel unwilling to change?* Very often, students who are initially unsuccessful at writing a new genre are rigidly repeating what they have done before, and engaging in what writing scholars Anis Bawarshi and Mary Jo Reiff call "boundary guarding." Ask yourself what you need to change, and what you are unwilling to change, and why that is the case.

When you write in new situations and in new genres, it's likely you won't succeed the first time (or at least, you might not immediately do as well as you had hoped). That is completely normal, and these "failures" can be seen as opportunities for reflection that can help you write more effectively the next time. Doctors engage in what they call "Morbidity and Mortality Conferences" ("M&Ms") where, according to surgeon Atul Gawande, they talk about "mistakes, untoward events, and deaths that occurred on their watch, determine responsibility, and figure out what to do differently next time" (qtd. in Robertson et al.). Other professionals, such as air traffic controllers, similarly dedicate time to "critical incident analyses." This reflective practice can be applied to writing, since we know that all writers have more to learn and that writing is not perfectible. As scholars Liane Robertson, Kara Taczak, and Kathleen Blake Yancey tell us, "even experts can revise their models when prompted to do so." You can conduct your own critical incident analysis or M&M after you write something that doesn't succeed as you want it to. We recommend you do this with someone else — a classmate or two, your roommate, or even your teacher. Here's a technique:

- First, present information about the "case": what you were writing, for whom, under what circumstances.
- Second, explain what happened, focusing specifically on what went wrong or what "mistakes" you think you made.
- Third, take questions from your partner or group members.

- With your partner or group, consider what you might have done to see the problems sooner, and how you might have avoided them. It's always helpful to get your thoughts in writing. What did you learn? Is there anything you learned from this critical incident review that you would like to do in the future? How can you see your apparent setbacks as opportunities?

In the rest of this book, we ask you to reflect quite a lot, and in many different ways. This is because we are trying to prompt and guide you to become mindful and meta-aware, not just in this class but in your life as a writer in and beyond school. Before each reading in Chapters 4–7, you will see questions that prompt you to reflect on what you already know about and know how to do that will be relevant to the reading. After each reading, you will be asked to answer some questions about what you have read and how the reading relates to your own experiences and knowledge. There are also "Meta Moments" in each chapter that really try to prompt you to reflect on what you have read and make connections. Keep in mind that all of these prompts are meant to help you learn, transfer, repurpose, and engage effectively in new writing situations.

Sources That Informed Chapter 1

Adler-Kassner, Linda, and Elizabeth Wardle, editors. *Naming What We Know: Threshold Concepts of Writing Studies*. Utah State UP, 2015.

Bransford, John D., James W. Pellegrino, and M. Suzanne Donovan, editors. *How People Learn: Brain, Mind, Experience, and School: Expanded Edition*. National Academies P, 2000.

Elon Statement on Writing Transfer. www.elon.edu/docs/e-web/academics/teaching/ers/writing _transfer/Elon-Statement-Writing-Transfer.pdf.

Lunsford, Andrea A. "Writing Is Informed by Prior Experience." Adler-Kassner and Wardle, pp. 54–55.

Meyer, Jan H. F., and Ray Land. "Threshold Concepts and Troublesome Knowledge (2): Epistemological Considerations and a Conceptual Framework for Teaching and Learning." *Higher Education*, vol. 49, no. 3, 2005, pp. 373–88.

Perkins, David N., and Gavriel Salomon. "Transfer of Learning." *International Encyclopedia of Education*. 2nd ed., Pergamon P, 1992. pp. 2–13.

Reiff, Mary Jo, and Anis Bawarshi. "Tracing Discursive Resources: How Students Use Prior Genre Knowledge to Negotiate New Writing Contexts in First-Year Composition." *Written Communication*, vol. 28, no. 3, 2011, pp. 312–37.

Robertson, Liane, Kara Taczak, and Kathleen Blake Yancey. "Notes Toward a Theory of Prior Knowledge and Its Role in College Composers' Transfer of Knowledge and Practice." *Composition Forum*, vol. 26, Fall 2012, compositionforum.com/issue/26/prior-knowledge -transfer.php.

Yancey, Kathleen Blake. "Writers' Histories, Processes, and Identities Vary." Adler-Kassner and Wardle, pp. 52–54.

Questions for Discussion and Journaling

1. What surprised you most in this chapter? Why?

2. What confused you most? Why?

3. Did anything you read give you a sense of relief, or lead you to have an "aha moment"? Why?

4. If you were going to pick one of the threshold concepts we have talked about in this chapter and study it in depth this semester, which would it be? Why? Look ahead to the chapter where that concept is explored in detail and list a few of the reading or writing assignments there that interest you. Why?

Applying and Exploring Ideas

1. Make a list of key terms from this chapter. (Key terms appear in bold type on the first mention.) If you aren't sure you understand them, reread the explanation and/or read their definitions in the glossary. Pick three that seem especially important and write a few paragraphs about why you think they are important to you as a writer or reader.

2. What are some threshold concepts that you've encountered in other fields or subjects, such as history or biology or art or math? In other words, what is an important idea from that area that you struggled with and may have misunderstood, but needed to learn in order to progress and understand the area better? (These would be concepts you might describe as "lights coming on" moments.) Describe the concept in about a paragraph, explain why it was difficult for you, what helped you finally understand it, and why it was important for you to understand. If you can't think of a threshold concept for a school subject, maybe you can think of a threshold concept for a hobby or interest that you have outside of school (for example, are there threshold concepts of gaming, or fanfiction, or baking?).

3. Explain in your own words why and how your ideas about something (your conceptions) can impact what you do. Given some examples of where and how this is the case in your life, in or outside of school.

4. What is one bad idea or misconception about writing that you feel has harmed you in some way? Where did that idea come from? How has it affected you? How would you like to "fight back" to change this idea and its impact on your life?

Writing about Threshold Concepts

- -

Assignment Option 1

CHALLENGING AND EXPLORING YOUR CONCEPTIONS ABOUT WRITING

In this assignment, you will revisit the ideas you had before reading this chapter, consider how they have changed (or not), and pick one that you would like to explore in more detail. You will then spend some time observing and talking with people around you in order to learn more about one of these ideas about writing or writers. Then you will write about this for an audience other than yourself, attempting to help them learn a more accurate conception of writing that can positively impact how they engage with writing.

Planning, Drafting, and Revising.   Begin by jotting down your ideas about the following:

- Writing is . . .
- Good writing is . . .
- Good writers do or are . . .
- Writers are influenced by . . .
- Learning to write involves . . .

Once you have done this, pull out what you wrote about these ideas in Activity 1.1 at the beginning of this chapter. Skim them quickly to see how they are similar and different.

Next, trade your pre- and post-reading ideas with another student and ask them to help you consider ways in which your ideas have changed or remained the same. Together, make lists of how your ideas have changed (or not). Do the same for them.

Pick one of the ideas about which your thinking has changed, and go back to your notes from throughout this chapter (including answers to the activities) and see if you wrote about this idea at all. Once you have those notes fresh in your mind, free-write for about one page, exploring how and why your idea has changed and why this matters. Don't worry right now about audience or organization or "getting it right," just get some ideas on paper.

Next, spend a few days gathering examples from your daily life and experiences, as well as those of your friends, parents, teachers, or other acquaintances in order to learn more. For example, if you suggested that "good" writers are those who keep trying, plan ahead, and don't let "failure" stop them from trying again, then pick a few people you know who you think are "good" writers. Ask them how they go about writing something new and difficult. Ask if you can see some examples of drafts they have written, or if you can watch them writing, etc.

Step back and see what you have gathered, observed, and learned from your notes, reflection, discussions, and observations. What you would like to write about now? What would you like to say about writing and writers? Who would you like to say it to? Why? What might be the best form (or "genre") in which to share your ideas with that audience?

Begin drafting. Be sure to explain the idea (or "conception") about writing that interests you and why it matters that learners have an accurate conception. Explain any aspect of this idea or conception that might conflict with common misconceptions about it that your readers might have or that you commonly see in school, movies, books, etc. Give examples to show what you mean (these can be examples from your own experience, from class discussions, from the observations and interviews you did), define your terms if your audience won't be familiar with them, and quote from or paraphrase any readings you've done in class that help you draw your conclusion. (For example, if you believe that school-based notions of "good writing" are too limited and do not stand up to what research and everyday experience show us about good writing, you will need to guide readers through that line of thinking, as if they haven't done the reading and thinking you've been doing in this chapter.)

Revise your draft to more specifically make it appropriate and meaningful for your audience. Who do you want to share your ideas and examples with? Why? What do those people expect? Where do they get their information? What are they likely to read? What do those texts look like? Make some decisions about the genre that you want to write (a letter to your teacher? a letter to the editor? a blog post? a Facebook post?). For example, you might decide that you would like to share your changing and research-based ideas about good writing with your high school English teacher, because she constantly marked up your paper for grammar and ignored your ideas. How would you communicate with her? Possibly in a letter or a formal e-mail, in which case you'd need to look at examples before writing up your final draft that way.

What Makes It Good? This writing task has two primary purposes. First, to help you deeply reflect and consider your ideas about writing and how they hold up to what you are learning in this class and what you do in your daily life and school. Second, to try to make a thoughtful claim that you can support through inquiry-based examples (we will talk more about inquiry in Chapter 2, but for now just know that you have been engaging in inquiry throughout this chapter by testing your ideas against your own experiences and observations). Ensuring that what you are writing is thoughtful and supported by meaningful examples is the first priority for writing well here. You will then need to decide who you want to communicate this information with, and why. If you write appropriately for the audience and purpose you have in mind, and if you reflect and make a thoughtful and well-supported claim, you will have accomplished your goals.

- -

Assignment Option 2

WHAT IS WRITING AND HOW DOES IT WORK IN THE WORLD? A COLLAGE AND ARTIST'S STATEMENT

For this assignment you will spend about a week keeping a log of all the ways that you use writing on a daily basis. Then you will create a collage using media of your choosing that answers the questions: *what is writing and how does it work in the world?* You will write a short "artist's statement" to accompany the collage, describing your message, your artistic intent, and why you chose the media that you did. Ideally, you will then present your collage to your class.

Planning, Drafting, and Revising.   Keep a notebook for the next week — it can be a small paper notebook or on your phone or on the computer. A paper notebook or your phone might be most effective, since you want to be able to make a note immediately any time you write. In this notebook, keep a log every day for a week. Every time you use writing for any purpose, write down:

- when and where you wrote (time, date, place)
- what you wrote
- what form you wrote in (for example, lists, texts, paragraphs, etc.)
- what technologies you used (for example, phone, pen, computer, etc.)
- the reason that you wrote
- the audience(s) for whom you wrote

At the end of the week, sit down with the complete log and begin to analyze what you have recorded. Makes lists of all the reasons you wrote, all of the forms in which you wrote, all of the technologies you used for writing, and all the kinds of audiences you wrote for. Then write down any other observations you have; for example, do you tend to write more in a particular place or time?

Next, take a look at the kinds of things you wrote and ask yourself what makes them "good" or "effective."

Now spend a little time just writing freely in answer to these questions: What is writing? How does writing work? What makes writing "good"? As you write, think about your log and the notes in your log. Don't worry about getting this answer right, just write freely about what comes to mind for about 10–15 minutes.

Your next task is to create a multimodal collage, using whatever media you find appropriate and useful. A collage is a work of art composed of any variety of materials from paper to photos to various found objects; the collage can be on paper or digital. The purpose of the collage is to illustrate what you have learned this week about writing, what it is, how it works, and what makes it effective. Spend some time looking at your log and notes and free-writing. Then decide what you want your collage to say and how you would like to express these ideas. You can use paper with images and ideas cut from magazines, you can use digital objects or electronic images, you can make 3D images — the choice is entirely yours. But be sure that what you create actually illustrates the ideas you have been researching this week.

Once you have a draft of your collage, write a short artist's statement. An artist's statement explains your message and your decision-making. It should be no more than one single-spaced page, and answer these questions:

- What is the message of this collage?
- Why did you use the materials that you used?
- How did you come to the ideas and conclusions in this collage?
- What do you want viewers to understand differently after viewing your collage?

When you turn in your work for peer review and evaluation, you should include the week's writing log, your analysis of the log, the collage, and the artist's statement.

What Makes It Good? This collage is an alternative to a traditional "paper." It asks you to share your research findings about writing using media beyond traditional alphabetic text. It is effective if the collage clearly reflects and shares what you learned during the week that you logged your writing practices, and if your choices in creating the collage are deliberate and thoughtfully explained. The final goal of this assignment is to change viewers' ideas about writing, and to prompt them to think and ask questions about how writing works in their lives. In other words, the goal is for both you and the viewers of your collage to engage deeply with threshold concepts about writing.

READERS, WRITERS, AND TEXTS
Understanding Genre and Rhetorical Reading

Two tourists study a Paris Metro map to better understand how to navigate the city. In this chapter, you'll learn how genres of writing serve as maps to new situations and communities.

Researchers have come to understand the threshold concepts introduced in the preceding chapter as a result of investigations into writing. In this chapter, we will dig into the idea of research as conversational inquiry — a process of participating in the scholarly discussion about a subject by seeking answers to open questions. We'll examine how to use conversational inquiry to seek answers to questions about writing. By studying how **genres** work, we will describe how texts are used in conversational inquiry, and finally, how readers make their own meaning of the texts they read and respond to through the process of rhetorical reading.

Reading and Writing for Conversational Inquiry

Most people are used to thinking of reading and writing as ways to convey *information*, things that some people already know and other people need or want to know. Reading and writing are also ways of being *entertained*, like when we read or write stories like *Harry Potter*. This chapter introduces another way of reading and writing: reading and writing to collaborate with others to seek answers to questions *nobody* knows the answers to yet — How can we prevent or cure breast cancer?

What are the effects of poverty on child development? Why do certain kinds of voters favor certain kinds of candidates? Where does language comes from and how does the brain process it?

Seeking answers to these kinds of questions entails participating in conversational inquiry, a kind of research that brings people together to talk, question, and cooperatively argue in order to better understand problems or questions that are not yet understood. Research often means *gathering existing information*: finding a lot of library books or web pages that have the information we need, and quoting or paraphrasing from them to pass on that existing knowledge to a teacher or a boss. That's not what we mean here. Nor do we mean the research you might have done or seen in high school speech and debate — collecting facts and statements of opinion in support of a one-sided argument for a particular policy. That's not a collaborative questioning and exploration of unknowns.

Conversational inquiry is mostly done through reading and writing, but in a more active and questioning way than you may have done research in the past. With conversational inquiry, the goal is to make new knowledge, rather than simply reporting on information you've gathered from a library or web search. By thinking about reading and writing as inquiry, you'll be better able to make sense of the *researched* story of writing discussed in this course, and to participate in all of your courses differently than you may have previously.

How does conversational inquiry work? We'll start with the example of how the threshold concepts informing this book were arrived at through conversational inquiry. In 2012, writing researchers Linda Adler-Kassner and Elizabeth Wardle (one of this book's co-authors) noticed that, while Writing Studies had been researching how writing, writers, and discourse work for over 50 years, the people working in this field of study had not yet tried to summarize what it had learned in that time. In other areas of study, this kind of synthesis and summary of research is quite common; there are many individual studies of heart valve replacements or water supply pollutants, for example, and researchers in those fields commonly pull all of them together to see what the larger, cumulative picture shows. At the same time, Wardle and Adler-Kassner had encountered a recent idea (or "theoretical frame") for explaining how people learn, called threshold concepts (see Chapter 1). What would happen, they wondered, if they asked writing scholars to draw together ideas we had come to believe about writing, beliefs that come from research (conversational inquiry) across many years, that function as threshold concepts — ideas that change the way people think about and engage in writing. This is a research problem or **research question**: Adler-Kassner and Wardle had identified an open question, so far unanswered, which left a gap (or niche) in the field's knowledge. The question was, "What are some core things we know from research about writing that impact how writers work and think?"

ACTIVITY 2.1 | Write Reflectively

List a few areas of study ("fields of inquiry") you're aware of — these might be subjects you studied in high school, or subjects of your college classes, or potential majors. For each area you list, try to then write some open questions the field might have. For example, if you were to list "Psychology," you might list "how does memory work?" or "why do people dream?" You don't need to be certain that the questions are actually unanswered by the field — just go with what seem like reasonable questions to you.

In conversational inquiry, once you have a research question, the next step is figuring out how to answer it. Remember, conversational inquiry is asking questions that other people haven't already answered, so you can't just look up the answers online. You have to do some kind of "primary" (original, first-hand) research to make new knowledge about the question. Researchers call ways of doing primary research methods.

Adler-Kassner and Wardle decided to try to answer the question using a method of *collaborative conversation*. (If you've ever seen a *focus group*, that would be much smaller but similar in spirit.) They emailed 45 other writing teachers (one of whom was Doug Downs, a co-author of this textbook); 29 of them responded with 51 suggestions for threshold concepts (TCs) in Writing Studies. They then made 139 comments on those suggestions. This work took place almost entirely via reading and writing, using a wiki (Wikipedia is an example of a wiki, which lets multiple writers contribute to and edit webpages, keeps a record of their edits, and creates separate discussion pages on the page being edited). As project leaders, Adler-Kassner and Wardle set up and directed the conversation, summarizing at appropriate points, joining up particular contributors to the conversation as co-authors on a given TC, and keeping track as the group discussed, added, shifted, combined, and deleted ideas. Finally, the group arrived at 37 threshold concepts about writing, organized under an overarching "meta"-concept plus 5 main TCs Adler-Kassner and Wardle identified from the conversation. The contributors then each wrote 500-word definitions of each TC, again editing each other's contributions in conversation.

The process of arriving at threshold concepts about writing illustrates some key points about conversational inquiry:

1. These researchers did not work alone. They used writing and reading to *create an ongoing conversation*, a discussion in which participants shaped each other's thinking.

2. Though this conversation drew on existing knowledge, its purpose wasn't just to retransmit that knowledge, but rather to *make new knowledge*.

3. To make new knowledge, this conversation used a kind of argument. Not the kind of argument you'd have with a sibling about whose turn it is to take out the trash,

or the kind two drivers would have after colliding at an intersection, or the kind political commentators with opposing views would have. Those kinds of arguments assert a fixed position in order to win — "you hit me and thus you are at fault," or "I took out the trash last week and now it is your turn." The kind of argument the researchers used was *consensus-seeking argument*, figuring things out together, rather than one person winning while others lose. Consensus-seeking argument is not the kind of argument we typically see on the news or in our daily lives.

4. While researchers based their argument on existing knowledge, they were not simply exchanging facts, they were *interpreting data and experience*. They were trying to develop informed, shared opinions about how to interpret and best express various observations and ideas.

5. They were asking genuinely *open questions without already knowing the answer*. No one knew in advance what those answers would be. This is what we mean by the term *inquiry*. It is a genuine *wondering* and *openness* to learning and creating new knowledge, to being surprised, and to having your expectations upended.

6. The *researchers treated possible answers as imperfect, incomplete, provisional (uncertain), revisable, and iterative*: they were open to suggesting answers that might prove to be wrong or not the best. They were open to having different answers offered in place of their own, and having this happen over and over until participants concluded that the best answers had been found. The point of such research is to propose a lot of possible answers to the same question, using conversation to settle on the best answer. In fact, even in the resulting book, *Naming What We Know*, Adler-Kassner and Wardle point out that the ideas conveyed in the book might and likely will change as we continue to learn more about writing.

In this chapter, we want to emphasize that reading and writing are central to conversational inquiry, and demonstrate how the reading and writing used to carry out conversational inquiry differ from other kinds of reading and writing. The first step is to understand the activity that scholarly researchers, including your own professors and fellow students, are engaged in: collaboratively seeking out new and provisional answers to open questions, arguing to build consensus about the best of many possible answers, creating new knowledge that adds to our understanding of whatever phenomenon is in question, in any field you might choose to study in college.

ACTIVITY 2.2 | Try Thinking Differently

How does the kind of research we've described here — "conversational inquiry" — differ from your own experience with research so far? Are there ways it resembles your experience? Compared with how you usually do research projects or papers that your teacher assigns, what would you have to change about how you write research papers in order to participate in the conversational-inquiry kind of research?

Genres and How Writers and Readers Depend on Them

Conversational inquiry happens through writing and reading; in order to engage in it yourself, you need to draw on and work with a variety of kinds of texts, some of which will be new to you. It will be easier for you to understand and learn new kinds of writing, including where they come from and how they're working, if you understand them as genres: recognizable forms of writing that respond to repeating situations. When you begin to engage in conversational inquiry, you will also engage with some new genres. In this section, we will first explain what genres are, and then show how they function to forward conversational inquiry.

WHAT GENRES ARE

Throughout life, you'll regularly encounter types of readings and texts new to you as you encounter new situations and groups of people who use writing in different ways to accomplish their goals. Sometimes this can be fun (learning a new social media app), sometimes it can be frustrating (reading a play from four centuries ago), and sometimes it can seem easy but then turn out to be difficult (as with resumes and cover letters).

Types of texts have recognizable names because they are kinds of writing that recur, happening over and over because they facilitate regularly occurring functions in life. Resumes, wedding invitations, birthday cards, parking tickets, textbooks, novels, text messages, magazine cover stories, eulogies, Instagram posts, feasibility reports, lyrics — these are all kinds of writing that help us participate in constantly recurring events. If a particular writing situation happens repeatedly, prompting writers to need to respond again and again (for example, the need to apply for a job), then certain kinds of writing come into existence to respond to that recurring situation (like resumes). These recurring text-types are genres, what scholar Carolyn Miller describes as typified rhetorical actions in response to recurrent situations or situation-types. *Typified* here means (and sounds) something like "typical" — the situation creates a habitual response (a recognizable text, a genre). Weddings keep happening and guests need to be invited, so a typical rhetorical action related to weddings evolved into what we understand as the genre of wedding invitations.

Genres help you tremendously as a writer. Consider this situation: People have to apply for jobs all the time, and they have a pretty good idea of how to do this through resumes and cover letters because so many other people before them have done the same thing. But what if there was no agreed-upon way for people to apply for jobs? What if no conventions for doing that had ever come into being? You as a job seeker would have no idea what you should do when you want a job;

actually, much worse, every single option would be open to you. You could sing a song, write a haiku, send a carrier pigeon, make a painting . . . really, you could do anything, and you'd have no way to know what option was best. It would take a long time to respond to the situation. This wouldn't be efficient, and it would be very stressful for you as a writer. And it would be at least as bad for the person trying to review job applications. They probably wouldn't know what do with a carrier pigeon.

So genres emerge because writers start to find ways to respond to the recurring situation that seem to work pretty well, and other writers keep using them and tweaking them. Because job seekers found that listing all their previous jobs on a piece of paper was helpful to potential employers, people kept doing it. There are a lot of ways to make a resume (check out the range of templates in your word-processing software), but there are some constraints that at least make it easier for you as a resume writer to know that you could, for example, organize by date or organize by skill, but not organize as haiku. Genres give you a limited area to aim for so that you have a better chance of success.

There are a lot of reasons to think about this phenomenon of genre — that writers over time create "typical" or expected responses to situations that come up over and over. Understanding genre helps you look for patterns when you encounter new situations and new kinds of texts. The genre might look strange and new to you, but if it's a typical or expected response to a recurring situation, it means you can find out what the recurring situation is and what previous responses have looked like.

When you encounter a new genre, you should try to discern the similarities in the situations calling for the genre you are encountering, and various versions of the genre constructed in response to them. According to Sonja Foss, there are four kinds of questions to ask when looking at a new or unfamiliar genre:

- *Questions about situational elements*: What conditions (situations) call for the genre? What prompts this sort of document to be written? What is the need or reason for a given action or communication?
- *Questions about substantive characteristics (content)*: What sort of content (substance) is typically contained in this genre? What do these texts tend to talk about or say?
- *Questions about stylistic characteristics (form)*: What form does this sort of genre take? What does it look like? How is it organized? What language does it use? What tone does it take?
- *Questions about the organizing principle*: What makes this genre what it is? What are the common denominators of the genre? What makes a resume a resume, for example? Of each characteristic that you identify in the first three questions above, you might ask, "If I took out this characteristic, would it still be recognizable as this genre?"

ACTIVITY 2.3 | Write Reflectively

Gather the syllabi that you've collected from your different classes during the first week or two of school this year. Look at them all and then answer these questions:

- What situation calls for a syllabus to be written?
- What content is typically contained in a syllabus?
- What does a syllabus look like; what shape does it take?
- How is a syllabus organized?
- What tone is used? Is the language formal or informal?

You'll notice that although syllabi are similar, they can be very different, too. Note some ways your syllabi differ from one another, and then consider the common denominators — what makes a syllabus a syllabus, even though individually they differ?

GENRES AS FLEXIBLE MAPS

When you encounter new writing situations and contexts, genres ensure that you aren't completely on your own in a strange world. Genres are helpful but flexible guides for understanding and approaching new writing situations. They provide maps, if you know to look for them and can figure out how to read them.

Think for a minute about the idea of genres as maps to new situations. For maps to work, you have to ask certain questions. Where am I and where do I want to go? If you don't know these things, you'll find yourself looking at a map of the entire world that is simply not helpful in your current situation. If you know that you are in Orlando and you want to go to Key West, then you know that there are maps for this situation. You'll want a map of Florida, particularly southeast Florida. But you also need to know what to look for on the map and what the various symbols mean. You'll need to know how to read this map. You'll need to know north from south, east from west, highways from back roads, toll roads from free roads. When you first start driving, you might end up getting lost a few times before you can make sense of the map.

The other thing to remember about maps is that they change — for all sorts of reasons, including technology. You might never have used a paper map before, since today's maps are on smartphones. You might never have had to look at a paper map and its key to figure out what you are seeing, because your smartphone does this for you. Maps change, and people have to figure out how to read new kinds of maps. Ask your parents or grandparents whether they find it easier to read paper maps or maps on their smartphones, and you'll see that what seems easy to you is not easy or obvious to everyone else. What's on the maps changes across time (as roads have been paved, as federal highways have been created) and for different purposes (sailors use completely different maps than vacationers, and both sailors and vacationers use maps that are completely different from those used by forest rangers).

Because maps (like genres), are changeable, they aren't entirely reliable. Relying on maps and cell-phone navigation systems without thinking for yourself (being able to tell what direction you're going, noticing when your mapping system is unwittingly telling you to drive into a lake) can leave you stranded and lost. Genres are the same way. They are maps, but not maps that you should rely on rigidly without thinking for yourself about what to do in any writing situation. Genres, just like maps, are extremely helpful if you know how to read them and remember that they change across time and for different purposes. But like maps, they aren't rigid and formulaic. You can always do something different with writing, just like you can choose a different kind of map, or a different route on your map: "Rules of a genre do not specify precisely how a rhetorical act is to be performed. A genre is not formulaic; there is always another strategy that a rhetor can use to meet the requirements of the situation. But a genre establishes bounded options for rhetors in situations" (Foss, 231).

ACTIVITY 2.4 | Try Thinking Differently

Many students have been taught the genre of the Five-Paragraph Essay as a rigid formula for how to write an essay for school. It has an intro, three body paragraphs, and a conclusion, and most students have received instructions (not always identical) about how many sentences each paragraph should have and what each should do. In a "Schaeffer" paragraph, for instance, you would use five sentences: topic, concrete detail, commentary, commentary, and closing / transition. We would suggest that this rigid formula is a misuse of a genre "map."

Consider whether you've been taught a specific formula for writing essays, and if so, try actively changing the formula, moving from a (false) universal "rule" about what the essay must contain to a more genre-like "map" that uses guidelines that can be modified to fit specific circumstances. For example, if you were taught a rule about where the "thesis statement" must go in an essay, think about how you could change that rule if you knew it didn't always apply. What guideline could you create if you wanted to be able to put the thesis statement someplace else, or replace it with a focusing question? What's your rule, how would you change it, and why?

SETS AND SYSTEMS: HOW GENRES CIRCULATE AND RESPOND TO OTHER GENRES

We can apply the principles of genre described in the preceding section to understanding the kinds of writing you'll encounter and use while participating in conversational inquiry about writing, in order to help you use and make sense of them. In order to do this, it first helps to think about how genres circulate in the world and respond to other genres.

Genres that support any given activity — finding a job, getting married, conducting conversational inquiry — don't usually occur in isolation. Rather, groups of genres that support an activity begin working together as an entire "ecosystem" of individual genres interacting, feeding into, and relying on one another. Groups of people, like tax attorneys, might use a particular genre set to get their daily work done; that is, they write one kind of genre (maybe an application for tax relief) in response to another type of genre (maybe a penalty letter from the IRS). Then, they interact regularly with other attorneys, as well as clients, accountants, and IRS agents through a variety of genres that make up a **genre system**. Writing scholar Amy Devitt describes these genre systems as "sets of genres interacting to achieve an overarching function within an activity system" (57). When you are thinking about genre systems, it's useful to start with a group of people and their shared goals: accountants or teachers or sorority members. These people and the work they do together constitute activity systems (groups of people working together to achieve a common goal) — doing taxes, educating students, engaging in community service, etc.

When scholars or researchers or other professionals set out to answer questions or solve problems or achieve shared goals, they engage with many genre sets and participate in many genre systems. Take an example from writing scholar Charles Bazerman: he "traces the system of interrelated genres that connect patent applications to patent grants, including the application, letters of correspondence, various forms, appeals, and potential court rulings, as well as the patent grant. The patent grant subsequently connects to other genre systems, such as funding corporations, and so on" (summarized in Bawarshi and Reiff, 88). In this case, if a person or company wants to acquire a patent, there is a system of genres that enables them to engage with others, demonstrate what they have done, and achieve the goal. Another scholar, Anthony Paré, has traced the genre sets used by hospital social workers: referral forms, initial assessments, ongoing assessments (progress reports), and closing / transfer reports (summarized in Bawarshi and Reiff, 88). The social workers are participating in a larger genre system in the hospital activity system. That hospital includes genre sets that are produced by doctors, nurses, radiologists, the billing office, etc. Together all of these create the genre system of the hospital.

The genres you will write and read as you engage in conversational inquiry in college will make more sense if you more fully understand the larger genre sets and systems in which they participate. You'll have an easier time understanding the "primary" genres of conversational inquiry, like journal articles and book chapters, if you know more about the genre systems those individual genres participate in, emerge from, and lead to. Books and journal articles that share research don't just spring out of nothingness. They are written by people working in discourse communities or activity systems (discussed further in Chapter 7) after scholars have *already* engaged in extensive conversational inquiry that is enabled by genre sets or systems that may be invisible to you as a reader.

For example, imagine a kinesiology researcher, Dr. Smith, who spends a lot of time in his lab looking at how and why older adults lose their balance, and whether chiropractic intervention can help them. He needs funding to do this research, because the equipment he uses is expensive. Thus, he writes grant proposals (one genre) in response to requests for proposals (RFPs) (another genre) from organizations like the National Institutes of Health. He may receive an award letter (a third genre). He writes regular reports to that funding agency to let them know he is using the money as he promised (a fourth genre). All together, this constitutes one *genre set* that is part of the larger *overall genre system* in which he is working.

Once Dr. Smith thinks he has some useful results, he wants to share them with other researchers working on the same research question, or similar ones. He might first do that at a conference with other professionals in his field, maybe the International Society of Electrophysiology & Kinesiology or the Association of Chiropractic Colleges Research Agenda Conference (ACC-RAC). The conference organizers put out a call for proposals (CFP) (one genre) and he responds with a conference proposal (another genre). If he receives an acceptance (a third genre), he travels to the conference and presents his work as a talk to a live audience (a fourth genre). The audience then asks him questions and provides feedback in a post-session question and answer session (a fifth genre). This conference and its texts represents a second genre set.

Sometimes, the conference organizers will ask attendees to submit possible papers for a book that represents the conference "proceedings," which they would do through a call for proposals (CFP) (one genre). Dr. Smith submits a draft paper to the editors of that conference proceedings book, which requires revising his conference presentation (another genre). The editors, if they accept the paper, will provide extensive feedback and notes about required revisions he needs to make (a third genre). If the paper is accepted with revisions, then it is included in the book (the end result of this genre set, and one of the most public genres of the entire system in which he is participating). Dr. Smith's students might end up reading his chapter as part of their coursework with him in the kinesiology program.

Together, these genre sets (lab funding, conference presenting, and edited conference proceedings) and many others make up a genre system in which the scholar is participating in order to engage in conversational inquiry with other scholars, journal and book editors, and even his students (see Figure 2.1).

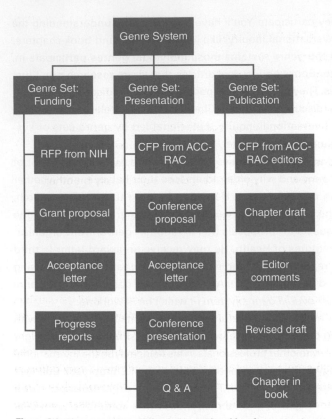

Figure 2.1 Genre system enabling conversational inquiry

Much of what you will read in Chapters 4–7 of this book was originally published as journal articles or book chapters, which report on research about writing. These are all "turns" in a larger conversation about writing in which the authors are participating (we will explore this idea further in Chapter 3). The conversations can take a long time, and many parts of them might be invisible to you. Just imagine if you were Dr. Smith's student, reading his chapter in class. Nearly every other genre in that system in which he participated on the road to publishing that chapter would be invisible to you.

We want you to keep in mind that the research articles and book chapters you will read (including later in this book) don't exist in a vacuum. They are parts of larger conversations in which scholars are inquiring about questions and problems that interest them. They generally have particular and consistent features that you can learn to recognize, because that is the nature of genres and how they respond to recurring situations. While those features may change, there are some consistent "moves" that scholarly texts tend to make, that you can look for as you engage with them.

ACTIVITY 2.5 | Write Reflectively

Consider a group (activity system) you regularly participate in where you can easily remember the genres that help facilitate conversation among members and participants. List three or four of the genre sets you engage in there. For example, if you are part of an activity system of fans who write fanfiction, think of genres that prompt you to write, genres in which others respond to you, forums for discussion, etc. Once you have a list, consider: How do the genres relate to each other and prompt additional genres in response? How does a genre rely on other genres? Who writes the various genres?

FEATURES OF THE SCHOLARLY RESEARCH ARTICLE GENRE

Journal articles are one genre of conversational inquiry that has a well-established genre map. One typical pattern of an article's parts is Introduction, Methods, Results, and Discussion (often called an IMRaD pattern). IMRaD research articles are very functional: They don't include unnecessary parts, because researchers have to read so many of them. (Though scholars in different fields of study have very different ideas about what these parts might look like and contain, and how long they might be). The introduction, which we'll discuss more in Chapter 3, is necessary because it tells readers what the piece will talk about and how it fits with previous conversational inquiry. The methods talk about how the researchers actually did their research. The results explain what data those methods resulted in, and the discussion talks about what the results *mean*. Such an article will conclude by summarizing the study's findings (the conclusions summed up from the results and discussion) and considering their implications for the ongoing conversation: If our research has found X, where then should the conversation go from here?

You'll encounter other organizational patterns in journal articles — older articles, especially, might not even have sections at all, but be a straight-through discussion. Some articles will include sections in or after the introduction like "Background" or "Review of Literature" that expand these functions of the introduction. Of course, not all articles you will read in different classes will be IMRaD articles. In philosophy, for example, articles do not take this form. However, they are still participating in conversational inquiry and often make similar "moves," such as setting up the importance of the question the author wants to address.

If there are headings in an article, skimming those can help you understand how the article is working. You can read all the headings before trying to read what's in each section; that way, you'll have your own map of where the article is going, which will help you not to get lost in it.

Rhetorical Reading: The Reader's Role in Conversational Inquiry

All these genres of conversational inquiry are written in order to be *read* by those people who will use them in the cycle of scholarly conversation. So to think about the nature of inquiry, we have to look not just at writing but at reading as well.

TWO STORIES ABOUT READING

Just as we can identify at least two notably different stories about writing (see Chapter 1), there are significantly divergent ways of imagining reading. One "story" of reading, which we expect you will be very familiar with, is that a text has a single fixed meaning, acting as a repository of information and making reading an act of pulling that information off the page. This *informational* view of reading tends to put readers in an accepting, "just tell me" position toward the text, which must always be "right" if it is made of facts and can mean only one thing. Further, if the text is simply information, it shouldn't matter who wrote it (factual information should be the same no matter who says it) and there shouldn't be any disagreement about what a text is saying.

The other story — the research-based story — is that texts are not disembodied vaults of factual information, but rather the opinions, perspectives, and voices of their writers — that *texts are people talking.* This matters because you wouldn't think to ask "who's talking" if you think it makes no difference — if a text is just undeniable fact. But if texts are people talking, then the sense you make of a text will depend in part on your sense of who is speaking, and *why* (what their motives are), and *from what perspective* they're speaking (no one is neutral). In reality, readers do not simply pull information off a page. Instead they **construct** or create meaning by reading — they *make* sense of texts. Readers do so by blending the words they encounter on the page with what they already know or think; they also use their understanding of the contexts in which the text was originally written and in which they're reading it, and their knowledge of who's talking in the text, and why they created the text to begin with. Because of these elements beyond the text that contribute to meaning, some of which only an individual reader can contribute, texts can and do mean different things to different readers; there is no "literal" meaning inherently fixed in the text. *People* are where the meaning in texts comes from — not from texts themselves.

How do we know that a fixed meaning isn't "in" written texts? Just as is the case with writing, reading is something people not only do, but study. Studying the biology of reading is pretty fascinating. For example, when we track readers' eyes moving across the page they're reading, we discover that fluent readers don't actually read word by word. They treat texts like parkour experts treat buildings, covering ground (encountering sentences) in big leaps (reading whole phrases or lines at a time) and using their momentum (fast reading) to glide over sketchy areas where the footing isn't good (where the meaning isn't immediately clear). Research also shows that readers fill in missing information in texts on their own. (If yo'v ncon- terd mems shwig ow ou an ead entnces evn wtih wrdos misng o tarsnposgn mny ltetrs, yu'voe sene hs fritshnd.) These are all evidence that readers don't simply take existing meaning *out of* a text, but make up meaning even when it's not there. If we didn't, we would all be reading like first-graders: one. word. at. a. time.

This is one example of how readers construct meaning from texts. But there are many other ways that texts don't "mean" on their own — that outside informa- tion, or knowledge readers bring *to* a text, will shape the meaning readers make of it. One term that helps us remember the actual nature of reading as construct- ing meaning rather than just absorbing information is *rhetorical reading*. The term *rhetorical* relates to *communication* — the ways that people interact, make up their minds, and change their minds. We want you to begin thinking of texts as *other people talking*, and to see yourself as a reader *interacting* with those people to make (construct) meaning.

ACTIVITY 2.6 | Write Reflectively

List one or two times recently when you have read something (it doesn't have to be for school) and you actually considered who the writer was. What were you reading, and what genre was it an example of? Why was the author important — why did you know about them, or try to find out about them? And what kinds of things do you wind up knowing about them? Next, list one or two times recently when you read something without paying attention to the author at all. What were you reading? Why did it seem less important, for these texts, to know who's speaking? What difference would it make to how you interpret or make meaning of the text to know who is talking and something about them, and what would be helpful to know?

ELEMENTS OF RHETORICAL READING

A rhetorical perspective on reading (or a rhetorical *way* of reading) emphasizes readers' and writers' *motives*, the *need* shared by readers and writers which called for the text to begin with, the specific *contexts* and moments in which the text was written and is read, and the *values and expectations* that readers bring to the text. These four elements shape the meaning a reader constructs from a text — which will be true of each text you read in this book. (You can learn more about rhetori- cal reading in Christina Haas and Linda Flower's "Rhetorical Reading Strategies" in Chapter 7, page 432.)

Writers and Readers Have Motives

It's easy for us to recognize people's motives during conversation, when we can see their faces or hear their tone of voice and the way they speak. When people write and read instead of speaking face to face, it's not as easy to tell, but they still have motives. Texts say what they say because their writers are **motivated** by a variety of purposes. If you've written a resume, you already know this: Your choices in what to include and how to design and edit the resume are motivated by your desire to impress a potential employer in order to get the job. So we say the resume is a "motivated" text. In fact, *every* nonfiction text you can think of is motivated. Readers can construct one meaning of a text if they're unaware of its writer's motives, and a wiser meaning when they know those motives. Imagine writing to a parent seeking money: their response may differ if they think your motive is partying versus if it's spending less time at work so you can study more. Notice too in this example how *readers* have motives: Your parents are probably motivated to see you do well in college and finish quickly. If they had different motives (like never ever wanting to see you lack for anything your heart desired), they would have different responses to *your* motives as a writer. Readers construct different interpretations of discourse if they ascribe different motivations to it. Does "It's cold in here!" mean the speaker is complaining, or asking for the heat to be turned up? Whether you think it means one, the other, or both will depend heavily on what you think motivates the statement to begin with. Motives are the first reason why a text is never "just the facts" — someone had a motive for telling you those facts to begin with.

When you are reading others' work in order to learn more about a question that interests you, make sure that you know, or take steps to learn, who wrote it, and what might have motivated them. It's often as simple as a quick web search of the author's name (you can learn a lot just by seeing what else they've written) and of the subject under discussion.

Texts Are Called into Being by a Need Shared between Writers and Readers

The next important concept for reading rhetorically (and one which Keith Grant-Davie's piece in Chapter 6 explains further) is **exigence**, the need or reason for a given act of communication. In conversational inquiry, the exigence for a text is usually that there's something we don't know and need to, and writing and reading the text will help more people fill in that missing knowledge. (For more on this idea, see Chapter 3, especially John Swales' "Create A Research Space" or CARS model of research articles, page 62.)

Consider, for example, the exigence for a Wikipedia article on "spaceflight": (1) spaceflight is a concept in need of explaining to a set of readers who are curious about it or need to know about it; (2) Wikipedia tries to be a thorough and complete source of explanations of concepts; so (3) Wikipedia needs an article on spaceflight. The rhetorical situation (a moment which calls for some kind of human interaction through language) in which people use Wikipedia to gain a quick understanding of a huge range of subjects "calls" the spaceflight article into being.

Exigence is distinct from a writer's motives, though exigence and motives can overlap. In this example, the motives of the writer of the spaceflight article might be (1) to show what the writer knows about spaceflight, (2) to write a really nicely done article on spaceflight, and (3) to make Wikipedia more complete. There are interesting gaps between the way the situation calls the article into being and the writer's motives for "answering" that call.

When you are reading a text on a question that interests you, seek out its exigence by asking: Why did this text need to be written? What problem or need would remain unfulfilled if it did not exist? What activities, knowledge-making, or conversations is it allowing to happen that could not happen without it? Why are we talking about this? Because texts don't write themselves, there will always be a reason for a text to exist, even if at first it's not clear. For example, during a campaign season when your TV channels are clogged with political ads, perhaps you notice one that says "Tell Senator Jiminy Cricket to vote against big polluters in our backyard!" The *exigence* of the ad is whatever answers the question, "Why are we talking about this?" and "Why does this text exist?" With further digging, you might discover that Senator Cricket is the swing vote on whether nuclear waste can be stored in your state. Storage of nuclear waste in your state, the coming vote, and voters' ability to pressure their representatives on how to vote are all parts of the exigence for the ad.

Just as when you have a sense of the writer's motives in creating the text, when you consider the exigence of the text you'll construct a different and fuller meaning of it.

Context Shapes How Readers Construct a Text's Meaning

Context refers to the circumstances surrounding a text's exigence, including where a text comes from and where it appears. Context can include other texts that the text is responding to, as well as the cultural and historical situation that gives rise to the text. In order for the reader's constructed meaning to reflect the writer's intended meaning, a reader has to be aware of the context the writer wrote in and any differences between it and the context in which the reader is encountering the text. These might be quite different. It is extremely difficult, for example, for a modern reader to make meanings of Harriet Beecher Stowe's *Uncle Tom's Cabin* or Harper Lee's *To Kill a Mockingbird* anything like readers of those text in the years they were actually published (1852 and 1960, respectively) because our contexts as readers now are so different, and because we are so far from the original contexts that they are very hard to comprehend. Context includes *things we take for granted*. Most readers today take for granted that people of all ethnicities in all parts of the United States can eat together and use the same hotels, theaters, bathrooms, swimming pools, and transportation. The first readers of Lee's book, in many parts of the country, took for granted the exact opposite. The first readers of Stowe's book wouldn't even have imagined people of color *using* hotels or pools or theaters.

The web of assumptions we gain from context contributes to the meaning we make of a text, which is why *the meaning we construct of texts depends in part on their contexts*. In the same way that the utterance "It's really cold in here" means "Please turn up the heat" in one context (a physically cold room where people have access to climate controls), "I wish we could turn up the heat" in another context (same room, but no access to climate controls), and "Wow, the people in this room really don't like each other!" in a third context (where the room is not cold at all but people are visibly "chilly" toward one another or have a public history of disliking one another), a text's context shapes the meaning we make of it.

Put in terms of conversational inquiry: Context shapes what the conversation means, and how the conversation happens. The context of a research article includes all the research on that subject that has preceded it. It also includes the scene and setting in which the current research takes place. For example, if you were researching public opinion about student writing ability, you would probably encounter news articles from the 1970s on "Why Johnny Can't Write," and articles from the present day raising concerns that texting and other social media are weakening student writing ability. The same conversation has continued even as its context has changed radically over the past forty years. As a participant in conversational inquiry, you have to be highly sensitive to contextual elements that are influencing the sense you make of texts. Much of inquiry is about trying to decide which parts of the conversation you agree and disagree with. Misunderstanding context, and thus the text itself, may lead you to think a writer is saying something they aren't, or to become confused about why a writer is making a given argument. A good way to make sure you're being sensitive to context is to actively ask yourself, "what am I assuming to be true of the time and place in which this text was written, relating to what the writer is talking about, and is my sense of that context accurate?"

Readers Bring Their Own Needs, Values, and Expectations to Texts

Readers of conversational inquiry, resumes, Wikipedia, or other genres meet those texts with at least four kinds of knowledge or ideas already formed. The first is simply the experiential background knowledge a given reader has of the world as a whole and of how texts and reading work. Circles are round, trees grow upward, there's no air in space, etc. And as with writing, your current practices and expectations of reading are shaped by your past reading experiences. If you are used to a particular genre being dull and loathsome, you will expect another example of that genre to keep being so — and your mind will make it so.

The other three kinds of knowledge readers bring to texts are much more specific to the interaction or conversation they and the text are taking part in:

- The reader has a particular need related to that text. They use a resume to screen job candidates, so they need the resume to convey a particular range of information in order to use the document. (You will remember that the rhetorical element of *exigence* is also about the needs for a text that readers and writers have in a given rhetorical situation. Thinking about an individual reader's needs is another way to understand the exigence in a situation and how particular readers fit into the situation.)
- The reader has specific sets of values — some readers, for example, might value conciseness while others might value depth of information. These values are, put most simply, what a reader thinks will make a given text good or not good. In conversational inquiry, some of the reader's values will concern how well the inquiry has been done, some will concern how well the writer has described that inquiry.
- The reader has specific expectations for what the text will do and be, many of which are genre-based. A research article should look like a research article, a resume should look like a resume, a Wikipedia article should work like a Wikipedia article. Some other reader expectations come with a given situation and context. If you're reading a Wikipedia article on spaceflight in 2019, you expect it to talk about not just the 1960s NASA moonflight program, but about current private endeavors like SpaceX and SpaceShipTwo.

Readers' needs, values, and expectations in a given situation or rhetorical activity are fairly stable and predictable. Readers of resumes will always value neatness and attention to detail, for example, and they'll always need to know what order you held previous jobs in, and for how long. The stability of readers' needs, values, and expectations helps establish genres, given that genres are typified responses to repeating situations. What this means for you as a reader of the pieces of conversational inquiry in this book is that you can better understand why a text does what it does if you take stock of what readers seem to need, value, and expect in the genre you're reading. Readers of research articles *need* to see, for example, clear description of how the research was actually conducted and what methods a writer used to address their research question. Knowing this, you should *expect* to find a clear description of those methods in what you're reading. And part of how much you *value* the article will depend on how well those methods are described. As you read for conversational inquiry, you'll learn what other needs, values, and expectations readers should have of genres that do such work.

ACTIVITY 2.7 | Try Thinking Differently

Most of us, in our everyday approaches to reading, assume that meaning "lives in" the text we're reading, and that we just "absorb" or "extract" or "see" the meaning that's there. When you read, try thinking instead that you're making the meaning of the text, building it from the ground up. To help you see from this perspective, ask these questions of what you're reading:

- Who is the writer of this text? What are the writer's motives for writing it?
- How does this text emerge from some "need" in the situation shared between you as the reader and the text's writer?
- What needs, values, and expectations do you bring to the text you're reading?
- How is context — the situation in which the text is written and that in which it will be read, its history, and your history as a reader — shaping the meaning you build from the text?
- How can this text be understood as a "turn" in a conversation? Can you see yourself as talking with, interacting with, its writer?

At this point, we expect you have a lot of new ideas about how "research" works — more inquiry, more conversation, more fact-making; less information, less objectivity, less regurgitating known facts. And you'll have some new ways of understanding how writing and reading work in research — the role and value of genres, and the importance of reading rhetorically rather than informationally. Probably you have more ideas than you can really keep track of right now. As you make your way through your writing class and Part 2 of this book, you'll be encountering each of these ideas repeatedly, and they'll begin to make more sense and fit together more fully. Keep them actively in mind as you continue reading and participating in conversational inquiry about writing, discourse, and literacy.

Sources That Informed Chapter 2

Bawarshi, Anis, and Mary Jo Reiff. *Genre: An Introduction to History, Theory, Research, and Pedagogy.* Parlor Press and WAC Clearinghouse, 2010 wac.colostate.edu/books/referenceguides/bawarshi-reiff/.

Devitt, Amy. *Writing Genres.* Southern Illinois UP, 2008.

Foss, Sonja. *Rhetorical Criticism: Exploration and Practice* 5th ed. Waveland Press, 2018.

Miller, Carolyn. "Genre as Social Action." *Quarterly Journal of Speech* vol. 70, 1984, 151–67.

GETTING THE MOST OUT OF THE READINGS IN THIS BOOK

Many of the texts in Part 2 of this book are written by expert researchers for other experts. These texts are not easy even for your instructors, and they won't be easy or quick reading for you at first, either. We believe that the time you spend with the readings will be worthwhile, leading you to new insights and more successful writing experiences, helping you cross the particular thresholds the texts lead you to encounter. To help you, we have some practical suggestions about how to approach these texts, as a companion to the more theoretical strategies of rhetorical reading.

- Leave plenty of time for reading. These aren't pieces that you'll be able to sit down and skim in fifteen minutes.
- Consciously connect at least some part of each piece you read to your own experience as a writer. The readings have been chosen specifically to allow you to do that.
- Read the backstory of each piece, which you'll find in the "Framing the Reading" sections. These introductions give you background knowledge necessary to understand the pieces themselves more fully.
- Look in the glossary for definitions of boldfaced words in the chapter introduction or the "Framing the Reading" section. These are specialized terms that you'll encounter in the readings.
- Use the "Getting Ready to Read" section to help you focus your reading and develop additional background knowledge to make sense of the texts.
- Look over the "Questions for Discussion and Journaling," "Applying and Exploring Ideas," and "Meta Moments" before you read, so that you can get a further sense of where to focus your attention while you read. This should help you be selective in your attention, rather than trying to read every word in the article in equal depth.
- Read with your favorite search engine and Wikipedia open so you can get instant definitions and background, and so that you can learn more about the authors by quickly researching them.
- Don't feel like you're doing poorly just because you don't understand the piece well. As we explained in Chapter 1, it is natural to be confused while you are learning new and difficult ideas.

Questions for Discussion and Journaling

1. This chapter thinks about research as *conversation*. You've seen conversations online in your social media applications. How do you think the conversations done in research might be the same, and how might they be different?

2. In earlier levels of school, were you taught anything that looks like the "rhetorical reading" described in this chapter? If so, what things were you encouraged to pay attention to that look similar to aspects of rhetorical reading?

3. This chapter argues that meaning is not "built into" texts, but that instead a reader *makes* meaning by bringing together what a text says and a number of other elements. What are those other elements? Can you suggest examples from your own experience that show this argument is accurate? Do other examples from your experience suggest it's not?

4. What do the writers mean when they say "texts are people talking"?

5. This chapter argues that writing is not something you should imagine doing alone. How does this ideal compare with your own experience? How comfortable are you with this assertion?

6. What do you know about the writers of this textbook? How is it a motivated text?

Applying and Exploring Ideas

1. This chapter thinks mostly about the kinds of scholarly writing you'll encounter in your college studies. But did you notice any key principles (such as those relating to research as conversation, genres of writing, or rhetorical reading) that also apply to writing you do on social media? If so, discuss what they are and how they are the same as (or a bit different from) the principles for scholarly research writing.

2. Based on the concepts in this chapter, create a list of questions that readers of conversational inquiry should ask of, or understand about, each text they encounter.

3. Often college doesn't differ as much as we'd like from high school, in terms of telling students what to think in various subjects, rather than making them co-inquirers with their professors. But if you're fortunate, you may be in some classes this term with professors who don't just want to lecture their subject matter to you, but who want to make you genuine inquirers into the subject. If you're in such a course besides this one, write a description of it and how the professor expects you to be actively contributing knowledge rather than just receiving it.

4. Try rhetorically reading a text that you might usually only read for information — like a chapter from one of your science textbooks, or a Wikipedia article, or even the nutrition information on a cereal box. How is the text *motivated*? What *exigence* brings it into existence to begin with? How do you hear the writer

talking to you? How does the *context* in which it was written shape it, and how does the context you're reading it in shape your construction of its meaning? How do your needs, values, and expectations of the text as a reader shape the meaning you make of it, and your reaction to it?

5. What are some questions you have about writing, writers, discourse, persuasion, or reading that you think would make good research questions? Remember that they should be *open* (there isn't an agreed upon answer yet) and interesting to you personally.

Genre Analysis

Your task in this assignment is to choose a genre of writing, explain its conventions, and relate those conventions to the work that the genre does for the people who use it. The main question your analysis should address is: Why does the genre take the shape(s) that it does given what people are trying to accomplish when they use that genre? If you can get used to doing this kind of analysis when you encounter new genres, you'll be able to create documents in those genres more quickly and successfully yourself, and become a better reader of them when you encounter other instances of them.

Planning, Drafting, and Revising. First, you'll need to select your genre. We recommend selecting a genre that uses relatively short documents, no longer than five to six pages each. Using a very short genre whose documents are a single page or only part of a page is fine. You could use one of the genres we've used as an example in this chapter (remember wedding invitations, resumes, thank-you notes, and eulogies?), but there are hundreds to choose from. Some tips:

- Choose a genre you can collect five to ten different instances of. (Beware: Some genres might be interesting but hard to collect samples of.)
- Don't choose a genre that is too "broad." "Webpage ads," for example, is much too broad, as there are many genres of advertisements that show up on the web. "Social media" is also too broad to be a genre; more useful would be Twitter posts or Facebook posts by individuals (or by companies, which are likely a related but different genre).
- Choose a genre where different instances of your genre demonstrate differences. No two resumes or cover letters look quite alike, which is good for an analysis like this.

Once you've assembled your sample of five to ten instances of your genre, you'll study them for what they have in common. You can use the categories and questions of analysis that Sonja Foss offers (we expand a little here):

- *Situational elements*: What conditions (situations) call for the genre? What prompts this sort of document to be written? What is the exigence — the need or reason for a given action or communication? And who usually creates this genre — people doing what?
- *Substantive characteristics (content)*: What sort of content (substance) is typically contained in this genre? What do these texts tend to talk about or say? Is there information that's typically present (or not present) in these texts?

- *Stylistic characteristics (form)*: What form does this sort of genre take and what does it look like (length, page layout, color, font)? How are its parts organized? What language does it use? Are there specialized terms? What tone does it take (formal, informal, friendly, stiff, casual, light)?

- *Organizing principles*: What elements make this genre what it is? What are the common denominators of the genre? What makes a resume a resume, for example? Of each characteristic that you identify in the first three questions above, you might ask, "If I took out this characteristic, would it still be recognizable as this genre?"

Your analysis should tell the story of this genre, emphasizing the overall question of how what it needs to accomplish leads to the shape it typically takes. How will you describe the scene in which this genre most often gets used? How will you differentiate between features your analysis suggests the genre *must* have in order to be recognizable and usable as that genre, and features that some of your samples have but others don't, making them optional in the genre? What will be the best order to work through the document's features in? And how will you *show* the document? It will likely be best not to rely on words alone — can you include an image or a screen-capture of a typical instance of the genre, and then refer back to that image as you describe the genre's various features and parts?

Your teacher may assign a specific length for your analysis, but you can expect to have between three and five pages worth of material to say about your genre. You might choose not to create a detailed outline of your analysis before you begin drafting, but we recommend at least creating headings for the major parts you decide your analysis will need to have.

What Makes It Good?   The best analyses will have

- an introduction that poses the assignment's main question, explains what genre is being studied, and previews both the most interesting findings of your analysis and the path your analysis will take

- a graphical example of the genre or part of it

- a clear explanation of who uses the genre and for what purposes

- conclusions built on comparison of several instances of the genre

- accurate assessments of the genre's elements

- a clear organizational structure including a logical progression through whatever elements of the genre the analysis highlights

- a conclusion that addresses the assignment's main question

CHAPTER 3

PARTICIPATING IN CONVERSATIONAL INQUIRY ABOUT WRITING

LeoPatrizi/Getty Images

A group gathers for a conversation about a book they're reading together. This chapter shows how much of the work you do in college is entering the "Burkean parlor," joining ongoing academic conversations about a question or problem.

In this class, you will engage in your own conversational inquiry on writing, writers, discourse, and literacy. One very sound (and fun) way to learn is to ask questions and then go in search of answers, in conversation with other people. Conversational inquiry is thus one kind of learning-by-doing: Everyone who participates in conversational inquiry is a learner, whether they are a student or a professor. This book, and your class, focus on helping you learn more about writing, discourse, and literacy, particularly the threshold concepts that Chapter 1 outlines and which other researchers explore in depth in Chapters 4–7. Engaging in conversational inquiry on those or other threshold concepts of writing will, as explained in Chapter 1, make it more likely that you will be able to transfer your learning from this class to later writing situations. You'll learn more about conversational inquiry, and how to make sense of the scholarly articles you'll read in this and other classes, by doing conversational inquiry yourself. And you'll have the opportunity to make a meaningful contribution to the field of Writing Studies.

This chapter offers you a guide to contributing to the conversational inquiry already happening in Writing Studies. You'll learn about why even as a student in a college composition course you can be in conversation with other researchers on writing, and the activities necessary to do so: formulating a research question by finding existing conversations and how your own interests intersect with them, making a plan to gather data that will address your research question, interpreting the data you collect to create a contribution to the conversation, and making that contribution by sharing your research with others.

Walking into the Party

As Chapter 2 demonstrated, conversational inquiry isn't just about your own learning; It's about making knowledge new to everyone studying a given subject. In 1941, an extremely well-known rhetoric scholar, Kenneth Burke, likened conversational inquiry to an evening gathering in someone's parlor (or living room). Today he might have called it a party. A crowd of people are clustered in small groups talking about various subjects of interest to them that are contested, not settled knowledge. You show up long after the party has begun, hear an interesting snippet of conversation, and join that group. After a while, when you've listened to a few turns in the conversation, you notice something no one is saying yet that would improve the conversation. You find a way to share your idea and people respond to you. Some of them support what you said while others question it, and your contribution becomes integrated into the conversation. As you talk, some people leave the conversation and several new people join it, as you did earlier. Eventually you decide to leave — maybe you hear another interesting snippet of conversation from across the room and step over to join it — but the conversation you were in continues on without you.

This "Burkean parlor" is what's taking place all around the college or university you're attending. You can imagine each of the readings in Part 2 of this book is a turn in a conversation, and the threshold concepts this book focuses on were arrived at through conversational inquiry. What might be surprising to you is that college students, especially first-years, can contribute meaningfully to the field's knowledge about writing, writers, discourse, and literacy.

WHAT CAN A STUDENT CONTRIBUTE?

There is a general belief in American culture that students (especially high school but also undergraduate college students) are in school to learn existing knowledge and are not yet able to make new knowledge. We expect you might have encountered some of this attitude along your way as a student, and thus it might seem strange to be invited to join in on knowledge-making activities. But you don't need a college degree to do the kind of conversational inquiry we've been describing because this kind of knowledge is based on having a question, trying to answer the question, and telling people about your investigation. From one perspective, conversational inquiry is storytelling. The storytelling that makes good conversational inquiry is systematic, precise, and structured — a "story" like an investigative news story, not fiction. To write research is to recount your experiences exploring a question or problem, and sharing experiences is something everyone can do.

Writing is a subject that particularly lends itself to conversational inquiry for a number of reasons. You've likely had years of experience with reading and writing, and a lot of questions and concerns that emerge from that experience. There is much about how writing works that no one understands — not you, nor longtime writing researchers. By virtue of your experience, your questions are important and valid. By virtue of being an everyday reader and writer, you are *already* positioned to ask good questions and become part of ongoing conversations about writing, writers, and discourse. Students like you are contributing to research publications in Writing Studies every semester. You can see their work in scholarly journals including *Young Scholars in Writing*, *Stylus*, *Xchanges*, and *The JUMP+*, and you'll encounter some of it in this book.

OPEN QUESTIONS, ACCESSIBLE METHODS

The field of Writing Studies is also relatively young, meaning that people haven't been formally researching it for very long. (Though they've been *talking about* it for millennia; many of the world's oldest written texts focus on writing, speech-making, persuasion, and the best ways to learn these.) Very few activities are as widely used or engaged with as discourse, writing, and persuasion, yet studied by such a relatively small number of people. This means that most of your own questions are likely to still be "open" — not yet have definitive answers.

Many of the ways to go about answering questions on writing, discourse, and persuasion are highly accessible to anyone who can observe, interact with others, read, and write. Most Writing Studies research projects require little in the way of specialized equipment; they don't require lab space, and they usually cost very little. Not everyone can build and conduct a billion-dollar physics experiment trying to detect gravitational waves, but many of us can conduct interviews with people who do a particular kind of writing, or set up an observation of writing in a particular situation.

In other words, there is a lot still to learn about writing, your questions about it are important, and you are likely able to engage in many of the methods used to answer those questions and share your findings with others.

Formulating a Research Question

Conducting your own conversational inquiry begins by explaining what you're wondering about — *your* open question — and looking for existing conversation on that question in research articles or books. The heart of the research is your curiosity, your desire for an answer to a question that doesn't yet seem to have one.

A student research project that one of us mentored began when a first-year college student who had served in the U.S. Navy, Angie Mallory, looked at her own college writing course and was surprised at how different it was from military service. Her experience in the Navy had led her to expect that, in order to succeed in college, she would need to listen carefully to what faculty were telling her to think and be very good at following orders. It was difficult for her to get comfortable in a college writing class where she had to decide for herself what to say and where her questions for instructions were met with "it depends on what you want to say." Given her own difficult transition from an order-driven to an open-thinking environment, she began to wonder how many other military veterans had similar challenges in college writing courses. In this example, you can see how personal experience and the perennial question, "I wonder if it's *usually* that way?" led to a clear research question. Sometimes, a question arises from your observation of other people. Sometimes, something you're already reading will raise a question that it doesn't answer. Part of what motivated Angie to do her research project was reading a call for chapter proposals for a book on military veterans' experiences in college writing courses. The proposal acknowledged the many open questions in the area she was interested in, which further stoked her curiosity.

Keep two principles in mind that Angie's experience demonstrates about where research questions come from: *curiosity* and *dissonance*. First, if you don't *wonder* about what you see around you or experience personally, if you're not curious, it will be harder to notice or develop research questions. Second, research questions usually arise from some kind of itch, discord, or sense that *something's not right*. This lack of harmony in your mind we call dissonance, and it's what alerts you to things out of place, problems, unresolved difficulties, complaints or frustrations with the status quo. These variances are where most research questions arise. Whether you're drawing on personal experience in arriving at your research question, as Angie did, or observing the world around you and other people's experiences, many research questions emerge from the same overall categories of dissonance or problem-recognizing. In Writing Studies, those categories include:

- Challenges, difficulties, complaints, frustrations, or problems you or others have with writing or reading
- Things you wish were different about writing or reading, for you or others
- Things that have puzzled you about writing or language and how they work (including the threshold concepts considered in this book, beginning in Chapter 1)
- Aspects of writing, discourse, or persuasion that fascinate you and you'd like to learn more about.

Another way to know whether a question is "open" is if other people feel the same dissonance you do when you call it to their attention. Conversational inquiry is meant to be conversational right from the start. When you have a truly open question, it's good to start talking about it with friends and teachers right away. They can tell you whether they share the same question, whether it seems valuable to them, and whether they're already aware of some answers to it. Often a teacher will also be able to tell you the names of researchers or articles that have done research on similar questions. A teacher may also be able to help you come up with names of the categories or subjects your research question fits into. Being able to name what you're wondering about is crucial for finding existing conversation on it. Angie, for example, needed to know that her research question fit in the areas of "writing pedagogy," "military veterans," "non-traditional students," and "higher education."

ACTIVITY 3.1 | Try Thinking Differently

In past experiences with informational research (where you write a report or an argument on a subject), you may have been allowed to choose your own "topic." Conversational inquiry works on questions rather than topics. Think of a research project you've done and write what its topic was. Now, think again about the project: What questions did you have about the topic? Were they genuine questions, things you really didn't know? Were they questions more like "Why is gun control bad?" when you already had a fixed opinion on gun control that you were not really going to change? List some of both kinds of questions that you can remember having. Of your genuine questions, things you really didn't know the answer to, were there any that no one else knew the answer to either? These were "open" questions. Finally, consider, in preparation for class discussion, why conversational inquiry wants you to think in terms of questions rather than topics. Why does the difference matter?

FINDING EXISTING CONVERSATIONS USING DATABASES AND SEARCH ENGINES

Researchers look for existing conversations in scholarly and professional journals and books by using search engines (like Google Scholar) and databases (like *CompPile*), which try to index (make a record of) every book and journal that publishes research on writing. Databases can be searched both by keywords you choose, by their own built-in subject terms, and/or by author and title. Such resources specialize in keeping track of all the scholarly conversation being published in a given field, and almost every field of study has at least one good database. Some databases incorporate work from *many* fields rather than just one. (Ebsco's *Academic Search Complete* is an excellent example of such a database — it's fairly likely your college gives you free access to it through your campus library website.) Search engines like Google Scholar are less specialized than databases, but powerful in their own right. All these resources tell you that a given article or book exists; often, though far from always, they will also link you directly to the resource. (As a college student, some of your student fees go to purchase access to scholarly material through your school's library. If you ever find a web page that has the article you want but asks you to pay for it, talk to your librarian instead — they'll get it for you for free.)

Writing Studies spans several disciplines (writing, linguistics, communication, English, psychology, education, and sociology, to name a few), so writing researchers routinely have to search more than one field's databases to make sure they're finding a wide range of existing conversation on their question. Angie's project on veterans in writing classes required her to search *ERIC*, an education database; *CompPile*; *PsycINFO*, a psychology database; and general databases like *Academic Search Complete* for military science research on veterans.

ACTIVITY 3.2 | Explore New Resources

Take a few minutes to explore the research resources your college library's website offers through the following questions:

- How many databases does your library give students access to, and can you find any that relate to Writing Studies specifically?
- Does your library offer research guides for various fields (like psychology or marketing)? Does it offer one for Writing Studies or a related field?
- What is the easiest way at your library to ask a librarian for assistance on your project?
- If you find an article you want to read but your library doesn't already have the article on its website, or a website asks you for money in order to access an article, how can your library send it to you for free?
- How does your library explain the difference between a search engine like Google Scholar and a database like *JSTOR*?

In reading through the existing research, Angie was quickly able to confirm that her question had not been talked about much yet, and that what talk there was so far wasn't focusing on what she was curious about. She found that most of the literature focusing on military veterans in college writing classes was concerned with how to cope with veterans who couldn't reacclimate well to non-military life or who came home from battle with PTSD. Very little of the conversation focused on veteran students' *abilities* rather than stereotypical *disabilities*. Angie's interest was a gap in the literature — as if she were standing in a Burkean parlor in a conversation on veterans and no one was saying what she thought needed to be said. But she was also able to use her reading to narrow her research question and build more precise language for it that the field already recognized. This is typical of inquiry projects: usually, reading the existing conversation will help you refine your research question, making it more specific and letting you put it in language the field uses. (See the box, "What Makes a Good Research Question?" below.)

In her reading of the existing conversation through scholarly articles and books, Angie had to remember that they weren't *information*; they were *claims* and *arguments*. You'll need to do the same as you explore the existing conversation on your research question. What you read won't give you the final answer to your question; instead, it will help you see how the conversation has moved forward and where there are gaps that your research question might address. Not everyone agrees with the research you're reading, though enough people came to consensus on the piece's value to publish it. If you think a piece doesn't make sense, ask yourself why others thought it did. Also remember that words you have a tough time with in such

---

WHAT MAKES A GOOD RESEARCH QUESTION?

- *Open*: The field your research contributes to, the community in conversation on your area of inquiry, does not consider the question already answered; you can argue that more (or any) research is needed on your question.
- *Personally interesting*: Your question should be one you yourself are curious about and are invested in; this will improve your motivation for the project.
- *Specific and Narrow*: Most research questions start out too broad, like "does procrastination help writers or hinder them?" You need a very narrow, tightly focused question because it's *small* enough to manage a research project on: "What are the outcomes when reporters at X newspaper procrastinate writing feature articles?"
- *Uses the field's language*: To locate existing conversation on your subject, match your question to the language the conversation is already in. For example, if you want to study how people write a first version of a text, you need to know that the field uses the terms *composing* and *drafting* differently.
- *Researchable*: It's easy to ask questions you lack the resources or access to answer. It's a good thing to brainstorm questions regardless of whether you can actually research them or not, but as you select from the questions you've brainstormed, you need to choose one you can actually study.

pieces aren't there because the writer thought the vocabulary made them sound smarter; rather, they are part of the specialized language of the field (something discussed further in Chapter 7). Look up the language so that you begin to understand it and can use it in your own inquiry. And don't forget to read not just for what the pieces *say*, but for the writer's motivation, the exigence, and the context. At this stage, you're trying to *make connections* and keep *asking questions*. That will help you get the big picture of the conversation you're exploring.

CREATING A RESEARCH SPACE (CARS)

All scholars and researchers must situate their own work in relation to the work of other researchers they have read as they solidify their research questions and begin to look for answers to them. They do this using the conventions of scholarly genres — journal articles, books, book chapters, and, increasingly, websites and video presentations. Genres, as Chapter 2 explains, are typical patterns for doing something with discourse in recurring situations; because there are patterns, once you know how scholarly articles work as a genre, they become much easier to interpret. Linguist and genre researcher John Swales has used a research method called corpus analysis to examine how introductions work in the genre of scholarly articles. His analysis of thousands of journal articles has shown that there are typical ways that scholars situate their research in relationship to the research of others.

Scholars typically situate their own research by making some common "moves" in the introductions to their written work. These moves are intended to convince readers that the piece is usefully participating in the scholarly conversation in which they are interested. In other words, these moves are the enactment, in written text form, of a scholar walking into a party and showing that they have heard what others are saying, are responding to them in appropriate ways, and have something of their own to say that others might want to hear and then, in turn, respond to.

These moves show up so frequently in the research articles that you will encounter in this book, and when you conduct research elsewhere in college, that it is helpful for you as a reader to able to identify them. It is equally important that you be able to make them yourself when you are writing about your own inquiry projects. Swales's model of these moves — known as the **CARS (Create A Research Space) model** is summarized in Figure 3.1.

Knowing to look for these moves when you are reading (even skimming) others' research will help you make quicker sense of any scholarly piece you come across. Seeing these moves at work in your readings for this class will also help you better understand what a good research question ultimately needs to be able to do: find the intersection of your own curiosity and the gap in the conversation, the niche in the field's knowledge that you can fill.

CREATING A RESEARCH SPACE

MOVE 1: ESTABLISHING A TERRITORY

In this move, the author sets the context for his or her research, providing necessary background on the topic. This move includes one or more of the following steps:

Step 1
Claiming Centrality. The author asks the discourse community (the audience for the paper) to accept that the research about to be reported is part of a lively, significant, or well-established research area. To claim centrality the author might write: "Recently there has been a spate of interest in . . ." or "Knowledge of X has great importance for . . . ." This step is used less in the physical sciences than in the social sciences and the humanities.

and/or

Step 2
Making Topic Generalizations. The author makes statements about current knowledge, practices, or phenomena in the field. For example: "X is a common finding in patients with . . ." or "The properties of X are still not completely understood."

and/or

Step 3
Reviewing Previous Items of Research. The author relates what has been found on the topic and who found it. For example: "Both Johnson and Morgan claim that the biographical facts have been misrepresented" or "Several studies have suggested that . . . (Gordon, 2003; Ratzinger, 2009)." In citing the research of others, the author may use integral citation (citing the author's name in the sentence, as in the first example above) or nonintegral citation (citing the author's name in parentheses only, as in the second example above). The use of different types of verbs (e.g., reporting verbs such as *shows* or *claims*) and verb tenses (past, present perfect, or present) varies across disciplines, as does the choice of citation style (MLA, APA, CMS, etc.).

MOVE 2: ESTABLISHING A NICHE

In this move, the author argues that there is an open "niche," or gap, in the existing research, a space that needs to be filled through additional research. Authors establish a niche in one of four ways:

Option 1
Counter-Claiming. The author refutes or challenges earlier research by making a counter-claim. For example: "While Jones and Riley believe X method to be accurate, a close examination demonstrates their method to be flawed."

Option 2
Indicating a Gap. The author demonstrates that earlier research does not sufficiently address all existing questions or problems. For example: "While existing studies have clearly established X, they have not addressed Y."

Option 3
Question-Raising. The author asks questions about previous research, suggesting that additional research needs to be done. For example: "While Jones and Morgan have established X, their findings raise a number of questions, including . . . ."

Option 4
Continuing a Tradition. The author presents the research as a useful extension of existing research. For example: "Earlier studies seemed to suggest X. To verify their findings, more work is urgently needed. . . ."

MOVE 3: OCCUPYING A NICHE

In this move, the author turns the niche established in Move 2 into the research space that he or she will fill; that is, the author demonstrates how he or she will substantiate the counter-claim made, fill the gap identified, answer the question(s) asked, or continue the research tradition. The initial step (1A or 1B) is obligatory, though many research articles stop after that step.

Step 1A
Outlining Purposes. The author indicates the main purpose(s) of the current article. For example: "In this article I argue . . ." or "The present research tries to clarify . . . ."

or

Step 1B
Announcing Present Research. The author describes the research in the current article. For example: "This paper describes three separate studies conducted between March 2008 and January 2009."

Step 2
Announcing Principal Findings. The author presents the main conclusions of his or her research. For example: "The results of the study suggest . . ." or "When we examined X, we discovered . . . ."

Step 3
Indicating the Structure of the Research Article. The author previews the organization of the article. For example: "This paper is structured as follows . . . ."

Figure 3.1 **Summary of John Swales's CARS model of a research article's introduction.**

Adapted from John M. Swales, *Genre Analysis: English in Academic and Research Settings.* Cambridge UP, 1990.

ACTIVITY 3.3 | Test These Ideas

Pick a scholarly piece in Part 2 of this book and flip to it now. Find its introduction, and look for the moves Swales describes, underlining or highlighting them. Recognize that they don't always come in order, that authors
can make a particular move more than once, and some authors (whether
wisely or not is up to you to decide) sometimes leave a move out.

Seeking Answers by Gathering Data

Once you have a research question and some sense of where it fits in the existing
conversation, your next move is to consider the kinds of data you need to collect
in order to explore your question. Most of the questions people think to ask
about writing, writers, discourse, and persuasion have to be addressed by studying people, by studying the texts people write and the language they use, or by
some combination of these. The data that you collect will enable you to engage in
inquiry-driven experiences that you will ultimately share with others in the kind of
conversation we have been describing in this and the preceding chapters.

When Angie settled on her research question — how do military veterans used to a
very constrained, order-driven environment adapt to the non-directive, open environment of the typical college writing class? — she could see that the most obvious way
to seek answers to her question would be to ask military-veteran college students
what their writing classes had been like. She could do that by interviewing them or
surveying them. (Interviews have more depth and make follow-up questions easy;
surveys are better for getting some information from a lot more people, because you
don't have to speak to everyone directly.) She also realized that she would learn different things from students' *reports of* their experiences (gained through interviewing or surveying) than she would by *observing them directly*. So she decided sit in on
some college writing classes being taken by veterans. She also asked the veterans in
the class she was observing to do some additional reflective writing on the experience, which opened another experience to her: that of *analyzing the texts* they wrote.

Each of these methods — interviewing, surveying, observation (in this instance,
a *case study*), and textual analysis (a kind of *discourse analysis*) — is a common
category of researching with people. Other categories include ethnography (a
much broader-scale kind of case study), focus groups (a kind of interviewing), and
experiments. Researchers are always matching the general kind of research they
choose to the question they're trying to answer. (See the box, "Research Methods in
Writing Studies," p. 64.) Angie *could* have tried answering her question via experiment — which means establishing a test or trial instance of an experience and comparing it to a "normal" (control) experience — but that simply wasn't an effective
way to study her question. Part of the way she knew this was by looking at the

methods which had been used in the articles and books that made up existing conversation on military veterans in college writing classes. They, too, were using case
studies, interviewing, analysis of students' writing, and surveying (of both students
and teachers) to build data on their questions.

RESEARCH METHODS IN WRITING STUDIES

Focused on Language and Texts

- Discourse Analysis — quantitative and qualitative detailed examination
  of language-in-use, including word counts, word choice, and prose
  structure
  - Textual Analysis — discourse analysis applied to specific texts
  - Rhetorical Analysis — discourse analysis focused on discourse or
    texts as rhetorical acts or performance, and thus analyzed through
    categories developed by rhetorical theory (see the readings in
    Chapter 5 for examples)
- Genre Analysis — discourse analysis focused on the genre functions of
  texts, discourse, or activities (see Chapter 2, "Genres and How Writers
  and Readers Depend on Them")
- Historiography and Archival Research — study of the history of writing,
  texts, discourse acts, or people, most often through interviews and
  oral histories or research in archives and other collections of old or
  ancient texts
- Theoretical Frames, Analysis, and Modeling — non-empirical, initially
  hypothetical explanations or accounts of how a phenomenon happens
  or how a system works. (In the sciences, theorizing and modeling is
  nearly always math-based and quantitative; in humanities and social
  sciences, it is mostly language-based and qualitative.)

Focused on People

- Survey — questions arranged on a form and distributed to large
  number of people
- Interview — conversation with an individual or small group using both
  predetermined questions and follow-up questions that emerge from
  the conversation
- Focus Group — conversation with a small or large group of people designed
  to elicit feedback on preselected questions through group conversation
- Case Study — intense observation of, interaction with, and description
  of an individual instance of a phenomenon under study
- Ethnography — long-term, intense observation of a situation or scene
  of activity that focuses on interrelations between all its elements

---

> ### *More Specialized Methods*
> - Experiment — carefully arranged test of a specific prediction by creating circumstances in which a specific variable can be manipulated while other potential variables are controlled
> - Big Data and Corpus Research — visual and statistical analysis of large data sets (e.g., a "corpus," or large body, of language or text, or numerical data on the behavior of hundreds or thousands of individuals, such as keystrokes while writing or step data from Fitbits)
> - Meta-Analysis — comparison of the findings of multiple previous studies, usually through statistical manipulation of the existing studies' results
>
> For more on methods, see Mary Sue MacNeally, *Strategies for Empirical Research in Writing*, and Joyce Kinkead, *Researching Writing: An Introduction to Research Methods*. This interactive graphic on data collection terminology is also helpful: https://methods .sagepub.com/methods-map.

Data simply means *things you experienced first-hand*. Everything that you sense (see, hear, smell, taste, feel) with your body is, from one perspective, data — even though we don't usually talk about it that way. Usually "data" also implies *application* to a specific question, and it also implies *organized collection*. So we don't usually call everything you saw on a trip to a zoo "data" because you didn't collect it in an organized way and you probably aren't trying to answer a single specific question with it. But what if you were? Suppose you read a report critical of treatment of big cats at a zoo you could go to, and you decided to check it out for yourself. Your research question would be, "How are they treating their cats?" And you would go looking for specific things: how they're fed, how much space they have, how much that space resembles a natural habitat for the species you're observing, how the zookeepers treat and handle the animals, and so on. Everything you saw that applied to those questions would be data; and if you were wise, you organized your observations by looking around with your specific questions in mind, and keeping careful notes (handwritten, typed, or voice-recorded) on what you were seeing, and taking photographs or video to have a record of some of what you saw and heard. All your recordings, photos, notes, and memories are data. The more careful your collection method — well-planned and organized, precise and accurate — the "better" those data are. And the more closely or directly the data apply to your question, the "better" they are. (Your question is on big cats, so data you collect on bobcats aren't "as good" — as applicable to your question — as data you collect on jaguars or tigers.)

Angie's study of veterans let her collect several kinds of data: interview transcripts, observation notes from class, and student writing. (But it didn't, for example, let her collect any information on what *faculty* thought, because she didn't talk to the students' teachers.) Her study was *qualitative* rather than *quantitative*. A quantitative study tries to answer questions with numbers. (Had she asked, "How many veterans earn high grades in college writing classes?" that would have been a quantitative study.) Quantitative studies are often good at helping researchers see *what* is happening, especially with large-scale phenomena (like species extinction due to climate change, or how smartphones are affecting teenagers' social lives). Qualitative studies use language rather than numbers to answer questions, as Angie's did. Qualitative studies aren't as good at addressing questions which require looking at huge numbers of instances, but they tend to be very good at helping researchers know *why* a given phenomenon is happening on a smaller scale. Most Writing Studies research is actually *mixed-method*, which usually (though not always) blends quantitative and qualitative methods. If a researcher gives a survey, for example, they'll analyze it both quantitatively (how many people answered a given question in a particular way?) and qualitatively (what language did people choose to use on an open-ended question?).

ANALYZING YOUR DATA

Once you have collected data to try to learn more about your question, then you have another big task in front of you: making sense of everything you have collected. This process is called data analysis, and it can be both the most exciting but also the messiest, most frustrating, and most unpredictable part of the inquiry process. Your data won't speak for itself; data always require interpretation. The researcher has to decide which data are most important, what they are indicating, and what is the best way to make sense of it all.

Returning to Angie's case: Once she collected her data — notes or video from observing writers, notes or video or audio from interviewing them — she needed to label and categorize it, and look for patterns or trends and exceptions to them. In qualitative research, this process is often called *coding* the data. (If Angie's data were quantitative rather than qualitative, she instead would be doing a lot of counting and statistical analysis.) Angie also needed to assess how what she *actually* saw in her data lined up with what she *expected* to see. Because Angie wasn't doing an experiment, she didn't make a formal hypothesis or prediction of what her study would find. But she *did* have some expectations. She thought that the non-directiveness of writing classes, where students were expected to decide for themselves what to write about and what to say, would be frustrating for the veterans coming from an order-driven environment. Her analysis centered on seeing whether her data bore out those expectations or not, and she had to be careful not to let her expectations color her interpretation of her data, which can often be a serious challenge. The results of her data analysis became her study's findings.

As Angie analyzed and interpreted her data, she was using an interpretive frame or "lens" to do so. Making sense of an experience through interpretive frameworks isn't unique to research; all of us are doing it all the time. Frames tell us which data to pay attention to and which to ignore, which are more important and less important, and how pieces fit together to make a sensible whole. For example, in the United States, some people frame poverty as individual failure, while others frame it as a failure of systems and society. The first frame expects individuals to be wholly responsible for taking care of themselves and asserts that in the United States, if people work hard, follow the rules, and exercise personal responsibility, they will not be in poverty. Any evidence to the contrary is ignored or explained as some other problem or failing. Framing poverty as a social problem, the second frame, requires believing instead that some reasons for poverty lie beyond the control of individuals (like place and circumstances of childhood, economic systems and government policies that favor those already having wealth, and systemic biases against particular personal characteristics including race and gender). In this frame, only public systems (larger than a single individual) can address causes of poverty that do not lie with the individual, and the frame is therefore likely to attend to public causes of and solutions to poverty rather than individual ones.

Angie's data analysis framed veteran composition students as inherently *able* rather than, as she saw in much of the existing conversation on the subject, inherently *disabled*. This choice shaped her sense of what was important in her data, what stood out; it also shaped her explanations of particular classroom events and student statements and her choice of what data to highlight in her chapter reporting her findings. Her interpretation of her data also imposed a frame of seeing military life as order-driven and seeing university life as choice-based. Again, her frame created a lens or filter that helped her choose what to emphasize in her data and what seemed less important. In writing about her research, Angie had to be very clear in explaining what frames she was using and how they shaped her interpretations of data, so that others in the conversation would be able to weigh her choices. (See the box, "Guiding Principles for Data Analysis," p. 68.)

CONDUCTING RESEARCH ETHICALLY

You need to exercise great care to design methods that treat your research participants ethically. Ethics, according to scholars Gretchen Rossman and Sharon Rallis, "are standards for conduct based on moral principles" (70). You need to design and implement a study that does not violate your participants' privacy or create any potential for physical or psychological harm to them. You also need their voluntary, informed consent to participate in your project. Federal law requires colleges and universities to maintain Institutional Review Boards (IRBs) which review research projects at the institution. If you use research methods that involve interacting with people (survey, interview, case study, ethnography, etc.), your teacher will help you work with your IRB on ethical and responsible research design. Rossman and Rallis

GUIDING PRINCIPLES FOR DATA ANALYSIS

- Read all your data and then make notes about your first overall impressions, including anything that stands out or is particularly interesting and any categories of phenomena or findings you can already tell you want to look more closely at. At this point you're just getting the "big picture" of your data.
- With caution, use your expectations to help form questions you ask of the data. Your expectations will lead you to "hunt through" your data for specific answers; at the beginning of your analysis, you should know what you may eventually "hunt" for in your data, but you should mostly be "gathering," browsing through the data to see what they make available.
- Sort and name your data sets. A data set is a collection of data all of one kind, which you'll keep and analyze separately from other data sets. For example, a study on people's writing habits might have data sets of 1) interviews with participants, 2) observations of participants, and 3) pieces of writing they've created.
- Use your interpretive framework to create categories to examine or to guide what aspects of your data you look at. For example, in research on attitudes toward required writing, previous research might lead you to look specifically at "Mood" as one category of interest.
- "Code" your data by labeling or tagging particular instances or pieces of data according to what categories they fit. For example, you would label (code) any instances in your data of people expressing or acting on their mood as "Mood."
- As you code, and as you then begin reviewing what you've coded, look for patterns and for instances that break those patterns. Expect to make several passes through your data, examining various codes and combinations of codes for these patterns and outliers. Keep notes on what you're seeing with each pass, and frequently reread your notes to see what stands out.
- Look for things that come up frequently and then not at all. Look for things that seem strange or inexplicable.

For more on data analysis, see Mary Sue MacNeally, *Strategies for Empirical Research in Writing,* and Joyce Kinkead, *Researching Writing: An Introduction to Research Methods.*

provide a list of questions that researchers can ask when working to ensure their research is ethical:

- Is the study competently conducted?
- Is it systematic and rigorous?

- Is it potentially useful?
- What happens as a result of this study? What are the possible consequences, and for whom?
- Are participants' rights and privacy protected?
- Are any groups of people left out whose voices or experiences should be included?
- Does the researcher reflect on his/her own role and biases?
- Could another researcher understand how this researcher came to his/her conclusions? Is the explanation of how the study was done clear?

Most importantly, they remind all researchers that "the ethical researcher does not exploit any person in any circumstances regardless of differences in status, race, gender, language, and other social identity considerations" (72). (See the box, "Tips for Conducting Ethical Research," below.)

TIPS FOR CONDUCTING ETHICAL RESEARCH

- Read and follow the CCCC Guidelines for the Ethical Conduct of Research in Composition Studies, found at https://cccc.ncte.org/cccc /resources/positions/ethicalconduct.
- Find and follow your institution's policies for ensuring ethical conduct of research. (Search your university website with the terms *Institutional Review Board* or *ethical conduct of research*.)
- Never work with minors (people under the age of eighteen) without permission from their parent or guardian.
- Obtain your participants' informed consent by explaining your project. (Your institution will have guidelines for how you should do so.) Get specific permission to quote any writing your participants share with you.
- Take care not to share information about your participants that they wish to remain private. If your participants want anonymity, use pseudonyms. However, think carefully about the impact on your participants of anything you say about them or share from them that might hurt them or cause embarrassment; don't rely only on anonymity to protect them.
- Do all you can to prevent unauthorized access to your data by keeping it physically or electronically locked (encrypted / password protected / stored offline).
- Offer to share the final draft of your research report with the research subject(s), when appropriate.

Telling Your Story: Sharing Your Research

If you're doing a research project like Angie did, you'll have been writing all the way through it and sharing your writing. First you're writing your research question, then your plan (sometimes a proposal) for your methods; then you'll be writing while you analyze your data. In the spirit of real conversational inquiry, you should be sharing with friends or teachers along the way, getting their feedback, considering their suggestions, and writing more (or differently) in response. But even though you're constantly writing and sharing your writing during research, the turn to telling your story by publicly sharing what you have learned is a new phase in your research. Not only do you have to explain your experience and what you learned from it to other people, but their responses to your work will take on a more critical edge. This is your moment to join the conversation, and at the same time, you must now expect that others will respond to your ideas, claims, and research methods. They might applaud what you have done even while asking questions about things you haven't considered.

As we noted earlier in this chapter, most of the genres through which you could present your research require you to cover the same basic questions in your writing; this is true whether you're presenting to your class, giving a presentation at a student research conference, publishing in an undergraduate research journal, or, as Angie did, writing a chapter for an edited collection. Even if you are presenting your research on a blog or vlogging via YouTube or Vimeo, you still need to cover certain bases in order to be taken seriously as a participant in the conversation. In all cases, you'll need to:

- Explain what you wanted to know (your research question) and convince others this was a question they, too should be curious about (show there is a gap in the conversation).
- Explain how you worked to answer the question by detailing what data you collected, and how you collected and analyzed it (show your research methods).
- Explain what you have learned, what you think you know now, based on your research (address or answer your question).
- Tell people why they should care, why this matters, what your research findings mean for others in the conversation (detail the implications of the work you've done).
- Explain what you still *don't* know or what you have more questions about. Very rarely does a single research study on any meaningful question result in definitive, complete knowledge that closes the question. Research presentations almost always discuss research that your own work shows is still required.

How much time you spend on each of these moves will differ greatly depending on your audience, purpose, genre, and medium. If you are sharing a video or letter for a nonacademic audience, you will probably spend more time on steps d and e and very little time on b. If you are writing to academics and researchers, you will need to be extremely diligent about steps a and b. But in general, your readers and respondents want to know what you learned, how you learned it, and why it matters.

BEING PEER-REVIEWED AND MANAGING FEEDBACK

While the basic subjects of discussion are the same no matter your mode of presenting your work, different audiences and venues (YouTube versus scholarly article) will have very different ways of responding. If you present to your class, it's likely your project will result in some interesting conversation among your classmates, but that they will probably not be too critical of your findings or your work. As you present to more and more specialized and expert audiences, the level of critique, both positive and negative, will increase. If you propose a conference presentation on your research, the proposal will be reviewed by the conference organizers and accepted if it looks likely to make a good contribution to the conference. (And rejected if not.) To merit space in a scholarly journal or book, your article or manuscript would be **peer-reviewed**, usually blind (you don't know who the reviewers are and they don't know who you are). Peer reviewers will make suggestions to the editors you submitted your work to on what's working well in your piece and on how to strengthen it.

You might be surprised to know that peer review doesn't just happen after you have a complete draft. In fact, in order to write a strong draft in the first place, you'll need to be sharing your writing with peers, friends, and teachers throughout the inquiry process. Remember, you are participating in conversational inquiry, engaging in the "Burkean parlor," and you don't walk into that party with a full written text for people to read. You work out ideas and problems with other people as you go along. There are many times to get feedback from others along the way, but some critical ones are:

- As you figure out what research conversation you want to participate in. Ask your peers: Does this conversation seem interesting? Would you want to know what happens here?
- As you write your guiding research question. Ask your peers: Does this question make sense? Is this question answerable? Does this question seem interesting?
- As you plan how to gather data. Ask your peers: Is this kind of data most effective for finding an answer to my question? Am I designing a project that seems ethical?
- As you analyze your data. Here, it's always a good idea to ask other people to analyze your data with you, and you can return the favor and help them make sense of their data.

As you begin to write about your project, you'll want to ask your peers and other readers to give you feedback on questions like:

- Is it clear what I was studying and why?
- Is it clear how I gathered and analyzed data?
- What argument do I seem to be making? Is it clear and compelling?
- Do you believe my argument? Why or why not?

In Chapter 4, you'll find a piece by Richard Straub that talks about ways of giving honest, effective feedback to other writers on their work. The more you're able to collaborate with other writers as a reader in these ways, the better a writer you'll be, *and* the better you'll be at taking other readers' feedback on your work and using it to strengthen your ideas.

CONVERSATIONAL INQUIRY IS COLLABORATIVE

Conversational inquiry involves collaboration and iteration. You have questions, which arise in response and in relation to others. As you seek answers to your questions, don't work alone. Keep in mind that you are in the "Burkean parlor," talking with others at a party where you are interested in exploring ideas and working out problems. Any problem worth exploring will require working in stages and making multiple attempts. Engaging in conversational inquiry and writing about your research doesn't happen quickly or in isolation. It is a social and collaborative process. It requires conversing with others throughout your process, drafting and composing your writing a bit at a time, returning to it many times, and strengthening it more with each pass. That's how the best conversational inquiry comes to be. And remember, as we said at the beginning of this chapter, when the subject is writing, anyone who has experienced reading and writing can engage in research about it.

If you would like to see a beautiful and quite literal illustration of one student's inquiry process, visit the University of Central Florida's peer-reviewed journal of first-year writing, *Stylus*. In Spring 2018 (volume 9, issue 1), Chelsea Harrison published a multimodal text that takes readers through her inquiry process. Her visual representation of the process illustrate all of the moves we've discussed in this chapter, including the CARS introduction described earlier. She describes her interest in the subject of social media, her survey of what other scholars had written, how and why she designed her own study, and what she found. Her visual representation of the inquiry process might help motivate you to start asking your own questions.

Sources That Informed Chapter 3

Burke, Kenneth. *The Philosophy of Literary Form*. U of California P, 1941.

Conference on College Composition and Communication. *CCCC Guidelines for the Ethical Conduct of Research in Composition Studies*. CCCC, 2015 https://cccc.ncte.org/cccc/resources/positions/ethicalconduct

Kinkead, Joyce. *Researching Writing: An Introduction to Research Methods*. Utah State UP, 2016.

MacNeally, Mary Sue. *Strategies for Empirical Research in Writing*. Allyn & Bacon, 1999.

Mallory, Angie, and Doug Downs. "Uniform Meets Rhetoric: Excellence through Interaction." In *Generation Vet: Composition, Student Veterans, and the Post-9/11 University*, edited by Sue Doe and Lisa Langstraadt, Utah State UP, 2015, pp. 51–72.

Rossman, Gretchen, and Sharon Rallis. *Learning in the Field: An Introduction to Qualitative Research*, 3rd edition. Sage, 2011.

SAGE ResearchMethods. *Methods Map*. Interactive Webpage. Sage Publications, 2018 https://methods.sagepub.com/methods-map.

Swales, John M. *Genre Analysis: English in Academic and Research Settings*. Cambridge UP, 1990.

Questions for Discussion and Journaling

1. Burke wrote his "parlor" metaphor in the 1940s, when most houses were built with parlors for entertaining guests. We've updated the metaphor to "party." What other metaphors might you use for the kind of interaction Burke seems to be describing?

2. What might make your perspective valuable as a researcher on writing and reading despite having little experience with this kind of research?

3. What are some ways that you can collaborate with other people as you work on a conversational inquiry project?

4. How do you treat a text differently when you recognize it as an argument than you do when you recognize it as information? Can you think of any texts that include only information and no argument?

5. Why does Swales call his analysis of research article introductions *"Creating* a research space"? (As opposed to "Finding" a research space or something similar?) How does he see research as *creative*?

6. Review Swales's CARS model again (p. 62). In your own research experience, have you done anything that resembled any of the steps Swales describes?

7. This chapter describes the process of analyzing data as one of letting findings *emerge* from multiple passes through (looks at) the data. What does that suggest about the nature of interpreting data?

8. What are some ways that interviewing fellow students on their processes for completing school writing assignments could put their privacy at risk?

Applying and Exploring Ideas

1. Build a list with your class of databases that would be useful to search on questions related to Writing Studies. Start with the *CompPile* database, and explore your library's database resources. Be sure to actually talk with a librarian about this question.

2. Write down three to four questions or subjects you find potentially interesting in the realms of writing, reading, and language. As a class, compare your lists and develop an overall list of conversations in Writing Studies your class seems interested in.

3. What research methods could you use to study the question of how people learn to write a genre that's brand new to them?

4. We assert that "data always require interpretation." Can you think of any cases where data don't? Why or why not?

5. How does the collaborative peer review we are advocating while working through the research process sound different from other kinds of peer review you've done in writing or English classes?

6. Reflecting on Harrison's example of conversational inquiry, does it seem possible to take on such questioning and research of your own? What would you have to learn, or do differently from research you've done in the past, in order to do research like Harrison's?

Participating in Conversational Inquiry

 Assignment Option 1

ENTERING THE BURKEAN PARLOR: EXPLORING A CONVERSATION ABOUT WRITING

In this project you'll choose a conversation about writing, reading, and literacy that interests you, "listen in" on it by tracing it through databases, and tell the story of the conversation to a friend, detailing what happened at this party.

What Conversations Will You "Listen In" On? Choosing a conversation is like making sure you're going to the right party, where there are like-minded people with similar interests. How do decide what research "parties" might interest you?

One way is to start with yourself. What are your experiences, frustrations, questions, problems with writing, reading, and literacy? Take about fifteen minutes to free-write about things that made you mad, upset you, or puzzled you.

As you read what you've written, know that everything there is most likely related to conversations already going on among writing and rhetoric scholars at the party you haven't arrived at yet.

Summarize each of the ideas you've brainstormed in the form of a statement or question or phrase that is a little broader than your own experience. For example, if you were frustrated by your high school English teacher's focus on grammar or rules, you might write "teachers, rules, writing" or "what makes writing teachers effective?" or "teaching grammar." If you were frustrated at the trouble you had learning to read, you might write "learning to read" or "how do children learn to read?"

With these phrases / statements / questions a little broader than your personal experience, you can begin looking around for what conversations are happening, and which one you might want to join. Visit https://wac.colostate.edu/comppile/ and begin searching the *CompPile* database. For each statement, phrase, or question you have written down, you will need several different tries. For example, you might type "teaching grammar" into the basic search feature, and then type "grammar" "teaching" and "school" into the advanced search boxes. If one search term doesn't work, try thinking up synonyms or connected words. *CompPile* also has a glossary you can search to try to see what words researchers use to refer to these ideas.

For each of your phrases / statements / questions, keep a list of the terms you've tried, and paste in any interesting results you find in *CompPile*. The database is acting like a webcam in the room of each party you're considering joining: you can overview parties and the conversations happening at them.

Pick One Conversation and See What Is Being Said. From the titles of your lists for each conversation you found, pick one conversation (list of search results on a topic) that seems most interesting. On the list of pieces in that conversation, choose four to six results that you want to read more deeply — perhaps because they sound most interesting or are most recent. Be sure the pieces you choose do all seem to be about a related idea or question, and that the idea or question is still interesting to you.

Now begin to read those results. As you do, remember all that you have learned in Chapters 2 and 3 about how to read in general, and how to read scholarly articles in particular. You can rely on the CARS moves to help you skim introductions and figure out what gap the authors are filling and how they plan to fill it. You can try to find the results or findings sections of the articles to get a good preview of what the authors are saying. Doing this first rather than deeply reading every word will save you time and energy.

Once you've skimmed to assure yourself that each of your choices seems to take a good "turn" in the conversation, settle in to read deeply. Look for the big ideas: What are the problems or questions the authors are taking up? What are their arguments or findings?

Having read and taken notes on all of these, look for connections between the texts. How are these authors speaking to each other? Might they actually cite each other? What conversation are they having? How do the turns they are taking, the pieces of the conversation they create, fit together? You'll have to attend to context: When was each article written? Who are the authors of each and what are their credentials, where do they work? What context does each piece provide for the issues it takes up?

Also pay attention, as you would in any party conversation, to who is talking and how. Consider the people talking in the texts you're reading. How does each sound to you? What would you like to ask each one if you were in the same room with them? (Or e-mailed them?) Which voices do you find yourself most in sympathy with or uncomfortable with? Who would you like to talk to further?

With your notes about findings, contexts, and connections, try summarizing the conversation. Your summary should sound something like this: *On the question of X (for example, how best to teach grammar), two scholars argue for A approach, while three others argue for B, an entirely different approach.*

Remember the big picture: You've chosen a party to go to and listened in on an interesting conversation at it, and started to get a sense of who's talking and saying what.

Tell a Friend What Happened at the Party. As would be the case at any party you went to, you would want to tell the story of a good conversation to roommates, family, or friends you're close to, after you've left the party. How you explain the conversation should depend on who you are talking to and should use media most appropriate for that end:

- Write your account as a letter or an e-mail.
- Create a blog or vlog post, including links to each of the pieces you read.
- Create a Snapchat or Instagram story by finding photos online of the participants in the conversation to go with summaries and snippets you write of what they said.
- Write a dialogue between the participants as a Facebook post.
- Write a narrative of the "event" of this conversation.
- Write a straightforward report.

Just don't go on too long sharing the conversation: 1,200 words of prose or two to three minutes of video will be plenty.

Think about what you might want to convey to your readers to help them share your sense of this conversation:

- Your questions and interests about writing and reading
- A quick sense of what other conversations you found while looking for the one you wanted to listen in on
- How the conversation you settled into actually took place. Who are the personalities in it, and what seemed to be of greatest concern to each? What alliances or conflicts formed during the conversation? What turns were taken — what order did it go in? How did people talk? Were there any particularly good or memorable lines anyone offered? If you've chosen electronic modes like blogging or vlogging for your account of the conversation, what can you *show* about the conversation rather than simply *saying* in words? What did the conversation *look* like?
- What you learned from the conversation. How did your understanding of the issue the conversation focused on change? What did you discover various conversants are interested in, and what did you learn from those interests and what was being argued about?
- Finally, given what you learned in that conversation, what interests you now? What might you want to know more about?

What Makes It Good?   This project asks you to take a few big steps:

- Move from your own experiences and interests to a larger questions.
- Search *CompPile* for relevant research on those questions.

- Use what you learned in Chapters 2 and 3 to help you skim and then more deeply read that research.

- Get a handle on what the scholars are saying to each other about the question.

If you can do these things, you've done a good job of trying out the Burkean parlor. If you can then explain what you did and found to someone else who wasn't there, in a clear and meaningful way, then you have succeeded in this project! This assignment isn't about reading all the research, or understanding everything perfectly, or explaining it in perfect academic prose. Rather, it's a chance for you to practice some of the preliminary moves of conversational inquiry, and see that it really is possible for you to join the party and take a turn in an interesting conversation.

- -

Assignment Option 2

DEVELOPING A RESEARCH QUESTION

In this project, you'll develop your own research question relating to writing, writers, discourse, or literacy. It combines brainstorming, source research, and strategic thinking about getting answers to questions you have.

Planning, Drafting, and Revising. The beginning of developing a research question is to *reflect on your own interests and curiosities* within the broad subject area of Writing Studies. What do you wonder about when it comes to these subjects? There are almost as many ways to brainstorm as there are people, but here are a few questions to help you mine your existing interests:

- What challenges, difficulties, or problems have you had in the past with writing or reading, and what kept you from having an easier time with them?

- Are there things that make you mad or upset you when you think about writing you've done in the past?

- Are there questions you've long wondered about and never heard a satisfactory answer to, or questions where you get inconsistent answers (answers in conflict with each other, or in conflict with your own experience, so you don't know what to think)?

- Are there aspects of writing, discourse, or persuasion that fascinate you and you'd like to learn more about?

What the above suggestions have in common is that they probe for *dissonance* in your thinking or experience: unresolved problems that make an "itch" in your brain that won't quit. Whatever your research question is, it will probably emerge from a dissonance of some kind, so part of finding good questions is looking for those dissonances.

Make a list of several possible questions that emerge from your brainstorming, and remember: *Write them in the form of a question*, as a sentence that can sensibly end with a question mark. We are not looking for "topics," except as very general categories in which you might pose questions (like "electronic writing" or "language I'm not allowed to use.") A topic is not a question and will not suffice for this project. If you can't say it in the form of a question, it's not a question.

When you find a question that's interesting to you, the work of making a good research question has just begun. You also need to find out whether it's a question that's interesting to anyone else and that other *experts in the field would agree is an open question* — one that has not yet been answered. To know this, you need to do some preliminary reading in the existing conversation on your question.

- In your draft research question, find keywords that will let you search for related articles in a search engine like Google Scholar or databases like *Academic Search Complete* or *CompPile*. You should also brainstorm a list of keywords that isn't necessarily in your research question itself, but relates to your area of inquiry. Keywords that will find the research you're looking for can be hard to guess, and it's not uncommon to initially not find the results you're looking for from the keywords you can think of on your own. Plan to ask a teacher, librarians, or friends to help you think of additional keywords. (Librarians have training and wide experience in choosing keywords that give good results — definitely plan on talking with one during your research, as early as possible.)

- In your search engine or database's list of hits, read results fairly quickly, just to get the lay of the land: Do any of the sources you find already answer your question? Is there considerable debate around your question? Or can you not find people addressing your question at all?

- For each source you find participating in the conversation you're seeking, write a short paragraph (just a hundred words or so) summarizing the contribution that source makes to the conversation. (Often the source itself will include an abstract that details this very point.)

- Reading over your summary paragraphs for each piece, create an overall account of the conversation you're finding so far by writing a brief (two- or three-paragraph) summary of the results of your preliminary source search that explains what the research you're finding talks about and how it relates to your question.

If your sense from preliminary research is that there are already plenty of good answers to your question, select another question from your previous brainstorming. Perhaps more likely, your initial source search will show you how to modify your first version of your question to make it narrower, more specific, and more answerable. Usually, first versions of research questions are too broad, and reading some of the existing literature on the subject helps you see how. One reason to do preliminary research before "locking in" your question is exactly to get a sense of your question's fit to the field and feasibility. You can expect to need to modify it some as you begin to compare it to existing research.

Once your preliminary search suggests that your question hasn't been answered yet by existing research and has helped you narrow and refine your question, you're ready for the final step for this project.

Your final product will be a medium-length paragraph that (1) states your research question, (2) explains why it's interesting to you, and (3) shows why you're confident that it is not yet sufficiently researched. Your question itself will be one sentence (one which makes sense when ended with a question mark); your own interest statement would be another few sentences; and your explanation of how it's an open question not yet sufficiently researched will take several more, drawing from the paragraphs you previously wrote summarizing the conversation you've found so far.

This paragraph should end with a list of works consulted that includes all the material you surveyed when you were honing your question.

What Makes It Good? You can refer to the "What Makes a Good Research Question?" box on page 60 for a refresher on this question. Don't forget to make sure your paragraph reads like a paragraph rather than a series of disjointed sentences, and make sure you respond to the three main points the assignment requests.

PART 2

Joining Conversations about Writing

CHAPTER 4

COMPOSING
Threshold Concept: Writing Is a Process, and All Writers Have More to Learn

Stephanie Pilick/picture-alliance/dpa/AP Images

An image of composing in the twenty-first century — digital, networked, collaborative, screen-based, and interactive.

This chapter looks at how people compose texts: the processes by which individuals put words on a page and attempt to make meaning — for themselves as well as for and with others. Questions about composing relate to several threshold concepts about writing that we noted in Chapter 1: Composing takes time and practice, our writing will never be perfect, and all writers always have more to learn.

Answering the question, "How do I write?" isn't as easy as it seems. How well do you really understand how you get things written? How would you describe your writing process if asked to do so right now? And is what you *think* you do *actually* what you do?

While many people are quite conscious of "what works for them" in order to get a text written, they tend to have more difficulty explaining *why* it works — or even what they're doing, beyond some basic details like "I write down a lot of ideas until I feel like I know what I want to say and then I just start typing it up." Such a description doesn't actually tell us a lot. Yet it would seem that if you want to become a more versatile, capable, powerful writer, you need to be pretty aware of which activities, behaviors, habits, and approaches lead to your strongest writing — and which ones don't.

Understanding yourself as a writer is complicated by popular conceptions (or misconceptions) of what writing is and how it gets done. As we discussed in Chapter 1, many of our conceptions related to writing (like imagining it to have universal rules, or cultural attitudes toward originality in writing) are inaccurate.

These misconceptions are not harmless; they can impact what we do and don't do, what we are willing to try or not, and how we feel about ourselves and our writing — our self-efficacy, how competent and powerful we feel at doing a given activity. In the case of writing processes, several popular but incorrect conceptions seem to be that good writers write alone, using "inspiration" or genius; that writing does not make new knowledge but rather simply transmits existing information; that some people are born writers and others are not; and that good writing is easy and "automatic" for good writers, who don't have to think about what they're doing. If we believe these things about writing, we might be less likely to try to write better, assuming that if we struggle we simply aren't "natural writers." Or we might not ask other people for feedback, assuming that good writers should be able to produce something by themselves without feedback from readers.

This chapter explores some more accurate threshold concepts about writing:

- Most good writers neither find writing easy nor "get it right the first time," because revision is central to developing writing and writing is imperfectible.
- Good writers are made, not born, through extensive practice and through circumstance. Writers always have more to learn.
- Writers always have more to learn in part because writing involves working with multiple **modes** (print, visual, numeric, and so on) that require them to address specific audiences and draw on different resources.
- Writing is enhanced by **mindfulness** and reflection — writers thinking about what they are actually doing and consciously controlling their process. Researchers on learning and thought call this *metacognition*, thinking about thinking.

Writing researchers have collected useful data on what people are doing when they write, so that they can show novice writers what experienced writers are doing, get them to practice doing similar things, and help them find their own writing groove along the way. Many writers in this chapter are concerned with **planning** and **revision**. Sondra Perl examines in great detail the many ways in which her research participants divide their time while writing — and how this influences the quality of what they write. Perl's work engages the threshold concepts of knowledge-making and the importance of revision. In addition, her attention to developing writers emphasizes the concept that all writers have more to learn and that writing *can be* learned. Perl demonstrates the influence of a writer's mindfulness and reflection on their writing. Jaydelle Celestine, a student researcher, illustrates this idea of mindfulness and reflection as he traces his growth as a writer and investigates where his ideas come from and how he gets writing done.

Mike Rose explores writers' awareness of rules they believe apply to writing and how those beliefs can actually block them *from* writing. Compared with writers who treat rules flexibly and say what they want before thinking about following rules, other writers are so busy trying not to break any rules that they have difficulty thinking of anything to say. Rose ultimately emphasizes that part of the way writers need to keep developing is to grow their awareness of the beliefs they have about writing and rules for writing, and to learn how "true" those rules are. Michael-John DePalma and Kara Poe Alexander examine a different way that students struggle — when they compose with many more **multimodal** resources than they typically have in school (with sounds, video, images, rather than strictly print, alphabetic text). They note a number of ways that these additional tools and resources can make it more difficult for students to imagine options that will be effective for their audiences.

Students aren't the only writers who struggle and find themselves sometimes unable to write. Professional, award-winning writers struggle as well. Carol Berkenkotter, in "Decisions and Revisions: The Planning Strategies of a Publishing Writer" observes Donald Murray at work with his writing. (And Murray responds with "Response of a Laboratory Rat — or, Being Protocoled.") Berkenkotter observes that Murray emphasizes the importance of personal investment in writing while still being able to accomplish serious work. The study shows the advantages of closely examining process in order to become mindful of how the various phases of a writing process — such as planning, drafting, reading, and revising — blend together and may not go in order. By studying Murray's process, Berkenkotter found that Murray was doing a lot of planning via revision — returning us to the threshold concept that writing is not easy even for award-winning professional writers, and writing by good writers rarely comes out "right" the first time. Anne Lamott speaks to the same concept in her very popular piece "Shitty First Drafts," insisting that as writers we have permission to write badly at first, as a necessary step in finding our way to better later drafts. The weight that these writers put on revision and their belief that meaning emerges through multiple drafts leads us to Nancy Sommers's finding that student writers often don't understand that ideas emerge through the act of writing, and thus they tend to see revision as changing words rather than as a chance to continue to find their ideas.

There are a number of other ways to understand the readings in this chapter as well, depending on what aspects of the writing process you are focusing on. For example, because writing is in the realm of thought and ideas, we're dealing in part with **cognition** — the mental aspect of writing — when we think about process. You'll see a number of the researchers in this chapter thinking about, theorizing about, modeling, and testing problem-solving patterns, or **heuristics,** and other guesses at how our brains process ideas in order to construct meaning in texts (both as writers and readers); see, for example, Rose (p. 158), Berkenkotter (p. 123), and Sommers (p. 143).

Along with the cognitive, some researchers consider the *affective* domain — that is, what goes on with the body and with emotions. Berkenkotter (p. 123), Lamott (p. 87), Perl (p. 93), and Celestine (p. 205) think about these issues.

This is where **context** comes in: Writing depends not only on the ideas in your brain, but on whether you're trying to write in a journal under a tree on a gorgeous sunny afternoon, or in a fluorescent-lit cubicle with a boss breathing over your shoulder who needs your memo on budget cuts right away. It also depends on the history of the writer (discussed in more detail in Chapter 5) and his or her previous experiences with writing, with the ideas currently under consideration, with the genre being written, etc. Our environment and **rhetorical situation** shape our thoughts, so the cognitive domain never stands apart from what's outside our brains and bodies.

Still, writing is ultimately the meaning we make in our heads, so to understand composing processes, we have to somehow look inside our heads. This is the tricky part of writing research, as you'll see reflected in the numerous **methodologies** (procedures for conducting research, which we discussed in Chapter 3) the studies in this chapter use and demonstrate. The basic problem is this: Researchers can't directly access what's happening in your brain; they have to infer what's happening by looking for external signs. You could *tell* researchers what you're thinking, although (1) you can't talk as fast as you think, and (2) the talking inevitably *changes* what you're thinking. Researchers could look at the mistakes you make and try to explain the rules you're following (which you're probably not even aware of). They could interview you and study the words you use to express yourself. They could ask you to draw about your processes and all of the resources on which you rely while writing. But they would still never know *exactly* what's going on in there. (Not even you know that, really.) So, in these readings, you'll see researchers working to get at something that we can't access directly.

CHAPTER GOALS

- Understand the threshold concept, *writing is a process, and all writers have more to learn.*
- Improve as a reader of complex, research-based texts.
- Acquire vocabulary for talking about writing processes and yourself as a writer.
- Actively consider your own writing processes and practices and shift them if you wish.
- Understand writing and research as processes requiring planning, incubation, and revision.

Shitty First Drafts

ANNE LAMOTT

Araya Diaz/WireImage/Getty Images

Framing the Reading

Anne Lamott is most people's idea and, perhaps, stereotype of a successful writer. She has published fourteen novels and nonfiction books since 1980, probably the best known of which is the book this excerpt comes from, *Bird by Bird: Some Instructions on Writing and Life*. She is known for her self-deprecating humor and openness (much of her writing touches on subjects such as alcoholism, depression, spirituality and faith, and motherhood). This piece is no exception. Characteristically, Lamott's advice in "Shitty First Drafts" draws extensively on her personal experience with writing (it was her sixth book). And you'll probably find it makes its arguments not only reasonably, but entertainingly. Not many writers would disagree with either her overall point or her descriptions in making it. Thus, it's become one of the most widely anthologized pieces of contemporary advice on the writing process. Few writers get more directly at the threshold concepts that writing is not perfectible, that writers always have more to learn, and that writing is a process of trying and trying again, not simply for "weak" writers but for *all* writers.

Getting Ready to Read

Before you read, do at least one of the following activities:

- Think back through your writing experiences and education, and make a list of the times you've been told it's okay to write badly, and who told you.
- What advice would you typically give someone who's having a hard time getting started writing?

As you read, consider the following questions:

- Can you imagine what the shitty first draft of *this piece itself* looked like? Reading the finished prose, can you make any guesses about what the second and third drafts changed from the first?
- How does this piece make you feel about writing?

Lamott, Anne. "Shitty First Drafts." *Bird by Bird: Some Instructions on Writing and Life.* Anchor Books, 1994, pp. 21–27.

NOW, PRACTICALLY EVEN BETTER news than that of short assignments is the idea of shitty first drafts. All good writers write them. This is how they end up with good second drafts and terrific third drafts. People tend to look at successful writers, writers who are getting their books published and maybe even doing well financially, and think that they sit down at their desks every morning feeling like a million dollars, feeling great about who they are and how much talent they have and what a great story they have to tell; that they take in a few deep breaths, push back their sleeves, roll their necks a few times to get all the cricks out, and dive in, typing fully formed passages as fast as a court reporter. But this is just the fantasy of the uninitiated. I know some very great writers, writers you love who write beautifully and have made a great deal of money, and not *one* of them sits down routinely feeling wildly enthusiastic and confident. Not one of them writes elegant first drafts. All right, one of them does, but we do not like her very much. We do not think that she has a rich inner life or that God likes her or can even stand her. (Although when I mentioned this to my priest friend Tom, he said you can safely assume you've created God in your own image when it turns out that God hates all the same people you do.)

Very few writers really know what they are doing until they've done it. Nor do they go about their business feeling dewy and thrilled. They do not type a few stiff warm-up sentences and then find themselves bounding along like huskies across the snow. One writer I know tells me that he sits down every morning and says to himself nicely, "It's not like you don't have a choice, because you do — you can either type or kill yourself." We all often feel like we are pulling teeth, even those writers whose prose ends up being the most natural and fluid. The right words and sentences just do not come pouring out like ticker tape most of the time. Now, Muriel Spark is said to have felt that she was taking dictation from God every morning — sitting there, one supposes, plugged into a Dictaphone, typing away, humming. But this is a very hostile and aggressive position. One might hope for bad things to rain down on a person like this.

For me and most of the other writers I know, writing is not rapturous. In fact, the only way I can get anything written at all is to write really, really shitty first drafts.

The first draft is the child's draft, where you let it all pour out and then let it romp all over the place, knowing that no one is going to see it and that you can shape it later. You just let this childlike part of you channel whatever voices and visions come through and onto the page. If one of the characters wants to say, "Well, so what, Mr. Poopy Pants?" you let her. No one is going to see it. If the kid wants to get into really sentimental, weepy, emotional territory, you let him. Just get it all down on paper, because there may be something great in those six crazy pages that you would never have gotten to by more rational, grown-up means. There may be something in the very last line of the very last paragraph on page six that you just love, that is so beautiful or wild that you now know what you're supposed to be writing about, more or less, or in what direction you might go — but there was no way to get to this without first getting through the first five and a half pages.

I used to write food reviews for *California* magazine before it folded. (My writing food reviews had nothing to do with the magazine folding, although every single review did cause a couple of canceled subscriptions. Some readers took umbrage at my comparing mounds of vegetable puree with various ex-presidents' brains.) These reviews always took two days to write. First I'd go to a restaurant several times with a few opinionated, articulate friends in tow. I'd sit there writing down everything anyone said that was at all interesting or funny. Then on the following Monday I'd sit down at my desk with my notes, and try to write the review. Even after I'd been doing this for years, panic would set in. I'd try to write a lead, but instead I'd write a couple of dreadful sentences, xx them out, try again, xx everything out, and then feel despair and worry settle on my chest like an x-ray apron. It's over, I'd think, calmly, I'm not going to be able to get the magic to work this time. I'm ruined. I'm through. I'm toast. Maybe, I'd think, I can get my old job back as a clerk-typist. But probably not. I'd get up and study my teeth in the mirror for a while. Then I'd stop, remember to breathe, make a few phone calls, hit the kitchen and chow down. Eventually I'd go back and sit down at my desk, and sigh for the next ten minutes. Finally I would pick up my one-inch picture frame, stare into it as if for the answer, and every time the answer would come: All I had to do was to write a really shitty first draft of, say, the opening paragraph. And no one was going to see it.

So I'd start writing without reining myself in. It was almost just typing, just making my fingers move. And the writing would be *terrible*. I'd write a lead paragraph that was a whole page, even though the entire review could only be three pages long, and then I'd start writing up descriptions of the food, one dish at a time, bird by bird, and the critics would be sitting on my shoulders, commenting like cartoon characters. They'd be pretending to snore, or rolling their eyes at my overwrought descriptions, no matter how hard I tried to tone those descriptions down, no matter how conscious I was of what a friend said to me gently in my early days of restaurant reviewing. "Annie," she said, "it is just a piece of *chicken*. It is just a bit of *cake*."

But because by then I had been writing for so long, I would eventually let myself trust the process — sort of, more or less. I'd write a first draft that was maybe twice as long as it should be, with a self-indulgent and boring beginning, stupefying descriptions of the meal, lots of quotes from my black-humored friends that made them sound more like the Manson girls than food lovers, and no ending to speak of. The whole thing would be so long and incoherent and hideous that for the rest of the day I'd obsess about getting creamed by a car before I could write a decent second draft. I'd worry that people would read what I'd written and believe that the accident had really been a suicide, that I had panicked because my talent was waning and my mind was shot.

The next day, though, I'd sit down, go through it all with a colored pen, take 8 out everything I possibly could, find a new lead somewhere on the second page, figure out a kicky place to end it, and then write a second draft. It always turned out fine, sometimes even funny and weird and helpful. I'd go over it one more time and mail it in.

Then, a month later, when it was time for another review, the whole process 9 would start again, complete with the fears that people would find my first draft before I could rewrite it.

Almost all good writing begins with terrible first efforts. You need to start 10 somewhere. Start by getting something — anything — down on paper. A friend of mine says that the first draft is the down draft — you just get it down. The second draft is the up draft — you fix it up. You try to say what you have to say more accurately. And the third draft is the dental draft, where you check every tooth, to see if it's loose or cramped or decayed, or even, God help us, healthy.

> Almost all good writing begins with terrible first efforts. You need to start somewhere. Start by getting something — anything — down on paper.

What I've learned to do when I sit down 11 to work on a shitty first draft is to quiet the voices in my head. First there's the vinegar-lipped Reader Lady, who says primly, "Well, *that's* not very interesting, is it?" And there's the emaciated German male who writes these Orwellian memos detailing your thought crimes. And there are your parents, agonizing over your lack of loyalty and discretion; and there's William Burroughs, dozing off or shooting up because he finds you as bold and articulate as a houseplant; and so on. And there are also the dogs: let's not forget the dogs, the dogs in their pen who will surely hurtle and snarl their way out if you ever *stop* writing, because writing is, for some of us, the latch that keeps the door of the pen closed, keeps those crazy ravenous dogs contained.

Quieting these voices is at least half the battle I fight daily. But this is bet- 12 ter than it used to be. It used to be 87 percent. Left to its own devices, my mind spends much of its time having conversations with people who aren't there. I walk along defending myself to people, or exchanging repartee with them, or rationalizing my behavior, or seducing them with gossip, or pretending I'm on their TV talk show or whatever. I speed or run an aging yellow light or don't come to a full stop, and one nanosecond later am explaining to imaginary cops exactly why I had to do what I did, or insisting that I did not in fact do it.

I happened to mention this to a hypnotist I saw many years ago, and he 13 looked at me very nicely. At first I thought he was feeling around on the floor for the silent alarm button, but then he gave me the following exercise, which I still use to this day.

Close your eyes and get quiet for a minute, until the chatter starts up. Then 14 isolate one of the voices and imagine the person speaking as a mouse. Pick it up by the tail and drop it into a mason jar. Then isolate another voice, pick it up by the tail, drop it in the jar. And so on. Drop in any high-maintenance parental units, drop in any contractors, lawyers, colleagues, children, anyone who is whining in your head. Then put the lid on, and watch all these mouse people clawing at the glass, jabbering away, trying to make you feel like shit because you won't do what they want — won't give them more money, won't be more successful, won't see them more often. Then imagine that there is a volume-control button on the bottle. Turn it all the way up for a minute, and listen to the stream of angry, neglected, guilt-mongering voices. Then turn it all the way down and watch the frantic mice lunge at the glass, trying to get to you. Leave it down, and get back to your shitty first draft.

A writer friend of mine suggests opening the jar and shooting them all in the head. 15 But I think he's a little angry, and I'm sure nothing like this would ever occur to you.

- -

Questions for Discussion and Journaling

1. Why is it so hard for many people (maybe you) to knowingly put bad writing on paper?

2. What are your own "coping strategies" for getting started on a piece of writing? Do you have particular strategies for making yourself sit down and start writing?

3. What would you say is the funniest line in this piece? Why did it make you laugh?

4. Most readers find that Lamott sounds very down-to-earth and approachable in this piece. What is she doing with language and words themselves to give this impression?

5. Lamott talks, toward the end of this piece, about all the critical voices that play in her mind when she's trying to write. Most, maybe all, writers have something similar. What are yours?

Applying and Exploring Ideas

1. Lamott obviously knows well what the weaknesses in her first drafts are likely to be. Are you aware yet of any patterns in your first-draft writing — places or ways in which you simply expect that the writing will need work once you actually have words on paper?

2. As you read other "process" pieces in this chapter, consider what makes Lamott's writing and advice different from, say, Rose or Sommers?

3. Lamott says: "There may be something in the very last line of the very last paragraph of page six that you just love . . . but there was no way to get to this without first getting through the first five and a half pages" (para. 4). We might explain this idea about revision with an analogy: When you drive at night, your headlights don't light the whole way to your destination, just the first couple hundred yards. When you drive that far, then you can see the next couple hundred yards — and so on. Drafting works exactly the same way: In your first draft, you write what you know so far. But you discover new ideas while you write, and so, just like being able to see more of the road in your headlights, after you've written one draft, what you wrote in it helps you know *more* to say in the second draft — and so on. What other metaphors or analogies could you make to explain this phenomenon?

- -

META MOMENT   Lamott gives you permission to write badly in order to write well. What else would you like permission to do with / in your writing?

- -

The Composing Processes of Unskilled College Writers

SONDRA PERL

Courtesy of Sondra Perl

Framing the Reading

Writing this article in 1979, Sondra Perl argued, "To date no examination of composing processes has dealt primarily with unskilled writers. As long as 'average' or skilled writers are the focus, it remains unclear as to how process research will [help unskilled writers]" (para. 4). Much of the nature of this article is captured in that brief passage.

With the study reported here, Perl attempted to accomplish two important and quite distinct projects in advancing writing research. The first was to create a brand-new way to study writers writing. In the first few pages you'll read Perl's description of the problem with previous research on the writing process: It relied almost entirely on stories researchers told about what they observed. Perl tried to create a more objective system for describing what writers were doing.

The second was to study a group of writers that previous research had ignored. Writers who aren't very good at writing probably aren't the best test subjects for "how writing works," and so they had not been studied much by researchers trying to learn about "the composing process" (which is how composition was described in those times — as a single kind of process writers either mastered or didn't). Yet, as Perl argued, studying people who are already proficient writers would probably not "provide teachers with a firmer understanding of the needs of students with serious writing problems" (para. 4). And what Perl saw her research participants doing connects to our threshold concepts that writing makes knowledge (often through revision) and that writers always have more to learn, no matter how strong or weak they are.

Like a few other articles in this chapter, Perl's is more than thirty years old. It reflects a time of great interest, among writing researchers, about processes writers use to compose texts. That interest waned by the end of the 1980s; even though there was still much to be discovered and understood (most process research findings were provisional at best and needed to

Perl, Sondra. "The Composing Processes of Unskilled College Writers." *Research in the Teaching of English*, vol. 13, no. 4, Dec. 1979, pp. 317–36.

be followed up with larger-scale studies that have never been done), the attention of writing researchers went in other directions. Thus there is a major gap between research on process conducted in the late 1970s and 1980s, like Perl's, and when interest in process research returned in the early 2000s, when a few researchers began to take up the question again, often motivated by the influence of technologies and social media on composing.

Perl's article had a particularly great impact on the field because of her combined focus on a standardized method for observing, recording, and reporting on writers' behaviors while writing and her attention to "basic" writers whose writing was difficult to read and understand. Work such as this has made Perl one of the most significant researchers the field has seen. She went on to study how writers imagine what to say before they quite *know* what they want to say. (In 2004 she published a book called *Felt Sense: Writing with the Body*, which includes a CD that offers "meditations" for writers. It's quite different from the work you'll read here, which we hope might motivate you to look it up.)

Getting Ready to Read

Before you read, do at least one of the following activities:

- Ask yourself how you view yourself as a writer. Do you think you are a skilled or unskilled writer? Is writing easy or hard for you?
- Write down exactly what you think you do when you have to write something for school. Have you ever consciously thought about this before?
- Watch a roommate or friend write something for school, and make note of the things he or she does while writing.

As you read, consider the following questions:

- What arguments does Perl make about what research methods are necessary for good studies of writing?
- How are Tony's processes as an "unskilled" writer different from those of skilled writers?

THIS PAPER PRESENTS the pertinent findings from a study of the composing 1 processes of five unskilled college writers (Perl, 1978). The first part summarizes the goals of the original study, the kinds of data collected, and the research methods employed. The second part is a synopsis of the study of Tony, one of the original five case studies. The third part presents a condensed version of the findings on the composing process and discusses these findings in light of current pedagogical practice and research design.

GOALS OF THE STUDY

This research addressed three major questions: (l) How do unskilled writers
write? (2) Can their writing processes be analyzed in a systematic, replicable
manner? and (3) What does an increased understanding of their processes suggest about the nature of composing in general and the manner in which writing
is taught in the schools?

In recent years, interest in the composing process has grown (Britton et al.,
1975; Burton, 1973; Cooper, 1974; Emig, 1967, 1971). In 1963, Braddock,
Lloyd-Jones, and Schoer, writing on the state of research in written composition, included the need for "direct observation" and case study procedures
in their suggestions for future research (pp. 24, 31–32). In a section entitled
"Unexplored Territory," they listed basic unanswered questions such as, "What
is involved in the act of writing?" and "Of what does skill in writing actually
consist?" (p. 51). Fifteen years later, Cooper and Odell (1978) edited a volume
similar in scope, only this one was devoted entirely to issues and questions
related to research on composing. This volume in particular signals a shift in
emphasis in writing research. Alongside the traditional, large-scale experimental
studies, there is now widespread recognition of the need for works of a more
modest, probing nature, works that attempt to elucidate basic processes. The
studies on composing that have been completed to date are precisely of this
kind; they are small-scale studies, based on the systematic observation of writers
engaged in the process of writing (Emig, 1971; Graves, 1973; Mischel, 1974;
Pianko, 1977; Stallard, 1974).

For all of its promise, this body of research has yet to produce work that
would insure wide recognition for the value of process studies of composing.
One limitation of work done to date is methodological. Narrative descriptions
of composing processes do not provide sufficiently graphic evidence for the
perception of underlying regularities and patterns. Without such evidence, it
is difficult to generate well-defined hypotheses and to move from exploratory
research to more controlled experimental studies. A second limitation pertains
to the subjects studied. To date no examination of composing processes has
dealt primarily with unskilled writers. As long as "average" or skilled writers
are the focus, it remains unclear as to how process research will provide teachers with a firmer understanding of the needs of students with serious writing
problems.

The present study is intended to carry process research forward by addressing
both of these limitations. One prominent feature of the research design involves
the development and use of a meaningful and replicable method for rendering
the composing process as a sequence of observable and scorable behaviors. A
second aspect of the design is the focus on students whose writing problems
baffle the teachers charged with their education.

DESIGN OF THE STUDY

This study took place during the 1975–1976 fall semester at Eugenio Maria 6 de Hostos Community College of the City University of New York. Students were selected for the study on the basis of two criteria: writing samples that qualified them as unskilled writers and willingness to participate. Each student met with the researcher for five 90-minute sessions (see Table 1). Four sessions were devoted to writing with the students directed to compose aloud, to externalize their thinking processes as much as possible, during each session. In one additional session, a writing profile on the students' perceptions and memories of writing was developed through the use of an open-ended interview. All of the sessions took place in a soundproof room in the college library. Throughout each session, the researcher assumed a noninterfering role.

The topics for writing were developed in an introductory social science 7 course in which the five students were enrolled. The "content" material they were studying was divided into two modes: extensive, in which the writer was directed to approach the material in an objective, impersonal fashion, and reflexive, in which the writer was directed to approach similar material in an affective, personalized fashion. Contrary to Emig's (1971) definitions, in this study it was assumed that the teacher was always the audience.

DATA ANALYSIS

Three kinds of data were collected in this study: the students' written products, 8 their composing tapes, and their responses to the interview. Each of these was studied carefully and then discussed in detail in each of the five case study presentations. Due to limitations of space, this paper will review only two of the data sets generated in the study.

Coding the Composing Process

One of the goals of this research was to devise a tool for describing the move- 9 ments that occur during composing. In the past such descriptions have taken the form of narratives which detail, with relative precision and insight, observable composing behaviors; however, these narratives provide no way of ascertaining the frequency, relative importance, and place of each behavior within an individual's composing process. As such, they are cumbersome and difficult to replicate. Furthermore, lengthy, idiosyncratic narratives run the risk of leaving underlying patterns and regularities obscure. In contrast, the method created in this research provides a means of viewing the composing process that is:

1. Standardized—it introduces a coding system for observing the composing process that can be replicated;
2. Categorical—it labels specific, observable behaviors so that types of composing movements are revealed;

TABLE 1   DESIGN OF THE STUDY

	SESSION 1 (S1)	SESSION 2 (S2)	SESSION 3 (S3)	SESSION 4 (S4)	SESSION 5 (S5)
Mode	Extensive	Reflexive		Extensive	Reflexive
Topic	Society & Culture	Society & Culture	Interview: Writing Profile	Capitalism	Capitalism
Directions	Students told to compose aloud; no other directions given	Students told to compose aloud; no other directions given		Students told to compose aloud; also directed to talk out ideas before writing	Students told to compose aloud; also directed to talk out ideas before writing

3. Concise — it presents the entire sequence of composing movements on one or two pages;

4. Structural — it provides a way of determining how parts of the process relate to the whole; and

5. Diachronic — it presents the sequences of movements that occur during composing as they unfold in time.

In total, the method allows the researcher to apprehend a process as it unfolds. It lays out the movements or behavior sequences in such a way that if patterns within a student's process or among a group of students exist, they become apparent.

The Code

The method consists of coding each composing behavior exhibited by the student 10 and charting each behavior on a continuum. During this study, the coding occurred after the student had finished composing and was done by working from the student's written product and the audiotape of the session. It was possible to do this since the tape captured both what the student was saying and the literal sound of the pen moving across the page. As a result, it was possible to determine when students were talking, when they were writing, when both occurred simultaneously, and when neither occurred.

The major categorical divisions in this coding system are talking, writing, 11 and reading; however, it was clear that there are various kinds of talk and various kinds of writing and reading operations, and that a coding system would need to distinguish among these various types. In this study the following operations were distinguished:

1. General planning [PL] — organizing one's thoughts for writing, discussing how one will proceed.

2. Local planning [PLL] — talking out what idea will come next.

3. Global planning [PLG] — discussing changes in drafts.

4. Commenting [C] — sighing, making a comment or judgment about the topic.

5. Interpreting [I] — rephrasing the topic to get a "handle" on it.

6. Assessing [A(+); A(−)] — making a judgment about one's writing; may be positive or negative.

7. Questioning [Q] — asking a question.

8. Talking leading to writing [T→W] — voicing ideas on the topic, tentatively finding one's way, but not necessarily being committed to or using all one is saying.

9. Talking and writing at the same time [TW] — composing aloud in such a way that what one is saying is actually being written at the same time.

10. Repeating [re] — repeating written or unwritten phrases a number of times.

11. Reading related to the topic:
    (a) Reading the directions [R_D]
    (b) Reading the question [R_q]
    (c) Reading the statement [R_s]

12. Reading related to one's own written product:
    (a) Reading one sentence or a few words [R^a]
    (b) Reading a number of sentences together [R^{a-b}]
    (c) Reading the entire draft through [R^{W1}]

13. Writing silently [W]

14. Writing aloud [TW]

15. Editing [E]
    (a) adding syntactic markers, words, phrases, or clauses [Eadd]
    (b) deleting syntactic markers, words, phrases, or clauses [Edel]
    (c) indicating concern for a grammatical rule [Egr]
    (d) adding, deleting, or considering the use of punctuation [Epunc]
    (e) considering or changing spelling [Esp]
    (f) changing the sentence structure through embedding, coordination or subordination [Ess]
    (g) indicating concern for appropriate vocabulary (word choice) [Ewc]
    (h) considering or changing verb form [Evc]

16. Periods of silence [s]

By taking specific observable behaviors that occur during composing and 12 supplying labels for them, this system thus far provides a way of analyzing the process that is categorical and capable of replication. In order to view the frequency and the duration of composing behaviors and the relation between one particular behavior and the whole process, these behaviors need to be depicted graphically to show their duration and sequence.

The Continuum

The second component of this system is the construction of a time line and a 13 numbering system. In this study, blank charts with lines like the following were designed:

```
----------------------------------------------------------------------
    10        20        30        40        50        60        70
```

A ten-digit interval corresponds to one minute and is keyed to a counter on a 14 tape recorder. By listening to the tape and watching the counter, it is possible to determine the nature and duration of each operation. As each behavior is heard on the tape, it is coded and then noted on the chart with the counter used as

99

a time marker. For example, if a student during prewriting reads the directions and the question twice and then begins to plan exactly what she is going to say, all within the first minute, it would be coded like this:

$$\overbrace{\text{R\textsc{d}R\textsc{q}R\textsc{d}R\textsc{q}PLL}}^{\text{Prewriting}}$$
$$\underset{10}{\rule{3cm}{0.4pt}}$$

If at this point the student spends two minutes writing the first sentence, during which time she pauses, rereads the question, continues writing, and then edits for spelling before continuing on, it would be coded like this:

$$\overbrace{\text{TW}_1\text{/s/R\textsc{q}} \qquad \text{TW}_1[\text{Esp}]\text{TW}_1}^{1}$$
$$\underset{20}{\rule{2.5cm}{0.4pt}} \qquad \underset{30}{\rule{2.5cm}{0.4pt}}$$

At this point two types of brackets and numbering systems have appeared. 15 The initial sublevel number linked with the TW code indicates which draft the student is working on. TW_1 indicates the writing of the first draft; TW_2 and TW_3 indicate the writing of the second and third drafts. Brackets such as [Esp] separate these operations from writing and indicate the amount of time the operation takes. The upper-level number above the horizontal bracket indicates which sentence in the written product is being written and the length of the bracket indicates the amount of time spent on the writing of each sentence. All horizontal brackets refer to sentences, and from the charts it is possible to see when sentences are grouped together and written in a chunk (adjacent brackets) or when each sentence is produced in isolation (gaps between brackets). (See Appendix for sample chart.)

The charts can be read by moving along the time line, noting which behav- 16 iors occur and in what sequence. Three types of comments are also included in the charts. In boldface type, the beginning and end of each draft are indicated; in lighter typeface, comments on the actual composing movements are provided; and in the lightest typeface, specific statements made by students or specific words they found particularly troublesome are noted.

From the charts, the following information can be determined: 17

1. the amount of time spent during prewriting;
2. the strategies used during prewriting;
3. the amount of time spent writing each sentence;
4. the behaviors that occur while each sentence is being written;

5. when sentences are written in groups or "chunks" (fluent writing);

6. when sentences are written in isolation (choppy or sporadic writing);

7. the amount of time spent between sentences;

8. the behaviors that occur between sentences;

9. when editing occurs (during the writing of sentences, between sentences, in the time between drafts);

10. the frequency of editing behavior;

11. the nature of the editing operations; and

12. where and in what frequency pauses or periods of silence occur in the process.

The charts, or *composing style sheets* as they are called, do not explain what students wrote but rather *how* they wrote. They indicate, on one page, the sequences of behavior that occur from the beginning of the process to the end. From them it is possible to determine where and how these behaviors fall into patterns and whether these patterns vary according to the mode of discourse.

It should be noted that although the coding system is presented before the 18 analysis of the data, it was derived from the data and then used as the basis for generalizing about the patterns and behavioral sequences found within each student's process. These individual patterns were reported in each of the five case studies. Thus, initially, a style sheet was constructed for each writing session on each student. When there were four style sheets for each student, it was possible to determine if composing patterns existed among the group. The summary of results reported here is based on the patterns revealed by these charts.

Analyzing Miscues in the Writing Process

Miscue analysis is based on Goodman's model of the reading process. Created 19 in 1962, it has become a widespread tool for studying what students do when they read and is based on the premise that reading is a psycholinguistic process which "uses language, in written form, to get to the meaning" (Goodman, 1973, p. 4). Miscue analysis "involves its user in examining the observed behavior of oral readers as an interaction between language and thought, as a process of constructing meaning from a graphic display" (Goodman, 1973, p. 4). Methodologically, the observer analyzes the mismatch that occurs when readers make responses during oral reading that differ from the text. This mismatch or miscueing is then analyzed from Goodman's "meaning-getting" model, based on the assumption that "the reader's preoccupation with meaning will show in his miscues, because they will tend to result in language that still makes sense" (Goodman, 1973, p. 9).

In the present study, miscue analysis was adapted from Goodman's model in 20 order to provide insight into the writing process. Since students composed aloud, two types of oral behaviors were available for study: encoding processes or what students spoke while they were writing and decoding processes or what students "read"[1] after they had finished writing. When a discrepancy existed between encoding or decoding and what was on the paper, it was referred to as miscue.

For encoding, the miscue analysis was carried out in the following manner: 21

1. The students' written products were typed, preserving the original style and spelling.
2. What students said while composing aloud was checked against the written products; discrepancies were noted on the paper wherever they occurred,
3. The discrepancies were categorized and counted.

Three miscue categories were derived for encoding: 22

1. Speaking complete ideas but omitting certain words during writing.
2. Pronouncing words with plural markers or other suffixes completely but omitting these endings during writing.
3. Pronouncing the desired word but writing a homonym, an approximation of the word or a personal abbreviation of the word on paper.

For decoding, similar procedures were used, this time comparing the words 23 of the written product with what the student "read" orally. When a discrepancy occurred, it was noted. The discrepancies were then categorized and counted.

Four miscue categories were derived for decoding: 24

1. "Reading in" missing words or word endings;
2. Deleting words or word endings;
3. "Reading" the desired word rather than the word on the page;
4. "Reading" abbreviations and misspellings as though they were written correctly.

A brief summary of the results of this analysis appears in the findings.

SYNOPSIS OF A CASE STUDY

Tony was a 20-year-old ex-Marine born and raised in the Bronx, New York. Like 25 many Puerto Ricans born in the United States, he was able to speak Spanish, but he considered English his native tongue. In the eleventh grade, Tony left high school, returning three years later to take the New York State high school equivalency exam. As a freshman in college, he was also working part-time to support a child and a wife from whom he was separated.

Behaviors

The composing style sheets provide an overview of the observable behaviors 26 exhibited by Tony during the composing process. (See Appendix for samples of Tony's writing and the accompanying composing style sheet.) The most salient feature of Tony's composing process was its recursiveness. Tony rarely produced a sentence without stopping to reread either a part or the whole. This repetition set up a particular kind of composing rhythm, one that was cumulative in nature and that set ideas in motion by its very repetitiveness. Thus, as can be seen from any of the style sheets, talking led to writing which led to reading which led to planning which again led to writing.

The style sheets indicated a difference in the composing rhythms exhibited 27 in the extensive and reflexive modes. On the extensive topics there was not only more repetition within each sentence but also many more pauses and repetitions between sentences, with intervals often lasting as long as two minutes. On the reflexive topics, sentences were often written in groups, with fewer rereadings and only minimal time intervals separating the creation of one sentence from another.

Editing occurred consistently in all sessions. From the moment Tony began 28 writing, he indicated a concern for correct form that actually inhibited the development of ideas. In none of the writing sessions did he ever write more than two sentences before he began to edit. While editing fit into his overall recursive pattern, it simultaneously interrupted the composing rhythm he had just initiated.

During the intervals between drafts, Tony read his written work, assessed his 29 writing, planned new phrasings, transitions or endings, read the directions and the question over, and edited once again.

Tony performed these operations in both the extensive and reflexive modes 30 and was remarkably consistent in all of his composing operations. The style sheets attest both to this consistency and to the densely packed, tight quality of Tony's composing process—indeed, if the notations on these sheets were any indication at all, it was clear that Tony's composing process was so full that there was little room left for invention or change.

Fluency

Table 2 provides a numerical analysis of Tony's writing performance. Here it is 31 possible to compare not only the amount of time spent on the various composing operations but also the relative fluency. For Sessions 1 and 2 the data indicate that while Tony spent more time prewriting and writing in the extensive

TABLE 2 TONY: SUMMARY OF FOUR WRITING SESSIONS (TIME IN MINUTES)

			S1 TW_1			S4 T→W
	Drafts	Words	Time	Drafts	Words	Time
Extensive mode			Prewriting: 7.8			Prewriting: 8.0
	W1	132	18.8	W1	182	29.0
	W2	170	51.0	W2	174	33.9
	Total	302	Total composing: 91.2*	Total	356	Total composing: 82.0*

			S2 TW_1			S5 T→W
	Drafts	Words	Time	Drafts	Words	Time
Reflexive mode			Prewriting: 3.5			Prewriting: 5.7
	W1	165	14.5	W1	208	24.0
	W2	169	25.0	W2	190	38.3
	W3	178	24.2	W3	152	20.8
	Total	512	Total composing: 76.0*	Total	550	Total composing: 96.0*

*Total composing includes time spent on editing and rereading, as well as actual writing.

mode, he actually produced fewer words. For Sessions 4 and 5, a similar pattern can be detected. In the extensive mode, Tony again spent more time prewriting and produced fewer words. Although writing time was increased in the reflexive mode, the additional 20 minutes spent writing did not sufficiently account for an increase of 194 words. Rather, the data indicate that Tony produced more words with less planning and generally in less time in the reflexive mode, suggesting that his greater fluency lay in this mode.

Strategies

Tony exhibited a number of strategies that served him as a writer whether the mode was extensive or reflexive. Given any topic, the first operation he performed was to focus in and narrow down the topic. He did this by rephrasing the topic until either a word or an idea in the topic linked up with something in his own experience (an attitude, an opinion, an event). In this way he established a connection between the field of discourse and himself and at this point he felt ready to write. 32

Level of Language Use

Once writing, Tony employed a pattern of classifying or dividing the topic 33
into manageable pieces and then using one or both of the divisions as the basis
for narration. In the four writing sessions, his classifications were made on the
basis of economic, racial, and political differences. However, all of his writing
reflected a low level of generality. No formal principles were used to organize
the narratives nor were the implications of ideas present in the essay developed.

In his writing, Tony was able to maintain the extensive / reflexive distinction. 34
He recognized when he was being asked directly for an opinion and when he was
being asked to discuss concepts or ideas that were not directly linked to his experience. However, the more distance between the topic and himself, the more difficulty he experienced, and the more repetitive his process became. Conversely,
when the topic was close to his own experience, the smoother and more fluent
the process became. More writing was produced, pauses were fewer, and positive
assessment occurred more often. However, Tony made more assumptions on the
part of the audience in the reflexive mode. When writing about himself, Tony
often did not stop to explain the context from which he was writing; rather, the
reader's understanding of the context was taken for granted.

Editing

Tony spent a great deal of his composing time editing. However, most of this time 35
was spent proofreading rather than changing, rephrasing, adding, or evaluating the
substantive parts of the discourse. Of a total of 234 changes made in all of the sessions,
only 24 were related to changes of content and included the following categories:

1. Elaborations of ideas through the use of specification and detail;
2. Additions of modals that shift the mood of a sentence;
3. Deletions that narrow the focus of a paper;
4. Clause reductions or embeddings that tighten the structure of a paper;
5. Vocabulary choices that reflect a sensitivity to language;
6. Reordering of elements in a narrative;
7. Strengthening transitions between paragraphs;
8. Pronoun changes that signal an increased sensitivity to audience.

The 210 changes in form included the following: 36

Additions	19	Spelling	95
Deletions	44	Punctuation	35
Word choice	13	Unresolved problems	89
Verb changes	4		

The area that Tony changed most often was spelling, although, even after completing three drafts of a paper, Tony still had many words misspelled.

Miscue Analysis

Despite continual proofreading, Tony's completed drafts often retained a look 37 of incompleteness. Words remained misspelled, syntax was uncorrected or over-corrected, suffixes, plural markers, and verb endings were missing, and often words or complete phrases were omitted.

The composing aloud behavior and the miscue analysis derived from it pro- 38 vide one of the first demonstrable ways of understanding how such seemingly incomplete texts can be considered "finished" by the student. (See Table 3 for

TABLE 3 TONY—MISCUE ANALYSIS

	ENCODING			
	Speaking complete ideas but omitting certain words during writing	Pronouncing words with plural markers or other suffixes completely but omitting these endings during writing	Pronouncing the desired word but writing a homonym, an approximation of the word or a personal abbreviation of the word on paper	Total
S1	1	4	11	16
S2	8	0	14	22
S4	4	0	16	20
S5	3	1	15	19
	16	5	56	77
	DECODING			
	Reading in missing words or word endings	Deleting words or word endings	Reading the desired word rather than the word on the page	Reading abbreviations and misspellings as though they were written correctly	Total
S1	10	1	1	15	27
S2	5	1	2	10	18
S4	3	3	0	13	19
S5	7	1	2	10	20
	25	6	5	48	84

a summary of Tony's miscues.) Tony consistently voiced complete sentences when composing aloud but only transcribed partial sentences. The same behavior occurred in relation to words with plural or marked endings. However, during rereading and even during editing, Tony supplied the missing endings, words, or phrases and did not seem to "see" what was missing from the text. Thus, when reading his paper, Tony "read in" the meaning he expected to be there which turned him into a reader of content rather than form. However, a difference can be observed between the extensive and reflexive modes, and in the area of correctness Tony's greater strength lay in the reflexive mode. In this mode, not only were more words produced in less time (1,062 vs. 658), but fewer decoding miscues occurred (38 vs. 46), and fewer unresolved problems remained in the text (34 vs. 55).

When Tony did choose to read for form, he was handicapped in another 39 way. Through his years of schooling, Tony learned that there were sets of rules to be applied to one's writing, and he attempted to apply these rules of form to his prose. Often, though, the structures he produced were far more complicated than the simple set of proofreading rules he had at his disposal. He was therefore faced with applying the rule partially, discarding it, or attempting corrections through sound. None of these systems was completely helpful to Tony, and as often as a correction was made that improved the discourse, another was made that obscured it.

Summary

Finally, when Tony completed the writing process, he refrained from comment- 40 ing on or contemplating his total written product. When he initiated writing, he immediately established distance between himself as writer and his discourse. He knew his preliminary draft might have errors and might need revision. At the end of each session, the distance had decreased if not entirely disappeared. Tony "read in" missing or omitted features, rarely perceived syntactic errors, and did not untangle overly embedded sentences. It was as if the semantic model in his head predominated, and the distance with which he entered the writing process had dissolved. Thus, even with his concern for revision and for correctness, even with the enormous amount of time he invested in rereading and repetition, Tony concluded the composing process with unresolved stylistic and syntactic problems. The conclusion here is not that Tony can't write, or that Tony doesn't know how to write, or that Tony needs to learn more rules: Tony is a writer with a highly consistent and deeply embedded recursive process. What he needs are teachers who can interpret that process for him, who can see through the tangles in the process just as he sees meaning beneath the tangles in his prose, and who can intervene in such a way that untangling his composing process leads him to create better prose.

SUMMARY OF THE FINDINGS

A major finding of this study is that, like Tony, all of the students studied dis-   41
played consistent composing processes; that is, the behavioral subsequences
prewriting, writing, and editing appeared in sequential patterns that were recognizable across writing sessions and across students.

This consistency suggests a much greater internalization of process than has   42
ever before been suspected. Since the written products of basic writers often
look arbitrary, observers commonly assume that the students' approach is also
arbitrary. However, just as Shaughnessy (1977) points out that there is "very
little that is random . . . in what they have written" (p. 5), so, on close observation, very little appears random in *how* they write. The students observed had
stable composing processes which they used whenever they were presented with
a writing task. While this consistency argues against seeing these students as
beginning writers, it ought not necessarily imply that they are proficient writers.
Indeed, their lack of proficiency may be attributable to the way in which
premature and rigid attempts to correct and edit their work truncate the flow of
composing without substantially improving the form of what they have written.
More detailed findings will be reviewed in the following subsections which treat
the three major aspects of composing: prewriting, writing, and editing.

Prewriting

When not given specific prewriting instructions, the students in this study   43
began writing within the first few minutes. The average time they spent on
prewriting in sessions 1 and 2 was four minutes (see Table 4), and the planning
strategies they used fell into three principal types:

1. Rephrasing the topic until a particular word or idea connected with the
   student's experience. The student then had "an event" in mind before
   writing began.
2. Turning the large conceptual issue in the topic (e.g., equality) into two
   manageable pieces for writing (e.g., rich vs. poor; black vs. white).
3. Initiating a string of associations to a word in the topic and then
   developing one or more of the associations during writing.

When students planned in any of these ways, they began to write with an   44
articulated sense of where they wanted their discourse to go. However, frequently students read the topic and directions a few times and indicated that
they had "no idea" what to write. On these occasions, they began writing without any secure sense of where they were heading, acknowledging only that
they would "figure it out" as they went along. Often their first sentence was

TABLE 4 OVERVIEW OF ALL WRITING SESSIONS

	PREWRITING TIME*				TOTAL WORDS / TOTAL COMPOSING TIME				EDITING CHANGES		UNRESOLVED PROBLEMS	MISCUES DURING READING
	S1	S2	S4	S5	S1	S2	S4	S5	Content	Form		
TONY	7.8	3.5	8.0	5.7	302 / 91.2	512 / 76.0	356 / 82.0	550 / 96.0	24	210	89	84
DEE	2.5	2.9	5.0	5.0	409 / 55.5	559 / 65.0	91 / 24.5	212 / 29.0	7	24	40	32
STAN	3.5	4.3	14.8	14.7	419 / 62.0	553 / 73.1	365 / 73.0	303 / 68.0	13	49	45	55
LUELLER	2.0	1.5	4.0	13.0	518 / 90.8	588 / 96.8	315 / 93.0	363 / 77.8	2	167	143	147
BEVERLY	5.5	7.0	32.0	20.0	519 / 79.0	536 / 80.3	348 / 97.4	776 / 120.0	21	100	55	30

*Due to a change in the prewriting directions, only Sessions 1 and 2 are used to calculate the average time spent in prewriting.

a rephrasing of the question in the topic which, now that it was in their own handwriting and down on paper in front of them, seemed to enable them to plan what ought to come next. In these instances, writing led to planning which led to clarifying which led to more writing. This sequence of planning and writing, clarifying and discarding, was repeated frequently in all of the sessions, even when students began writing with a secure sense of direction.

Although one might be tempted to conclude that these students began writ- 45 ing prematurely and that planning precisely what they were going to write ought to have occurred before they put pen to paper, the data here suggest:

1. that certain strategies, such as creating an association to a key word, focusing in and narrowing down the topic, dichotomizing and classifying, can and do take place in a relatively brief span of time; and

2. that the developing and clarifying of ideas is facilitated once students translate some of those ideas into written form. In other words, seeing ideas on paper enables students to reflect upon, change and develop those ideas further.

Writing

Careful study revealed that students wrote by shuttling from the sense of what 46 they wanted to say forward to the words on the page and back from the words on the page to their intended meaning. This "back and forth" movement appeared to be a recursive feature: at one moment students were writing, moving their ideas and their discourse forward; at the next they were backtracking, rereading, and digesting what had been written.

Recursive movements appeared at many points during the writing process. 47 Occasionally sentences were written in groups and then reread as a "piece" of discourse; at other times sentences and phrases were written alone, repeated until the writer was satisfied or worn down, or rehearsed until the act of rehearsal led to the creation of a new sentence. In the midst of writing, editing occurred as students considered the surface features of language. Often planning of a global nature took place: in the midst of producing a first draft, students stopped and began planning how the second draft would differ from the first. Often in the midst of writing, students stopped and referred to the topic in order to check if they had remained faithful to the original intent, and occasionally, though infrequently, they identified a sentence or a phrase that seemed, to them, to produce a satisfactory ending. In all these behaviors, they were shuttling back and forth, projecting what would come next and doubling back to be sure of the ground they had covered.

A number of conclusions can be drawn from the observations of these stu- 48 dents composing and from the comments they made: although they produced inadequate or flawed products, they nevertheless seemed to understand and perform some of the crucial operations involved in composing with skill. While it cannot be stated with certainty that the patterns they displayed are shared by other writers, some of the operations they performed appear sufficiently sound to serve as prototypes for constructing two major hypotheses on the nature of their composing processes. Whether the following hypotheses are borne out in studies of different types of writers remains an open question:

> *Composing does not occur in a straightforward, linear fashion. The process is one of accumulating discrete bits down on the paper and then working from those bits to reflect upon, structure, and then further develop what one means to say.*

1. Composing does not occur in a straightforward, linear fashion. The process is one of accumulating discrete bits down on the paper and then working from those bits to reflect upon, structure, and then further develop what one means to say. It can be thought of as a kind of "retrospective structuring"; movement forward occurs only after one has reached back, which in turn occurs only after one has some sense of where one wants to go. Both aspects, the reaching back and the sensing forward, have a clarifying effect.

2. Composing always involves some measure of both construction and discovery. Writers construct their discourse inasmuch as they begin with a sense of what they want to write. This sense, as long as it remains implicit, is not equivalent to the explicit form it gives rise to. Thus, a process of constructing meaning is required. Rereading or backward movements become a way of assessing whether or not the words on the page adequately capture the original sense intended. Constructing simultaneously affords discovery. Writers know more fully what they mean only after having written it. In this way the explicit written form serves as a window on the implicit sense with which one began.

Editing

Editing played a major role in the composing processes of the students in 49 this study (see Table 5). Soon after students began writing their first drafts, they began to edit, and they continued to do so during the intervals between drafts, during the writing of their second drafts and during the final reading of papers.

While editing, the students were concerned with a variety of items: the 50 lexicon (i.e., spelling, word choice, and the context of words); the syntax

TABLE 5 EDITING CHANGES

	TONY	DEE	STAN	LUELLER	BEVERLY	TOTALS
Total number of words produced	1720	1271	1640	1754	2179	8564
Total form	210	24	49	167	100	550
Additions	19	2	10	21	11	63
Deletions	44	9	18	41	38	150
Word choice	13	4	1	27	6	51
Verb changes	4	1	2	7	12	26
Spelling	95	4	13	60	19	191
Punctuation	35	4	5	11	14	69
Total content	24	7	13	2	21	67

(i.e., grammar, punctuation, and sentence structure); and the discourse as a whole (i.e., organization, coherence, and audience). However, despite the students' considered attempts to proofread their work, serious syntactic and stylistic problems remained in their finished drafts. The persistence of these errors may, in part, be understood by looking briefly at some of the problems that arose for these students during editing.

Rule Confusion

(1) All of the students observed asked themselves, "Is this sentence [or feature] correct?" but the simple set of editing rules at their disposal was often inappropriate for the types of complicated structures they produced. As a result, they misapplied what they knew and either created a hypercorrection or impaired the meaning they had originally intended to clarify; (2) The students observed attempted to write with terms they heard in lectures or class discussions, but since they were not yet familiar with the syntactic or semantic constraints one word placed upon another, their experiments with academic language resulted in what Shaughnessy (1977, p. 49) calls, "lexical transplants" or "syntactic dissonances"; (3) The students tried to rely on their intuitions about language, in particular the sound of words. Often, however, they had been taught to mistrust what "sounded" right to them, and they were unaware of the particular feature in their speech codes that might need to be changed in writing to match the standard code. As a result, when they attempted corrections by sound, they became confused, and they began to have difficulty differentiating between what sounded right in speech and what needed to be marked on the paper.

Selective Perception

These students habitually reread their papers from internal semantic or mean- 52
ing models. They extracted the meaning they wanted from the minimal cues on
the page, and they did not recognize that outside readers would find those cues
insufficient for meaning.

A study of Table 6 indicates that the number of problems remaining in the 53
students' written products approximates the number of miscues produced
during reading. This proximity, itself, suggests that many of these errors persisted because the students were so certain of the words they wanted to have on
the page that they "read in" these words even when they were absent; in other
words, they reduced uncertainty by operating as though what was in their heads
was already on the page. The problem of selective perception, then, cannot be
reduced solely to mechanical decoding; the semantic model from which students read needs to be acknowledged and taken into account in any study that
attempts to explain how students write and why their completed written products end up looking so incomplete.

TABLE 6 THE TALK-WRITE PARADIGM MISCUES—DECODING BEHAVIORS

	TONY	DEE	STAN	LUELLER	BEVERLY	TOTALS
Unresolved problems	89	40	45	143	55	372
"Reading in" missing words or word endings	25	13	11	44	11	104
Deleting words or word endings	6	2	4	14	9	35
"Reading" the desired word rather than the word on the page	5	6	18	15	8	52
"Reading" abbreviations and misspellings as though they were written correctly	48	11	22	74	2	157
Miscues during reading	84	32	55	147	30	348

Egocentricity

The students in this study wrote from an egocentric point of view. While they 54 occasionally indicated a concern for their readers, they more often took the reader's understanding for granted. They did not see the necessity of making their referents explicit, of making the connections among their ideas apparent, of carefully and explicitly relating one phenomenon to another, or of placing narratives or generalizations within an orienting, conceptual framework.

On the basis of these observations one may be led to conclude that these 55 writers did not know how to edit their work. Such a conclusion must, however, be drawn with care. Efforts to improve their editing need to be based on an informed view of the role that editing already plays in their composing processes. Two conclusions in this regard are appropriate here:

1. Editing intrudes so often and to such a degree that it breaks down the rhythms generated by thinking and writing. When this happens the students are forced to go back and recapture the strands of their thinking once the editing operation has been completed. Thus, editing occurs prematurely, before students have generated enough discourse to approximate the ideas they have, and it often results in their losing track of their ideas.

2. Editing is primarily an exercise in error-hunting. The students are prematurely concerned with the "look" of their writing; thus, as soon as a few words are written on the paper, detection and correction of errors replaces writing and revising. Even when they begin writing with a tentative, flexible frame of mind, they soon become locked into whatever is on the page. What they seem to lack as much as any rule is a conception of editing that includes flexibility, suspended judgment, the weighing of possibilities, and the reworking of ideas.

IMPLICATIONS FOR TEACHING AND RESEARCH

One major implication of this study pertains to teachers' conceptions of 56 unskilled writers. Traditionally, these students have been labeled "remedial," which usually implies that teaching ought to remedy what is "wrong" in their written products. Since the surface features in the writing of unskilled writers seriously interfere with the extraction of meaning from the page, much class time is devoted to examining the rules of the standard code. The pedagogical soundness of this procedure has been questioned frequently,[2] but in spite of the debate, the practice continues, and it results in a further complication, namely that students begin to conceive of writing as a "cosmetic" process where concern for correct form supersedes development of ideas. As a result, the excitement of composing, of constructing and discovering meaning, is cut off almost before it has begun.

More recently, unskilled writers have been referred to as "beginners," implying that 57 teachers can start anew. They need not "punish" students for making mistakes, and they need not assume that their students have already been taught how to write. Yet this view ignores the highly elaborated, deeply embedded processes the students bring with them. These unskilled college writers are not beginners in a *tabula rasa* sense, and teachers err in assuming they are. The results of this study suggest that teachers may first need to identify which characteristic components of each student's process facilitate writing and which inhibit it before further teaching takes place. If they do not, teachers of unskilled writers may continue to place themselves in a defeating position: imposing another method of writing instruction upon the students' already internalized processes without first helping students to extricate themselves from the knots and tangles in those processes.

A second implication of this study is that the composing process is now 58 amenable to a replicable and graphic mode of representation as a sequence of codable behaviors. The composing style sheets provide researchers and teachers with the first demonstrable way of documenting how individual students write. Such a tool may have diagnostic as well as research benefits. It may be used to record writing behaviors in large groups, prior to and after instruction, as well as in individuals. Certainly it lends itself to the longitudinal study of the writing process and may help to elucidate what it is that changes in the process as writers become more skilled.

A third implication relates to case studies and to the theories derived from 59 them. This study is an illustration of the way in which a theoretical model of the composing process can be grounded in observations of the individual's experience of composing. It is precisely the complexity of this experience that the case study brings to light. However, by viewing a series of cases, the researcher can discern patterns and themes that suggest regularities in composing behavior across individuals. These common features lead to hypotheses and theoretical formulations which have some basis in shared experience. How far this shared experience extends is, of course, a question that can only be answered through further research.

A final implication derives from the preponderance of recursive behaviors in 60 the composing processes studied here, and from the theoretical notion derived from these observations: retrospective structuring, or the going back to the sense of one's meaning in order to go forward and discover more of what one has to say. Seen in this light, composing becomes the carrying forward of an implicit sense into explicit form. Teaching composing, then, means paying attention not only to the forms or products but also to the explicative process through which they arise.

APPENDIX

Composing Style Sheet

Name:	Tony	Mode:	Extensive TW₁	Date:	October 31, 1975
Session:	1	Topic:	Society & Culture	Time:	11:00 AM - 12:30 PM

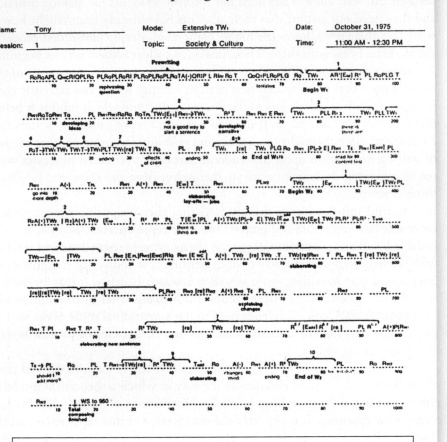

Writing Sample

TONY

Session 1

W1

All men can't be consider equal in a America base on financial

situation.[1] Because their are men born in rich families that will

never have to worry about any financial difficulties.[2] And then

theyre / ~~the~~ another type of Americans that is born to a poor fam-

ily and alway / have some kind of fina—difficulty.[3] Espeicaly nowadays in New York city With the bugdit Crisis / $\overset{\text{and all}}{}$.[4]

$\overset{\text{If he is able}}{\text{~~He may~~}}$ be able To get a job.[5] But are now he lose the job just as easy as he got it.[6] So when he loses his job he'll have to try to get some fina—assistance.[7] ~~A~~ Then he'll probley have even more fin—diffuicuty.[8] So right here / $\overset{\text{here}}{}$ you can't see that In Ameri~~an~~, all men are not create equal in the fin—sense.[9]

Writing Sample

TONY

Session 1

W2

All men can not be consider equal in America base on financial situations.[1] Because their are men born in rich families that will never have to worry about any finan~~cial diffuel~~ diffuliculties.[2] And then there are $\overset{\text{the}}{}$ / another type of ameicans that are born to a poor familty.[3] And This is the type of Americans that ~~will~~ / $\overset{\text{may}}{}$ alway have some kind of finanical diffuliculty.[4] Espeical today ~~today the~~in new york The way the city has fallen ~~has fallen~~ into fin—debt.[5] It has become such a big crisis for the $\overset{\text{working}}{\text{~~people~~}}$ people, in the [6] If the working man is able to find a job, espeicaly ~~for~~ / $\overset{\text{with the}}{\text{~~city a~~}}$ city The way ~~the way~~ $\overset{\text{the}}{}$ city / fin—sitionu $\overset{\text{is}}{}$ is set up now, ~~h~~He'll prob-lely lose the job a whole lot faster than what he got it.[7] When he loses his job he'll ~~p~~ have even more fin—difficulty.[8] And then he'll be force to ~~got~~ to the city for some fini—assi—.[9] So right here you can see that all men in America are not create equal in the fin—sense.[10]

Notes

1. The word "read" is used in a particular manner here. In the traditional sense, reading refers to accurate decoding of written symbols. Here it refers to students' verbalizing words or endings even when the symbols for those words are missing or only minimally present. Whenever the term "reading" is used in this way, it will be in quotation marks.

2. For discussions on the controversy over the effects of grammar instruction on writing ability, see the following: Richard Braddock, Richard Lloyd-Jones, and Lowell Schoer, *Research in Written Composition* (Urbana, Ill.: National Council of Teachers of English, 1963); Frank O'Hare, *Sentence Combining* (NCTE Research Report No. 15, Urbana, Ill.: National Council of Teachers of English, 1973); Elizabeth F. Haynes, "Using Research in Preparing to Teach Writing," *English Journal,* 1978, 67, 82–89.

References

Braddock, R., Lloyd-Jones, R., & Schoer, L. *Research in written composition.* Urbana, Ill.: National Council of Teachers of English, 1963.

Britton, J., Burgess, T., Martin, N., McLeod, A., & Rosen, H. *The development of writing abilities (11–18).* London: Macmillan Education Ltd., 1975.

Burton, D. L. Research in the teaching of English: The troubled dream. *Research in the Teaching of English,* 1973, *1,* 160–187.

Cooper, C. R. Doing research/reading research. *English Journal,* 1974, *63,* 94–99.

Cooper, C. R., & Odell, L. (Eds.) *Research on composing: Points of departure.* Urbana, Ill.: National Council of Teachers of English, 1978.

Emig, J. A. On teaching composition: Some hypotheses as definitions. *Research in the Teaching of English,* 1967, *1,* 127–135.

Emig, J. A. *The composing processes of twelfth graders.* Urbana, Ill.: National Council of Teachers of English, 1971. (Research Report No. 13) (Ed. D. Dissertation, Harvard University, 1969).

Goodman, K. S. (Ed.) *Miscue analysis: Applications to reading instruction.* Urbana, Ill.: NCTE and ERIC, 1973.

Graves, D. H. Children's writing: Research directions and hypotheses based upon an examination of the writing process of seven year old children (Doctoral dissertation, State University of New York at Buffalo, 1973). *Dissertation Abstracts International,* 1974, *34,* 6255A.

Haynes, E. F. Using research in preparing to teach writing. *English Journal,* 1978, *67,* 82–89.

Mischel, T. A case study of a twelfth-grade writer. *Research in the Teaching of English,* 1974, *8,* 303–314.

O'Hare, F. *Sentence-combining: Improving student writing without formal grammar instruction.* Urbana, Ill.: National Council of Teachers of English, 1973. (Research Report No. 15).

Perl, S. *Five writers writing: Case studies of the composing processes of unskilled college writers.* Unpublished doctoral dissertation, New York University, 1978.

Pianko, S. *The composing acts of college freshmen writers.* Unpublished Ed.D. dissertation, Rutgers University, 1977.

Shaughnessy, M. P. *Errors and expectations: A guide for the teacher of basic writing.* New York: Oxford University Press, 1977.

Stallard, C. K. An analysis of the writing behavior of good student writers. *Research in the Teaching of English,* 1974, *8,* 206–218.

Questions for Discussion and Journaling

1. Perl notes that Tony's writing process and resulting text were markedly different when he was writing about his own experience and when he was trying to write less personally. Describe this difference and explain whether it makes sense to you.

2. Why does Perl take it as such a positive sign that Tony and her other research participants' composing processes are "consistent" rather than scattered or random?

3. Find the section of the article where Perl discusses how she developed her "code" of composing behaviors. What is your sense of how she put it together, and at what point in her research did she do so?

4. Build a list of reasons Perl is critical of previous writing-process research, and explain each of them. How well would you say her research here overcomes or eliminates those problems?

5. Do you think Perl's research methods might have actively shaped the writing her participants produced? That is, if she had changed the design of her study, is it possible she would have gotten different writing from her participants? Explain.

6. Perl appears not to count changes made while drafting sentence-by-sentence as "editing"; instead, she reserves that term for changes made between drafts. Why do you think she makes that distinction?

7. Do you see your own composing as "the carrying forward of an implicit sense into explicit form" (para. 60)? How so, and how not?

8. How does Perl's "retrospective structuring" (para. 60) apply to the threshold concepts emphasized in this chapter — that writing makes new knowledge, and that writers don't usually "get it right the first time"?

Applying and Exploring Ideas

1. Put together a list of the problems Tony had with composing and editing — for example, his tendency to say a sentence one way but write down something else. As you review the list, do you see problems that you've had trouble with in the past, or any you still have trouble with? If so, how did you solve them — or what have you tried that hasn't worked? Discuss this question with one or more classmates: Have they encountered the problem of selective perception, for example? If so, how have they dealt with it?

2. Perl argues that it's a good thing when people don't wait to write until they know everything they want to say — rather, she wants writers to use the clarifying power of the act of writing itself to help them figure out what they want to say. To what extent does this strategy resemble your own writing process?

3. Perl was researching in a time before easy video recording. Today, to do the same research, we would not only set up a camera (thus recording the participant's speech, behaviors, and writing activity simultaneously and in real time) but

possibly also capture their keystrokes (assuming they composed at a computer) for a microscopically accurate record of exactly how the participant was writing. If you have a device to record video, try recording yourself or a volunteer while he or she writes, and then use the recording to help you devise a code to explain the processes you recorded. If that's not possible, consider: If you were doing Perl's study today, how would you design it to take advantage of current technology and your own ideas about the writing process? What kind of code would you devise to explain the activity that your technology recorded?

- -

META MOMENT   Name one thing you now understand about the writing process or will do differently in your own writing after reading about Tony's process.

- -

Decisions and Revisions: The Planning Strategies of a Publishing Writer

CAROL BERKENKOTTER

and

Response of a Laboratory Rat — or, Being Protocoled

DONALD M. MURRAY

Courtesy of Carol Berkenkotter

© Gary Samson, University of New Hampshire

Framing the Readings

Earlier in this chapter, you may have read Sondra Perl's 1979 study of "unskilled college writers," which used a "think-aloud" or "talk-aloud" protocol, a technique that at the time was very popular among psychology researchers. This method solved a very basic problem of research on mental operations — that is, how we know what thoughts people are having that lead them to write certain things — by proposing the following simple solution: Have them talk while they think. Another aspect of Perl's design, a "laboratory" setting where students came to the researcher and wrote in response to specific prompts the researcher provided, was quite common in this time and style of research on writing processes. Most researchers publishing studies on writers' processes, including Carol Berkenkotter, author of one of the pieces you are about to read, used such methods.

Berkenkotter, Carol. "Decisions and Revisions: The Planning Strategies of a Publishing Writer." *College Composition and Communication*, vol. 34, no. 2, May 1983, pp. 156–69.

Murray, Donald M. "Response of a Laboratory Rat — or, Being Protocoled." *College Composition and Communication*, vol. 34, no. 2, May 1983, pp. 169–72.

But there are real problems with this kind of research, chief among them the artificiality of the setting and the writing tasks. In the following selection, you will read Berkenkotter's account of how she engaged a professional writer, Donald Murray, as a participant for a different kind of research, one that tried to keep the writer in his own context — normal surroundings, real projects — rather than bringing him into a lab. Like Perl's article, then, Berkenkotter's has two focuses: a test of a particular methodology and a question about a particular aspect of composing — in this case, the revision process of a professional writer.

Berkenkotter and Murray did something else uncharacteristic of research on writing in the era: Murray was given the opportunity to write a reflection on the experience of being a research subject, his thoughts on what Berkenkotter's study found, and observations on the methodology. For this reason, we strongly recommend that you read the pieces back-to-back; the experience of reading Berkenkotter isn't complete without Murray's rejoinder and the interplay between the two pieces.

While you should pay close attention to any researcher's methods and context, the most interesting part of this article for you will likely be what you can learn about how a professional and award-winning writer goes about writing. His processes are odd, and you likely don't write like Murray did. In 1981, when Berkenkotter and Murray undertook the study, cell phones, the Internet, and personal computers were not in widespread use. Pay close attention, though, to how Murray invents things to say, how he learns from his writing, how he writes for his audience, and how he revises, and ask yourself what his writing gains from his complex planning, drafting, and revising. Consider how his process links to the threshold concepts that this chapter has stressed: that writing makes knowledge, that it often doesn't come out well the first time for experienced writers, that even experienced writers can find themselves struggling to put words on a page, and that writers always have more to learn about writing and how their writing is working.

Carol Berkenkotter passed away in 2016, after teaching for many years, most recently in the University of Minnesota's Department of Writing Studies. At the time she wrote this piece, about 30 years ago, she was teaching at Michigan Technological University. Over that span of time, her research shifted from the kinds of writing-process questions that shaped this article to extensive focus on **genre** theory (a topic we discussed at length in Chapter 2). A great deal of what we understand about genre is influenced by Berkenkotter. One of her most significant works is her 1995 book with Thomas Huckin, *Genre Knowledge in Disciplinary Communication: Cognition / Culture / Power.* Her research subject and co-author here, Donald Murray, has an article of his own in this book, "All Writing Is Autobiography" in Chapter 6.

Getting Ready to Read

Before you read, do at least one of the following activities:

- Take fifteen minutes and write in response to this prompt: "Explain death to an eleven-year-old." Then consider how it felt to write this. Was it easy? Hard?

What did you wonder or think about while you were writing? Set this aside and come back to it after you have read this article.

- Consider whether you have any writing rituals. For example, do you have to have a cup of coffee while you write? Do you need to write on paper before typing? Do you have to take a nap or clean the house?

As you read, consider the following questions:

- What discoveries do Berkenkotter and Murray make that contradict their expectations?
- What are strengths and weaknesses of this particular way of studying writing processes?
- What have you learned about writing from reading this article that you didn't know before?

DECISIONS AND REVISIONS: THE PLANNING STRATEGIES OF A PUBLISHING WRITER

Carol Berkenkotter

THE CLEAREST MEMORY I have of Donald M. Murray is watching him 1
writing at a long white wooden table in his study, which looks out on the New Hampshire woods. Beside his desk is a large framed poster of a small boy sitting on a bed staring at a huge dragon leaning over the railing glowering at him. The poster is captioned, "Donald imagined things." And so he did, as he addressed the problems writers face each time they confront a new assignment. During the summer of 1981, as I listened to him daily recording his thoughts aloud as he worked on two articles, a short story, and an editorial, I came to understand in what ways each writer's processes are unique and why it is important that we pay close attention to the setting in which the writer composes, the kind of task the writer confronts, and what the writer can tell us of his own processes. If we are to understand *how* writers revise, we must pay close attention to the context in which revision occurs.

Janet Emig, citing Eliot Mishler, has recently described the tendency of writ- 2
ing research toward "context stripping."[1] When researchers remove writers from their natural settings (the study, the classroom, the office, the dormitory room, the library) to examine their thinking processes in the laboratory, they create "a context of a powerful sort, often deeply affecting what is being observed and assessed."[2] Emig's essay points to the need to examine critically the effects of these practices.

The subject of the present study is not anonymous, as are most subjects, nor 3 will he remain silent. I began the investigation with a critical eye regarding what he has said about revision, he with an equally critical attitude toward methods of research on cognitive processes. To some extent our original positions have been confirmed — yet I think each of us, researcher and writer, has been forced to question our assumptions and examine our dogmas. More important, this project stirs the dust a bit and suggests a new direction for research on composing processes.

I met Mr. Murray at the Conference on College Composition and Commu- 4 nication meeting in Dallas, 1981. He appeared at the speaker's rostrum after my session and introduced himself, and we began to talk about the limitations of taking protocols in an experimental situation. On the spur of the moment I asked him if he would be willing to be the subject of a naturalistic study. He hesitated, took a deep breath, then said he was very interested in understanding his own composing processes, and would like to learn more. Out of that brief exchange a unique collaborative research venture was conceived.

To date there are no reported studies of writers composing in natural (as 5 opposed to laboratory) settings that combine thinking-aloud protocols with the writers' own introspective accounts. Recently, researchers have been observing young children as they write in the classroom. In particular, we have seen the promising research of Donald Graves, Lucy Calkins, and Susan Sowers, who have worked intimately with children and their teachers in the Atkinson Schools Project.[3] By using video tapes and by actively working in the classroom as teachers and interviewers, these researchers were able to track the revising processes of individual children over a two-year period. Studies such as these suggest that there may be other ways of looking at writers' composing processes than in conventional research settings.

There remains, however, the question: to what extent can a writer's subjective 6 testimony be trusted? I have shared the common distrust of such accounts.[4] There is considerable cognitive activity that writers cannot report because they are unable to compose and monitor their processes simultaneously. Researchers have responded to this problem by taking retrospective accounts from writers immediately after they have composed,[5] or have studied writers' cognitive activity through the use of thinking-aloud protocols.[6] These protocols have been examined to locate the thoughts verbalized by the subjects while composing, rather than for the subjects' analysis of what they said. Typically, subjects were instructed to "say everything that comes to mind no matter how random or crazy it seems. Do not analyze your thoughts, just say them aloud." The effect of these procedures, however, has been to separate the dancer from the dance, the subject from the process. Introspective accounts made in medias res have not been possible thus far because no one has developed techniques that would allow a subject to write and comment on his or her processes between composing episodes. For this reason I had begun to entertain the idea of asking a professional writer to engage in a lengthy naturalistic study. When Donald Murray introduced himself, I knew I wanted him to be the subject.

METHODOLOGY

The objectives that I began with are modifications of those Sondra Perl iden- 7 tified in her study of five unskilled writers.[7] I wanted to learn more about the planning and revising strategies of a highly skilled and verbal writer, to discover how these strategies could be most usefully analyzed, and to determine how an understanding of this writer's processes would contribute to what we have already discovered about how skilled writers plan and revise.

The project took place in three stages. From June 15th until August 15th, 8 1981 (a period of 62 days), Mr. Murray turned on the tape recorder when he entered his study in the morning and left it running during the day wherever he happened to be working. in his car waiting in parking lots, his university office, restaurants, the doctor's office, etc. This kind of thinking-aloud protocol differs from those taken by Linda Flower and John R. Hayes since the subject's composing time is not limited to a single hour; in fact, during the period of time that Mr. Murray was recording his thoughts, I accumulated over one hundred and twenty hours of tape. The writer also submitted photocopies of all text, including notes and drafts made prior to the study. Thus I was able to study a history of each draft.

In the second stage, during a visit to my university, I gave the writer a task 9 which specified audience, subject, and purpose. I asked him to think aloud on tape as he had previously, but this time for only one hour. Between the second and third stages, Mr. Murray and I maintained a dialogue on audiotapes which we mailed back and forth. On these tapes he compared his thoughts on his composing in his own environment over time to those on giving a one-hour protocol in a laboratory setting.

During the third stage of the study, I visited the writer at his home for two 10 days. At this time I observed him thinking aloud as he performed a writing task which involved revising an article for a professional journal. After two sessions of thinking aloud on tape for two and one-half hours, Mr. Murray answered questions concerning the decisions he had made. Over the two-day period we taped an additional four hours of questions and answers regarding the writer's perceptions of his activities.

Another coder and I independently coded the transcripts of the protocols 11 made in the naturalistic and laboratory settings. Using the same procedure I employed in my study of how writers considered their audience (i.e., first classifying and then counting all audience-related activities I could find in each protocol), my coder and I tallied all planning, revising, and editing activities, as well as global and local evaluations of text[8] that we agreed upon. I was particularly interested in Murray's editing activities. Having listened to the tapes I was aware that editing (i.e., reading the text aloud and making word- and sentence-level changes) sometimes led to major planning episodes, and I wanted to keep track of that sequence.

The study was not conducted without problems. The greatest of these arose 12 from how the writer's particular work habits affected the gathering of the data and how he responded to making a one-hour protocol. Unlike most writers who hand draft or type, Mr. Murray spends much time making copious notes in a daybook, then dictates his drafts and partial drafts to his wife, who is an accomplished typist and partner in his work. Later, he reads aloud and edits the drafts. If he determines that copy-editing (i.e., making stylistic changes in the text) is insufficient, he returns to the daybook, makes further notes, and prepares for the next dictation. The revision of one of the articles he was working on went through eight drafts before he sent it off. Two days later he sent the editor an insert.

Murray's distinctive work habits meant that all of the cognitive activity 13 occurring during the dictation that might ordinarily be captured in a protocol was lost since he processed information at a high speed. During these periods I could not keep track of the content of his thoughts, and became concerned instead with the problem of why he frequently would find himself unable to continue dictating and end the session. There turned out to be considerable value in following the breakdowns of these dictations. I was able to distinguish between those occasions when Murray's composing was, in Janet Emig's terms, "extensive," and when it was "reflexive,"[9] by comparing the relative ease with which he developed an article from well-rehearsed material presented at workshops with the slow evolution of a conceptual piece he had not rehearsed. According to Emig, "The extensive mode . . . focuses upon the writer's conveying a message or communication to another. . . . the style is assured, impersonal, and often reportorial." In contrast, reflexive composing " . . . focuses on the writer's thoughts and feelings. . . . the style is tentative, personal, and exploratory."[10] In the latter case the writer is generating, testing, and evaluating new ideas, rather than reformulating old ones. I could observe the differences between the two modes of composing Emig describes, given Murray's response to the task in which he was engaged. When the writer was thoroughly familiar with his subject, he dictated with great fluency and ease. However, when he was breaking new ground conceptually, his pace slowed and his voice became halting; often the drafts broke down, forcing him to return to his daybook before attempting to dictate again.[11]

A more critical problem arose during the giving of the one-hour protocol. 14 At the time he came to my university, the writer had been working on tasks he had selected, talking into a tape recorder for two months in a familiar setting. Now he found himself in a strange room, with a specific writing task to perform in one short hour. This task was not simple; nor was it familiar. He was asked to "explain the concept of death to the ten- to twelve-year-old readers of *Jack and Jill* magazine." Under these circumstances, Murray clutched, producing two lines of text: "*Dear 11 year old. You're going to die. Sorry. Be seeing you. P. Muglump, Local Funeral Director.*" Both the transcript and later retrospective testimony of the writer indicated that he did not have pets as a child and his memories of death were not of the kind that could be described to an audience of ten- to twelve-year-old children. He also had difficulty forming a picture of his audience, since he suspected the actual audience was grandparents in Florida who send their children subscriptions to *Jack and Jill*. Toward the end of the hour, he was able to imagine a reader when he remembered the daughter of a man he had met the previous evening. The protocol, however, is rich with his efforts to create rhetorical context—he plotted repeated scenarios in which he would be asked to write such an article. Nevertheless, it seems reasonable to conclude that Mr. Murray was constrained by what Lester Faigley and Stephen Witte call "situational variables":[12] the knowledge that he had only one hour in which to complete a draft, his lack of familiarity with the format of *Jack and Jill* (he had never seen the magazine), his doubts that an audience actually existed, and finally, the wash of unhappy memories that the task gave rise to. "So important are these variables," Faigley and Witte contend, "that writing skill might be defined as the ability to respond to them."[13]

One final problem is intrinsic to the case study approach. Although the tapes are rich in data regarding the affective conditions under which the writer composed (he was distracted by university problems, had to contend with numerous interruptions, encountered family difficulties that he had to resolve, not to mention experiencing his own anxiety about his writing), as Murray reported, the further away he was in time from what he had done, the less able he was to reconstruct decisions he had made. 15

RESULTS

Planning and Revising

In this study I was primarily concerned with the writer's planning, revising, and editing activities. I had to develop a separate code category for the evaluation of text or content, since the writer frequently stopped to evaluate what he had written. Figure 1 indicates the percentage of coded activities devoted to planning, revising, and editing for three pieces of discourse.[14] These three pieces were among the projects Murray worked on over the two-month period when he was making the protocols. 16

	JOURNAL OF BASIC WRITING	COLLEGE COMPOSITION AND COMMUNICATION	EDITORIAL FOR CONCORD MONITOR
Planning	45%	56%	35%
Evaluating	28%	21%	18%
Revising	3.0%	3.0%	.0%
Editing	24%	20%	47%

Figure 1 Percentage of Coded Activities Devoted to Planning, Evaluating, Revising, and Editing for Three Pieces of Discourse

The coded data (taken from the transcripts of the tapes he made during this time) showed that up to 45%, 56%, and 35% of the writer's activities were concerned with planning, 28%, 21%, and 18% with either global or local evaluation, 3.0%, 3.0%, and .0% with revising (a finding which surprised me greatly, and to which I shall return), and 24%, 20%, and 47% with editing. 17

Murray's planning activities were of two kinds: the first were the stating of "process goals" — mentioning procedures, that is, that he developed in order to write (e.g., "I'm going to make a list of titles and see where that gets me," or "I'm going to try a different lead.").[15] Frequently, these procedures (or "thinking plans" as they are also called)[16] led the writer to generate a series of sub-plans for carrying out the larger plan. The following excerpt is from the first draft of an article on revision that Murray was writing for *The Journal of Basic Writing*. He had been reading the manuscript aloud to himself and was nearly ready to dictate a second draft. Suddenly he stopped, took his daybook and began making copious notes for a list of examples he could use to make the point that the wise editor or teacher should at first ignore sentence-level editing problems to deal with more substantive issues of revision (this excerpt as well as those which follow are taken from the transcript of the tape and the photocopied text of the daybook): 18

> Let me take another piece of paper here. Questions, ah . . . examples, and ah set up . . . situation . . . *frustration of writer. Cooks a five course dinner and gets response only to the table setting . . . or to the way the napkins are folded* or to the . . . *order of the forks.* All right. I can see from the material I have how that'll go. I'll weave in. Okay. *Distance in focus. Stand back. Read fast. Question writer.* Then *order doubles advocate. Then voice. Close in. Read aloud.* Okay, I got a number of different things I can see here that I'm getting to. I'm putting different order because that may be, try to emphasize this one. May want to put the techniques of editing and teaching first and the techniques of the writer second. So I got a one and a two to indicate that. [Italics identify words written down.]

In this instance we can see how a writing plan (taking a piece of paper and developing examples) leads to a number of sub-plans: "I'll weave in," "I'm putting in different order because that may be, try to emphasize this one," "May want to put the techniques of editing and teaching first and the techniques of the writer second," etc.

A second kind of planning activity was the stating of rhetorical goals, i.e., 19 planning how to reach an audience: "I'm making a note here, job not to explore the complexities of revision, but simply to show the reader how to do revision." Like many skilled writers, Murray had readers for his longer pieces. These readers were colleagues and friends whose judgment he trusted. Much of his planning activity as he revised his article for *College Composition and Communication* grew out of reading their responses to his initial draft and incorporating his summary of their comments directly onto the text. He then put away the text, and for the next several days made lists of titles, practiced leads, and made many outlines and diagrams in his daybook before dictating a draft. Through subsequent drafts he moved back and forth between the daybook and his edited dictations. He referred back to his readers' comments twice more between the first and last revised drafts, again summarizing their remarks in his notes in the daybook.

To say that Mr. Murray is an extensive planner does not really explain the 20 nature or scope of his revisions. I had initially developed code categories for revising activities; however, my coder and I discovered that we were for the most part double-coding for revising and planning, a sign the two activities were virtually inseparable. When the writer saw that major revision (as opposed to copy-editing) was necessary, he collapsed planning and revising into an activity that is best described as *reconceiving*. To "reconceive" is to scan and rescan one's text from the perspective of an external reader and to continue redrafting until all rhetorical, formal, and stylistic concerns have been resolved, or until the writer decides to let go of the text. This process, which Nancy Sommers has described as the resolution of the dissonance the writer senses between his intention and the developing text,[17] can be seen in the following episode. The writer had been editing what he thought was a final draft when he saw that more substantive changes were in order. The flurry of editing activity was replaced by reading aloud and scanning the text as the writer realized that his language was inadequate for expressing a goal which he began to formulate as he read:

(reading from previous page)[18] *It was E. B. White who reminded us, "Don't write about Man. Write about a man."* O.K. I'm going to cut that paragraph there . . . I've already said it. *The conferences when the teacher listens to the student can be short. When the teacher listens to the student in conference . . . when the teacher listens to the student* . . . the conference is, well, *the conference can be short.*

The student learns to speak first of what is most important to the student at the point. To mention first what is most important . . . what most concerns . . . the student about the draft or the process that produced it. The teacher listens . . . listens, reads the draft through the student's eyes then reads the draft, read or rereads . . . reads or . . . scans or re-scans the draft to confirm, adjust, or compromise the student's concerns. *The range of student response includes the affective and the cognitive . . . It is the affective that usually controls the cognitive, and the affective responses usually have to be dealt with first* . . . (continues reading down the page) *Once the feelings of inadequacy, overconfidence, despair or elation are dealt with, then the conference teacher will find the other self speaking in more cognitive terms. And usually these comments* . . . O.K. that would now get the monitor into, into the phrase. All right. Put this crisscross cause clearly that page is going to be retyped . . . I'll be dictating so that's just a note. (continues reading on next page) *Listening to students allows the teacher to discover if the student's concerns were appropriate to where the student is in the writing process. The student, for example, is often excessively interested in language at the beginning of the process. Fragmentary language is normal before there is a text.* Make a comment on the text, (writes *intervention*) Now on page ten scanning . . . my God, I don't . . . I don't think I want to make this too much a conference piece. I'm going to echo back to that . . . monitor and also to the things I've said on page two and three. O.K. Let's see what I can do . . . The biggest question that I have is how much detail needs to be on conferences. I don't think they're, I don't think I can afford too much. Maybe some stronger sense of the response that ah . . . students make, how the other self speaks. They've got to get a sense of the other self speaking.

The next draft was totally rewritten following the sentence in the draft: 21 "When the teacher listens to the student, the conference can be short." The revision included previously unmentioned anecdotal reports of comments students had made in conferences, a discussion of the relevant implications of the research of Graves, Calkins, and Sowers, and a section on how the writing workshop can draw out the student's "other self" as other students model the idealized reader. This draft was nearly three pages longer than the preceding one. The only passage that remained was the final paragraph.

Granted that Mr. Murray's dictation frees him from the scribal constraints 22 that most writers face, how can we account for such global (i.e., whole text) revision? One answer lies in the simple, yet elegant, principle formulated by Linda Flower and John R. Hayes.[19] In the act of composing, writers move back and forth between planning, translating (putting thoughts into words), and reviewing their work. And as they do, they frequently "discover" major rhetorical goals.[20] In the episode just cited we have seen the writer shifting gears from editing to planning to reconceiving as he recognized something missing from the text and identified a major rhetorical goal—that he had to make the concept of the other self still more concrete for his audience: "They've got to get a sense of the other self speaking." In this same episode we can also see the cognitive basis for alterations in the macrostructure, or "gist," of a text, alterations Faigley and Witte report having found in examining the revised drafts of advanced student and expert adult writers.[21]

Planning and Incubation

This discussion of planning would be incomplete without some attention to the role of incubation. Michael Polanyi describes incubation as "that persistence of heuristic tension through . . . periods of time in which problems are not consciously entertained."[22] Graham Wallas and Alex Osborn agree that incubation involves unconscious activity that takes place after periods of intensive preparation.[23]

23

Given the chance to observe a writer's processes over time, we can see incubation at work. The flashes of discovery that follow periods of incubation (even brief ones) are unexpected, powerful, and catalytic, as the following episode demonstrates. Mr. Murray was revising an article on revision for the *Journal of Basic Writing*. He had begun to review his work by editing copy, moving to more global issues as he evaluated the draft:

> *Given the chance to observe a writer's processes over time, we can see incubation at work. The flashes of discovery that follow periods of incubation (even brief ones) are unexpected, powerful, and catalytic. . . .*

24

> The second paragraph may be . . . Seems to me I've got an awful lot of stuff before I get into it. (Counting paragraphs) 1, 2, 3, 4, 5, 6, 7, 8, 9, 10, ten paragraphs till I really get into the text. Maybe twelve or thirteen. I'm not going to try to hustle it too much. That might be all right.

The writer then reread the first two paragraphs, making small editorial changes and considering stylistic choices. At that point he broke off and noted on the text three questions, *"What is the principle? What are the acts? How can it be taught?"* He reminded himself to keep his audience in mind. "The first audience has got to be the journal, and therefore, teachers." He took a five-minute break and returned to report,

> But, that's when I realized . . . the word hierarchy ah, came to me and that's when I realized that in a sense I was making this too complicated for myself and simply what I have to do is show the reader . . . I'm making a note here . . . *Job not to explore complexities of revision, but simply to show the reader how to do revision.*

131

From a revision of his goals for his audience, Murray moved quickly into plan- 25
ning activity, noting on his text,

> Hierarchy of problems. O.K. What I'm dealing with is a hierarchy of problems.
> *First, focus / content, second, order / structure, third, language / voice* . . . O.K. Now,
> let's see. I need to ah, need to put that word, hierarchy in here somewhere. Well,
> that may get into the second paragraph so put an arrow down there (draws
> arrow from hierarchy to second paragraph), then see what we can do about the
> title if we need to. Think of things like 'first problems first' (a mini-plan which
> he immediately rejects). It won't make sense that title, unless you've read the
> piece. Ah well, come up with a new title.

Here we can observe the anatomy of a planning episode with a number of 26
goals and sub-goals generated, considered, and consolidated at lightning speed:
"O.K. What I'm dealing with is a hierarchy of problems." " . . . I need to ah,
need to put that word, hierarchy in here somewhere." " . . . so put an arrow
down there, then see what we can do about the title . . ." " . . . 'first problems
first.' It won't make sense that title . . . Ah well, come up with a new title."
We can also see the writer's process of discovery at work as he left his draft
for a brief period and returned having identified a single meaning-laden word.
This word gave Murray an inkling of the structure he wanted for the article—a
listing of the problems writers face before they can accomplish clear, effective
revision. In this case, a short period of incubation was followed by a period of
intense and highly concentrated planning when Murray realized the direction
he wanted the article to take.

Introspection

One of the most helpful sources in this project was the testimony of the writer 27
as he paused between or during composing episodes. Instead of falling silent, he
analyzed his processes, providing information I might have otherwise missed.
The following segments from the protocols will demonstrate the kinds of
insights subjects can give when not constrained by time. At the time of the first,
Mr. Murray had completed the tenth list of titles he had made between June
26th and July 23rd while working on the revision of his article for *College Composition and Communication*. Frequently, these lists were made recursively, the
writer flipping back in his daybook to previous lists he had composed:

> I think I have to go back to titles. *Hearing the student's other self.* Hold my place
> and go back and see if I have any that hit me in the past. *Teaching the reader and
> the writer. Teaching the reader in the writer. Encouraging the internal dialogue.*
> I skipped something in my mind that I did not put down. *Make your students
> talk to themselves. Teaching the writer to read.*

At this point he stopped to evaluate his process:

> All that I'm doing is compressing, ah, compressing is, ah, why I do a title . . . it
> compresses a draft for the whole thing. Title gives me a point of view, gets the tone,
> the difference between teaching and teach. A lot of time on that, that's all right.

The following morning the writer reported, "While I was shaving, I thought of 28 another title. *Teaching the other self: the writer's first reader.* I started to think of it as soon as I got up." This became the final title for the article and led to the planning of a new lead.

Later that day, after he had dictated three pages of the fourth of eight drafts, 29 he analyzed what he had accomplished:

> Well, I'm going to comment on what's happened here . . . this is a very
> complicated text. One of the things I'm considering, of course, is incorporating
> what I did in Dallas in here . . . ah, the text is breaking down in a constructive
> way, um, it's complex material and I'm having trouble with it . . . very much
> aware of pace of proportion; how much can you give to the reader in one part,
> and still keep them moving on to the next part. I have to give a little bit of head
> to teaching. . . . As a theatrical thing I am going to have to put some phrases in
> that indicate that I'm proposing or speculating, speculating as I revise this . . .

This last summation gave us important information on the writer's global 30 and local evaluation of text as well as on his rhetorical and stylistic plans. It is unique because it shows Murray engaged in composing and introspecting at the same time. Generally speaking, subjects giving protocols are not asked to add the demands of introspection to the task of writing. But, in fact, as Murray demonstrated, writers *do* monitor and introspect about their writing simultaneously.

SUMMARY

Some of the more provocative findings of this study concern the sub-processes 31 of planning and revising that have not been observed in conventional protocols (such as those taken by Flower and Hayes) because of the time limitations under which they have been given. When coding the protocols, we noted that Mr. Murray developed intricate style goals:

> It worries me a little bit that the title is too imperative. When I first wrote, most
> of my articles were like this; they pound on the table, do this, do that. I want
> this to be a little more reflective.

He also evaluated his thinking plans (i.e., his procedures in planning): "Ah, reading through, ah, hmm . . . I'm just scanning it so I really can't read it. If I read it, it will be an entirely different thing."

133

Most important, the writer's protocols shed new light on the great and 32 small decisions and revisions that form planning. These decisions and revisions form an elaborate network of steps as the writer moves back and forth between planning, drafting, editing, and reviewing.[24] This recursive process was demonstrated time after time as the writer worked on the two articles and the editorial, often discarding his drafts as he reconceived a major rhetorical goal, and returned to the daybook to plan again. Further, given his characteristic habit of working from daybook to dictation, then back to daybook, we were able to observe that Donald Murray composes at the reflexive and extensive poles described by Janet Emig. When working from material he had "rehearsed" in recent workshops, material with which he was thoroughly familiar, he was able to dictate virtually off the top of his head. At other times he was unable to continue dictating as he attempted to hold too much in suspension in short-term memory. On these occasions the writer returned to the daybook and spent considerable time planning before dictating another draft.

One final observation: although it may be impolitic for the researcher to con- 33 tradict the writer, Mr. Murray's activity over the summer while he was thinking aloud suggests that he is wrong in his assertion that writers only consider their audiences when doing external revision, i.e., editing and polishing. To the contrary, his most substantive changes, what he calls "internal revision," occurred as he turned his thoughts toward his audience. According to Murray, internal revision includes

> everything writers do to discover and develop what they have to say, beginning with the reading of a completed first draft. They read to discover where their content, form, language, and voice have led them. They use language, structure, and information to find out what they have to say or hope to say. The audience is one person: the writer.[25]

The writer, however, does not speak in a vacuum. Only when he begins to discern what his readers do not yet know can he shape his language, structure, and information to fit the needs of those readers. It is also natural that a writer like Murray would not be aware of how significant a role his sense of audience played in his thoughts. After years of journalistic writing, his consideration of audience had become more automatic than deliberate. The value of thinking-aloud protocols is that they allow the researcher to eavesdrop at the workplace of the writer, catching the flow of thought that would remain otherwise unarticulated.

However, *how* the writer functions when working in the setting to which he 34 or she is accustomed differs considerably from how that writer will function in an unfamiliar setting, given an unfamiliar task, and constrained by a time period over which he or she has no control. For this reason, I sought to combine the methodology of protocol analysis with the techniques of naturalistic inquiry.

This project has been a first venture in what may be a new direction. 35 Research on single subjects is new in our discipline; we need to bear in mind that each writer has his or her own idiosyncrasies. The researcher must make a trade-off, forgoing generalizability for the richness of the data and the qualitative insights to be gained from it. We need to replicate naturalistic studies of skilled and unskilled writers before we can begin to infer patterns that will allow us to understand the writing process in all of its complexity.

Notes

1. Janet Emig, "Inquiry Paradigms and Writing," *College Composition and Communication*, 33 (February, 1982), p. 55.

2. Emig, "Inquiry Paradigms and Writing," p. 67.

3. Donald Graves, "What Children Show Us About Revision," *Language Arts*, 56 (March, 1979), 312–319; Susan Sowers, "A Six Year Old's Writing Process: The First Half of the First Grade," *Language Arts*, 56 (October, 1979), 829–835; Lucy M. Calkins, "Children Learn the Writer's Craft," *Language Arts*, 57 (February, 1980), 207–213.

4. Janet Emig, *The Composing Processes of Twelfth-Graders* (Urbana, IL: National Council of Teachers of English, 1971), pp. 8–11; Linda Flower and John R. Hayes, "A Cognitive Process Theory of Writing," *College Composition and Communication*, 32 (December, 1981), 368.

5. See Janet Emig, *The Composing Processes of Twelfth-Graders*, p. 30; Sondra Perl, "Five Writers Writing: Case Studies of the Composing Processes of Unskilled College Writers," Diss. New York University, 1978, pp. 48, 387–391; "The Composing Processes of Unskilled College Writers," *Research in the Teaching of English*, 13 (December, 1979), 318; Nancy I. Sommers, "Revision Strategies of Student Writers and Experienced Adult Writers," paper delivered at the Annual Meeting of the Modern Language Association, New York, 28 December, 1978. A slightly revised version was published in *College Composition and Communication*, 32 (December, 1980), 378–388.

6. See Linda Flower and John R. Hayes, "Identifying the Organization of Writing Processes," in *Cognitive Processes in Writing*, ed. Lee W. Gregg and Erwin R. Steinberg (Hillsdale, NJ: Lawrence Erlbaum Associates, 1981), p. 4; "The Cognition of Discovery: Defining a Rhetorical Problem," *College Composition and Communication*, 32 (February, 1980), 23; "The Pregnant Pause: An Inquiry into the Nature of Planning," *Research in the Teaching of English*, 19 (October, 1981), 233; "A Cognitive Process Theory of Writing," p. 368; Carol Berkenkotter, "Understanding a Writer's Awareness of Audience," *College Composition and Communication*, 32 (December, 1981), 389.

7. Perl, "Five Writers Writing: Case Studies of the Composing Processes of Unskilled College Writers," p. 1.

8. Evaluations of text were either global or local. An example of global evaluation is when the writer says, "There's a lack of fullness in the piece." When the writer was evaluating locally he would comment, " . . . and the ending seems weak."

9. Emig, *The Composing Processes of Twelfth-Graders*, p. 4.

10. *Ibid.* See also "Eye, Hand, and Brain," in *Research on Composing: Points of Departure*, ed. Charles R. Cooper and Lee Odell (Urbana, IL: National Council of Teachers of English), p. 70. Emig raises the question, "What if it is the case that classical and contemporary rhetorical terms such as . . . extensive and reflexive may represent centuries old understandings that the mind deals differentially with different speaking and writing tasks. To put the matter declaratively, if hypothetically, modes of discourse may represent measurably different profiles of brain activity."

11. Janet Emig, observing her subject's writing processes, noted that "the *nature of the stimulus*" did not necessarily determine the response. Emig's students gave extensive responses to a reflexive task (*The Composing Processes of Twelfth-Graders*, pp. 30–31, 33). Similarly, Murray gave a reflexive response to an extensive task. Such a response is not unusual when we consider what the writer himself has observed: "The deeper we get into the writing process the more we may discover how affective concerns govern the cognitive, for writing is an intellectual activity carried on in an emotional environment, a precisely engineered sailboat trying to hold course in a vast and stormy Atlantic" ("Teaching the Other Self: The Writer's First Reader," *College Composition and Communication*, 33 [May, 1982], p. 142). For a writer as deeply engaged in his work as Murray, drafting a conceptual piece was as personal and subjective as describing a closely felt experience.

12. Lester Faigley and Stephen Witte, "Analyzing Revision," *College Composition and Communication*, 32 (December, 1981), 410–411.

13. Faigley and Witte, p. 411.

14. These three pieces of discourse were chosen because their results are representative of the writer's activities.

15. Linda Flower and John R. Hayes describe "process goals" as "instructions and plans the writer gives herself for directing her own composing process." See "The Pregnant Pause: An Inquiry into the Nature of Planning," p. 242. However, this definition is not always agreed upon by cognitive psychologists studying problem-solvers in other fields. On one hand, Allen Newell, Herbert A. Simon, and John R. Hayes distinguish between the goals and plans of a problem-solver, considering a goal as an end to be achieved and a plan as one kind of method for reaching that end. See John R. Hayes, *Cognitive Psychology* (Homewood, IL: The Dorsey Press, 1978), p. 192; Allen Newell and Herbert A. Simon, *Human Problem Solving* (Englewood Cliffs, NJ: Prentice-Hall, Inc. 1972), pp. 88–92, 428–429. On the other hand, George Miller, Eugene Galanter, and Karl H. Pribram use the term "plan" inclusively, suggesting that a plan is "any hierarchical process in the organism that can control the order in which a sequence of operations is to be performed." See *Plans and the Structure of Human Behavior* (New York: Holt, Rinehart, and Winston, Inc., 1960), p. 16.

16. Flower and Hayes use these terms interchangeably, as have I. "Thinking plans" are plans for text that precede drafting and occur during drafting. Thinking plans occur before the movements of a writer's hand. Because of the complexity of the composing process, it is difficult to separate thinking plans from "process goals." It is possible, however, to distinguish between *rhetorical goals* and *rhetorical plans*. Murray was setting a goal when he remarked, "The biggest thing is to . . . what I've got to get to satisfy the reader . . . is that point of what do we hear the other self saying and how does it help?" He followed this goal with a plan to "Probe into the other self. What is the other self? How does it function?"

17. Sommers, "Revision Strategies," pp. 385, 387. (See note 5, above.)

18. The material italicized in the excerpts from these transcripts is text the subject is writing. The material italicized and underlined is text the subject is reading that has already been written.

19. Flower and Hayes, "A Cognitive Process Theory of Writing," 365–387.

20. Berkenkotter, "Understanding a Writer's Awareness of Audience," pp. 392, 395.

21. Faigley and Witte, pp. 406–410.

22. Michael Polanyi, *Personal Knowledge: Toward a Post-Critical Philosophy* (Chicago: The University of Chicago Press, 1958), p. 122.

23. Graham Wallas, *The Art of Thought* (New York: Jonathan Cape, 1926), pp. 85–88; Alex Osborn, *Applied Imagination: Principles and Procedures of Creative Problem-Solving*, 3rd rev. ed. (New York: Charles F. Scribner and Sons), pp. 314–325.

24. For a description of the development of a writer's goal structure, see Flower and Hayes, "A Cognitive Process Theory of Writing."

25. Donald M. Murray, "Internal Revision: A Process of Discovery," *Research on Composing: Points of Departure* (see note 10), p. 91.

RESPONSE OF A LABORATORY RAT — OR, BEING PROTOCOLED

Donald M. Murray

1.

First a note on self-exposure, a misdemeanor in most communities. I have long felt the academic world is too closed. We have an ethical obligation to write and to reveal our writing to our students if we are asking them to share their writing with us. I have felt writers should, instead of public readings, give public workshops in which they write in public, allowing the search for meaning to be seen. I've done this and found the process insightful — and fun.

I have also been fascinated by protocol analysis research. It did seem a fruitful way (a way, there is no one way) to study the writing process. I was, however, critical of the assignments I had seen given, the concentration on inexperienced students as subjects, and the unrealistic laboratory conditions and time limitations.

And, in the absence of more proper academic resources, I have made a career of studying myself while writing. I was already without shame. When Carol Berkenkotter asked me to run in her maze I gulped, but I did not think I could refuse.

2.

The one-hour protocol was far worse than I had expected. If I had done that 4 first there would have been no other protocols. I have rarely felt so completely trapped and so inadequate. I have gone through other research experiences, but in this case I felt stronger than I ever had the need to perform. That was nothing that the researcher did. It was a matter of the conditions. I had a desperate desire to please. I thought of that laboratory experiment where subjects would push a button to cause pain to other people. I would have blown up Manhattan to get out of that room. To find equivalent feelings from my past I would have to go back to combat or to public school. I have developed an enormous compassion and respect for those who have performed for Masters and Johnson.

3.

The process of a naturalistic study we have evolved (Can a rat be a colleague? Since 5 a colleague can be a rat, I don't see why not.) soon became a natural process. I do not assume, and neither did my researcher, that what I said reflected all that was taking place. It did reflect what I was conscious of doing, and a bit more. My articulation was an accurate reflection of the kind of talking I do to myself while planning to write, while writing, and while revising. At no time did it seem awkward or unnatural. My talking aloud was merely a question of turning up the volume knob on the muttering I do under my breath as I write.

> Writing is an intellectual activity, and I do not agree with the romantics who feel that the act of writing and the act of thinking are separate.

I feel that if there was any self-consciousness in the process it was helpful. I 6 was, after all, practicing a craft, not performing magic. Writing is an intellectual activity, and I do not agree with the romantics who feel that the act of writing and the act of thinking are separate.

Having this researcher, who had earned my trust, waiting to see what I wrote 7 was a motivating factor. While the experiment was going on she was appropriately chilly and doctoral. But I still knew someone was listening, and I suspect that got me to the writing desk some days.

It is certainly true that debriefing by the researcher at some distance from 8 the time of writing was virtually useless. I could not remember why I had done what. In fact, the researcher knows the text better than I do. I am concentrating almost entirely on the daily evolving text, and yesterday's page seems like last year's. I intend to try some teaching experiments in the future that make it possible for me to be on the scene when my students are writing. I'm a bit more suspicious now than I had been about the accounts that are reconstructed in a conference days after writing. They are helpful, the best teaching point I know, but I want to find out what happens if we can bring the composing and the teaching closer together.

4.

I certainly agree with what my researcher calls introspection. I am disappointed, however, that she hasn't included the term that I overheard the coders use. Rats aren't all that dumb, and I think there should be further research into those moments when I left the desk and came back with a new insight. They called them: "Bathroom epiphanies." 9

5.

I was surprised by: 10

1. The percentage of my time devoted to planning. I had realized the pendulum was swinging in that direction, but I had no idea how far it had swung. I suspect that when we begin to write in a new genre we have to do a great deal of revision, but that as we become familiar with a genre we can solve more writing problems in advance of a completed text. This varies according to the writer but I have already changed some of my teaching to take this finding into account by allowing my students much more planning time and introducing many more planning techniques.

2. The length of incubation time. I now realize that articles that I thought took a year in fact have taken three, four, or five years.

3. The amount of revision that is essentially planning, what the researcher calls "reconceiving." I was trying to get at that in my chapter, "Internal Revision: A Process of Discovery," published in *Research on Composing: Points of Departure*, edited by Charles R. Cooper and Lee Odell. I now understand this process far better, and much of my revision is certainly a planning or prewriting activity.

6.

I agree with my researcher (what rat wouldn't?) that affective conditions are import- ant in writing. I do think the affective often controls the cognitive, and I feel strongly that much more research has to be done, difficult as it may be, into those conditions, internal and external, that make effective writing possible or impossible. 11

7.

I was far more aware of audience than I thought I was during some of the writing. My sense of audience is so strong that I have to suppress my conscious awareness of audience to hear what the text demands. 12

Related to this is the fact that I do need a few readers. The important role 13
of my pre-publication readers was clear when my revisions were studied. No
surprise here. I think we need more study of the two, or three, or four readers
professional writers choose for their work in process. It would be helpful for
us as teachers to know the qualities of these people and what they do for the
writer. I know I choose people who make me want to write when I leave them.

8.

I worry a bit about the patterns that this research revealed have been laid down in my 14
long-term memory. The more helpful they are the more I worry about them. I fear
that what I discover when I write is what I have discovered before and forgotten, and
that rather than doing the writing that must be done I merely follow the stereotypes
of the past. In other words, I worry that the experienced writer can become too glib,
too slick, too professional, too polished—can, in effect, write too well.

9.

The description of working back and forth from the global to the particular 15
during the subprocesses of planning and revising seems accurate to me.

There is a great deal of interesting research and speculation about this pro- 16
cess, but we need much more. I find it very difficult to make my students aware
of the layers of concern through which the writing writer must oscillate at such
a speed that it appears the concerns are dealt with instantaneously.

Too often in my teaching and my publishing I have given the false impres- 17
sion that we do one thing, then another, when in fact we do many things simultaneously. And the interaction between these things is what we call writing.
This project reaffirmed what I had known, that there are many simultaneous
levels of concern that bear on every line.

10.

I realize how eccentric my work habits appear. I am aware of how fortunate 18
I am to be able to work with my wife. The process of dictation of non-fiction
allows a flow, intensity, and productivity that is quite unusual. It allows me to
spend a great deal of time planning, because I know that once the planning is
done I can produce copy in short bursts. It is not my problem but the researcher's,
however, to put my eccentric habits into context.

If I am the first writer to be naked, then it is up to those other writers who do 19
not think they look the same to take off their clothes. I hope they do not appear
as I do; I would be most depressed if I am the model for other writers. I hope, and
I believe, that there must be a glorious diversity among writers. What I think we
have done, as rat and ratee, is to demonstrate that there is a process through which
experienced writers can be studied under normal working conditions on typical

writing projects. I think my contribution is not to reveal my own writing habits but to show a way that we can study writers who are far better writers than I.

11.

Finally, I started this process with a researcher and have ended it with a col- 20
league. I am grateful for the humane way the research was conducted. I have learned a great deal about research and about what we have researched. It has helped me in my thinking, my teaching, and my writing. I am grateful to Dr. Carol Berkenkotter for this opportunity.

Questions for Discussion and Journaling

1. What was your impression of Murray's writing processes as they're described by Berkenkotter? How do they compare to yours? What do you do the same or differently?

2. Murray's relationship with his audience seems complicated. Try to describe it, and then compare it with your own sense of audience: How much are *you* thinking about *your* audience while you write?

3. How did this study change Berkenkotter's understanding of writing processes, particularly planning and revision?

4. What problems with existing methods for studying writing process does Berkenkotter identify? If you read Perl (p. 93), did you notice any of these problems in her methods? What do you think they might mean for Perl's findings? In what ways is Berkenkotter's newer approach to studying writing processes able to solve the weaknesses in other methods? Do any weaknesses remain?

5. Why do you suppose Berkenkotter often refers to Murray as "the writer" and in his response Murray calls Berkenkotter "the researcher"? Why not just use each other's names, since the audience knows them anyway?

6. What do you think of the apparent back-and-forth between the researcher and the researched that occurred as Berkenkotter analyzed her data and drew conclusions? Was it good? Bad? Necessary? Irrelevant? Did anything about it surprise you?

7. As you read this account of Murray's writing, how much (to what extent, or, how often) does he seem to be aware of writing as making new knowledge (one of this chapter's threshold concepts)? Does he seem to imagine all his writing as doing this, or just some pieces?

Applying and Exploring Ideas

1. Less-experienced writers, especially when writing for school, tend to spend comparatively little time on revision (by which we mean *developing the ideas* in a piece rather than **editing**, which is the sentence-level work that improves

the style and correctness of a text). Explore your own writing habits: How do you spend your writing time? How would you characterize your level of writing experience? How do you think your level of experience relates to the amount of time you spend on various parts of the writing process? In making these estimates, keep the following in mind: Murray, a highly professional and quite reflective writer, had an erroneous impression of how much time he spent on various aspects of his writing process.

2. Begin a writing log in which you list all the writing situations you find yourself in on a day-to-day basis: Every time you write over two weeks, note what you write, the audience for that writing, the genre, the technologies employed, and the skills used. At the end of the period, reflect on what you learned about your writing habits.

3. Try your own brief experiment, recreating Berkenkotter and Murray's dynamic: Pair with a class partner and designate one of you as research*er* and the other as research*ed*. Have the researcher observe the researched's writing process on a short (approximately one-page) piece of writing, and then have the researcher write a brief description of that process while the researched writes a piece of similar length on the experience of doing the writing. Compare these descriptions and negotiate the findings: What, put together, do the two accounts reveal about the writer's process?

- -
META MOMENT   Name one thing you learned from the Berkenkotter and Murray readings that you could use to help you write more effectively.
- -

Revision Strategies of Student Writers and Experienced Adult Writers

NANCY SOMMERS

Framing the Reading

For twenty years, Nancy Sommers led Harvard University's Expository Writing Program, and established and directed the Harvard Writing Project. She now teaches in Harvard's Graduate School of Education. Sommers conducted the Harvard Study of Undergraduate Writing, which tracked four hundred students throughout their college experience in order to investigate what they were writing and how.

Throughout her career, Sommers's work has focused on the development of high school and college students' literacies and writing. She has been a significant advocate and practitioner of empirical research on writing: interviewing writers directly, getting them to write about writing, studying what they say, and collecting (often at great expense) and reading the writing they actually produce. Her work has been of tremendous value to other writing researchers. In this piece Sommers investigates how writers handle revision, or further developing drafts or sections of a text that have been drafted. She wrote this article when she worked at the University of Oklahoma and at New York University in the late 1970s and early 1980s, long before she moved to Harvard.

This study is one of the most widely anthologized articles in the field (meaning that it is very frequently reprinted in a variety of collections about the study of writing and writing process — including the book you are reading now), and it won a major award. Sommers's basic research question is whether there are differences in how student writers talk about and implement revision in their writing compared with how experienced professional writers do so. The need for this research, she argued in 1980, was that while other aspects of

Sommers, Nancy. "Revision Strategies of Student Writers and Experienced Adult Writers." *College Composition and Communication*, vol. 31, no. 4, Dec. 1980, pp. 378–88.

the writing process were being studied quite carefully, revision wasn't being studied in the same detail. She attributed this lack of research to definitions of the writing process that were dominant at the time — definitions that imagined revision as almost an afterthought to writing. So Sommers studied revision and reached the conclusions you'll read here, finding that revision is central to writing, and that professional and experienced writers understand revision differently than most student writers.

Sommers's work showed us how to think of revision as something like driving with headlights (our metaphor, not hers): Headlights only let you see a couple hundred yards, but once you've driven those, you see new ground that you couldn't at the beginning. Revision lets you write what you know at the beginning, find out what new ground you can see having written that much, and then write again saying what you would have if you'd known in the beginning what you learned while writing the first draft. Revision, Sommers's research shows, isn't a punishment or something writers need to do when they've done badly; the better a writer you are, the more likely you are to revise, because it's so powerful a way to find out what you want to say. This reality again leads us to the threshold concept that writing is not perfectible and that writing is a process in which writers learn more about what they're writing about.

Something you want to keep in mind while reading this piece: Context is important. Remember, for example, that the composing and revising Sommers observed *was not* happening on word-processors, because those largely didn't exist in 1980. Whatever you think of revision today, however you do it, unless you're writing with pencil / pen and paper, you're not experiencing revision the same way that the people Sommers interviewed in 1980 did. (And you're probably aware how different drafting on a computer is from drafting on paper.) Be sure that you're attending to these kinds of contextual differences between a more than 35-year-old study and how you write today, and keep an eye out for others. Still, part of the reason Sommers's article is still so widely read is because it suggested something that all of us involved in the study of writing should look out for as we think about writing process. See if you can get a feel for the importance of this subject as you're reading.

Getting Ready to Read

Before you read, do at least one of the following activities:

- Make a list of words you use to describe the process of changing what you've written to improve it. What do you call this kind of changing? Do you use different terms for the changing that you do at different times (for example, changes you make to a sentence while you're finishing writing it, changes you make after you finish an entire draft of what you're writing, or changes you make as you're getting ready to turn a draft in for grading or give your final version to readers)?

- Think about where revision fits in your writing process: At what points do you do it? How much, usually?

As you read, consider the following question:

- At what moments in the piece does Sommers's discussion of principles lead to clear, straightforward statements of differences between the student and experienced writers? Make a list of these statements.

ALTHOUGH VARIOUS ASPECTS of the writing process have been studied 1 extensively of late, research on revision has been notably absent. The reason for this, I suspect, is that current models of the writing process have directed attention away from revision. With few exceptions, these models are linear; they separate the writing process into discrete stages. Two representative models are Gordon Rohman's suggestion that the composing process moves from prewriting to writing to rewriting and James Britton's model of the writing process as a series of stages described in metaphors of linear growth, conception—incubation—production.[1] What is striking about these theories of writing is that they model themselves on speech: Rohman defines the writer in a way that cannot distinguish him from a speaker ("A writer is a man who . . . puts [his] experience into words in his own mind"—p. 15); and Britton bases his theory of writing on what he calls (following Jakobson) the "expressiveness" of speech.[2] Moreover, Britton's study itself follows the "linear model" of the relation of thought and language in speech proposed by Vygotsky, a relationship embodied in the linear movement "from the motive which engenders a thought to the shaping of the thought, *first* in inner speech, *then* in meanings of words, and *finally* in words" (quoted in Britton, p. 40). What this movement fails to take into account in its linear structure—"first . . . then . . . finally"—is the recursive shaping of thought by language; what it fails to take into account is *revision*. In these linear conceptions of the writing process revision is understood as a separate stage at the end of the process—a stage that comes after the completion of a first or second draft and one that is temporally distinct from the prewriting and writing stages of the process.[3]

The linear model bases itself on speech in two specific ways. First of all, 2 it is based on traditional rhetorical models, models that were created to serve the spoken art of oratory. In whatever ways the parts of classical rhetoric are described, they offer "stages" of composition that are repeated in contemporary models of the writing process. Edward Corbett, for instance, describes the "five parts of a discourse"—*inventio, dispositio, elocutio, memoria, pronuntiatio*—and, disregarding the last two parts since "after rhetoric came to be concerned mainly with written discourse, there was no further need to deal with them,"[4] he produces a model very close to Britton's conception [*inventio*], incubation [*dispositio*], production [*elocutio*]. Other rhetorics also follow this procedure, and they do so not simply because of historical accident. Rather, the process represented in the linear model is based on the irreversibility of speech. Speech, Roland Barthes says, "is irreversible":

> "A word cannot be retracted, except precisely by saying that one retracts it. To cross out here is to add: if I want to erase what I have just said, I cannot do it without showing the eraser itself (I must say: '*or rather . . .*' "*I expressed myself badly . . .*"); paradoxically, it is ephemeral speech which is indelible, not monumental writing. All that one can do in the case of a spoken utterance is to tack on another utterance."[5]

What is impossible in speech is *revision:* like the example Barthes gives, revision in speech is an afterthought. In the same way, each stage of the linear model must be exclusive (distinct from the other stages) or else it becomes trivial and counterproductive to refer to these junctures as "stages."

By staging revision after enunciation, the linear models reduce revision in 3 writing, as in speech, to no more than an afterthought. In this way such models make the study of revision impossible. Revision, in Rohman's model, is simply the repetition of writing; or to pursue Britton's organic metaphor, revision is simply the further growth of what is already there, the "preconceived" product. The absence of research on revision, then, is a function of a theory of writing which makes revision both superfluous and redundant, a theory which does not distinguish between writing and speech.

What the linear models do produce is a parody of writing. Isolating revision 4 and then disregarding it plays havoc with the experiences composition teachers have of the actual writing and rewriting of experienced writers. Why should the linear model be preferred? Why should revision be forgotten, superfluous? Why do teachers offer the linear model and students accept it? One reason, Barthes suggests, is that "there is a fundamental tie between teaching and speech," while "writing begins at the point where speech becomes *impossible.*"[6] The spoken word cannot be revised. The possibility of revision distinguishes the written text from speech. In fact, according to Barthes, this is the essential difference between writing and speaking. When we must revise, when the very idea is subject to recursive shaping by language, then speech becomes inadequate. This is a matter to which I will return, but first we should examine, theoretically, a detailed exploration of what student writers as distinguished from experienced adult writers *do* when they write and rewrite their work. Dissatisfied with both the linear model of writing and the lack of attention to the process of revision,

I conducted a series of studies over the past three years which examined the revision processes of student writers and experienced writers to see what role revision played in their writing processes. In the course of my work the revision process was redefined as *a sequence of changes in a composition—changes which are initiated by cues and occur continually throughout the writing of a work.*

METHODOLOGY

I used a case study approach. The student writers were twenty freshmen at 5 Boston University and the University of Oklahoma with SAT verbal scores ranging from 450–600 in their first semester of composition. The twenty experienced adult writers from Boston and Oklahoma City included journalists, editors, and academics. To refer to the two groups, I use the terms *student writers* and *experienced writers* because the principal difference between these two groups is the amount of experience they have had in writing.

Each writer wrote three essays, expressive, explanatory, and persuasive, and 6 rewrote each essay twice, producing nine written products in draft and final form. Each writer was interviewed three times after the final revision of each essay. And each writer suggested revisions for a composition written by an anonymous author. Thus extensive written and spoken documents were obtained from each writer.

The essays were analyzed by counting and categorizing the changes made. 7 Four revision operations were identified: deletion, substitution, addition, and reordering. And four levels of changes were identified: word, phrase, sentence, theme (the extended statement of one idea). A coding system was developed for identifying the frequency of revision by level and operation. In addition, transcripts of the interviews in which the writers interpreted their revisions were used to develop what was called a *scale of concerns* for each writer. This scale enabled me to codify what were the writer's primary concerns, secondary concerns, tertiary concerns, and whether the writers used the same scale of concerns when revising the second or third drafts as they used in revising the first draft.

REVISION STRATEGIES OF STUDENT WRITERS

Most of the students I studied did not use the terms *revision* or *rewriting*. In 8 fact, they did not seem comfortable using the word *revision* and explained that revision was not a word they used, but the word their teachers used. Instead, most of the students had developed various functional terms to describe the type of changes they made. The following are samples of these definitions:

> *Scratch Out and Do Over Again:* "I say scratch out and do over, and that means what it says. Scratching out and cutting out. I read what I have written and I cross out a word and put another word in; a more decent word or a better word.

Then if there is somewhere to use a sentence that I have crossed out, I will put it there."

Reviewing: "Reviewing means just using better words and eliminating words that are not needed, I go over and change words around."

Reviewing: "I just review every word and make sure that everything is worded right. I see if I am rambling; I see if I can put a better word in or leave one out. Usually when I read what I have written, I say to myself, 'that word is so bland or so trite,' and then I go and get my thesaurus."

Redoing: "Redoing means cleaning up the paper and crossing out. It is looking at something and saying, no that has to go, or no, that is not right."

Marking Out: "I don't use the word rewriting because I only write one draft and the changes that I make are made on top of the draft. The changes that I make are usually just marking out words and putting different ones in."

Slashing and Throwing Out: "I throw things out and say they are not good. I like to write like Fitzgerald did by inspiration, and if I feel inspired then I don't need to slash and throw much out."

The predominant concern in these definitions is vocabulary. The students 9 understand the revision process as a rewording activity. They do so because they perceive words as the unit of written discourse. That is, they concentrate on particular words apart from their role in the text. Thus one student quoted above thinks in terms of dictionaries, and, following the eighteenth century theory of words parodied in *Gulliver's Travels*, he imagines a load of things carried about to be exchanged. Lexical changes are the major revision activities of the students because economy is their goal. They are governed, like the linear model itself, by the Law of Occam's razor that prohibits logically needless repetition: redundancy and superfluity. Nothing governs speech more than such superfluities; speech constantly repeats itself precisely because spoken words, as Barthes writes, are expendable in the cause of communication. The aim of revision according to the students' own description is therefore to clean up speech; the redundancy of speech is unnecessary in writing, their logic suggests, because writing, unlike speech, can be reread. Thus one student said, "Redoing means cleaning up the paper and crossing out." The remarkable contradiction of cleaning by marking might, indeed, stand for student revision as I have encountered it.

The students place a symbolic importance on their selection and rejection of 10 words as the determiners of success or failure for their compositions. When revising, they primarily ask themselves: can I find a better word or phrase? A more impressive, not so clichéd, or less hum-drum word? Am I repeating the same word or phrase too often? They approach the revision process with what could be labeled as a "thesaurus philosophy of writing"; the students consider the thesaurus a harvest of lexical substitutions and believe that most problems in their essays can be solved by rewording. What is revealed in the students' use of the thesaurus is a governing attitude toward their writing: that the meaning to be communicated is already there, already finished, already produced, ready to be communicated, and all that is necessary is a better word "rightly worded." One student defined revision as "redoing"; "redoing" meant "just using better words and eliminating words that are not needed." For the students, writing is translating: the thought to the page, the language of speech to the more formal language of prose, the word to its synonym. Whatever is translated, an original text already exists for students, one which need not be discovered or acted upon, but simply communicated.[7]

The students list repetition as one of the elements they most worry about. 11 This cue signals to them that they need to eliminate the repetition either by substituting or deleting words or phrases. Repetition occurs, in large part, because student writing imitates—transcribes—speech: attention to repetitious words is a manner of cleaning speech. Without a sense of the developmental possibilities of revision (and writing in general) students seek, on the authority of many textbooks, simply to clean up their language and prepare to type. What is curious, however, is that students are aware of lexical repetition, but not conceptual repetition. They only notice the repetition if they can "hear" it; they do not diagnose lexical repetition as symptomatic of problems on a deeper level. By rewording their sentences to avoid the lexical repetition, the students solve the immediate problem, but blind themselves to problems on a textual level; although they are using different words, they are sometimes merely restating the same idea with different words. Such blindness, as I discovered with student writers, is the inability to "see" revision as a process: the inability to "re-view" their work again, as it were, with different eyes, and to start over.

The revision strategies described above are consistent with the students' 12 understanding of the revision process as requiring lexical changes but not semantic changes. For the students, the extent to which they revise is a function of their level of inspiration. In fact, they use the word *inspiration* to describe the ease or difficulty with which their essay is written, and the extent to which the essay needs to be revised. If students feel inspired, if the writing comes easily, and if they don't get stuck on individual words or phrases, then they say that they cannot see any reason to revise. Because students do not see revision as an activity in which they modify and develop perspectives and ideas, they feel that if they know what they want to say, then there is little reason for making revisions.

The only modification of ideas in the students' essays occurred when they 13 tried out two or three introductory paragraphs. This results, in part, because the students have been taught in another version of the linear model of composing to use a thesis statement as a controlling device in their introductory paragraphs. Since they write their introductions and their thesis statements even before they have really discovered what they want to say, their early close attention to the

149

thesis statement, and more generally the linear model, function to restrict and circumscribe not only the development of their ideas, but also their ability to change the direction of these ideas.

Too often as composition teachers we conclude that students do not will- 14 ingly revise. The evidence from my research suggests that it is not that students are unwilling to revise, but rather that they do what they have been taught to do in a consistently narrow and predictable way. On every occasion when I asked students why they hadn't made any more changes, they essentially replied, "I knew something larger was wrong, but I didn't think it would help to move words around." The students have strategies for handling words and phrases and their strategies helped them on a word or sentence level. What they lack, however, is a set of strategies to help them identify the "something larger" that they sensed was wrong and work from there. The students do not have strategies for handling the whole essay. They lack procedures or heuristics to help them reorder lines of reasoning or ask questions about their purposes and readers. The students view their compositions in a linear way as a series of parts. Even such potentially useful concepts as "unity" or "form" are reduced to the rule that a composition, if it is to have form, must have an introduction, a body, and a conclusion, or the sum total of the necessary parts.

The students decide to stop revising when they decide that they have not vio- 15 lated any of the rules for revising. These rules, such as "Never begin a sentence with a conjunction" or "Never end a sentence with a preposition," are lexically cued and rigidly applied. In general, students will subordinate the demands of the specific problems of their text to the demands of the rules. Changes are made in compliance with abstract rules about the product, rules that quite often do not apply to the specific problems in the text. These revision strategies are teacher-based, directed towards a teacher-reader who expects compliance with rules — with pre-existing "conceptions" — and who will only examine parts of the composition (writing comments about those parts in the margins of their essays) and will cite any violations of rules in those parts. At best the students see their writing altogether passively through the eyes of former teachers or their surrogates, the textbooks, and are bound to the rules which they have been taught.

REVISION STRATEGIES OF EXPERIENCED WRITERS

One aim of my research has been to contrast how student writers define revi- 16 sion with how a group of experienced writers define their revision processes. Here is a sampling of the definitions from the experienced writers:

Rewriting: "It is a matter of looking at the kernel of what I have written, the content, and then thinking about it, responding to it, making decisions, and actually restructuring it."

Rewriting: "I rewrite as I write. It is hard to tell what is a first draft because it is not determined by time. In one draft, I might cross out three pages, write two, cross out a fourth, rewrite it, and call it a draft. I am constantly writing and rewriting. I can only conceptualize so much in my first draft—only so much information can be held in my head at one time; my rewriting efforts are a reflection of how much information I can encompass at one time. There are levels and agenda which I have to attend to in each draft."

Rewriting: "Rewriting means on one level, finding the argument, and on another level, language changes to make the argument more effective. Most of the time I feel as if I can go on rewriting forever. There is always one part of a piece that I could keep working on. It is always difficult to know at what point to abandon a piece of writing. I like this idea that a piece of writing is never finished, just abandoned."

Rewriting: "My first draft is usually very scattered. In rewriting, I find the line of argument. After the argument is resolved, I am much more interested in word choice and phrasing."

Revising: "My cardinal rule in revising is never to fall in love with what I have written in a first or second draft. An idea, sentence, or even a phrase that looks catchy, I don't trust. Part of this idea is to wait a while. I am much more in love with something after I have written it than I am a day or two later. It is much easier to change anything with time."

Revising: "It means taking apart what I have written and putting it back together again. I ask major theoretical questions of my ideas, respond to those questions, and think of proportion and structure, and try to find a controlling metaphor. I find out which ideas can be developed and which should be dropped. I am constantly chiseling and changing as I revise."

The experienced writers describe their primary objective when revising as 17 finding the form or shape of their argument. Although the metaphors vary, the experienced writers often use structural expressions such as "finding a framework," "a pattern," or "a design" for their argument. When questioned about this emphasis, the experienced writers responded that since their first drafts are usually scattered attempts to define their territory, their objective in the second draft is to begin observing general patterns of development and deciding what should be included and what excluded. One writer explained, "I have learned from experience that I need to keep writing a first draft until I figure out what I want to say. Then in a second draft, I begin to see the structure of an argument and how all the various sub-arguments which are buried beneath the surface of all those sentences are related." What is described here is a process in which the writer is both agent and vehicle. "Writing," says Barthes, unlike speech, "develops like a seed, not a line,"[8] and like a seed it confuses beginning and end, conception and production. Thus, the experienced writers say their drafts are "not determined by time," that rewriting is a "constant process," that they feel as if (they) "can go on forever." Revising confuses the beginning and end, the agent and vehicle; it confuses, *in order to find*, the line of argument.

After a concern for form, the experienced writers have a second objective: a concern for their readership. In this way, "production" precedes "conception." The experienced writers imagine a reader (reading their product) whose existence and whose expectations influence their revision process. They have abstracted the standards of a reader and this reader seems to be partially a reflection of themselves and functions as a critical and productive collaborator — a collaborator who has yet to love their work. The anticipation of a reader's judgment causes a feeling of dissonance when the writer recognizes incongruities between intention

> . . . experienced writers say their drafts are "not determined by time," that rewriting is a "constant process," that they feel as if (they) "can go on forever."

and execution, and requires these writers to make revisions on all levels. Such a reader gives them just what the students lacked: new eyes to "re-view" their work. The experienced writers believe that they have learned the causes and conditions, the product, which will influence their reader, and their revision strategies are geared towards creating these causes and conditions. They demonstrate a complex understanding of which examples, sentences, or phrases should be included or excluded. For example, one experienced writer decided to delete public examples and add private examples when writing about the energy crisis because "private examples would be less controversial and thus more persuasive." Another writer revised his transitional sentences because "some kinds of transitions are more easily recognized as transitions than others." These examples represent the type of strategic attempts these experienced writers use to manipulate the conventions of discourse in order to communicate to their reader.

But these revision strategies are a process of more than communication; they are part of the process of *discovering meaning* altogether. Here we can see the importance of dissonance; at the heart of revision is the process by which writers recognize and resolve the dissonance they sense in their writing. Ferdinand de Saussure has argued that meaning is differential or "diacritical," based on differences between terms rather than "essential" or inherent qualities of terms. "Phonemes," he said, "are characterized not, as one might think, by their own positive quality but simply by the fact that they are distinct."[9] In fact, Saussure bases his entire *Course in General Linguistics* on these differences, and such differences are dissonant; like musical dissonances which gain their significance from their relationship to the "key" of the composition which itself is determined by the whole language, specific language (parole) gains its meaning from the system of language (langue) of which it is a manifestation and part. The musical composition—a "composition" of parts—creates its "key" as in an overall structure which determines the value (meaning) of its parts. The analogy with music is readily seen in the compositions of experienced writers: both sorts of composition are based precisely on those structures experienced writers seek in their writing. It is this complicated relationship between the parts and the whole in the work of experienced writers which destroys the linear model; writing cannot develop "like a line" because each addition or deletion is a reordering of the whole. Explicating Saussure, Jonathan Culler asserts that "meaning depends on difference of meaning."[10] But student writers constantly struggle to bring their essays into congruence with a predefined meaning. The experienced writers do the opposite: they seek to discover (to create) meaning in the engagement with their writing, in revision. They seek to emphasize and exploit the lack of clarity, the differences of meaning, the dissonance, that writing as opposed to speech allows in the possibility of revision. Writing has spatial and temporal features not apparent in speech—words are recorded in space and fixed in time—which is why writing is susceptible to reordering and later addition. Such features make possible the dissonance that both provokes revision and promises, from itself, new meaning.

For the experienced writers the heaviest concentration of changes is on the 20 sentence level, and the changes are predominantly by addition and deletion. But, unlike the students, experienced writers make changes on all levels and use all revision operations. Moreover, the operations the students fail to use—reordering and addition—seem to require a theory of the revision process as a totality—a theory which, in fact, encompasses the *whole* of the composition. Unlike the students, the experienced writers possess a non-linear theory in which a sense of the whole writing both precedes and grows out of an examination of the parts. As we saw, one writer said he needed "a first draft to figure out what to say," and "a second draft to see the structure of an argument buried beneath the surface." Such a "theory" is both theoretical and strategical; once again, strategy and theory are conflated in ways that are literally impossible for the linear model. Writing appears to be more like a seed than a line.

Two elements of the experienced writers' theory of the revision process are 21 the adoption of a holistic perspective and the perception that revision is a recursive process. The writers ask: what does my essay as a *whole* need for form, balance, rhythm, or communication. Details are added, dropped, substituted, or reordered according to their sense of what the essay needs for emphasis and proportion. This sense, however, is constantly in flux as ideas are developed and modified; it is constantly "re-viewed" in relation to the parts. As their ideas change, revision becomes an attempt to make their writing consonant with that changing vision.

The experienced writers see their revision process as a recursive process — a 22 process with significant recurring activities — with different levels of attention and different agenda for each cycle. During the first revision cycle their attention is primarily directed towards narrowing the topic and delimiting their ideas. At this point, they are not as concerned as they are later about vocabulary and style. The experienced writers explained that they get closer to their meaning by not limiting themselves too early to lexical concerns. As one writer commented to explain her revision process, a comment inspired by the summer 1977 New York power failure: "I feel like Con Edison cutting off certain states to keep the generators going. In first and second drafts, I try to cut off as much as I can of my editing generator, and in a third draft, I try to cut off some of my idea generators, so I can make sure that I will actually finish the essay." Although the experienced writers describe their revision process as a series of different levels or cycles, it is inaccurate to assume that they have only one objective for each cycle and that each cycle can be defined by a different objective. The same objectives and sub-processes are present in each cycle, but in different proportions. Even though these experienced writers place the predominant weight upon finding the form of their argument during the first cycle, other concerns exist as well. Conversely, during the later cycles, when the experienced writers' primary attention is focused upon stylistic concerns, they are still attuned, although in a reduced way, to the form of the argument. Since writers are limited in what they can attend to during each cycle (understandings are temporal), revision strategies help balance competing demands on attention. Thus, writers can concentrate on more than one objective at a time by developing strategies to sort out and organize their different concerns in successive cycles of revision.

It is a sense of writing as discovery — a repeated process of beginning over 23 again, starting out new — that the students failed to have. I have used the notion of dissonance because such dissonance, the incongruities between intention and execution, governs both writing and meaning. Students do not see the incongruities. They need to rely on their own internalized sense of good writing and to see their writing with their "own" eyes. Seeing in revision — seeing beyond hearing — is at the root of the word *revision* and the process itself; current dicta on revising blind our students to what is actually involved in revision. In fact, they blind them to what constitutes good writing altogether. Good writing disturbs: it creates dissonance. Students need to seek the dissonance of discovery, utilizing in their writing, as the experienced writers do, the very difference between writing and speech — the possibility of revision.

Notes

1. D. Gordon Rohman and Albert O. Wlecke, "Pre-writing: The Construction and Application of Models for Concept Formation in Writing," Cooperative Research Project No. 2174,

U.S. Office of Education, Department of Health, Education, and Welfare; James Britton, Anthony Burgess, Nancy Martin, Alex McLeod, Harold Rosen, *The Development of Writing Abilities (11–18)* (London: Macmillan Education, 1975).

2. Britton is following Roman Jakobson, "Linguistics and Poetics," in T. A. Sebeok, *Style in Language* (Cambridge, Mass: MIT Press, 1960).

3. For an extended discussion of this issue see Nancy Sommers, "The Need for Theory in Composition Research," *College Composition and Communication*, 30 (February 1979), 46–49.

4. *Classical Rhetoric for the Modern Student* (New York: Oxford University Press, 1965), p. 27.

5. Roland Barthes, "Writers, Intellectuals, Teachers," in *Image-Music-Text*, trans. Stephen Heath (New York: Hill and Wang, 1977), pp. 190–191.

6. "Writers, Intellectuals, Teachers," p. 190.

7. Nancy Sommers and Ronald Schleifer, "Means and Ends: Some Assumptions of Student Writers," *Composition and Teaching*, II (in press).

8. *Writing Degree Zero* in *Writing Degree Zero and Elements of Semiology*, trans. Annette Lavers and Colin Smith (New York: Hill and Wang, 1968), p. 20.

9. *Course in General Linguistics*, trans. Wade Baskin (New York, 1966), p. 119.

10. Jonathan Culler, *Saussure* (Penguin Modern Masters Series; London: Penguin Books, 1976), p. 70.

Acknowledgment

The author wishes to express her gratitude to Professor William Smith, University of Pittsburgh, for his vital assistance with the research reported in this article and to Patrick Hays, her husband, for extensive discussions and critical editorial help.

- -

Questions for Discussion and Journaling

1. Sommers says that the language students use to describe revision is about *vocabulary*, suggesting that they "understand the revision process as a rewording activity" (para. 9). How is that different from the way she argues that revision *should* be understood?

2. Is it important that Sommers elected to identify her two groups of writers as *student* and *experienced* writers rather than as, for example, *novice* and *professional* writers? What alternative terms might *you* choose to identify these groups? Do the terms make a difference?

3. In her introduction and in analyzing students' descriptions of revision, Sommers focuses quite a lot on the difference between speech and writing. In your words, what is she saying that difference is between the two, and why is this difference relevant to how we understand revision?

4. In paragraph 19, Sommers writes that for experienced writers, revision strategies are "a process of more than communication; they are a part of the process of *discovering meaning* altogether." What does she seem to mean by "discovering meaning"? How is "discovering meaning" different from "communication"? Does Sommers's emphasis on writing as an act of making meaning relate to anything else you've encountered in this book?

5. What do you think Sommers means when she says that for experienced writers, revision is based on a non-linear theory in which a sense of the whole writing both precedes and grows out of an examination of the parts? What does she mean by "the whole writing"? What does it mean for writing processes to be non-linear (not a straight line of progress from beginning to end)? And why do you think that experienced writers see writing as non-linear but student writers tend to see writing as linear (prewrite → write → edit)?

6. One of the experienced writers that Sommers interviews talks about having an "editing generator" and an "idea generator." What do you think that means? Can you think about your own writing experiences and identify any kinds of mental "generators" that help you come up with ideas, edit, etc.? If you haven't had the experience of an "idea generator," why do you think that is?

7. Sommers's research, she says, makes her believe that student revision practices don't reflect a *lack* of engagement, "but rather that they do what they have been taught to do in a consistently narrow and predictable way" (para. 14). Where do you think students got the idea that they should see writing as transcribing and revising as changing words? Does this match what you have been taught about writing and revising? If not, what has been different in your experience?

8. In the closing lines of her article, Sommers asserts that "good writing disturbs; it creates dissonance." What does that mean? Do you think that is always true? Can you think of good writing that *doesn't* disturb, create dissonance, or try to resist other ideas? Sommers is really making a claim about what counts as "good" writing. How does her definition here of good writing compare to those of other scholars you've read in this book? How does it compare to your own idea of good writing?

9. Sommers contrasts writing with a "predefined meaning" (para. 19) versus "writing as discovery" (para. 23). How are these two understandings of writing different? Why does she claim that these are opposing? What does writing as discovery seem to allow that writing with a predefined meaning doesn't? Can you think of examples where you've done each? Was one kind of experience better than the other?

Applying and Exploring Ideas

1. Create a one- to two-paragraph summary of Sommers's report on what student writers say about revision, gathering up her main points about what the students she interviewed thought about revision. Then compare it with your own ideas about revision. How much do these students sound like you? Where your ideas

about revision sound different, do they sound more like the professional writers' ideas, or like something else altogether?

2. Sommers begins her article by looking at research by Rohman and Wlecke and Britton that imagines writing as happening in linear *stages*. By the end of her article, she describes research suggesting that writers seem to be concerned with most stages of writing (coming up with ideas, composing text, revising ideas, editing, etc.) all at the same time (see para. 22). Explain each of these views and then argue for one of these views (or a combination of the two) that best explains how you write.

3. Look up the word *recursive* and get a sense of its various definitions. Based on that, and on how you typically think about writing, write an explanation for the class of why writing is a recursive activity. Then stop and think: How is *your* typical writing process *actually* recursive? What does that recursivity look like in your own writing?

4. Sommers identifies four "levels of change" in revision: word, phrase, sentence, and theme — "the extended statement of one idea" (by which she seems to mean, when a single sentence doesn't express a "complete thought" but rather when a couple or several sentences or even a paragraph are required to express an idea). Find two pieces of writing you've completed recently which you revised before submitting, and examine what you actually changed between the first draft and the last. Do you see any changes that aren't accounted for by Sommers's four levels — any levels "higher" than theme, or different from *sentence structure* (which basically contains all her levels)? Write a report on your analysis that focuses specifically on this question.

- -

META MOMENT   Can you think of things you can do, and ways you can imagine writing differently, so that you revise more like an experienced writer and less like the student writers in Sommers's study?

- -

Rigid Rules, Inflexible Plans, and the Stifling of Language

A Cognitivist Analysis of Writer's Block

Mike Rose

MIKE ROSE

Framing the Reading

All of the readings in this chapter focus on aspects of how writers compose — that is, how they walk through the process of actually producing a text, from coming up with ideas for it to finalizing the piece. Some selections pay more attention to elements or functions of composing (like planning, prewriting, drafting, and revising); others focus on the **constraints** and rules — audiences, situations, grammar rules — that writers must navigate. Mike Rose's study of writer's block brings these elements together by asking what's happening when writers are literally incapable of writing the next sentence.

Rose's career has been one of studying, teaching, and helping writers who have a difficult time writing. Currently Research Professor in the UCLA Graduate School of Education and Information Studies, Rose has taught for nearly forty years at many levels of education, including kindergarten and adult literacy programs. Some of his earliest research involved problems of writers block, and the article you're reading here eventually became part of his 1984 book *Writer's Block: The Cognitive Dimension*. More broadly, Rose has worked throughout his career on problems of literacy and access to education. His most widely recognized book is 1989's *Lives on the Boundary*, and he has since published many works dealing with access to education and the opportunities it provides.

At the time Rose wrote this article, the dominant approach to understanding writing problems was to consider them to be *thinking* problems — problems of cognition, or

mental operation. If we could understand how writers *think*, how their brains process information, the theory was, we would be able to teach writing more effectively because we could understand and teach the mental operations that lead to good writing.

Rose, Mike. "Rigid Rules, Inflexible Plans, and the Stifling of Language: A Cognitivist Analysis of Writer's Block." *College Composition and Communication*, vol. 31, no. 4, Dec. 1980, pp. 389–401.

Some proponents of cognitive analysis seemed to want to reduce human thinking to machine processing. They ignored everything going on *outside* a writer's head — that is, the rhetorical situation and context — and assumed that situation had nothing to do with the rules by which brains process information and thus generate writing. Like other critics of this position, Rose suspected that other rules — cultural rules, school rules — might need more study and critique. Trained in psychological counseling, he applied a different set of cognitivist ideas to this problem of cultural rules and their negative effect on some people's writing. You'll read the results in this article.

Perhaps most importantly, Rose's work gives us a powerful example of the ways in which what a writer *thinks is true about writing* can shape their experience with writing because it constrains how a writer goes about writing to begin with. This reminds us of two main threshold concepts in this chapter. First, that good writers are made, not born, and someone who does not start out as a strong and confident writer can become stronger by changing their ideas about writing. And second, that writing is enhanced by mindfulness — careful consideration of what you're actually doing.

It's worth noting that writer's block is a technical term that American culture tends to overuse. In the same way that anyone who finds focusing for more than ten seconds difficult might claim they have "ADHD" when in fact most people don't, too many writers who can't think of what to say next are likely to claim, jokingly or seriously, that they have "writer's block." Rose is talking about a rarer, more serious problem.

Getting Ready to Read

Before you read, do at least one of the following activities:

- Quickly make a list of rules that seem to always be in your mind when you are writing for school.
- Make a short list of things that make it hard for you to write.
- Write one paragraph about a person or event that negatively impacted your ability to write.

As you read, consider the following questions:

- What kinds of rules seem to keep people from writing, and what kinds of rules seem to enable people to write?
- What are the relationships among heuristics, plans, rules, algorithms, set, and perplexity?
- Where do you see yourself, if anywhere, among the various writers Rose describes?

RUTH WILL LABOR OVER the first paragraph of an essay for hours. She'll 1
write a sentence, then erase it. Try another, then scratch part of it out. Finally, as
the evening winds on toward ten o'clock and Ruth, anxious about tomorrow's
deadline, begins to wind into herself, she'll compose that first paragraph only to
sit back and level her favorite exasperated interdiction at herself and her page:
"No. You can't say that. You'll bore them to death."

Ruth is one of ten UCLA undergraduates with whom I discussed writer's 2
block, that frustrating, self-defeating inability to generate the next line, the
right phrase, the sentence that will release the flow of words once again. These
ten people represented a fair cross-section of the UCLA student community:
lower-middle-class to upper-middle-class backgrounds and high schools, third-
world and Caucasian origins, biology to fine arts majors, C+ to A− grade point
averages, enthusiastic to blasé attitudes toward school. They were set off from
the community by the twin facts that all ten could write competently, and all
were currently enrolled in at least one course that required a significant amount
of writing. They were set off among themselves by the fact that five of them
wrote with relative to enviable ease while the other five experienced moderate
to nearly immobilizing writer's block. This blocking usually resulted in rushed,
often late papers and resultant grades that did not truly reflect these students'
writing ability. And then, of course, there were other less measurable but probably more serious results: a growing distrust of their abilities and an aversion
toward the composing process itself.

What separated the five students who blocked from those who didn't? It 3
wasn't skill; that was held fairly constant. The answer could have rested in the
emotional realm—anxiety, fear of evaluation, insecurity, etc. Or perhaps blocking in some way resulted from variation in cognitive style. Perhaps, too,
blocking originated in and typified a melding of emotion and cognition not
unlike the relationship posited by Shapiro between neurotic feeling and neurotic thinking.[1] Each of these was possible. Extended clinical interviews and
testing could have teased out the answer. But there was one answer that sur-
faced readily in brief explorations of these students' writing processes. It was
not profoundly emotional, nor was it embedded in that still unclear construct
of cognitive style. It was constant, surprising, almost amusing if its results
weren't so troublesome, and, in the final analysis, obvious: the five students
who experienced blocking were all operating either with writing rules or with
planning strategies that impeded rather than enhanced the composing process. The five students who were not hampered by writer's block also utilized
rules, but they were less rigid ones, and thus more appropriate to a complex
process like writing. Also, the plans these non-blockers brought to the writing
process were more functional, more flexible, more open to information from
the outside.

These observations are the result of one to three interviews with each stu- 4
dent. I used recent notes, drafts, and finished compositions to direct and hone
my questions. This procedure is admittedly non-experimental, certainly more
clinical than scientific; still, it did lead to several inferences that lay the foundation for future, more rigorous investigation: (a) composing is a highly complex problem-solving process[2] and (b) certain disruptions of that process can be
explained with cognitive psychology's problem-solving framework. Such investigation might include a study using "stimulated recall" techniques to validate
or disconfirm these hunches. In such a study, blockers and non-blockers would
write essays. Their activity would be videotaped and, immediately after writing, they would be shown their respective tapes and questioned about the rules,
plans, and beliefs operating in their writing behavior. This procedure would
bring us close to the composing process (the writers' recall is stimulated by their
viewing the tape), yet would not interfere with actual composing.

In the next section I will introduce several key concepts in the problem- 5
solving literature. In section three I will let the students speak for themselves.
Fourth, I will offer a cognitivist analysis of blockers' and non-blockers' grace or
torpor. I will close with a brief note on treatment.

SELECTED CONCEPTS IN PROBLEM SOLVING: RULES AND PLANS

As diverse as theories of problem solving are, they share certain basic assumptions 6
and characteristics. Each posits an *introductory period* during which a problem
is presented, and all theorists, from Behaviorist to Gestalt to Information
Processing, admit that certain aspects, stimuli, or "functions" of the problem
must become or be made salient and attended to in certain ways if successful
problem-solving processes are to be engaged. Theorists also believe that some
conflict, some stress, some gap in information in these perceived "aspects" seems
to trigger problem-solving behavior. Next comes a *processing period*, and for all
the variance of opinion about this critical stage, theorists recognize the necessity
of its existence — recognize that man, at the least, somehow "weighs" possible
solutions as they are stumbled upon and, at the most, goes through an elaborate
and sophisticated information-processing routine to achieve problem solution.
Furthermore, theorists believe — to varying degrees — that past learning and
the particular "set," direction, or orientation that the problem solver takes in
dealing with past experience and present stimuli have critical bearing on the
efficacy of solution. Finally, all theorists admit to a *solution period*, an end-state
of the process where "stress" and "search" terminate, an answer is attained, and a
sense of completion or "closure" is experienced.

These are the gross similarities, and the framework they offer will be use- 7
ful in understanding the problem-solving behavior of the students discussed in
this paper. But since this paper is primarily concerned with the second stage of

problem-solving operations, it would be most useful to focus this introduction on two critical constructs in the processing period: rules and plans.

Rules

Robert M. Gagné defines "rule" as "an inferred capability that enables the indi- 8 vidual to respond to a class of stimulus situations with a class of performances."[3] Rules can be learned directly[4] or by inference through experience.[5] But, in either case, most problem-solving theorists would affirm Gagné's dictum that "rules are probably the major organizing factor, and quite possibly the primary one, in intellectual functioning."[6] As Gagné implies, we wouldn't be able to function without rules; they guide response to the myriad stimuli that confront us daily, and might even be the central element in complex problem-solving behavior.

Dunker, Polya, and Miller, Galanter, and Pribram offer a very useful 9 distinction between two general kinds of rules: algorithms and heuristics.[7] Algorithms are precise rules that will always result in a specific answer if applied to an appropriate problem. Most mathematical rules, for example, are algorithms. Functions are constant (e.g., pi), procedures are routine (squaring the radius), and outcomes are completely predictable. However, few day-to-day situations are mathematically circumscribed enough to warrant the application of algorithms. Most often we function with the aid of fairly general heuristics or "rules of thumb," guidelines that allow varying degrees of flexibility when approaching problems. Rather than operating with algorithmic precision and certainty, we search, critically, through alternatives, using our heuristic as a divining rod — "if a math problem stumps you, try working backwards to solution"; "if the car won't start, check x, y, or z," and so forth. Heuristics won't allow the precision or the certitude afforded by algorithmic operations; heuristics can even be so "loose" as to be vague. But in a world where tasks and problems are rarely mathematically precise, heuristic rules become the most appropriate, the most functional rules available to us: "a heuristic does not guarantee the optimal solution or, indeed, any solution at all; rather, heuristics offer solutions that are good enough most of the time."[8]

Plans

People don't proceed through problem situations, in or out of a laboratory, 10 without some set of internalized instructions to the self, some program, some course of action that, even roughly, takes goals and possible paths to that goal into consideration. Miller, Galanter, and Pribram have referred to this course of action as a plan: "A plan is any hierarchical process in the organism that can control the order in which a sequence of operations is to be performed" (p. 16). They name the fundamental plan in human problem-solving behavior the TOTE, with the initial T representing a *test* that matches a possible solution against the perceived end-goal of problem completion. O represents the clearance to *operate* if the comparison between solution and goal indicates that the solution is a sensible one. The second T represents a further, post-operation, *test* or comparison of solution with goal, and if the two mesh and problem solution is at hand the person *exits* (E) from problem-solving behavior. If the second test presents further discordance between solution and goal, a further solution is attempted in TOTE-fashion. Such plans can be both long-term and global and, as problem solving is underway, short-term and immediate.[9] Though the mechanicality of this information-processing model renders it simplistic and, possibly, unreal, the central notion of a plan and an operating procedure is an important one in problem-solving theory; it at least attempts to metaphorically explain what earlier cognitive psychologists could not—the mental procedures underlying problem-solving behavior.

Before concluding this section, a distinction between heuristic rules and plans should be attempted; it is a distinction often blurred in the literature, blurred because, after all, we are very much in the area of gestating theory and preliminary models. Heuristic rules seem to function with the flexibility of plans. Is, for example, "If the car won't start, try x, y, or z" a heuristic or a plan? It could be either, though two qualifications will mark it as heuristic rather than plan. (A) Plans subsume and sequence heuristic and algorithmic rules. Rules are usually "smaller," more discrete cognitive capabilities; plans can become quite large and complex, composed of a series of ordered algorithms, heuristics, and further planning "sub-routines." (B) Plans, as was mentioned earlier, include criteria to determine successful goal-attainment and, as well, include "feedback" processes—ways to incorporate and use information gained from "tests" of potential solutions against desired goals. 11

One other distinction should be made: that is, between "set" and plan. Set, also called "determining tendency" or "readiness,"[10] refers to the fact that people often approach problems with habitual ways of reacting, a predisposition, a tendency to perceive or function in one way rather than another. Set, which can be established through instructions or, consciously or unconsciously, through experience, can assist performance if it is appropriate to a specific problem,[11] but much of the literature on set has shown its rigidifying, dysfunctional effects.[12] Set differs from plan in that set represents a limiting and narrowing of response alternatives with no inherent process to shift alternatives. It is a kind of cognitive habit that can limit perception, not a course of action with multiple paths that directs and sequences response possibilities. 12

The constructs of rules and plans advance the understanding of problem solving beyond that possible with earlier, less developed formulations. Still, critical problems remain. Though mathematical and computer models move one 13 toward more complex (and thus more real) problems than the earlier research, they are still too neat, too rigidly sequenced to approximate the stunning complexity of day-to-day (not to mention highly creative) problem-solving behavior. Also, information-processing models of problem-solving are built on logic theorems, chess strategies, and simple planning tasks. Even Gagné seems to feel more comfortable with illustrations from mathematics and science rather than with social science and humanities problems. So although these complex models and constructs tell us a good deal about problem-solving behavior, they are still laboratory simulations, still invoked from the outside rather than self-generated, and still founded on the mathematico-logical.

Two Carnegie Mellon researchers, however, have recently extended the above 14 into a truly real, amorphous, unmathematical problem-solving process—writing. Relying on protocol analysis (thinking aloud while solving problems), Linda Flower and John Hayes have attempted to tease out the role of heuristic rules and plans in writing behavior.[13] Their research pushes problem-solving investigations to the real and complex and pushes, from the other end, the often mysterious process of writing toward the explainable. The latter is important, for at least since Plotinus many have viewed the composing process as unexplainable, inspired, infused with the transcendent. But Flower and Hayes are beginning, anyway, to show how writing generates from a problem-solving process with rich heuristic rules and plans of its own. They show, as well, how many writing problems arise from a paucity of heuristics and suggest an intervention that provides such rules.

> Blockers may well be stymied by possessing rigid or inappropriate rules, or inflexible or confused plans. Ironically enough, these are occasionally instilled by the composition teacher or gleaned from the writing textbook.

This paper, too, treats writing as a 15 problem-solving process, focusing, however, on what happens when the process dead-ends in writer's block. It will further suggest that, as opposed to Flower and Hayes' students who need more rules and plans, blockers may well be stymied by possessing rigid or inappropriate rules, or inflexible or confused plans. Ironically enough, these are occasionally instilled by the composition teacher or gleaned from the writing textbook.

"ALWAYS GRAB YOUR AUDIENCE" — THE BLOCKERS

In high school, *Ruth* was told and told again that a good essay always grabs 16 a reader's attention immediately. Until you can make your essay do that, her teachers and textbooks putatively declaimed, there is no need to go on. For Ruth, this means that beginning bland and seeing what emerges as one generates prose is unacceptable. The beginning is everything. And what exactly is the audience seeking that reads this beginning? The rule, or Ruth's use of it, doesn't provide for such investigation. She has an edict with no determiners. Ruth operates with another rule that restricts her productions as well: if sentences aren't grammatically "correct," they aren't useful. This keeps Ruth from toying with ideas on paper, from the kind of linguistic play that often frees up the flow of prose. These two rules converge in a way that pretty effectively restricts Ruth's composing process.

The first two papers I received from *Laurel* were weeks overdue. Sections 17 of them were well written; there were even moments of stylistic flair. But the papers were late and, overall, the prose seemed rushed. Furthermore, one paper included a paragraph on an issue that was never mentioned in the topic paragraph. This was the kind of mistake that someone with Laurel's apparent ability doesn't make. I asked her about this irrelevant passage. She knew very well that it didn't fit, but believed she had to include it to round out the paper, "You must always make three or more points in an essay. If the essay has less, then it's not strong." Laurel had been taught this rule both in high school and in her first college English class; no wonder, then, that she accepted its validity.

As opposed to Laurel, *Martha* possesses a whole arsenal of plans and rules 18 with which to approach a humanities writing assignment, and, considering her background in biology, I wonder how many of them were formed out of the assumptions and procedures endemic to the physical sciences.[14] Martha will not put pen to first draft until she has spent up to two days generating an outline of remarkable complexity. I saw one of these outlines and it looked more like a diagram of protein synthesis or DNA structure than the time-worn pattern offered in composition textbooks. I must admit I was intrigued by the aura of process (vs. the static appearance of essay outlines) such diagrams offer, but for Martha these "outlines" only led to self-defeat: the outline would become so complex that all of its elements could never be included in a short essay. In other words, her plan locked her into the first stage of the composing process. Martha would struggle with the conversion of her outline into prose only to scrap the whole venture when deadlines passed and a paper had to be rushed together.

Martha's "rage for order" extends beyond the outlining process. She also 19 believes that elements of a story or poem must evince a fairly linear structure and thematic clarity, or—perhaps bringing us closer to the issue—that analysis of a story or poem must provide the linearity or clarity that seems to be absent in the text. Martha, therefore, will bend the logic of her analysis to reason ambiguity out of existence. When I asked her about a strained paragraph in her paper on Camus' "The Guest," she said, "I didn't want to admit that it [the story's conclusion] was just hanging. I tried to force it into meaning."

Martha uses another rule, one that is not only problematical in itself, but one 20 that often clashes directly with the elaborate plan and obsessive rule above. She believes that humanities papers must scintillate with insight, must present an array of images, ideas, ironies gleaned from the literature under examination. A problem arises, of course, when Martha tries to incorporate her myriad "neat little things," often inherently unrelated, into a tightly structured, carefully sequenced essay. Plans and rules that govern the construction of impressionistic, associational prose would be appropriate to Martha's desire, but her composing process is heavily constrained by the non-impressionistic and non-associational. Put another way, the plans and rules that govern her exploration of text are not at all synchronous with the plans and rules she uses to discuss her exploration. It is interesting to note here, however, that as recently as three years ago Martha was absorbed in creative writing and was publishing poetry in high school magazines. Given what we know about the complex associational, often non-neatly-sequential nature of the poet's creative process, we can infer that Martha was either free of the plans and rules discussed earlier or they were not as intense. One wonders, as well, if the exposure to three years of university physical science either established or intensified Martha's concern with structure. Whatever the case, she now is hamstrung by conflicting rules when composing papers for the humanities.

Mike's difficulties, too, are rooted in a distortion of the problem-solving pro- 21 cess. When the time of the week for the assignment of writing topics draws near, Mike begins to prepare material, strategies, and plans that he believes will be appropriate. If the assignment matches his expectations, he has done a good job of analyzing the professor's intentions. If the assignment *doesn't* match his expectations, however, he cannot easily shift approaches. He feels trapped inside his original plans, cannot generate alternatives, and blocks. As the deadline draws near, he will write something, forcing the assignment to fit his conceptual procrustian bed. Since Mike is a smart man, he will offer a good deal of information, but only some of it ends up being appropriate to the assignment. This entire situation is made all the worse when the time between assignment of topic and generation of product is attenuated further, as in an essay examination. Mike believes (correctly) that one must have a plan, a strategy of some sort in order to solve a problem. He further believes, however, that such a plan, once formulated, becomes an exact structural and substantive blueprint that cannot be violated. The plan offers no alternatives, no "subroutines." So, whereas Ruth's, Laurel's, and some of Martha's difficulties seem to be rule-specific ("always catch your audience," "write grammatically"), Mike's troubles are more global. He may have strategies that are appropriate for various writing situations (e.g., "for this kind of political science assignment write a compare / contrast essay"), but his entire approach to formulating plans and carrying them through to problem solution is too mechanical. It is probable that Mike's behavior is governed by an explicitly learned or inferred rule: "Always try to 'psych out' a professor." But in this case this rule initiates a problem-solving procedure that is clearly dysfunctional.

While Ruth and Laurel use rules that impede their writing process and Mike 22
utilizes a problem-solving procedure that hamstrings him, *Sylvia* has trouble
deciding which of the many rules she possesses to use. Her problem can be
characterized as cognitive perplexity: some of her rules are inappropriate, others are functional; some mesh nicely with her own definitions of good writing,
others don't. She has multiple rules to invoke, multiple paths to follow, and that
very complexity of choice virtually paralyzes her. More so than with the previous four students, there is probably a strong emotional dimension to Sylvia's
blocking, but the cognitive difficulties are clear and perhaps modifiable.

Sylvia, somewhat like Ruth and Laurel, puts tremendous weight on the craft- 23
ing of her first paragraph. If it is good, she believes the rest of the essay will be
good. Therefore, she will spend up to five hours on the initial paragraph: "I
won't go on until I get that first paragraph down." Clearly, this rule — or the
strength of it — blocks Sylvia's production. This is one problem. Another is that
Sylvia has other equally potent rules that she sees as separate, uncomplementary
injunctions: one achieves "flow" in one's writing through the use of adequate
transitions; one achieves substance to one's writing through the use of evidence.
Sylvia perceives both rules to be "true," but several times followed one to the
exclusion of the other. Furthermore, as I talked to Sylvia, many other rules,
guidelines, definitions were offered, but none with conviction. While she *is*
committed to one rule about initial paragraphs, and that rule is dysfunctional,
she seems very uncertain about the weight and hierarchy of the remaining rules
in her cognitive repertoire.

"IF IT WON'T FIT MY WORK, I'LL CHANGE IT" — THE NON-BLOCKERS

Dale, Ellen, Debbie, Susan, and Miles all write with the aid of rules. But their 24
rules differ from blockers' rules in significant ways. If similar in content, they
are expressed less absolutely — e.g., "*Try* to keep audience in mind." If dissimilar, they are still expressed less absolutely, more heuristically — e.g., "I can use
as many ideas in my thesis paragraph as I need and then develop paragraphs
for each idea." Our non-blockers do express some rules with firm assurance,
but these tend to be simple injunctions that free up rather than restrict the
composing process, e.g., "When stuck, write!" or "I'll write what I can." And
finally, at least three of the students openly shun the very textbook rules that
some blockers adhere to: e.g., "Rules like 'write only what you know about' just
aren't true. I ignore those." These three, in effect, have formulated a further rule
that expresses something like: "If a rule conflicts with what is sensible or with
experience, reject it."

On the broader level of plans and strategies, these five students also differ 25
from at least three of the five blockers in that they all possess problem-solving

plans that are quite functional. Interestingly, on first exploration these plans seem to be too broad or fluid to be useful and, in some cases, can barely be expressed with any precision. Ellen, for example, admits that she has a general "outline in [her] head about how a topic paragraph should look" but could not describe much about its structure. Susan also has a general plan to follow, but, if stymied, will quickly attempt to conceptualize the assignment in different ways: "If my original idea won't work, then I need to proceed differently." Whether or not these plans operate in TOTE-fashion, I can't say. But they do operate with the operate-test fluidity of TOTEs.

True, our non-blockers have their religiously adhered-to rules: e.g., "When 26 stuck, write," and plans, "I couldn't imagine writing without this pattern," but as noted above, these are few and functional. Otherwise, these non-blockers operate with fluid, easily modified, even easily discarded rules and plans (Ellen: "I can throw things out") that are sometimes expressed with a vagueness that could almost be interpreted as ignorance. There lies the irony. Students that offer the least precise rules and plans have the least trouble composing. Perhaps this very lack of precision characterizes the functional composing plan. But perhaps this lack of precision simply masks habitually enacted alternatives and sub-routines. This is clearly an area that needs the illumination of further research.

And then there is feedback. At least three of the five non-blockers are an 27 Information-Processor's dream. They get to know their audience, ask professors and T.A.s specific questions about assignments, bring half-finished products in for evaluation, etc. Like Ruth, they realize the importance of audience, but unlike her, they have specific strategies for obtaining and utilizing feedback. And this penchant for testing writing plans against the needs of the audience can lead to modification of rules and plans. Listen to Debbie:

> In high school I was given a formula that stated that you must write a thesis paragraph with *only* three points in it, and then develop each of those points. When I hit college I was given longer assignments. That stuck me for a bit, but then I realized that I could use as many ideas in my thesis paragraph as I needed and then develop paragraphs for each one. I asked someone about this and then tried it. I didn't get any negative feedback, so I figured it was o.k.

Debbie's statement brings one last difference between our blockers and 28 non-blockers into focus; it has been implied above, but needs specific formu- lation: the goals these people have, and the plans they generate to attain these goals, are quite mutable. Part of the mutability comes from the fluid way the goals and plans are conceived, and part of it arises from the effective impact of feedback on these goals and plans.

ANALYZING WRITER'S BLOCK

Algorithms Rather Than Heuristics

In most cases, the rules our blockers use are not "wrong" or "incorrect"—it is 29
good practice, for example, to "grab your audience with a catchy opening" or
"craft a solid first paragraph before going on." The problem is that these rules
seem to be followed as though they were algorithms, absolute dicta, rather than
the loose heuristics that they were intended to be. Either through instruction,
or the power of the textbook, or the predilections of some of our blockers for
absolutes, or all three, these useful rules of thumb have been transformed into
near-algorithmic urgencies. The result, to paraphrase Karl Dunker, is that these
rules do not allow a flexible penetration into the nature of the problem. It is this
transformation of heuristic into algorithm that contributes to the writer's block
of Ruth and Laurel.

Questionable Heuristics Made Algorithmic

Whereas "grab your audience" could be a useful heuristic, "always make three 30
or more points in an essay" is a pretty questionable one. Any such rule, though
probably taught to aid the writer who needs structure, ultimately transforms a
highly fluid process like writing into a mechanical lockstep. As heuristics, such
rules can be troublesome. As algorithms, they are simply incorrect.

Set

As with any problem-solving task, students approach writing assignments with 31
a variety of orientations or sets. Some are functional, others are not. Martha
and Jane (see footnote 14), coming out of the life sciences and social sciences
respectively, bring certain methodological orientations with them—certain sets
or "directions" that make composing for the humanities a difficult, sometimes
confusing, task. In fact, this orientation may cause them to misperceive the
task. Martha has formulated a planning strategy from her predisposition to see
processes in terms of linear, interrelated steps in a system. Jane doesn't realize
that she can revise the statement that "committed" her to the direction her essay
has taken. Both of these students are stymied because of formative experiences
associated with their majors—experiences, perhaps, that nicely reinforce our
very strong tendency to organize experiences temporally.

The Plan That Is Not a Plan

If fluidity and multi-directionality are central to the nature of plans, then 32
the plans that Mike formulates are not true plans at all but, rather, inflexible
and static cognitive blueprints.[15] Put another way, Mike's "plans" represent a

restricted "closed system" (vs. "open system") kind of thinking, where closed system thinking is defined as focusing on "a limited number of units or items, or members, and those properties of the members which are to be used are known to begin with and do not change as the thinking proceeds," and open system thinking is characterized by an "adventurous exploration of multiple alternatives with strategies that allow redirection once 'dead ends' are encountered."[16] Composing calls for open, even adventurous thinking, not for constrained, no-exit cognition.

Feedback

The above difficulties are made all the more problematic by the fact that [33] they seem resistant to or isolated from corrective feedback. One of the most striking things about Dale, Debbie, and Miles is the ease with which they seek out, interpret, and apply feedback on their rules, plans, and productions. They "operate" and then they "test," and the testing is not only against some internalized goal, but against the requirements of external audience as well.

Too Many Rules — "Conceptual Conflict"

According to D. E. Berlyne, one of the primary forces that motivate [34] problem-solving behavior is a curiosity that arises from conceptual conflict — the convergence of incompatible beliefs or ideas. In *Structure and Direction in Thinking*,[17] Berlyne presents six major types of conceptual conflict, the second of which he terms "perplexity":

> This kind of conflict occurs when there are factors inclining the subject toward each of a set of mutually exclusive beliefs. (p. 257)

If one substitutes "rules" for "beliefs" in the above definition, perplexity becomes a useful notion here. Because perplexity is unpleasant, people are motivated to reduce it by problem-solving behavior that can result in "disequalization":

> Degree of conflict will be reduced if either the number of competing . . . [rules] or their nearness to equality of strength is reduced. (p. 259)

But "disequalization" is not automatic. As I have suggested, Martha and Sylvia hold to rules that conflict, but their perplexity does *not* lead to curiosity and resultant problem-solving behavior. Their perplexity, contra Berlyne, leads to immobilization. Thus "disequalization" will have to be effected from without. The importance of each of, particularly, Sylvia's rules needs an evaluation that will aid her in rejecting some rules and balancing and sequencing others.

A NOTE ON TREATMENT

Rather than get embroiled in a blocker's misery, the teacher or tutor might interview 35 the student in order to build a writing history and profile: How much and what kind of writing was done in high school? What is the student's major? What kind of writing does it require? How does the student compose? Are there rough drafts or outlines available? By what rules does the student operate? How would he or she define "good" writing? etc. This sort of interview reveals an incredible amount of information about individual composing processes. Furthermore, it often reveals the rigid rule or the inflexible plan that may lie at the base of the student's writing problem. That was precisely what happened with the five blockers. And with Ruth, Laurel, and Martha (and Jane) what was revealed made virtually immediate remedy possible. Dysfunctional rules are easily replaced with or counter-balanced by functional ones if there is no emotional reason to hold onto that which simply doesn't work. Furthermore, students can be trained to select, to "know which rules are appropriate for which problems."[18] Mike's difficulties, perhaps because plans are more complex and pervasive than rules, took longer to correct. But inflexible plans, too, can be remedied by pointing out their dysfunctional qualities and by assisting the student in developing appropriate and flexible alternatives. Operating this way, I was successful with Mike. Sylvia's story, however, did not end as smoothly. Though I had three forty-five minute contacts with her, I was not able to appreciably alter her behavior. Berlyne's theory bore results with Martha but not with Sylvia. Her rules were in conflict, and perhaps that conflict was not exclusively cognitive. Her case keeps analyses like these honest; it reminds us that the cognitive often melds with, and can be overpowered by, the affective. So while Ruth, Laurel, Martha, and Mike could profit from tutorials that explore the rules and plans in their writing behavior, students like Sylvia may need more extended, more affectively oriented counseling sessions that blend the instructional with the psychodynamic.

Notes

1. David Shapiro, *Neurotic Styles* (New York: Basic Books, 1965).

2. Barbara Hayes-Ruth, a Rand cognitive psychologist, and I are currently developing an information-processing model of the composing process. A good deal of work has already been done by Linda Flower and John Hayes (see para. 14 of this article). I have just received—and recommend—their "Writing as Problem Solving" (paper presented at American Educational Research Association, April 1979).

3. *The Conditions of Learning* (New York: Holt, Rinehart and Winston, 1970), p. 193.

4. E. James Archer, "The Psychological Nature of Concepts," in H. J. Klausmeier and C. W. Harris, eds., *Analysis of Concept Learning* (New York: Academic Press, 1966), pp. 37–44; David P. Ausubel, *The Psychology of Meaningful Verbal Behavior* (New York: Grune and Stratton, 1963); Robert M. Gagné, "Problem Solving," in Arthur W. Melton, ed., *Categories of Human Learning* (New York: Academic Press, 1964), pp. 293–317; George A. Miller, *Language and Communication* (New York: McGraw-Hill, 1951).

5. George Katona, *Organizing and Memorizing* (New York: Columbia Univ. Press, 1940); Roger N. Shepard, Carl I. Hovland, and Herbert M. Jenkins, "Learning and Memorization of Classifications," *Psychological Monographs*, 75, No. 13 (1961) (entire No. 517); Robert S. Woodworth, *Dynamics of Behavior* (New York: Henry Holt, 1958), chs. 10–12.

6. *The Conditions of Learning*, pp. 190–91.

7. Karl Dunker, "On Problem Solving," *Psychological Monographs*, 58, No. 5 (1945) (entire No. 270); George A. Polya, *How to Solve It* (Princeton: Princeton University Press, 1945); George A. Miller, Eugene Galanter, and Karl H. Pribram, *Plans and the Structure of Behavior* (New York: Henry Holt, 1960).

8. Lyle E. Bourne, Jr., Bruce R. Ekstrand, and Roger L. Dominowski, *The Psychology of Thinking* (Englewood Cliffs, N.J.: Prentice-Hall, 1971).

9. John R. Hayes, "Problem Topology and the Solution Process," in Carl P. Duncan, ed., *Thinking: Current Experimental Studies* (Philadelphia: Lippincott, 1967), pp. 167–81.

10. Hulda J. Rees and Harold E. Israel, "An Investigation of the Establishment and Operation of Mental Sets," *Psychological Monographs*, 46 (1925) (entire No. 210).

11. Ibid.; Melvin H. Marx, Wilton W. Murphy, and Aaron J. Brownstein, "Recognition of Complex Visual Stimuli as a Function of Training with Abstracted Patterns," *Journal of Experimental Psychology*, 62 (1961), 456–60.

12. James L. Adams, *Conceptual Blockbusting* (San Francisco: W. H. Freeman, 1974); Edward DeBono, *New Think* (New York: Basic Books, 1958); Ronald H. Forgus, *Perception* (New York: McGraw-Hill, 1966), ch. 13; Abraham Luchins and Edith Hirsch Luchins, *Rigidity of Behavior* (Eugene: Univ. of Oregon Books, 1959); N. R. F. Maier, "Reasoning in Humans. I. On Direction," *Journal of Comparative Psychology*, 10 (1920), 115–43.

13. "Plans and the Cognitive Process of Writing," paper presented at the National Institute of Education Writing Conference, June 1977; "Problem Solving Strategies and the Writing Process," *College English*, 39 (1977), 449–61.

14. Jane, a student not discussed in this paper, was surprised to find out that a topic paragraph can be rewritten after a paper's conclusion to make that paragraph reflect what the essay truly contains. She had gotten so indoctrinated with Psychology's (her major) insistence that a hypothesis be formulated and then left untouched before an experiment begins that she thought revision of one's "major premise" was somehow illegal. She had formed a rule out of her exposure to social science methodology, and the rule was totally inappropriate for most writing situations.

15. Cf. "A plan is flexible if the order of execution of its parts can be easily interchanged without affecting the feasibility of the plan . . . the flexible planner might tend to think of lists of things he had to do; the inflexible planner would have his time planned like a sequence of cause-effect relations. The former could rearrange his lists to suit his opportunities, but the latter would be unable to strike while the iron was hot and would generally require considerable 'lead-time' before he could incorporate any alternative sub-plans" (Miller, Galanter, and Pribram, p. 120).

16. Frederic Bartlett, *Thinking* (New York: Basic Books, 1958), pp. 74–76.

17. *Structure and Direction in Thinking* (New York: John Wiley, 1965), p. 255.

18. Flower and Hayes, "Plans and the Cognitive Process of Writing," p. 26.

Questions for Discussion and Journaling

1. Create a list of all the rules that, according to Rose, interfere with "the blockers" writing. What rules, if any, do you find yourself forced to follow that seem to get in the way of your writing?

2. Describe the difference between the rules that blockers in Rose's study were following and those that non-blockers were following. What accounts for the difference?

3. What's the difference between an *algorithm* and a *heuristic*? Give a couple of examples of each that you use on an everyday basis.

4. Based on Rose's study and descriptions of writers and their rules, write a "rule" explaining what makes a rule good for writers, and what makes a rule bad for writers. You'll get bonus points if you can tell whether your rule is an algorithm or a heuristic.

5. Can you think of mutually exclusive rules that you've tried to follow in your writing? If you can't easily or quickly think of any, comb through the rules that you follow for writing, and see if they're consistent with each other.

6. Rose writes that the attitude of the non-blocking writers he interviewed is, "If it won't fit my work, I'll change it!" Is it a threshold concept for you that writers can have, or take, this kind of power?

Applying and Exploring Ideas

1. Find the origins of the rules you follow. Start by listing the ten rules that most powerfully impact your writing, whether good or bad. Now stop and think. Where, and when, did you learn each rule? Did it come from personal experience? Teachers? Parents? Observation of what other people were doing? Are there any rules you follow that you *don't* like? What would happen if you abandoned them?

2. Stop and think: Do you encounter rules in writing that flatly contradict your experience as a writer or reader? (For example, we're aware of a rule against beginning a sentence with "and." And we see good, professional writers do it all the time.) Describe one or two of these rules that you know of.

3. Rose concludes his article with a discussion of the difference between *knowing* a rule is ineffective and *acting* on that knowledge. If you find yourself following a rule that Rose suggests has a negative impact on writing, reflect on these questions: If you had permission to, would you stop following this rule? What is the risk of setting aside one rule and starting to use another? Is it possible that, rather than setting aside a rule completely, you might simply treat it more flexibly and have the best of both worlds?

- -

META MOMENT   Has anyone ever talked to you about *blocking* before? How might understanding this concept and knowing how to actively deal with it be useful to you in your life?

- -

A Bag Full of Snakes

Negotiating the Challenges of Multimodal Composition

**MICHAEL-JOHN DePALMA AND
KARA POE ALEXANDER**

Framing the Reading

We mentioned in the introduction to this chapter that after a sustained interest in studying composing in the 1970s and 1980s, there was a lull until the 2000s, when researchers became interested in this topic again because of the many changes that technologies and other media were playing in people's writing processes. This article, published in 2015, is one of those pieces of research. In it, Michael-John DePalma and Kara Poe Alexander described findings from a study they conducted of undergraduate and graduate students' multimodal composing. DePalma and Alexander are both associate professors in the English Department at Baylor University, where they direct the Professional Writing and Rhetoric Program and the Writing Center, respectively.

In this study, DePalma and Alexander want to know whether and how students are able to transfer and use what they know from traditional print- and alphabetic composing to multimodal composing. This might be a good time to revisit the discussion of transfer in Chapter 1 (p. 19), or read it for the first time. Here, DePalma and Poe talk about the idea of "adaptive transfer," or "reshaping, adapting, re-situating, extending, and recontextualizing writing and genre knowledge" in new writing situations. Scholars disagree about how different or similar traditional alphabetic, print composition and multimodal composition are — and thus, how writers' processes are similar or different when composing in each.

Some of the terms the authors use likely won't be familiar to you and might sound intimidating — *semiotic modes, multimodal, alphabetic rhetorical knowledge, print-based rhetorical knowledge, rhetorical skills*. While they sound unfamiliar, they all refer to ideas you know but likely don't describe in this way. For example, *semiotic modes* refers to the means available for communicating; *multimodal,* combinations of semiotic modes such as aural, visual, gestural, linguistic, and

DePalma, Michael-John, and Kara Poe Alexander. "A Bag Full of Snakes: Negotiating the Challenges of Multimodal Composition." *Computers and Composition*, vol. 37, 2015, pp. 182–200.

technological; *alphabetic,* the traditional writing you do every day; *rhetorical knowledge,* your knowledge about that writing; *rhetorical skills*, your skill set for communicating effectively. Despite the vocabulary, the overall approach and ideas in this study are not complicated. The authors are wondering how students approach communicative tasks that use multiple modes that tend to be uncommon in academic settings (at least after primary school).

This study emphasizes all of the threshold concepts of this chapter: writers always have more to learn, composing (in any mode) entails a process, and our compositions are not perfectible.

Getting Ready to Read

Before you read, do at least one of the following activities:

- Visit the Stony Brook University Libraries online page defining "Digital Composition, Storytelling, and Multimodal Literacy" (https://guides.library. stonybrook.edu/digital-storytelling) and read the short definitions of composing, digital literacy, and multimodal literacy.
- Open an online dictionary and keep it handy to search terms that are new to you.
- Skim the article headings so that you know where the piece is going.

As you read, consider the following questions:

- What are your own experiences doing the kind of composing that the authors are studying?
- What choices did the researchers make regarding research questions, methods, and analysis?

"Your project is in a controlled space with traditional academic writing. I have these thoughts, but I know the box I'm going to put them in. But this other thing—multimodal composing—is like having a bag full of snakes. It's like I don't know what I'm doing with all this. I'm not in control of any of it . . . The problem here is that nothing is the same."

— Duncan, graduate student in study

1. INTRODUCTION

FOR WELL OVER TWO DECADES, the field of computers and writing has been 1 interested in the ways that digital composing technologies shape and re-shape the way literacy is defined, valued, investigated, and learned (e.g., Gee, 2003;

Hawisher & Selfe, 1999; Kress, 2003; Selber, 2004; Selfe & Hawisher, 2004). This rich body of scholarship has emphasized the social nature of multimodal writing (Barton & Hyman, 2012); how rhetorical concepts transfer to multimodal composition (Ball, 2006; Powell, Alexander, & Borton, 2011); the need for assignments that utilize a range of semiotic resources (Fulwiler & Middleton, 2012; Sheppard, 2009; Shipka, 2011); and practical ways to implement multiliteracies pedagogies into writing classrooms (Bowen & Whithaus, 2013; Selber, 2004; Selfe, 2007; Sorapure, 2006).

These advances in digital writing research present new questions for scholars and teachers, including two questions central to discussions of multimodal writing[1] pedagogies: 1) To what extent does students' alphabetic rhetorical knowledge enable or inhibit their ability to successfully navigate multimodal composition tasks? And 2) Which aspects of students' print-based rhetorical knowledge enable and inhibit composers' attempts to successfully navigate multimodal composition tasks? 2

Questions concerning the transfer of writing knowledge have been central to discussions in rhetoric and composition studies for nearly three decades (Bergmann & Zepernick, 2007; Carroll, 2002; Dias, Freedman, Medway, & Pare, 1999; McCarthy, 1987; Russell, 1995; Smit, 2004; Walvoord & McCarthy, 1990; Wardle, 2007, 2009). Of longstanding interest for transfer researchers has been understanding the extent to which writers transfer what they learn from one task to another, from one class to another, from one school year to the next, and from school to the workplace. One important development in recent transfer research has been the reconceptualization of traditional notions of transfer (see, for example, DePalma & Ringer, 2011; Nowacek, 2011). Such work has demonstrated that while transfer does involve applying past writing knowledge to new situations, it also entails reshaping, adapting, re-situating, extending, and recontextualizing writing and genre knowledge (Adler-Kassner et al., 2012; Artemeva & Fox, 2010; Devitt, 2007; Reiff & Bawarshi, 2011; Robertson, Taczak, & Yancey, 2012; Tardy, 2009). This emerging interest in processes of adaptive transfer has prompted transfer researchers to begin to consider the ways writers mobilize and transform print-based writing knowledge and skills while engaging in multimodal composing tasks (see, for example, DePalma, 2015). 3

Not surprisingly, writing scholars hold a range of views concerning the extent to which print-based rhetorical knowledge and composing processes transfer to multimodal contexts. Some scholars posit that multimodal composition teaches students many of the same rhetorical skills that they learn in print-based composing tasks (Alexander, 2013; Takayoshi & Selfe, 2007). Those working from this view assert that writers composing multimodally still must analyze an audience, choose a purpose, craft rhetorical appeals, and negotiate many of the same decision-making processes required in print-based writing situations. In addition, 4 they argue that the stages of the alphabetic writing process are applicable to multimodal composition—students must invent, draft, revise, and edit when composing a multimodal text just like they do when composing a written essay.

Others resist this view and assert that the conventional work of composition 5 teaching must be reimagined to suit the exigencies of multimodal composing situations. In "Looking for Sources of Coherence in a Fragmented World: Notes toward a New Assessment Design," Kathleen Blake Yancey (2004) articulated this need clearly:

> If we are to value this new composition . . . we will need to invent a language that allows us to speak to these new values. Without a new language, we will be held hostage to the values informing print, values worth preserving for that medium, to be sure, but values incongruent with those informing the digital, (pp. 89–90)

One context that illuminates this tension is in the assessment of multimodal 6 texts. For a number of scholars, the criteria for assessing student learning in multimodal composing can be derived from the theoretical frameworks and pedagogical practices best suited to assessing student learning in print-based texts. Borton and Huot (2007), for example, stated, "In assessing multimodal texts . . . [s]mart teachers will use what they already know about rhetorical theory and practice to assess multimodal texts effectively" (p. 110). In line with this view, Elizabeth A. Murray, Hailey A. Sheets, and Nicole A. Williams (2010) asserted that "we can use the same rubric during the grading process regardless of if students are being asked to complete a single-mode or multiple-mode assignment." Others, however, have rejected such claims. Madeleine Sorapure (2006), for example, argued that using a broad rhetorical approach to assess multimodal compositions is problematic because "it doesn't in itself offer any specific guidance or criteria for handling the multimodal aspects of the composition" (p. 3).

Another layer of the discussion shaping much of the discourse surrounding 7 multimodal composition pedagogy is the assumption that students—as "digital natives" (Prensky, 2001) who have been immersed in technology since their early years—have a high-level of facility with and knowledge of digital composing practices. Though it is likely true that students' extensive exposure to new media technologies has allowed them to develop particular capacities for navigating new technologies, the extent to which these literacies have prepared students *to produce* rhetorically sophisticated texts is a different question altogether. Furthermore, although particular kinds of print-based rhetorical knowledge and composing experiences will enable students to successfully engage in multimodal composing tasks, some of their knowledge and experiences might possibly hinder their efforts. The goal for researchers, then, is to understand which aspects of their rhetorical knowledge and experiences as alphabetic composers might apply to their work as multimodal composers and which aspects of their knowledge and experiences must be reshaped or ignored altogether.

Although scholars in composition studies have persuasively argued for 8 the value of multimodal composing practices (i.e., Ball, 2004; Bickmore & Christiansen, 2010; Bowen & Whithaus, 2013; Sheridan, Ridolfo, & Michel, 2012; Takayoshi & Selfe, 2007; Wysocki, Johnson-Eilola, Selfe, & Sirc, 2004) and illustrated the valuable learning that occurs when students engage in multimodal composing activities (Alexander, 2013; Fulwiler & Middleton, 2012; Sheppard, 2009), little research has examined how students negotiate multimodal composing processes: what knowledge, skills, and semiotic resources[2] they draw from and what challenges they face as they engage in multimodal composing tasks. This study, therefore, explores the following questions:

- How does multimodal composition reinforce and / or challenge students' rhetorical knowledge and composing processes?
- What kinds of rhetorical frameworks and rhetorical decision-making processes do instructors need to cultivate in order to mitigate the challenges of multimodal composing?
- What kinds of pedagogical approaches might composition instructors utilize to help students negotiate the conceptual challenges of multimodal composition?

Drawing on case studies that include data from students' digital projects, 9 written reflections, and interviews, we discuss the challenges writers encountered while engaged in multimodal composing tasks. These challenges included how to conceptualize an audience and how to negotiate the semiotic resources afforded through multimodal texts. We also offer several pedagogical strategies for assisting composition instructors in their efforts to help students navigate the conceptual challenges of multimodal composing. In doing so, our goal is to provide writing instructors with approaches that might prepare students to thrive in a range of rapidly-changing contexts.

2. METHODS

To understand more about students' experiences as they engaged in multimodal 10 composition tasks, we collected a range of data from undergraduate and graduate students who had composed multimodal and digital compositions. Data included final digital / multimodal projects, written reflections composed at the end of the project, and focus group interviews.

2.1. Participants

Twenty-four students from a mid-sized private religious institution participated 11 in this study. Fifteen were undergraduate students, and nine were graduate students. Seventeen of the students were female, and seven were male.

The undergraduate students came from a variety of majors, including professional writing, English, journalism, biology, history, and business. The graduate students were all enrolled in a doctoral program in English literature, and all but two of them were currently working in the writing center or teaching first-year writing. All of the participants reported that this was their first time composing a multimodal text in the classroom, and none of the graduate students who were teaching (or had taught) a writing course had assigned a multimodal composition before.

2.2. Data Collection

The students came from four writing courses—three undergraduate courses 12 and one graduate course—and data were collected over a period of three semesters. Alexander taught two of the courses—one graduate course titled "Digital Writing and Literacy" and one upper-level undergraduate special topics course called "Writing in the Digital Age." In the graduate course, students composed two multimodal projects. First, they composed a five to six minute audio literacy narrative in which they explored the role of literacy, education, and / or technology in their lives and provided some reflective insight for an audience of their choosing. In addition to the audio essay, the graduate students also composed a six to ten minute scholarly digital video documentary in which they chose a discourse community to examine and then made an argument about the way literacy was used, practiced, and / or valued in that community. Students were asked to create a research space for their topic, incorporate primary research (i.e., interviews, observation, surveys) about the discourse community, and include secondary research to frame their work for a scholarly academic audience. In the undergraduate course taught by Alexander, students composed multimodal compositions for professional audiences, including an audio or video PSA about a topic and a digital video for a community partner. In both courses and with each assignment, students were asked to flesh out their audience and purpose—in accordance with the assignment guidelines—and to compose with those audiences in mind. These students were also provided multiple opportunities to conceptualize, analyze, and further define their audience through a "pitch proposal," storyboards, studio review workshops, and instructor feedback. Alexander also asked students to describe their audience in their final written reflective letters.

DePalma taught two undergraduate "Advanced Expository Writing" courses 13 where students composed a three to five minute "digital story" about a critical moment in their literacy development. In conveying the significance of this primary moment of transition, students were asked to reflect on the ways in which their experiences might be brought to bear on the wider academic, professional, communal, and civic discussions with which they were engaged. Students were also instructed to identify and define their audiences for their digital stories. To prepare students to analyze and adapt to the particular audiences they aimed to address, DePalma introduced students to Ede and Lunsford's (1984) heuristic for thinking about audience. Students were also provided multiple opportunities to conceptualize then-audiences during peer workshops about their proposals and digital stories, as well as during conferences with DePalma. In addition to constructing a digital story and a proposal, students also wrote a storyboard and a two-page reflection letter that discussed the choices they made in designing their texts.

At the end of the semester, students submitted their final projects and writ- 14 ten reflections to the researchers. After these data were collected, focus group interviews were conducted with the twenty-four students who participated in the study in order to discuss their experiences with multimodal composing. Each focus group interview lasted approximately one and a half hours. Interviews were video-recorded and transcribed.

2.3. Data Analysis

The data were analyzed using grounded theory methods (see Glaser & Strauss, 15 1967). Grounded theory allowed us to identify common themes and categories that emerged from the data and to make generalizations. All policies regarding human subjects were followed. All names used here are pseudonyms.

3. RESULTS

Results show that students attempted to draw on their rhetorical knowledge of 16 print-based composing as they approached multimodal composing tasks. This approach worked well for students when they perceived aspects of print-based and multimodal composing tasks as similar, but it did not work as well when they perceived aspects of multimodal tasks as different from their print-based composing experiences. In fact, when students conceived of the task as different yet still attempted to statically apply their print-based rhetorical knowledge and composing practices to aspects of multimodal composing, they faced significant difficulties conceptualizing an audience and negotiating semiotic resources. Furthermore, because multimodal composing often required more complex notions of audience and processes of inventing meaning than the print-based composing tasks students had previously undertaken, students experienced frustration, anxiety, and feelings of failure.

In what follows, we first describe the challenges related to audience adaptation 17 that students faced in carrying out multimodal composition activities. We then discuss the difficulties students encountered in their attempts to coordinate and transfer semiotic resources in multimodal composing. After highlighting these obstacles, we discuss the implications of our findings and outline several pedagogical recommendations in response to these concerns.

3.1. The Challenges of Conceptualizing an Audience in Multimodal Composition

In their multimodal composition projects, students had difficulty conceiv- 18
ing of an audience for their texts. This difficulty came primarily because they
viewed multimodal composition as oppositional to "academic" writing. Several
students viewed multimodal composition as a "public" practice—an activity
that seeks to reach a nontechnical (i.e., a lay, general, or public) audience for
the purposes of entertaining, humoring, or expressing interesting ideas—rather
than as an academic practice—an activity that aims to engage with specialists
in particular disciplinary contexts for the purpose of advancing knowledge or
disseminating information. Although imagining an audience beyond that of
teachers and classmates certainly has the potential to be beneficial to students
in several regards, in this case, it functioned reductively. Rather than enrich-
ing students' notions of audience by invoking a diverse range of viewers, the
"public" or "average person" became a substitute term for an ill-defined mass. In
other words, "public" was offered as a default term that represented anyone and
everyone who might happen upon students' multimodal texts while browsing
the Web. As Arielle noted, "I wasn't sure [who my audience was]. I guess the
audience would be . . . generally people who were watching it."

Part of the reason for this imprecision may be that students mistook the invi- 19
tation to make their work public through YouTube, the DALN, or their blogs
as license to define their audiences in the broadest possible terms, even though
classroom instruction emphasized a specific audience. Another possible reason
is that many of the multimodal texts with which students were familiar were
created for the purposes of entertaining public audiences. They had few models
of multimodal texts that seek to engage in scholarly work for purpose of advancing knowledge or disseminating information. Thus, when students attempted
to compose their multimodal projects, they did not know how to address or
invoke such an audience, assume the role of a public intellectual, or create a
nuanced, accessible, and sophisticated discussion of a complex issue in the form
of a multimodal text. In response to this challenge, students thus disassociated
their notions of print-based academic genres from their ideas about multimodal
composing as they attempted to make sense of their rhetorical situations in
their multimodal composition projects. In doing so, several students set up a
dichotomy between formal, print-based academic writing and creative, multimodal composing for public audiences. Duncan, for example, stated, "I don't
think that the digital essay is like the print essay. I think the digital—the film,
the audio, whatever you want to do—is more like a creative project." Though
he acknowledged that "academic writing is creative," he explained that it is
"creativity in a controlled space." Nick, too, expressed that in multimodal composing "there's an aesthetic creativity, um, that is missing in, um, some academic

writing." Nora drew a similar distinction between print-based, academic writing and multimodal composing when she declared:

> I think about writing poetry as composition in some form but not academic papers, really, like, then I'm writing or making an argument, so during these projects where you use different modes and mediums, to convey an argument, but it is more like a narrative, and it's creative and it's more fun.

As a result of setting up this dichotomy between print-based, academic writing and creative, multimodal composing for a public audience, students had difficulty understanding how to create a sophisticated and interesting discussion of a complex subject in the form of a multimodal text. Put otherwise, the binary constructed between academic print-based texts and multimodal public texts prevented students from seeing how they might address a knowledgeable and specialized audience in creative and engaging ways. For these students, an "academic" audience for print-based texts was extremely narrow and expected obscure and straightforward transactional discourse, whereas a public audience for multimodal texts was a vast, indefinable mass that required creative and interesting material. Most students had the latter audience in mind as they composed their multimodal texts. Nora and Jennifer, who composed a video on the collaborative writing process of a folk band, illustrated the limitations of thinking in these terms. Throughout the course of the project, they had difficulty deciding on their audience and actually resisted composing for an academic audience. They wanted the digital video to be useful and interesting to the band — not just an assignment for a class — but they could not figure out how to compose a text for both the band and a scholarly audience. Nora stated in her interview:

> I felt like I had to make [the video] far more interesting to the average person doing a project like this. Because with academic writing, academics read it, but no one else really reads it. So you have this captive audience that likes their titles to look a certain way and they like a thesis to come, and you know how to do things, and they will be interested regardless. But making a movie, like anyone could watch it. So, I tried to think about, "What is actually inherently interesting to humans?" It was broader instead of this captive narrow audience.

Nora and Jennifer did not see writing for an academic audience as appropriate for multimodal composing. They wanted their videos to be "creative," "entertaining" and "relevant," and they viewed these characteristics as conflicting with the expectations of an academic audience. This was true for nearly all of the students in this study. In fact, almost all of the final projects failed to make a data-driven argument that was situated within the discourse. Students wanted their interview data to "speak for itself," so they resisted framing the information, theorizing their findings, and providing viewers a context to inter-pret their texts, because they viewed such moves as "too academic." Instead, many felt strongly that the voices of their interview subjects would organically convey their arguments. As Jack noted, "When I'm writing a story, there's a certain point where the character takes over and that person tells the story, and then I'm just the vehicle for it being put on paper. And that's exactly how a documentary is." Students like Jack, then, view scholarly multimodal writing as more similar to fiction than to the writing that occurs in composition courses.

Related to the difficulties students faced conceptualizing an audience was 22 the challenge of understanding how their audiences would interact with and understand their multimodal texts. In describing the ways her understanding of composing for an audience was tested during the multimodal composition project, Jessie, for example, stated,

> You have to think about how the audience is going to be experiencing your
> [multimodal composition]. You can't just think about it from your own
> perspective. You want them to relate. You don't want them to walk out of there
> confused . . . and you do have to make so many more decisions about what
> you keep and how you convey [something]. So you have to experience it from
> the perspective of the audience before you give it to someone else to partake in.
> Otherwise, they might not get it. You might not be meeting the needs of your
> audience if you're only thinking about how the author perceives something.

Here, Jessie emphasized the need for the audience to "get it" and made 23 implicit comparisons between this composing experience and her prior print-based composing experiences.

The challenge of anticipating how viewers might interact with and interpret 24 the multimodal texts students crafted stemmed from their lack of experience composing multimodal texts for a well-defined audience. Such difficulties were also rooted in their attempts to apply an understanding of audiences that had been shaped primarily by print-based composing experiences to multimodal composing tasks. As Jessie noted, prior to carrying out the multimodal com-position project, she generally perceived her audiences as passive consumers of texts who simply processed information on an intellectual level. In compos-ing her digital story, however, Jessie's notion of audience as mere onlookers, decoding language and processing ideas, was challenged, as the genre compelled her to consider her audience as active participants, partaking in an experience that was relational, embodied, responsive, and interactive. This was true of sev-eral students in this study. Rather than thinking about the relationships among writers, audiences, and texts as static and unidirectional, they were forced to address the dynamic ways that these elements interacted. Related to this, they were also confronted with the material, relational, emotional, sensational, and volitional dimensions of textual production, as well as the ways in which multimodal texts might powerfully act on audiences to establish an exigence, evoke concern, and create identification. Many, however, felt unprepared to handle these complex rhetorical challenges.

3.2. The Challenges of Negotiating Multiple Semiotic Resources

In addition to the challenge students faced negotiating their assumptions about 25 writing and audience in multimodal composition, students also had difficulty negotiating multiple semiotic domains. Specifically, they struggled to incorporate multiple semiotic resources into their projects and to navigate the rhetorical constraints presented in multimodal composing tasks.

3.2.1. Incorporating Multiple Modes to Make Meaning

A major challenge for students in multimodal composing was determining how 26 to coordinate interactions among semiotic resources. Students experienced difficulty determining how to best utilize multiple semiotic modes, such as the aural, visual, gestural, linguistic, and technological, to fulfill their rhetorical objectives. This challenge was particularly noteworthy because students tended to contrast their multimodal composing experiences with composing in the print. Mallory remarked, for instance: "Pen to paper is so natural now, but moving into those kinds of [multimodal composing] projects, there just seems to be so many more factors that you have to consider." Arielle similarly reflected:

> I think a lot of times when you're writing an academic paper, your focus isn't on how you're delivering the message, it's the message itself, or the argument itself, whereas when you're composing something multimodally you're also thinking about how to make it visually interesting as well as communicating, so you're thinking about how you're presenting it as well as what you're presenting.

Nick, too, remarked that "the same sorts of [academic writing] standards don't 27 hold true in multimodal composition" because you have to consider so many other elements. "Ideas," he stated, "need to take center stage, not the shape of the document necessarily. But when you bring in the other media, then it can't just be about the ideas because you're going to lose your audience otherwise."

These comments indicate that students viewed multimodal composing as 28 more complex and challenging because of the multiple modes they had to negotiate when composing. Part of this complexity was because students typically had not had to negotiate the demands of integrating multiple modes into print-based compositions. Although there are multiple modes in print-based writing (words and images, visual features of words, paragraphing, and so forth), the emphasis in the classroom is on words — alphabetic literacy. Many of the visual elements are decided for them: one-inch margins, MLA format, double-spacing, and page numbers. In multimodal composing, however, the multiple modes became more apparent and students were required to attend to all of them, which proved difficult.

Reflecting on the difficulty of this process in composing her digital story, 29 Elisabeth, an undergraduate biology major, explained:

> There are so many things to think about. It's not just, "I am talking about [my fiance Dave] in this voiceover, so I am going to put a picture of Dave there." It's, "What kind of picture do I want to put of Dave? Do I definitely want to put a picture of Dave, or do I want to put a picture of something that is representative of our relationship at that point? What kind of music do I want to use? And not only what kind of music do I want and what song, but at what point in the song? Are there rises and falls in the song? Is there a part where the tempo picks up? What kind of effect will that make?" So you constantly have to think about the visual things, the textual things, the audio things, the words in the song, and the words in my audio voiceover. It's just so much to think about.

Elisabeth articulated the distinction between print-based composing and 30 multimodal composing using the terms *saying* and *conveying*. When asked to clarify this distinction, she explained:

> When you say, "I am *saying* something," you're thinking words. When I am trying to *convey* meaning, it's abstract. There aren't necessarily words. If I am trying to convey something, I might not use words at all. I might use a look, or the tone of my voice even might contradict what I am saying.

Rather than focusing only on *what* was being communicated as she was 31 composing, Elisabeth noted that she was forced to consider *how* information was communicated. Put otherwise, in the process of crafting her multimodal project, the once clear line between form and content was blurred.

This fusing of form and content was true for several students in our study. 32 Instead of seeing a text's meaning as linked primarily to *content* — to words taken at face value — through their work as digital composers, students were confronted by the fact that form and content could not be separated — that both shape an audience's interpretation of a text in vital ways. Rather than understanding communication as primarily word-driven, these students came to see the ways that multiple modes of communication shape a text's meaning. The following remarks by Elisabeth are representative of the ways several students' notions of rhetorical practice were challenged:

> One of the things that [multimodal composition] does is it forces you to remove the text from what you're trying to say. How can you convey something without

even using words? . . . There were points in my digital story where I was saying something in my voiceover, and I had the picture to go with it, and I had the timing, but the song at that point wasn't right, and it was distracting from my meaning, and so I had to rearrange it. That's what the digital story makes you do. You have to take a step back. You can't just rely on your words. You have to think about what every single piece of your digital story is saying to your audience. Conveying, not saying [laughs].

Overall, students in this study were accustomed to thinking about language 33 in specific, narrow ways—as a vehicle for transmitting thought through clear and concrete transactions—but composing multimodal projects that asked them to integrate multiple semiotic resources to convey meaning challenged their assumptions, understandings, and approaches to composing texts.

3.2.2. Rhetorical Constraints

Students in our study also had difficulty negotiating the affordances of differ- 34 ent modes and media, particularly those affordances that were connected to their assumptions about what kind of argument could be made in a multimodal composition. The research on visual and multimodal communication—and even how the Center for Digital Storytelling taught digital storytelling—argues that you should "show, not tell" (see Ball, 2004, for instance). In other words, readers / viewers of multimodal composition should be able to discern what the author is saying without the writer explicitly stating the point. Nora, for instance, approached her multimodal composition in this way:

The idea is that you kind of show instead of just tell like in an essay and that because it's audio you're able to show things that you couldn't show in a written essay. So you want to pick a subject that you can do that with.

This show-don't-tell approach to multimodal composition made it difficult 35 for some students to decide what they should say and how they should say it. Because they were not aware of the affordances of these modes and media—for instance, what decisions a composer must make to effectively "show, not tell"—students' final products were not as rhetorically effective as they might have been. An example is that students often included interview footage without framing it in a way that would allow their audience to understand it. They edited the interview data—including and excluding what they thought fit with their message—but they rarely included their own "voice" in the mix of the footage. Students assumed the audience would understand the point they were trying to make solely based on the quotations they included from their interview subjects. Nick noted that he wanted to make an implicit argument and did not want his voice to interrupt or change the perspectives offered by his interview subjects. He remarked:

> I think, letting them tell their story and get across what they want to get across [is important]. They'll be more authentic, and you won't be putting words in their mouth. And then you just shape it with the editing. I think that's where really the composition comes together is arranging the parts.

Duncan also seemed to rely on the affordances of digital media too heavily 36 when he decided to place the impetus of understanding completely on the reader / hearer. He composed an audio literacy narrative in which the entire text was a meditation recorded during a jog. When Duncan first brought his draft for studio review, the essay was entirely implicit, a conversation at points. The feedback Duncan received was about how to make the significance of his subject clearer to readers. Duncan pushed back against this feedback, saying that he didn't want to be heavy-handed by explicitly revealing his message to readers; instead, he wanted them to infer it. But, as listeners of his story, we didn't understand his meaning. Duncan thus was faced with the dilemma of determining how he could maintain his rhetorical aims and still convey his meaning in a way that readers would understand his message. In reflecting on this issue in the interview, Duncan stated:

> Peer review was a challenge for me. [My draft] was not exactly everything I wanted it to be. I mean it was a rough draft, but it had all the wildness that I wanted. But, like, I don't think anyone in the class got it. I knew we'd present it again, and so, what I turned in is a really dumbed down and tame version of what I hope to actually do with this. I wanted you to hear what goes on in my head. Instead of like me telling you what I think. After the peer review, I was like, I don't want them to hear what's in my head. I'm going to just give them what they want . . . and then, yeah, save that for something else.

In the end, Duncan chose to convey his literacy narrative implicitly by 37 embedding his literacy practices in the narrative itself rather than explicitly reflecting aurally. He remarked, "Hopefully, I am showing you that I have a literate life that depends heavily on technology without saying so."

Relating to difficulties with implicit and explicit decisions, students also felt 38 that they lost so much control of the argument they were trying to make in multimodal composition. Jack, for instance, stated:

> In [traditional academic] forms, I have the control. I really have control of the language. When we moved into these multimodal compositions, I thought it was harder to have control. One, you're depending on someone else's voice to say what you want to say. But also the story is just a lot more slippery.

Nora, likewise, noted how she couldn't just make an argument and write that 39
argument; instead, she had to rely on her research participants to give her the
information she needed. She and her collaborator went in with a plan of what
they wanted from the interview, but the responses from the participants completely took it in a different direction. Nora reflected on this experience:

> We had to completely rewrite the whole thing. We kind of had this shape we
> wanted it to take . . . but then after we interviewed them, it just, we could not
> figure out how to piece it together, so we typed up all the things they said, cut
> out the strips, and tried to rearrange it until it made sense. It wasn't like how we
> planned it.

The students' challenges in this project might be attributed in part to the fact 40
that the assignment was an empirical research project that relied on interview data.
Nora's comment also brings up an interesting point, though, about how integrating technology can make such projects more complicated. Specifically, her remarks
highlight the fact that revising and editing can be increasingly difficult in multimodal composing than in alphabetic writing. In some cases, students thought
the constraints of editing and revising were almost insurmountable in multimodal
composing. Part of their perceptions resulted from the sheer amount of time revising and editing an audio or video required.[3] Carrie, for instance, noted:

> A big challenge for me was time. And that has something to do with not really
> knowing . . . the medium that you're working with and the program, and just the
> consumption of time that it took to piece, to piece things together and to find things
> and place them in a particular order and then match them with the other elements.

Simon also told a story of how he spent five hours looking for dialogue from 41
video clips only to later realize that he was going to narrate over the dialogue. This
time spent inventing and drafting was lost and the ideas were never used. As a
result of such experiences, the affordances of revising and editing in multimodal
composing were viewed by several students as constraints, and these constraints
prevented students from successfully using the semiotic resources at their disposal.

In addition to the time required for such work, several students also viewed 42
editing and revising in multimodal texts as more complex than in the print-
based writing. Nick noted, "We have so much footage and we could edit that
footage in a thousand different ways. . . . Deciding how to edit is very difficult."
Likewise, Jennifer stated:

> We're so used to writing now that, you know, moving from one paragraph to
> the next seems so natural and easy. But with the audio and visual, you know,
> timing and how much you space things out, that can make a big difference in
> your communication.

Lola, too, remarked:

> transitions between paragraphs in writing is so simple, and like we don't really
> think about it, but like how do you visually and auditorily make that same kind
> of shift come across? Like that was, I think, the hardest consideration.

Though students like David pointed out that "the more time we spend with 44
it the easier it will become," students generally viewed the multimodal composing process as more complex. Jack, for instance, noted that revising and editing
was not as automatic as it was in a word-processing program. In multimodal
composing, he explained, writers can't "just fix a word." Instead, they must

> go into the program, find the piece, or maybe it's just like trimming a word, or
> adding a word, and it's very detailed. It's not as automatic as, and maybe, if you
> did a bunch of these, it would be. But it's not as automatic as just "fixing."

A final challenge that students faced with regard to semiotic resources involved 45
a lack of understanding about the intense role technology would play in the composing and rhetorical decision-making processes. Even though students had been
bombarded with these kinds of media as consumers, they did not necessarily reflect
on the complexity of composing such texts, perhaps because the tools and skills
involved in composing a print text had virtually been erased (see Haas, 1996;
Wysocki, 2003). That is, although students knew that technology was going to play
a major role in their final products and that they would have to learn new technologies to complete those texts, students did not feel prepared for the ways that
technology was integrated into the writing process from beginning to end.[4] This
reality was a problem for Nolan who remarked that he "was not aware of how much
work actually goes into these things we consume" and noted that "it's difficult to . . .
conquer that learning curve with the technology and produce something good."

As a result of this difficulty, when students were required to use mostly new 46
technologies in the composing process, they failed to anticipate how technology
would impact their work as writers. Many students, for example, shared experiences of losing saved files or having to re-record or re-shoot footage because
an aspect of their projects did not work out as planned. These proved to be
enormous interruptions for students during the composing process. Carrie, for
instance, stated, "One of the great challenges was my proficiency with technology. This was my first time to use these programs, and so my ability to portray
what I wanted to portray just wasn't as good." Students who were familiar with
the technologies used in the multimodal composition projects likewise experienced technical difficulties. Stephanie, for instance, explained:

> I wish I had known better how to, like, transfer certain principles I had learned
> earlier into my PSA. I took a photography class the semester before, and we made

a video project and we got to use the journalism department equipment. . . . And when I went to do the PSA. I tried to re-learn everything when I should have used . . . everything I had used before."

Although technical problems also occur when composing print essays, 47 these challenges are increased in multimodal composing projects due to the multiple modes, media, and semiotic resources involved and because of the all-encompassing role of technology in data collection, drafting, and editing. When students were interrupted or had to redo work because of technological challenges, their composing processes were stifled. In many cases, such experiences forced to writers to redirect their attention from an emphasis on generating ideas to a focus on solving problems with technology. Such issues detrimentally influenced the overall quality of students' projects.

In spite of the challenges presented by learning a range of technologies, stu- 48 dents valued learning how to navigate a range of new technologies and semiotic resources. We should also note that students were resourceful in seeking out resources to help them learn. They went to YouTube and Google or asked their friends and co-workers. Simon summed it up best in his reflective letter: "Learning how to learn a program or digital tool is a transferable skill that I will use in the future when I need to learn something new." Thus, incorporating multiple semiotic resources could be challenging, but it also had immense value to students.

4. IMPLICATIONS

In carrying out their multimodal composition projects, students encountered a 49 range of challenges related to audience, ethics, composing processes, rhetorical constraints, technology, and collaboration. Due to spatial constraints, we have focused only on challenges related to audience, semiotic resources, and transfer in this essay. Based on students' remarks concerning these challenges, several issues deserve consideration when guiding students' multimodal composing processes.

First, students had difficulty conceptualizing a multidimensional audience 50 when composing multimodally. As a result, they often resorted to defining their audience in broad and imprecise terms such as "public," "humans," "the average person," and "people generally." Students thus dissociated their prior knowledge of print-based academic audiences and genres from their processes of multimodal composition. As such, many were working from a binary opposition that constructed print-based academic texts in opposition to multimodal "general" texts. These findings point to a need for more explicit discussion of and reflection on the relationships among students' genre knowledge and assumptions about audience in print-based composing and their genre knowledge and assumptions about composing multimodally. Related to this, our findings illustrate the need to provide students with rich examples of multimodal scholarship that they might model. These models can be used in the classroom to analyze the audience and purpose envisioned by the author, the semiotic resources available to the author, and the rhetorical techniques used to accomplish their goals.

Second, a key challenge that writers encountered in multimodal composing was determining which aspects of their print-based genre knowledge and composing experiences might enable them to create a nuanced, accessible, and sophisticated multimodal text for a diverse audience and which aspects might stifle their ability to do so. Said differently, students had difficulty understanding how to use the multiple semiotic resources afforded through multimodal composition to their advantage. Given this fact, an important role for instructors to consider is how we can help students see which aspects of their print-based genre knowledge and composing experience might allow them to think in more complex ways about the audiences they address. 51

A third challenge for students in carrying out these activities was deciding which semiotic resources they might reuse, reshape, add, or omit when moving from a print-based text to a multimodal text. Though it is not surprising that many had difficulty moving from print-based to multimodal composition (due to their lack of experience producing multimodal texts), our findings provide insight into the particular kinds of difficulties students faced in multimodal composing. As such, they offer a starting point for thinking about the kinds of pedagogical strategies that might be developed to help students coordinate semiotic resources and utilize affordances to suit their rhetorical objectives in multimodal composition projects. 52

Fourth, students experienced difficulties at the revising and editing stages of the composing process. One of the reasons that revising and editing might have seemed more difficult to students was the degree to which their notions of revising and editing print-based texts differed from the processes of revising and editing multimodal texts. Though scholars have persuasively argued that revising and editing in alphabetic writing is a recursive process that happens throughout the composing process, applying print-based notions of these terms in multimodal composition resulted in confusion for students. That is, *transfer* between contexts did not always or easily occur. What we discovered was that the term *editing* in audio and video, for instance, was actually *inventing* and *drafting* as it has been traditionally defined. Students used the software to *edit* a piece together, but this editing was really part of the invention stage where students decided what they were going to say and how they were going to say it, rather than something they did after they had a near final product. Given this fact, it seems explicit discussion with students concerning the ways composing processes must be rethought and reshaped in multimodal composition could be valuable. 53

Finally, students also faced major challenges with technology. Though they expected technology to play a significant role in the writing process, they were unprepared for how much it would impact their ability to compose rhetorically 54 effective projects. Many students, in fact, felt that the technology and their inexperience composing multimodally prevented them from drafting the kinds of projects they envisioned and were surprised by some of the rhetorical constraints regarding technology. Even though they were excited to compose in new ways, they were disappointed with the constraints technology placed on their work as composers. With this in mind, we need to continue to research ways that technology can enhance students' composing processes rather than inhibit them, as well as ways we might continue to develop technological literacy in our students.

In some respects, the challenges students faced as multimodal composers 55 were not unique to multimodal composing tasks. The kinds of rhetorical challenges we describe are to some extent inherent in any writing situation wherein students are learning a new genre, adapting to an unfamiliar audience, or navigating a novel context. Transfer research has been particularly adept at illustrating this complexity and has provided a range of ways to productively navigate these challenges. In Elizabeth Wardle's (2007) two-year longitudinal study, for example, she suggested that cultivating meta-awareness about writing, language, and rhetorical strategies might positively impact the ways students assess and adapt to writing demands across disciplines. Mary Jo Reiff and Anis Bawarshi's (2011) longitudinal study of how writers access and make use of prior genre knowledge when they encounter new writing tasks offered metacognitive reflection on writing tasks as a strategy for helping students apply and repurpose their prior genre knowledge. We view such strategies as highly valuable for assisting students in their efforts to draw upon and repurpose their print-based writing knowledge in multimodal composing. At the same time, though, our findings here illustrate the need to develop strategies for helping students negotiate the particular complexities of multimodal composing. Specifically, students need more guidance conceptualizing audience and coordinating semiotic and technical resources in multimodal writing tasks. As Andrea Lunsford and Lisa Ede (2012) noted, "changes in technology and other material conditions that have brought us to the present moment have opened avenues for audiences to take on agency and to become participants and shapers / creators of discourse in more profound ways than ever" (p. 251). As such, our notions of audience require a more expansive set of considerations than those traditionally associated with print-based media. This claim also holds true for the ways writers are trained to use the semiotic resources at their disposal when engaging in multimodal composing practices. Cynthia Selfe (2007), Jennifer

> The kinds of rhetorical challenges we describe are to some extent inherent in any writing situation wherein students are leaning a new genre, adapting to an unfamiliar audience, or navigating a novel context.

Sheppard (2009), and Kathleen Blake Yancey (2004) all made particularly persuasive arguments along these lines.

5. PEDAGOGICAL RECOMMENDATIONS

Having outlined the challenges related to audience and the coordination of 56 semiotic resources in multimodal composing, along with the implications of those challenges for composition teaching, we close our article by offering several pedagogical strategies that we have developed for helping students productively navigate the rhetorical complexities of audience and meaning-making in multimodal writing.

5.1. Mitigating Audience-Related Challenges through Reflection

In reviewing students' reflections on their experiences composing multimodally, it is apparent that their audience-related difficulties stemmed from their assumptions about multimodal texts and from a lack of examples for carrying out such work. Even though students composed proposals in which they analyzed their audience(s) and purpose(s) for the multimodal composition projects, we as instructors did not spend much time unpacking assumptions about genre and audience, nor did we attempt to complicate students' notions *of public* and *academic* audiences. Given the range of material that we attempted to cover during these projects, attention to these important rhetorical dimensions was not dealt with extensively. As we assign multimodal compositions in the future, however, we will spend increased time discussing students' assumptions about the particular genres of multimodal composition that they are working in, as well as the audiences for those genres. In doing so, we will begin by asking students to spend time reflecting on their assumptions about audience in print-based writing and multimodal composition genres. These reflections will serve as an entry point for class discussion about what constitutes a public and an academic audience in multimodal genres.

Another key facet of this reflective work will be to provide students with example 58 multimodal texts that are aimed at multidimensional audiences and that illustrate the possibility of doing sophisticated intellectual work in creative and interesting ways. A genre particularly well suited for modeling multimodal texts of this kind are documentary films, which could illustrate well for students the possibility of dealing with complex academic issues in engaging and creative ways. Critical discussion of such texts would also likely challenge students to move beyond flat distinctions in their notions of audience. In addition, written texts by public intellectuals might also productively enter such discussions as a means of rupturing the binaries between academic and public discourses, texts, and audiences.

An additional part of this reflective work might be to ask students to compile 59 effective examples of multimodal genres that have a purpose and an audience similar to those that they have defined for the multimodal texts they are composing. Students could then perform a rhetorical analysis of those texts in an effort to examine the various audiences they might address. Such work might allow students to more precisely define the ways the affordances of the genre and medium that they are using constrain and enable their work as composers.

5.2. Analyzing (Dis)connections between Print-based and Multimodal Genre Knowledge

Another way that composition instructors might assist students in their efforts 60 to conceptualize a multidimensional audience for multimodal composing projects is to provide students with opportunities to reflect on their genre knowledge in print-based composing in relation to their genre knowledge in multimodal composition. In our courses, we asked students to engage in genre analysis for each composing task. We asked students to apply Bawarshi's (2004) framework for analyzing genres to their composing task, thereby providing a means for students to consider diverse and multifaceted audiences in precise and generative terms. Bawarshi's analytical guide also provided students with a meta-language for discussing which audiences were appropriate for different genres of writing and a lens for considering the connections and disparities among audiences for various genres. Work of this kind offered a means of helping students determine which aspects of their print-based genre knowledge and composing experience might enable them to create a nuanced, accessible, and sophisticated multimodal text for multidimensional audiences and which aspects of that genre knowledge and experience might hinder their ability to do so.

In an effort to help students reflect on these relationships, we have con- 61 structed an activity that asks students to consider their print-based genre knowledge in relation to their multimodal genre knowledge. We imagine this activity as a starting point for talking with students about the genres they are working in and the audiences they envision for their particular projects. For each question, we've listed a range of genres in brackets, so that instructors can adapt this activity to the particular writing projects they teach.

5.3. Taking Stock of Semiotic Resources in Processes of Remediation

In reflecting on the particular challenges of negotiating semiotic resources and 62 affordances in multimodal composition, we developed two strategies for helping students engage in remediation from print-based texts to multimodal texts and from multimodal texts to print-based texts. First, instructors might provide students with low stakes writing opportunities to practice remediation. Work of this kind could begin by asking students to analyze a written text and make decisions about how they would adapt that text to a digital medium. For such an assignment, instructors might ask students to imagine that they are the screenwriters or directors responsible for adapting a written text to fit the screen. In this process of adaptation, it would be useful to encourage students to consider the kinds of semiotic resources that they would use to fulfill the purposes they have identified in the written text. In carrying out this process, students might consider the following questions: What literal images should be used in adapting the written text to a visual medium? What symbolic or metaphorical images should be used? What film or video clips might be effective? What music might be selected for the soundtrack? What lines should be kept for the voiceover narration? What parts of the essay need to be cut for the film adaptation of this essay? What kinds of visual and verbal transitions might work well?

Students could also be asked to engage in this process of remediation in the 63 opposite direction, moving from multimodal text to alphabetic text. For such an assignment, students might be asked to think about how the dramatic tension conveyed through visual images might be reconstructed in the written text, how the mood established by the multimodal text's soundtrack might be recreated in language, or how the pacing of the multimodal text might be similarly established through the structuring of sentences, paragraphs, and the design of the written text.

Assignments of this kind encourage students to take stock of the various 64 components that contribute to a text's rhetorical qualities, and they position writers to develop an enlarged perspective regarding the shapes that those components might take. For example, in analyzing the way a writer's voice is constructed in a written essay, students might discuss a writer's stylistic choices, use of qualifiers, selection of terms, choice of subject matter, questions, arrangement of ideas, and so forth. Similar features might be noted when students examine the way(s) a writer's voice is constructed in multimodal writing projects; however, additional qualities are apt to be revealed as well, some of which include the writer's use of silence and pauses, accent, rate of speech, intonation, volume, and inflection. In the case of constructing a text's mood, a similar pattern might be revealed. Students will often suggest that mood is created in a written text through sensory details, vivid description (or a lack thereof), the kinds of reflection a writer offers, the writer's language and stylistic choices, and so on. When analyzing the rhetorical features that contribute to the mood of a multimodal text, they are also likely to observe these features, but they will often offer several others, too, some of which include the importance of the images a writer selects, the musical soundtrack selected, the cutaways and overlays of video footage, the qualities of the writer's voiceover narration, the sound effects used by the writer, and the visual transitions that a writer uses. When students are encouraged to engage in this kind of analysis and textual reshaping, they begin to consider the full range of semiotic and rhetorical resources at their disposal.

After students engage in these decision-making processes by analyzing the 65
texts of others, they might then engage in similar processes with texts that they
are composing. Such activities would position students to weigh the limits and
possibilities of various modes of communication, serve to deepen their rhetorical knowledge, and enrich the ways they are able to talk about the choices
they make as writers and revisers. Work of this kind would also provide students a means by which to reconsider their text-based writing knowledge in
light of their experiences as multimodal composers. In asking students to adapt
a written text to suit a digital medium or a digital text to suit a print-based
medium, students would be provided the opportunity to engage in complex
decision-making processes regarding the rhetorical resources they might reuse
and reshape. Through such processes, students are challenged to think about the
purposes that each portion of their texts serves and about the rhetorical devices
that might allow them to accomplish those purposes in another medium.

Table 1 provides instructors a resource that might be used to help students 66
think about available rhetorical resources when engaging in processes of remediation. In the first column is a list of example rhetorical qualities that are fea-
tured in a range of text-types. The second column includes the rhetorical tools
used in alphabetic texts to construct the rhetorical qualities listed in column
one, and the third column lists additional rhetorical tools used in multimodal
composition to construct the rhetorical qualities listed in column one. This
table could provide students a starting point for thinking through processes of
remediation when analyzing the texts of others and making rhetorical choices
about texts they are crafting. This table is not intended to be extensive (there
are, of course, numerous other rhetorical qualities that might be added); rather,
it is meant to provide instructors with a flexible tool that can be adapted to suit
a range of instructional needs.

5.4. Reflecting on Inventional Possibilities while Remediating Texts

Another means of helping students negotiate semiotic resources and affordances 67
in multimodal composing is a strategy we call *semiotic mapping*.[5] Semiotic mapping provides students opportunities to examine the possibilities and limits of
the semiotic resources available in each particular writing situation (e.g., images,
video, written text, visual tensions, oral transitions, voiceover narration), along
with the relationships they might forge among those resources to achieve their
rhetorical purposes. Semiotic mapping begins with writers defining the purpose
of a text and reflecting on the rhetorical moves, semiotic modes, and media
affordances they have utilized to achieve their purposes. They can reflect on
these various elements individually in writing or with peers through "distributed invention" techniques as outlined by Alexander and Williams (2015).

TABLE 1 RHETORICAL RESOURCES FOR REMEDIATION

RHETORICAL QUALITIES	PERSONAL ESSAY	MULTIMODAL OR DIGITAL COMPOSITION
Theme / Argument	• Genre of Writing • Simile / Metaphor • Narrative Structure • Juxtaposition of Scenes • Narrative Arc • Narrative Tension • Point of View	• Genre of Music • Symbolic / Literal Images • Arrangement of Images • Arrangement of Music • Visual Transitions • Voiceover Narration • Camera Angles • Zoom or Pan Images
Voice	• Content • Sentence Structure • Word Choice • Style • Punctuation	• Tone • Inflection • Volume • Pace • Pauses • Silence
Mood	• Vivid Description • Sensory Details • Reflection • Emotional Appeals • Language Choices	• Soundtrack • Sound Effects • Images • Voiceover Narration
Pacing	• Arrangement • Sentence Structure • Paragraph Construction • Written Transitions	• Soundtrack • Duration of Images • Pauses and Silences • Visual Transitions • Spoken Transitions

In taking stock of the ways the semiotic resources are functioning in relation to their overarching rhetorical objectives, writers are then well-positioned to consider additional inventional possibilities. This mapping might involve drawing upon additional semiotic resources, utilizing different media affordances, integrating other literacies, or remediating existing texts to suit writers' rhetorical goals. Table 2 outlines the two stages of semiotic mapping, along with guiding questions for helping direct writers through each stage of this process.

TABLE 2 SEMIOTIC MAPPING ACTIVITY

STAGE 1: MAPPING THE DRAFT	GUIDING QUESTIONS
Define your purpose	What is the overarching purpose of this text?
Identify the rhetorical moves in the text	What rhetorical moves do you make in the text to fulfill your purpose?
Mark the places where the text shifts from one kind of rhetorical work to another	How is each segment of the text functioning? What rhetorical work is each segment of text doing in relation to your larger purpose?
Take stock of semiotic resources	What semiotic resources are being utilized to do this rhetorical work? What semiotic resources and media affordances are being effectively utilized? Which might be better utilized?
Take stock of literacies	What literacies have you integrated to shape the content of these segments of text? Which literacies have informed your composing process in shaping this segment?
STAGE 2: INVENTING AND REMEDIATING	GUIDING QUESTIONS
Consider inventional possibilities	What additional rhetorical resources might be drawn upon to do this work? What additional semiotic resources and media affordances might be utilized to engage in this rhetorical work?
Consider additional literacies	What additional literacies might you integrate to fulfill your rhetorical objectives? What other literacies might inform your composing process in shaping this segment?
Remediating alphabetic text to fit a digital medium	Which portions of the written text are essential for communicating the central ideas in the multimodal text? Where might portions of the alphabetic text be cut and communicated through other modes? In which places of the alphabetic essay might images or video replace written text? Which music selections might best convey the ideas that are being communicated in the written text? How might you best coordinate interactions among voiceover narration, images, written text, and visual transitions to serve your intended purpose?

(continued)

TABLE 2 SEMIOTIC MAPPING ACTIVITY (*continued*)

Remediating digital texts to suit a print-based medium	How might the visuals used in the multimodal text be repurposed to suit the medium of an alphabetic text? How might the tone established by the interactions of semiotic resources in the multimodal text be recreated in the written text? How might prose in the written essay be structured in such a way that the mood of the alphabetic essay is consistent with the mood in the multimodal text? What semiotic resources might be used in the written essay to create an ethos that is consistent with that established in the multimodal text? In what ways might the structure of the multimodal text align with and depart from the arrangement of the written text?

We see semiotic mapping as an effective means of helping students develop 68 a greater awareness of the ways they are using semiotic resources to construct a text's larger trajectory. This awareness is invaluable in that it provides a sound basis for decision-making as writers consider the rhetorical possibilities available to them during processes of revising, remediating, and inventing texts. Reflection of this kind not only positions writers to make thoughtful rhetorical choices and encourages revision, but it also prompts writers to consider possible ways that they might utilize literacies from various domains and coordinate interactions among available semiotic resources to achieve their rhetorical goals. In sharing this heuristic, our goal is to provide writers with a framework that might allow them to navigate the complex rhetorical decisions they will be required to make as they move among contexts, genres, media, and modes in multimodal composing tasks.

As new technologies steadily and incrementally reshape students' notions of 69 rhetorical practice and composing processes, the need to understand writers' experiences in multimodal composition projects is increasingly apparent. Through research of this kind, we are better positioned to determine if the methods utilized in composition teaching are those best apt to help students develop and transfer the kinds of literacies they will need to thrive in a range of twenty-first century contexts. Ultimately, we hope that the insights and pedagogical tools offered in this study better equip multimodal composition instructors to guide students as they make their way through this bag full of snakes.

Notes

1. In our view, multimodal compositions are texts that employ multiple semiotic resources to purposefully convey meaning. Our understanding of the term "multimodal composition" draws from both the New London Group's (1996) definition of combining modes of meaning into a single composition (p. 84) and Kress and van Leeuwen's (2001) definition: "the use of several semiotic modes in the design of a semiotic product or event, together with the particular way in which these modes are combined" (p. 20).

2. We define "semiotic resources" as "the actions, materials and artifacts we use for communicative purposes . . . together with the ways in which these resources can be organized" (van Leeuwen, 2004, p. 285). Semiotic resources are thus the communicative and rhetorical options writers have available to them when they combine multiple semiotic modes (i.e., aural, visual, gestural, linguistic, technological, material, spatial).

3. Nora and Jennifer had over 4 hours of video footage to for a 6–10 minute video documentary. Duncan and Nick had 129 minutes of footage. Duncan commented that every time he needed to cull footage it was another 129 minutes: "So that's probably just 6 hours of watching it and then trying to cut it and find what I needed." Even those students who did not use video footage expressed surprise over how long it took to compose a video.

4. Students were used to composing print-based texts where the tools and technologies used to write are virtually invisible. Sure, students have to learn word-processing software to write, but they use the computer so often that it has become second nature to many of them.

5. Semiotic mapping intersects with the notion of *tracing* (see DePalma, 2015); semiotic mapping, however, was conceived in relation to a broad range of remediation activities, one of which includes moving between print-based essays and digital stories.

References

Adler-Kassner, Linda, Majewski, John. & Koshnick, Damian (2012). The value of troublesome knowledge: Transfer and threshold concepts in writing and history. *Composition Forum: A Journal of Pedagogical Theory in Rhetoric and Composition, 26*(Fall). Retrieved from http://compositionforum.com/issue/26.

Alexander, Kara Poe. (2013). Material affordances: The potential of scrapbooks in the composition classroom. *Composition Forum: A Journal of Pedagogical Theory in Rhetoric and Composition, 27*(Spring). Retrieved from http://compositionforum.com/issue/27/.

Alexander, Kara Poe, & Williams, Danielle. (2015). DMAC after dark: Distributed invention at and beyond DMAC. *Computers and Composition: An International Journal, 36,* 32–43.

Artemeva, Natasha, & Fox, Janna. (2010). Awareness versus production: Probing students' antecedent genre knowledge. *Journal of Business and Technical Communication, 24*(4), 476–515.

Ball, Cheryl E. (2004). Show, not tell: The value of new media scholarship. *Computers and Composition, 21*(4), 403–425.

Ball, Cheryl E. (2006). Designerly ≠ Readerly: Re-assessing multimodal and new media rubrics for use in writing studies. *Convergence: The International Journal of Research into New Media Technologies, 12*(4), 393–412.

Bawarshi, Anis. (2004). *Guidelines for analyzing genres. Genre and the invention of the writer: Reconsidering the place of invention in composition.* Logan, UT: Utah State University Press.

Bergmann, Linda S., & Zepernick, Janet. (2007). Disciplinarity and transfer: Students' perceptions of learning to write. *WPA: Writing Program Administration, 31*(1/2), 124–149.

Bickmore, Lisa, & Christiansen, Ron. (2010). "Who will be the inventors? Why not us?" Multimodal composition in the two-year college classroom. *Teaching English in the Two-Year College, 37*(3), 230–242.

Borton, Sonya, & Huot, Brian. (2007). Responding, Assessing. In Cynthia L. Selfe (Ed.), *Multimodal composition: Resources for teachers* (pp. 99–111). Cresskill, NJ: Hampton Press.

Bowen, Tracey, & Whithaus, Carl. (Eds.). (2013). *Multimodal literacies and emerging genres.* Pittsburgh, PA: University of Pittsburgh Press.

Carroll, Lee Ann. (2002). *Rehearsing new roles: How college students develop as writers.* Carbondale, IL: Southern Illinois University Press.

DePalma, Michael-John. (2015). Tracing transfer across media: Writers' perceptions of cross-contextual and rhetorical reshaping in processes of remediation. *College Composition and Communication, 66*(4), 615–642.

DePalma, Michael-John, & Ringer, Jeffrey M. (2011). Toward a theory of adaptive transfer: Expanding disciplinary discussions of "transfer" in second-language writing and composition studies. *Journal of Second Language Writing, 20*(2), 134–147.

Dias, Patrick, Freedman, Aviva, Medway, Peter, & Paré, Anthony. (1999). *Worlds apart: Acting and writing in academic and workplace contexts.* Mahwah, NJ: Lawrence Erlbaum Associates.

Ede, Lisa, & Lunsford, Andrea. (1984). Audience addressed/audience invoked: The role of audience in composition theory and pedagogy. *College Composition and Communication, 35*(2), 155–171.

Fulwiler, Meagan, & Middleton, Kim. (2012). After digital storytelling: Video composing in the new media age. *Computers and Composition, 29*(1), 39–50.

Gee, James Paul. (2003). *What video games have to teach us about learning and literacy.* New York, NY: Palgrave Macmillan.

Glaser, Barney G., & Strauss, Anselm L. (1967). *The discovery of grounded theory: Strategies for qualitative research.* Chicago, IL: Aldine Publishing Company.

Haas, Christina. (1996). *Writing technology: Studies on the materiality of literacy.* Mahwah, NJ: Lawrence Erlbaum Associates.

Hawisher, Gail E., & Selfe, Cynthia L. (Eds.). (1999). *Passions, pedagogies, and 21st century technologies.* Logan, UT: Utah State University Press and National Council of Teachers of English.

Kress, Gunther. (2003). *Literacy in the new media age.* London, UK: Routledge.

Kress, Gunther, & van Leeuwen, Theo. (2001). *Multimodal discourse: The modes and media of contemporary communication.* New York, NY: Oxford University Press.

Leeuwen, Theo. (2004). *Introducing social semiotics: An introductory textbook.* London, UK: Routledge.

McCarthy, Lucille P. (1987). A stranger in strange lands: A college student writing across the curriculum. *Research in the Teaching of English, 21*(3), 233–265.

Murray, Elizabeth A., Sheets, Hailey A., & Williams, Nicole A. (2010). The new work of assessment: Evaluating multimodal compositions. *Computers and Composition Online,* (Spring). Retrieved from http://www2.bgsu.edu/departments/english/cconline/virtualc.htm.

New London Group. (1996). A pedagogy of multiliteracies: Designing social futures. *Harvard Educational Review, 66*(1), 60–92.

Nowacek, Rebecca S. (2011). *Agents of integration: Understanding transfer as a rhetorical act.* Carbondale, IL: Southern Illinois University Press.

Powell, Beth, Alexander, Kara Poe, & Borton, Sonya. (2011). Interaction of author, audience, and purpose in multimodal texts: Students' discovery of their role as composer. *Kairos: A Journal of Rhetoric, Technology, and Pedagogy: PraxisWiki, 15*(2). Retrieved from http://technorhetoric.com/praxis/tiki-index.php?page=Student_Composers.

Prensky, Marc. (2001). Digital natives, digital immigrants part 1. *On the horizon, 9*(5), 1–6.

Reiff, Mary Jo, & Bawarshi, Anis. (2011). Tracing discursive resources: How students use prior genre knowledge to negotiate new writing contexts in first-year composition. *Written Communication, 28*(3), 312–337.

Robertson, Liane, Taczak, Kara, & Yancey, Kathleen Blake. (2012). Notes toward a theory of prior knowledge and its role in college composers' transfer of knowledge and practice. *Composition Forum, 26*(Fall). Retrieved from http://compositionforum.com/issue/26.

Russell, David R. (1995). Activity theory and its implications for writing instruction. In Joseph Petraglia (Ed.), *Reconceiving writing, rethinking writing instruction* (pp. 51–77). Mahwah, NJ: Lawrence Erlbaum Associates.

Selber, Stuart. (2004). *Multiliteracies for a digital age.* Carbondale, IL: Southern Illinois University Press.

Selfe, Cynthia L. (Ed.). (2007). *Multimodal composition: Resources for teachers.* Cresskill, NJ: Hampton Press.

Selfe, Cynthia L., & Hawisher, Gail E. (2004). *Literate lives in the information age: Narratives of literacy from the United States.* Mahwah, NJ: Lawrence Erlbaum Associates.

Sheppard, Jennifer. (2009). The rhetorical work of multimedia production practices: It's more than just technical skill. *Computers and Composition, 26*(2), 122–131.

Sheridan, David M., Ridolfo, Jim, & Michel, Anthony J. (Eds.). (2012). *The available means of persuasion: Mapping a theory and pedagogy of multimodal public rhetoric.* West Lafayette, IN: Parlor Press.

Shipka, Jody. (2011). *Toward a composition made whole.* Pittsburgh, PA: University of Pittsburgh Press.

Smit, David W. (2004). *The end of composition studies.* Carbondale, IL: Southern Illinois University Press.

Sorapure, Madeleine. (2006). Between modes: Assessing student new media compositions. *Kairos: A Journal of Rhetoric, Technology, and Pedagogy, 10*(2). Retrieved from http://english.ttu.edu/KAIROS/10.2/binder2.html?coverweb/sorapure/index.html.

Takayoshi, Pamela, & Selfe, Cynthia L. (2007). Thinking about multimodality. In Cynthia L. Selfe (Ed.), *Multimodal composition: Resources for teachers* (pp. 1–12). Cresskill, NJ: Hampton Press.

Tardy, Christina. (2009). *Building genre knowledge.* West Lafayette, IN: Parlor Press.

Walvoord, Barbara E., & McCarthy, Lucille P. (1990). *Thinking and writing in college: A naturalistic study of students in four disciplines.* Urbana, IL: National Council of Teachers of English.

Wardle, Elizabeth. (2007). Understanding "transfer" from FYC: Preliminary results of a longitudinal study. *WPA: Writing Program Administration, 31*(1/2), 65–85.

Wardle, Elizabeth. (2009). "Mutt genres" and the goal of FYW: Can we help students write the genres of the university? *College Composition and Communication, 60*(4), 765–789.

Wysocki, Anne Frances. (2003). With eyes that think, and compose, and think: On visual rhetoric. In Pamela Takayoshi & Brian Huot (Eds.), *Teaching writing with computers* (pp. 182–201). Boston, MA: Houghton Mifflin Harcourt.

Wysocki, Anne Frances, Johnson-Eilola, Johndan, Selfe, Cynthia L., & Sirc, Geoffrey (Eds.). (2004). *Writing new media: Theory and applications for expanding the teaching of composition.* Logan, UT: Utah State University Press.

Yancey, Kathleen Blake. (2004). Looking for sources of coherence in a fragmented world: Notes toward a new assessment design. *Computers and Composition, 21*(1), 89–102.

- -

Questions for Discussion and Journaling

1. Find the research questions that DePalma and Poe outline. Explain in your own words what they were looking for.

2. What research methods did DePalma and Poe use to explore those questions? Referring back to the discussion of questions and methods in Chapter 3, can you think of other methods they might have used to explore these questions? Consider, for example, that DePalma and Poe studied students enrolled in academic courses in a university. What other populations or contexts might they have studied, and why?

3. How would you summarize DePalma and Poe's most interesting findings?

4. How is the idea of "audience" complicated by multimodal composing?

5. Why did students in this study have difficulty drawing on all the modes and resources available to them when composing multimodal texts?

6. DePalma and Poe note that although students are constantly exposed to technologies and multiple modes, they do not have experience using technology to create such texts themselves. What do they mean by this? Do you agree?

Applying and Exploring Ideas

1. Consider where and how you compose regularly using various modes. Do you regularly compose multimodal texts? If so, for what contexts? Does a school setting ever require you to create multimodal texts? As you answer these questions, think carefully about how you are defining what counts as "multimodal."

2. List some of the differences the research participants described between multimodal and "print essays" or "academic writing." What do you understand as some differences and similarities between these modes?

3. DePalma and Poe argue that "the binary constructed between academic print-based texts and multimodal public texts prevented students from seeing how they might address a knowledgeable and specialized audience in creative and engaging ways" (para. 20). Consider what situations might call for addressing specialized audiences in "creative and engaging ways" and what those "creative" ways might be (what genres a writer could use); make as complete a list of possibilities as you can.

4. One of the students, Jessie, argues that composing a multimodal text is difficult because audiences could easily "walk out of there confused." Students also had difficulty knowing how to use the various modes (for example, video or

voiceover). Why do you think the students in this study felt it was harder to communicate with audiences via multimodal texts? Do you share this feeling? Why or why not?

5. DePalma and Poe list some strategies that they believe teachers should incorporate into writing classrooms to help students compose effective multimodal texts. What are these strategies? Do you agree that you would benefit if teachers used these? In particular, take a look at Table 2, the "semiotic mapping activity." How might these mapping and questioning activities assist you in your own composing?

- -
META MOMENT   After reading this and other texts, what does it mean to "write" or to compose a "text"? How might it help you be a more effective communicator to broaden your ideas of these terms?
- -

Did I Create the Process? Or Did the Process Create Me?

JAYDELLE CELESTINE

Samantha Nash, Courtesy of Jaydelle Celestine

Framing the Reading

Jaydelle Celestine was a student at the University of Central Florida when he wrote this essay for his first-year composition course. In this piece, you will learn a lot about his personal history, including his upbringing on the island of Grenada, his literacy experiences at an all-boys school, and the voice of the teacher he continues to hear today when he writes. Celestine was majoring in Event Management at UCF and hopes to own an event planning agency. In the meantime, he is now active on campus and in his community, serving as a member of the National Society of Minorities in Hospitality and on the Leadership Council for UCF's Rosen College of Hospitality. He also models and acts when he can.

In this essay, Celestine reviews his varied writing processes, noting people, experiences, and changing contexts that have influenced his writing. He examines factors that both help and hinder his writing. His experiences illustrate the threshold concepts that writing is a process, writers always have more to learn, and writing is not perfectible.

Getting Ready to Read

Before you read, do at least one of the following activities:

- Search the Internet to learn about the island of Grenada, where Celestine was raised.
- Research the current size, location, and student makeup at the University of Central Florida, where one of Celestine's vignettes takes place.

As you read, consider the following questions:

- What choices does Celestine make in terms of organization and focus? What genre of text is he writing?
- How are your own writing experiences similar to — or different from — his?

Stylus: A Journal of First-Year Writing, Department of Writing and Rhetoric, University of Central Florida

stylus
a journal of first-year writing

Galaxy-Wide Writing Strategies Used by Official *Star Wars* Bloggers
ARIELLE FELDMAN

Did I Create the Process? Or Did the Process Create Me?
JAYDELLE CELESTINE

Changing Scenes: The Rise and Success of Diversity on Broadway
KATT GENTRY

The Language Transition Process and Its Influence on Language Use
LETICIA LENKIU

Liking in Group Messaging: Perception versus Meaning
CHLOE LAROCHELLE

The Extent of Influence that Genre Conventions Have on TED Talks
PRISCILLA SAMATOA

Volume 8 | Issue 2 | Fall 2017

Celestine, Jaydelle. "Did I Create the Process? Or Did the Process Create Me?" *Stylus,* vol. 8, no. 2, Fall 2017, pp. 1–12.

I'M AT MY DESK in my dorm finishing breakfast and I don't really know 1
where to start. It is a beautiful Friday morning, and navigating my thoughts
as to the best way to proceed with this essay proves much more difficult than I
anticipated. I never gave much thought to the habits and factors that influenced
my writing process, and now I've been challenged to do so. My approach needs
to be specific, different to what I've already been taught. As I get lost in my
thoughts and explore the patterns of my earliest pieces of literary work from
the earliest parts of my childhood, slowly, each piece falls into place. I surprise
myself as to the memories that I uncover, the emotions I felt and the break-
throughs I've made. What is happening, I soon realize, is the beginning of a
beautiful story that culminates at this stage in my life and reveals the factors of
which make me the writer I am today.

At this moment I have the entire dorm to myself. This is the ideal setting 2
for me. Over the years I have definitely been able to produce most of my best
work this way, in seclusion. I raise my hands to type, and a truck pulls up rum-
bling loudly outside for what seems like forever. I could *never* focus in uproar,
especially when I remember how my process started as a child and the role my
mother had in that process.

I believe my mom is the primary catalyst as to the affinity I've developed 3
when it comes to both reading and writing. At that point in time, she worked
at our local library, which was very close to our school. Once classes ended, I'd
make my way straight to the library to wait on her to finish work so we could
go home.

In the earlier stages, she would sit me down in a room at the back, give me 4
a book to make my company until she was ready, and close the door. It was
always just me in that room, and reading without any distraction was amazing.
I was my own company; I could concentrate and disappear into my own little
world of wild imagination until 4 o'clock. I really enjoyed that space she created
for me, and it definitely stayed with me more than I thought throughout my
life as well.

As I got older, I chose my books while I waited in that same room and my 5
imagination slowly broadened. You would think it stopped there, but it didn't.
Most of my gifts as a young boy growing up included toys, but it mainly consisted of books. A book then became my favorite gift. I preferred it above all
else (well, not counting the occasional twenty-dollar bill that would fall out of
my birthday and Christmas cards). As time progressed, it was books like *Goose-
bumps, Robin Hood, Frankenstein, Dr. Jekyll and Mr. Hyde, The Time Machine*
and countless others that inspired me to become a storyteller of my own one
day. Those books had me writing all sorts of idle short stories whenever I could
as a result.

THE PROFOUND EFFECT OF MY FACEBOOK STORY

It was a warm Thursday morning in May 2014, and I was on the computer in 6 our study room at home. Our study room was very cozy. A dark green carpet that lined the floor, a thick, sturdy mahogany desk near the window, as well as a huge shelf on the left that climbed upwards of four levels, housing books, board games and VMS cassettes of my early childhood.

I literally had nothing to do on the computer that day: I opened and closed 7 browsers, googled all sorts of nonsense that came to mind, found nothing interesting on YouTube. And so I made my way to Facebook. Well that was initially an effort in futility as well; there was nothing fascinating happening there either. Generally, it was just people complaining about life and asking questions to engage comments, such as, "Who'd you rather, Rihanna or Beyoncé?" and a couple of interesting pictures sprinkled in between the timeline to break up the monotony.

I remember hearing cheesy music playing, looking around at the TV, and 8 saw that it was a rerun on one of our local channels of the soap opera, *The Young & the Restless*. I watched for a bit, intrigued as this lady was crying hysterically begging this old guy not to leave her and him telling her rather directly that he couldn't do *this* anymore (whatever *this was*). After snapping myself out of watching that tragedy, I was gazing at our airport out of the study window at the lone British Airways flight that remained the night prior, and my mind ran on my family in England.

Turning around at the TV once more, there was an advertisement now of a 9 new *Beauty & the Beast* DVD in HD or something like that. I told myself that women always needed saving, that they were always perceived as "damsels in distress" and someone needs to do something about that. Men are not always the bad guys, or the "beasts" they're most times made out to be.

That was all it took. I closed the study door to rid myself of distractions, 10 opened up the note portion of my Facebook page, and started writing the ideas that came to my mind. This consisted of a prince and a princess, dancing at a ball after their marriage ceremony in their English palace. This story would be different, the woman would be the bad guy and no one would be the wiser. I set it all up so that it all it appeared to be her dream come true after growing up poor and marrying into royalty, but included a mass murder at said ball with her trying to escape for her life, only to reveal that she orchestrated the entire thing. It took me a while to really get it all together. I knew what I wanted to do, but I had never done a written piece in that format and especially on a forum like Facebook.

I would usually try to isolate myself away from any distraction, give myself 11 a time frame to work with, draft my thoughts via pen and paper, proofread, type out my final product, review and do whatever necessary after. This was different, and a new turning point happened that would slightly alter how

I approached writing. I just typed as the words came, paused occasionally, read it over and made slight changes. What eventually continued happening in that moment was I tried to type so fast as the ideas came. It was like I didn't want to stop for fear of losing the ideas through the momentum.

Inevitably I stopped, and stopped a lot, because I ran out of ideas. I found   12
myself stretching, staring at my screen, playing with our dog or going outside, and walking around idly and finding stuff to do in the kitchen that I wouldn't normally do. I was trying to find some sort of inspiration, or unconsciously giving myself a break. The longer I stayed away, the more I heard my secondary school English teacher, Ms. Patrick, in my head saying, "Paint their minds with your creativity, Jaydelle. Be descriptive, reel them in."

Ms. Patrick is always in my head now, anytime I write something, always   13
coaching and constantly criticizing. I always try to live up to her expectations because she always believed and fed my potential. However, I would then head back to the computer and find myself googling stuff again, trying to listen to music (which helped, but later on in life would just become a distraction), and then heading back in an attempt to finish the piece. I did finish. I started around 9 A.M. and was able to post it a little before noon. That has always affected me in my writing going forward, as that ritualistic fashion of starting and then straying or procrastinating has stayed with me to this day, a process that was nowhere near the habits I had in secondary school.

After all was said and done, I was able to hit the post button of my short   14
story, and received much more feedback than I anticipated. People actually read it and I felt pretty good. They didn't just hit the "like" button, but some commented too, on my seven-paragraph story born out of idleness. Ms. Patrick would be proud. It felt much longer after having read the finished product, but the feedback encouraged me to do a second piece in July of that same year. All because of my imagination from those damn books as a child, with a little nudge from a soap opera, a *Beauty & the Beast* commercial, and some time on my hands. It made me continue writing more short stories after that, but what was even stranger was that whereas before I would have written drafts down with pen and paper, I now begun typing it via Microsoft Word. My primary and secondary school processes were somewhat abandoned and this new one now formed. It still remains a huge part of who I am in my writing, to this day.

THE WOMAN WHO CHANGED THE PROCESS

Here enters this professionally clad lady on a sunny morning in January of 2001.   15
She was about 5'7", walking slowly but proudly, holding the edges of her black jacket. She wore a hairstyle reminiscent of Scary Spice from the Spice Girls, and had way too much makeup on. She chewed her gum vigorously as though

anxiously awaiting something to happen and wore a smile that accentuated how badly she had lined her lips. Her mouth opened and surprised everyone with a deep and boisterous, "Good Morning, boys!" and received the echoes of us all in the room as we stood and greeted her back. "I am Angela Patrick, your English A Teacher. Please have your seats."

Ms. Patrick was both the *worst* and the *best* English teacher I've ever had. 16 She pushed you to your limit, especially as far as being creative was concerned. Not only did she love a good piece of writing, she spoke and breathed it as well. Anyone from the class of '06 could tell you that she could beat a metaphor to death. She encouraged us differently than any other teacher I had up until that point: write a draft, read and make corrections, produce the final piece, but verify one last time. Having to do all that and be timed in 40-minute class sessions helped make us some of the most efficient writers of the 2006 graduating class. It became so natural after the initial stress of it passed, and a lot of us had her to thank as it helped us in time management as well. Her grading scheme was particularly rigid, even for the simplest of assignments. If any student got as much as an 18 / 25, it was cause for mass celebration. Her main gripe was never punctuation; rather, it was pulling out of us the potential she knew was there. She emphasized content, helping the audience live vicariously through our work. She expected nothing less.

There was one instance I remember her coming to class in her usual 17 mid-morning slot and spontaneously giving us one of her infamous "Short Story" assignments. However, this experience was different, because generally what accompanied those assignments were at least five topics to choose from. This time, we were on our own to choose whatever we wanted, and have it completed by the end of our 40-minute class session. Knowing what Ms. Patrick expected, the pressure was on. Everything had to be perfect, from introduction through the body and wrapping it up at the end.

This was a bit difficult to do. As a 15- or 16-year-old student, you were 18 already accustomed to having been spoon-fed your creative direction, and now you felt like a fish out of water when it was left up to you. I had no topic and no idea what I wanted to write about. Plus, attending an all boy school was the worst as far as distraction was concerned; it made it so difficult to focus at times. I always wanted to escape and gather my thoughts as I usually do, but I couldn't. Here it was again, this pesky noise issue following me, and I had no control over it. I couldn't come up with anything.

Before we knew it, the bell rung and students started fussing about who 19 wasn't finished, who had nothing and if we could complete it for homework. Unknown to everyone, the joke was on us and Ms. Patrick was going to have the last laugh. She told us that this wasn't a graded assignment, and we all stared in shock. Her response in turn was this: "You boys have to learn that there would be times when you're asked to pull from you, not have someone pull from your-selves, for you." In hindsight it made sense, but back then it felt like the worst thing ever. She asked something very simple of us, yet none of could do it effec-tively (and, at 16, that's a bit embarrassing. I bet it made for a good staffroom joke though). We had to learn to expect the unexpected and be prepared for anything, and that didn't apply only for her class, but for life in general.

PUTTING THE PIECES TOGETHER

I've realized while typing this that what it means for me to produce an effec- 20
tive written piece has changed over time and has been heavily tied in part to my environment, which in turn affects my writing habits. From writing short stories as a child in a primary school of over three hundred, that lacked parti-tions between classes and having no sense of strict time for the assignments. To essays and assessments of varying degrees in a more organized secondary school, but with three times the students, a stricter time rule and set revision pattern. To now, an actually structured research essay, rigid citation guidelines and projects while at the mammoth of a school that is UCF, but where you as the student have more control as to what your environment is and how it affects your output. I honestly don't know the exact reason why those habits changed, but I'm sure it has something to do with what each of my teachers required at those various stages of my life. However, back then, each stage would have served me as some sort of guide as to how I should go about writing each required piece of text, thus culminat-ing into what my writing habits and preferred environment are at this point in my life.

> I've realized while typing this that what it means for me to produce an effective written piece has changed over time and has been heavily tied in part to my environment, which in turn affects my writing habits.

In primary school we didn't know better, but we had more freedom to 21
express ourselves with just a tad bit of guidance into associating with the norm. I was never as productive as I could be surrounded by distraction, though, as I remember my mom clearly telling me that my teachers back then said. I would rip my paper up and put my hand over my ears when I wrote something; noise and I just weren't the best of friends. My teachers would, however (with the best of intentions I'm sure), tell me how it's supposed to be done and make sure I did so accordingly.

In secondary school, a defined structure was given, and we had to navigate 22
how to produce our best piece of work within a more firm time frame and very formal setting. That period of time in particular was annoying because there

wasn't only chaos to worry about in an all boy school; you had to satisfy what your teacher wanted and still inject a part of you into that work.

My two years at the T.A. Marryshow Community College were also very 23 revealing to me; the game changed drastically. No teacher paid you the time of day, like they did back in secondary school. Nobody had time to run after students begging them to turn in work, or give them pep talks. You were in charge of you, and the environment was much different now as you returned to a mix of co-ed students, who were free to skip class at their choosing and a host of other unproductive choices to choose from. As spacious as the campus was, noise was still everywhere. By now you would think I'd be able to navigate through the distraction of others given I've been prepped for it all of my life, but I still wasn't. You would also think that being from a culture whereby the people naturally talk at more elevated levels, I could deal with that too, but it proved challenging.

As a culture in the Caribbean, we tend to be loud, dramatic and very descrip- 24 tive with how we communicate, and it rolled over into teachings at home and in the classroom. To give you a better idea, we don't just say, "Take a left and around the corner there's a red building, that's your destination." We might say, "Take a left and look for a tall tree that's bent slightly as though it has scoliosis, then around the corner you would find a bright red building, made completely of bricks, and you usually have to enter where there's an exit sign." Both ways are effective, but one more memorable than the other. This innate trait of who we are as a people, coupled with my imagination and love of film, always resulted in me writing short stories.

HOW MY CULTURE IMPACTED THE PROCESS

My island itself—Grenada—is rather small. We're about 133 square miles and 25 our population is approximately 106,000. We have sparkling blue waters, clear skies, sunny days and friendly people. We are but one of the many gems the Caribbean has to offer. Coming from a small island, you tend to either run the risk of (1) not being heard of, (2) mistaken for somewhere else, or (3) having to find some trait that stands out so you can inject yourself into a conversation to let people know that they may in fact know who you are.

Our families and communities are tight-knit. Everyone knows everyone 26 (both a gift and a curse) and in the rare instances you don't know someone, they know you (generally by parentage). Coming from a smaller island in the Caribbean also affords a loose version of the "Napoleon Complex." We feel the need to overcompensate, as we aren't recognized on the same level as everyone else. Growing up in this environment instilled a sense of pride whenever an islander received positive international recognition, and reinforced that no matter how small we might be that we should always be especially proud of our heritage.

My life changed when I got accepted to one of the largest universities in 27 Florida, for the fall semester of 2016. The University of Central Florida boasts a student population of approximately 60,000. This in itself was overwhelming. On my first official day of school, I saw so many different people of all shapes and sizes, colors and creeds from various walks of life that it left me in awe. I've been to New York and I've traveled to many other Caribbean islands, but obviously nothing compares to the institution that is UCF. As Dorothy would tell me, I was definitely not in Kansas anymore.

Walking through the Student Union was the best feeling for me; I saw the 28 flags of countries that represented the nationalities of UCF's student population. Anxiously looking for mine (I couldn't be the only Grenadian here); I was left with the disappointment that my flag wasn't there. I probably looked like a madman pacing back and forth looking through each row just to be certain, and taking pictures on top of that too. After confirming what was inevitably true, I walked away and decided I would fix that. But how would I? I would fix it through one of my most favorite mediums: writing.

In January 2017, I spoke to a polite young lady at the Guest Services Desk at 29 the Student Union, and asked her who the best person was to speak to regarding the issue of my flag. She pointed me in the direction of Jamie Morales (the Associate Director in charge of Maintenance and Operations for the Student Union). So, in transit to my next class, I crafted a formal inquiry that praised the diversity of UCF, how happy I was to be there, and its efficiency that was displayed to me in any aspect when I needed it. Ms. Patrick taught me back home that to be successful in conveying an effective message one must know how to appeal to the senses of whom they are speaking to. This allowed me through my email, to further confirm the good work that UCF has been doing over the years by touching on its efficiency, as well as acknowledging how large and diverse a school it indeed is and the people that continue to make it that way by how helpful they are. However, I also conveyed the absence I felt from that diversity when I noticed my flag wasn't there, and that I felt my culture wasn't recognized on the level it should be with everyone else. Being able to speak up helped serve as a catalyst to effect this change I wanted, through a written piece.

Maybe if I wasn't literate enough, or didn't have the experience of writing so 30 many essays in the past, I would not have known what was alright to say or not in this circumstance, but my experience taught me better. Mr. Morales messaged me back within minutes, thanking me for my email and explaining why I may not have seen it there, as well as a link of the flag to ensure that had the correct one for when they had to place the order. He assured me my flag would be there very soon, and I felt that he understood my message and was going to do his best to address it.

Imagine my surprise and the happiness I felt a week or two later, when, while walking through the Student Union, I found my country's flag. I immediately felt a sense of accomplishment. *I* did that. I texted my mom and then my best friends back home, and I posted it on my social media to overwhelmingly positive, private and public feedback. This was a writing success for me, one that I would never forget; I automatically look up every time I pass through the Student Union at my flag, smiling every time. Had it not been for the way I was taught to write growing up, or the pride I grew up with, I may have been less likely to care and make a difference. Now here is my flag, proudly hanging with the others, a part of that international community that makes up the bulk of UCF. This is simply amazing!

The process of that experience, however, was different than what I was used 32 to. When I wrote about my country's flag being missing from the display of flags in the Student Union, that wasn't in a formal environment. I was actually typing that email in transit to my next class, timing myself as I typed and I still produced an effective piece that got me what I wanted. Before, I needed absolute quiet to focus and produce my best work. Now that didn't even apply for me to effectively get what I wanted. I was surrounded by students and chatter, but what made that situation different than the rest? Maybe this was Ms. Patrick at work again, taking lessons learned from her class about time management and efficiency. At this university, most correspondence is sent via email during the day. One may not have the time to get to a library or a controlled environment, sit, and gather their thoughts and type. One has to be flexible enough to do it on the go sometimes, maximizing both time and efficiency, especially to effectively attain the result they want.

I don't know why I prefer being in complete solitude when it isn't needed to 33 necessarily produce my best work. In university, being in total quiet is a huge challenge and distractions are everywhere. It still seems unfortunate that I can't read textbooks or accomplish anything that requires real thought in the main campus library (so if you ever see me there with a book open, you know it's a ruse of some sort). People, chatter, and movement distract me. At the Rosen campus, the library on the right day is all mine, but I would always prefer my dorm room's privacy.

However, if not in isolation, just like the day I created my short story on 34 Facebook, I find myself easily sidetracked, getting up ever so often and looking for excuses to procrastinate. Does that help? Sometimes it does and I focus much better, but other times I can't and I don't really know why. Now I understand it to a degree. Presently, I am adjusting to working in varied noise levels and am making progress. I won't always find absolute seclusion as experienced in the past, so that habit may not be the best for maximizing efficiency. I don't like the fact that I completely abandon whatever I'm doing whenever I get stuck in general either, but I've been doing it for so long that it's become ...t of who I am. It just feels like I waste so much time when I do so, and I must improve that before it consumes me.

***

Why am I so easily distracted? I still can't give a concrete answer for that no 35 matter how many times I ask it, and you know what? That's okay. I've come to the realization that, regardless of how I went about the many writing experiences I've had over the years and how I've been taught, that I can efficiently produce content that is meant to be understood through my desired mode of communication. Typing this now, I know that back then I was trying to please someone specific at that point in time regarding my content. It was about what *they* wanted, how *they* thought they could get the best out of me, and not how *I* could get the best out of *me* but still satisfy them. There is an ideal situation for my writing processes, but I've found that I adapt to suit. Do I have a preference? Of course I do, and as I'm learning right now as there are people chatting in the living room and listening to music, I modify, but won't forsake the quality of my work because of it.

It's phenomenal coming to the realization that the seed for me preferring the 36 silence of my environment may have been planted from the days of when I visited my mom after primary school. That helped cultivate my reading, thinking, and writing habits. It has apparently been a common denominator throughout various aspects of my writing life as well. It played a huge part in my Facebook short story's success, but it made me struggle in my secondary school life because the environment wasn't in my control. When I wrote my short story, it also helped add another layer to my habit, which was typing my thoughts instead of jotting by pen, and allowing me to free my thought process by abandoning the desk whenever I chose.

What secondary school helped incorporate in my process, to some extent, 37 was time management and efficiency. It has helped me at every point from then until now. That has allowed me to hone my own methods even further by doing things on my own time and knowing how to take breaks. As I've matured, I've learned how long those breaks should be, and allow myself to be rejuvenated creatively; so, I am in control.

In primary school and college, I was still constrained by my environment. 38 I was even more frustrated with the latter, because here I was in a situation where I should be able to change it, but couldn't. In a funny way, it's as though I was trying to rebel. I've been doing things by the standard of others for too long, even if it has helped me to some extent create my own process and become a better writer.

At UCF, I've discovered I can be effective without being tied to a chair, or ꞏ with what I identified as a distraction for the majority of my life: noise. I can write effectively on the go and not in the ideal surroundings, because I choose to. Where I am also influences how I write and my thought process. With my Facebook story I had no one in authority judging me. I did it according to my own standards and was successful at it because in part my audience was different. I may still hear Ms. Patrick from time to time, but that's alright. Her influence will forever be etched in my life. She is a big part of the reason that I am who I am today.

Learning how to bring both my environment as well as how I've been taught 40 together works better for me than against me. I am at that stage in life where responsibility sneaks itself into almost anything I do. Writing and my environment is no exception. It's interesting looking back at my growth process to see what it means in the grander scheme of things for me as a young adult. As much as the demands of my process can hold me back, it has made me better, and as much as it frustrates me, it relieves me. I am a bit more conscious of it now than I was then. It will never stay stagnant. I know that as I continue to grow, it will continue to change. It is undoubtedly part of who I am as a writer today, and now instead of fearing the journey, I embrace it and what it's done for me.

I have many more questions than answers right now. When will I see new 41 writing habits form? Have they already started and I don't know? Will it be more challenging now than before? How much of it will affect what I've learned up until now? Is my environment going to help me or hold me back as a result? Not knowing what the answers are for these questions puts the fear of God in me, yet excites me at the same time. It makes me more cognizant of my current habits and behavioral patterns every time I'm about to engage in a piece of writing. What fascinates me even more is that I may have started to form new habits and probably don't even know. This has birthed one of the most important lessons I've probably taken away from any composition class: understanding the process is just as important as anything else when it comes to crafting an effective written piece. I need to understand who I am as a writer and what influences me during that process, and then use that to my advantage to take my work to the next level.

- -

Questions for Discussion and Journaling

1. Describe the relationship Celestine outlines between reading and writing in his experience, and how reading prompted him to write.

2. What environments or contexts does Celestine describe as being necessary for him to write?

...e fact that Celestine describes his ideal writing environment, he also ...onstrates that different types of writing might require different writing environments. Why might this be the case?

4. Celestine describes the various ways he looks for inspiration. What are they?

5. Celestine notes that for many years he wrote to please others, considering "what *they* wanted" and "how *they* thought they could get the best" out of him, rather than how he could get the best out of himself. What do you think he means by this? How does that compare to your own experience of writing for yourself versus writing for others?

Applying and Exploring Ideas

1. Celestine describes in a somewhat stream of consciousness way how he comes up with ideas when he writes (his sources of invention). Write a few paragraphs that similarly recall a time when you were motivated to write, and how your ideas were invented.

2. Celestine explores the writing environments that best help him compose, and he explains why this might be the case. Spend a few minutes free-writing about your ideal writing environment, and the experiences you have had that make that the sort of environment that is ideal for you.

3. Celestine talks about the voice of Ms. Patrick who is always in his head when he writes, "coaching and constantly criticizing." Whose voices are in your head when you write, and what are they saying?

4. Celestine says that fifteen- and sixteen-year olds are "accustomed to having been spoon-fed . . . creative direction" and not being given one left him with "no idea" what to write about. What is your experience with being told what to write about? Is your writing process more or less successful with direction from others? Why do you think that is the case?

5. Celestine claims that in his composition course he learned that "understanding the process is just as important as anything else when it comes to crafting an effective written piece." Do you agree with him? What are some aspects of your own writing process(es) that you would like to learn more about?

- -

META MOMENT   Think about the voices and influences in your head that impact you as you write, and decide which ones you want to encourage and which ones you don't want to listen to any more.

- -

Responding — Really Responding — to Other Students' Writing

RICHARD STRAUB

Framing the Reading

Richard Straub was an associate professor of English at Florida State University prior to his untimely death in 2002. His special area of research interest was responding to student writing. He wrote a number of articles and books on how teachers can respond effectively to student writing in order to help students grow and improve. The short piece you will read here takes what Straub learned about responding to writing and explains it directly to students. It was originally published in a textbook for first-year students, so you'll see that he speaks directly to you, giving you explicit advice about how to best give feedback on your fellow students' writing as it develops. As you read the texts drafted by your classmates during the semester or quarter, remember to read them as turns in a conversation that are attempting to make meaning with others, including with you, as we discussed in Chapters 2 and 3.

The question of how writers respond to each other's writing during its development from **invention** through final copyediting is not well studied in our field, except with regard to college students' writing. Yet if we mean to study and understand writing processes, then the question of how writers are influenced, while developing their writing, by other readers' feedback on their in-process drafts is a hugely important one. This is all the more true given that writing outside classrooms looks almost nothing like writing you do for school with respect to *who works on it*. In professional and civic settings, writing is almost always shared between many collaborators and stakeholders (people who will ultimately *use* the resulting text) as it develops. We expect that as a student you're more used to being the only person to work on your writing, and getting just some limited feedback from fellow students before you submit a draft to your teacher for a grade.

We include Straub's piece, then, because we think it will be valuable for you to see an ideal description of, and extensive

Straub, Richard. "Responding—Really Responding—to Other Students' Writing." *The Subject Is Writing*, edited by Wendy Bishop and James Strickland, Heinemann / Boynton-Cook Publishers, 2005, pp. 136–46.

w to help other writers develop their writing through your own com-
on their drafts. If you've commented on your fellow students' writing before,
you probably know that it can be difficult to know *what* to say (what to comment on
and what to say about it) and *how* to say it — balancing kindness and supportiveness
with necessary criticism. Straub helps us think about this aspect of the writing process *as writers who must also be readers.*

Getting Ready to Read

Before you read, do at least one of the following activities:

* Consider your experiences with responding to other students' writing. (Often
  this is called *peer response* or *peer-reviewing*.) What has gone wrong? What
  has gone well? What is your attitude toward it?
* Think of a time peer response has gone well for you, or for a friend. What was
  it about the experience that made it go well?

As you read, consider the following questions:

* Does Straub's advice set up peer-responding differently than your previous
  experiences did?
* How can you understand and better participate in peer response if you
  understand your task as reading rhetorically and making meaning with
  another author?

OKAY. YOU'VE GOT a student paper you have to read and make comments 1
on for Thursday. It's not something you're looking forward to. But that's alright,
you think. There isn't really all that much to it. Just keep it simple. Read it
quickly and mark whatever you see. Say something about the introduction.
Something about details and examples. Ideas you can say you like. Mark any
typos and spelling errors. Make your comments brief. Abbreviate where possible: *awk. Good intro, give ex, frag.* Try to imitate the teacher. Mark what he'd
mark and sound like he'd sound. But be cool about it. Don't praise anything
really, but no need to get harsh or cut throat either. Get in and get out. You're
okay. I'm okay. Everybody's happy. What's the problem?

This is, no doubt, a way of getting through the assignment. Satisfy the teacher 2
and no surprises for the writer. It might just do the trick. But say you want to
do a *good* job. Say you're willing to put in the time and effort — though time is
tight and you know it's not going to be easy — and help the writer look back on
the paper and revise it. And maybe in the process learn something more yourself

about writing. What do you look for? How do you sound? How much do you take up? What exactly are you trying to accomplish? Here are some ideas.

HOW SHOULD YOU LOOK AT YOURSELF AS A RESPONDER?

Consider yourself a friendly reader. A test pilot. A roommate who's been asked 3 to look over the paper and tell the writer what you think. Except you don't just take on the role of The Nice Roommate or The Ever-faithful Friend and tell her what she wants to hear. *This all looks good. I wouldn't change a thing. There are a couple places that I think he might not like, but I can see what you're doing there. I'd go with it. Good stuff.* You're supportive. You give her the benefit of the doubt and look to see the good in her writing. But friends don't let friends think their writing is the best thing since *The Great Gatsby* and they don't lead them to think that all is fine and well when it's not. Look to help this friend, this room-mate writer — okay, this person in your class — to get a better piece of writing. Point to problems and areas for improvement but do it in a constructive way. See what you can do to push her to do even more than she's done and stretch herself as a writer.

WHAT ARE YOUR GOALS?

First, don't set out to seek and destroy all errors and problems in the writing. 4 You're not an editor. You're not a teacher. You're not a cruise missile. And don't rewrite any parts of the paper. You're not the writer; you're a reader. One of many. The paper is not yours; it's the writer's. She writes. You read. She is in charge of what she does to her writing. That doesn't mean you can't make sug-gestions. It doesn't mean you can't offer a few sample rewrites here and there, as models. But make it clear they're samples, models. Not rewrites. Not edits. Not corrections. Be reluctant at first even to say what you would do if the paper were yours. It's not yours. Again: Writers write, readers read and show what they're understanding and maybe make suggestions. What to do instead: Look at your task as a simple one. You're there to play back to the writer how you read the paper: what you got from it; what you found interesting; where you were confused; where you wanted more. With this done, you can go on to point out problems, ask questions, offer advice, and wonder out loud with the writer about her ideas. Look to help her improve the writing or encourage her to work on some things as a writer.

HOW DO YOU GET STARTED?

Before you up and start reading the paper, take a minute (alright, thirty sec- 5 onds) to make a mental checklist about the circumstances of the writing, the context. You're not going to just read a text. You're going to read a text within a certain context, a set of circumstances that accompany the writing and that you bring to your reading. It's one kind of writing or another, designed for one audience and purpose or another. It's a rough draft or a final draft. The writer is trying to be serious or casual, straight or ironic. Ideally, you'll read the paper with an eye to the circumstances that it was written in and the situation it is looking to create. That means looking at the writing in terms of the assignment, the writer's particular interests and aims, the work you've been doing in class, and the stage of drafting.

- *The assignment:* What kind of writing does the assignment call (or allow) for? Is the paper supposed to be a personal essay? A report? An analysis? An argument? Consider how well the paper before you meets the demands of the kind of writing the writer is taking up.

- *The writer's interests and aims:* What does the writer want to accomplish? If she's writing a personal narrative, say, is she trying to simply recount a past experience? Is she trying to recount a past experience and at the same time amuse her readers? Is she trying to show a pleasant experience on the surface, yet suggest underneath that everything was not as pleasant as it seems? Hone in on the writer's particular aims in the writing.

- *The work of the class:* Try to tie your comments to the concepts and strategies you've been studying in class. If you've been doing a lot of work on using detail, be sure to point to places in the writing where the writer uses detail effectively or where she might provide richer detail. If you've been working on developing arguments through examples and sample cases, indicate where the writer might use such methods to strengthen her arguments. If you've been considering various ways to sharpen the style of your sentences, offer places where the writer can clarify her sentence structure or arrange a sentence for maximum impact. The best comments will ring familiar even as they lead the writer to try to do something she hasn't quite done before, or done in quite the same way. They'll be comforting and understandable even as they create some need to do more, a need to figure out some better way.

- *The stage of drafting:* Is it an early draft? A full but incomplete draft? A nearly final draft? Pay attention to the stage of drafting. Don't try to deal with everything all at once if it's a first, rough draft. Concentrate on the large picture: the paper's focus; the content; the writer's voice. Don't worry about errors and punctuation problems yet. There'll be time for them later. If it's closer to a full draft, go ahead and talk, in addition to the overall content, about arrangement, pacing, and sentence style. Wait till the final draft to give much attention to fine-tuning sentences and dealing in detail with proofreading. Remember: You're not an editor. Leave these sentence revisions and corrections for the writer. It's her paper. And she's going to learn best by detecting problems and making her own changes.

WHAT TO ADDRESS IN YOUR COMMENTS?

Try to focus your comments on a couple of areas of writing. Glance through the paper quickly first. Get an idea whether you'll deal mostly with the overall content and purpose of the writing, its shape and flow, or (if these are more or less in order) with local matters of paragraph structure, sentence style, and correctness. Don't try to cover everything that comes up or even all instances of a given problem. Address issues that are most important to address in this paper, at this time. 6

WHERE TO PUT YOUR COMMENTS?

Some teachers like to have students write comments in the margins right next to the passage. Some like to have students write out their comments in an end note or in a separate letter to the writer. I like to recommend using both marginal comments and a note or letter at the end. The best of both worlds. Marginal comments allow you to give a quick moment-by-moment reading of the paper. They make it easy to give immediate and specific feedback. You still have to make sure you specify what you're talking about and what you have to say, but they save you some work telling the writer what you're addressing and allow you to focus your end note on things that are most important. Comments at the end allow you to provide some perspective on your response. This doesn't mean that you have to size up the paper and give it a thumbs up or a thumbs down. You can use the end comment to emphasize the key points of your response, explain and elaborate on issues you want to deal with more fully, and mention additional points that you don't want to address in detail. One thing to avoid: plastering comments all over the writing; in between and over the lines of the other person's writing — up, down, and across the page. Write in your space, and let the writer keep hers. 7

HOW TO SOUND?

Not like a teacher. Not like a judge. Not like an editor or critic or shotgun. (Wouldn't you want someone who was giving you comments not to sound like a teacher's red pen, a judge's ruling, an edi-

> *Even when you're tough and demanding you can still be supportive.*

8

tor's impatience, a critic's wrath, a shotgun's blast?) Sound like you normally sound when you're speaking with a friend or acquaintance. Talk to the writer.

You're not just marking up a text; you're responding to the writer. You're a reader, a helper, a colleague. Try to sound like someone who's a reader, who's helpful, and who's collegial. Supportive. And remember: Even when you're tough and demanding you can still be supportive.

HOW MUCH TO COMMENT?

Don't be stingy. Write most of your comments out in full statements. Instead 9 of writing two or three words, write seven or eight. Instead of making only one brief comment and moving on, say what you have to say and then go back over the statement and explain what you mean or why you said it or note other alternatives. Let the writer know again and again how you are understanding her paper, what you take her to be saying. And elaborate on your key comments. Explain your interpretations, problems, questions, and advice.

IS IT OKAY TO BE SHORT AND SWEET?

No. At least not most of the time. Get specific. Don't rely on general statements 10 alone. How much have generic comments helped you as a writer? "Add detail." "Needs better structure." "Unclear." Try to let the writer know what exactly the problem is. Refer specifically to the writer's words and make them a part of your comments. "Add some detail on what it was like working at the beach." "I think we'll need to know more about your high school crowd before we can understand the way you've changed." "This sentence is not clear. Were *you* disappointed or were *they* disappointed?" This way the writer will see what you're talking about, and she'll have a better idea what to work on.

DO YOU PRAISE OR CRITICIZE OR WHAT?

Be always of two (or three) minds about your response to the paper. You like the 11 paper, but it could use some more interesting detail. You found this statement interesting, but these ideas in the second paragraph are not so hot. It's an alright paper, but it could be outstanding if the writer said what was really bothering her. Always be ready to praise. But always look to point to places that are not working well or that are not yet working as well as they might. Always be ready to expect more from the writer.

HOW TO PRESENT YOUR COMMENTS?

Don't steer away from being critical. Feel free—in fact, feel obliged—to tell 12 the writer what you like and don't like, what is and is not working, and where you think it can be made to work better. But use some other strategies, too.

Try to engage the writer in considering her choices and thinking about possible ways to improve the paper. Make it a goal to write two or three comments that look to summarize or paraphrase what the writer is saying. Instead of *telling* the reader what to do, *suggest* what she might do. Identify the questions that are raised for you as you the reader:

- Play back your way of understanding the writing:
    This seems to be the real focus of the paper, the issue you seem most interested in.
    So you're saying that you really weren't interested in her romantically?

- Temper your criticisms:
    This sentence is a bit hard to follow.
    I'm not sure this paragraph is necessary.

- Offer advice:
    It might help to add an example here.
    Maybe save this sentence for the end of the paper.

- Ask questions, especially real questions:
    What else were you feeling at the time?
    What kind of friend? Would it help to say?
    Do you need this opening sentence?
    In what ways were you "daddy's little girl"?

- Explain and follow up on your initial comments:
    You might present this episode first. This way we can see what you mean when you say that he was always too busy.
    How did you react? Did you cry or yell? Did you walk away?
    This makes her sound cold and calculating. Is that what you want?

- Offer some praise, and then explain to the writer why the writing works:
    Good opening paragraph. You've got my attention.
    Good detail. It tells me a lot about the place.
    I like the descriptions you provide—for instance, about your grandmother cooking, at the bottom of page 1; about her house, in the middle of page 2; and about how she said her rosary at night: "quick but almost pleading, like crying without tears."

HOW MUCH CRITICISM? HOW MUCH PRAISE?

Challenge yourself to write as many praise comments as criticisms. When you 13 praise, praise well. Think about it. Sincerity and specificity are everything when it comes to a compliment.

HOW MUCH SHOULD YOU BE INFLUENCED
BY WHAT YOU KNOW ABOUT THE WRITER?

Consider the person behind the writer when you make your comments. If 14
she's not done so well in class lately, maybe you can give her a pick-me-up in
your comments. If she's shy and seems reluctant to go into the kind of personal detail the paper seems to need, encourage her. Make some suggestions
or tell her what you would do. If she's confident and going on arrogant, see
what you can do to challenge her with the ideas she presents in the paper.
Look for other views she may not have thought about, and find ways to lead
her to consider them. Always be ready to look at the text in terms of the
writer behind the text.

Good comments, this listing shows, require a lot from a reader. But you 15
don't have to make a checklist out of these suggestions and go through each one
methodically as you read. It's amazing how they all start coming together when
you look at your response as a way of talking with the writer seriously about
the writing, recording how you experience the words on the page and giving
the writer something to think about for revision. The more you see examples of
thoughtful commentary and the more you try to do it yourself, the more you'll
get a feel for how it's done.

Here's a set of student comments on a student paper. They were done 16
in the last third of a course that focused on the personal essay and concentrated on helping students develop the content and thought of their writing. The class had been working on finding ways to develop and extend the
key statements of their essays (by using short, representative details, full-
blown examples, dialogue, and multiple perspectives) and getting more
careful about selecting and shaping parts of their writing. The assignment
called on students to write an essay or an autobiographical story where
they looked to capture how they see (or have seen) something about one
or both of their parents — some habits, attitudes, or traits their parents
have taken on. They were encouraged to give shape to their ideas and experiences in ways that went beyond their previous understandings and try
things they hadn't tried in their writing. More a personal narrative than an
essay, Todd's paper looks to capture one distinct difference in the way his
mother and father disciplined their children. It is a rough draft that will
be taken through one or possibly two more revisions. Readers were asked
to offer whatever feedback they could that might help the writer with the
next stage of writing (Figure 1).

This is a full and thoughtful set of comments. The responder, Jeremy, 17
creates himself not as a teacher or critic but first of all as a reader, one who

Figure 1

Jeremy
Todd
ENG 1
Rick Straub
Assign 8b

"Uh, oh"

When I called home from the police station I was praying that my father would answer the phone. He would listen to what I had to say and would react comely, logical, and in a manner that would keep my mother from screaming her head off. If my Mother was to answer the phone, I would have to explain myself quickly in order to keep her from having a heart attached.

I like this paragraph. It immediately lets the reader relate to you and also produces a picture in the reader's mind

When I was eleven years old I hung out with a group of boys that were almost three years older than me. The five of us did all the things that young energetic kids did playing ball, riding bikes, and getting in to trouble. [Because they were older they worried less about getting in trouble and the consequences of there actions than I did.]

Good point, makes it more unlikely that you should be the one to get caught

My friends and I would always come home from school, drop our backpacks off and head out in the neighborhood to find something to do. Our favorite thing to do was to find construction cites and steal wood to make tree forts in the woods or skateboard ramps. So one day, coming home from school, we noticed a couple new houses being built near our neighborhood. It was a prime cite for wood, nails, and anything else we could get our hands on. We discussed our plan on the bus and decided that we would all meet there after dropping our stuff off at home. [I remember being a little at hesitant first because it was close to my house but beyond the boundaries my parents had set for me. Of course I went because I didn't want to be the odd man out and have to put up with all the name calling.] I dropped my bag off and I headed to the construction cite.

What other things did you do to get into trouble? Or is it irrelevant?

great passage really lets the reader know what you were thinking

I meet my friends there and we began to search the different houses for wood and what not. We all picked up a couple of things and were about to leave when one of my friends noticed what looked to be a big tool shed off behind of the houses. It looked promising so we decided that we should check it out. Two of the boys in the group said that they had all the wood they could carry and said they were going home. The rest of us headed down to the shed to take a look.

was there a reason you were there first or did it just happen that way

Once there we noticed that the shed had been broken in to previously. The lock on it had been busted on the hinges were bent. I opened the door to the shed and stepped inside to take a look around while my friends waited outside. It was dark inside but I could tell the place had been ransacked, there was nothing to take so I decided to leave. I heard my friends say something so turned back around to site of them running away.

(continued)

is intent on saying how he takes the writing and what he'd like to hear more about:

> Good point. Makes it more unlikely that you should be the one to get caught. Great passage. Really lets the reader know what you were thinking. Was there a reason you were first or did it just happen that way? Would he punish you anyway or could you just get away with things?

He makes twenty-two comments on the paper—seventeen statements in the margins and five more in the end note. The comments are written out in full statements, and they are detailed and specific. They make his response into a lively exchange with the writer, one person talking with another about what

18

(continued)

Figure 1

I thought that they were playing a joke on me so I casually walked out only to see a cop car parked near one of the houses under construction. As soon as I saw that cop car I took off but was stopped when a big hand pulled at the back of my shirt. I watched my friends run until they were out of cite and then I turned around.

The cop had me sit in the cop car while he asked my questions. He asked me if I know those kids that ran off and I said "Nnnnnooooooooo". He asked me if I had broken into that shed and I said "Nnnnnoooooo". The cop wrote down what I was saying all the while shaking his head. Then he told me that I wasn't being arrested but I would have to go down to the station to call parents and have them pick me up. Upon hearing that I nearly soiled my undershorts. "My God, I'm dead. My mom is going to kill me".

what else happened at the police station? how long were you there?

At the station the officer showed me the whole station, jail cells and everything. An obvious tactic to try and scare me, which worked. That plus the thought of my mom answering the phone and my trying to explain what happened nearly made me sick.

"Wwwwhhhaatttt! You're where?" She would say.

"The police station mom," uh oh, hear it comes.

"Ooooohhhh my God, my son is a criminal," so loud I would have to pull the phone away from my ear.

maybe you could say more as to why you think your mom is like this

She had this uncanny ability to blow things out of proportion right from the start. She would assume the worse and then go from there. This was a classic example of why I could never go to her if I had any bad news. She would start screaming, get upset, and then go bitch at my father. My father is a pretty laid back but when ever my mother started yelling at him about me, he would get angry and come chew me out worse than if I had just gone to him in the first place.

If my father were to answer the phone he would respond with out raising his voice. He would examine the situation in a logical manner and make a decision from there.

"Uhmmm (long pause). You're at the police station."

"Yeah dad. I didn't get arrested they just had me come down here so I had to tell you."

Did your Dad get into trouble as a kid so he knows what it's like? Explain why he reacts as he does

"Uhm, so you didn't get arrested (long pause). Well (long pause), I'll come pick you up and will talk about then."

I feel like I can relate to my father much better than I can to my mother. He has a cool and collective voice that can take command of any situation. I always feel like he understands me, like he knows what I'm thinking all the time. This comes in real handy when I get in trouble.

would he punish you anyway or could you just get away with things

I like the way you use dialogue in this section to illustrate how each of your parents would react and then explain to the reader what each of them are like, it works well.

(continued)

---

he's said. Well over half of the comments are follow-up comments that explain, illustrate, or qualify other responses.

The comments focus on the content and development of the writing, in line with the assignment, the stage of drafting, and the work of the course. They also view the writing rhetorically, in terms of how the text has certain effects on readers. Although there are over two dozen wording or sentence-level errors in the paper, he decides, wisely, to stick with the larger matters of writing. Yet even as he offers a pretty full set of comments he doesn't ever take control over the text. His comments are placed unobtrusively on the page, and he doesn't try to close things down or decide things for the writer. He offers (*continued*)   **Figure 1**

I called home. Sweet beading on my lip.

"Hello," my mom said. Oh geez, I'm dead.

"Mom can I talk to dad?"

"Why, what's wrong?"

"Oh, nothing, I just need to talk to him," yes, this is going to work!

"Hold on," she said.

"Hello," my father said.

"Dad, I'm at the police station," I told him the whole story of what happened. He reacted exactly as I expect he would.

"Uhmm (long pause). You're at the police station...........

I really like the ending, it tells the reader what is going to happen without having to explain it step, by step. Good paper, I like the use of dialogue. Perhaps more on your understanding of why your parents react as they do.

praise, encouragement, and direction. What's more, he pushes the writer to do more than he has already done, to extend the boundaries of his examination. In keeping with the assignment and the larger goals of the course, he calls on Todd in several comments to explore the motivations and personalities behind his parents' different ways of disciplining:

> Maybe you could say more as to why you think your mom is like this. Did your dad get into trouble as a kid so he knows what it's like? Explain why he reacts as he does.

He is careful, though, not to get presumptuous and make decisions for the writer. Instead, he offers options and points to possibilities:

> Perhaps more on your understanding of why your parents react as they do.
> What other things did you do to get into trouble? Or is it irrelevant?

From start to finish he takes on the task of reading and responding and leaves the work of writing and revising to Todd.

Jeremy's response is not in a class by itself. A set of comments to end all commentary on Todd's paper. He might have done well, for instance, to recognize how much this paper works because of the way Todd arranges the story. He could have done more to point to what's not working in the writing or what could be made to work better. He might have asked Todd for more details about his state of mind when he got caught by the policeman and while he was being held at the police station. He might have urged him more to make certain changes. He might even have said, if only in a brief warning, something about the number of errors across the writing. But this is moot and just. Different readers are always going to pick up on different things and respond in different ways, and no one reading or response is going to address everything that

20

227

might well be addressed, in the way it might best be addressed. All responses are incomplete and provisional—one reader's way of reading and reacting to the text in front of him. And any number of other responses, presented in any number of different ways, might be as useful or maybe even more useful to Todd as he takes up his work with the writing.

All this notwithstanding, Jeremy's comments are solid. They are full. They are thoughtful. And they are respectful. They take the writing and the writer seriously and address the issues that are raised responsibly. His comments do what commentary on student writing should optimally do. They turn the writer back into his writing and lead him to reflect on his choices and aims, to consider and reconsider his intentions as a writer and the effects the words on the page will have on readers. They help him see what he can work on in revision and what he might deal with in his ongoing work as a writer.

21

- -

Questions for Discussion and Journaling

1. Straub advocates that readers see themselves *as readers* rather than as writers of what they're reading, so that "you're there to play back to the writer how you read the paper" (para. 4). What are some ways readers can "play back" their experience of reading a piece to its writer?

2. A very common concern students have with peer response is that they're being asked to help another student write well for an assignment when the peer responders might not understand the assignment very well themselves. What advice does Straub offer that can help address this difficulty?

3. What does Straub mean when he writes "you're not a cruise missile" (para. 4)? What are some better metaphors for what you are, as a responder to others' writing?

4. If you've done peer-responding (or received peer response) before, it's likely you've had mixed experiences (both good and bad) with it. If there have been times peer response hasn't worked well for you, do you think following Straub's advice in this chapter would address the reasons it didn't go well? In your experiences, have there been difficulties with peer response that Straub *doesn't* discuss here? If so, what are they?

Applying and Exploring Ideas

1. Imagine yourself writing a tremendously important text — an application essay for a full-ride scholarship, a statement of support for a child-custody claim, a legal defense, or a letter to a dying relative from whom you've been estranged — something important that you *really want help* with. Write a paragraph about what kind of help you want. If a friend could read a draft, how would you want

them to respond and talk with you about it? If the situation were reversed and your friend had written this kind of text, what are some ways you could try to respond helpfully? Write your ideas as a list of five to eight items detailing "how to respond effectively to your friend's ideas."

2. Straub's piece was published in 2005, just as writing courses were beginning to assign multimodal projects (such as those discussed by DePalma and Poe earlier in this chapter). But Straub doesn't seem to be thinking beyond traditional paper-based essays in giving his advice on responding. Write down five of Straub suggestions for responding to drafts, and then imagine yourself giving feedback on a fellow student's website or short video. How would you modify Straub's advice in order to give good feedback on such texts?

3. Team up with two friends or classmates to make a two-minute video demonstrating your ideas of what it looks like to give helpful responses to other people's writing. To make this more fun, you might start with a short segment showing what happens when peer response goes badly.

- -

META MOMENT   After you leave school and are responding to other people's writing in workplaces and other settings, what are some approaches you would like to use?

- -

Writing about Processes

Assignment Option 1

AUTOETHNOGRAPHY

For this assignment, you will conduct a study similar to those conducted by Perl and Berkenkotter, but instead of looking at someone else, you will examine yourself and your own writing processes and write an **autoethnography** in which you describe them. Your method will be to record (preferably with video and audio) your complete writing process as you complete a writing assignment for a class. Your purpose is to try to learn some things about your actual writing practices that you might not be aware of and to reflect on what you learn using the terms and concepts you've read about in this chapter.

Determining Your Object of Study and Collecting Data   To make this assignment as useful as possible, you need to plan ahead, so figure out what you will be writing for this or other classes in the next few weeks, and make a decision about what you will study. Consider the following:

- What kinds of assignments are easiest or most difficult for you to write?
- What kinds of assignments would be the most useful to examine yourself writing?

Before beginning your project, make sure that you know how to use your computer or other device's audio and / or video recording programs.

As you write the assignment that you will study, record yourself every time that you work on it — this includes even times when you are thinking and planning for it, or when you are revising. Keep the following in mind:

- You may not be near your recording device(s) when you are planning; if that is the case, then keep a log in which you note your thoughts about the assignment.
- When you sit down to type the paper, think out loud the entire time. This will feel strange, and it will take some effort. Do your best.
- Try to externalize everything you are thinking. If you have trouble knowing what to say, go back to Perl and to Berkenkotter and look at the kinds of things that Tony and Donald Murray said aloud when they were being studied.

When you have completely finished the writing process for your assignment, listen to or view the recording of yourself and transcribe it. This means typing everything that you said on the tape, even the "ums" and "ahs." It will be helpful to double space (or even triple space) the transcript so that you can make notes on it, if you plan to do so by hand. You might also find Track Changes or its equivalent useful for note-taking as you transcribe.

Analyzing Your Data   Alone or with your class, as your teacher directs, come up with a code to help you study your transcript. To see how to make a code, return to Berkenkotter or Perl for their descriptions of how they came up with their codes. To consider what categories or elements of the writing process you might want to include in your code, look back through the readings you've done in this chapter. What did the various authors choose to study about people's writing processes? Some suggestions for things you might include would be notes about context (where and when you wrote, what distractions you faced, your attitude, any deadlines, etc.), codes for planning, brainstorming, large-scale revision, small-scale revision, pausing, and so on.

What you want is a code that will help you understand what's happening when you write. Beware of the following potential pitfalls:

- If the code is too vague, you won't learn anything at all.
- If the code is too detailed (for example, if you try to do what Perl did and record the exact amount of time you took for each action), you might never get done coding.

We recommend coming up with a code with the rest of your class, and then trying to use that code on a practice transcript that your teacher provides. This will help you see if the code is useful.

Once you have settled on a code, use it to analyze your transcript.

- You might get a box of highlighters of different colors, and use each color to highlight the parts of the text that correspond to parts of the code (for example, pink is for planning).
- You could simply underline parts of the transcript and label them in shorthand (P = planning).
- If you used a computer, you could search for key phrases in the text and mark each occurrence by using the software's "reviewing" feature to insert a comment in the margin.
- You could use free or low-cost coding and data analysis software such as Dedoose to upload your transcript and label different parts of it with codes you input, which allows you to generate helpful visualizations of how your various codes interact with the data.

Once you have coded the transcript, go back and consider these questions:

- What is interesting about what you found? What immediately jumps out at you?
- Did you do some things a lot and other things rarely or never? Which codes do you see frequently or little at all?
- How does your analysis suggest you compare with Tony or with Murray?

Like some of the authors in this chapter, you might make some charts or tables for yourself in order to visually explore what percentage of time you spent on various activities.

Planning and Drafting   What are you going to write about? You don't need to go into excruciating detail about everything you coded. Instead, you should decide what you want to claim about what you found. For example:

- How would you describe your writing process?
- What are the most important take-home points from your analysis?
- Are there aspects of your process that are definitively impacted by technologies like instant messaging, social networking, Skype, or even word-processing?

Based on the patterns that emerge from your analysis of data, decide what your claims will be and then return to your analysis to select data that give evidence of those claims.

By now, from discussions in class and with your teacher you should have a sense of what genre you'll write your report in, and in deciding that, you should know your audience, purpose, and exigence as well. Will you write about your findings in an informal reflective essay in which you discuss your process and compare yourself to some of the writers in the chapter or write a more formal, researched argument like Perl or Berkenkotter did, using an intro / background / methods / analysis / discussion structure? Or are you inspired by DePalma and Poe to try your hand at a multimodal essay?

You'll definitely want to plan your genre before you begin drafting, since your drafting processes will vary by genre. If you are writing the reflective essay, you are most likely writing for yourself (writing to learn) and to share what you learn with fellow student writers and your teacher, for the purpose of improving your writing processes and abilities. Such reflection is often best "drafted toward" by knowing the main claims you want to make and striking out on your writing, understanding that you'll be discovering and learning along the way and will probably revise extensively in order to reach a consistent message from beginning to ending of your piece.

If you will be writing a more scholarly research article, you might begin by outlining the various sections of your paper: In your introduction, what other research will you cite? Whose work provides important background information for your study? What is the gap or niche that your study fills? How will you describe your research methods? What are the main claims you want to make in the findings? One trick that some writers use is to write headings for each section, with main claims underneath. Then the writer can go back and write one section at a time in order to break up the writing.

Once you have a "shitty first draft," revise it to make it a little more coherent. Then share it with classmates, being sure to tell them what genre you wrote and what concerns or issues you'd like them to read for.

What Makes It Good? The purpose of this assignment was for you to try to learn some things about your actual writing practices that you might not have been aware of, and to reflect on what you learned using the terms and concepts you've read about in this chapter. Does your text demonstrate that this purpose was achieved? In addition, your readers will want to learn something from having read your paper. Does your finished text clearly convey your insights and findings?

A caveat: We have found that some students just go through the motions when they complete this assignment, but don't make an attempt to learn something about themselves as writers. When those students write their papers, they have very little to say about "results" or "insights." They tend to say pretty clichéd things like "I am distracted when I write. I should try to write with fewer distractions." In general, if the "insights" of the paper were obvious to you before you ever conducted the autoethnography, then you have not fully engaged in the project and are unlikely to receive a good grade on it.

Alternative Assignment Instead of studying yourself writing one assignment, compare yourself writing two very different kinds of texts (maybe in school and out of school, or humanities and science) and analyze them to see whether — or how — your process changes depending on what you're writing.

- -

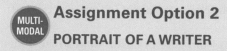

Assignment Option 2

PORTRAIT OF A WRITER

The various authors in this chapter clearly believe that good writing takes hard work and multiple drafts, and that many of us are hampered from being better writers by the "rules" and misconceptions we have been taught about writing.

This is true even of very famous people who write a lot every day. For example, U.S. Supreme Court Justice Sonia Sotomayor has been widely criticized for her writing. She even criticizes herself, saying, "Writing remains a challenge for me even today — everything I write goes through multiple drafts — I am not a natural writer."[1] Here she conflates being a "good" writer with being a "natural" writer; she seems to believe that some people are born good writers and some people aren't. Her conception is that a "good" writer only has to write one draft; anyone who has to write multiple drafts must be a "bad" writer. Even from this one short quotation, you can see that Justice Sotomayor's conceptions of writing are limiting and would not hold up if closely examined by the researchers and professional writers in this chapter.

Use what you have read in this unit to consider the story you have to tell about yourself as a writer. How do you see yourself as a writer? Is that self-perception helping you be the best writer you can be? The purpose of this assignment is for you

---

[1]Gerstein, Josh. "Sotomayor: Writing a Challenge 'Even Today.'" *POLITICO*, 4 June 2009, www.politico.com/blogs/under-the-radar/2009/06/sotomayor-writing-a-challenge-even -today-018902.

to apply what you have learned in this chapter to help you better understand why and how you write — and how you might write differently.

Brainstorming and Planning Try the following to generate material for your assignment:

- Go back to the discussion and activity questions you completed as you read the articles in this chapter. What did you learn about yourself and your writing processes here?
- Consider what you write and don't write.
- Consider how you prepare — or don't prepare — to write a paper.
- Think of any kinds of writing that you enjoy and any kinds of writing that you dread.
- Free-write about the writing rules that block you and the writing rules that aid you.
- Make a list of all the metaphors or similes about writing and revision that you and your friends use.

You should spend a substantial amount of time reflecting on yourself as a writer, using the concepts and ideas that you learned in this chapter. Even if some or most of your brainstorming doesn't end up in your paper, the act of reflecting should be useful to you as a writer.

Looking at all the notes and free-writing from your brainstorming so far, consider what's interesting here. What catches your interest the most? What is new or surprising to you? Settle on a few of these surprises or "aha!" moments as the core of what you will write for this assignment. For each of these core elements of your essay, brainstorm examples, details, and explanations that would help your reader understand what you are trying to explain about yourself.

Creating an Essay Write a three- to five-page essay in which you describe your view of yourself as a writer, using examples and explanations to strengthen your description. As appropriate, you might refer to the authors of texts in this chapter to help explain your experiences, processes, or feelings. Conclude the essay by considering how or whether the things you've learned in this chapter might change your conception of yourself as a writer or your writing behaviors. Your class should discuss potential audiences for this essay:

- Are you writing to the teacher, to demonstrate what you've learned in this chapter?
- Are you writing for yourself, to help solidify what you've learned?
- Would you like to adapt your essay to write for someone else — maybe your parents, to demonstrate who you are as a writer and what influences you can identify? Maybe to a teacher who had an impact, positive or negative, on who you are as a writer?

Of course, this choice of audience and purpose will have a significant impact on your essay — its form, content, tone, language, level of formality, and so on. You might also talk with your teacher about more creative ways to paint your self-portrait:

- Try writing a play outlining your writing process.

- Transform a metaphor about writing into a visual description — for example, a collage — of who you are as a writer or what you think "good writing" is.

- Create a hypertext essay where readers can look at pictures, watch video, listen to songs, even listen to your own voice, as you describe yourself and your conceptions of writers, the writing process, and "good writing."

Try to get readers for your piece as early in your composing process as possible, and use their feedback on their reading experience to revise for the most reader-friendly document possible. Pay particular attention to whether your readers seem to be experiencing all the ideas you want them to — or whether some of what you want to say is clear in your thoughts but not in what you've composed.

Creating a Multimodal Project   Instead of writing the traditional print / alphabetic essay described above, use other modes available to you in order to share your portrait. What could your project be? Options are endless, but could include collage, video, podcast, scrapbook, map, or other projects. If you choose this option, you and your teacher and classmates should discuss in detail your audience, purpose, and the resources available to you. Consider what DePalma and Poe demonstrated about some of the challenges students face when drafting multimodal texts, and be willing to experiment and accept an imperfect final product. You'll probably find a multimodal project takes much more time to complete than a traditional essay, but you'll also likely find that it allows you to illustrate ideas in ways that an essay cannot.

What Makes It Good?   The purpose of this assignment is for you to step back and consider yourself as a writer, applying what you learned in this chapter to help you better understand why and how you write — and how you might write differently, or perhaps even understand yourself differently as a writer. When you've finished it, ask yourself:

- Were you able to apply what you learned in this chapter to understand yourself better? (If not, that will likely show up in the depth of your writing.)

- Did you successfully identify an audience for your piece and compose appropriately for those readers?

Assignment Option 3

MULTI-MODAL

ILLUSTRATING WRITERS' PROCESSES

The purpose of the project will be to discover what professional writers of various kinds have to say about an aspect of their writing processes that intrigues you, and what your own experiences of that aspect have been. To present your findings in ways that help readers visualize them, we suggest you create a poster, slide deck (such as in PowerPoint, Prezi, or similar), or map.

To create your process visualization, you'll need to specify a research question about writing processes, search archives of interviews of writers talking about their processes in order to select at least two other writers whose interviews speak to your research question, and examine your own writing processes for your personal responses to your research question. Then you'll need to decide how to verbally and visually organize your findings about an aspect of the writing process in a way that addresses your research question.

Create a Research Question on Writing Processes What would you like to know, that you don't already, about some aspect of writing processes? Review the readings you've done in this chapter, and read the preceding two assignment guides (Autoethnography and Writer's Portrait) to get a sense of some of the available questions on process. Consider as well the unanswered questions about process you brought into the class, and those that have arisen in your conversations with classmates and friends. Some sample questions that would work well for this project:

- How do writers *prepare* to write? What do they do before they start drafting, and how do they know when it's time to start drafting?

- Do writers do other activities (such as listen to music, watch TV, or eat) while they write?

- How does what they're writing about impact a writer's process? Do different subjects or genres require different processes? Do some subjects make writing more difficult than other subjects do?

- At what point do writers show their developing writing to other people? Who do they choose to show it to? How do writers use reader feedback to develop their pieces?

Researching Other Writers' Processes One of the most common questions asked of famous writers (journalists, essayists, novelists, poets, cultural commentators, sportswriters, etc.) is "how do you do it?" — that is, how do you write such good stuff? This is a process question, and frequently such writers are willing to try to explain their own approaches to writing. A number of archives have been created of such interviews. We suggest you search these archives in order to find the kinds of writers you're interested in featuring in your visualization, and in order to find discussion of the particular aspect of composing processes that you're interested in.

While many catalogs and archives of interviews exist (along with an even greater number of interviews locatable through a general web search), we suggest looking at these five:

The Paris Review, "Interviews," theparisreview.org/interviews

The Paris Review is a journal of literary writing (fiction, poetry, and essays) that also publishes some literary criticism. Since the mid-1950s it has run interviews with about a half-dozen contemporary writers every year. The site is searchable by author or by decade. This site often asks for a subscription to see full articles. Rather than buying a subscription, ask your librarian if they have access or can request interviews through interlibrary loan.

The New York Times — Books, "Writers on Writing," nytimes.com/books/specials/writers.html

In the *New York Times* column "Writers on Writing," writers provide short essays on a topic related to writing. The essays are thematic, such as, taking a break from writing in order to have more to say (Richard Ford), selecting music for writing (Edmund White), the relationship between writing and living (Gish Jen), how running assists writing (Joyce Carol Oates), or the role of rewriting in writing (Susan Sontag). In order to use this archive well, you'll need time to skim the opening of many essays, to see what the theme of each is. (They are only listed by author name.)

Songwriters on Process, songwritersonprocess.com

This website archives interviews with song-writing musicians. The interviews are conducted by site author Benjamin Opipari, who asks questions of the writers about "their creative process, from beginning to end." Opipari demonstrates an eclectic taste in music genres and interview subjects. Interviews focus on the processes by which songwriters get ideas for lyrics and music, and how they move those ideas along to become finished songs. The site is arranged by the name of the interviewee and their band, and access is open / free.

Writers on Writing, http://writersonwriting.blogspot.com/

A weekly radio program hosted by Barbara DeMarco-Barrett and Marrie Stone, *Writers on Writing* interviews writers on the art and business of writing. Aired on KUCI, audio of each show is archived at the blog above. In some cases, audio of full interviews with writers is also archived when the show itself edited the interview for length.

The New York Times, "Why I Write: Q & A with Seven Times Journalists," learning.blogs.nytimes.com/2011/10/17/why-i-write-q-and-a-with-seven-times -journalists/

This "Learning Network" blog post in the *New York Times* focused on a short list of journalists and asked each the same questions. Writers responded to questions on (among others) how they became a reporter, what outside forces influence their writing, what their writing process looks like, and why they write. The whole set of interviews can be read in about half an hour and is extremely valuable for seeing less famous but very professional writers talk in down-to-earth ways about how they experience writing.

Your Writing Process   While you do not need to complete a full autoethnography of your writing process in order to address the research question you're asking for your process visualization here, we do recommend that you read the autoethnography assignment guide (p. 230) to get a sense of how to carefully study your own experiences with the aspect of the writing process that your research question considers. We recommend writing a one- to three-page description detailing how the aspect of the writing process which you're studying appears in your own experiences with writing.

Comparing and Analyzing Your Data   Once you have a stack of interviews that relate to your subject of inquiry, analyze that data in the same way you do for many other projects in this book:

- Watch for patterns that emerge — what gets said repeatedly? — but also be prepared for there to be no pattern. If writers disagree or do things in wildly different ways, that is just as much a finding as discovering that there are similarities across writers. Writing is a very individual process, so finding a single pattern might be difficult. You might also see several patterns — people might do A, B, or C rather than mostly doing A.

- Watch for outliers: Is there something just one writer says? Is it striking or unusual in comparison to the emerging patterns?

- Look closely at details in language. When a writer refers to revision as "polishing" versus as "honing," for example, the terms engage different metaphors that show different assumptions about the nature of revision and how it works.

- Compare what you're reading with your own experience. What are these writers saying that sounds "normal" and what are they saying that sounds unusual to you?

Again, as in other projects requiring analysis of observations or a **corpus** of textual data, take careful notes to keep track of the patterns and interesting ideas you're seeing, and after you've reviewed your interviews at least twice, step back and see what you have to say on your question. Now might also be a good time to do more general web searching to see if other people have written and commented on the question you're working on.

Planning, Drafting, and Revising   Your process visualization should illustrate your comparison of an aspect of writers' processes and offer evidence for whatever findings you wish to present. This evidence might be, for example, specific quotations from interviews or counts of how often a given concept appears. Remember that what the interviewees said is your data, and your readers need to be able to see examples of your data in order to judge for themselves how much sense the conclusions that you're drawing from the data make. If your instructor has given you a choice of projects (a poster, a slide deck, a map, or something else) and you're not sure which to create, begin by assembling the materials you have to *show* the writers' processes. You might have created timelines of processes writers describe, or gathered images of the writing or the activity you're studying that illustrate what you've read, heard, or seen in interviews, gathered images of your own settings and scenes of writing, collected long or short quotations from the interviews that you want to set off as text blocks that stand out, or made diagrams or flowcharts of your own workflows. You might have material that lends itself to counting or data visualization (like a circle graph showing how much of a writer's total time is spend on revising). You might have audio of an interview that you wish to play, or even video of yourself writing that you want to embed in your piece. You might wish to graphically represent an aspect of process by drawings or images of something analogous to it — for example, maybe you wish to represent the aspect of process you studied in comparison to baking a cake or hiking up a mountain.

The material you have will guide the type of project to create. If you need to *embed audio or video*, a slide deck will likely be a better fit for your project than a poster. If you have comparisons that would be presented in three *side-by-side columns*, a poster might be ideal. If you want to show *pathways* or workflows through a project, a map might work best. Your decision should allow you to 1) state your research question, 2) describe the findings you wish to emphasize, and 3) visualize your findings and the data that support them.

Revise, as always, by getting reader feedback on how much sense the piece makes, how readable it is (in terms of flow and organization, clarity of statements of ideas, and editing quality), and what would improve their experience of the piece.

What Makes It Good?   The best versions of this project will do the following:

- Explain your research question and the sources of it precisely and clearly.
- Make a clear point or series of points about your subject of inquiry.
- Balance use of quotations as examples with analysis of them.
- Create an interesting, usable visualization of your arguments (research question, data, and findings) that helps make your points understandable and convincing to readers of your piece.

CHAPTER 5

LITERACIES
Threshold Concept: Writing Is Impacted by Identities and Prior Experiences

Mike Burley/Telegraph Herald/Associated Press

All of us have what Deborah Brandt will call "literacy sponsors." You see here a barber from Iowa who gave free back-to-school haircuts to kids who would read him a book. In this way, he helped them engage in and value reading, even if they hadn't found this same value at home.

If you are reading this textbook, you are a literate person. You went to school, learned to read and write, and were admitted to the college where you are now being asked to write new and different kinds of texts. Experts who study **literacy** typically think about more than the ability to read and write. They refer broadly to fluency or expertise in communicating and interacting with other people in many different ways. Thus, it's more accurate to speak about *literacies* when thinking about what it means to be a literate person.

This book asks you to think broadly about what it means to be literate. What is writing? What is reading? How do you communicate and compose? How have you been taught to engage with texts, and how has this influenced your understanding of writing and your relationship with writing? This chapter focuses on how individuals develop literacies and become literate learners. It asks you to think about what your literacies and your attitudes about literacies are, how they developed, how they influence one another, and who you are as a literate person. The purpose of doing so is to help you deeply engage with one of the *threshold concepts* we discussed in Chapter 1 — that our prior experiences deeply impact our writing and literacy practices.

In thinking about literacies, it might help you to start by considering your daily life. For example, every day you read and write all kinds of things that you probably rarely talk about in school and that you might not think about as literacy practices or forms of literacy: You check your Facebook account, you text friends, you Skype. You interpret thousands of visual images every time you turn on the television, read a magazine, or go to the mall. You also have literacies particular to your interests — you may know everything there is to know about a particular baseball player's RBIs, for example, or you may have advanced to an impressively high level in a complex, massively multiplayer online role-playing game like *World of Warcraft*. And, of course, you have home literacies that may be very different from school or hobby-related literacies. You may come from a family where languages other than English are spoken, or you may live in a community that values collaborative literacy practices (such as storytelling) that school often does not.

Researchers in the discipline of Writing Studies are particularly interested in these more complex ideas about literacy because they want to understand how people acquire literacies and what literacies a society should assist people in acquiring. Over the past decade, for example, we've seen a marked shift in public attitudes toward texting, from people believing it would be the death of writing (because, commentators worried, we might forget that *you* is not spelled *u* in formal writing) to a certain tolerance as texting has become ubiquitous while society as we know it has not crumbled around us. (As a result of texting, at least, though the jury's still out on Twitter.) With time, it's fairly likely that schools will move from banning texting to teaching it.

The readings in this chapter ask you to consider what counts as "literacy," how people become literate, how their prior experiences inform that literacy, how cultures support and value various forms of literacy, and how we use (or adapt and change) literacy practices across contexts (or what Chapter 7 will describe as *discourse communities*). Deborah Brandt's "Sponsors of Literacy" will provide some starting definitions of literacy and some questions about how we acquire the literacies that we do. All of the other readings in the chapter can be understood in some ways as demonstrating the ideas that Brandt talks about in her piece — literacy, access to literacy, and the power that literacy can provide. The excerpts from Sandra Cisneros's and Victor Villanueva's autobiographies are short but poignant examples of how an individual's family life, finances, race, home language and culture, gender, and similar experiences, identities, and influences impact lifelong literacies, access to education, economic status, and the like. Arthur Tejada et al., a group of students who were labeled as "remedial" writers, ask you to consider how labels influence who you believe you are and what you believe you can do; they illustrate the power that institutions and teachers have in encouraging or discouraging students from all backgrounds to embrace their literacy and language practices. Joseph Williams then opens the question of what counts as error in language and which readers notice which writers' errors, furthering Tejada et al.'s discussion of the power of labels in perceptions of language use. In two other selections, Vershawn Ashanti Young and Barbara Mellix specifically ask you to consider language use and how and why various forms of English are valued differently — and how those values affect writers. The chapter closes with Julie Wan's literacy narrative (written in response to one of this chapter's main assignments) illustrating how identity and literacy experiences shape one another and how both shape writing experiences.

Pieces like Wan's, Mellix's, and Villanueva's will also help you think about how people use what they have learned in one setting when they are interacting in another setting — ways that our identities and experiences inform what we write, how we write, and how we think of things to write in the first place. This threshold concept is important for a number of reasons related to what scholars might talk about as agency, or having the ability to take some ownership over your experiences and decide what they mean and how you want to value them. As you'll see in several readings in this chapter, the experiences we have growing up, especially our formal education, can leave us with many ideas that are other people's but not ours — about what we should read, or how we should sound, or what counts as good writing or whether our accents or language use are more or less "valuable" as determined by our larger culture. Reflecting on the threshold concept of this chapter can prompt us to examine what we value or dismiss in our own experiences, abilities, values, and literacy practices; we can ask whether we are taking on other people's — our culture's — ideas about ourselves and whether we want to accept or reject those ideas. We are never completely in control of our experiences, but we can gain some greater control over our *understanding* of them and of ourselves as we reflect on conceptions of writing, literacy, and language; where these ideas came from and who decides what is valuable; and which ideas we want to retain or transform going forward.

Before you begin reading, take a few minutes to consider how you became the literate person you are today. No two people have exactly the same literacies, and yours are peculiar to your own personal history — your family, your geographic location, your culture, your hobbies, your religious training, your schooling, and so on. Consider, for example, the following questions:

- When and how did you learn to read?
- What did you read?
- Were there things you were not allowed to read?
- Where did you first or most memorably encounter texts as a child — for example, at home, at school, at a church or synagogue, at day care, at a friend's or relative's house?
- Did you write or draw as a child? Was this encouraged or discouraged?
- What languages or different forms of the same language did you speak at home and elsewhere?
- What technologies (from pencils to phones to social media platforms and computer software) impact your literacy practices?

Because your experiences have shaped your literacy practices — both what they are, and what they are not — your answers will not be the same as other people's. All of us were shaped by what Brandt calls **literacy sponsors** — people, ideas, or institutions that helped us become literate, but literate in specific ways. Students who attend private high schools instead of public school, for example, often have different literate experiences than public school students. As you reflect on your own experiences, consider both the texts you were exposed to and those you were not exposed to, or the ones that you were explicitly denied. When you learned to write, what motivated you to want to write? Who helped you — or did not? What kinds of things did you write, and for whom? As you grew older, did your interest in writing change? What factors impacted those changes — friends? teachers? parents? new hobbies?

This brief reflection on your literacy history should illustrate the point we are trying to make: You are a literate person; you are an expert on your own literacy practices and history; you have been shaped by many factors including home language(s), class, race, geographical location, and much more. You come to this chapter knowing a lot, and through the readings and activities you'll find here, we hope to help you uncover more of what you know, in addition to learning some things that you did not know before. We hope you will be able to see your past experiences living in your current experiences and draw on them in creative and useful ways. We hope you will consciously consider what it means to be literate (and who decides what "literate" means), and what it means to read and write in various contexts and cultures — and by so doing broaden your understandings in new ways.

CHAPTER GOALS

- Understand the threshold concept, *writing is impacted by identities and prior experiences.*
- Improve as a reader of complex, research-based texts.
- Acquire vocabulary for talking about literacies and your experiences as a writer.
- Come to greater awareness of the forces that have shaped you as a writer and reader.
- Consider how you use your literacy practices across different settings, what that means for you, and what it reveals about our culture at large.
- Understand ways of conducting contributive research and writing about literacy that can be shared with an audience.

Sponsors of Literacy

DEBORAH BRANDT

Framing the Reading

Deborah Brandt is a professor emerita in the Department of English at the University of Wisconsin–Madison. She has written several books about literacy, including *Literacy as Involvement: The Acts of Writers, Readers and Texts* (1990); *Literacy in American Lives* (2001); and *Literacy and Learning: Reading, Writing, Society* (2009). Her most recent book is *The Rise of Writing: Redefining Mass Literacy* (2015). She has also written a number of scholarly articles about literacy, including the one you are about to read here, "Sponsors of Literacy," which describes some of the data she collected when writing *Literacy in American Lives*. In that book, Brandt examined the way literacy learning changed between 1895 and 1985, noting that literacy standards have risen dramatically. In "Sponsors of Literacy" she discusses the forces that shape our literacy learning and practices.

Brandt's breakthrough idea in this piece is that people don't become literate on their own; rather, literacy is *sponsored* by people, institutions, and circumstances that both make it possible for a person to become literate and shape the way the person actually acquires literacy. And this is, of course, part of the threshold concept this chapter is emphasizing. In interviewing a large number of people from all ages and walks of life, Brandt began recognizing these **literacy sponsors** everywhere, and thus her article here (and the book her research led to) is crammed with examples, ranging from older siblings to auto manufacturers and World War II.

While we think of the term *sponsor* as suggesting support or assistance, Brandt doesn't confine her discussion to the supportive aspects of literacy sponsors. Her research shows ways in which, while opening some doors, literacy sponsors may close others: Their sponsorship is selective. Literacy sponsors are not always altruistic — they have self-interested reasons for sponsoring literacy, and very often only some kinds of literacy will support their goals. (If you've ever wondered why schools encourage you to read but seem less than thrilled if you'd rather read the *Hunger Games* series than Ernest Hemingway, Brandt's explanation of literacy sponsorship may provide an answer.) Brandt also discusses cases where people "misappropriate" a literacy sponsor's intentions by using a particular literacy for their own ends rather than for the sponsor's.

Brandt, Deborah. "Sponsors of Literacy." *College Composition and Communication*, vol. 49, no. 2, May 1998, pp. 165–85.

Brandt's portrayal of the tension between people and their literacy sponsors illustrates one more important point in thinking about literacy acquisition and how each of us has become literate. We claim in the chapter introduction that you have a combination of literacies that make you unique. While this is true, people also share many of the *same* literacy experiences. Brandt can help us understand this, too. Some literacy sponsors are organizations or institutions, such as a public school system or a major corporation, whose sponsorship affects large numbers of people. During the Middle Ages prior to the invention of the printing press, the biggest literacy sponsor in Western civilization was the Roman Catholic Church, which shaped the literacies of virtually every person in feudal Europe as well as vast native populations around the world. Remember, literacy sponsors are not necessarily empowering; they can also disempower and *prevent* people from becoming literate in some ways while fostering other literacies. "Big" literacy sponsors such as these have likely influenced your literacy narrative in the same way they've influenced many others, giving you something in common with others around you even as your particular literacies are unique to you.

Getting Ready to Read

Before you read, do at least one of the following activities:

- Compare notes with a roommate or friend about what your school literacy experience was like. What books did the school encourage you to read and discourage you from reading? What events and activities supported reading?
- Make a list of the ways you've seen U.S. culture and your own local community encourage and emphasize reading. What are the reasons usually given for being a good reader and writer, and who gives those reasons?

As you read, consider the following questions:

- What are Brandt's primary terms, in addition to *literacy sponsor*, and how do they apply to you?
- Where do you see yourself in the examples Brandt gives, and where do you not? Keep your early literacy experiences in mind as you read.
- What are some implications of Brandt's idea of literacy sponsors for your education *right now* as a college student?

IN HIS SWEEPING HISTORY of adult learning in the United States, Joseph 1
Kett describes the intellectual atmosphere available to young apprentices who worked in the small, decentralized print shops of antebellum America. Because printers also were the solicitors and editors of what they published, their workshops served as lively incubators for literacy and political discourse. By the

mid-nineteenth century, however, this learning space was disrupted when the invention of the steam press reorganized the economy of the print industry. Steam presses were so expensive that they required capital outlays beyond the means of many printers. As a result, print jobs were outsourced, the processes of editing and printing were split, and, in tight competition, print apprentices became low-paid mechanics with no more access to the multi-skilled environment of the craft-shop (Kett 67–70). While this shift in working conditions may be evidence of the deskilling of workers induced by the Industrial Revolution (Nicholas and Nicholas), it also offers a site for reflecting upon the dynamic sources of literacy and literacy learning. The reading and writing skills of print apprentices in this period were the achievements not simply of teachers and learners nor of the discourse practices of the printer community. Rather, these skills existed fragilely, contingently within an economic moment. The pre-steam press economy enabled some of the most basic aspects of the apprentices' literacy, especially their access to material production and the public meaning or worth of their skills. Paradoxically, even as the steam-powered penny press made print more accessible (by making publishing more profitable), it brought an end to a particular form of literacy sponsorship and a drop in literate potential.

The apprentices' experience invites rumination upon literacy learning and teaching today. Literacy looms as one of the great engines of profit and competitive advantage in the 20th century: a lubricant for consumer desire; a means for integrating corporate markets; a foundation for the deployment of weapons and other technology; a raw material in the mass production of information. As ordinary citizens have been compelled into these economies, their reading and writing skills have grown sharply more central to the everyday trade of information and goods as well as to the pursuit of education, employment, civil rights, status. At the same time, people's literate skills have grown vulnerable to unprecedented turbulence in their economic value, as conditions, forms, and standards of literacy achievement seem to shift with almost every new generation of learners. How are we to understand the vicissitudes of individual literacy development in relationship to the large-scale economic forces that set the routes and determine the worldly worth of that literacy? 2

The field of writing studies has had much to say about individual literacy development. Especially in the last quarter of the 20th century, we have theorized, researched, critiqued, debated, and sometimes even managed to enhance the literate potentials of ordinary citizens as they have tried to cope with life as they find it. Less easily and certainly less steadily have we been able to relate what we see, study, and do to these larger contexts of profit making and competition. This even as we recognize that the most pressing issues we deal with — tightening associations between literate skill and social viability, the breakneck pace of change in communications technology, persistent inequities in access and 3 reward — all relate to structural conditions in literacy's bigger picture. When economic forces are addressed in our work, they appear primarily as generalities: contexts, determinants, motivators, barriers, touchstones. But rarely are they systematically related to the local conditions and embodied moments of literacy learning that occupy so many of us on a daily basis.[1]

This essay does not presume to overcome the analytical failure completely. 4 But it does offer a conceptual approach that begins to connect literacy as an individual development to literacy as an economic development, at least as the two have played out over the last ninety years or so. The approach is through what I call sponsors of literacy. Sponsors, as I have come to think of them, are any agents, local or distant, concrete or abstract, who enable, support, teach, model, as well as recruit, regulate, suppress, or withhold literacy — and gain advantage by it in some way. Just as the ages of radio and television accustom us to having programs *brought* to us by various commercial sponsors, it is useful to think about who or what underwrites occasions of literacy learning and use. Although the interests of the sponsor and the sponsored do not have to converge (and, in fact, may conflict) sponsors nevertheless set the terms for access to literacy and wield powerful incentives for compliance and loyalty. Sponsors are a tangible reminder that literacy learning throughout history has always required permission, sanction, assistance, coercion, or, at minimum, contact with existing trade routes. Sponsors are delivery systems for the economies of literacy, the means by which these forces present themselves to — and through — individual learners. They also represent the causes into which people's literacy usually gets recruited.[2]

For the last five years I have been tracing sponsors of literacy across the 20th 5 century as they appear in the accounts of ordinary Americans recalling how they learned to write and read. The investigation is grounded in more than 100 in-depth interviews that I collected from a diverse group of people born roughly between 1900 and 1980. In the interviews, people explored in great detail their memories of learning to read and write across their lifetimes, focusing especially on the people, institutions, materials, and motivations involved in the process. The more I worked with these accounts, the more I came to realize that they were filled with references to sponsors, both explicit and latent, who appeared in formative roles at the scenes of literacy learning. Patterns of sponsorship became an illuminating site through which to track the different cultural attitudes people developed toward writing vs. reading as well as the ideological congestion faced by late-century literacy learners as their sponsors proliferated and diversified (see my essays on "Remembering Reading" and "Accumulating Literacy"). In this essay I set out a case for why the concept of sponsorship is so richly suggestive for exploring economies of literacy and their effects. Then, through use of extended case examples, I demonstrate the practical application of this approach for interpreting current conditions of literacy teaching and learning, including persistent stratification of opportunity and escalating standards for literacy achievement. A final section addresses implications for the teaching of writing.

SPONSORSHIP

Intuitively, *sponsors* seemed a fitting term for the figures who turned up most typically in people's memories of literacy learning: older relatives, teachers, priests, supervisors, military officers, editors, influential authors. Sponsors, as we ordinarily think of them, are powerful figures who bankroll events or smooth the way for initiates. Usually richer, more knowledgeable, and more entrenched than the sponsored, sponsors nevertheless enter a reciprocal relationship with those they underwrite. They lend their resources or credibility to the sponsored but also stand to gain benefits from their success, whether by direct repayment or, indirectly, by credit of association. *Sponsors* also proved an appealing term in my analysis because of all the commercial references that appeared in these 20th-century accounts — the magazines, peddled encyclopedias, essay contests, radio and television programs, toys, fan clubs, writing tools, and so on, from which so much experience with literacy was derived. As the 20th century turned the abilities to read and write into widely exploitable resources, commercial sponsorship abounded.

In whatever form, sponsors deliver the ideological freight that must be borne for access to what they have. Of course, the sponsored can be oblivious to or innovative with this ideological burden. Like Little Leaguers who wear the logo of a local insurance agency on their uniforms, not out of a concern for enhancing the agency's image but as a means for getting to play ball, people throughout history have acquired literacy pragmatically under the banner of others' causes. In the days before free, public schooling in England, Protestant Sunday Schools warily offered basic reading instruction to working-class families as part of evangelical duty. To the horror of many in the church sponsorship, these families insistently, sometimes riotously demanded of their Sunday Schools more instruction, including in writing and math, because it provided means for upward mobility.[3] Through the sponsorship of Baptist and Methodist ministries, African Americans in slavery taught each other to understand the Bible in subversively liberatory ways. Under a conservative regime, they developed forms of critical literacy that sustained religious, educational, and political movements both before and after emancipation (Cornelius). Most of the time, however, literacy takes its shape from the interests of its sponsors. And, as we will see below, obligations toward one's sponsors run deep, affecting what, why, and how people write and read.

> *Obligations toward one's sponsors run deep, affecting what, why, and how people write and read.*

The concept of sponsors helps to explain, then, a range of human rela- 8
tionships and ideological pressures that turn up at the scenes of literacy learning—from benign sharing between adults and youths, to euphemized coercions
in schools and workplaces, to the most notorious impositions and deprivations
by church or state. It also is a concept useful for tracking literacy's material: the
things that accompany writing and reading and the ways they are manufactured and distributed. Sponsorship as a sociological term is even more broadly
suggestive for thinking about economies of literacy development. Studies of
patronage in Europe and *compadrazgo* in the Americas show how patron-client
relationships in the past grew up around the need to manage scarce resources
and promote political stability (Bourne; Lynch; Horstman and Kurtz). Pragmatic, instrumental, ambivalent, patron-client relationships integrated otherwise antagonistic social classes into relationships of mutual, albeit unequal
dependencies. Loaning land, money, protection, and other favors allowed the
politically powerful to extend their influence and justify their exploitation of
clients. Clients traded their labor and deference for access to opportunities for
themselves or their children and for leverage needed to improve their social
standing. Especially under conquest in Latin America, *compadrazgo* reintegrated
native societies badly fragmented by the diseases and other disruptions that followed foreign invasions. At the same time, this system was susceptible to its
own stresses, especially when patrons became clients themselves of still more
centralized or distant overlords, with all the shifts in loyalty and perspective that
entailed (Horstman and Kurtz 13–14).

In raising this association with formal systems of patronage, I do not wish to 9
overlook the very different economic, political, and educational systems within
which U.S. literacy has developed. But where we find the sponsoring of literacy, it will be useful to look for its function within larger political and economic arenas. Literacy, like land, is a valued commodity in this economy, a key
resource in gaining profit and edge. This value helps to explain, of course, the
lengths people will go to secure literacy for themselves or their children. But it
also explains why the powerful work so persistently to conscript and ration the
powers of literacy. The competition to harness literacy, to manage, measure,
teach, and exploit it, has intensified throughout the century. It is vital to pay
attention to this development because it largely sets the terms for individuals'
encounters with literacy. This competition shapes the incentives and barriers
(including uneven distributions of opportunity) that greet literacy learners in
any particular time and place. It is this competition that has made access to the
right kinds of literacy sponsors so crucial for political and economic well-being.
And it also has spurred the rapid, complex changes that now make the pursuit
of literacy feel so turbulent and precarious for so many.

In the next three sections, I trace the dynamics of literacy sponsorship through 10
the life experiences of several individuals, showing how their opportunities for

literacy learning emerge out of the jockeying and skirmishing for economic and political advantage going on among sponsors of literacy. Along the way, the analysis addresses three key issues: (1) how, despite ostensible democracy in educational chances, stratification of opportunity continues to organize access and reward in literacy learning; (2) how sponsors contribute to what is called "the literacy crisis," that is, the perceived gap between rising standards for achievement and people's ability to meet them; and (3) how encounters with literacy sponsors, especially as they are configured at the end of the 20th century, can be sites for the innovative rerouting of resources into projects of self-development and social change.

SPONSORSHIP AND ACCESS

A focus on sponsorship can force a more explicit and substantive link between 11 literacy learning and systems of opportunity and access. A statistical correlation between high literacy achievement and high socioeconomic, majority-race status routinely shows up in results of national tests of reading and writing performance.[4] These findings capture yet, in their shorthand way, obscure the unequal conditions of literacy sponsorship that lie behind differential outcomes in academic performance. Throughout their lives, affluent people from high-caste racial groups have multiple and redundant contacts with powerful literacy sponsors as a routine part of their economic and political privileges. Poor people and those from low-caste racial groups have less consistent, less politically secured access to literacy sponsors — especially to the ones that can grease their way to academic and economic success. Differences in their performances are often attributed to family background (namely education and income of parents) or to particular norms and values operating within different ethnic groups or social classes. But in either case, much more is usually at work.

As a study in contrasts in sponsorship patterns and access to literacy, consider 12 the parallel experiences of Raymond Branch and Dora Lopez, both of whom were born in 1969 and, as young children, moved with their parents to the same, mid-sized university town in the midwest.[5] Both were still residing in this town at the time of our interviews in 1995. Raymond Branch, a European American, had been born in southern California, the son of a professor father and a real estate executive mother. He recalled that his first-grade classroom in 1975 was hooked up to a mainframe computer at Stanford University and that, as a youngster, he enjoyed fooling around with computer programming in the company of "real users" at his father's science lab. This process was not interrupted much when, in the late 1970s, his family moved to the midwest. Raymond received his first personal computer as a Christmas present from his parents when he was twelve years old, and a modem the year after that. In the 1980s, computer hardware and software stores began popping up within a bicycle-ride's distance from where he lived. The stores were serving the university community and, increasingly, the high-tech industries that were becoming established in that vicinity. As an adolescent, Raymond spent his summers roaming these stores, sampling new computer games, making contact with founders of some of the first electronic bulletin boards in the nation, and continuing, through reading and other informal means, to develop his programming techniques. At the time of our interview he had graduated from the local university and was a successful freelance writer of software and software documentation, with clients in both the private sector and the university community.

Dora Lopez, a Mexican American, was born in the same year as Raymond 13 Branch, 1969, in a Texas border town, where her grandparents, who worked as farm laborers, lived most of the year. When Dora was still a baby her family moved to the same midwest university town as had the family of Raymond Branch. Her father pursued an accounting degree at a local technical college and found work as a shipping and receiving clerk at the university. Her mother, who also attended technical college briefly, worked part-time in a bookstore. In the early 1970s, when the Lopez family made its move to the midwest, the Mexican-American population in the university town was barely one per cent. Dora recalled that the family had to drive seventy miles to a big city to find not only suitable groceries but also Spanish-language newspapers and magazines that carried information of concern and interest to them. (Only when reception was good could they catch Spanish-language radio programs coming from Chicago, 150 miles away.) During her adolescence, Dora Lopez undertook to teach herself how to read and write in Spanish, something, she said, that neither her brother nor her U.S.-born cousins knew how to do. Sometimes, with the help of her mother's employee discount at the bookstore, she sought out novels by South American and Mexican writers, and she practiced her written Spanish by corresponding with relatives in Colombia. She was exposed to computers for the first time at the age of thirteen when she worked as a teacher's aide in a federally-funded summer school program for the children of migrant workers. The computers were being used to help the children to be brought up to grade level in their reading and writing skills. When Dora was admitted to the same university that Raymond Branch attended, her father bought her a used word processing machine that a student had advertised for sale on a bulletin board in the building where Mr. Lopez worked. At the time of our interview, Dora Lopez had transferred from the university to a technical college. She was working for a cleaning company, where she performed extra duties as a translator, communicating on her supervisor's behalf with the largely Latina cleaning staff. "I write in Spanish for him, what he needs to be translated, like job duties, what he expects them to do, and I write lists for him in English and Spanish," she explained.

In Raymond Branch's account of his early literacy learning we are able to see 14 behind the scenes of his majority-race membership, male gender, and high-end socioeconomic family profile. There lies a thick and, to him, relatively accessible economy of institutional and commercial supports that cultivated and subsidized his acquisition of a powerful form of literacy. One might be tempted to say that Raymond Branch was born at the right time and lived in the right place — except that the experience of Dora Lopez troubles that thought. For Raymond Branch, a university town in the 1970s and 1980s provided an information-rich, resource-rich learning environment in which to pursue his literacy development, but for Dora Lopez, a female member of a culturally unsubsidized ethnic minority, the same town at the same time was information- and resource-poor. Interestingly, both young people were pursuing projects of self-initiated learning, Raymond Branch in computer programming and Dora Lopez in biliteracy. But she had to reach much further afield for the material and communicative systems needed to support her learning. Also, while Raymond Branch, as the son of an academic, was sponsored by some of the most powerful agents of the university (its laboratories, newest technologies, and most educated personnel), Dora Lopez was being sponsored by what her parents could pull from the peripheral service systems of the university (the mail room, the bookstore, the second-hand technology market). In these accounts we also can see how the development and eventual economic worth of Raymond Branch's literacy skills were underwritten by late-century transformations in communication technology that created a boomtown need for programmers and software writers. Dora Lopez's biliterate skills developed and paid off much further down the economic-reward ladder, in government-sponsored youth programs and commercial enterprises, that, in the 1990s, were absorbing surplus migrant workers into a low-wage, urban service economy.[6] Tracking patterns of literacy sponsorship, then, gets beyond SES shorthand to expose more fully how unequal literacy chances relate to systems of unequal subsidy and reward for literacy. These are the systems that deliver large-scale economic, historical, and political conditions to the scenes of small-scale literacy use and development.

This analysis of sponsorship forces us to consider not merely how one social group's literacy practices may differ from another's, but how everybody's literacy practices are operating in differential economies, which supply different access routes, different degrees of sponsoring power, and different scales of monetary worth to the practices in use. In fact, the interviews I conducted are filled with examples of how economic and political forces, some of them originating in quite distant corporate and government policies, affect people's day-to-day ability to seek out and practice literacy. As a telephone company employee, Janelle Hampton enjoyed a brief period in the early 1980s as a fraud investigator, pursuing inquiries and writing up reports of her efforts. But when the breakup of the telephone utility reorganized its workforce, the fraud division was moved two states away and she was returned to less interesting work as a data processor. When, as a seven-year-old in the mid-1970s, Yi Vong made his way with

15

his family from Laos to rural Wisconsin as part of the first resettlement group of Hmong refugees after the Vietnam War, his school district—which had no ESL programming—placed him in a school for the blind and deaf, where he learned English on audio and visual language machines. When a meager retirement pension forced Peter Hardaway and his wife out of their house and into a trailer, the couple stopped receiving newspapers and magazines in order to avoid cluttering up the small space they had to share. An analysis of sponsorship systems of literacy would help educators everywhere to think through the effects that economic and political changes in their regions are having on various people's ability to write and read, their chances to sustain that ability, and their capacities to pass it along to others. Recession, relocation, immigration, technological change, government retreat all can—and do—condition the course by which literate potential develops.

SPONSORSHIP AND THE RISE IN LITERACY STANDARDS

As I have been attempting to argue, literacy as a resource becomes available 16 to ordinary people largely through the mediations of more powerful sponsors. These sponsors are engaged in ceaseless processes of positioning and repositioning, seizing and relinquishing control over meanings and materials of literacy as part of their participation in economic and political competition. In the give and take of these struggles, forms of literacy and literacy learning take shape. This section examines more closely how forms of literacy are created out of competitions between institutions. It especially considers how this process relates to the rapid rise in literacy standards since World War II. Resnick and Resnick lay out the process by which the demand for literacy achievement has been escalating, from basic, largely rote competence to more complex analytical and interpretive skills. More and more people are now being expected to accomplish more and more things with reading and writing. As print and its spinoffs have entered virtually every sphere of life, people have grown increasingly dependent on their literacy skills for earning a living and exercising and protecting their civil rights. This section uses one extended case example to trace the role of institutional sponsorship in raising the literacy stakes. It also considers how one man used available forms of sponsorship to cope with this escalation in literacy demands.

The focus is on Dwayne Lowery, whose transition in the early 1970s from 17 line worker in an automobile manufacturing plant to field representative for a major public employees union exemplified the major transition of the post-World War II economy—from a thing-making, thing-swapping society to an information-making, service-swapping society. In the process, Dwayne Lowery had to learn to read and write in ways that he had never done before. How his experiences with writing developed and how they were sponsored—and distressed—by institutional struggle will unfold in the following narrative.

A man of Eastern European ancestry, Dwayne Lowery was born in 1938 18
and raised in a semi-rural area in the upper midwest, the third of five children
of a rubber worker father and a homemaker mother. Lowery recalled how, in his
childhood home, his father's feisty union publications and left-leaning newspapers and radio shows helped to create a political climate in his household. "I was
sixteen years old before I knew that goddamn Republicans was two words," he
said. Despite this influence, Lowery said he shunned politics and newspaper reading as a young person, except to read the sports page. A diffident student, he graduated near the bottom of his class from a small high school in 1956 and, after a
stint in the Army, went to work on the assembly line of a major automobile man-
ufacturer. In the late 1960s, bored with the repetition of spraying primer paint on
the right door checks of 57 cars an hour, Lowery traded in his night shift at the
auto plant for a day job reading water meters in a municipal utility department. It
was at that time, Lowery recalled, that he rediscovered newspapers, reading them
in the early morning in his department's break room. He said:

> At the time I guess I got a little more interested in the state of things within
> the state. I started to get a little political at that time and got a little more
> information about local people. So I would buy [a metropolitan paper] and I
> would read that paper in the morning. It was a pretty conservative paper but
> I got some information.

At about the same time Lowery became active in a rapidly growing pub- 19
lic employees union, and, in the early 1970s, he applied for and received a
union-sponsored grant that allowed him to take off four months of work and
travel to Washington, D.C., for training in union activity. Here is his extended
account of that experience:

> When I got to school, then there was a lot of reading. I often felt bad. If I
> had read more [as a high-school student] it wouldn't have been so tough.
> But they pumped a lot of stuff at us to read. We lived in a hotel and we had
> to some extent homework we had to do and reading we had to do and not
> make written reports but make some presentation on our part of it. What
> they were trying to teach us, I believe, was regulations, systems, laws. In case
> anything in court came up along the way, we would know that. We did a
> lot of work on organizing, you know, learning how to negotiate contracts,
> contractual language, how to write it. Gross National Product, how that
> affected the Consumer Price Index. It was pretty much a crash course. It was
> pretty much crammed in. And I'm not sure we were all that well prepared
> when we got done, but it was interesting.

After a hands-on experience organizing sanitation workers in the west, Lowery
returned home and was offered a full-time job as a field staff representative for

the union, handling worker grievances and contract negotiations for a large, active local near his state capital. His initial writing and rhetorical activities corresponded with the heady days of the early 1970s when the union was growing in strength and influence, reflecting in part the exponential expansion in information workers and service providers within all branches of government. With practice, Lowery said he became "good at talking," "good at presenting the union side," "good at slicing chunks off the employer's case." Lowery observed that, in those years, the elected officials with whom he was negotiating often lacked the sophistication of their Washington-trained union counterparts. "They were part-time people," he said. "And they didn't know how to calculate. We got things in contracts that didn't cost them much at the time but were going to cost them a ton down the road." In time, though, even small municipal and county governments responded to the public employees' growing power by hiring specialized attorneys to represent them in grievance and contract negotiations. "Pretty soon," Lowery observed, "ninety percent of the people I was dealing with across the table were attorneys."

This move brought dramatic changes in the writing practices of union reps, 20 and, in Lowery's estimation, a simultaneous waning of the power of workers and the power of his own literacy. "It used to be we got our way through muscle or through political connections," he said. "Now we had to get it through legalistic stuff. It was no longer just sit down and talk about it. Can we make a deal?" Instead, all activity became rendered in writing: the exhibit, the brief, the transcript, the letter, the appeal. Because briefs took longer to write, the wheels of justice took longer to turn. Delays in grievance hearings became routine, as lawyers and union reps alike asked hearing judges for extensions on their briefs. Things went, in Lowery's words, "from quick, competent justice to expensive and long term justice."

In the meantime, Lowery began spending up to 70 hours a week at work, 21 sweating over the writing of briefs, which are typically fifteen- to thirty-page documents laying out precedents, arguments, and evidence for a grievant's case. These documents were being forced by the new political economy in which Lowery's union was operating. He explained:

> When employers were represented by an attorney, you were going to have a
> written brief because the attorney needs to get paid. Well, what do you think
> if you were a union grievant and the attorney says, well, I'm going to write
> a brief and Dwayne Lowery says, well, I'm not going to. Does the worker
> somehow feel that their representation is less now?

To keep up with the new demands, Lowery occasionally traveled to major cities for two- or three-day union-sponsored workshops on arbitration, new legislation, and communication skills. He also took short courses at a historic

School for Workers at a nearby university. His writing instruction consisted mainly of reading the briefs of other field reps, especially those done by the college graduates who increasingly were being assigned to his district from union headquarters. Lowery said he kept a file drawer filled with other people's briefs from which he would borrow formats and phrasings. At the time of our interview in 1995, Dwayne Lowery had just taken an early and somewhat bitter retirement from the union, replaced by a recent graduate from a master's degree program in Industrial Relations. As a retiree, he was engaged in local Democratic party politics and was getting informal lessons in word processing at home from his wife.

Over a 20-year period, Lowery's adult writing took its character from a particular juncture in labor relations, when even small units of government began wielding (and, as a consequence, began spreading) a "legalistic" form of literacy in order to restore political dominance over public workers. This struggle for dominance shaped the kinds of literacy skills required of Lowery, the kinds of genres he learned and used, and the kinds of literate identity he developed. Lowery's rank-and-file experience and his talent for representing that experience around a bargaining table became increasingly peripheral to his ability to prepare documents that could compete in kind with those written by his formally-educated, professional adversaries. Face-to-face meetings became occasions mostly for a ritualistic exchange of texts, as arbitrators generally deferred decisions, reaching them in private, after solitary deliberation over complex sets of documents. What Dwayne Lowery was up against as a working adult in the second half of the 20th century was more than just living through a rising standard in literacy expectations or a generalized growth in professionalization, specialization, or documentary power—although certainly all of those things are, generically, true. Rather, these developments should be seen more specifically, as outcomes of ongoing transformations in the history of literacy as it has been wielded as part of economic and political conflict. These transformations become the arenas in which new standards of literacy develop. And for Dwayne Lowery—as well as many like him over the last 25 years—these are the arenas in which the worth of existing literate skills become degraded. A consummate debater and deal maker, Lowery saw his value to the union bureaucracy subside, as power shifted to younger, university-trained staffers whose literacy credentials better matched the specialized forms of escalating pressure coming from the other side. 22

In the broadest sense, the sponsorship of Dwayne Lowery's literacy experiences lies deep within the historical conditions of industrial relations in the 20th century and, more particularly, within the changing nature of work and labor struggle over the last several decades. Edward Stevens Jr. has observed the rise in this century of an "advanced contractarian society" (25) by which formal relationships of all kinds have come to rely on "a jungle of rules and 23 regulations" (139). For labor, these conditions only intensified in the 1960s and 1970s when a flurry of federal and state civil rights legislation curtailed the previously unregulated hiring and firing power of management. These developments made the appeal to law as central as collective bargaining for extending employee rights (Heckscher 9). I mention this broader picture, first, because it relates to the forms of employer backlash that Lowery began experiencing by the early 1980s and, more important, because a history of unionism serves as a guide for a closer look at the sponsors of Lowery's literacy.

These resources begin with the influence of his father, whose membership in 24 the United Rubber Workers during the ideologically potent 1930s and 1940s grounded Lowery in class-conscious progressivism and its favorite literate form: the newspaper. On top of that, though, was a pragmatic philosophy of worker education that developed in the U.S. after the Depression as an anti-communist antidote to left-wing intellectual influences in unions. Lowery's parent union, in fact, had been a central force in refocusing worker education away from an earlier emphasis on broad critical study and toward discrete techniques for organizing and bargaining. Workers began to be trained in the discrete bodies of knowledge, written formats, and idioms associated with those strategies. Characteristic of this legacy, Lowery's crash course at the Washington-based training center in the early 1970s emphasized technical information, problem solving, and union-building skills and methods. The transformation in worker education from critical, humanistic study to problem-solving skills was also lived out at the school for workers where Lowery took short courses in the 1980s. Once a place where factory workers came to write and read about economics, sociology, and labor history, the school is now part of a university extension service offering workshops—often requested by management—on such topics as work restructuring, new technology, health and safety regulations, and joint labor-management cooperation.[7] Finally, in this inventory of Dwayne Lowery's literacy sponsors, we must add the latest incarnations shaping union practices: the attorneys and college-educated co-workers who carried into Lowery's workplace forms of legal discourse and "essayist literacy."[8]

What should we notice about this pattern of sponsorship? First, we can 25 see from yet another angle how the course of an ordinary person's literacy learning—its occasions, materials, applications, potentials—follows the transformations going on within sponsoring institutions as those institutions fight for economic and ideological position. As a result of wins, losses, or compromises, institutions undergo change, affecting the kinds of literacy they promulgate and the status that such literacy has in the larger society. So where, how, why, and what Lowery practiced as a writer—and what he didn't practice—took shape as part of the post-industrial jockeying going on over the last thirty years by labor, government, and industry. Yet there is more to be seen in this inventory of literacy sponsors. It exposes the deeply textured history that lies within the literacy practices of institutions and within any individual's literacy experiences. Accumulated layers of sponsoring influences—in families, workplaces, schools, memory—carry forms of literacy that have been shaped out of ideological and economic struggles of the past. This history, on the one hand, is a sustaining resource in the quest for literacy. It enables an older generation to pass its literacy resources onto another. Lowery's exposure to his father's newspaper-reading and supper-table political talk kindled his adult passion for news, debate, and for language that rendered relief and justice. This history also helps to create infrastructures of opportunity. Lowery found crucial supports for extending his adult literacy in the educational networks that unions established during the first half of the 20th century as they were consolidating into national powers. On the other hand, this layered history of sponsorship is also deeply conservative and can be maladaptive because it teaches forms of literacy that oftentimes are in the process of being overtaken by new political realities and by ascendent forms of literacy. The decision to focus worker education on practical strategies of recruiting and bargaining—devised in the thick of Cold War patriotism and galloping expansion in union memberships—became, by the Reagan years, a fertile ground for new forms of management aggression and cooptation.

It is actually this lag or gap in sponsoring forms that we call the rising stan- 26 dard of literacy. The pace of change and the place of literacy in economic competition have both intensified enormously in the last half of the 20th century. It is as if the history of literacy is in fast forward. Where once the same sponsoring arrangements could maintain value across a generation or more, forms of literacy and their sponsors can now rise and recede many times within a single life span. Dwayne Lowery experienced profound changes in forms of union-based literacy not only between his father's time and his but between the time he joined the union and the time he left it, twenty-odd years later. This phenomenon is what makes today's literacy feel so advanced and, at the same time, so destabilized.

SPONSORSHIP AND APPROPRIATION IN LITERACY LEARNING

We have seen how literacy sponsors affect literacy learning in two power- 27 ful ways. They help to organize and administer stratified systems of opportunity and access, and they raise the literacy stakes in struggles for competitive advantage. Sponsors enable and hinder literacy activity, often forcing the formation of new literacy requirements while decertifying older ones. A somewhat different dynamic of literacy sponsorship is treated here. It pertains to the potential of the sponsored to divert sponsors' resources toward ulterior projects, often projects of self-interest or self-development. Earlier I mentioned how Sunday School parishioners in England and African Americans in slavery appropriated church-sponsored literacy for economic and psychic survival.

"Misappropriation" is always possible at the scene of literacy transmission, a reason for the tight ideological control that usually surrounds reading and writing instruction. The accounts that appear below are meant to shed light on the dynamics of appropriation, including the role of sponsoring agents in that process. They are also meant to suggest that diversionary tactics in literacy learning may be invited now by the sheer proliferation of literacy activity in contemporary life. The uses and networks of literacy crisscross through many domains, exposing people to multiple, often amalgamated sources of sponsoring powers, secular, religious, bureaucratic, commercial, technological. In other words, what is so destabilized about contemporary literacy today also makes it so available and potentially innovative, ripe for picking, one might say, for people suitably positioned. The rising level of schooling in the general population is also an inviting factor in this process. Almost everyone now has some sort of contact, for instance, with college-educated people, whose movements through workplaces, justice systems, social service organizations, houses of worship, local government, extended families, or circles of friends spread dominant forms of literacy (whether wanted or not, helpful or not) into public and private spheres. Another condition favorable for appropriation is the deep hybridity of literacy practices extant in many settings. As we saw in Dwayne Lowery's case, workplaces, schools, families bring together multiple strands of the history of literacy in complex and influential forms. We need models of literacy that more astutely account for these kinds of multiple contacts, both in and out of school and across a lifetime. Such models could begin to grasp the significance of re-appropriation, which, for a number of reasons, is becoming a key requirement for literacy learning at the end of the 20th century.

The following discussion will consider two brief cases of literacy diversion. 28 Both involve women working in subordinate positions as secretaries, in print-rich settings where better-educated male supervisors were teaching them to read and write in certain ways to perform their clerical duties. However, as we will see shortly, strong loyalties outside the workplace prompted these two secretaries to lift these literate resources for use in other spheres. For one, Carol White, it was on behalf of her work as a Jehovah's Witness. For the other, Sarah Steele, it was on behalf of upward mobility for her lower-middle-class family.

Before turning to their narratives, though, it will be wise to pay some atten- 29 tion to the economic moment in which they occur. Clerical work was the largest and fastest-growing occupation for women in the 20th century. Like so much employment for women, it offered a mix of gender-defined constraints as well as avenues for economic independence and mobility. As a new information economy created an acute need for typists, stenographers, bookkeepers, and other office workers, white, American-born women and, later, immigrant and minority women saw reason to pursue high school and business-college educations. Unlike male clerks of the 19th century, female secretaries in this century had little chance for advancement. However, office work represented a step up from the farm or the factory for women of the working class and served as a respectable occupation from which educated, middle-class women could await or avoid marriage (Anderson, Strom). In a study of clerical work through the first half of the 20th century, Mary Christine Anderson estimated that secretaries might encounter up to 97 different genres in the course of doing dictation or transcription. They routinely had contact with an array of professionals, including lawyers, auditors, tax examiners, and other government overseers (52–53). By 1930, 30% of women office workers used machines other than typewriters (Anderson 76) and, in contemporary offices, clerical workers have often been the first employees to learn to operate CRTs and personal computers and to teach others how to use them. Overall, the daily duties of 20th-century secretaries could serve handily as an index to the rise of complex administrative and accounting procedures, standardization of information, expanding communication, and developments in technological systems.

With that background, consider the experiences of Carol White and Sarah 30 Steele. An Oneida, Carol White was born into a poor, single-parent household in 1940. She graduated from high school in 1960 and, between five maternity leaves and a divorce, worked continuously in a series of clerical positions in both the private and public sectors. One of her first secretarial jobs was with an urban firm that produced and disseminated Catholic missionary films. The vice-president with whom she worked most closely also spent much of his time producing a magazine for a national civic organization that he headed. She discussed how typing letters and magazine articles and occasionally proofreading for this man taught her rhetorical strategies in which she was keenly interested. She described the scene of transfer this way:

> [My boss] didn't just write to write. He wrote in a way to make his letters
> appealing. I would have to write what he was writing in this magazine too.
> I was completely enthralled. He would write about the people who were in
> this [organization] and the different works they were undertaking and people
> that died and people who were sick and about their personalities. And he
> wrote little anecdotes. Once in a while I made some suggestions too. He was
> a man who would listen to you.

The appealing and persuasive power of the anecdote became especially important to Carol White when she began doing door-to-door missionary work for the Jehovah's Witnesses, a pan-racial, millennialist religious faith. She now uses colorful anecdotes to prepare demonstrations that she performs with other women at weekly service meetings at their Kingdom Hall. These demonstrations, done in front of the congregation, take the form of skits designed to explore daily problems through Bible principles. Further, at the time of our interview, Carol White was working as a municipal revenue clerk and had recently enrolled in an on-the-job training seminar called Persuasive Communication, a two-day class offered free to public employees. Her motivation for taking the course stemmed from her desire to improve her evangelical work. She said she wanted to continue to develop speaking and writing skills that would be "appealing," "motivating," and "encouraging" to people she hoped to convert.

Sarah Steele, a woman of Welsh and German descent, was born in 1920 into a large, working-class family in a coal mining community in eastern Pennsylvania. In 1940, she graduated from a two-year commercial college. Married soon after, she worked as a secretary in a glass factory until becoming pregnant with the first of four children. In the 1960s, in part to help pay for her children's college educations, she returned to the labor force as a receptionist and bookkeeper in a law firm, where she stayed until her retirement in the late 1970s. 31

Sarah Steele described how, after joining the law firm, she began to model her household management on principles of budgeting that she was picking up from one of the attorneys with whom she worked most closely. "I learned cash flow from Mr. B_____," she said. "I would get all the bills and put a tape in the adding machine and he and I would sit down together to be sure there was going to be money ahead." She said that she began to replicate that process at home with household bills. "Before that," she observed, "I would just cook beans when I had to instead of meat." Sarah Steele also said she encountered the genre of the credit report during routine reading and typing on the job. She figured out what constituted a top rating, making sure her husband followed these steps in preparation for their financing a new car. She also remembered typing up documents connected to civil suits being brought against local businesses, teaching her, she said, which firms never to hire for home repairs. "It just changes the way you think," she observed about the reading and writing she did on her job. "You're not a pushover after you learn how business operates." 32

The dynamics of sponsorship alive in these narratives expose important elements of literacy appropriation, at least as it is practiced at the end of the 20th century. In a pattern now familiar from the earlier sections, we see how opportunities for literacy learning — this time for diversions of resources — open up in the clash between long-standing, residual forms of sponsorship and the new: between the lingering presence of literacy's conservative history and its pressure for change. So, here, two women — one Native American and both working-class — filch contemporary literacy resources (public relations techniques and accounting practices) from more-educated, higher-status men. The women are emboldened in these acts by ulterior identities beyond the workplace: Carol White with faith and Sarah Steele with family. These affiliations hark back to the first sponsoring arrangements through which American women were gradually allowed to acquire literacy and education. Duties associated with religious faith and child rearing helped literacy to become, in Gloria Main's words, 33 "a permissible feminine activity" (579). Interestingly, these roles, deeply sanctioned within the history of women's literacy—and operating beneath the newer permissible feminine activity of clerical work—become grounds for covert, innovative appropriation even as they reinforce traditional female identities.

Just as multiple identities contribute to the ideologically hybrid character of 34 these literacy formations, so do institutional and material conditions. Carol White's account speaks to such hybridity. The missionary film company with the civic club vice president is a residual site for two of literacy's oldest campaigns—Christian conversion and civic participation—enhanced here by 20th-century advances in film and public relations techniques. This ideological reservoir proved a pleasing instructional site for Carol White, whose interests in literacy, throughout her life, have been primarily spiritual. So literacy appropriation draws upon, perhaps even depends upon, conservative forces in the history of literacy sponsorship that are always hovering at the scene of acts of learning. This history serves as both a sanctioning force and a reserve of ideological and material support.

At the same time, however, we see in these accounts how individual acts 35 of appropriation can divert and subvert the course of literacy's history, how changes in individual literacy experiences relate to larger-scale transformations. Carol White's redirection of personnel management techniques to the cause of the Jehovah's Witnesses is an almost ironic transformation in this regard. Once a principal sponsor in the initial spread of mass literacy, evangelism is here rejuvenated through late-literate corporate sciences of secular persuasion, fundraising, and bureaucratic management that Carol White finds circulating in her contemporary workplaces. By the same token, through Sarah Steele, accounting practices associated with corporations are, in a sense, tracked into the house, rationalizing and standardizing even domestic practices. (Even though Sarah Steele did not own an adding machine, she penciled her budget figures onto adding-machine tape that she kept for that purpose.) Sarah Steele's act of appropriation in some sense explains how dominant forms of literacy migrate and penetrate into private spheres, including private consciousness. At the same time, though, she accomplishes a subversive diversion of literate power. Her efforts to move her family up in the middle class involved not merely contributing a second income but also, from her desk as a bookkeeper, reading her way into an understanding of middle-class economic power.

TEACHING AND THE DYNAMICS OF SPONSORSHIP

It hardly seems necessary to point out to the readers of *CCC* that we haul a 36 lot of freight for the opportunity to teach writing. Neither rich nor powerful enough to sponsor literacy on our own terms, we serve instead as conflicted brokers between literacy's buyers and sellers. At our most worthy, perhaps, we show the sellers how to beware and try to make sure these exchanges will be a little fairer, maybe, potentially, a little more mutually rewarding. This essay has offered a few working case studies that link patterns of sponsorship to processes of stratification, competition, and reappropriation. How much these dynamics can be generalized to classrooms is an ongoing empirical question.

I am sure that sponsors play even more influential roles at the scenes of lit- 37 eracy learning and use than this essay has explored. I have focused on some of the most tangible aspects—material supply, explicit teaching, institutional aegis. But the ideological pressure of sponsors affects many private aspects of writing processes as well as public aspects of finished texts. Where one's sponsors are multiple or even at odds, they can make writing maddening. Where they are absent, they make writing unlikely. Many of the cultural formations we associate with writing development—community practices, disciplinary traditions, technological potentials—can be appreciated as make-do responses to the economics of literacy, past and present. The history of literacy is a catalogue of obligatory relations. That this catalogue is so deeply conservative and, at the same time, so ruthlessly demanding of change is what fills contemporary literacy learning and teaching with their most paradoxical choices and outcomes.[9]

In bringing attention to economies of literacy learning I am not advocating 38 that we prepare students more efficiently for the job markets they must enter. What I have tried to suggest is that as we assist and study individuals in pursuit of literacy, we also recognize how literacy is in pursuit of them. When this process stirs ambivalence, on their part or on ours, we need to be understanding.

Acknowledgments

This research was sponsored by the NCTE Research Foundation and the Center on English Learning and Achievement. The Center is supported by the U.S. Department of Education's Office of Educational Research and Improvement, whose views do not necessarily coincide with the author's. A version of this essay was given as a lecture in the Department of English, University of Louisville, in April 1997. Thanks to Anna Syvertsen and Julie Nelson for their help with archival research. Thanks too to colleagues who lent an ear along the way: Nelson Graff, Jonna Gjevre, Anne Gere, Kurt Spellmeyer, Tom Fox, and Bob Gundlach.

Notes

1. Three of the keenest and most eloquent observers of economic impacts on writing, teaching, and learning have been Lester Faigley, Susan Miller, and Kurt Spellmeyer.

2. My debt to the writings of Pierre Bourdieu will be evident throughout this essay. Here and throughout I invoke his expansive notion of "economy," which is not restricted to literal and ostensible systems of money making but to the many spheres where people labor, invest, and exploit energies—their own and others'—to maximize advantage; see Bourdieu and Wacquant, especially 117–120 and Bourdieu, Chapter 7.

3. Thomas Laqueur (124) provides a vivid account of a street demonstration in Bolton, England, in 1834 by a "pro-writing" faction of Sunday School students and their teachers. This faction demanded that writing instruction continue to be provided on Sundays, something that opponents of secular instruction on the Sabbath were trying to reverse.

4. See, for instance, National Assessments of Educational Progress in reading and writing (Applebee et al.; and "Looking").

5. All names used in this essay are pseudonyms.

6. I am not suggesting that literacy that does not "pay off" in terms of prestige or monetary reward is less valuable. Dora Lopez's ability to read and write in Spanish was a source of great strength and pride, especially when she was able to teach it to her young child. The resource of Spanish literacy carried much of what Bourdieu calls cultural capital in her social and family circles. But I want to point out here how people who labor equally to acquire literacy do so under systems of unequal subsidy and unequal reward.

7. For useful accounts of this period in union history, see Heckscher; Nelson.

8. Marcia Farr associates "essayist literacy" with written genres esteemed in the academy and noted for their explicitness, exactness, reliance on reasons and evidence, and impersonal voice.

9. Lawrence Cremin makes similar points about education in general in his essay "The Cacophony of Teaching." He suggests that complex economic and social changes since World War II including the popularization of schooling and the penetration of mass media, have created "a far greater range and diversity of languages, competencies, values, personalities, and approaches to the world and to its educational opportunities" than at one time existed. The diversity most of interest to him (and me) resides not so much in the range of different ethnic groups there are in society but in the different cultural formulas by which people assemble their educational — or, I would say, literate — experience.

Works Cited

Anderson, Mary Christine. "Gender, Class, and Culture: Women Secretarial and Clerical Workers in the United States, 1925–1955." Diss. Ohio State U, 1986.

Applebee, Arthur N., Judith A. Langer, and Ida V. S. Mullis. *The Writing Report Card: Writing Achievement in American Schools.* Princeton: ETS, 1986.

Bourdieu, Pierre. *The Logic of Practice.* Trans. Richard Nice. Cambridge: Polity, 1990.

Bourdieu, Pierre, and Loic J. D. Wacquant. *An Invitation to Reflexive Sociology.* Chicago: Chicago UP, 1992.

Bourne, J. M. *Patronage and Society in Nineteenth-Century England.* London: Edward Arnold, 1986.

Brandt, Deborah. "Accumulating Literacy: Writing and Learning to Write in the 20th Century." *College English* 57 (1995): 649–68.

____. "Remembering Reading, Remembering Writing." *CCC* 45 (1994): 459–79.

Cornelius, Janet Duitsman. '*When I Can Ready My Title Clear': Literacy, Slavery, and Religion in the Antebellum South.* Columbia: U of South Carolina P, 1991.

Cremin, Lawrence. "The Cacophony of Teaching." *Popular Education and Its Discontents.* New York: Harper, 1990.

Faigley, Lester. "Veterans' Stories on the Porch." *History, Reflection and Narrative: The Professionalization of Composition, 1963–1983.* Eds. Beth Boehm, Debra Journet, and Mary Rosner. Norwood: Ablex, 1999. 23–38.

Farr, Marcia. "Essayist Literacy and Other Verbal Performances." *Written Communication* 8 (1993): 4–38.

Heckscher, Charles C. *The New Unionism: Employee Involvement in the Changing Corporation.* New York: Basic, 1988.

Horstman, Connie, and Donald V. Kurtz. *Compadrazgo in Post-Conquest Middle America.* Milwaukee: Milwaukee-UW Center for Latin America, 1978.

Kett, Joseph F. *The Pursuit of Knowledge Under Difficulties: From Self Improvement to Adult Education in America 1750–1990.* Stanford: Stanford UP, 1994.

Laqueur, Thomas. *Religion and Respectability: Sunday Schools and Working Class Culture 1780–1850.* New Haven: Yale UP, 1976.

Looking at How Well Our Students Read: The 1992 National Assessment of Educational Progress in Reading. Washington: US Dept. of Education, Office of Educational Research and Improvement, Educational Resources Information Center, 1992.

Lynch, Joseph H. *Godparents and Kinship in Early Medieval Europe.* Princeton: Princeton UP, 1986.

Main, Gloria L. "An Inquiry into When and Why Women Learned to Write in Colonial New England." *Journal of Social History* 24 (1991): 579–89.

Miller, Susan. *Textual Carnivals: The Politics of Composition.* Carbondale: Southern Illinois UP, 1991.

Nelson, Daniel. *American Rubber Workers and Organized Labor, 1900–1941.* Princeton: Princeton UP, 1988.

Nicholas, Stephen J., and Jacqueline M. Nicholas. "Male Literacy, 'Deskilling,' and the Industrial Revolution." *Journal of Interdisciplinary History* 23 (1992): 1–18.

Resnick, Daniel P., and Lauren B. Resnick. "The Nature of Literacy: A Historical Explanation." *Harvard Educational Review* 47 (1977): 370–85.

Spellmeyer, Kurt. "After Theory: From Textuality to Attunement with the World." *College English* 58 (1996): 893–913.

Stevens, Jr., Edward. *Literacy, Law, and Social Order.* DeKalb: Northern Illinois UP, 1987.

Strom, Sharon Hartman. *Beyond the Typewriter: Gender, Class, and the Origins of Modern American Office Work, 1900–1930.* Urbana: U of Illinois P, 1992.

- -

Questions for Discussion and Journaling

1. How does Brandt define *literacy sponsor*? What are the characteristics of a literacy sponsor?

2. How does Brandt support her claim that sponsors always have something to gain from their sponsorship? Can you provide any examples from your own experience?

3. How do the sponsored sometimes "misappropriate" their literacy lessons?

4. Consider Brandt's claim that literacy sponsors "help to organize and administer stratified systems of opportunity and access, and they raise the literacy stakes in struggles for competitive advantage" (para. 27). What does Brandt mean by the term *stratified*? What "stakes" is she referring to?

5. Giving the examples of Branch and Lopez as support, Brandt argues that race and class impact how much access people have to literacy sponsorship. Summarize

the kinds of access Branch and Lopez had — for example, in their early education, access to books and computers, and parental support — and decide whether you agree with Brandt's claim.

Applying and Exploring Ideas

1. Compare your own literacy history with that of Branch and of Lopez, using categories like those in discussion Question 5 above. Then consider who your primary literacy sponsors were (people, as well as institutions such as churches or clubs or school systems) and what literacies they taught you (academic, civic, religious, and so on). Would you consider the access provided by these sponsors adequate? What literacies have you not had access to that you wish you had?

2. Have you ever had literacy sponsors who withheld (or tried to withhold) certain kinds of literacies from you? For example, did your school ban certain books? Have sponsors forced certain kinds of literacies on you (for example, approved reading lists in school) or held up some literacies as better than others (for example, saying that certain kinds of books didn't "count" as reading)? Were you able to find alternate sponsors for different kinds of literacy?

3. Interview a classmate about a significant literacy sponsor in their lives, and then discuss the interview in an entry on a class wiki or blog, a brief presentation, or a one-page report. Try to cover these questions in your interview:

    a. Who or what was your literacy sponsor?

    b. What did you gain from the sponsorship?

    c. Did you "misappropriate" the literacy in any way?

    d. What materials, technologies, and so forth were involved?

    In reflecting on the interview, ask yourself the following:

    a. Did the sponsorship connect to larger cultural or material developments?

    b. Does the sponsorship let you make any hypotheses about the culture of your interviewee? How would you test that hypothesis?

    c. Does your classmate's account have a "So what?" — a point that might make others care about it?

- -
META MOMENT Review the goals for this chapter (p. 243): For which goals is Brandt's article relevant? Are there experiences you're currently having that Brandt's ideas help to explain?
- -

Only Daughter

SANDRA CISNEROS

David Livingston/Getty Images
Entertainment/Getty Images

Framing the Reading

Sandra Cisneros is a successful and prolific writer of poetry, novels, stories, children's books, and even a picture book for adults. Some of her best-known work includes *The House on Mango Street* (1984) and *Woman Hollering Creek and Other Stories* (1991). She returns frequently to the theme of Chicana identity in her writing. She has won numerous awards, including the MacArthur Fellowship, two National Endowment for the Arts fellowships, a 2016 National Medal of Arts, and, in 2017, one of twenty-five Ford Foundation Art of Change fellowships. Born to Mexican American parents, she grew up in Chicago with six brothers and, as a dual citizen of the United States and Mexico, now lives in San Miguel de Allende.

The following short narrative describes the struggle she faced to gain her father's approval for her writing. This narrative illustrates Brandt's idea of literacy sponsorship, including ways that sponsors seek to promote certain kinds of literacy experiences and not others, and the way that the sponsored can "misappropriate" the literacy experiences available to them toward ends other than those intended by the sponsor. Cisneros's text also asks you to think about what it means to be multilingual, and how literacy experiences differ (and are valued differently) across different cultural contexts. These ideas will be taken up in other ways later in this chapter. Ultimately Cisneros's piece helps exemplify and explain both how this chapter's threshold concept works, and why it matters.

Getting Ready to Read

Before you read, do at least one of the following activities:

- Refresh your memory regarding Brandt's definition of *literacy sponsor* in the previous reading.
- Google Sandra Cisneros and learn a little more about what she has written.

As you read, consider the following questions:

- How do Cisneros's experiences illustrate the idea of literacy sponsorship?
- In what ways are your experiences with literacy and family similar to and different from Cisneros's?

Cisneros, Sandra. "Only Daughter." *Glamour*, Nov. 1990, pp. 256–57.

ONCE, SEVERAL YEARS AGO, when I was just starting out my writing 1
career, I was asked to write my own contributor's note for an anthology I was
part of. I wrote: "I am the only daughter in a family of six sons. *That* explains
everything."

Well, I've thought about that ever since, and yes, it explains a lot to me, but 2
for the reader's sake I should have written: "I am the only daughter in a *Mexican*
family of six sons." Or even: "I am the only daughter of a Mexican father and
a Mexican American mother." Or: "I am the only daughter of a working-class
family of nine." All of these had everything to do with who I am today.

I was / am the only daughter and *only* a daughter. Being an only daughter in 3
a family of six sons forced me by circumstance to spend a lot of time by myself
because my brothers felt it beneath them to play with a *girl* in public. But that
aloneness, that loneliness, was good for a would-be writer — it allowed me time
to think and think, to imagine, to read and prepare myself.

Being only a daughter for my father meant my destiny would lead me to 4
become someone's wife. That's what he believed. But when I was in fifth grade
and shared my plans for college with him, I was sure he understood. I remember my father saying, "*Que bueno, mi'ja*, that's good." That meant a lot to me,
especially since my brothers thought the idea hilarious. What I didn't realize was
that my father thought college was good for girls — for finding a husband. After
four years in college and two more in graduate school, and still no husband, my
father shakes his head even now and says I wasted all that education.

In retrospect, I'm lucky my father believed daughters were meant for 5
husbands. It meant it didn't matter if I majored in something silly like English.
After all, I'd find a nice professional eventually, right? This allowed me the
liberty to putter about embroidering my little poems and stories without my
father interrupting with so much as a "What's that you're writing?"

But the truth is, I wanted him to interrupt. I wanted my father to under- 6
stand what it was I was scribbling, to introduce me as "My only daughter, the
writer." Not as "This is my only daughter.
She teaches." *El maestra* — teacher. Not
even *profesora*.

> I wanted my father to
> understand what it was I
> was scribbling, to introduce
> me as "My only daughter,
> the writer."

In a sense, everything I have ever writ- 7
ten has been for him, to win his approval
even though I know my father can't read
English words, even though my father's
only reading includes the brown-ink *Esto*
sports magazines from Mexico City and
the bloody *¡Alarma!* magazines that feature yet another sighting of *La Virgen
de Guadalupe* on a tortilla or a wife's revenge on her philandering husband by
bashing his skull in with a *molcajete* (a kitchen mortar made of volcanic rock).

Or the *fotonovelas*, the little picture paperbacks with tragedy and trauma erupting from the characters' mouths in bubbles.

My father represents, then, the public majority. A public who is uninterested 8 in reading, and yet one whom I am writing about and for, and privately trying to woo.

When we were growing up in Chicago, we moved a lot because of my father. 9 He suffered periodic bouts of nostalgia. Then we'd have to let go our flat, store the furniture with mother's relatives, load the station wagon with baggage and bologna sandwiches, and head south. To Mexico City.

We came back, of course. To yet another Chicago flat, another Chicago 10 neighborhood, another Catholic school. Each time, my father would seek out the parish priest in order to get a tuition break, and complain or boast: "I have seven sons."

He meant *siete hijos*, seven children, but he translated it as "sons." "I have 11 seven sons." To anyone who would listen. The Sears Roebuck employee who sold us the washing machine. The short-order cook, where my father ate his ham-and-eggs breakfasts. "I have seven sons." As if he deserved a medal from the state.

My papa. He didn't mean anything by that mistranslation, I'm sure. But 12 somehow I could feel myself being erased. I'd tug my father's sleeve and whisper: "Not seven sons. Six! and *one daughter*."

When my oldest brother graduated from medical school, he fulfilled my 13 father's dream that we study hard and use this — our heads, instead of this — our hands. Even now my father's hands are thick and yellow, stubbed by a history of hammer and nails and twine and coils and springs. "Use this," my father said, tapping his head, "and not this," showing us those hands. He always looked tired when he said it.

Wasn't college an investment? And hadn't I spent all those years in college? 14 And if I didn't marry, what was it all for? Why would anyone go to college and then choose to be poor? Especially someone who had always been poor.

Last year, after ten years of writing professionally, the financial rewards 15 started to trickle in. My second National Endowment for the Arts Fellowship. A guest professorship at the University of California, Berkeley. My book, which sold to a major New York publishing house.

At Christmas, I flew home to Chicago. The house was throbbing, same as 16 always; hot *tamales* and sweet *tamales* hissing in my mother's pressure cooker, and everybody — mother, six brothers, wives, babies, aunts, cousins — talking too loud and at the same time, like in a Fellini film, because that's just how we are.

I went upstairs to my father's room. One of my stories had just been trans- 17 lated into Spanish and published in an anthology of Chicano writing, and I wanted to show it to him. Ever since he recovered from a stroke two years ago, my father likes to spend his leisure hours horizontally. And that's how I found him, watching a Pedro Infante movie on Galavision and eating rice pudding.

There was a glass filmed with milk on the bedside table. There were several 18
vials of pills and balled Kleenex. And on the floor, one black sock and a plastic
urinal that I didn't want to look at but looked at anyway. Pedro Infante was
about to burst into song, and my father was laughing.

I'm not sure if it was because my story was translated into Spanish, or because 19
it was published in Mexico, or perhaps because the story dealt with Tepeyac, the
colonia my father was raised in, but at any rate, my father punched the mute
button on his remote control and read my story.

I sat on the bed next to my father and waited. He read it very slowly. As if he 20
were reading each line over and over. He laughed at all the right places and read
lines he liked out loud. He pointed and asked questions: "Is this So-and-so?"
"Yes," I said. He kept reading.

When he was finally finished, after what seemed like hours, my father looked 21
up and asked: "Where can we get more copies of this for the relatives?"

Of all the wonderful things that happened to me last year, that was the most 22
wonderful.

- -

Questions for Discussion and Journaling

1. At the beginning of this piece, Cisneros writes several sentences about herself that she says "explain everything." List those sentences. Why does she
   think these aspects of her identity and experience are so powerful? Now write
   several sentences about yourself that you think might "explain everything"
   in a similar way. Why are these aspects of your identity and experience so
   powerful?

2. Cisneros's father supported her in attending college, but for very different reasons than her own. Explain how her father and college were what Brandt terms
   "literacy sponsors," and how Cisneros "misappropriated" the college literacy
   sponsorship that her father intended.

3. Cisneros's father had his own literacy sponsors, some of which are mentioned in
   this reading. What are they? How do you think they impacted what he expected
   of his daughter? How do they differ from his daughter's literacy sponsors?

4. Cisneros and her father have different ideas about what it means to be successful. How and why do they differ?

5. Cisneros has achieved extensive recognition for her writing, but she says that
   her father's approval of one story was "the most wonderful" thing that happened
   to her the year before she wrote this narrative (para. 22). Why? What about that
   particular story helped her bridge the divide between what she valued and what
   her father valued?

6. Cisneros speaks one language with her family and uses another language in her professional life and writing, at least most of the time. What does this multilingual experience provide Cisneros that a monolingual experience would not? What challenges does it present her?

Applying and Exploring Ideas

1. In your own family, how is literacy understood? Which literacy practices are frequently engaged in? Which literacy practices are valued, and which are not?

2. In Question 4 above, you listed some of Cisneros's father's literacy sponsors. Now think about your own parents and list some of their literacy sponsors. How are these similar to or different from your own? How did those sponsors show up in your house and impact your own literacy?

3. Do you speak different languages at home, school, and work? If so, what language(s) do you speak in which settings? What do you think you gain from being able to draw on these various languages in different contexts? Are there any times when these multiple languages present a challenge for you? If you speak the same language in all contexts, reach out to a classmate or friend who is multilingual, and ask them the above questions.

- -
META MOMENT   How does Cisneros's experience help you understand yourself and your own literacy sponsors differently?
- -

Excerpt from *Bootstraps: From an American Academic of Color*

Victor Villanueva

VICTOR VILLANUEVA

Framing the Reading

You've probably noticed, consciously or unconsciously, that some languages or dialects tend to be dominant in particular settings, while others seem marginalized. In many cases, language users have the ability to change their language for different audiences and purposes — that is, to "code switch" or "code mesh" (ideas taken up in more detail by Young later in this chapter, and by Gee in Chapter 7). Changing language use in this way might be as simple as speaking differently in a place of worship versus at work or school. Or it could be as complicated as speaking one language with your parents and grandparents, and another with your friends and teachers. There are many variations of a language; there is not just one "English" but many Englishes that are spoken and written to great effect by people from different countries, regions of a country, ethnicities, classes, and even genders.

The ability to move among different versions of a language, or different languages altogether, can be helpful in communicating effectively and powerfully in different circumstances. But moving and changing language like this can also require speakers and writers to give up something that is important to who they are. This is because to be human is to be aware of the interplay among languages and how they mark power, identity, status, and potential. In circumstances where individuals use a form of language that is not the dominant or powerful one in that context, they have choices to make: Should they use (or learn to use) the dominant and powerful language? Can they do so effectively (a question that Gee also takes up [p. 507])? If so, when, where, and how much should they use it? What do they give up and gain by doing so (a question taken up by Young; see p. 325)? Making decisions about what language practices to use is not just a matter of learning something new, but of becoming someone else.

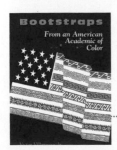

Villanueva, Victor. *Bootstraps: From an American Academic of Color*. National Council of Teachers of English, 1993, pp. 66–77.

Victor Villanueva's book *Bootstraps: From an American Academic of Color* is a narrative and an analysis of his own experience with this struggle. Villanueva, a Puerto Rican American, grew up in the Hell's Kitchen area of New York City, with parents who had emigrated from Puerto Rico with Spanish as their first language. As an adult, he became a successful professor of rhetoric, focusing on questions of race, language, and power. *Bootstraps* tells the story of his evolution, and the excerpt that you'll read here focuses specifically on his movement from the U.S. Army into an English degree and graduate school. It's a literacy narrative that captures the feelings of confusion and frustration, as well as elation and satisfaction, experienced by one member of a group whose language and ethnicity are not dominant as he learns to participate in an academic community that requires its participants to use very different language practices. Villanueva's story, like the other literacy narratives included in this chapter, demonstrates the complexity of what it means to be "literate" — and who has the authority to decide what forms of literacy are understood as powerful or "legitimate." Villanueva's experiences illustrate what it might look like to try out both old and new language practices in a new place; it also describes the frustrations of learning to write in school settings like the one you are in now.

Villanueva is Regents Professor and Edward R. Meyer Distinguished Professor of Liberal Arts at Washington State University. In his work, he describes and theorizes the relationship between language and power, especially the ways that language is used as a tool of racism. He has won a wide range of honors and awards both from the field of writing studies and the universities in which he's taught, researched, and administered.

Getting Ready to Read

Before you read, do at least one of the following activities:

- Find out more about this writer and his experiences through a quick online search.
- Think back to when you first considered going to college, whatever age that was. Did you think, back then, you could do it? If you didn't feel confident, what prevented that confidence?

As you read, consider the following questions:

- What school-writing experiences have you encountered that resemble any described by Villanueva?
- What do you know about affirmative action in higher education, and how is this reading matching up with that knowledge?

I WANTED TO TRY my hand at college, go beyond the GED. But college   1
scared me. I had been told long ago that college wasn't my lot.

He drives by the University District of Seattle during his last days in the military   2
and sees the college kids, long hair and sandals, baggy short pants on the men, long,
flowing dresses on the women, some men in suits, some women in high heels, all
carrying backpacks over one shoulder. There is both purpose and contentment in
the air. Storefronts carry names like Dr. Feelgood and Magus Bookstore, reflecting the good feelings and magic he senses. A block away is the University, red tiles
and green grass, rolling hills and tall pines, apple and cherry blossoms, the trees
shading modern monoliths of gray concrete and gothic, church-like buildings of
red brick. And he says to himself, "Maybe in the next life."

He must be content with escaping a life at menial labor, at being able to   3
bank on the skills in personnel management he had acquired in the Army. But
there are only two takers. The large department-store chain would hire him as
a management trainee—a shoe salesman on commission, no set income, but a
trainee could qualify for GI Bill benefits as well as the commissions. Not good
enough, not getting paid beyond the GI Bill; and a sales career wasn't good
enough either, the thought of his mother's years as a saleslady, years lost, still in
memory. A finance corporation offers him a job: management trainee. The title:
Assistant Manager. The job: bill collector, with low wage, but as a trainee, qualified to supplement with the GI Bill. The combined pay would be good, but he
would surely lose his job in time, would be unable to be righteously indignant
like the bill collectors he has too often had to face too often are, unable to
bother people like Mom and Dad, knowing that being unable to meet bills isn't
usually a moral shortcoming but most often an economic condition.

The GI Bill had come up again, however, setting the "gettinover" wheels in   4
motion. The nearby community college charges ninety dollars a quarter tuition, would accept him on the strength of his GED scores. That would mean
nearly four hundred dollars a month from the GI Bill, with only thirty dollars
a month for schooling ("forgetting" to account for books and supplies). What a
get-over! There would be immediate profit in simply going to school. And if he
failed, there would be nothing lost. And if he succeeded, an Associate degree in
something. He'd be better equipped to brave the job market again.

So he walks onto the community college campus in the summer of 1976.   5
It's not the campus of the University of Washington. It's more like Dominguez
High School in California. But it is a college. Chemistry: a clumsiness at the
lab, but relative grace at mathematical equations and memorization. French is
listening to audiotapes and filling out workbooks. History is enjoyable stories,
local lore from a retired newsman, easy memorization for the grade.

Then there is English. There are the stories, the taste he had always had for   6
reading, now peppered with talk of philosophy and psychology and tensions

and textures. Writing is 200 words on anything, preceded by a sentence outline. He'd write about Korea and why *The Rolling Stone* could write about conspiracies of silence, or he'd write about the problems in trying to get a son to understand that he is Puerto Rican when the only Puerto Ricans he knows are his grandparents; he'd write about whatever seemed to be on his mind at the time. The night before a paper would be due, he'd gather pen and pad, and stare. Clean the dishes. Stare. Watch an "I Love Lucy" rerun. Stare. Then sometime in the night the words would come. He'd write; scratch something out; draw arrows shifting paragraphs around; add a phrase or two. Then he'd pull out the erasable bond, making changes even as he typed, frantic to be done before school. Then he'd use the completed essay to type out an outline, feeling a little guilty about having cheated in not having produced the outline first.

The guilt showed one day when Mrs. Ray, the Indian woman in traditional 7 dress with a Ph.D. in English from Oxford, part-time instructor at the community college, said there was a problem with his writing. She must have been able to tell somehow that he was discovering what to write while writing, no prior thesis statement, no outline, just a vague notion that would materialize, magically, while writing. In her stark, small office she hands him a sheet with three familiar sayings mimeoed on it; instructs him to write on one, right there, right then. He writes on "a bird in the hand is worth two in the bush." No memory of what he had written, probably forgotten during the writing. Thirty minutes or so later, she takes the four or five pages he had written; she reads; she smiles; then she explains that she had suspected plagiarism in his previous writings. She apologizes, saying she found his writing "too serious," too abstract, not typical of her students. He is not insulted; he is flattered. He knew he could read; now he knew he could write well enough for college.

English 102, Mr. Lukens devotes a portion of the quarter to Afro-Ameri- 8 can literature. Victor reads Ishmael Reed, "I'm a Cowboy in the Boat of Ra." It begins,

> I am a cowboy in the boat of Ra,
> sidewinders in the saloons of fools
> bit my forehead   like   O
> the untrustworthiness of Egyptologists
> Who do not know their trips. Who was that
> dog faced man? they asked, the day I rode
> from town.
>
> School marms with halitosis cannot see
> the Nefertiti fake chipped on the run by slick
> germans, the hawk behind Sonny Rollins' head or
> the ritual beard of his axe; a longhorn winding
> its bells thru the Field of Reeds.

There was more, but by this point he was already entranced and excited. Poetry has meaning, more than the drama of Mark Antony's speech years back.

Mr. Lukens says that here is an instance of poetry more for effect (or maybe 9 *affect*) than for meaning, citing a line from Archibald MacLeish: "A poem should not mean / But be." But there *was* meaning in this poem. Victor writes about it. In the second stanza, the chipped Nefertitti, a reference to a false black history, with images from "The Maltese Falcon" and war movies. The "School marms" Reed mentions are like the schoolmasters at Hamilton, unknowing and seeming not to know of being unknowing. Sonny Rollins' axe and the Field of Reeds: a saxophone, a reed instrument, the African American's links to Egypt, a history whitewashed by "Egyptologists / Who do not know their trips." He understood the allusions, appreciated the wordplay. The poem had the politics of Bracy, the language of the block, TV of the fifties, together in the medium Mr. D had introduced to Victor, Papi, but now more powerful. This was fun; this was politics. This was Victor's history, his life with language play.

Years later, Victor is on a special two-man panel at a conference of the 10 Modern Language Association. He shares the podium with Ishmael Reed. Victor gives a talk on "Teaching as Social Action," receives applause, turns to see Ishmael Reed looking him in the eye, applauding loudly. He tries to convey how instrumental this "colleague" had been in his life.

He'll be an English major. Mr. Lukens is his advisor, sets up the community 11 college curriculum in such a way as to have all but the major's requirements for a BA from the University of Washington out of the way. The University of Washington is the only choice: it's relatively nearby, tuition for Vietnam veterans is $176 a quarter. "Maybe in this life."

His AA degree in his back pocket, his heart beating audibly with exhilaration 12 and fear, he walks up the campus of the University of Washington, more excited than at Disneyland when he was sixteen. He's proud: a regular transfer student, no special minority waivers. The summer of 1977.

But the community is not college in the same way the University is. The 13 community college is torn between vocational training and preparing the unprepared for traditional university work. And it seems unable to resolve the conflict (see Cohen and Brawer).[1] His high community-college GPA is no measure of what he is prepared to undertake at the University. He fails at French 103, unable to carry the French conversations, unable to do the reading, unable to do the writing, dropping the course before the failure becomes a matter of record. He starts again. French 101, only to find he is still not really competitive with the white kids who had had high school French. But he cannot fail, and he does not fail, thanks to hour after hour with French tapes after his son's in bed.

---

[1]Cohen, Arthur M., and Florence B. Brawer. *The American Community College.* 2nd ed., Jossey-Bass, 1989.

English 301, the literature survey, is fun. Chaucer is a ghetto boy, poking fun 14
at folks, the rhyming reminding him of when he did the dozens on the block;
Chaucer telling bawdy jokes: "And at the wyndow out she putte hir hole . . .
'A berd, a berd!; quod hende Nicholas." So this is literature. Chaucer surely ain't
white. At least he doesn't sound white, "the first to write poetry in the vernacular," he's told. Spenser is exciting: images of knights and damsels distressing,
magic and dragons, the *Lord of the Rings* that he had read in Korea paling in the
comparison. Donne is a kick: trying to get laid when he's Jack Donne, with a
rap the boys from the block could never imagine; building church floors with
words on a page when he's Dr. John Donne. Every reading is an adventure,
never a nod, no matter how late into the night the reading. For his first paper,
Victor, the 3.8 at Tacoma Community College, gets 36 out of a possible 100 —
"for your imagination," written alongside the grade.

I was both devastated and determined, my not belonging was verified but I 15
was not ready to be shut down, not so quickly. So to the library to look up what
the Professor himself had published: *Proceedings of the Spenser Society.* I had no
idea what the Professor was going on about in his paper, but I could see the
pattern: an introduction that said something about what others had said, what
he was going to be writing about, in what order, and what all this would prove;
details about what he said he was going to be writing about, complete with
quotes, mainly from the poetry, not much from other writers on Spenser; and a
"therefore." It wasn't the five-paragraph paper Mr. Lukens had insisted on, not
just three points, not just repetition of the opening in the close, but the pattern
was essentially the same. The next paper: 62 out of 100 and a "Much better."
Course grade: B. Charity.

I never vindicated myself with that professor. I did try, tried to show that 16
I didn't need academic charity. Economic charity was hard enough. I took
my first graduate course from him. This time I got an "All well and good, but
what's the point?" alongside a "B" for a paper. I had worked on that paper all
summer long.

I have had to face that same professor, now a Director of Freshman Writ- 17
ing, at conferences. And with every contact, feelings of insecurity well up from
within, the feeling that I'm seen as the minority (a literal term in academics for
those of us of color), the feeling of being perceived as having gotten through
because I am a minority, an insecurity I face often. But though I never got over
the stigma with that professor (whether real or imagined), I did get some idea
on how to write for the University.

Professorial Discourse Analysis became a standard practice: go to the library; 18
see what the course's professor had published; try to discern a pattern to her
writing; try to mimic the pattern. Some would begin with anecdotes. Some
would have no personal pronouns. Some would cite others' research. Some
would cite different literary works to make assertions about one literary work.

> *I was both devastated and determined, my not belonging was verified but I was not ready to be shut down, not so quickly. So to the library to look up what the Professor himself had published: Proceedings of the Spenser Society. I had no idea what the Professor was going on about in his paper, but I could see the pattern.*

Whatever they did, I would do too. And it worked, for the most part, so that I could continue the joy of time travel and mind travel with those, and within those, who wrote about things I had discovered I liked to think about: Shakespeare and work versus pleasure, religion and the day-to-day world, racism, black Othello and the Jewish Merchant of Venice; Dickens and the impossibility of really getting into the middle class (which I read as "race," getting into the white world, at the time), pokes at white folks (though the Podsnaps were more likely jabs at the middle class); Milton and social responsibility versus religious mandates; Yeats and being assimilated and yet other (critically conscious with a cultural literacy, I'd say now); others and other themes. And soon I was writing like I had written in the community college: some secondary reading beforehand, but composing the night before a paper was due, a combination of fear that nothing will come and faith that something would eventually develop, then revising to fit the pattern discovered in the Professorial Discourse Analysis, getting "A's" and "B's," and getting comments like "I never saw that before."

There were failures, of course. One professor said my writing was too formulaic. One professor said it was too novel. Another wrote only one word for the one paper required of the course: "nonsense." But while I was on the campus I could escape and not. I could think about the things that troubled me or intrigued me, but through others' eyes in other times and other places. I couldn't get enough, despite the pain and the insecurity. 19

School becomes his obsession. There is the education. But the obsession is as much, if not more, in getting a degree, not with a job in mind, just the degree, just because he thinks he can, despite all that has said he could not. His marriage withers away, not with rancor, just melting into a dew. The daily routine has him taking the kid to a daycare / school at 6:00 A.M., then himself to school, from school to work as a groundskeeper for a large apartment complex; later, a maintenance man, then a garbage man, then a plumber, sometimes coupled with other jobs: shipping clerk for the library, test proctor. From work to pick up the kid from school, prepare dinner, maybe watch a TV show with the kid, tuck him into bed, read. There are some girlfriends along the way, and he studies them too: the English major who won constant approval from the same professor who had given him the 36 for being imaginative; the art major who had traveled to France (French practice); the fisheries major whose father was 20 an executive vice president for IBM (practice at being middle class). Victor was going to learn—quite consciously—what it means to be white, middle class. He didn't see the exploitation; not then; he was obsessed. There were things going on in his classes that he did not understand and that the others did. He didn't know what the things were that he didn't understand, but he knew that even those who didn't do as well as he did, somehow did not act as foreign as he felt. He was the only colored kid in every one of those classes. And he hadn't the time nor the racial affiliation to join the Black Student Union or Mecha. He was on his own, an individual pulling on his bootstraps, looking out for number one. He's not proud of the sensibility, but isolation—and, likely, exploitation of others—are the stuff of racelessness.

There were two male friends, Mickey, a friend to this day, and Luis el Loco. 21 Luis was a *puertoriceño*, from Puerto Rico, who had found his way to Washington by having been imprisoned in the federal penitentiary at MacNeal Island, attending school on a prison-release program. Together, they would enjoy talking in Spanglish, listening to *salsa*. But Luis was a Modern Languages major, Spanish literature. Nothing there to exploit. It's a short-lived friendship. Mickey was the other older student in Victor's French 101 course, white, middle class, yet somehow other, one who had left the country during Vietnam, a disc jockey in Amsterdam. The friendship begins with simply being the two older men in the class, longer away from adolescence than the rest; the friendship grows with conversations about politics, perceptions about America from abroad, literature. But Victor would not be honest with his friend about feeling foreign until years later, a literary bravado. Mickey was well read in the literary figures Victor was coming to know. Mickey would be a testing ground for how Victor was reading, another contact to be exploited. Eventually, Mickey and his wife would introduce Victor to their friend, a co-worker at the post office. This is Carol. She comes from a life of affluence, and from a life of poverty, a traveler within the class system, not a journey anyone would volunteer for, but one which provides a unique education, a path not unlike Paulo Freire's. From her, there is the physical and the things he would know of the middle class, discussed explicitly, and there is their mutual isolation. There is love and friendship, still his closest friend, still his lover.

But before Carol there is simply the outsider obsessed. He manages the BA. He 22 cannot stop, even as the GI Bill reaches its end. He will continue to gather credentials until he is kicked out. Takes the GRE, does not do well, but gets into the graduate program with the help of references from within the faculty—and with the help of minority status in a program decidedly low in numbers of minorities. "Minority," or something like that, is typed on the GRE test results in his file, to be seen while scanning the file for the references. His pride is hurt, but he remembers All Saints, begins to believe in the biases of standardized tests: back in the eighth grade, a failure top student; now a near-failure, despite a 3.67 at the competitive Big University of State. Not all his grades, he knew, were matters of charity. He had earned his GPA, for the most part. Nevertheless, he is shaken.

More insecure than ever, there are no more overnight papers. Papers are writ- 23 ten over days, weeks, paragraphs literally cut and laid out on the floor to be pasted. One comment appears in paper after paper: "Logic?" He thinks, "Yes." He does not understand. Carol cannot explain the problem. Neither can Mickey. He does not even consider asking the professors. To ask would be an admission of ignorance, "stupid spic" still resounding within. This is his problem.

Then by chance (exactly how is now forgotten), he hears a tape of a confer- 24 ence paper delivered by the applied linguist Robert Kaplan. Kaplan describes contrastive rhetoric. Kaplan describes a research study conducted in New York City among Puerto Ricans who are bilingual and Puerto Ricans who are mono- lingual in English, and he says that the discourse patterns, the rhetorical patterns which include the logic, of monolingual Puerto Ricans are like those of Puerto Rican bilinguals and different from Whites, more Greek than the Latin-like prose of American written English. Discourse analysis takes on a new intensity. At this point, what this means is that he will have to go beyond patterns in his writing, become more analytical of the connections between ideas. The impli- cations of Kaplan's talk, for him at least, will take on historical and political significance as he learns more of rhetoric.

About the same time as that now lost tape on Kaplan's New York research 25 (a study that was never published, evidently), Victor stumbles into his first rhet- oric course.

The preview of course offerings announces a course titled "Theories of 26 Invention," to be taught by Anne Ruggles Gere. His GRE had made it clear that he was deficient in Early American Literature. Somewhere in his mind he recalls reading that Benjamin Franklin had identified himself as an inventor; so somehow, Victor interprets "Theories of Invention" as "Theories of Inventors," an American lit course. What he discovers is Rhetoric.

Not all at once, not just in that first class on rhetoric, I discover some things 27 about writing, my own, and about the teaching of writing. I find some of mod- ern composition's insights are modern hindsights. I don't mind the repetition. Some things bear repeating. The repetitions take on new significance and are elaborated upon in a new context, a new time. Besides, not everyone who teaches writing knows of rhetoric, though I believe everyone should.

I read Cicero's *de Inventione*. It's a major influence in rhetoric for centuries. The 28 strategies he describes on how to argue a court case bears a remarkable resemblance to current academic discourse, the pattern I first discovered when I first tried to figure out what I had not done in that first English course at the University.

Janet Emig looks to depth psychology and studies on creativity and even 29 neurophysiology, the workings of the brain's two hemispheres, to pose the case that writing is a mode of learning. She explains what I had been doing with my first attempts at college writing, neither magic nor a perversion. Cicero had said much the same in his *de Oratore* in the first century BCE (Before the Common Era, the modern way of saying BC):

> *Writing* is said to be *the best and most excellent modeler and teacher of oratory;* and not without reason; for if what is meditated and considered easily surpasses sudden and extemporary speech, a constant and diligent habit of writing will surely be of more effect than meditation and consideration itself; since all the arguments relating to the subject on which we write, whether they are suggested by art, or by a certain power of genius and understanding, will present themselves, and occur to us, while we examine and contemplate it in the full light of our intellect and all the thoughts and words, which are the most expressive of their kind, must of necessity come under and submit to the keenness of our judgment while writing; and a fair arrangement and collocation of the words is effected by writing, in a certain rhythm and measure, not poetical, but oratorical. (*de Oratore* I.cxxxiv)

Writing is a way of discovering, of learning, of thinking. Cicero is arguing the case for literacy in ways we still argue or are arguing anew.

David Bartholomae and Anthony Petrosky discuss literary theorists like Jona- 30 than Culler and the pedagogical theorist Paulo Freire to come up with a curriculum in which reading is used to introduce basic writers, those students who come into the colleges not quite prepared for college work, to the ways of academic discourse. Quintilian, like others of his time, the first century CE, and like others before his time, advocates reading as a way to come to discover the ways of language and the ways of writing and the ways to broaden the range of experience.

Kenneth Bruffee, Peter Elbow, and others, see the hope of democratizing the 31 classroom through peer-group learning. So did Quintilian:

> But as emulation is of use to those who have made some advancement of learning, so, to those who are but beginning and still of tender age, to imitate their schoolfellows is more pleasant than to imitate their master, for the very reason that it is more easy; for they who are learning the first rudiments will scarcely dare to exalt themselves to the hope of attaining that eloquence which they regard as the highest; they will rather fix on what is nearest to them, as vines attached to trees fain the top by taking hold of the lower branches first (23–24).

Quintilian describes commenting on student papers in ways we consider new:

> [T]he powers of boys sometimes sink under too great severity in correction; for they despond, and grieve, and at last hate their work; and what is most

> prejudicial, while they fear everything; they cease to attempt anything. . . .
> A teacher ought, therefore, to be as agreeable as possible, that remedies, which
> are rough in their nature, may be rendered soothing by gentleness of hand; he
> ought to praise some parts of his pupils' performances, tolerate some, and to
> alter others, giving his reasons why the alterations are made. (100)

Richard Haswell recommends minimal scoring of student papers, sticking to one or two items in need of correction per paper. Nancy Sommers warns against rubber-stamp comments on student papers, comments like "awk;" she says comments ought to explain. Both have more to say than Quintilian on such matters, but in essence both are Quintilian revisited.

Edward P. J. Corbett looks to Quintilian, Cicero, and others from among the 32 ancients, especially Aristotle, to write *Classical Rhetoric for the Modern Student*. In some ways, the book says little that is different from other books on student writing. But the book is special in its explicit connections to ancient rhetorical traditions.

Without a knowledge of history and traditions, we risk running in circles 33 while seeking new paths. Without knowing the traditions, there is no way of knowing which traditions to hold dear and which to discard. Self evident? Maybe. Yet the circles exist.

For all the wonders I had found in literature — and still find — literature 34 seemed to me self-enveloping. What I would do is read and enjoy. And, when it was time to write, what I would write about would be an explanation of what I had enjoyed, using words like *Oedipal complex* or *polyvocal* or *anxiety* or *unpacking*, depending on what I had found in my discourse-analytical journeys, but essentially saying "this is what I saw" or "this is how what I read took on a special meaning for me" (sometimes being told that what I had seen or experienced was nonsense). I could imagine teaching literature — and often I do, within the context of composition — but I knew that at best I'd be imparting or imposing one view: the what I saw or the meaning for me. The reader-response theorists I would come to read, Rosenblatt, Fish, Culler, and others, would make sense to me, that what matters most is what the reader finds. Bakhtin's cultural and political dimension would make even more sense: that all language is an approximation, generated and understood based on what one has experienced with language. In teaching literature, I thought, there would be those among students I would face who would come to take on reading, perhaps; likely some who would appreciate more fully what they had read. But it did not seem to me that I could somehow make someone enjoy. Enjoyment would be a personal matter: from the self, for the self.

And what if I did manage a Ph.D. and did get a job as a professor? I would 35 have to publish. A guest lecturer in a medieval lit course spoke of one of the important findings in his new book: medieval scribes were conscious of the thickness of the lozenge, the medieval version of the comma. He found that thinner lozenges would indicate a slight pause in reading; thicker lozenges, longer pauses. Interesting, I reckon. Surely of interest to a select few. But so what, in some larger sense? What would I write about?

Then I stumbled onto rhetoric. Here was all that language had been to me. 36 There were the practical matters of writing and teaching writing. There were the stylistic devices, the tricks of language use that most people think about when they hear the word *rhetoric;* "Let's cut through the rhetoric." It's nice to have those devices at one's disposal—nice, even important, to know when those devices are operating. But there is more. Rhetoric's classic definition as the art of persuasion suggests a power. So much of what we do when we speak or write is suasive in intent. So much of what we receive from others—from family and friends to thirty-second blurbs on TV—is intended to persuade. Recognizing how this is done gives greater power to choose. But rhetoric is still more.

Rhetoric is the conscious use of language: "observing in any given case 37 the available means of persuasion," to quote Aristotle (I.ii). As the conscious use of language, rhetoric would include everything that is conveyed through language: philosophy, history, anthropology, psychology, sociology, literature, politics—"the use of language as a symbolic means of inducing cooperation in beings that by nature respond to symbols," according to modern rhetorician Kenneth Burke.[2] The definition says something about an essentially human characteristic: our predilection to use symbols. Language is our primary symbol system. The ability to learn language is biologically transmitted. Burke's definition points to language as ontological, part of our being. And his definition suggests that it is epistemological, part of our thinking, an idea others say more about (see Leff).[3]

So to study rhetoric becomes a way of studying humans. Rhetoric becomes 38 for me the complete study of language, the study of the ways in which peoples have accomplished all that has been accomplished beyond the instinctual. There were the ancient greats saying that there was political import to the use of language. There were the modern greats saying that how one comes to know is at least mediated by language, maybe even constituted in language. There were the pragmatic applications. There was the possibility that in teaching writing and in teaching rhetoric as conscious considerations of language use I could help others like myself: players with language, victims of the language of failure.

---

[2] Burke, Kenneth. *A Rhetoric of Motives.* U of California P, 1969, p. 46.
[3] Leff, Michael C. "In Search of Ariadne's Thread: A Review of the Recent Literature on Rhetorical Theory." *Central States Speech Journal*, no. 29, 1978, pp. 73–91.

Questions for Discussion and Journaling

1. This account shifts back and forth between the first person (*I*) and the third person (*Victor*, *he*). What effects does that shifting create? Does it break any rules you've been taught?

2. How does Villanueva define *rhetoric*? What else does he say that studying rhetoric helps you study?

3. Have you ever tried observing and imitating the writing moves that other writers make, as Villanueva describes doing with his English teachers ("Professorial Discourse Analysis")? If so, what was your experience doing so? If not, what would you need to look for in order to do the kind of imitation Villanueva describes?

4. In paragraph 6, Villanueva describes his college writing process as, "The night before a paper was due, he'd gather pen and pad, and stare. Clean the dishes. Stare. Watch an 'I Love Lucy' rerun. Stare. Then sometime in the night the words would come." What elements of this process resemble your own? How is yours different?

5. Villanueva describes his own experience of encountering affirmative action — how he benefited from it, and how it also had some negative effects. Was this an account you might have expected to hear? If not, how did it differ from your perceptions of affirmative action?

6. In telling the story of his writing process and being called into Mrs. Ray's office (para. 7), Villanueva suggests that he expected Mrs. Ray would take issue with his writing style of "discovering what to write while writing, no prior thesis statement, no outline, just a vague notion of what would materialize, magically, while writing." What are some of your own experiences of being taught how you are supposed to plan and write?

7. Did you attend other colleges before attending the one at which you're using this book? Villanueva describes the difference between his community college and the University of Washington (paras. 5–21). If you've attended both two-year and four-year schools, what differences do you see? If you've attended different schools of the same sort, what were the differences? Can you see your experiences at different schools as acquiring different "literacies"?

8. In a number of places in this excerpt, Villanueva talks not just about "literacy sponsors" but about authors whose ideas about writing and teaching writing shaped his own. Before coming to college, what authors had you read that shaped your thinking about writing?

Applying and Exploring Ideas

1. Villanueva writes that "school became my obsession," and yet he describes struggling with writing for school. In other words, he ran the risk of being barred from doing the thing he loved because of his writing. Consider the activities you

most love being part of: Was there ever a moment where language or writing threatened to (or did) bar your access to them? Or where language or writing provided your gateway to them? Write a two- to three-page descriptive narrative (imitate Villanueva's style, if you like) about that situation.

2. Analyze Villanueva's piece using Brandt's notion of literacy sponsorship. What literacy sponsors appear in Villanueva's literacy narrative? (Start by making as complete a list as you can.) What did these sponsors allow and limit?

3. Do some Professorial Discourse Analysis of two college or high school teachers you've had. What did they each expect from your writing? Did they agree or differ in their expectations? Describe their expectations in two to three pages, and give specific examples of what each expected.

4. Look up information about Robert Kaplan's "contrastive rhetoric." Write a two- to three-page paper describing contrastive rhetoric and explaining why it might have helped a student like Villanueva make sense of his own experiences in college.

- -
META MOMENT   After reading Villanueva, what is your understanding of the relationship between language, identity, and power? How can this understanding help you better understand your own experiences or those of other people you know?
- -

Challenging Our Labels

Rejecting the Language of Remediation

ARTURO TEJADA JR.
ESTHER GUTIERREZ
BRISA GALINDO
DeSHONNA WALLACE
SONIA CASTANEDA

Framing the Reading

This article was written by five first-year composition students at California State University, San Bernardino, as part of their "rebellion" against being labeled "remedial" writers due to the results of a standardized, timed test they took prior to entering college.

The issues these students raise here should be ones with which you can relate. Even if you were never labeled remedial, you likely had to take (and be judged by your performance on) timed writing tests. You've probably been labeled in some form, and then encountered specific treatment and experience based on those labels. You've probably encountered teachers whose perceptions of you colored your feelings about yourself and your ability. And certainly the type of school you attended determined the kinds of experiences and resources to which you were exposed.

This article illustrates many of the threshold concepts discussed in this book, and also many of the claims made by other scholars in this chapter. For example, Tejada

et al. talk a great deal about how words, ideas, and labels made them who they are, both as people and as writers. In other words, thoughts and ideas make reality, as we explained in Chapter 1 (p. 7). Their experiences illustrate what happens to students when the two stories about writing that we discussed in that chapter collide: Their administrators and high school

Tejada, Arturo, Jr., et al. "Challenging Our Labels: Rejecting the Language of Remediation." *Young Scholars in Writing*, vol. 11, 2014, pp. 5–16.

teachers seem to be acting out of a traditional story about writing as error avoidance, while their college writing teacher seems to see writing as much richer than that. These writers illustrate repeatedly the ways that their writing (and their sense of themselves) is impacted by their prior experiences, that it is possible to see writing as a powerful way to get things done and take action (in this case, as rebellion against labels they don't want to accept), and that all writers have more to learn — thus, it's problematic to label any particular group of students as "remedial."

Getting Ready to Read

Before you read, do at least one of the following activities:

- Do you have any experience being tested and then "placed" into a writing or English class? If so, what was that experience like?
- Conduct an Internet search for "remediation" and "remedial writer" and see what you find.

As you read, consider the following questions:

- Where do you relate to the authors' feelings and experiences?
- Are there any unfamiliar terms, particularly those related to testing, placement, and orientation at their school? You may want to bring these up in class.

EVEN THOUGH MOST California State University campuses no longer offer 1 remedial English courses, the university's system-wide English Placement Test (EPT) continues to designate between 50–80% of first-year students enrolled on its twenty-three campuses as remedial writers, although sometimes using the label "not yet proficient." English departments have resisted these categories in various ways, and now most of them have adopted local enactments of what Arizona State University calls "stretch" programs (Glau) in which students do substantive text work that is not, and is not named, remedial. On our campus, students are directed to one-, two-, or three-quarter first-year writing (FYW) courses in which they are taught in the same cohort by the same instructor.

However, on our campus, as on many others, despite these curricular and 2 pedagogical changes, the language of remediation has continued to be imposed by institutional structures in both official communications and campus conversation — again, even though our English department has not offered remedial writing courses for several years.

Based on our EPT scores, we five FYW students were categorized as reme- 3 dial. The implications of that assessment became clear to us in unexpected and conflicting ways. For example, although documents from the Chancellor's

Office as well as communications from our home campus personnel used the term *remedial*, we were assigned to a three-quarter (thirty-week) FYW "stretch" course, listed by the English department as nonremedial. In fact, far from being remedial in either its topics or its pedagogy, our coursework helped us to challenge the language of remediation that continues to mark students like us and our writing.

Elizabeth Wardle and Doug Downs's *Writing about Writing* unmasked the 4 language of remediation for us and for our professors, class TAs, and writing center tutors, pushing us all not only to stretch our own ideas about labeled writing populations but also to speak out to the academic community about how institutional language constructs students and shapes their relationships with their families, with other students, with professors, and within the professions they plan to enter.

As we read Deborah Brandt's work on literacy sponsorship and Jean Anyon's 5 descriptions of socioeconomic-status (SES) differentiated high school curricula and pedagogy, we began to challenge CSU's administrative labeling practices, showing how these labels isolate and limit students. This has come to matter enormously to us, and thus we offer the following narratives, which have helped us to better understand the importance of language and labels. We hope to challenge others to think about how the language they use each day shapes writers and the writing that takes place in their spaces. We begin by explaining how we came to *feel* remedial and how that constructed us as students and writers, then show how those perceptions clashed with our experiences in our FYW class. Next we describe our research into labels and labeling. We conclude by showing some of the impact we believe our work has had locally and by challenging others to join in this work in their own spaces. We especially hope that we can encourage students who have been labeled remedial to realize that they are not alone and that they don't have to accept someone else's label.

WHY DID WE FEEL REMEDIAL WHEN WE WERE NOT IN A REMEDIAL COURSE?

Even "remedial" students can read signs! Even before we arrived on campus, 6 we knew that we were remedial. And if we didn't, we quickly learned who we "really" were, and it wasn't pretty.

Sonia: As a first-generation college student, I had been told by my parents 7 that they would always try their best to support me and to help me reach my goals, so receiving an acceptance letter from a four-year university was the best feeling ever. My parents were beyond excited and proud of me. Any chance they had, they told people that I got accepted to a four-year university and that not many people can get in, but I did because I worked hard for it. Two weeks later, when I received my EPT results, I was confused. I didn't know what my scores meant until I went to orientation and found out that I was placed in what they called a remedial course for English. I was speechless. The word *remedial* hit me like a brick. I knew I was being accepted by Cal State, but when I found out that I was placed in a remedial English course I began to question myself—if I were worthy of their sponsorship. I didn't have the courage to tell my parents that their daughter needed to take a "remedial" course. Just the word itself was disappointing and made me feel embarrassed. That was two years ago. Even though I have successfully passed my English course and Cal State no longer labels me remedial, my parents still don't know that I was in a remedial class, and I don't know if they ever will.

Esther: Like Sonia, once I received my acceptance letter I was proud of 8 myself that I had made it—against all odds I had made it. In fact, I was not aware of what the term *remedial* even meant until I came to orientation at CSUSB. But I quickly learned. As I sat through the dean of the natural sciences' speech, I heard him use it about classes that were not "college level." I remember the dean making specific remarks about these courses, that if you had to take any remedial classes you were already behind on being able to graduate in four years. This meant if you were not enrolled in Math 110 or English 107, you were behind. As I sat there looking at my paper that had on it the classes I was eligible to enroll in, I felt ashamed. My paper had 102 for English, while everyone around me had a 107 on theirs. I felt so embarrassed. I had never wanted to run and hide so much as I did at this moment. Already behind, and I had not even started? Hearing this come from someone of such power made me feel as though I was no match for all the other students who had placed into "college-level" English. My first thought after hearing this was, "Oh, great, now I must take high school English all over again." Being labeled remedial shook my confidence as a student because all my life I had been told that going to college was basically not an option for me. Then once I finally made it, I had to carry with me this "remedial" label which shows people that I wasn't good enough to be a regular college student, that I was underprepared and needed fixing. Feeling accepted and welcomed to the university is very important as an incoming freshman. Once I left that orientation, I knew I would still have to demonstrate to the university administrators as well as myself that I belonged at CSUSB. The feeling of not belonging created an unnecessary barrier for me as a student because of the negative impact the label "remedial" carries.

Arturo: When I went to orientation, I was extremely confident because my 9 hard work in high school, resulting in a high GPA, allowed me to gain acceptance into every school I applied to, and I chose Cal State, San Bernardino. When I received my schedule, I saw that I had an English 102 class and a Math 90 class. I had no idea what those meant, but the orientation instructor told us that students who were placed below Math 110 or below English 107 were in "remedial classes" and had one year to pass them or else they were kicked off the campus. Like the others here, these words stung so much because I had worked so hard to get here, only to find myself at the bottom of the food chain, which meant being looked down upon by everyone. I felt like I did not belong at this school.

As soon as I got home and told others about my classes, they scrutinized me intensely. My father even told me to go to a community college because he thought that I should not be in Cal State if I was a "remedial" student and that I would be discriminated against there. However, when he left me at my Cal State dorm, he said, "I know you are better than the label, but now you just have to prove to them how much you want it." 10

My first reaction to the orientation adviser's warning about finishing our "remedial" classes within one year or being kicked out was shock. The next was shame. But then I began to feel afraid—afraid that he was right to segregate me, that I would never be good enough to fit in. This fear either makes or breaks students because they can carry it for the rest of their college career, creating a sense of helplessness that may ultimately cause them to drop out: if they'll never measure up, what point is there in continuing? Luckily, I instead used fear as motivation. I allowed it to consume me and become an obsession, the reason I got up every morning. My fear and anger of never measuring up in the eyes of my peers and superiors, due to the discrimination that came with the "remedial" label, made me want to do my absolute best to prove them wrong by working that much more on my craft—because in my eyes, failure was not an option. 11

Being discriminated against is painful, especially when it jeopardizes people's futures. It's been three years since I was labeled, and I've accomplished so much during that time. However, despite my accomplishments, the label still stings as much as it did at first. That fear of never measuring up, never being good enough, still consumes me to my very core. It shows up in my school-work, even in my day-to-day behavior. I'm constantly second-guessing myself; the question *Do I belong here?* will probably be in the back of my mind for the rest of my college career and maybe even my professional career. Much like so many others, no matter how much I fight against it, trying to prove that I'm not "remedial," that label has become part of my identity because of the internal scars it's inflicted. Not everyone has the good fortune to be stubborn in facing and enduring the label, in trying to prove it wrong, which is why all of us feel so keenly about this project. 12

Brisa: When I started college, I did know what remediation meant because of an explanation from my high school AVID (Advancement via Individual Determination, a college-readiness program) teacher. He said, "When you place in remedial it means that you have to take extra English classes in order to be considered a 'real college student.'" That shocked me because I had worked so hard to get into a university, only to find out that I was not a "real college 13 student" after all. Like Sonia, I was too embarrassed to tell anyone in my family that I was remedial because I felt guilty. I almost felt ashamed when I told people what school I was going to because I didn't know if one small move could jeopardize my university standing. I couldn't enjoy my first year in college because the thought of being kicked out of the university followed my every move. If I had any doubts about what the university thought about me, they flew out the window when I was sitting in my philosophy class and another student asked the professor a question about the *Crito*. He answered, "It's not like you are remedial!" That made me feel ashamed, lower than the other philosophy majors. I'm not saying that professors should watch every word they say in their classes, but it was another reminder that even though I was sitting in the same classroom with "regular" students, I would still be looked down upon if anyone discovered that I was remedial. I hoped no one would find out, and I wondered whether the philosophy major was off limits to people like me. It made me sad but also mad. I never knew how much a simple word could affect me until I was labeled remedial; I still feel the loss of that pride I had when I was first admitted. Instead of identifying as a legitimate student with my school—which is an important element in persistence—I still sometimes feel like a fake, as if someone will discover that I don't really belong. I think that even when I receive my diploma, I'll still be looking for the attachment that reads "provisional" or somehow not-real.

DeShonna: When I was graduating from high school, the majority of the   14
teachers pushed students into going to a junior college not only because of price but because we would learn more there in order to transfer to a four-year university as "equals." Already I felt remedial because I could see that going into college meant going into a hierarchy. You take a placement test and find out where you fall in that hierarchy. Then once I got my results and saw that I would be taking remedial courses, I knew for sure that I was not considered college level. Shocking, because no one had said that this test would rank us as remedial or not; it was instead described as showing whether or not students should take a freshman English class. I did not want to skip that class and didn't think that I would be looked down on for taking it.

Having graduated high school with honors and thus gained admission to   15
any CSU campus I chose, I thought as time went on that maybe I had escaped CSUSB's hierarchy. But once I got to campus, the orientation session let me know that although I may have had a great past, the EPT made me remedial now. The counselors placed me in a thirty-week English class and emphasized that failing to complete remedial classes in my first year would get me kicked out of school. As a pre-nursing student, they stressed, I had no room for failure. I began to feel less and less sure of myself. They actually told me that because I had to take remedial courses, most likely I would in fact not even make it into the nursing major. This bothered me because the orientation staff, without

knowing anything about me, judged my lifetime capabilities by one inaccurately described placement test. Although they may have thought they were doing a good deed in being realistic and welcoming students to "the real world," they were only increasing the odds that I would fail by *predicting* that I would fail. The remedial title somehow also entered into the social fabric of the school, so that even in places like the writing center, I felt that some tutors treated me differently from other students once they found out what English class I was in — even if I came with work from another class like philosophy. So for most of that year, I went into the writing center only to fulfill assignments for my English class.

So — we all had plenty of people to tell us that we were remedial and exactly what that meant: not-good, fake, damaged, unlikely to succeed. We were embarrassed; we felt marginal, inferior, and alienated. Some of us were angry, but more of us just decided that we had to play the university's game. However, the labels mattered so much to our identities that when other students asked us what "English" we were taking, we avoided the questions or we lied. 16

AND THEN WE SHOWED UP FOR OUR FIRST "NOT-REMEDIAL REMEDIAL" ENGLISH CLASS

We came through the door not knowing what to expect, but expecting it not to be good — and again we were confused. Our professor didn't seem to have heard that we were remedial. When we began reading and writing, she kept pestering us about "exigency," which didn't seem like something we remedial students should have. It didn't seem like something that went along with the Google definition of *remedial* as "1. Giving or intended as a remedy or cure. 2. Provided or intended for students who are experiencing learning difficulties." What we were called and what we were actually doing in class just didn't add up, so we spent a lot of time wondering what we were being cured of, and exactly what "learning difficulties" had placed us in what the university, at least, thought was a remedial English course. 17

Sonia: I can still remember how nervous I was that first day of our class; my heart was pounding so fast that I thought I might explode as I sat there looking around. The classroom little by little started to fill in, and the professor came in and gave us our syllabus and explained what we would be doing for the quarter. I was shocked when I started reading the syllabus. I thought it would have a lot of grammar lessons or basic instructions on how to do an essay, but it didn't. It had a lot of reading passages and articles by scholars like Michel Foucault, Peter Elbow, James Paul Gee, and many more. Why were we reading these scholars if this was a remedial course? 18

What surprised me the most was the professor. She never treated us like 19 remedial students. She believed in us and knew from the beginning that we had a lot of potential. She gave us work that many other professors wouldn't give their first-year students. At the end of class, I knew that I wasn't a remedial student and neither were my classmates. We were labeled by the school, but our work said something else. It showed that we were capable of being scholars.

Arturo: Coming into my FYW class, I was so furious that the only thing 20 I was interested in was proving to Professor Hanson that I could write just as well as, if not better than, any one of her students in the non-"remedial" ten-week course. I refused to accept the mediocrity, the failure, the being looked down on that I felt the university was assigning me. I was determined to prove not just to my professors and everyone around me but especially to myself that I belonged, that I was an equal, normal college student. But as we began to read John Swales, James Paul Gee, Deborah Brandt, Ann Johns, Sherman Alexie, bell hooks, Mike Rose,

> At the end of the class I knew that I wasn't a remedial student and neither were my classmates. We were labeled by the school, but our work said something else. It showed that we were capable of being scholars.

and others, I noticed that Professor Hanson believed in us, saw us as normal, and challenged us. One way she did this—beyond having us read difficult, "real" work—was by asking us, surprisingly, what we would say back to them, and how they might speak to us in response. She challenged us to prove we were not the label by first using the work to prove it to ourselves. She assigned us work that even graduate students did, and then had us apply those concepts in everyday life in order to prove to others that we were not "remedial." I started to feel more confident—even proud. My dad was right: we were better than our labels, and now we had to work harder to challenge the entire structure of academia and prove who we really were—which, ironically enough, we discovered in our "remedial" class.

Esther: As I stepped into my remedial English class, I was so sure I 21 would be going over exactly the same material I had gone through in high school—because obviously I did not learn it the first time and I needed to go over it some more in order to be ready for "college-level" English. I was shocked when our professor did not hand out a grammar book and start teaching us how to construct sentences or how to properly use a comma. Instead she began by having us read scholarly journals and think critically about them. These journals were a new genre of writing we had never been exposed to. It was difficult to understand exactly what the authors were saying, but class discussion brought the meaning clearer and clearer as we began to adapt.

I was even more surprised when we began to read Jean Anyon's essay "Social 22 Class and the Hidden Curriculum of Work." She writes about the difference in the teaching methods elementary teachers use, differences that depend on the economic status and social class of the community in which a school is placed. The "executive elite" method of teaching is for schools in wealthy communities, where students are imagined as leaders, to learn to challenge and remake others' rules rather than just follow them. "In the executive elite school," Anyon writes, "work is developing one's analytical intellectual powers" (83). As we read Anyon, I could see that in K-12 I had been taught to be a follower, an obeyer; but in my FYW class, I was finally being challenged to think in more depth about the assignments, not just follow grammar rules. As the class proceeded and the level at which I was being challenged increased, I began to wonder who exactly decided this class was remedial. No one in our class needed to be cured of anything, and as far as I could see, no one had learning difficulties. We were all able to keep up, and we all worked together to unpack the readings. The term *remedial* implies that we are not at the college level, but in my "remedial" class all we ever did from the first day was college-level work.

Brisa: I took the remedial class, but to me it felt nothing like I thought a 23 remedial class would be. We were reading everything from Gee to Foucault, and we were breaking the high school habit of Jane Schaffer paragraphs by writing college essays. I didn't feel like a remedial student because of all the difficult reading that I was doing; when I asked my peers, none of them were reading what I was. I began to enjoy doing difficult work, to read in between the lines, to think critically, and to feel confident in my writing. I no longer felt that my essay was controlling me. I knew what I wanted to say, and I knew how to translate it into my paper; I controlled what I wrote.

DeShonna: When I entered the opening ten weeks of our thirty-week 24 English course, I thought this would be easy, especially since I had graduated high school with honors. However, my professor did not do the expected grammar drills but instead told us this class would be no different from the English class that any incoming college students take, except that our class was stretched over a longer span. We would get a chance to learn in more depth, she said, which would help us excel in college. As the weeks went by, we learned a lot about the academic community and read articles that graduate students said they were having difficulty with. This led me to question why we were considered "not yet proficient" by the English department and remedial by everyone else, especially when my English class pedagogy was more advanced than some of the classes I saw "proficient" students taking. After icebreakers in class, I finally felt that I could speak on remediation without feeling ashamed. I began to wonder why over half of Cal State students were being labeled remedial, why the majority of the students who are defined as remedial are minorities, and why students who start off being classified as remedial and not yet proficient end up with lower retention rates (Tierney and Garcia 2).

However, exigency took on life when our professor offered us extra credit 25 to attend the Celebration of Writing for FYW and said that she hoped we might get excited about entering the contest ourselves. Us? Remedial students earning writing awards? It became even more confusing when during the awards ceremony, one of her colleagues in the composition department gave a speech celebrating the successful elimination of remedial classes on our campus. "What?" we demanded during our next class. How could she make that claim when we were all acutely aware of our own remedial status and the remedial status of our stretch class? Yes, we had begun not to feel remedial while we were actually in class, but we sure knew we were outside of it.

WE DID RESEARCH ON LABELS AND REMEDIATION AND BECAME EVEN MORE CONFUSED

Our professor didn't have any answers that satisfied us, but she agreed that we 26 could take it on for our winter-quarter research project. Because we found the disjunction between what the institution said about us, what we were learning in class, and what we thought about ourselves puzzling, irritating, and at times enraging, we decided that we needed to look beyond our own experiences to the work of those we were now describing as "other scholars." We were especially attracted to Brandt's work on literacy sponsors, Gee's on identity kits, Anyon's on how different educations prepare and predestine students, Elbow's and Rose's on the effects of remediation and labeling, and that of some of our fellow CSUSB students.

Brisa: Things just didn't add up. I learned while researching my remedia- 27 tion paper that over 60% of students place into some kind of remedial class in CSUSB. This shocked me when I thought about my philosophy professor's comment about remedial students: didn't he know about the 60%? Had my adviser missed the prerequisite for philosophy majors that said, "No remedial students permitted"?

I also was confused when I read Elbow's comment that "the teachers of reme- 28 dial classes are often the least well paid and the least respected" (588). When we discussed this in class, it seemed to us that if professors had the option of teaching a remedial class or a "regular" writing class, most often they would pick the regular class. How is that supposed to help us with our confidence, knowing we aren't usually first choice? We enter as remedial students, so since we are considered unprepared, wouldn't it make sense to have the most prepared professors teaching us? Although our professor was new, we were lucky in the sense that she actually wanted to teach our class. She wanted to teach our class because she was excited about us all learning together. Had she and my philosophy professor ever met?

Arturo: I was so furious when I began our class that I hardly could believe 29 Professor Hanson when she told us that she did not see any of us as "remedial students." I was amazed when she asked us if we wanted to do a paper on the topic of "remediation" for our term paper. I thought if I was going to prove that I wasn't a remedial student, I would need to interview as many students, professors, and administrators that were directly associated with the label as I could, so I did just that. I interviewed over a hundred college students, most of whom said a lot of the same things that my peers and I said: remediation means that you don't really belong, are doing "basic" work, and are less smart and less likely to succeed. When I asked the composition professors who have direct contact with students, they said that they don't look at incoming freshmen as anything but developing writers. Even the chair said, "The content of the courses in our stretch program is university level and not remedial." So why were we being labeled?

To find out I spoke to one of the college deans. He argued that, while it is 30 not good that there is a negative connotation to being in certain classes, "the fact of the matter is that students in these classes need additional help in these subjects." When I asked him whether the EPT is flawed, he said that every test has some flaw in it, but the EPT is an "adequate" test that has been working for a long time, and there is no reason to discontinue its use. He said that there could be improvements to better evaluate students coming out of high school, but he had to work within the framework of the budget, and as of now the EPT is the best way to evaluate students.

The EPT was created many years ago to help the university place students in 31 FYW classes that would give them the best chance to succeed as college students; that was its only purpose. However, this two-part exam—a multiple-choice grammar, usage, and critical thinking test, plus a thirty-minute essay—has become much more than that. Now it is seen as a proficiency test, one students can fail. Worse, it uses predicted outcomes to designate a system-wide "failure" rate of 50% or higher, depending on the population of individual campuses.

Further, the language the Educational Testing Service (ETS) website uses and 32 the way the CSU system interprets the test conflict in how they present information about the test to incoming students. ETS tells students that the test is not for admission but simply helps determine which courses best match their level of performance in English (ETS). Prior to the test, I was told how insignificant and easy it was. The ETS website even tells people not to stress about the test, so when I went to take it, I was extremely confident. I followed the advice and relaxed—until none of the test was as I expected. The multiple-choice section asked questions unlike anything that I had seen before, even on the SATs and AP tests. The essay question took awhile just to figure out what I was being asked to write about—which wasn't even being looked at by the graders, who were looking more at grammar. I did not finish the test because it took me a long time to figure out how I wanted to tackle the topic. When I write, it takes me hours just to write the first draft, which usually has numerous grammatical errors. How could I have been accurately evaluated by a test that eliminated that normal, extended writing process? Even more irritating was how my results hinged on the performance of others taking the test that day via the system's predetermined "failure" rate.

Only after I had taken the test did I realize the importance of the very differ- 33 ent language employed by the CSU campuses. They look at it as an evaluation as opposed to how the ETS presents it. There the language of remediation and the costs of failure are alive and well. I learned that EPT scores like mine result in students being unjustly labeled and prejudged prior to stepping foot inside a classroom of the university—to which they were already admitted prior to the test.

I was astonished to find out that even on our campus there was a huge dif- 34 ference in opinion regarding the topic of remediation depending on who you talked to and their ranking in academe. However, I was less surprised when I read Rose's statements about how academics get their ideas about students:

> There's not a lot of close analysis of what goes on in classrooms, [and] the cognitive give and take of instruction and what students make of it. . . . We don't get much of a sense of the texture of students' lives . . . but even less of a sense of the power of learning things and through that learning redefining who you are. Student portraits when we do get them are too often profiles of failure rather than of people with dynamic mental lives. (12)

Maybe the administrators should talk to the professors and the students and get some of that texture into their definitions. And maybe they should be reading what we read in our research.

Sonia: College students see themselves partly through the images and frame- 35 works that are constructed by their literacy sponsors. Brandt defines literacy sponsors as "any agents, local or distant, concrete or abstract, who enable, support, teach, model, as well as recruit, regulate, suppress, or withhold literacy—and gain advantage by it in some way" (334). Students might be sponsored by a scholarship, a sport, or their parents. The support they receive varies depending on the type of sponsors they have. Reading Brandt helped us reflect on our sponsors. Our families believed in us, but when they learned that we were remedial (that is, if we told them), some were afraid and warned us to scale down our hopes. They didn't want us to take on higher goals until we were ready for them. Many family members and friends assumed that our placement was remedial for a reason. Most of our high school sponsors were like DeShonna's, who said that after high school we were meant to either get jobs or go to community colleges. Brandt argues that some kinds of literacy sponsorship, in privileging one kind of literacy, actually suppress others. Cal State's sponsorship was mixed: the administration was sponsoring us as somehow special or different, which wasn't a vote of confidence, but our professor saw us as smart and capable. At first we weren't sure whether to believe her, but since Professor Hanson was pretty powerful in her belief, we began to trust in what she and other scholars said about us. So our parents supported us in our literacy goals even though the EPT shook their faith; our high school and college administrators regulated and in some ways suppressed or even withheld literacy; and our professor and her colleagues and department modeled literacy and enabled us as literate persons.

Esther: Reading Anyon's "Social Class and the Hidden Curriculum of Work" 36 was shocking and revealing. It was discouraging to discover that social and economic class differentiates teaching, so the school you attend can determine how well you become prepared to either go into the workforce or attend college. Anyon spent a full year researching five schools with different economic backgrounds. She found that although the same material was being taught throughout the five different schools, *how* the students were being taught had a huge impact. Coming from a "working-class" school, I have been taught since I was a child how to follow rules and regulations. These are the steps working-class students are taught because we are expected to go into the workforce once we are done with high school as opposed to attending college. We especially don't learn that we are on the bottom rung of a ladder on which some other students are taught to become our thinkers and managers.

Students who come from a working-class school face a hard battle every day. 37 By the ways we are taught and labeled, we face the oppression of being told we will not make it to college. Ever since I was little, I was told that people like me will find a job after high school, ending their schooling. When a high school teacher asked what I planned to do after high school, I told him I was hoping to go to CSU. He looked at me and said that if I wanted to go to a four-year university, I was in the wrong school. Our high school prepares students to go into the workforce or community college.

DeShonna: The disjunction between schools that Esther's high school 38 teacher was pointing out is a function of what Gee calls "Discourses," and these differences also help explain validity problems with the EPT. A Discourse, according to Gee, "is a sort of 'identity kit,' which comes complete with instructions on how to talk, act, and write as taking on a particular social role that others will recognize" (484). High school and college are two very different Discourses. When I entered college it bothered me that the community identified students as remedial based on invalid reasons—invalid because the EPT measures of critical thinking and college writing skills can, as Esther uses Anyon to point out, also be shaped by your socioeconomic status. As Anyon says, a major difference between elite and working-class schools can be instruction in critical thinking and writing. Working-class students may not be prepared to write as college students because they are not expected to go to college, having instead mostly been taught to follow directions so they can join the workforce. These different ways of teaching are creating students who work within different Discourses, and why would we expect valid test results on potential for accomplishment in a Discourse many students haven't even been taught yet?

There are two other reasons that labeling incoming college students remedial 39 is a bad idea. First, many universities, including some Ivy League schools, offer all students thirty weeks of writing instruction without any negative connotation. However, for many public schools, budget cuts discourage any course over ten weeks, which resonates with Anyon's assertions about socioeconomic status and education. This limitation contributes to the negative stereotype of students in the stretch programs. Second, psychology suggests that a critical period of identity formation occurs between the ages of thirteen and twenty, during which people (including the majority of first-year college students) clarify their values and try to experience success. They are also developing a sense of individuality, connectedness, and critical thinking. It's not the time to critically undermine student self-efficacy with spurious labels.

In my own case, the remedial label affected my identity formation in that 40 the university's doubt whether I was a "real" college student weakened my own sense of identity and belonging as a college student. I started to feel like I had not accomplished anything in high school, and I felt powerless and confused, lacking confidence — and silenced, as I worried about telling other students and campus offices that I was in the stretch program. Gee argues that an identity kit for a role includes clothes, attitudes, language — both oral and print — and ways of interacting with others. Labeled a remedial writer, I started to wonder, "Well, am I remedial in my other classes as well? Will the teachers be able to tell I am a remedial writer? Can I even write a paper and get a good grade?"

OUR REBELLION

Scholarship had helped us understand the issues. However, all the work we 41 read was written by professors and other scholars, not by students who have actually lived with the stigma of being labeled remedial. We wanted our voices heard, so first we presented our work at the 2012 International Writing Centers Association (IWCA) Conference, which helped us complicate our thinking about institutional, tutor, and student language. Then Arturo entered his remediation research project into our campus's FYW Celebration of Writing and took home the first prize, which helped us believe in ourselves and our words. And then we proposed and presented a session at the 2013 Conference on College Composition and Communication (CCCC), where the audience response encouraged us to reach farther with our ideas. So we began writing, hoping to someday publish our work. That was our rebellion against the unfair label. In rebelling we came to believe we do belong in college. We believe that our work shows how student-initiated and carefully theorized resistance to institutional language helped us, and our professors, to reexamine our own acceptance of institutional labeling as well as to challenge administrators and faculty to label students accurately: as writers.

One of our favorite class quotes is from Albert Einstein: "Everybody is a 42 genius. But if you judge a fish by its ability to climb a tree, it will live its whole life believing that it is stupid." Gee's theory of identity formation speaks powerfully to labeling students as remedial, and it is why a university should put extra effort into understanding the effects of remedial labels on its writers. This could go a long way toward keeping students from feeling put down; they would be more motivated to meet the common goals of the other students in the university and not feel they are worth less than their colleagues. After all, college writing is very different from high school writing. There is no way students should be condemned for not exhibiting characteristics of a style they have never been taught.

Fortunately for the incoming students who followed us, prior to our speaking 43 out, numerous faculty members had already been laying the foundation to resolve the injustice done to us; all we did was bring it out in the open. In a sense, it was the perfect storm. The following year, things did end up changing at CSUSB, due in part to the implementation of a new initiative, directed self-placement (DSP), which gave students the opportunity to choose their own English placement. So throughout that year, our sophomore year, we asked numerous first-year students if any of them felt a "remedial" stigma related to writing; much to our surprise, they had no idea what we were talking about. Some even asked us to define the term. When we explained it and the effect it has had on us as university students, many were shocked. In speaking to them about the past, we felt as if we were telling a mythical tale because to them, last year was a page in an old history book. It was hard for them to believe because the present is so different.

Also in our sophomore year, though, the CSU system implemented the Early 44 Start Program, a mandatory experience for students designated as "underprepared" by the EPT. They are required to attend a four-day class to "prepare" them for college-level writing. When we came to college, our university told us that our four years of high school hadn't prepared us for college writing, yet they now believe four days will prepare new students. According to the composition faculty who have been working with us on this project, CSUSB and other CSU campuses with Stretch Composition and DSP have asked to be exempt from Early Start, but their requests have been denied. So now, even though several professors have commented that the work that came out of our class unmasked the harmful language regarding remediation and influenced both the professor-training materials and the ways Early Start classes are conducted on our campus, students in this year's Early Start are still being discriminated against based on their EPT scores. Although they seem to have no awareness of the remedial label, they do know that their EPT scores were what required them to come to campus in the summer for the Early Start session. And while our faculty has worked hard to find and erase the language of remediation in our campus documents, it remains unchanged on the CSU and ETS websites.

We have helped to change the landscape, and even though Early Start may be 45 the new obstacle that keeps students from equality, we are optimistic that it can be overcome as long as people keep speaking up. We hope that our class doing so will have some effect on other universities' use of the remedial label. Seeing the interest in our presentations at the 2012 IWCA and the 2013 CCCC conferences gave us courage, and we encourage others to speak out. Being engaged as FYW students doing research that matters to us positioned us not just as research subjects for "real" writing scholars to study, but as scholars ourselves who can create knowledge and rewrite the terms of our own education.

As more of us let our voices be heard, there may come a time when all stu- 46 dents are treated as normal. The scarring of the past need not continue in the future—a future which will be determined not just by administrators but by brave students who speak out and start making a difference.

Works Cited

Anyon, Jean. "Social Class and the Hidden Curriculum of Work." *Journal of Education* 162.1 (1980): 67–92. Print.

Brandt, Deborah. "Sponsors of Literacy." *College Composition and Communication* 49 (1998): 165–85. Rpt. in Wardle and Downs 332–50. Print.

The California State University (CSU). "Analytic Studies: CSU Proficiency." 15 April 2013. Web. 8 Oct. 2013.

Elbow, Peter. "Response to Glynda Hull, Mike Rose, Kay Losey Fraser, and Marisa Castellano, 'Remediation as Social Construct.'" *College Composition and Communication* 44 (1993): 587–88. Print.

ETS. "CSU: About the CSU Placement Tests." 2013. Web. 8 Oct. 2013.

Gee, James Paul. "Literacy, Discourse, and Linguistics: Introduction." *Journal of Education* 171.1 (1989): 5–17. Rpt. in Wardle and Downs 482–95. Print.

Glau, Gregory. "The 'Stretch Program': Arizona State University's New Model of University-Level Basic Writing Instruction." *WPA: Writing Program Administration* 20.1–2 (1996): 79–91. Print.

Rose, Mike. "Rethinking Remedial Education and the Academic-Vocational Divide." *Mind, Culture, and Activity* 19 (2012): 1–16. Print.

Tierney, William G., and Lisa D. Garcia. "Preparing Underprepared Students for College: Remedial Education and Early Assessment Programs." *Journal of At-Risk Issues* 14.2 (2008): 1–7. Print.

Wardle, Elizabeth, and Doug Downs. *Writing about Writing: A College Reader.* Boston: Bedford/St. Martin's, 2011. Print.

Questions for Discussion and Journaling

1. What is a "remedial" writer, according to the definitions you researched prior to reading, and according to Tejada et al.?

2. What do you think Tejada et al. mean when they say that reading this book (*Writing about Writing*) "unmasked the language of remediation" for them? Is there anything in your experience of reading this book so far that might help you to understand and question what it means to be called a "remedial" writer?

3. The writers talk about the shame of what Esther calls "carrying this remedial label" (para. 8). Arturo's father warned him that this label would cause him to be discriminated against at the university, and told him that he had to prove to university administrators that he was "better than the label" (para. 10). And Arturo argues that no matter how many successes he has had, the label of remedial has become a part of his identity. Why do you think labels have so much power to shape how people feel about themselves and even who they are?

4. Tejada and the other writers here were placed into their college writing course based on the California EPT placement test. How were you placed into your writing class? If you don't know, do a little research to find out.

5. DeShonna talks about the "hierarchy" in education. Think back to your experiences with reading and writing throughout your school experience. What hierarchies were at play? How were you slotted into reading and writing groups, experiences, and classes? How did those experiences serve as "literacy sponsors" for you? Did these experiences increase the odds that you would fail or succeed by predicting that you would do so, as DeShonna argues?

6. The student writers here talk about the power of their teacher, who seemed not to have heard that they were remedial and who assigned them difficult work that showed they "were capable of being scholars" (para. 19). What experiences have you had with the power of teachers who either believed in you or did not? How have those experiences impacted you?

7. Brisa says that in her college writing class she finally felt that her essay was no longer controlling her. What do you think she means? Can you relate to her feeling of being "controlled" by your writing?

8. These authors demonstrate the difficulty of completing a timed essay. What's your own experience with timed writing? Do you think such tests are a good way to judge your abilities as a writer? Why or why not?

Applying and Exploring Ideas

1. Bring a set of index cards to class. With your classmates, fill the index cards with any of the labels that you have been given in your life, both academic and nonacademic. Post the labels on the board. Then as a class engage in the following activities:

   • Discuss who has had the power to assign these labels and write their names on the cards.

- Consider how the labels have impacted what you could do, were willing to do, and have become. Next to each label write terms to explain how those labels affected you (for example, *limited, encouraged, hurt, created self-doubt*).
- Decide which labels you would like to reject and then remove them from the board.
- Decide which new labels you might want to name and choose for yourselves, and add them to the board.

2. Write a short manifesto about the power of labels, how labels impact your identity and your writing, and the labels you would like to claim for yourself.

3. Google and read the Jean Anyon article, "Social Class and the Hidden Curriculum of Work" that the writers mention here. Write a short explanation of her argument, and then identify the social-class designation of the schools you have attended using her categories (working class, middle-class, affluent professional, or executive elite). Then explain whether the kinds of tasks engaged in at your schools were similar to the kinds of tasks Anyon outlines (for example, "following steps of a procedure" or "getting the right answer," "creative activity carried out independently," or "developing one's analytical intellectual powers"). Finally, consider how the type of school you attended and its activities have "sponsored" your literacy and expanded or limited what you were asked to do and learned to do.

4. Do some research on the relationship of remediation to social class and race. What do you find? Given what you have learned so far from this book and from the activities you engaged in above, try to write an explanation of why so many minority students are classified as remedial.

- -

META MOMENT   How would you like to label yourself as a writer? What labels have been given to you by others that you want to reject?

- -

The Phenomenology of Error

JOSEPH M. WILLIAMS

Framing the Reading

Be forewarned: Your teacher will know if you do not read beyond the first three pages of Joseph Williams's "The Phenomenology of Error." Once you reach the end you'll understand why.

Error, in composition theory, is a technical term, referring to a specific set of mistakes that writers make with syntax and the mechanics and **conventions** of writing. Errors include using *I* where we normally use *me*, incorrect spelling, or ending a sentence with a comma instead of a period. If you follow baseball, you might think of errors in writing just as you do in baseball, as mistakes in a standard, almost automatic, procedure that most people usually get right.

The interesting thing about error in writing is that many people believe the things you can make errors on — grammar, punctuation, spelling — are *all that writing is*. They think that if they learn grammar, punctuation, and spelling, they've learned to write. It's true that numerous errors can really drag down a piece of writing. But the fact is that the vast majority of what it takes to make writing good has nothing to do with "surface" correctness. Most writing that has some errors is still entirely understandable, and most readers who aren't already predisposed to criticize a piece of writing care *much* more about what it says than whether it's completely mistake-free.

So the question is, why does our education system think so differently? Where do millions of American students year after year get the idea that the most important, and the hardest part, of writing is making sure it has no spelling mistakes or punctuation errors? Did you ever wish that teachers would have paid a little more attention to what you were trying to say and a little less attention to how you messed up in getting it said? Did you ever feel like maybe they cared a little too much about the errors and not nearly enough about everything else there was to care about in your writing? Did you ever feel the difference between having your writing *read* and having it *corrected*?

In this piece, Joseph Williams, whose career was spent researching and teaching rhetoric, argument, and style in writing, studies American readers' assumptions about the importance and prevalence of error in writing. We include his piece

Williams, Joseph M. "The Phenomenology of Error." *College Composition and Communication*, vol. 32, no. 2, May 1981, pp. 152–68.

in this chapter on "Literacies" because the assumptions about writing that Williams studies relate directly to the ideas that many people are taught about what literacy fundamentally *is*. This is also true of Vershawn Young's piece following this one. The threshold concept that your writing is impacted by your identities and your prior experiences is directly related to how you were taught to think about making mistakes or errors; many people come away from their early education believing that error in writing is completely avoidable and that mistakes in writing make them bad writers and even bad (or at least failing) people (think about Tejada et al.'s experience in the previous reading). To understand your own relationship with writing and feelings about yourself as a writer, it can be helpful to better understand the cultural constructs of "error" that Williams studies in this piece.

Getting Ready to Read

Before you read, do at least one of the following activities:

- Make a list of the errors you most commonly make in your writing. What makes avoiding them difficult for you — why do you still make them even though you know about them?
- Look up the word *phenomenology.*

As you read, consider the following questions:

- What does Williams mean by the *phenomenology of error*? Why use this term rather than something more obvious or straightforward?
- Judging from his introduction, what would you say are the *research problem* and *question* that Williams means to address?

I AM OFTEN PUZZLED by what we call errors of grammar and usage, errors 1 such as *different than, between you and I*, a *which* for a *that,* and so on. I am puzzled by what motive could underlie the unusual ferocity which an *irregardless* or a *hopefully* or a singular *media* can elicit. In his second edition of *On Writing Well* (New York, 1980), for example, William Zinsser, an otherwise amiable man I'm sure, uses, and quotes not disapprovingly, words like *detestable vulgarity* (p. 43), *garbage* (p. 44), *atrocity* (p. 46), *horrible* (p. 48); *oaf* (p. 42), *idiot* (p. 43), and *simple illiteracy* (p. 46), to comment on usages like *OK, hopefully,* the affix *-wise,* and *myself* in *He invited Mary and myself to dinner.*

The last thing I want to seem is sanctimonious. But as I am sure Zinsser 2 would agree, what happens in Cambodia and Afghanistan could more reasonably be called horrible atrocities. The likes of Idi Amin qualify as legitimate oafs. Idiots we have more than enough of in our state institutions. And while simply illiteracy is the condition of billions, it does not characterize those who use *disinterested* in its original sense.[1]

I am puzzled why some errors should excite this seeming fury while others, 3 not obviously different in kind, seem to excite only moderate disapproval. And I am puzzled why some of us can regard any particular item as a more or less serious error, while others, equally perceptive, and acknowledging that the same item may in some sense be an "error," seem to invest in their observation no emotion at all.

At first glance, we ought to be able to explain some of these anomalies by 4 subsuming errors of grammar and usage in a more general account of defective social behavior, the sort of account constructed so brilliantly by Erving Goffman.[2] But errors of social behavior differ from errors of "good usage": Social errors that excite feelings commensurate with judgments like "horrible," "atrocious," "oaf(ish)," and "detestable" are usually errors that grossly violate our personal space: We break wind at a dinner party and then vomit on the person next to us. We spill coffee in their lap, then step on a toe when we get up to apologize. It's the Inspector Clouseau routine. Or the error metaphorically violates psychic space: We utter an inappropriate obscenity, mention our painful hemorrhoids, tell a racist joke, and snigger at the fat woman across the table who turns out to be our hostess. Because all of these actions crudely violate one's personal space we are justified in calling them "oafish"; all of them require that we apologize, or at least offer an excuse.

This way of thinking about social error turns our attention from error as a 5 discrete entity, frozen at the moment of its commission, to error as part of a flawed transaction, originating in ignorance or incompetence or accident, manifesting itself as an invasion of another's personal space, eliciting a judgment ranging from silent disapproval to "atrocious" and "horrible," and requiring either an explicit "I'm sorry" and correction, or a simple acknowledgment and a tacit agreement not to do it again.[3]

To address errors of grammar and usage in this way, it is also necessary to 6 shift our attention from error treated strictly as an isolated item on a page, to error perceived as a flawed verbal transaction between a writer and a reader. When we do this, the matter of error turns less on a handbook definition than on the reader's response, because it is that response — "detestable," "horrible" — that defines the seriousness of the error and its expected amendment.

> How can we not be puzzled over why so much heat is invested in condemning a violation whose consequence impinges not at all on our personal space?

But if we do compare serious nonlinguistic gaffes to errors of usage, how can we 7 not be puzzled over why so much heat is invested in condemning a violation whose consequence impinges not at all on our personal space? The language some use to condemn linguistic error seems far more intense than the language they use to describe more consequential social errors—a hard bump on the arm, for example—that require a sincere but not especially effusive apology. But no matter how "atrocious" or "horrible" or "illiterate" we think an error like *irregardless* or a *like* for an *as* might be, it does not jolt my ear in the same way an elbow might; a *between you and I* does not offend me, at least not in the ordinary sense of offend. Moreover, unlike social errors, linguistic errors do not ordinarily require that we apologize for them.[4] When we make *media* a singular or dangle a participle, and are then made aware of our mistake, we are expected to acknowledge the error, and, if we have the opportunity, to amend it. But I don't think that we are expected to say, "Oh, I'm sorry!" The objective consequences of the error simply do not equal those of an atrocity, or even of clumsiness.

It may be that to fully account for the contempt that some errors of usage 8 arouse, we will have to understand better than we do the relationship between language, order, and those deep psychic forces that perceived linguistic violations seem to arouse in otherwise amiable people.[5] But if we cannot yet fully account for the psychological source of those feelings, or why they are so intense, we should be able to account better than we do for the variety of responses that different "errors" elicit. It is a subject that should be susceptible to research. And indeed, one kind of research in this area has a long tradition: In this century, at least five major surveys of English usage have been conducted to determine how respondents feel about various matters of usage. Sterling Leonard, Albert Marckwardt, Raymond Crisp, the Institute of Education English Research Group at the University of Newcastle upon Tyne, and the *American Heritage Dictionary* have questioned hundreds of teachers and editors and writers and scholars about their attitudes toward matters of usage ranging from *which* referring to a whole clause to split infinitives to *enthuse* as a verb.[6]

The trouble with this kind of research, though, with asking people whether 9 they think *finalize* is or is not good usage, is that they are likely to answer. As William Labov and others have demonstrated,[7] we are not always our own best informants about our habits of speech. Indeed, we are likely to give answers that misrepresent our talking and writing, usually in the direction of more rather than less conservative values. Thus when the editors of the *American Heritage Dictionary* asks its Usage Panel to decide the acceptability of *impact* as a verb, we can predict how they will react: Merely by being asked, it becomes manifest to them that they have been invested with an institutional responsibility that will require them to judge usage by the standards they think they are supposed to uphold. So we cannot be surprised that when asked, Zinsser rejects *impact* as a verb, despite the fact that *impact* has been used as a verb at least since 1601.

The problem is self-evident: Since we can ask an indefinite number of questions about an indefinite number of items of usage, we can, merely by asking, 10 accumulate an indefinite number of errors, simply because whoever we ask will feel compelled to answer. So while it may seem useful for us to ask one another whether we think X is an error, we have to be skeptical about our answers, because we will invariably end up with more errors than we began with, certainly more than we ever feel on our nerves when we read in the ways we ordinarily do.

In fact, it is this unreflective feeling on the nerves in our ordinary reading 11 that interests me the most, the way we respond — or not — to error when we do not make error a part of our conscious field of attention. It is the difference between reading for typographical errors and reading for content. When we read for typos, letters constitute the field of attention; content becomes virtually inaccessible. When we read for content, semantic structures constitute the field of attention; letters — for the most part — recede from our consciousness.

I became curious about this kind of perception three years ago when I was 12 consulting with a government agency that had been using English teachers to edit reports but was not sure they were getting their money's worth. When I asked to see some samples of editing by their consultants, I found that one very common notation was "faulty parallelism" at spots that only by the most conservative interpretation could be judged faulty. I asked the person who had hired me whether faulty parallelism was a problem in his staff's ability to write clearly enough to be understood quickly, but with enough authority to be taken seriously, He replied, "If the teacher says so."

Now I was a little taken aback by this response, because it seemed to me 13 that one ought not have to appeal to a teacher to decide whether something like faulty parallelism was a real problem in communication. The places where faulty parallelism occurred should have been at least felt as problems, if not recognized as a felt difficulty whose specific source was faulty parallelism.

About a year later, as I sat listening to a paper describing some matters of 14 error analysis in evaluating compositions, the same thing happened. When I looked at examples of some of the errors, sentences containing alleged dangling participles, faulty parallelism, vague pronoun reference, and a few other items,[8] I was struck by the fact that, at least in some of the examples, I saw some infelicity, but no out-and-out grammatical error. When I asked the person who had done the research whether these examples were typical of errors she looked for to measure the results of extensive training in sentence combining, I was told that the definition of error had been taken from a popular handbook, on the assumption, I guess, that that answered the question.

About a year ago, it happened again, when a publisher and I began circu- 15 lating a manuscript that in a peripheral way deals with some of the errors I've mentioned here, suggesting that some errors are less serious than others. With one exception, the reviewers, all teachers at universities, agreed that an intelligent treatment of error would be useful, and that this manuscript was at least in the ballpark. But almost every reader took exception to one item of usage that they thought I had been too soft on, that I should have unequivocally condemned as a violation of good usage. Unfortunately, each of them mentioned a different item.

Well, it is all very puzzling: Great variation in our definition of error, great variation in our emotional investment in defining and condemning error, great variation in the perceived seriousness of individual errors. The categories of error all seem like they should be yes-no, but the feelings associated with the categories seem much more complex.   16

If we think about these responses for a moment we can identify one source of the problem: We were all locating error in very different places. For all of us, obviously enough, error is in the essay, on the page, because that is where it physically exists. But of course, to be in the essay, it first has to be in the student. But before that, it has to be listed in a book somewhere. And before that in the mind of the writer of the handbook. And finally, a form of the error has to be in the teacher who resonated—or not—to the error on the page on the basis of the error listed in the handbook.   17

This way of thinking about error locates error in two different physical locations (the student's paper and the grammarian's handbook) and in three different experiences: the experience of the writer who creates the error; in the experience of the teacher who catches it; and in the mind of the grammarian—the E. B. White or Jacques Barzun or H. W. Fowler—who proposes it. Because error seems to exist in so many places, we should not be surprised that we do not agree among ourselves about how to identify it, or that we do not respond to the same error uniformly.   18

But we might be surprised—and perhaps instructed—by those cases where the two places occur in texts by the same author—and where all three experiences reside in the same person. It is, in fact, these cases that I would like to examine for a moment, because they raise such interesting questions about the experience of error.   19

For example, E. B. White presumably believed what he (and Strunk) said in *Elements of Style* (New York, 1979) about faulty parallelism and *which* vs. *that*:   20

> Express coordinate ideas in similar form. This principle, that of parallel construction, requires that expressions similar in content and function be outwardly similar. (p. 26)
>
> *That, which. That* is the defining or restrictive pronoun, *which* the non-defining or non-restrictive . . . The careful writer . . . removes the defining *whiches,* and by so doing improves his work. (p. 59)

Yet in the last paragraph of "Death of a Pig,"[9] White has two faulty parallelisms, and according to his rules, an incorrect *which:*

> . . . the premature expiration of a pig is, I soon discovered, a departure which the community marks solemnly on its calendar . . . I have written this account in penitence and in grief, as a man who failed to raise his pig,

and to explain my deviation from the classic course of so many raised pigs. The grave in the woods is unmarked, but Fred can direct the mourner to it unerringly and with immense good will, and I know he and I shall often revisit it, singly and together, . . .

Now I want to be clear: I am not at all interested in the trivial fact that E. B. 21 White violated one or two of his own trivial rules. That would be a trivial observation. We could simply say that he miswrote in the same way he might have mistyped and thereby committed a typographical error. Nor at the moment am I interested in the particular problem of parallelism, or of *which* vs. *that,* any more than I would be interested in the particular typo. What I am interested in is the fact that no one, E. B. White least of all, seemed to notice that E. B. White had made an error. What I'm interested in here is the noticing or the not noticing by the same person who stipulates what should be noticed, and why anyone would surely have noticed if White had written,

I knows me and him will often revisit it, . . .

Of course, it may be that I am stretching things just a bit far to point out a 22 trivial error of usage in one publication on the basis of a rule asserted in another. But this next example is one in which the two co-exist between the same covers:

Were (sing.) is, then, a recognizable subjunctive, & applicable not to past facts, but to present or future non-facts. (p. 576)

Another suffix that is not a living one, but is sometimes treated as if it was, is *-al* . . . (p. 242)

H. W. Fowler. *A Dictionary of Modern English Usage.* Oxford, 1957.

Now again, Fowler may have just made a slip here; when he read these entries, certainly at widely separate intervals, the *was* in the second just slipped by. And yet how many others have also read that passage, and also never noticed?

The next example may be a bit more instructive. Here, the rule is asserted in 23 the middle of one page:

In conclusion, I recommend using *that* with defining clauses except when stylistic reasons interpose. Quite often, not a mere pair of *that's* but a threesome or foursome, including the demonstrative *that,* will come in the same sentence and justify *which* to all writers with an ear. (p. 68)

and violated at the top of the next:

Next is a typical situation which a practiced writer corrects for style virtually by reflex action. (p. 69)

Jacques Barzun. *Simple and Direct.* New York, 1976.

Now again, it is not the error as such that I am concerned with here, but rather the fact that after Barzun stated the rule, and almost immediately violated it, no one noticed — not Barzun himself who must certainly have read the manuscript several times, not a colleague to whom he probably gave the manuscript before he sent it to the publisher, not the copy editor who worked over the manuscript, not the proof reader who read the galleys, not Barzun who probably read the galleys after them, apparently not even anyone in the reading public, since that *which* hasn't been corrected in any of the subsequent printings. To characterize this failure to respond as mere carelessness seems to miss something important.

This kind of contradiction between the conscious directive and the unreflex- 24 ive experience becomes even more intense in the next three examples, examples that, to be sure, involve matters of style rather than grammar and usage:

Negative constructions are often wordy and sometimes pretentious.

1. wordy   Housing for married students is not unworthy of consideration.

   concise   Housing for married students is worthy of consideration.

   better   The trustees should earmark funds for married students' housing. (Probably what the author meant)

2. wordy   After reading the second paragraph you aren't left with an immediate reaction as to how the story will end.

   concise   The first two paragraphs create suspense.

The following example from a syndicated column is not untypical:

Sylvan Barnet and Marcia Stubbs. *Practical Guide to Writing.* Boston, 1977, p. 280.

Now Barnet and Stubbs may be indulging in a bit of self-parody here. But I don't think so. In this next example, Orwell, in the very act of criticising the passive, not only casts his proscription against it in the passive, but almost all the sentences around it, as well:

I list below, with notes and examples, various of the tricks by means of which the work of prose construction is habitually dodged . . . *Operators* or *verbal false limbs.* These save the trouble of picking out appropriate verbs and nouns, and at the same time pad each sentence with extra syllables which give it an appearance of symmetry . . . the passive voice is wherever possible used in preference to the active, and noun constructions are used instead of gerunds . . . The range of verbs is further cut down . . . and the banal statements are given an appearance of profundity by means of the *not un* formation. Simple conjunctions are replaced by . . . the ends of sentences are saved by . . .

   "Politics and the English Language"

Again, I am not concerned with the fact that Orwell wrote in the passive or used nominalizations where he could have used verbs.[10] Rather, I am bemused by the apparent fact that three generations of teachers have used this essay without there arising among us a general wry amusement that Orwell violated his own rules in the act of stating them.

And if you want to argue (I think mistakenly) that Orwell was indulging in 25 parody, then consider this last example—one that cannot possibly be parodic, at least intentionally:

> Emphasis is often achieved by the use of verbs rather than nouns formed from them, and by the use of verbs in the active rather than in the passive voice.
>
> *A Style Manual for Technical Writers and Editors*, ed. S. J. Reisman. New York, 1972. pp. 6–11.

In this single sentence, in a single moment, we have all five potential locations of error folded together: As the rule is stated in a handbook, it is simultaneously violated in its text; as the editor expresses in the sentence that is part of the handbook a rule that must first have existed in his mind, in his role as writer he simultaneously violates it. And in the instant he ends the sentence, he becomes a critical reader who should—but does not—resonate to the error. Nor, apparently, did anyone else.

The point is this: We can discuss error in two ways: we can discuss it at a 26 level of consciousness that places that error at the very center of our consciousness. Or we can talk about how we experience (or not) what we popularly call errors of usage as they occur in the ordinary course of our reading a text.

In the first, the most common way, we separate the objective material text 27 from its usual role in uniting a subject (us) and that more abstract "content" of the object, the text, in order to make the sentences and words the objects of consciousness. We isolate error as a frozen, instantiated object. In the second way of discussing error, a way we virtually never follow, we must treat error not as something that is simply on the surface of the page, "out there," nor as part of an inventory of negative responses "in here," but rather as a variably experienced union of item and response, controlled by the intention to read a text in the way we ordinarily read texts like newspapers, journals, and books. If error is no longer in the handbook, or on the page, or in the writer—or even purely in the reader—if instead we locate it at an intersection of those places, then we can explain why Barzun could write—or read—one thing and then immediately experience another, why his colleagues and editors and audience could read about one way of reflexively experiencing language and then immediately experience it in another.

But when I decided to intend to read Barzun and White and Orwell and 28 Fowler in, for all practical purposes, the way they seem to invite me to read—as an editor looking for the errors they have been urging me to search out—then I inform my experience, I deliberately begin reading with an intention to experience the material constitution of the text. It is as if a type-designer invited me to look at the design of his type as he discussed type-design.

In short, if we read any text the way we read freshman essays, we will find 29 many of the same kind of errors we routinely expect to find and therefore do find. But if we could read those student essays unreflexively, if we could make the ordinary kind of contract with those texts that we make with other kinds of texts, then we could find many fewer errors.

When we approach error from this point of view, from the point of view of 30 our pre-reflexive experience of error, we have to define categories of error other than those defined by systems of grammar or a theory of social class. We require a system whose presiding terms would turn on the nature of our response to violations of grammatical rules.

At the most basic level, the categories must organize themselves around two 31 variables: Has a rule been violated? And do we respond? Each of these variables has two conditions: A rule is violated or a rule is not violated. And to either of those variables, we respond, or we do not respond. We thus have four possibilities:

1a. A rule is violated, and we respond to the violation.

1b. A rule is violated, and we do not respond to its violation.

2a. A rule is not violated, and we do not respond.

2b. A rule is not violated, and we do respond.

	[+ response]	[− response]
[+ violation]		
[− violation]		

Now, our experiencing or noticing of any given grammatical rule has to be 32 cross-categorized by the variable of our noticing or not noticing whether it is or is not violated. That is, if we violate rule X, a reader may note it or not. But we must also determine whether, if we do not violate rule X, the same reader will or will not notice that we have violated it. Theoretically, then, this gives us four possible sets of consequences for any given rule. They can be represented on a feature matrix like this:

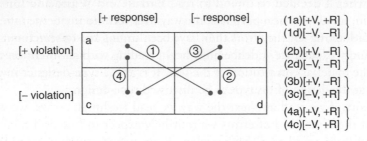

That is, the first kind of rule, indicated by the line marked ①, is of the following kind: When violated, [+V], we respond to the violation, [+R]. When it is not violated, [−V], we do not respond, [−R]. Thus the same rule results in combinations of features indicated by (a–d). Rule type ② is characterized by a rule that when violated, [+V], we do not notice, [−R]. But when we do not violate it, [−V], we do not notice it either, [−R]. Thus the single rule combines features indicated by (b–d). The other rules follow the same kind of grid relationships. (As I will point out later, the problem is actually much more complex than this, but this will do as a first approximation.)

I do not assert that the particular items I will list as examples of these rules ₃₃ are universally experienced in the way indicated. These categories are based on personal responses, and it is possible that your responses are quite different than mine. But in fact, on the basis of some preliminary research that I shall report later, I would argue that most readers respond in the ways reflected by these categories, regardless of how they might claim they react.

The most obviousest set of rules be those whose violation we instantly notes, but ₃₄ whose observation we entirely ignore. They are the rules that define bedrock standard English. No reader of this journal can fail to distinguish these two passages:

> There hasn't been no trainees who withdrawed from the program since them and the Director met to discuss the instructional methods, if they met earlier, they could of seen that problems was beginning to appear and the need to take care of them immediate. (+V, +R)

> There haven't been any trainees who have withdrawn from the program since they and the Director met to discuss the instructional methods. If they had met earlier, they could have seen that problems were beginning to appear and that they needed to take care of them immediately. (−V, −R)

Among the rules whose violation we readily note but whose observance we do not are double negatives, incorrect verb forms, many incorrect pronoun forms, pleonastic subjects, double comparatives and superlatives, most subject-verb disagreements, certain faulty parallelisms,[11] certain dangling modifiers,[12] etc.

The next most obvious set of rules are those whose observation we also 35 entirely ignore, but whose violation we ignore too. Because we note neither their observation nor their violation, they constitute a kind of folklore of usage, rules which we can find in some handbook somewhere, but which have, for the most part, lost their force with our readers. For most readers, these two passages differ very little from one another; for many readers, not at all:

> Since the members of the committee had discussed with each other all of the questions which had been raised earlier, we decided to conduct the meeting as openly as possible and with a concern for the opinions of everyone that might be there. And to ensure that all opinions would be heard, it was suggested that we not limit the length of the meeting. By opening up the debate in this way, there would be no chance that someone might be inadvertently prevented from speaking, which has happened in the past. (+V, −R)

> Because the members of the committee had discussed with one another all the questions that had been raised earlier, we decided to conduct the meeting in a way that was as open as possible and concerned with the opinion of everyone who might be there. To ensure that all opinions would be heard, someone suggested that we not limit the length of the meeting. By opening up the debate in this way, we would not take the chance that someone might be inadvertently prevented from speaking, something which has happened in the past. (−V, −R)

I appreciate the fact that some readers will view my lack of sensitivity to some of these errors as evidence of an incorrigibly careless mind. Which errors go in which category, however, is entirely beside the point.[13] The point is the existence of a *category* of "rules" to whose violation we respond as indifferently as we respond to their observance.

A third category of rules includes those whose violation we largely ignore but 36 whose observance we do not. These are rules which, when followed, impose themselves on the reader's consciousness either subliminally, or overtly and specifically. You can sense the consequence of observing these rules in this next "minimal pair":

> I will not attempt to broadly defend specific matters of evidence that one might rest his case on. If it was advisable to substantially modify the arguments, he would have to re-examine those patients the original group treated and extend the clinical trials whose original plan was eventually altered. (+V, −R)

> I shall not attempt broadly to defend specific matters of evidence on which one might rest one's case. Were it advisable substantially to modify the arguments, one should have to re-examine those patients whom the original research group treated and extend the clinical trials the original plan of which was eventually altered. (−V, +R)

I appreciate that many of you believe that you notice split infinitives as quickly 37
as you notice a subject-verb error, and that both should be equally condemned in
careful prose. At the end of this paper, I will try to offer an argument to the contrary—that in fact many—not all—of you who make that claim are mistaken.

The exceptions are probably those for whom there is the fourth category 38
of error, that paradoxical but logically entailed category defined by those rules
whose violation we note, and whose observance we also note. I think that very
few of us are sensitive to this category, and I think for those very few, the number of items that belong in the category must, fortunately, be very small. Were
the number of items large, we would be constantly distracted by noticing that
which should not be noticed. We would be afflicted with a kind of linguistic
hyperesthesia, noticing with exquisite pleasure that every word we read is spelled
correctly, that every subject agrees with its verb, that every article precedes its
noun, and so on. Many of us may be surprised when we get a paper with no
mispelled words, but that pleasure does not derive from our noticing that each
word in turn is correctly spelled, but rather in the absence of mispelled words.

In my own case, I think I note equally when an infinitive is split, and when it 39
is not. In recent months, I also seem to be noticing when someone uses *that* in
the way that the "rule" stipulates, and I notice when a writer uses *which* in the
way which the "rule" prohibits. I hope I add no more.

I suspect that some readers put into this category the *regardless/irregardless* 40
pair, *media* as a singular and as a plural, perhaps *disinterested/uninterested*. I
offer no pair of contrasting examples because the membership of the category is
probably so idiosyncratic that such a pair would not be useful.

Now in fact, all this is a bit more complicated than my four categories sug- 41
gest, albeit trivially so. The two-state condition of response: [+/−], is too crude
to distinguish different qualities of response. Responses can be unfavorable, as
the ordinary speaker of standard English would respond unfavorably to

> Can't nobody tell what be happening four year from now.

if it appeared in a text whose conventions called for standard English. A
response can be favorable, as in the right context, we might regard as appropriate the formality of

> Had I known the basis on which these data were analyzed, I should not have
> attempted immediately to dissuade those among you whom others have . . .

(We could, of course, define a context in which we would respond to this
unfavorably.)

Since only the category of [+response] can imply a type of response, we 42
categorize favorable and unfavorable response, [+/−favorable], across only
[+response]. This gives us four more simple categories:

> [+violate, −favorable]
> [−violate, +favorable]
> [+violate, +favorable]
> [−violate, −favorable]

The first two I have already illustrated:

> [+v, −f]: He knowed what I meaned.
> [−v, +f]: Had I known the basis on which . . . I should not etc.

This leaves two slightly paradoxical categories, which, like Category IV: 43 those rules whose violations we notice and whose observations we notice too, are populated by a very small number of items, and function as part of our responses only idiosyncratically. In the category [−violate, −favorable], I suspect that many of us would place *It is I,* along with some occurrences of *whom,* perhaps.

The other paradoxical category, [+violate, +favorable] is *not* illustrated by 44 *It's me,* because for most of us, this is an unremarked violation. If it elicits a response at all, it would almost invariably be [−favorable], but only among those for whom the *me* is a bête noir. In fact, I can only think of one violation that I respond to favorably: It is the *than* after *different(ly)* when what follows is a clause rather than a noun:

> This country feels differently about the energy crisis than it did in 1973.

I respond to this favorably because the alternative,

> This country feels differently about the energy crisis from the way it did in 1973.

is wordier, and on principles that transcend idiosyncratic items of usage, I prefer the two less words and the more certain and direct movement of the phrase. My noticing any of this, however, is entirely idiosyncratic.

As I said, though, these last distinctions are increasingly trivial. That is 45 why I refrain from pursuing another yet more finely drawn distinction: Those responses, favorable or unfavorable, that we consciously, overtly, knowingly experience, and those that are more subliminal, undefined, and unspecific. That is, when I read

> It don't matter.

I know precisely what I am responding to. When most of us read a *shall* and a shifted preposition, I suspect that we do not consciously identify those items as the source of any heightened feeling of formality. The response, favorable or unfavorable, is usually less specific, more holistic.

Now what follows from all this? One thing that does not follow is a rejection 46
of all rules of grammar. Some who have read this far are undoubtedly ready to
call up the underground grammarians to do one more battle against those who
would rip out the Mother Tongue and tear down Civilized Western Values. But
need I really have to assert that, just because many rules of grammar lack practical force, it is hardly the case that none of them have substance?

Certainly, how we mark and grade papers might change. We need not believe 47
that just because a rule of grammar finds its way into some handbook of usage,
we have to honor it. Which we honor and which we do not is a problem of
research. We have to determine in some unobtrusive way which rules of grammar the significant majority of careful readers notice and which they do not.
One way to do this research is to publish an article in a journal such as this,
an article into which have been built certain errors of grammar and usage. The
researcher would then ask his readers to report which errors jumped out at them
on the first reading. Those that you did not notice should then not be among
those we look for first when we read a student's paper.

One curious consequence of this way of thinking about error is that we no 48
longer have to worry about defining, rejecting, quibbling over the existence
of a rule. We simply accept as a rule anything that anyone wants to offer, no
matter how bizarre or archaic. Should anyone re-assert the 19th-century rule
against the progressive passive, fine. Upon inspection it will turn out that the
rule belongs in the category of those rules whose violation no one notices, and
whose observation no one notices either. As I said, it may be that you and I
will find that for any particular rule, we experience its violation in different
ways. But that is an empirical question, not a matter of value. Value becomes
a consideration only when we address the matter of which errors we should
notice.

Done carefully, this kind of classification might also encourage some dictio- 49
nary makers to amend their more egregious errors in labeling points of usage.
The *AHD,* for example, uses "non-standard" to label

> . . . forms that do not belong in any standard educated speech. Such
> words are recognized as non-standard not only by those whose speech is
> standard, but even by those who regularly use non-standard expressions.

The *AHD* staff has labeled as non-standard, *ain't, seen* as the past tense of *see,*
and *don't* with a singular subject. It has also labeled as non-standard *irregardless,*
like for *as, disinterested for uninterested,* and *see where,* as in the construction,
I see where . . . Thus we are led to believe that a speaker who would utter this:

> I see where the President has said that, irregardless of what happens with the
> gasoline shortage, he'll still be against rationing, just like he has been in the
> past. He seems disinterested in what's going on in the country.

would be just as likely to continue with this:

> I ain't sure that he seen the polls before he said that. He don't seem to know that people are fed up.

Indeed, we would have to infer from this kind of labeling that a speaker who said "I ain't sure he seen . . ." would also be sensitive to mistakes such as *disinterested* for *uninterested* or *like* for *as*. In matters such as this, we see too clearly the very slight scholarly basis upon which so much of this labeling rests.

Finally, I think that most of this essay is an exercise in futility. In these matters, the self-conscious report of what should be counted as an error is certainly an unreliable index to the unself-conscious experience. But it is by far a more satisfying emotion. When those of us who believe ourselves educated and literate and defenders of good usage think about language, our zealous defense of "good writing" feels more authentic than our experience of the same items in unreflective experience of a text. Indeed, we do not experience many of them at all. And no matter how wrong we might discover we are about our unreflective feelings, I suspect we could be endlessly lectured on how we do not respond to a *less* in front of a count noun, as in *less people*, but we would still express our horror and disgust in the belief that *less* is wrong when used in that way. It simply feels more authentic when we condemn error and enforce a rule. And after all, what good is learning a rule if all we can do is obey it?   50

If by this point you have not seen the game, I rest my case. If you have, I invite you to participate in the kind of research I suggested before. I have deposited with the Maxine Hairston of the University of Texas at Austin (Austin, Texas 78712), a member of the Editorial Board of this journal, a manuscript with the errors of grammar and usage that I deliberately inserted into this paper specifically marked. How can I ask this next question without seeming to distrust you? If you had to report right now what errors you noticed, what would they be? Don't go back and reread, looking for errors, at least not before you recall what errors you found the first time through. If you would send your list (better yet, a copy of the article with errors noted on first reading circled in red) to Professor Hairston, she will see that a tally of the errors is compiled, and in a later issue will report on who noticed what.   51

If you want to go through a second time and look for errors, better yet. Just make clear, if you would, that your list is the result of a deliberate search. I will be particularly interested in those errors I didn't mean to include. There are, incidentally, about 100 errors.   52

Notes

1. I don't know whether it is fair or unfair to quote Zinsser on this same matter:

> OVERSTATEMENT. "The living room looked as if an atomic bomb had gone off there," writes the inexperienced writer, describing what he saw on Sunday morning

after a Saturday night party that got out of hand. Well, we all know that he's exaggerating to make a droll point, but we also know that an atomic bomb didn't go off there, or any other bomb except maybe a water bomb. . . . These verbal high jinks can get just so high—and I'm already well over the limit—before the reader feels an overpowering drowsiness. . . . Don't overstate. (p. 108)

2. Erving Goffman, *Frame Analysis: An Essay on the Organization of Experience.* (New York: Harper and Row, 1974).

3. Some social errors are strictly formal and so ordinarily do not require an apology, even though some might judge them "horrible": a white wedding gown and a veil on a twice-divorced and eight-month pregnant bride, brown shoes with a dinner jacket, a printed calling card.

4. Some special situations do require an apology: When we prepare a document that someone else must take responsibility for, and we make a mistake in usage, we are expected to apologize, in the same way we would apologize for incorrectly adding up a column of figures. And when some newspaper columnists violate some small point of usage and their readers write in to point it out, the columnists will often acknowledge the error and offer some sort of apology. I think William Safire in *The New York Times* has done this occasionally.

5. Two other kinds of purely linguistic behavior do arouse hostile feelings. One kind includes obscenities and profanities. It may be that both are rooted in some sense of fouling that which should be kept clean: obscenities foul the mouth, the mouth fouls the name of a deity. The other kind of linguistic behavior that arouses hostility in some includes bad puns and baby talk by those who are too old for it. Curiously, Freud discusses puns in his *Wit and the Relation to the Unconscious* (under "Technique of Wit") but does not in "The Tendencies of Wit" address the faint sense of revulsion we feel at a bad pun.

6. Sterling Leonard, *Current English Usage,* English Monograph No. 1 (Champaign, Ill.; National Council of Teachers of English. Chicago, 1932); Albert H. Marckwardt and Fred Walcott, *Facts About Current English Usage,* English Monograph No. 7 (Champaign, Ill.: National Council of Teachers of English. New York, 1938); Raymond Crisp. "Changes in Attitudes Toward English Usage," Ph.D. dissertation, University of Illinois, 1971; W. H. Mittins, Mary Salu, Mary Edminson, Sheila Coyne, *Attitudes to English Usage* (London: Oxford University Press, 1970); *The American Heritage Dictionary of the English Language* (New York: Dell, 1979). Thomas J. Cresswell's *Usage in Dictionaries and Dictionaries of Usage,* Publication of the American Dialect Society, Nos. 63–64 (University, Alabama: University of Alabama Press 1975), should be required reading for anyone interested in these matters. It amply demonstrates the slight scholarly basis on which so much research on usage rests.

7. William Labov, *The Social Stratification of English in New York City* (Washington, D.C.: Center for Applied Linguistics, 1966), pp. 455–81.

8. Elaine P. Maimon and Barbara F. Nodine, "Words Enough and Time: Syntax and Error One Year After," in *Sentence Combining and the Teaching of Writing,* eds. Donald Daiker, Andrew Kerek, Max Morenberg (Akron, Ohio: University of Akron Press, 1979) pp. 101–108. This is considered a dangling verbal: *For example, considering the way Hamlet treats Ophelia, there is almost corruptness in his mind.* Clumsy yes, but *considering* is an absolute, or more exactly, meta-discourse. See footnote 12. This is considered a vague pronoun reference: *The theme of poisoning begins with the death of old King Hamlet, who was murdered by his brother when a leperous distillment was poured into his ear while he slept.* Infelicitous, to be sure, but who

can possibly doubt who's pouring what in whose ear (p. 103)? Counting items such as these as errors and then using those counts to determine competence, progress, or maturity would seem to raise problems of another, more substantive, kind.

9. *Essays of E. B. White* (New York: Harper and Row, 1977), p. 24.

10. Orwell's last rule: *Break any of these rules sooner than say anything outright barbarous,* does not apply to this passage. Indeed, it would improve if it had conformed to his rules:

> I list below, with notes and examples, various of the tricks by means of which a writer can dodge the work of prose construction . . . such writers prefer wherever possible the passive voice to the active, and noun constructions instead of gerunds . . . they further cut down the range of verbs . . . they make their banal statements seem profound by means of the *not un-*formation. They replace simple conjunctions by . . . they save the ends of sentences . . .

Should anyone object that this is a monotonous series of sentences beginning with the same subject, I could point to example after example of the same kind of thing in good modern prose. But perhaps an example from the same essay, near the end, will serve best (my emphasis):

> When *you* think of a concrete object, *you* think wordlessly and then, if *you* want to describe the thing *you* have been visualizing, *you* probably hunt about till *you* find the exact *words that* seem to fit it. When *you* think of something abstract *you* are more inclined to use words from the start, and unless *you* make a conscious effort to prevent it, the existing dialect will come rushing in and do the job for you . . .

Nine out of ten clauses begin with *you,* and in a space much more confined than the passage I rewrote.

11. Virtually all handbooks overgeneralize about faulty parallelism. Two "violations" occur so often in the best prose that we could not include them in this Category I. One is the kind illustrated by the E. B. White passage: the coordination of adverbials: . . . *unerringly and with immense good will.* The other is the coordination of noun phrases and WH-clauses: *We are studying the origins of this species and why it died out.* Even that range of exceptions is too broadly stated, but to explain the matter adequately would require more space than would be appropriate here.

12. Handbooks also overgeneralize on dangling constructions. The generalization can best be stated like this: When the implied subject of an introductory element is different from the overt subject of its immediately following clause, the introductory element dangles. Examples in handbooks are always so ludicrous that the generalization seems sound:

> Running down the street, the bus pulled away from the curb before I got there.

> To prepare for the wedding, the cake was baked the day before.

Some handbooks list exceptions, often called absolutes:

> Considering the trouble we're in, it's not surprising you are worried.

> To summarize, the hall is rented, the cake is baked, and we're ready to go.

These exceptions can be subsumed into a more general rule: When either the introductory element *or* the subject of the sentence consists of meta-discourse, the introductory element will not always appear to dangle. By meta-discourse I mean words and phrases that refer not to the primary content of the discourse, to the reference "out there" in the world, the writer's subject matter, but rather to the process of discoursing, to those directions that steer a reader through a discourse, those filler words that allow a writer to shift emphasis (*it, there, what*), and so on, words such as *it is important to note, to summarize, considering these issue, as you know, to begin with, there is,* etc. That's why an introductory element such as the following occurs so often in the prose of educated writers, and does not seem to dangle (meta-discourse is in bold face):

> To succeed in this matter, **it is important** for you to support as fully as possible . . .

> Realizing the seriousness of the situation, **it can be seen** that we must cut back on . . .

As I will point out later, the categories I am suggesting here are too broadly drawn to account for a number of finer nuances of error. Some violations, for example, clearly identify social and educational background:

> He didn't have no way to know what I seen.

But some violations that might be invariably noted by some observers do not invariably, or even regularly, reflect either social or educational background. Usages such as *irregardless, like* for *as, different than,* etc. occur so often in the speech and writing of entirely educated speakers and writers that we cannot group them with double negatives and non-standard verb forms, even if we do unfailingly respond to both kinds of errors. The usage note in the *American Heritage Dictionary* (Dell Paperback Edition, 1976; third printing, November, 1980) that *irregardless* is non-standard and "is only acceptable when the intent is clearly humorous" is more testimony to the problems of accurately representing the speech and writing of educated speakers. On February 20, 1981, the moderator on *Washington Week in Review,* a Public Broadcasting System news program, reported that a viewer had written to the program, objecting to the use of *irregardless* by one of the panelists. To claim that the person who used *irregardless* would also use *knowed* for *knew* or an obvious double negative would be simply wrong. (I pass by silently the position of *only* in that usage note. See footnote 13, item 9.) The counter-argument that the mere occurrence of these items in the speech and writing of some is sufficient testimony that they are not in fact educated is captious.

13. Here are some of the rules which I believe belong in this Category II: (1) Beginning sentences with *and* or *but;* (2) beginning sentences with *because* (a rule that appears in no handbook that I know of, but that seems to have a popular currency); (3) *which/that* in regard to restrictive relative clauses; (4) *each other* for two, *one another* for more than two; (5) *which* to refer to a whole clause (when not obviously ambiguous); (6) *between* for two, *among* for more than two. These next ones most readers of this journal may disagree with personally; I can only assert on the basis of considerable reading that they occur too frequently to be put in any other category for most readers: (7) *less* for *fewer;* (8) *due to* for *because;* (9) the strict placement of *only;* (10) the strict placement of *not only, neither,* etc. before only that phrase or clause that perfectly balances the *nor.* The usage of several disputed words must also suggest this category for most readers: *disinterested/uninterested, continuous/continual, alternative* for more than two. Since I have no intention of arguing which rules should go into any category, I offer these only as examples of my observations. Whether they are accurate for you is in principle irrelevant to the argument. Nor is it an exhaustive list.

14. The rules that go into Category III would, I believe, include these. Again, they serve only to illustrate. I have no brief in regard to where they should go. (1) *shall will,* (2) *who/whom,*

(3) unsplit infinitives, (4) fronted prepositions, (5) subjunctive form of *be*, (6) *whose/of which* as possessives for inanimate nouns, (7) repeated *one* instead of a referring pronoun *he/his/him*, (8) plural *data* and *media*, singular verb after *none*.

Questions for Discussion and Journaling

1. Return to our earlier question about the title: What does Williams mean by the *phenomenology of error*? Why do you think he chose that term?

2. What have been some of your own experiences with the construct of *error*? Why do they stand out in your mind? How might you react to those experiences now, having read Williams's piece?

3. What, if anything, did you disagree with in this article? Did Williams make any arguments that conflict with your experience or with your sense, as a writer, of how things should be done?

4. Two of Williams's claims are that (a) if we read expecting to find errors, we tend to find them, whereas if we aren't looking for them we are less likely to notice them, and (b) if we were to read student papers as we read non-student texts, we would find far fewer errors in them. If you take these two ideas together, what does Williams seem to be saying? What do you think of what he's saying?

5. How would you describe Williams's **tone** in this piece — that is, if he were reading it aloud, how would he sound? Note how often he repeats the words *puzzled* and *puzzling*. Do you think he really was puzzled?

6. What would you say Williams's text *does*? It might be helpful for you to think about why Williams wrote it, where it was published, and who was meant to read it. We think that Williams's article *indicts* someone or something. (If you aren't sure what *indict* means, look it up.) If this is true, then what or whom does it indict, and why?

7. Of the various observations that Williams makes in this article, what was most *surprising* to you? Which did you *like* most? Why?

Applying and Exploring Ideas

1. Compile your own list of writing errors that people criticize in others while ignoring in themselves. What will you use to come up with this list? Will you look in handbooks or in the writing of other students? Or will you think back to errors that your teachers have emphasized? Though this is a short assignment, gathering the information for your list can be considered a mini research project.

2. See how many errors you can find in Williams's piece: Mark it up with a red pen — and then make a list of the errors you find. Next, compare your list with those of three of your classmates. Which errors did you all notice? Which ones did only some, or just one, of you notice? Do these results tell you anything

about one of Williams's main questions — which errors are bigger problems than others?

3. Write a few informal paragraphs to share with your classmates regarding the research Williams did for this article. What did he study? What data did he collect? How did he analyze the data he collected? Now brainstorm a few research questions of your own that would prompt you to collect and analyze data like these. Why are these interesting questions to you?

4. Write a two-page memoir of your relationship, as a writer, to error and the school expectation of correctness in your writing. For example, do you remember particular writing or school experiences relating to error or correctness in your writing — for worse or for better? Do you remember particular moods or attitudes around writing related to expectations of correctness? If you have thought of yourself as a particularly strong or comfortable writer, or as a weak or nervous writer, does that self-concept connect in any way to errors and correctness? As you create this memoir, consider (and conclude with) what it helps you see about your prior experiences with literacy and how they shape your identity and your relationship with writing.

- -

META MOMENT   What might be different about your attitude toward writing and how you experience writing if you had been raised with the idea not that writing has to be perfectly correct to be good, but rather that error is not the most important factor in what makes good writing?

- -

Should Writers Use They Own English?

VERSHAWN ASHANTI YOUNG

Vershawn Ashanti Young

Framing the Reading

Vershawn Ashanti Young has described himself as a trans-disciplinary scholar and teacher working in African American studies, with research crossing language studies and performance studies. He studies and writes about the language issues that he discusses in this article, as well as about masculinity and representations of race in art, film, and literature. He has written and performed plays, and served as an anti-racism consultant, and he has been a high school teacher, an elementary school principal, and a school board administrator. He is currently professor of drama and speech communication at the University of Waterloo in Canada.

In this piece, Young argues against the traditional practice of teaching (and allowing) only one form of English, "standard English," in school and college. He asserts instead that we should include many versions of whatever language we're teaching, and that we should teach people how to understand and embed multiple versions of a language in whatever writing or speaking they're doing. Young calls this form of multilingualism *code meshing*, which "blend dialects, international languages, local idioms, chat-room lingo, and the rhetorical styles of various ethnic and cultural groups in both formal *and* informal speech acts" (para. 25) — as his definition itself does. In doing so, he joins a long-standing scholarly conversation among linguists and language teachers over whether we should *prescribe* what correct language is and try to make everyone's language use match that prescription, or whether we should instead look at how people actually use language and use our observations to *describe* how our language works.

In making his argument, Young points out severe problems with the "standard English" expectation in schools, demonstrating it as racist, unrealistic, and crippling — even for people who are used to using it (or thinking they do). If you also read Joseph Williams's piece in this chapter (p. 304), you'll see both writers describing how prescriptive language requirements lead to double standards that discriminate against some language users and not others. How Young arrives at these conclusions — the evidence he

Young, Vershawn Ashanti. "Should Writers Use They Own English?" *Iowa Journal of Cultural Studies*, vol. 12, no. 1, 2010, pp. 110–18.

offers and the ways in which he carefully considers the arguments of those supporting a "standard English only" approach to education — is a masterpiece of
argument structure and style in that he recognizes that you may repeatedly find
his claims difficult to accept, and as a result he works to bring you to his point of
view through careful examples and reasons.

You will immediately notice that Young writes his piece in a different version (or
dialect) of English than most pieces in this book. He's writing in what he calls "black
vernacular" (also called African American English or Black English Vernacular). Therefore, not only does this piece make its argument in favor of code meshing in part
by *performing* and thus demonstrating how code meshed scholarly arguments can
work; it also pushes you as a reader to encounter a version of English that has not
traditionally been allowed in the space you're encountering it here, and therefore to
wonder about the meaning and value of why it likely seems strange to you to see it in
a college writing course or a scholarly journal.

Getting Ready to Read

Before you read, do at least one of the following activities:

- Google "African American English" and write your own short description of it.
- Google "Stanley Fish What Should Colleges Teach Part 3" and read first-hand
  Fish's arguments that Young responds to in this piece.

As you read, consider the following questions:

- What experiences have you had being advantaged or disadvantaged by the
  school expectation of "standard English"?
- Is there a point where you stop noticing that Young writes in black vernacular?

---

*What would a composition course based on the method I urge look like? [. . .]
First, you must clear your mind of [the following. . .]: "We affirm the students'
right to their own patterns and varieties of language—the dialects of their
nurture or whatever dialects in which they find their own identity and style."*
— Stanley Fish, "What Should Colleges Teach? Part 3."

CULTURAL CRITIC STANLEY FISH COME TALKIN bout—in his three-piece 1
New York Times "What Should Colleges Teach?" suit—there only one way to
speak and write to get ahead in the world, that writin teachers should "clear [they]
mind of the orthodoxies that have taken hold in the composition world" ("Part 3").
He say dont no student have a rite to they own language if that language make
them "vulnerable to prejudice"; that "it may be true that the standard language

is [. . .] a device for protecting the status quo, but that very truth is a reason for teaching it to students" (Fish "Part 3").

Lord, lord, lord! Where do I begin, cuz this man sho tryin to take the nation back to a time when we were less tolerant of linguistic and racial differences. Yeah, I said racial difference, tho my man Stan be talkin explicitly bout language differences. The two be intertwined. Used to be a time when a black person could get hanged from the nearest tree just cuz they be black. And they fingers and heads (double entendre intended) get chopped off sometimes. Stanley Fish say he be appalled at blatant prejudice, and get even madder at prejudice exhibited by those who claim it dont happen no mo (Fish "Henry Louis Gates"). And it do happen — as he know — when folks dont get no jobs or get fired or whatever cuz they talk and write Asian or black or with an Applachian accent or sound like whatever aint the status quo. And Fish himself acquiesce to this linguistic prejudice when he come saying that people make theyselves targets for racism if and when they dont write and speak like he do.

But dont nobody's language, dialect, or style make them "vulnerable to prejudice." It's ATTITUDES. It be the way folks with some power perceive other people's language. Like the way some view, say, black English when used in school or at work. Black English dont make it own-self oppressed. It be negative views about other people usin they own language, like what Fish expressed in his *NYT* blog, that make it so.

This explain why so many bloggers on Fish's *NYT* comment page was tryin to school him on why teachin one correct way lend a hand to choppin off folks' tongues. But, let me be fair to my man Stan. He prolly unware that he be supportin language discrimination, cuz he appeal to its acceptable form–standard language ideology also called "dominant language ideology" (Lippi-Green). Standard language ideology is the belief that there is one set of dominant language rules that stem from a single dominant discourse (like standard English) that all writers and speakers of English must conform to in order to communicate effectively. Dominant language ideology also say peeps can speak whateva the heck way they want to — BUT AT HOME!

Dont get me wrong, Fish aint all wrong. One of his points almost on da money — the one when he say teachers of writin courses need to spend a lot of time dealin straight with writin, not only with topics of war, gender, race, and peace. But he dont like no black English and Native American rhetoric mixing with standard English. Yeah, he tell teachers to fake like students have language rites. He say,

> If students infected with the facile egalitarianism of soft multi-culturalism declare, "I have a right to my own language," reply, "Yes, you do, and I am not here to take that language from you; I'm here to teach you another one." (Who could object to learning a second language?) And then get on with it. (Fish "Part 3")

Besides encouraging teachers to be snide and patronizing, Fish flat out confusin 6 (I would say he lyin, but Momma say be nice). You cant start off sayin, "disabuse yo'self of the notion that students have a right to they dialect" and then say to tell students: "Y'all do have a right." That be hypocritical. It further disingenuous of Fish to ask: "Who could object to learning a second language?" What he really mean by this rhetorical question is that the "multiculturals" should be thrilled to leave they own dialect and learn another one, the one he promote. If he meant everybody should be thrilled to learn another dialect, then wouldnt everybody be learnin everybody's dialect? Wouldnt we all become multidialectal and pluralingual? And that's my exact argument, that we all should know everybody's dialect, at least as many as we can, and be open to the mix of them in oral and written communication (Young).

See, dont nobody all the time, nor do they in the same way subscribe to or 7 follow standard modes of expression. Everybody mix the dialect they learn at home with whateva other dialect or language they learn afterwards. That's how we understand accents; that's how we can hear that some people are from a Polish, Spanish, or French language background when they speak English. It's how we can tell somebody is from the South, from Appalachia, from Chicago or any other regional background. We hear that background in they speech, and it's often expressed in they writin too. It's natural (Coleman).

But some would say, "You cant mix no dialects at work; how would peeps 8 who aint from yo hood understand you?" They say, "You just gotta use standard English." Yet, even folks with good jobs in the corporate world dont follow no standard English. Check this out: Reporter Sam Dillon write about a survey conducted by the National Commission on Writing in 2004. He say "that a third of employees in the nation's blue-chip companies wrote poorly and that businesses were spending as much as $3.1 billion annually on remedial training" (A23).

Now, some peeps gone say this illustrate how Fish be rite, why we need to be 9 teachin mo standard grammar and stuff. If you look at it from Fish view, yeah it mean that. But if you look at it from my view, it most certainly dont mean that. Instead, it mean that the one set of rules that people be applyin to everybody's dialects leads to perceptions that writers need "remedial training" or that speakers of dialects are dumb. Teachin speakin and writin prescriptively, as Fish want, force people into patterns of language that aint natural or easy to understand. A whole lot of folk could be writin and speakin real, real smart if Fish and others stop using one prescriptive, foot-long ruler to measure the language of peeps who use a yard stick when they communicate.

Instead of prescribing how folks should write or speak, I say we teach lan- 10 guage descriptively. This mean we should, for instance, teach how language functions within and from various cultural perspectives. And we should teach what it take to understand, listen, and write in multiple dialects simultaneously.

We should teach how to let dialects comingle, sho nuff blend together, like blending the dialect Fish speak and the black vernacular that, say, a lot—certainly not all—black people speak.

See, people be mo pluralingual than we wanna recognize. What we need to do is enlarge our perspective about what good writin is and how good writin can look at work, at home, and at school. The narrow, prescriptive lens be messin writers and readers all the way up, cuz we all been taught to respect the dominant way to write, even if we dont, cant, or wont ever write that one way ourselves. That be hegemony. Internalized oppression. Linguistic self-hate. But we should be mo flexible, mo acceptin of language diversity, language expansion, and creative language usage from ourselves and from others both in formal and informal settings. Why? Cuz nobody can or gone really master *all* the rules of any language or dialect.

So, what happen when peeps dont meet the dominant language rules? Well, some folks can get away with not meeting those rules while others get punished, sometimes severely, for not doing so. Let me go a lil mo way with this: Even university presidents and highly regarded English professors dont always speak and write in the dominant standard, even when they believe they do.

Remember when Fish put former Harvard President Lawrence Summers on blast in 2002? What had happened was, Summers called professor Cornell West to his office and went straight off on the brotha for writin books everybody could read, for writin clear, accessible scholarship. Summers apologized after the media got involved, sayin: "I regret any faculty member leaving a conversation feeling they are not respected" (qtd. in Fish, "Say It Ain't So"). Fish say: "In a short, 13-word sentence, the chief academic officer of the highest ranked university in the country, and therefore in the entire world, has committed three grammatical crimes, failure to mark the possessive case, failure to specify the temporal and the causal relationships between the conversations he has and the effects he regrets, and failure to observe noun-pronoun agreement" ("Say It Ain't So").

But get this: Fish's correction of Summers is suspect, according to a grammar evaluation by linguist Kyoko Inoue (2002). Inoue say, "What the writer / speaker says (or means) often controls the form of the sentence." She say Summers' *intent* make his sentence clear and understandable, not rules from the grammar police-man.

But Fish gone ignore Inoue again, as he did back then in 2002. Fish gone say that the examples of Summers and the corporate workers show reasons why we should teach mo standard grammar, that if corporations and high ranked universities got folks who cant write rite, we gotta do a better job of teachin the rules. And since most of those workers are white, he gone also say he not supportin prejudice. He dont like it when whites dont speak rite, just the same as he dont like it when Latinos not speakin rite. Race aint got nothin to do with

11

12

13

14

15

it, he gone add. It be only about speakin and writin standard English. He say his words apply to everybody not just to those who be wantin "a right to they own language."

But here what Fish dont get: Standard language ideology insist that minority 16 people will never become an Ivy League English department chair or president of Harvard University if they dont perfect they mastery of standard English. At the same time the ideology instruct that white men will gain such positions, even with a questionable handle of standard grammar and rhetoric (I think here of the regular comments made about former President Bush's bad grammar and poor rhetoric). Fish respond that this the way our country is so let's accept it. I say: "No way, brutha!"

Also, Fish use his experience teachin grad students as evidence for his claim. 17 He say his grad students couldnt write a decent sentence. Well, they wrote good enuff in they essays to get into grad school, didnt they? And most grad schools admit students by committee, which mean some of his colleagues thought the grad students could write rite. But it sound like Fish sayin he the only one who could judge what good writin is — not his colleagues. What is Fish really on, what is he really tryin to prove?

> I dont believe the writin problems of graduate students is due to lack of standard English; they problems likely come from learnin new theories and new ways of thinkin. . . .

I, for one, sho aint convinced by Fish. 18 I dont believe the writin problems of graduate students is due to lack of standard English; they problems likely come from learnin new theories and new ways of thinkin and tryin to express that clearly, which take some time. New ideas dont always come out clear and understandable the first few times they expressed. And, further, grad students also be tryin too hard to sound smart, to write like the folk they be readin, instead of usin they own voices.

In my own experience teachin grad students, they also tend to try too hard 19 to sound academic, often using unnecessary convoluted language, using a big word where a lil one would do, and stuff. Give them students some credit, Fish! What you should tell them is there be more than one academic way to write rite. Didnt yo friend Professor Gerald Graff already school us on that in his book *Clueless in Academe* (2003)? He say he tell his students to be bilingual. He say, say it in the technical way, the college-speak way, but also say it the way you say it to yo momma — in the same paper. Now that's some advice!

But Fish must dont like this advice. He say that we should have students to 20 translate the way they talk into standard English on a chalk board. He say, leave the way they say it to momma on the board and put the standard way on paper.

This is wrongly called code switching. And many teachers be doin this with they students. And it dont work. Why? Cuz most teachers of code switching dont know what they be talkin bout. Code switching, from a linguistic perspective, is not translatin one dialect into another one. It's blendin two or mo dialects, languages, or rhetorical forms into one sentence, one utterance, one paper. And not all the time is this blendin intentional, sometime it unintentional. And that's the point. The two dialects sometime naturally, sometime intentionally, co-exist! This is code switching from a linguistic perspective: two languages and dialects co-existing in one speech act (Auer).

But since so many teachers be jackin up code switching with they "speak 21 this way at school and a different way at home," we need a new term. I call it CODE MESHING!

Code meshing is the new code switching; it's multidialectalism and pluralin- 22 gualism in one speech act, in one paper.

Let me drop some code meshing knowledge on y'all. 23

Code meshing what we all do whenever we communicate—writin, speakin, 24 whateva.

Code meshing blend dialects, international languages, local idioms, chat- 25 room lingo, and the rhetorical styles of various ethnic and cultural groups in both formal *and* informal speech acts.

This mode of communication be just as frequently used by politicians and 26 professors as it be by journalists and advertisers. It be used by writers of color to compose full-length books; and it's sometimes added intentionally to standard English to make the point that there aint no one way to communicate.

Code meshing also be used to add flavor and style, like journalist Tomas 27 Palermo do in the excerpt below from his interview with Jamal Cooks, professor of Education. In his online article "Rappin about Literacy Activism," Palermo write:

> Teachers frequently encounter him on panels with titles like "The Expanding Canon: Teaching Multicultural Literature In High School." But the dude is also hella down to earth. He was in some pretty successful "true-school" era hip-hop recording groups [. . .]. Meet the man who made it his passion to change the public education game, one class at a time.

With vernacular insertions such as "but the dude is also hella down to earth" (not to mention beginning a sentence with the conjunction *but*) and adding the colloquial *game* to "public education," the article, otherwise composed in mono-dialect standard English, shift into a code meshed text.

Here some mo examples:

(1) Iowa Republican Senator Chuck Grassley sent two tweets to Pres- 28 ident Obama in June 2009 (Werner). His messages blend together common

txtng abbrvs., standard English grammar and a African American rhetorical technique:

> First Tweet: "Pres Obama you got nerve while u sightseeing in Paris to tell us 'time to deliver' on health care. We still on skedul / even workinWKEND."

> Second Tweet: "Pres Obama while u sightseeing in Paris u said 'time to delivr on healthcare' When you are a 'hammer' u think evrything is NAIL I'm no NAIL."

(2) Professor Kermit Campbell uses multiple dialects to compose *Gettin' Our* 29 *Groove On* (2005), a study of college writing instruction. In it he say:

> Middle class aspirations and an academic career have rubbed off on me, fo sho, but all hell or Texas gotta freeze over befo you see me copping out on a genuine respect and love for my native tongue. [. . .] That's from the heart, you know. But I don't expect a lot of folks to feel me. (3)

(3) Chris Ann Cleland, a real estate agent from Virginia, express disap- 30 pointment about President Obama's economic plan in an interview with the *Washington Post* (Rich):

> "Nothing's changed for the common guy," she said. "I feel like I've been punked."

(4) Referencing Cleland's remark, the title of *New York Times* columnist 31 Frank Rich's Op-ed article asks: "Is Obama Punking Us?" Rich writes in the last paragraph of his article:

> "The larger fear is that Obama might be just another corporatist, punking voters much as the Republicans do when they claim to be all for the common guy."

The contraction "nothing's," the colloquial phrase "common guy," and the vernacular expression "punked," are neither unusual nor sensational. Yet, when these examples get compared to the advice giving about code switching, you get a glaring contradiction.

Students be told that vernacular language should be reserved for the play- 32 ground with friends or at a picnic with neighbors, and that standard English be used by professionals at work, in academic writing, and when communicating with important officials. However, the colloquial language of two white, middle-aged professionals (Cleland and Rich), which appears in two of our nations most highly regarded newspapers prove this aint so, at least not no mo and prolly never was. The BIG divide between vernacular and standard, formal and informal be eroding, if it aint already faded. And for many, it's a good thing. I know it sho be for me.

The Internet, among other mass media, as well as the language habits of 33
America's ever-growing diverse ethnic populations be affecting how everybody
talk and write now, too. A term like "punked," which come from black culture
to describe someone getting tricked, teased, or humiliated, used to be taboo in
formal communication as was black people wearin braided hair at work in the
1980s. The professional world has become more tolerant of black hair styles.
And that same world not only toleratin but incorporatin, and appropriatin,
black language styles.

Actor Ashton Kutcher popularized the term "punked" with his hit TV show 34
of the same title. That's probably how the word seeped into the parlance of sub-
urban professionals ("I feel punked"; "Obama [. . .] punking voters"), although
it still retains it colloquial essence.

Fish may reply, "But these examples be from TV and journalism; those expres- 35
sions wont fly in academic or scholarly writing." But did you read Campbell's
book, Fish? What about Geneva Smitherman's *Talkin and Testifyin* (1977)? Is
you readin this essay? Campbell blends the grammars and rhetorical styles of
both black English and so-called standard English, along with the discourse of
Rap and Hip Hop. He also blend in oral speech patterns (with the phonological
representation of words like "fo sho" and "befo"). And his book is published
by an academic press and marketed to teachers of English. Campbell just one
of many academics — professors of language and writin studies, no less — who
code mesh.

Still, Fish may say, "Yeah, but look, they paid their dues. Those professors 36
knew the rules of writin before they broke them." To this objection, Victor
Villanueva, a Puerto Rican scholar of American studies, as well as language and
literacy, point to "writers of color who have been using the blended form [. . .]
from the get-go" (351). As he put it, "The blended form is our dues" (351).
They dont have to learn to the rules to write rite first; the blended form or code
meshing is writin rite.

This brings us back to Senator Grassley's tweets. It's obvious he learned some 37
cool techno-shorthand (e.g., "WKEND" and "delivr"). He also uses both the
long spelling of *you* and the abbrv. "u" in the same line. "We still on skedul" is
a complete sentence; the backslash ("/") that follow it function like a semicolon
to connect the emphatic fragment to the previous thought. And the caps in
"WKEND" and "NAIL" pump up the words with emphasis, which alleviates
the need for formal exclamation marks.

Grassley's message be a form of loud-talking — a black English device where 38
a speaker indirectly insults an authority figure. The authority figure is meant to
overhear the conversation (thus loud-talking) so that the insult can be defended
as unintentional. Grassley sent the message over his Twitter social network but
he address Obama. He wanna point out what seem like a contradiction: If
healthcare reform is so important to Obama, why is he sightseeing in Paris?

Grassley didnt send no standard English as a tweet. Twitter allow messages 39 with 140 characters. The standard English question—If healthcare reform is so important to Obama, why is he sightseeing in Paris?—is 80 characters. Why didnt Grassley use this question or compose one like it? Cuz all kinds of folks know, understand, and like code meshing. So Grassley code meshed.

Code meshing be everywhere. It be used by all types of people. It allow writ- 40 ers and speakers to bridge multiple codes and modes of expression that Fish say disparate and unmixable. The metaphorical language tool box be expandin, baby.

Plus code meshing benefit everybody. 41

In the 1970's linguist William Labov noted that black students were ostra- 42 cized because they spoke and wrote black dialect. Yet he noted that black speakers were more attuned to argumentation. Labov say that "in many ways [black] working-class speakers are more effective narrators, reasoners, and *debaters* than many middle-class [white] speakers, who temporize, qualify, and lose their argument in a mass of irrelevant detail" (qtd in Graff 37).

So when we teach the rhetorical devices of blacks we can add to the writing 43 proficiency of whites and everybody else. Now, that's something, aint it? Code meshing use the way people already speak and write and help them be more rhetorically effective. It do include teaching some punctuation rules, attention to meaning and word choice, and various kinds of sentence structures and some standard English. This mean too that good writin gone look and sound a bit different than some may now expect.

And another real, real, good result is we gone help reduce prejudice. Yes, 44 mam. Now that's a goal to reach for.

Works Cited

Auer, Peter. *Code-Switching in Conversation: Language, Interaction and Identity.* New York: Routledge, 1988.

Campbell, Kermit. *Gettin' Our Groove On: Rhetoric, Language, and Literacy for The Hip Hop Generation.* Detroit: Wayne State University Press, 2005.

Coleman, Charles F. "Our Students Write with Accents. Oral Paradigms for ESD Students." *CCC* 48.4 (1997): 486–500.

Dillon, Sam. "What Corporate America Can't Build: A Sentence." *New York Times* 7 Dec. 2004: A23.

Fish, Stanley. "Henry Louis Gates: Déjà Vu All Over Again." *Opinionator: Exclusive Online Commentary From The Times.* The New York Times, 24 July 2009. <http://opinionator.blogs.nytimes.com/2009/07/24/henry-louis-gates-deja-vu-all-over-again/>.

——. "Say It Ain't So." *Chronicle of Higher Education.* 21 June 2002. <http://chronicle.com/article/Say-It-Ain-t-So/46137/>.

——. "What Should Colleges Teach?" *Opinionator: Exclusive Online Commentary From The Times.* The New York Times, 24 Aug. 2009. <http://fish.blogs.nytimes.com/2009/08/24/what-should-colleges-teach/>.

———. "What Should Colleges Teach? Part 2." *Opinionator: Exclusive Online Commentary From The Times.* The New York Times, 31 Aug. 2009. <http://fish.blogs.nytimes.com/2009/08/31/what-should-colleges-teach-part-2/>.

———. "What Should Colleges Teach? Part 3." *Opinionator: Exclusive Online Commentary From The Times.* The New York Times, 7 Sept. 2009. <http://fish.blogs. nytimes.com/2009/09/07/what-should-colleges-teach-part-3/>.

Graff, Gerald. *Clueless in Academe: How Schooling Obscures the Life of the Mind.* New Haven: Yale University Press, 2003.

Inoue, Kyoko. "A Linguist's Perspective on Teaching Grammar." Unpublished paper. University of Illinois at Chicago. Oct. 2002.

Lippi-Green, Rosina. *English with an Accent: Language, Ideology and Discrimination in the United States.* London: Routledge, 1997.

Palermo, Tomas. "Rappin about Literacy Activism." *WireTap Online Magazine.* 13 July 2007. <http://www.wiretapmag.org/education/43160/>.

Rich, Frank. "Is Obama Punking Us?" *New York Times* 9 Aug. 2009: WK8.

Smitherman, Geneva. *Talkin and Testifyin: The Language of Black America.* Detroit: Wayne State University Press, 1977.

Villanueva, Victor. "Personally Speaking: Experience as Evidence in Academic Discourse." *Rhetoric Review* 25.3 (2006): 348–352.

Werner, Erica. "Grassley Lashes Out at Obama Via Twitter." *Gazette* [Cedar Rapids-Iowa City, IA] 8 June 2009, F: 1A.

Young, Vershawn. *Your Average Nigga: Performing Race, Literacy, and Masculinity.* Detroit: Wayne State University Press, 2007.

- -

Questions for Discussion and Journaling

1. Young argues in "black vernacular" English against Fish's assertion of the necessity of "standard English." How powerful or effective do you find this strategy of Young's to be, and why?

2. In his opening line, Young characterizes Fish's editorial as "Cultural critic Stanley Fish come talkin about — in his three-piece *New York Times* . . . suit." What does Young's language play here show about the relationship between language or speech and class or social standing?

3. In paragraph 5, Young details his "exact argument." How would it apply to you personally?

4. Young argues that almost no one actually succeeds in using "standard English" even when they're trying to (para. 7). Do his examples to support this claim persuade you?

5. Young asserts that Fish's desire for everyone to know how to use one "correct" English is ultimately racist. How does Young reach that conclusion?

6. Why does Young want us to use the term *code meshing* rather than *code switching*?

7. Young describes several features of code meshing. What are three?

Applying and Exploring Ideas

1. Linguists classify versions of a language as "dialects" when they have regular rules consistently used by speakers that differentiate them from the rules of other dialects of the language. Find three regularly followed rules in Young's African American English dialect here that you recognize as different from the dialect of English usually taught in schools. (For example, where school-English uses "their" to show possession, AAE uses "they," as Young does consistently throughout his piece.)

2. Instead of believing that most people can't use English correctly, Young asserts, we should describe "correct English" as the English people *actually use*. Why do you think we don't already do this?

3. Young wants to demonstrate that the penalties for violating prescriptive English rules are not equal for all speakers or writers. What are some examples you've seen of unequal consequences for different kinds of people breaking the rules of "standard English"?

4. Name the first way you can think of that even writers who feel proficient at "standard English" would benefit from Young's argument against prescriptive English. Then list other ways that come to mind. Why do you think you thought of the first one first?

5. Young offers several extended examples of code meshing (beginning in para. 26). From your college classes or texts, find three extended examples of your own. From your "home" or "work" or personal life (including your social media), find three more.

6. One of Young's most common styles of argument in this piece is to imagine how Fish would respond to one of Young's objections to Fish's thinking. Find four instances, and use them to explain what effect this argument style has on you as a reader, and whether you think it would have a similar affect for most readers.

7. Write a long paragraph explaining to a friend or parent what benefits Young sees to everyone learning, or being taught, code meshing. Finish it by explaining, from your perspective, how we would have to change the ways we do education in order to do so.

- -
META MOMENT   How does Young's concern with writers using they own English relate to this chapter's threshold concept, writing is impacted by our identities and prior experiences?
- -

From Outside, In

BARBARA MELLIX

Leroy Mellix

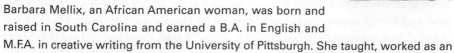

Framing the Reading

Barbara Mellix, an African American woman, was born and
raised in South Carolina and earned a B.A. in English and
M.F.A. in creative writing from the University of Pittsburgh. She taught, worked as an
assistant dean, and served as director of the advising center there.

In this essay, Mellix explores her experiences and conflicts with black English and
standard English. We have included her essay here because she illustrates many of
the conflicts and experiences that led Young, in the previous essay (p. 325), to argue
against requiring minority speakers to engage in "code switching" and instead that all
students should be taught "code meshing" to blend multiple languages or versions
of a language. (If you haven't read Young, we recommend that you do so before reading Mellix.) Mellix's essay illustrates the many ways that language is bound up with
identity, and how literacy practices are always informed by prior experiences. Who she
is as a writer, and how she feels about writing and the language she uses when she
writes, are all colored by her experiences in a particular place and time — experiences
that include home, school, extended family, geographical location, race, class, and
more.

Getting Ready to Read

Before you read, do at least one of the following activities:

- Think about the different ways you speak and write in different situations.
- Consider the ways that your family and schooling have shaped how you
  speak, and what kind of speech is considered "correct" in school and
  professional settings.

> *As you read,* consider the following questions:

- How do Mellix's experiences relate to Young's claims in the
  previous article?
- Which part of Mellix's experiences can you identify with, and
  which seem difficult to identify with?

Mellix, Barbara. "From Outside, In." *The Georgia Review*, vol. 41, no. 2, Summer 1987,
pp. 258–67.

TWO YEARS AGO, when I started writing this paper, trying to bring order 1 out of chaos, my ten-year-old daughter was suffering from an acute attack of boredom. She drifted in and out of the room complaining that she had nothing to do, no one to "be with" because none of her friends were at home. Patiently I explained that I was working on something special and needed peace and quiet, and I suggested that she paint, read, or work with her computer. None of these interested her. Finally, she pulled up a chair to my desk and watched me, now and then heaving long, loud sighs. After two or three minutes (nine or ten sighs), I lost my patience. "Looka here, Allie," I said, "you too old for this kinda carryin' on. I done told you this is important. You wronger than dirt to be in here haggin' me like this and you know it. Now git on outta here and leave me off before I put my foot all the way down."

I was at home, alone with my family, and my daughter understood that this 2 way of speaking was appropriate in that context. She knew, as a matter of fact, that it was almost inevitable; when I get angry at home, I speak some of my finest, most cherished black English. Had I been speaking to my daughter in this manner in certain other environments, she would have been shocked and probably worried that I had taken leave of my sense of propriety.

Like my children, I grew up speaking what I considered two distinctly dif- 3 ferent languages — black English and standard English (or as I thought of them then, the ordinary everyday speech of "country" coloreds and "proper" English) — and in the process of acquiring these languages, I developed an understanding of when, where, and how to use them. But unlike my children, I grew up in a world that was primarily black. My friends, neighbors, minister, teachers — almost everybody I associated with every day — were black. And we spoke to one another in our own special language: *That sho is a pretty dress you got on. If she don't soon leave me off I'm gon tell her head a mess. I was so mad I could'a pissed a blue nail. He all the time trying to low-rate somebody. Ain't that just about the nastiest thing you ever set ears on?*

Then there were the "others," the "proper" blacks, transplanted relatives 4 and one-time friends who came home from the city for weddings, funerals, and vacations. And the whites. To these we spoke standard English. "Ain't?" my mother would yell at me when I used the term in the presence of "others." "You *know* better than that." And I would hang my head in shame and say the "proper" word.

I remember one summer sitting in my grandmother's house in Greeleyville, 5 South Carolina, when it was full of the chatter of city relatives who were home on vacation. My parents sat quietly, only now and then volunteering a comment or answering a question. My mother's face took on a strained expression when she spoke. I could see that she was being careful to say just the right words in just the right way. Her voice sounded thick, muffled. And when she finished speaking, she would lapse into silence, her proper smile on her face. My father was more articulate, more aggressive. He spoke quickly, his words sharp and clear. But he held his proud head higher, a signal that he, too, was uncomfortable. My sisters and brothers and I stared at our aunts, uncles, and cousins, speaking only when prompted. Even then, we hesitated, formed our sentences in our minds, then spoke softly, shyly.

My parents looked small and anxious during those occasions, and I waited 6 impatiently for leave-taking when we would mock our relatives the moment we were out of their hearing. "Reeely," we would say to one another, flexing our wrists and rolling our eyes, "how dooo you stan' this heat? Chile, it just too h*yooo*-mid for words." Our relatives had made us feel "country," and this was our way of regaining pride in ourselves while getting a little revenge in the bargain. The words bubbled in our throats and rolled across our tongues, a balming.

As a child I felt this same doubleness in uptown Greeleyville where the 7 whites lived. "Ain't that a pretty dress you're wearing!" Toby, the town police-man, said to me one day when I was fifteen. "Thank you very much," I replied, my voice barely audible in my own ears. The words felt wrong in my mouth, rigid, foreign. It was not that I had never spoken that phrase before — it was common in black English, too — but I was extremely conscious that this was an occasion for proper English. I had taken out my English and put it on as I did my church clothes, and I felt as if I were wearing my Sunday best in the middle of the week. It did not matter that Toby had not spoken grammatically correct English. He was white and could speak as he wished. I had something to prove. Toby did not.

Speaking standard English to whites was our way of demonstrating that we 8 knew their language and could use it. Speaking it to standard-English-speaking blacks was our way of showing them that we, as well as they, could "put on airs." But when we spoke standard English, we acknowledged (to ourselves and to others — but primarily to ourselves) that our customary way of speaking was inferior. We felt foolish, embarrassed, somehow diminished because we were ashamed to be our real selves. We were reserved, shy in the presence of those who owned and/or spoke *the* language.

My parents never set aside time to drill us in standard English. Their forms of instruction were less formal. When my father was feeling particularly expansive, he would regale us with tales of his exploits in the outside world. In almost flawless English, complete with dialogue and fla-vored with gestures and embellishment, he told us about his attempt to get a haircut at

> *When we spoke standard English we acknowledged . . . that our customary way of speaking was inferior. We felt . . . diminished because we were ashamed to be our real selves.* 9

a white barbershop; his refusal to acknowledge one of the town merchants until the man addressed him as "Mister"; the time he refused to step off the sidewalk uptown to let some whites pass; his airplane trip to New York City (to visit a sick relative) during which the stewardesses and porters—recognizing that he was a "gentleman"—addressed him as "Sir." I did not realize then—nor, I think, did my father—that he was teaching us, among other things, standard English and the relationship between language and power.

My mother's approach was different. Often, when one of us said, "I'm 10 gon wash off my feet," she would say, "And what will you walk on if you wash them off?" Everyone would laugh at the victim of my mother's "proper" mood. But it was different when one of us children was in a proper mood. "You think you are so superior," I said to my oldest sister one day when we were arguing and she was winning. "Superior!" my sister mocked. "You mean I'm acting 'biggidy'?" My sisters and brothers sniggered, then joined in teasing me. Finally, my mother said, "Leave your sister alone. There's nothing wrong with using proper English." There was a half-smile on her face. I had gotten "uppity," had "put on airs" for no good reason. I was at home, alone with the family, and I hadn't been prompted by one of my mother's proper moods. But there was also a proud light in my mother's eyes; her children were learning English very well.

Not until years later, as a college student, did I begin to understand our 11 ambivalence toward English, our scorn of it, our need to master it, to own and be owned by it—an ambivalence that extended to the public school classroom. In our school, where there were no whites, my teacher taught standard English but used black English to do it. When my grammar-school teachers wanted us to write, for example, they usually said something like, "I want y'all to write five sentences that make a statement. Anybody git done before the rest can color." It was probably almost those exact words that led me to write these sentences in 1953 when I was in the second grade:

> The white clouds are pretty.
> There are only 15 people in our room.
> We will go to gym.
> We have a new poster.
> We may go out doors.

Second grade came after "Little First" and "Big First," so by then I knew the implied rules that accompanied all writing assignments. Writing was an occasion for proper English. I was not to write in the way we spoke to one another: The white clouds pretty; There ain't but fifteen people in our room; We going to gym; We got a new poster; We can go out in the yard. Rather I was to use the language of "other": clouds *are,* there *are,* we *will,* we *have,* we *may.*

My sentences were short, rigid, perfunctory, like the letters my mother wrote 12
to relatives:

> Dear Papa,
> How are you? How is Mattie? Fine I hope. We are fine. We will come
> to see you Sunday. Cousin Ned will give us a ride.
> Love,
> Daughter

The language was not ours. It was something from outside us, something we
used for special occasions.

But my coloring on the other side of that second-grade paper is different. I drew 13
three hearts and a sun. The sun has a smiling face that radiates and envelops everything it touches. And although the sun and the world are enclosed in a circle, the
colors I used—red, blue, green, purple, orange, yellow, black—indicate that I was
less restricted with drawing and coloring than I was with writing standard English.
My valentines were not just red. My sun was not just a yellow ball in the sky.

By the time I reached the twelfth grade, speaking and writing standard 14
English had taken on new importance. Each year, about half of the newly graduated seniors of our school moved to large cities—particularly in the North—to
live with relatives and find work. Our English teacher constantly corrected our
grammar: "Not 'ain't,' but 'isn't.'" We seldom wrote papers, and even those few
were usually plot summaries of short stories. When our teacher returned the
papers, she usually lectured on the importance of using standard English: "I *am;*
you *are;* he, she, or it *is,*" she would say, writing on the chalkboard as she spoke.
"How you gon git a job talking about 'I is,' or 'I isn't' or 'I ain't'?"

In Pittsburgh, where I moved after graduation, I watched my aunt and 15
uncle—who had always spoken standard English when in Greeleyville—switch
from black English to standard English to a mixture of the two, according to
where they were or who they were with. At home and with certain close relatives, friends, and neighbors, they spoke black English. With those less close,
they spoke a mixture. In public and with strangers, they generally spoke standard English.

In time, I learned to speak standard English with ease and to switch smoothly 16
from black to standard or a mixture, and back again. But no matter where I was,
no matter what the situation or occasion, I continued to write as I had in school:

> Dear Mommie,
> How are you? How is everybody else? Fine I hope. I am fine. So are
> Aunt and Uncle. Tell everyone I said hello. I will write again soon.
> Love,
> Barbara

At work, at a health insurance company, I learned to write letters to customers. I studied form letters and letters written by co-workers, memorizing the phrases and the ways in which they were used. I dictated:

> Thank you for your letter of January 5. We have made the changes in your coverage you requested. Your new premium will be $150 every three months. We are pleased to have been of service to you.

In a sense, I was proud of the letters I wrote for the company: they were proof of my ability to survive in the city, the outside world — an indication of my grow-ing mastery of English. But they also indicated that writing was still mechanical for me, something that didn't require much thought.

17 Reading also became a more significant part of my life during those early years in Pittsburgh. I had always liked reading, but now I devoted more and more of my spare time to it. I read romances, mysteries, popular novels. Look-ing back, I realize that the books I liked best were simple, unambiguous: good versus bad and right versus wrong with right rewarded and wrong punished, mysteries unraveled and all set right in the end. It was how I remembered life in Greeleyville.

18 Of course I was romanticizing. Life in Greeleyville had not become very uncomplicated. Back there I had been — first as a child, then as a young woman with limited experience in the outside world — living in a relatively closed-in society. But there were implicit and explicit principles that guided our way of life and shaped our relationships with one another and the people outside — principles that a newcomer would find elusive and baffling. In Pitts-burgh, I had matured, become more experienced. I had worked at three differ-ent jobs, associated with a wider range of people, married, had children. This new environment with different prescripts for living required that I speak stan-dard English much of the time and slowly, imperceptibly, I had ceased seeing a sharp distinction between myself and "others." Reading romances and myster-ies, characterized by dichotomy, was a way of shying away from change, from the person I was becoming.

19 But that other part of me — that part which took great pride in my ability to hold a job writing business letters — was increasingly drawn to the new develop-ments in my life and the attending possibilities, opportunities for even greater change. If I could write letters for a nationally known business, could I not also do something better, more challenging, more important? Could I not, perhaps, go to college and become a school teacher? For years, afraid and a little embar-rassed, I did no more than imagine this different me, this possible me. But six-teen years after coming north, when my youngest daughter entered kindergarten, I found myself unable — or unwilling — to resist the lure of possibility. I enrolled in my first college course: Basic Writing, at the University of Pittsburgh.

For the first time in my life, I was required to write extensively about myself. 20
Using the most formal English at my command, I wrote these sentences near
the beginning of the term:

> One of my duties as a homemaker is simply picking up after others. A day
> seldom passes that I don't search for a mislaid toy, book, or gym shoe, etc.
> I change the Ty-D-Bol, fight "ring around the collar," and keep our laundry
> smelling "April fresh." Occasionally, I settle arguments between my children
> and suggest things to do when they're bored. Taking telephone messages for
> my oldest daughter is my newest (and sometimes most aggravating) chore.
> Hanging the toilet paper roll is my most insignificant.

My concern was to use "appropriate" language, to sound as if I belonged in a
college classroom. But I felt separate from the language — as if it did not and
could not belong to me. I couldn't think and feel genuinely in that language,
couldn't make it express what I thought and felt about being a housewife.
A part of me resented, among other things, being judged by such things as the
appearance of my family's laundry and toilet bowl, but in that language I could
only imagine and write about a conventional housewife.

For the most part, the remainder of the term was a period of adjustment, a 21
time of trying to find my bearings as a student in a college composition class,
to learn to shut out my black English whenever I composed, and to prevent it
from creeping into my formulations; a time for trying to grasp the language
of the classroom and reproduce it in my prose; for trying to talk about myself
in that language, reach others through it. Each experience of writing was like
standing naked and revealing my imperfection, my "otherness." And each
new assignment was another chance to make myself over in language, reshape
myself, make myself "better" in my rapidly changing image of a student in a
college composition class.

But writing became increasingly unmanageable as the term progressed, and 22
by the end of the semester, my sentences sounded like this:

> My excitement was soon dampened, however, by what seemed like a small
> voice in the back of my head saying that I should be careful with my long
> awaited opportunity. I felt frustrated and this seemed to make it difficult to
> concentrate.

There is a poverty of language in these sentences. By this point, I knew that the
clichéd language of my Housewife essay was unacceptable, and I generally recognized trite expressions. At the same time, I hadn't yet mastered the language
of the classroom, hadn't yet come to see it as belonging to me. Most notable is
the lifelessness of the prose, the apparent absence of a person behind the words.
I wanted those sentences — and the rest of the essay — to convey the anguish of

yearning to, at once, become something more and yet remain the same. I had the sensation of being split in two, part of me going into a future the other part didn't believe possible. As that person, the student writer at that moment, I was essentially mute. I could not—in the process of composing—use the language of the old me, yet I couldn't imagine myself in the language of "others."

I found this particularly discouraging because at midsemester I had been 23 writing in a much different way. Note the language of this introduction to an essay I had written then, near the middle of the term:

> Pain is a constant companion to the people in "Footwork." Their jobs are physically damaging. Employers are insensitive to their feelings and in many cases add to their problems. The general public wounds them further by treating them with disgrace because of what they do for a living. Although the workers are as diverse as they are similar, there is a definite link between them. They suffer a great deal of abuse.

The voice here is stronger, more confident, appropriating terms like "physically damaging," "wounds them further," "insensitive," "diverse"—terms I couldn't have imagined using when writing about my own experience—and shaping them into sentences like, "Although the workers are as diverse as they are similar, there is a definite link between them." And there is the sense of a personality behind the prose, someone who sympathizes with the workers: "The general public wounds them further by treating them with disgrace because of what they do for a living."

What caused these differences? I was, I believed, explaining other people's 24 thoughts and feelings, and I was free to move about in the language of "others" so long as I was speaking *of* others. I was unaware that I was transforming into my best classroom language my own thoughts and feelings about people whose experiences and ways of speaking were in many ways similar to mine.

The following year, unable to turn back or let go of what had become some- 25 thing of an obsession with language (and hoping to catch and hold the sense of control that had eluded me in Basic Writing), I enrolled in a research writing course. I spent most of the term learning how to prepare for and write a research paper. I chose sex education as my subject and spent hours in libraries, searching for information, reading, taking notes. Then (not without messiness and often-demoralizing frustration) I organized my information into categories, wrote a thesis statement, and composed my paper—a series of paraphrases and quotations spaced between carefully constructed transitions. The process and results felt artificial, but as I would later come to realize I was passing through a necessary stage. My sentences sounded like this:

> This reserve becomes understandable with examination of who the abusers are. In an overwhelming number of cases, they are people the victims know

and trust. Family members, relatives, neighbors and close family friends commit seventy-five percent of all reported sex crimes against children, and parents, parent substitutes and relatives are the offenders in thirty to eighty percent of all reported cases. While assault by strangers does occur, it is less common, and is usually a single episode. But abuse by family members, relatives and acquaintances may continue for an extended period of time. In cases of incest, for example, children are abused repeatedly for an average of eight years. In such cases, "the use of physical force is rarely necessary because of the child's trusting, dependent relationship with the offender. The child's cooperation is often facilitated by the adult's position of dominance, an offer of material goods, a threat of physical violence, or a misrepresentation of moral standards."

The completed paper gave me a sense of profound satisfaction, and I read 26 it often after my professor returned it. I know now that what I was pleased with was the language I used and the professional voice it helped me maintain. "Use better words," my teacher had snapped at me one day after reading the notes I'd begun accumulating from my research, and slowly I began taking on the language of my sources. In my next set of notes, I used the word "vacillating"; my professor applauded. And by the time I composed the final draft, I felt at ease with terms like "overwhelming number of cases," "single episode," and "reserve," and I shaped them into sentences similar to those of my "expert" sources.

If I were writing the paper today, I would of course do some things differ- 27 ently. Rather than open with an anecdote—as my teacher suggested—I would begin simply with a quotation that caught my interest as I was researching my paper (and which I scribbled, without its source, in the margin of my notebook): "Truth does not do so much good in the world as the semblance of truth does evil." The quotation felt right because it captured what was for me the central idea of my essay—an idea that emerged gradually during the making of my paper—and expressed it in a way I would like to have said it. The anecdote, a hypothetical situation I invented to conform to the information in the paper, felt forced and insincere because it represented—to a great degree—my teacher's understanding of the essay, *her* idea of what in it was most significant. Improving upon my previous experiences with writing, I was beginning to think and feel in the language I used, to find my own voices in it, to sense that how one speaks influences how one means. But I was not yet secure enough, comfortable enough with the language to trust my intuition.

Now that I know that to seek knowledge, freedom, and autonomy means 28 always to be in the concentrated process of becoming—always to be venturing into new territory, feeling one's way at first, then getting one's balance, negotiating, accommodating, discovering one's self in ways that previously defined "others"—I sometimes get tired. And I ask myself why I keep on participating in this highbrow form of violence, this slamming against perplexity. But there is no real futility in the question, no hint of that part of the old me who stood outside standard English, hugging to herself a disabling mistrust of a language she thought could not represent a person with her history and experience. Rather, the question represents a person who feels the consequence of her education, the weight of her possibilities as a teacher and writer and human being, a voice in society. And I would not change that person, would not give back the good burden that accompanies my growing expertise, my increasing power to shape myself in language and share that self with "others."

"To speak," says Frantz Fanon, "means to be in a position to use a certain syntax, to grasp the morphology of this or that language, but it means above all to assume a culture, to support the weight of a civilization."* To write means to do the same, but in a more profound sense. However, Fanon also says that to achieve mastery means to "get" to a position of power, to "grasp," to "assume." This, I have learned—both as a student and subsequently as a teacher—can involve tremendous emotional and psychological conflict for those attempting to master academic discourse. Although as a beginning student writer I had a fairly good grasp of ordinary spoken English and was proficient at what Labov calls "code switching" (and what John Baugh in *Black Street Speech* terms "style shifting"), when I came face to face with the demands of academic writing, I grew increasingly self-conscious, constantly aware of my status as a black and a speaker of one of the many black English vernaculars, a traditional outsider. For the first time, I experienced my sense of doubleness as something menacing, a built-in enemy. Whenever I turned inward for salvation, the balm so available during my childhood, I found instead this new fragmentation which spoke to me in many voices. It was the voice of my desire to prosper, but at the same time it spoke of what I had relinquished and could not regain: a safe way of being, a state of powerlessness which exempted me from responsibility for who I was and might be. And it accused me of betrayal, of turning away from blackness. To recover balance, I had to take on the language of the academy, the language of "others." And to do that, I had to learn to imagine myself a part of the culture of that language, and therefore someone free to manage that language, to take liberties with it. Writing and rewriting, practicing, experimenting, I came to comprehend more fully the generative power of language. I discovered—with the help of some especially sensitive teachers—that through writing one can continually bring new selves into being, each with new responsibilities and difficulties, but also with new possibilities. Remarkable power, indeed. I write and continually give birth to myself.

Black Skin, White Masks (1952, rpt. New York: Grove Press, 1967), pp. 17–18.

Questions for Discussion and Journaling

1. Mellix argues that Toby, the Greeleyville town policeman, did not need to speak grammatically correct English because "He was white and could speak as he wished." Mellix herself, on the other hand, "had something to prove. Toby did not" (para. 7). Explain what she means.

2. Mellix says that "speaking standard English to whites was our way of demonstrating that we knew their language and could use it.. . . . But when we spoke standard English, we acknowledged . . . that our customary way of speaking was inferior" (para. 8). What does she mean by this? How would Young explain the damage this dual speaking was causing?

3. Young talked about the ways that school teaches children standard English. Where did Mellix learn standard English? Where have you learned standard English? Do you speak it in every situation or just some?

4. For many years, having to write in standard English made writing feel "mechanical" to Mellix, and she says she "felt separate from the language" (paras. 16, 20). Do you feel like your spoken, home, or social English is the same as the kind of English you are expected to use in school and workplace writing? If not, do you think that has an impact on your writing, as it did on Mellix's writing? Is there anything about your home/social and spoken language(s) you feel you have to "shut out" when you write?

5. Go back to Young and review his idea of "code meshing." Predict how Mellix's school experiences could have been different had her school, and American culture more broadly, valued the principles that code meshing relies on.

Applying and Exploring Ideas

1. Mellix says she was "shy in the presence of those who owned and/or spoke *the* language" (para. 8). Drawing on what you've learned from Young, Williams, and/or others in this chapter, write two to three pages in which you explain what "*the* language" is, why it is seen as "*the* language," how that is determined, and why certain people are seen to own it.

2. Young argues that linguistic differences and racial differences are intertwined. Write one to two pages about ways in which Mellix's experiences help Young's argument make more sense to you or ways in which they don't.

3. Most of Mellix's essay seems to suggest she would agree with Young's argument that students should not have to learn standard English in order to succeed in American culture; however, at the end she seems to change her position. How do you think Mellix would respond to Young's claims? Write a short dialogue between Young and Mellix on the subject of "standard English" and code meshing.

4. Conduct short interviews with three people you know from different areas of your life. Try to ensure these people are as different from one another as possible. Ask those people the following questions:

   • Do you speak the same way in every situation?

   • Do you feel like the way you speak at home with your family is the way you speak at school and/or at work?

- If not, what are some of the differences? Can you give examples?
- Do you feel like one of the ways you speak is valued more highly than the others? How do you know?

Summarize your results in two to three pages, and then share them with your classmates. What are some themes or trends that you find as a class? What questions does this raise for you? Do any of the answers you received relate to any of the readings you've done so far in this book?

META MOMENT   How can Mellix help you understand your feelings about the way that you and others speak? When your feelings or judgments about language varieties (your own or others') arise in the future, how can you respond to and reflect on them differently as a result of reading Mellix?

Chinks in My Armor: Reclaiming One's Voice

JULIE WAN

Framing the Reading

Julie Wan wrote this piece in her first-year composition course at the University of Central Florida, where she was majoring in computer science and minoring in creative writing. As Wan explains, she was "transplanted" from China to America at age three, and her literacy has been powerfully shaped by her sense of marginalization and non-ownership of English.

If you've read other pieces in Chapter 5, you're likely to recognize how Wan is weaving together many theories of literacy, particularly those of Young and Brandt, and how her literacy experiences both embody those principles and, perhaps, demonstrate them even more directly and powerfully than the original writers do. To understand the threshold concept that writing is shaped by identity and prior literacy experiences, you need only read Wan's explanation of how, and why, "Even after forfeiting my mother tongue and spending two decades ostensibly assimilating English, I still can't assume the American psyche of being an unequivocal, unified whole. My early Chinese socialization continues to frame and disrupt my literacy."

Wan's piece is one student's response to the Literacy Narrative assignment on p. 362 at the end of this chapter. Wan achieves the "What Makes It Good?" goals for the assignment by telling stories about her literacy history, talking about where she is now as a reader and writer and how her past has shaped that present, and making a (very powerful) point about her literacy experiences — and what they might mean to the rest of us.

Getting Ready to Read

Østylus
a journal of first-year writing

Volume 9 | Issue 1 | Spring 2018
The Journal of the First-Year Writing Program at the University of Central Florida

Before you read, do at least one of the following activities:

- Wan's title plays on multiple meanings of the word *chink*. Acquaint yourself with the history of the word *chink* as a racial slur by looking the word up in Wikipedia.

Wan, Julie. "Chinks in My Armor: Reclaiming One's Voice." *Stylus*, vol. 9, no. 1, Spring 2018, pp. 1–6.

- Read or review Vershawn Young's piece "Should Writers Use They Own English?" earlier in this chapter (p. 325).

As you read, consider the following questions:

- If you are reading this in the United States, does Wan's discussion remind you of any experiences you have either of being considered un-American because of your use of English, or of judging someone's belonging in America based on their use of English?
- Was there someone growing up who served as your "translator," helping you be understood by other people?

THOUGH I WAS TOO YOUNG to grasp shame in all its shades and magnitude, my early English transactions can only be described as humiliating, isolating, and fraught with cultural dissimilitude. At a tender three years of age, I was transplanted from rural China to the more urban United States and my nascent literacy was abruptly, vertiginously redefined. After twenty years of persistently conditioning my English writing and speaking, I developed an armor around my person to facilitate my integration and educational advancement. Though restrictive and unnatural at first, it became more fitted and authentic with time. But there remain chinks in the armor even now: eccentricities in my speech that I can't iron out, or certain idioms and pronunciations that continue to elude me because they were unheard-of in my ethnic household. Though unapparent, the chinks glare egregiously once noticed. When I bumble, it isn't absolved as a momentary slip or attributed to mild illiteracy. Rather, it's tantamount to being *un-American*. Even after forfeiting my mother tongue and spending two decades ostensibly assimilating in English, I still can't assume the American psyche of being an unequivocal, unified whole. My early Chinese socialization continues to frame and disrupt my literacy.

When learning English, I had studiously emulated how *White* people spoke because I'd wanted to sound impeccable. But I've since encountered many great orators that collectively broadened the faces and terms I associate with "native" English speaker. Code-meshing advocate Vershawn Young refuted the notion of a standardized English, performed invariably by White Americans, by exhibiting the dismaying illiteracy of even the most affluent, purportedly educated, public officials (164–5). As it stands, White Americans benefit from inflated perceptions of their literacy while non-Whites are linguistically marginalized and devalued.

I've had the distinct impression throughout my life that my literacy was held to a separate, lower standard. Not uncommonly, it won't be initially assumed or even tacitly acknowledged that I'm fluent in, let alone speak, English. If I delay to respond within nanoseconds of appropriate timing, or am a few decibels shy of hearability, it'll be tersely deduced that I "don't speak English." Within my radius, presumptions take precedence and my tenuous self-identity can be revoked. I've startled people in many parts of the world when I spoke a common phrase in English without a perceptible accent. I recall an incident in Johannesburg, South Africa, where I aroused a woman's sudden fascination in my singular upbringing. Forgetting that *I* approached her, she bypassed my inquiry and demanded, "Where are you from?" She might've been alarmed that I, an outsider, had breached her Western-born stronghold. Conversely, I've discovered that I can set people at ease with a Chinese affectation. I have a White, Asian Studies friend that always laughs, red and breathlessly, when I reproduce my mother's accent. Even though I capably speak it, English is still regarded as a White language and, owed to how others perceive me, I have to constantly re-negotiate and defend against lower estimations of my literacy.

From thirteen months until the age of three, I'd lived in a purely Chinese 4 vacuum under my grandmother's care in Guilin, China. Though the city is touted for its picturesque caves, mountains and rivers, my baby photos depict squalor and filth. In one of my earliest photos, I am squatting beside sewage and litter on a dirt road, with smudged cheeks, inflamed mosquito bites and half of a rice flour biscuit in my hand. I spoke my first words unabashedly and uninhibitedly, in an accepting, shared language fabric of close family and friends. Though affectionately monikered "Guilinese" by my mother and its people, the Guilin dialect is unbearably doltish. The mouth is kept agape and elongated, syllables are rhythmically pitched and unceremoniously dropped, and sudden volume spikes at sentences' end are characteristic. The people who speak it are unflinchingly uncouth. As an example, if my grandmother half-heartedly tried to discipline me, I'd squawk (in Chinese), "I'll throw uh cawck atcha!" And out of love or ignorance, my grandparents didn't wish or teach me differently.

Across the world in New York City, my parents had completed advanced 5 degrees and were industriously, financially situating themselves, wanting their only child to have a formal, first-world education. They calculated that geographical proximity to esteemed American powerhouses like Yale and Princeton would ensure my ascension, but a grand metamorphosis seemed unlikely. I was a scrawny, unrefined kid in an intimidating, new world. As ghetto as Queens was during the '90s, it remained utterly unrelatable from provincial Guilin. We were comparably much poorer, and it never felt like there was room for us. Our one bedroom apartment was confining and nightmarish. The walls teemed with the ghostly pitter-patter of mice and roaches. The summer months sweltered without the costly indulgence of air conditioning. I was disoriented by and unaccustomed to the thick fat crowds, the ear-numbing roar of the LIRR and tall seated toilets. When people spoke to me, they might have well just spoken *at* me. I would press a nervous finger against my lips in ponderance. My father was rarely present during this tumultuous transition. It felt that I'd only see him every few

> *Even though I capably speak it, English is still regarded as a White language and, owed to how others perceive me, I have to constantly re-negotiate and defend against lower estimations of my literacy.*

weekends. As English was one of his weaker languages, he had to take a job in another city. I orbited around the only remaining constant, my mother, who served as my de facto translator and literacy sponsor.

When first familiarizing myself with 6 English, my mother and I were already busied with converting my Guilinese to Mandarin, so my mispronunciations and malapropisms of English were enabled and concretized. My parents spoke the bougie, standard Mandarin of prodigious Beijing. They'd met while attending Peking University (China's Harvard). Because my provincial dialect wasn't dissimilar, I could organically decode and mimic them. English, on the other hand, was irreconcilable. When contoured around my tongue, the sounds were graceless, either too drawled or blunted. Any word I became acquainted with would be reproduced incongruously. I used "sweetheart" often, even though it was very mid-century and sounded incredulous and mismatched for a small, brutish child. Rather, the terminology befitted someone more charming, perhaps a fuller, rosy-cheeked Southern woman, a Western ideal of a deep and capable resource of love. In actuality, and completely opposite my adult reticence, I was once an incredibly loving and effusive child that always gravitated towards my mother. Despite its myriad of hybridizations, my most spoken words retained one message: "妈妈 I love you," or "我爱你 mama!"

My English vocabulary inherited meanings through comparable Chinese 7 precedents and was initially given a minor or supplementary role. If I wasn't confident that my English sample alone would successfully convey what I wanted to say, I'd resort to a select arsenal of Mandarin with designated meanings. The McDonald's golden arches looked like pigtails to me (ours was beside a Wendy's, so I might've associated both logos with hairstyles). Whenever we walked by I would ask, "Can we go My Donna 辫子地方 (pigtail place)?" I was decipherable if my mother only circumvented the obtusely accented English and focused on my Mandarin. She alone understood me without question so we failed to address my corrupt language use. I'd pulled heavily from Chinese to draw associations and comparable meanings, so my English was, at its bones, an impure derivative that flailed without context. Linguists have studied the language learning processes of young children and concluded that it's impossible to remove one's first language from the target language (Young 160). Because my English was birthed ancillary to and reliant on my mother tongue, they were intertwined in spite of them being two strikingly different languages.

For a few reluctant weeks, I was placed in day-care even though my mother 8 wasn't working. The experience may have served to gently prod my immersion, but it proved distressing and intolerable. Allegedly, I lacked commonalities with the other children and fundamental, preschool level intelligence. I truly can't remember any friends but can vaguely recall the impatience and insensitivity of the teachers. I was untranslatable and boring, my reality too austere when compared to the grandiose fictions the children worshipped. My unrushed, lifelike drawings of bowls of rice and squat toilets starkly contrasted with other kids' castles, princesses, and heroes. And somehow, even though I'd practically lived on a farm in China, I wasn't at all advantaged when it came to animals. I didn't know that cows incontrovertibly "mooed" or that pigs could never be the color green. And most offensively, I couldn't use seated toilets. I had to be lifted onto the ivory perch, where I'd ritually squat and splatter pee everywhere.

Though I was hastily removed, I was already knocked out of the safety of my 9 mother's orbit during those lonely, debasing weeks. Exposed to the world, I was suddenly made aware of the edges of my inherent otherness, a deformity and depreciation of my being. My revelation was a kind of double consciousness — a constant duality and tension between my living self and the outward perception that was stigmatized and made inferior — that propelled me to furiously learn English and abate my differences (Young 151). The very next year, I entered Kindergarten with same age peers. Because English wasn't my first language and America didn't feel like "home," I nursed a habit of overcompensating in order to obtain my literacy and some semblance of normalcy.

I was extremely self-conscious of my diction and how I enunciated. Owed to 10 my anxieties about my speech and general lack of friends, I rarely socialized and turned inward, honing my writing as a means to assimilate. I was never taught how to read or write in Chinese, so the act of putting pen to paper served as immaculate soil for cultivating my English literacy. At our first parent-teacher conference, my mother felt a momentary wave of disbelief followed by immense pride when my teacher declared that I was *good* at writing. After briefly showcasing the notebook to prove that it was indeed my handwriting (my lettering identifiable by its tidy assembly and modelesque stature), she commended my heavily borrowed retelling of the *Three Little Pigs*. I'd apparently absorbed the tale from somewhere and regurgitated the main plot points during free writing. The lack of ingenuity was obvious, and excused, by my command of sentence structure, paragraphing, and overall grammar. But I question that teacher's judgment because I never considered it a triumphant piece. I knew in my heart that the story was not mine, and that my writing was not good when compared to the enthralling storytelling of the original.

Though that was meant to be a pivotal moment in my life where my literacy 11 first and finally garnered approval and notice from someone with an educative purview, it felt undeserved. She was likely swayed by my mediocre piece because I wore the same clothes day to day, had a fresh off the boat bob cut and an Asiatic monosyllabic surname. Her being impressed was contingent on my being a Chinese immigrant from an impoverished background. The public school was in a multicultural blue-collar sect and I don't believe that the literacy standard would be up to par with those of a more expensive, privileged curriculum. In "Sponsors of Literacy," Deborah Brandt discusses the systemic distribution of literacy and its impacts: as education is democratized and made accessible, its requirements are increasingly stratified and escalated (89). My teacher's expectations were adjusted according to our collectively lower proficiency. In addition to my own vacillation between English and Mandarin, the classroom was filled with the varied dialects of Black, Muslim, and Hispanic students. Most likely, none of us had access to reliable sources of "standard" English.

I improved my faculty of English by emphasizing my reading and writing 12 throughout grade school and was affirmed when my appealing, formulaic essays tested me into challenging, specialized programs in more affluent districts. When I was accepted into a high school for the intellectually gifted on the Upper East Side, my mother became complacent with matters regarding my education and intervened less. We ceased our private, intimate exchanges and gradually drifted further apart with every passing school year. As my performance in English served as precious currency for advancement, it became my predominant, then *only* language. In the mornings, I'd take the Manhattan-bound train to new English speaking territories, while my mother remained in ethnic Queens. All these years, she's kept biased towards her native tongue while working at the same Citibank in Chinese-concentrated "Falasheng" (Flushing). And yet she coddled my bumbling Mandarin by conversing with me in her lesser English to help me along.

When I'd stopped using bilingual options to convey exclusive nuances with 13 my mother, a monumental portion of my literacy became void. Alarmingly, my writing began deteriorating. It scattered with misdirection, bloated with redundancy, and read jarringly. I fixated on my sentences, composing, re-arranging, and protracting until they lost direction. And though I strained for the right words, they always proved lofty or inaccurate. I grew frustrated with writing and became reluctant towards papers. Teachers' comments felt abrasive, like lashes on tender flesh, but the failure resided in my own work. I couldn't produce clear expressions to explain myself because my thought processes were fundamentally rooted in Chinese, my faculty of which was so lost by then that the memories could've been a remnant from another lifetime. I've yet to develop adequate English equivalents to fill or transition over the vacancies. Without my native speech saturating, supporting, and connecting my ideas, my writing became dissociated, tedious, and ineffectual.

As someone who code-switched and converted, rather than code-meshed and 14 integrated, I lost the raw, expressive quality in my communication (Young 162). I compromised my literacy by letting my Chinese go out of practice and evaporate. I can only manage forced, short exchanges in a language I should naturally, competently speak. I have disappointed expectant relatives and visitors by failing to confidently address them in our once shared dialogue. My parents and grandparents are disheartened by my negligent, vaporous Mandarin. Though they'd wanted me to have an American education, they hadn't expected the brunt of cultural divide. I've attempted to re-learn Mandarin with flashcards, beginner's books, and Chinese dramas, but the characters are unfamiliar and rebound from memory. Having obtusely abandoned the only language tethering me, I became estranged from my heritage and lost a sense of belonging and clarity.

> And yet, all this time, I've been envisioning a perfect, American English that doesn't exist.

When I ascribe idiosyncrasies or lapses in my speech to the fact that I am 15 Chinese, I receive an impatient dismissal: "You are Asian *American* and you don't have an accent." Perhaps I've conveniently and too often used my ethnicity as a crutch to allow myself some cultural leeway whenever I rubbed off as abnormal. But it truly is the reason why I speak and write the way that I do. If anyone has a prolonged conversation with me, they'll discern my unusual vocabulary and locutions, my pre-mediated evasions of certain pronunciations, and the underlying tremors that exacerbate my inarticulateness. Nancy Sommers, with her own displaced heritage, aptly describes in "I Stand Here Writing" that "only children of immigrant parents can understand the embarrassing moments of inarticulateness, the missed connections that come from learning to speak a language from parents who claim a different mother tongue" (217). I began intentionally collecting my mother's peculiarities of speech over the years, as mementos, hoping that I might also inherit her resilience. English is her fourth language. She's managed through two widely disparate continents and marriages. Despite our distinct histories — hers by comparison so weighted with strife — we're united and alike. We both suffer from our respective neuroses (I'm bipolar) but my hypercritical approach, where I overthink and over-strive, also stems from the double consciousness surrounding my incurable otherness.

And yet, all this time, I've been envisioning a perfect, American English that 16 doesn't exist. The threshold concept of writing is that text and language aren't static. Any transmission, regardless of its form, is an attempt in flux and never assured. Its interpretation is based on the audience and the totality of *their* experiences. On the last day of ENC 1101, first year Composition, we watched Jamila Lyiscott's TED performance on her three languages, all beautiful flavors of *English*. After someone implied that they hadn't, on account of her race, expected her to be "articulate," she rebuffed, "I may not come always before you with excellency of speech, but do not judge me by my language" (Lyiscott). Even if the delivery deviates from what's considered "standard" according to the dominant ideology imposed by those that speak only a single variant, there's a rich, gorgeous quality inherent in the wording of the marginalized (Young 164). Sommers, who argued that every person is a capable source of information, encouraged a more receptive audience, "to be open to other voices, untranslatable as they might be" (220). Even if the conveyance is hard to understand or relate to, there is still something worth a modicum of patience and reflection. Within every transaction, every written or spoken word, is a dynamic, evolving reconvergence of meaning. Just as Young advocated a multi-dialectical society that would benefit from the contributions of everyone's native intelligence by embracing and empowering their multitudes of self-expression, I've begun to appreciate aspects of my literacy that are far adrift from the norm and make my voice inimitable (161). Successful or not, my obsessive method, with its immeasurable layers of wandering, analysis and devotion, produces and contributes my own poetic wisdom.

When a kid summarily hissed "chink" in my direction in 2nd grade, it came 17 into place that being Chinese was a permanent, irrevocable condition — no matter if I didn't speak any Chinese at all. He'd employed its negative connotation, but I've since reexamined and reassigned its meaning. Wardle and Downs preface their reasons for studying writing by reporting that most people have painful literacy beginnings that permeate into their later lives as writers, and that while those initial feelings can adjust over time, we remain "an accumulation of everything we have experienced" (9). My own process of learning English wasn't without difficulty and sacrifice. Adapting and functioning in a social capacity in order to further my education required building an armor around my person. I relied so heavily on the armor that I forgot to take it off and converse with my grandmother on the phone from time to time. I didn't reclaim and secure my heritage, so the armor became hollow, fragile, and developed chinks. But the chinks in my armor are intrinsic and meaningful. My literacy is the culmination of my singular life experiences, and my chinks are the acquired, distinctive scars that allow the light from within to shine through.

Works Cited

Brandt, Deborah. "Sponsors of Literacy." Wardle and Downs, pp. 68–99. Originally published in *College Composition and Communication,* vol. 49, no. 2, 1998, pp. 165–85.

Lyiscott, Jamila. "What Does It Mean To Be 'Articulate'?" *TED Radio Hour,* NPR, 14 Nov. 2014, npr.org/templates/transcript/transcript.php?storyId=362372282.

Sommers, Nancy. "I Stand Here Writing." Wardle and Downs, pp. 212–22. Originally published in *College English,* vol. 55, no. 4, 1993, pp. 420–28.

Wardle, Elizabeth, and Doug Downs, editors. *Writing about Writing: A College Reader.* 3rd ed., Bedford/St. Martin's, 2017.

Young, Vershawn Ashanti. '"Nah, We Straight': An Argument Against Code Switching." Wardle and Downs, pp. 148–71. Originally published in *JAC,* vol. 29, no. 1, 2009, pp. 49–76.

Questions for Discussion and Journaling

1. How is Wan's statement that "my early Chinese socialization continues to frame and disrupt my literacy" an example of the threshold concept that writing is impacted by identities and prior experiences?

2. Wan writes that "English is still regarded as a White language" (para. 3). How does she explain this statement through her lived experience? To what extent are you aware of regarding English as a White language?

3. What are some instances that make Wan suspect that native speakers of American English expected her to be able to accomplish less in English because she was Chinese? Does her description remind you of any experiences of your own (or others around you) with having lower expectations imposed because of your nationality, race, class, or other identity markers?

4. Wan asserts that "even if the conveyance is hard to understand or relate to, there is still something worth a modicum of patience and reflection" with less fluent speakers of a language. How are you patient with others in this way, and can you name an instance of language-use or literacy where you wish others would be more patient with you?

5. Wan builds her narrative around two meanings of the word *chink*, both of which have negative connotations (one being a racial slur). How does she work to turn *chink* to have a positive meaning? Does she succeed?

Applying and Exploring Ideas

1. Wan is able to neatly interweave ideas from authors she's read (such as Young, Brandt, and Sommers) throughout her literacy narrative. Note how she uses those ideas to help interpret specific experiences (for example, paras. 9, 11, 14, and 15), and try it yourself: for each reading that you've done in Chapter 5, try to think of an experience that the principles in that reading help explain. Write a paragraph about each.

2. What responsibility do native speakers of a dominant language or dialect have to ensure that language does not become, as Wan describes (para. 12), a "precious currency for advancement"?

3. If you also read Young (p. 325), you've now read two explanations of how requiring everyone to learn a single, prescriptive "standard English" can strip speakers of other languages or English dialects of their "home" language. Which description and explanation did you find more convincing? Why? What does that suggest about strategies writers can use when they want to persuade their readers of a complex position?

- -
META MOMENT How does Wan's literacy narrative help you think differently about your own writing and speaking experiences?
- -

Writing about Literacies

Assignment Option 1

LITERACY NARRATIVE

Drawing on what you have read in this chapter, examine your own literacy history, habits, and processes. The purpose of this inquiry is to get to know yourself better as a reader and writer. Awareness gives power and purpose: The more you know about yourself as a reader and writer, the more control you are likely to have over these processes. This is why we consider the threshold concept that writing is impacted by identity and prior experiences so important.

Invention, Research, and Analysis.   Start your literacy narrative by considering your history as a reader and writer. Try to get at what your memories and feelings about writing/reading are and how you actually write/read now. Take bland generalizations ("I really love to write") into detailed, concrete description and examples of why, and of how you learned to write/read. Mine your memory, thinking carefully about where you've been and where you are as a reader and writer. You might begin by answering questions such as these:

- How did you learn to write and/or read?

- What kinds of writing/reading have you done in the past?

- How much have you enjoyed the various kinds of writing/reading you've done?

- What are particularly vivid memories that you have of reading, writing, or activities that involved them?

- What is your earliest memory of reading and of writing?

- What sense did you get, as you were learning to read and write, of the *value* of reading and writing, and where did that sense come from?

- What frustrated you about reading and writing as you were learning and then as you progressed through school? By the same token, what pleased you about them?

- What kind of writing and reading do you do most commonly?

- What is your favorite kind of writing and reading?

- What are your current attitudes, feelings, or stance toward reading and writing?

- Where do you think your feelings about and habits of writing and reading come from? How did you get to where you are as a writer/reader? What in your past has made you the kind of writer/reader you are today?

- Who are some people in your life who have acted as literacy sponsors?

- What are some institutions and experiences in your life that have acted as literacy sponsors?

- What technologies impact you as a writer? When, where, and why did you start using them?

- What have any of the readings in this chapter reminded you about from your past or present as a reader and writer?

Questions such as these help you start thinking deeply about your literate past. You should try to come up with some answers for all of them, but it's unlikely that you'll actually include all the answers to all those questions in your literacy narrative itself. Right now you're just thinking and writing about what reading and writing was like for you. When you plan the narrative, you'll select from among all the material you've been remembering and thinking about. The question then becomes, how will you decide what to talk about out of everything you *could* talk about? This depends in part on your analysis of what you're remembering.

As you consider what all those memories and experiences suggest, you should be looking for an overall "so what?" — a main theme, a central "finding," an overall conclusion that your consideration leads you to draw. It might be an insight about why you read and write as you do today based on past experience. It might be an argument about what works or what doesn't work in literacy education, on the basis of your experience. It might be a resolution to do something differently, or to *keep* doing something that's been working. It might be a description of an ongoing conflict or tension you experience when you read and write — or the story of how you resolved such a conflict earlier in your literacy history. (It could also be a lot of other things.)

Planning and Drafting. Your consideration and analysis of your previous experience, one way or another, will lead you to a *main point* that your literacy narrative will demonstrate and support. That main point is what you've learned in your analysis; the literacy narrative then explains why you think what you do about that main point. It draws in whatever stories, experiences, moments, and descriptions help explain the point. Because your literacy narrative tells the particular story of a particular person — you — its shape will depend on the particular experiences you've had and the importance you attach to them. Therefore, it's difficult to suggest a single structure for the literacy narrative that will work for all writers. The structure that you use should support your particular intention and content.

Headings or sections (such as Part I or Act I or "Early Literacy Memories") may be helpful, but your content may better lend itself to write one coherent, unbroken essay. Do what works for you, given the material you want to include. Just be sure to organize and make some sort of point (or points).

Because your literacy narrative is about you, you may find it difficult to write without talking about yourself in the first person. Using "I" when you need to may make the piece feel somewhat informal, which is appropriate to this kind of writing.

If you wish, include pictures or artifacts with your narrative. You could bring in your first spelling test or the award you won for the essay contest or the article in the school newspaper about your poem. If your circumstances make it appropriate, write this narrative in some mode other than alphabet-on-paper: For example, write it as a blog entry on your website and incorporate multimedia, or write it as a performed or acted presentation, or make it a PowerPoint presentation, a YouTube video, a poster, or whatever else works to reach the audience you want to and to help you make your point.

What Makes It Good? This assignment asks you to carefully think about your history as a reader and writer, to tell a clear story that helps make a point, and to write a readable piece. So, be sure your piece (1) tells a story or stories about your literacy history, (2) talks about where you are now as a writer and reader and how your past has shaped your present, and (3) makes some overall point about your literacy experiences. Of course, this essay should also be clear, organized, interesting, and well-edited. The strongest literacy narratives will incorporate ideas and concepts from the readings in this chapter to help frame and explain your experiences.

- -

Assignment Option 2
GROUP ANALYSIS OF LITERACY HISTORY

Collaborate with a team of classmates on a formal research study of some theme that emerges when everyone's literacy experiences are compared. You can use the following instructions to guide the writing of this kind of study, which lends itself to answering "bigger" questions or making larger points than a single literacy narrative usually can.

Conduct a Self-Study. Think about your history as a reader and writer, using the questions provided for the invention stage of a Literacy Narrative (p. 358). Post your answers to your class blog, wiki, website, or learning management system.

Discuss and Code the Self-Studies. In your group, read the answers to the self-interviews. Look together for common themes, recurring trends, or unique experiences, and determine which of these might be most interesting to further research and write about. What data will you need to collect to explore these themes? (For example, do you need to interview some classmates further? Interview people outside the class?) Common themes that emerge from this sort of study might include the role of technology in literacy, hobbies as literacy sponsors, motivations for literacy learning, privilege and access, and help overcoming literacy struggles.

Collaborate to Write about Emergent Themes. Pair up with another student by choosing an emergent theme to write a paper about. As a pair, pinpoint a specific research question related to your theme and gather whatever further data is necessary. Drawing on terms and ideas from this chapter's readings, you can then write your analysis of and findings on this theme.

Planning and Drafting.   Before beginning to write, the group as a whole should consider the audience and genre appropriate for this paper. Discuss the following questions together:

- Who should be the audience for what you write? How can you best reach them?
- How would you like to write about your findings? In a somewhat formal, scholarly way? In a more storytelling, narrative way?
- What content and format would make this narrative most effective? Paper, text-only? Paper, text, and images? Online text and images? Online text, images, and video?

As you analyze and begin to write with your partner, you should consider the following questions:

- What is your research question?
- What answers to this question do your research and analysis suggest?
- What data support each of these answers?

These questions will actually help you arrange your paper, too, in most cases. The paper will include an introduction that poses your research question and explains the value of it, and go on to explain how you attempted to answer the question — what methods you used to gather the data you gathered to try to reach answers. Next, you can talk about that data and what answers they led you to. The paper would conclude with your sense of "so what?" — the implications that your findings seem to suggest. What have you learned about this emergent theme from your research, and what does it mean for the rest of us?

If you haven't written collaboratively before, you may find it a bit of a challenge to coordinate schedules with your co-author, to decide how to break up the work of writing the piece, and to make sure you both always have current information and the other writer's most up-to-date ideas so that you can write the part of the piece you need to when you need to. You'll also find that you rewrite each other's material a bit — this will help it sound like the piece was written by a single voice or mind rather than two people.

What Makes It Good?   A good analysis of an issue emerging from your group's literacy history may take a number of different shapes but will tend to have these traits in common:

- A clear, directly stated research question
- A detailed description of what methods you used to try to answer the question

- A clear explanation of what you found in your research and what conclusions it led you to

- An explanation of "so what?" — why your findings might matter

- The usual: readable, fluent prose; transitions that make the paper easy to follow; and editing and proofreading that keep the paper from distracting readers with typos and goofs

- -

Assignment Option 3

LINGUISTIC OBSERVATION AND ANALYSIS

In this chapter, Young and Mellix illustrate that there are a variety of "Englishes," and that different varieties of English are valued differently. People who learn and speak the dominant "standard" version of English at home have power, authority, and privilege that those who learn other versions do not. However, Young also argues that different versions of English really aren't so different, and that in our culture people are more often than not borrowing freely from different forms of English in their daily interactions, resulting in what he calls *code meshing*. If you read Young and Mellix, you likely conducted some quick field research in order to test their claims. Here, you will continue that research in order to reach some conclusions about what it means to "speak English" and what forms of English have power — and in what settings.

Observations and Interviews.   First, choose three different sites where you can expect to find people of different ages, occupations, genders, races, interests, linguistic backgrounds, etc. — for example, outside a movie theater, in your sorority, at a convenience store, at a bar or restaurant, in an office. Consult with your teacher and classmates about sites that would be appropriate for observation. You want to be cautious about conducting observations in sites where you might make people uncomfortable. As a result, it might be easiest to choose sites where you already regularly interact.

Arrange for one to two hours where you can sit in each setting and listen and observe people interacting. Get permission if the site isn't public. Take careful notes. Who are you seeing? What are you hearing? Write down phrases, words, notes about tone and loudness, etc.

Next, conduct interviews with three people who are different from one another in some significant ways — age, race, gender, class, occupation, where they were raised, how they identify, etc. Be respectful of people and their time when you set up the interviews. Ask them these questions:

- Do you speak the same way in every situation?

- Do you feel like the way you speak at home with your family is the way you speak at school and/or at work?

- If not, what are some of the differences? Can you give examples?
- Do you feel like one of the ways you speak is valued more highly than the others? How do you know?

Caution: When you interview and observe, record *what people actually say*, not what you *expect* them to say. It will be easy to stereotype and to turn stereotypes into expectations. Listening to people and really hearing them must precede making conclusions or judgments. Ask yourself as you are listening to people whether your stereotypes and expectations (we all have them) are getting in the way of collecting data.

Analyzing Data. Look at the data that you collected by laying out your interview notes and transcripts and reading them carefully, annotating as you go. Then ask yourself the following questions:

- What are you seeing?
- Do you see everyone (or anyone) speaking one clear version of a standard English? If not, what are some of the variations?
- Do you see people switching back and forth between different versions of English? Do they do this within one setting, or in different settings? What are some examples?
- Do you think they are code switching, code meshing, or both?
- What do your interviewees say about their experiences changing language forms?
- What forms of language seem to have power or authority, and in what situations? How do you know?

Considering What You Think. Given what you read in this chapter, what you saw in your research, and what you've experienced in your own life, what do you have to say about the following questions:

- Is there one standard form of English?
- Are some forms of English inherently "superior" to other forms? If not, are some forms of English *treated as though* they are inherently "superior" to other forms?
- How can you tell when a certain form of English has power and authority? What happens to suggest that this is the case?
- How do you think those forms of English gained that power and authority?
- How have you personally been impacted by people's attitudes about appropriate and dominant forms of English?
- What did you *expect* to hear and find going into this study?

- Did your expectations make it difficult for you to really listen to people without stereotyping them?

- What does your experience trying to listen and observe suggest about the difficulties of conducing "unbiased" research?

Write a Reflection. It will not be possible or desirable for you to write a definitive argument-driven research essay about what you found. In order to do that, you would need much more data, collected across wider varieties of sites, and much more training in how to conduct linguistic analysis. Instead, we want you to engage in a formal, data- and research-driven *reflection* about what *you* are learning, thinking, and struggling with around issues of language use. (Don't write to persuade others; write to explain your thinking to yourself.)

Write a five- to six-page reflection that explores your growing understanding of what it means to "speak English," what it means in practice for people to speak different forms of English, how power is enacted through various versions of English, and how your own expectations and experiences impact your ability to conduct research.

As you reflect and take positions, draw on the data that you've collected, as well as your own experiences. As you've learned in this chapter, your own experiences are always going to shape what you think and understand, and will inevitably shape your writing. This is why it's important for you to also reflect on yourself, your expectations of what you would find, and how your expectations impacted your ability to collect and analyze data.

In a project like this, you should be cautious about trying to speak authoritatively about other people's experience. The purpose of this assignment is to grow and expand your thinking on difficult questions by gathering data and reflecting on what you find when you really listen to other people in order to interrogate your ideas and assumptions. Be cautious about assuming that your language variation is "normal" or superior to what you are hearing from the people you observe and speak with.

What Makes It Good? This is what writing scholars would call a "writing to learn" assignment. The primary goal is for you to think about, reflect on, and grapple with ideas about language that you may not have considered before, and to learn how to collect some data in order to test out ideas and assumptions.

In assessing whether your completed reflection is successful, consider the following questions:

- Have you integrated ideas and terms from relevant readings in this chapter?

- Have you collected data and used them to inform your ideas?

- Have you written about your ideas and reflected on them in ways that readers (likely your classmates and teacher) will be able to follow?

- Have you supported your thinking with data from readings and from your research?

- Have you been careful to reflect on what you actually heard when you listened to others and to avoid stereotyping people and their languages?

- Have you thought about your own position (what your own language habits are, your relationship to the language practices you're studying, and the social and cultural places you speak from) and the history and expectations you brought to this project?

If you've done these things and demonstrated that you are trying hard to think through questions that are difficult, then you've written a good reflection.

CHAPTER 6

RHETORIC

Threshold Concept: "Good" Writing Is Contextual

What does this sign say to you? Does it suggest children and adults? Walking or running? Does it invite such behavior, or warn against it? Could it mark a crosswalk, or show the way to a park? Why can't you immediately tell what it means? What's missing is *context*. This warning sign (a red border and white center with black figures on it) is used in the Netherlands to signify "Caution, Children At Play." We put it here to show how "good" writing is specific to its context, and that meaning itself always depends on context.

This chapter introduces you to rhetoric and **rhetorical theory** in order to help you understand the threshold concept that "good" writing is contextual. Rhetoric can be a difficult term to understand because it is used quite negatively in popular culture, and even when scholars use it, they can use it to mean a variety of things. Rhetoric is a field of study in which people examine how persuasion and communication work, and it is also the art of human interaction, communication, and persuasion.

The first reading in this chapter, Doug Downs's "Rhetoric: Making Sense of Human Interactions and Meaning-Making" will offer a broad overview of rhetoric and define it in detail. There you will learn more about how humans interact with one other through language and other symbols. A **symbol** is anything people make "stand for" something else. For example, a red light hanging in the street does not literally mean "stop," but humans have given it symbolic value so that in many cultures people understand it to mean "stop." Even letters themselves are just shapes and **inscriptions**. The letters *d-o-g* do not inherently mean anything, but English-speaking humans have made meaning of those letters, understanding them to refer to a four-legged creature that barks. **Rhetoric**, then, is the process by which humans communicate with one another through symbols. It is also the study of how humans do that.

A **rhetor** (any person interacting with others) uses mostly routine principles of rhetoric in order to try to make meaning. However, meaning depends not just on the person who initially uses the symbols, but also on how those who then hear or read or see the symbols understand and interpret them, guided by their culture's shared rhetorical principles. Someone from a culture where a red light does not mean "stop" will bring a quite different meaning to that symbol.

This chapter considers what this understanding of rhetoric means. In it you will learn that meaning depends on **context** and situation, including people, events, circumstances, objects, history, time, place, and bodies. Keith Grant-Davie in this chapter defines this **rhetorical situation** and gives an extended example of it. Downs, in his selection, discusses context as **rhetorical ecology**, so that we can consider rhetorical situations where participants might not even intend to communicate with one other or might do so over extended time and space (think of online comment threads where people share ideas over many months and after additional events have taken place).

The idea of context for rhetorical interactions is also taken up by James Porter, who examines the idea of **intertextuality**, or how texts speak to or implicitly refer to other texts, and how this happens within and across discourse communities (a concept discussed further in Chapter 7). How rhetors use and understand texts is complicated, and taken up by Margaret Kantz as well as by Christina Haas and Linda Flower. Kantz considers how students, in particular, understand texts and whether they are persuasive, while Haas and Flower look in more detail at how readers (including students) make meaning from the texts they read.

All of these scholars emphasize that texts don't simply *contain* meaning. Instead, both readers and writers interact (whether they know it or not) to build their own meanings from texts (and they can often miscommunicate or misunderstand one another). Donald Murray even points out that writers bring their own experiences and meaning to every text they write, whether they mean to do so or not. Those experiences certainly influence how they make meaning of texts. Different readers and observers can have different interpretations of the same symbolic action, as you will see in student Julie Arbutus's piece, where she looks at three writers who understand a photo of actress Emma Watson in very different ways. As readers and writers engage with texts, they don't just pass on existing knowledge; they actually make new knowledge. As a writer, this is important for you to understand. You will do different things when you believe "writing is just transcribing ideas you already have" versus when you believe "writing is building new knowledge, understanding ideas you didn't understand before."

All of this helps explain the underlying threshold concept of this chapter: "good" writing is context-specific. How readers and writers use and interpret symbols and work to make meaning together depends on context, purpose, time, participants, and the communities and networks in which they're all positioned. The conventions of writing a text message to your best friend about meeting you later will work very well for that purpose, but not at all for your history essay or your job application cover letter. Thus, there are few rules for what makes all communicative acts "good." Your best strategy is to understand more principles of rhetoric, how they work, and thus what to look for when you are trying to communicate in a new situation or when others are trying to communicate with you. The study of rhetoric offers a systematic explanation of how people make knowledge and meaning from interaction through language and other symbols, and helps us see how we make up our minds, change them, and try to convince others of our ideas. Thus, it is excellent for helping writers figure out how to communicate in a given situation, when there are no universal rules that will tell them what to do.

CHAPTER GOALS

- Understand the threshold concept, *"good" writing is contextual.*
- Improve as a reader of complex, research-based texts.
- Acquire vocabulary for understanding the basic outlines of rhetorical theory and its relation to writing and human interaction.
- Understand the concept of rhetorical situation and ecology and be able to apply it to reading and writing situations.
- Understand how writers construct texts persuasively (or not).
- Understand how readers construct meaning from texts.
- Understand what it means to say that knowledge is constructed.

Rhetoric: Making Sense of Human Interaction and Meaning-Making

DOUG DOWNS

Courtesy of Nayelly Barrios

Framing the Reading

There is a genre within rhetoric studies that summarizes thousands of years of rhetorical theory into relatively compact, coherent accounts. This selection by Doug Downs — one of the editors of *Writing about Writing* — is an example. It was composed specifically for this book to create a guide to rhetoric that would work for readers new to the study of rhetorical theory. This means that unlike most other pieces in this book, this selection is primarily addressed to readers like you — not writing scholars.

Downs's article uses an extended example of grant writers for a nonprofit organization to walk readers through many of rhetoric's main principles. It integrates concepts from classical (Greek) rhetoric such as rhetorical situation, the rhetorical canons, **kairos**, and the **pisteis** (you might know them as **logos**, **ethos**, and **pathos**) with late twentieth and twenty-first century rhetorical principles such as rhetorical ecology, embodiment and felt sense, **narrative** ways of knowing, informal logic, and **identification**. (To the extent the paper's subject is interesting to you, you may want to pay more attention than normal to the footnotes, which include suggestions for additional reading on these various principles.)

Many of the ideas overviewed in this piece are addressed in greater depth in other readings in the chapter. If you find yourself losing track, in some other readings, of how what they talk about relates to rhetoric and writing as a whole, you may find it helpful to turn back to this reading and see how the concept fits in to the larger whole of rhetorical theory. Two particular ideas in this paper — **rhetorical ecology** and **embodiment** — aren't addressed as such in other readings. Take in what you can about them here so you'll be able to see how these ideas connect to those you'll encounter later in the chapter.

Downs is an associate professor of writing studies at Montana State University, where he serves as editor of *Young Scholars in Writing*, the national journal of undergraduate research in rhetoric and writing studies. He studies the teaching of reading and research in writing classes, and he has published widely on writing-about-writing pedagogy.

Getting Ready to Read

Before you read, do at least one of the following activities:

- Write a definition of *rhetoric* as you understand it right now. What does the word mean to you? How do you usually hear it used?
- Look up the word *ecology.* Your definition will probably talk about relationships between organisms and their surroundings. Make a list of the ecologies that you personally participate in. Start thinking about what it means to be a part of an ecology — what kind of networks you participate in and how the various elements of that network influence each other.
- Think about someone you know who is famous for their rhetoric or their abilities with oratory. What is that person famous for? What is memorable about their rhetoric?

As you read, consider the following questions:

- How does what Downs is saying connect with what you already knew about rhetoric?
- What concepts discussed in this selection do you wish you could learn more about right away?

THIS GUIDE WALKS YOU through *rhetoric,* a set of principles for human 1 interaction that most people know unconsciously but don't think much about. Rhetorical principles organize and explain much of human communication, interaction, and experience. But most high school and college students don't study them in much depth, and in fact, often, earlier schooling teaches ideas that conflict with principles of rhetoric. Many come to believe, for example, that there are rules of writing that are true in all writing situations; rhetoric suggests there are not.

When you know rhetoric, you know how people make up their minds and 2 how they change them. You know how people make meaning of the world around them. You know how people come to believe that an idea is true, that it counts as "knowledge." When you know rhetoric, you gain a kind of "signal intelligence" that makes you a more powerful reader and writer.

Usually, by the term *rhetoric* western cultures mean something different than 3 any of that. Common conceptions of rhetoric include these:

- *"Calculated political BS"* (as in, "The congressman's rhetoric is just grandstanding to make it look like his opponents want to kill puppies")

- *"Dressing up a bad idea in convincing words"* (as did Hitler)
- *"Style lacking in substance"* (as in "That environmental activist's speech is very moving but it's just rhetoric")
- *Asking a rhetorical question* that everyone already knows the answer to just to make a point (as in, "You took my car out and now the fender's crumpled — how do you think that happened?")
- *Persuasive tactics* (as when Aristotle said that rhetoric is the art of seeing "the available means of persuasion in each case")

Those five uses of the word *rhetoric* constitute the total knowledge of most people on the subject. This guide will cover different ground about what rhetoric is.

Rhetoric explains why I started this piece by saying what it isn't. There's a 4 principle of human interaction that if readers have one idea about a concept (like "rhetoric is political BS") and a writer wants to present a contrasting idea, she needs to first explain that her idea comes from a much different place than where the readers are starting. Otherwise, readers may not realize the writer is using a different "lens" and, trying to interpret the writer's text just through their own existing lens, may not get a good understanding of what she's trying to say. "Rhetoric" refers both to such principles of meaning-making, and to the use of those principles in a given interaction.

WHAT DOES THE TERM *RHETORIC* APPLY TO?

One frustrating aspect of studying rhetoric is that the word has so many mean- 5 ings. That makes it hard to get a grip on what "rhetoric" refers to. This fuzziness is normal, and it does gradually diminish. In the beginning, it helps to think about what rhetoric "does."

Consider this comparison: The term *rhetoric* acts like the term *gravity*. 6 "Gravity" denotes a set of principles that explain and predict how chunks of matter interact. (Remember Newton's laws of gravity?) But "gravity" also refers to that interaction itself, the universal condition ("force") in which matter is attracted to other matter. In computer or gamer terms, we could say that gravity is an "operating system" for the interaction of matter — it sets the rules and structures for how everything will interact. Now, a lot of people — skiers, sky-divers, astronauts, auto racers, high-jumpers, airplane pilots, gymnasts, scuba divers — aren't just "subject to" gravity but are *artful users* of gravity. They take this independently existing force that is written into the nature of matter and which all matter, including humans, is thus subject to — and they strategically navigate it to make their activities possible.

In a similar way, the term *rhetoric* refers to *a set of principles that explain* 7 *and predict how people make meaning and interact.* But like "gravity," "rhetoric" applies not only to the principles for human interaction but to that interaction itself, the embodied expression of those principles. So, *rhetoric is an operating system for human interaction and meaning-making*. But rhetoric also refers to the *artful use* of those ever-present rhetorical principles. Some people learn to be rhetorical experts who can take those underlying principles shaping human interaction and finesse them in specific activities. The most obvious of these experts include counselors, comedians, lawyers, judges, advertisers, journalists, writers, and diplomats. But there are almost no human activities that don't involve interaction with other humans, which means that there is almost no activity you might be involved in that you can't do better as an aware user of rhetoric. Nurses and surgeons specialize in working on and healing people's bodies, but insofar as that work requires communicating with other doctors and nurses and with their patients, a nurse or surgeon who is a rhetoric super-user will probably get better results than those who aren't. Engineers? Same story. They aren't hired for their communication ability, but the engineers who can't write wind up working for the ones who can. Mathematicians are in the same situation. Much of what they do with math is rhetorical — including debating with other mathematicians about the best ways of doing math.

So start here: Rhetoric is pervasive. Given that it is an operating system for 8 human meaning-making and interaction, any time we are making meaning and interacting — otherwise known as "being human" — we are using rhetoric. There isn't any way to communicate without using rhetoric or "being rhetorical." Communication is inevitably rhetorical. You can't choose whether or not to use rhetoric. The only question is *how* you'll use it when you're more aware of how it works.

Another good place to begin is recognizing the ways rhetoric can help us. 9 Since rhetoric helps us understand human communication, there are a variety of problems or questions that rhetoric can help us make sense of. From its ancient roots as a study of persuasive speech, rhetoric offers explanations for *how we make up our minds and how we change them*. Because rhetoric has to do with how we make meaning of our experiences, it also gives us some keys to understanding *how we know what we know*. (The technical term for this subject is *epistemology*.) The rhetorical principles discussed here can even reveal something about *who we are likely to admire and befriend*. In its narrowest application, rhetoric lets us study *how we can most effectively communicate*. In its broadest, it shows us *ways of being* and ways of *recognizing the being of others*.

> Given that it is an operating system for human meaning-making and interaction, any time we are making meaning and interacting — otherwise known as "being human" — we are using rhetoric.

BEGINNING WITH BODIES

Rhetoric begins in the biology of how sentient bodies[1] experience 10 information and interaction via signals and symbols. Kenneth Burke, one of the premier rhetorical theorists of the twentieth century, showed that rhetoric always involves symbolic acts, in which meaning is made when one idea or object stands for another. Such substitution is the entire basis of language, in which sounds stand for (symbolize) ideas and objects. But language, of course, is not the only symbol system we encounter as humans; people can turn *anything* into a symbol. We make symbols of clothing, jewelry, objects like cars and homes, animals (mascots), and human behaviors from winks to jumps. (Like in *Game of Thrones* where "bending the knee" symbolizes kneeling, and kneeling symbolizes accepting a ruler.) As babies leave infanthood they learn that crying symbolizes physical needs (food, warmth, changing, comfort) to their caretakers. Children quickly associate one particular stomach sensation with hunger (we say that feeling is "a sign of" hunger) and a different stomach feeling with illness. You use symbols every time you encounter a green light hanging above the intersection of two streets, and know that this means "go," or a red octagon on a street corner, and know that this means "stop." Making one object or concept stand for some otherwise unrelated concept or object is one of our most basic human ways of making meaning.

Rhetoric begins with this very basic element of sentient (self-aware) embod- 11 iment. While we most often focus on *language* as the vehicle for symbolizing, communication scholars have shown that the majority of human communication and nearly the entirety of human / animal communication is nonverbal. Eyes, faces, the tilt of a head, hands, limbs, stance, posture, gait, demeanor, perspiration, voice and tone — our bodies create myriad signals that reveal to others a wide range of information about us. Add to this list the signals your body creates that can only be sensed by you — like the butterflies in your stomach when you show up for a first date. But to the extent you attend to your felt senses throughout an experience, those feelings and sensations are a crucial root of the meaning you make of each moment.[2]

Our bodies not only generate the signals which we and others interpret, 12 but also contain our sensory apparatus for perceiving and filtering both those

---

[1] We usually think of rhetoric as a human activity, but it's not difficult to identify rhetorical activity among a wide variety of animal species, as both George Kennedy and Natasha Seegart have demonstrated.

[2] Perhaps the most extensive writing on this subject is by Sondra Perl in her 2004 book *Felt Sense*.

signals and all the other signals our physical surroundings generate. What in an everyday sense we take as first-hand, direct experience is in fact filtered by our limited senses and then by perceptual interpretation of the resulting signal. Does cilantro taste like soap? We actually don't know. About 10 percent of the population thinks so, and the rest don't perceive it that way. The reality that is cilantro is impossible for us to encounter except through the filters of our senses. Our ears and eyes similarly give us access to only a portion of reality. Our eyes, which account for about 40 percent of our brains' sensory processing bandwidth, have a "frame rate" of 16 to 20 images per second—we don't actually see "continuously" as it appears to us that we do. Instead, our eyes see a limited number of still images per second and our brains "fill in" the gaps to create our perception of seeing moving images.

Our senses, then, are essentially filters that give us partial information, which   13
our brains must interpret into a sensible whole. Happily, our brains are pretty good at stitching that incomplete information together. We do that through another basic brain operation, *association*: we make sense of new information by connecting it to (associating it with) known information. If a friend tells you they're going to go "deposit a check," you can reasonably infer that they're going to a bank—because prior knowledge and past experience tell you (1) what "deposit" is, (2) what "check" is, and (3) where one usually needs to go in order to "deposit" a "check." If it weren't for your brain's ability to create vast "neural networks" that make and recall associations between new objects and ideas and those you've previously learned, you wouldn't be able to accomplish much. All this perception and interpretation, though, wreaks havoc with tasks like eyewitness testimony in courtrooms. Study after study has demonstrated that in high-stress situations like witnessing a crime, what people report seeing afterward is usually more what they would have *expected* to see (that business about making sense of new information by associating it with and interpreting it in light of prior knowledge) than what they could actually have witnessed.

Not all of our interpretation of signals is driven by our bodies, but much of   14
the meaning we make ultimately is. Linguists George Lakoff and Mark Johnson use a study of metaphor to show just how much of our everyday language is driven by bodily, physical comparisons. For example, our culture believes that *a mind is a brittle object*, as exemplified by language like "His ego is very *fragile*," "She just *snapped*," "He *broke* under cross-examination," "she is easily *crushed*," "the experience *shattered* him," and "I'm *going to pieces*" (28). Metaphor links our bodily experience to many concepts. Bodily, *up* is generally good and *down* is generally bad, as we associate "down" with illness, depression, unconsciousness, and death, and "up" with health, energy, vigor, "sharpness," and vitality. Lakoff and Johnson then show that we also associate *up* with having control, force, or power: "I have control *over* her. I am *on top of* the situation. He's in a *superior* position. He's at the *height* of his power. . . . He is *under* my control.

He *fell* from power. His power is on the *decline*. . . . He is *low man* on the totem pole" (15). This everyday metaphorical function of language is evidence that much of our meaning-making relates to bodily experience.

Human interaction and meaning-making is at heart, then, the experience of encountering a vast range of sensory signals and interpreting them by associating them with networks of our existing knowledge. Your average human is a genius at assembling a stream of disparate signals into a sensible whole, and this is the physical reality that rhetoric works with. A colleague of mine, Kimberly Hoover, accordingly describes rhetoric as "signal intelligence," because rhetoric is ultimately about the ways that we make sense of and respond to the many signals in our experience of a moment—signals from other people, from our surroundings, and from our own bodies. Rhetorical theorist George Kennedy suggests the parallel term *energy*: "the emotional energy that impels the speaker to speak, the physical energy expended in the utterance, the energy level encoded in the message, and the energy experienced by the recipient in decoding the message" (106).

All this biology and physics together have the following implications for rhetoric: First, *bodies matter* to knowing, meaning-making, and interaction. So *rhetoric must be about bodies as much as minds*, and about the material as much as the conceptual. This may be counterintuitive, because western culture since at least Descartes ("I think, therefore I am") has a tradition of, incorrectly, radically separating the mind and body. Contemporary rhetoric, particularly feminist rhetorical theory, makes clear the centrality of the body in making meaning, knowledge, and rhetoric (Kirsch and Royster, Wenger).

Second, because our knowledge, filtered through sensory perception, can only ever be partial and selective, *human interaction can never be based on complete, objective knowledge.* Objectivity is not physically or biologically possible for humans: We are limited to selectivity and partiality, which makes bias (literally "slanting") inevitable. We can be *more* or *less* objective by trying to get the most complete view of a situation or experience possible, and by being as open about our partialities as possible, but we can never achieve objectivity. Rhetoric cannot rely on, or be about the achievement of, objectivity. Rather, it allows people to interact and make sense of one another *without* objectivity—as subjective beings.

Third, because we make meaning by interpreting filtered sensory information, we cannot think about events directly; we can only think about our *interpretation of* events. You can experience a moment, but as soon as you reflect on that moment, try to put it in language, or look at a picture of it, you're no longer in that moment or talking about that moment; you're talking about your interpretation of it. The implication is that human interaction is always interpreted: What I say *next* depends on my *interpretation* of what you said *last*, and only unreflected-upon bodily experience can be very (briefly) uninterpreted. So *rhetoric must be a system for and art of interpreting other people's actions.*

15

16

17

18

Fourth, our bodies' ways of making meaning by putting new information in 19 terms of known information (symbolism) or figuring out its relation to known information (association) suggest that *rhetoric is always a matter of the symbolic.* If a phenomenon is, or can be made into, a symbol, it is rhetorical. *Where there are people, there is, inevitably, rhetoric.*

A RHETORICAL GUIDE TO HUMAN INTERACTION

Most moments of rhetorical action stem from people trying to do things with or 20 to each other, cooperatively or in competition. People work on a Golden Gate bridge or a rocket to the moon. People farm a field or run cattle on a ranch. People clean up tidal marshes after an oil spill. People try to impose their religion on others by war. People become lovers. People run a school board. In every such scene, people work with, for, through, and against each other, all of that work happening according to a web of rhetorical principles entangled with and always leading back to one another. In this section, I'll overview some of those principles and how they fit with one another by telling the story of Maria, Ian, and Jayla, grant writers at Reading Rivers, a nonprofit center for children's literacy in the rural West.

Rhetorical Elements

Motivation
Ecology
    Rhetors / Network
    Context
    Exigence
    Kairos / The Moment
    Interaction and Collaboration
Knowledge-Making
    Narrative / Making Present
    Values (Pathos Appeals and Mythos)
    Reasoning (Logos Appeals)
Identification
    Ethos Appeals
    Adherence
Canons (Rhetorical Arts)

Motivation

As grant writers, Maria, Ian, 21 and Jayla come to Reading Rivers each day with a particular motive: to raise money from government agencies, charitable donors, and corporations — money to buy books for children, to support local libraries, and to host literacy events for kids from poor families in remote areas of the western United States that lack much funding for public arts and social services. The entirety of the grant writer's fundraising work is done through rhetorical interaction with people all over the country, and one starting point of that interaction is always the team members' motives *for* interacting. *Rhetoric is always motivated.* People in rhetorical interactions — writers and readers — are always having those interactions for particular reasons that relate to what they want or need from the interaction. As discussed in the previous section, human biology makes objectivity impossible; we are always subjective, partial, and biased. Our *motives* are another aspect of that subjectivity.

In this case, the grant team's most obvious motives are to raise money for the 22
cause they work for: helping children in poverty to become better readers and writers. But other motives are in play as well. The team members are paid by Reading Rivers to bring in funds; if they don't succeed in doing so, they might lose their jobs. Suppose that Maria grew up in poverty, and she sees literacy as a powerful way to combat it; one of her motives might be getting children out of poverty. Perhaps Jayla cares about social justice and is trying to provide poor people the same opportunities as wealthier people. Ian might like developing public funding for the arts and can use this job as a way to do so.

We cannot attend only to the motives of the writers in the interaction, 23
though. With some reflection, it should be obvious that a listener's or reader's purposes or desires and the reasons for them (motives) shape the interaction, too. Our grant writers have to care about their readers' motives and resulting subjectivities. Grant reviewers are motivated to follow the correct process in awarding grants; they're also motivated by their interpretations of what will make the best use of grant funds to meet the purpose of the grant. And beyond writers and readers, there will be other nonhuman agents that bring motives to the interaction. The shared root of *motive*, *motivate*, *motivation*, and *motion* (Latin *motivus*) is *to move*. To say that rhetorical interaction is always "motivated" is to say that it is always moved by forces, causes, and desires. Some of these may be human and conscious; others may be human and unconscious. Others may not be human at all. In the same way that we can say water "wants" to run downhill, or that water is "motivated" (forced) to run downhill, we could for example say that government funds "want" (by nature of being what they are) to be spent rather than be saved. This motive of the funds themselves matters for grant writers. If our writers are applying for a grant for a library, it matters that libraries have particular motives (for example, to build collections of books). In this way, rhetorical theorists like Laura Micciche argue that it is not just human rhetors who have agency in rhetorical interactions; other entities that influence and constrain interactions can be understood as motivated and controlling as well.

Ultimately, the motives in rhetorical interaction are extremely complex, and 24
many will be hidden or unknown — but all are central to the interaction. The better you understand all of the motives playing into a given interaction, the more likely you are to be an effective rhetor in that interaction.

Ecology

It's obvious that a rhetorical interaction has to take place somewhere (or mul- 25
tiple somewheres) in space and time. We could call it a scene (invoking a sense of drama, as Burke does), a site (invoking a bounded sense of physical space),

a setting (invoking a sense of story), or a situation (invoking a sense of "state of affairs" or circumstances). The most common term is *rhetorical situation*, used by theorists like Lloyd Bitzer and Keith Grant-Davie. But probably the best current term for rhetorical situations, pioneered by a number of scholars, including Marilyn Cooper and Jenny Edbauer, is *rhetorical ecology*, because it invokes a sense of a place defined by a *network of myriad interconnecting and almost inseparable elements* that all shape the rhetorical interaction and meaning that emerges from them.

In the case of Jayla, Maria, and Ian at Reading Rivers, any given grant pro- 26 posal they write has its own ecology. Common elements across all their grants would be the writers and Reading Rivers itself. Each element is a rhetor, an actor in a given rhetorical ecology who influences, creates, encounters, or reads the text or discourse in question.[3] One grant proposal Jayla and Maria are working on is a U.S. Department of Education grant for after-school programs. Those two writers are the main producers of the grant proposal. But the proposal has many other contributing rhetors who are, in essence, also authors. The first of these are the people in the USDE who created the grant program, solicited proposals, and will read them during proposal review. These are the people who wrote the instructions for how the grant proposal is to be completed — so in many respects they are telling Jayla and Maria *what to write, and how.* They aren't the "authors," per se, but as the proposal's readers, they help constitute the ecology, the network of influences and actors, that is the environment in which Jayla and Maria are writing. Writers and readers — you might imagine that's the end of the list of rhetors. But also in this rhetorical ecology are the people whom the grant is meant to assist, rural schoolchildren and their teachers and families. If Reading Rivers is doing its job well, the organization has asked these people exactly what they need and would like in their after-school program — so these kids and parents have contributed to the design of what Jayla and Maria are seeking funds for, and that makes them "writers" of the grant proposal as well. Even if they hadn't contributed, that they will be *affected by* the grant proposal makes them a part of the rhetorical ecology and therefore rhetors just the same. What emerges in any

---

[3]Traditionally, rhetorical theory separates *rhetors* into "speaker" and "audience." The shortcoming of these terms is in suggesting that speakers don't listen while they speak and audiences don't speak while they listen, when in fact people in rhetorical interaction are constantly simultaneously speaking and listening. It's more accurate to speak of all involved as rhetors and emphasize their various *roles* of writing and reading, or speaking and listening, as needed.

rhetorical ecology, then, is a *network* of rhetors, many people with a variety of connections to each other.

Using the term *ecology* reminds us to look beyond *people* for even more 27 agents that influence writing. Can machines be rhetors? Imagine Maria's computer crashing as she drafts, the hard drive eating itself and taking her draft and supporting documents with it. Maria has to start over—which we can expect will lead to writing of a different shape than it would otherwise have been. So in the rhetorical ecology leading to a given text or discourse, yes, a machine is a rhetor. Scholars like Thomas Rickert in his work on "ambient rhetoric" trace a wide range of environmental conditions that contribute to a rhetorical interchange, all interacting to give our discourse whatever shape it ends up taking. In a rhetorical ecology there may be pets, food and drink, furniture, even lights, colors, and music which become rhetorical agents in this fashion.

Another way of understanding a rhetorical ecology is as the overall context in 28 which a rhetorical interaction (or set of interactions) takes place. Importantly, this context includes the exigence of the interaction, which Keith Grant-Davie defines as the *need* for a given rhetorical interaction to occur to begin with. What needs, desires, and motives in the rhetorical ecology, we can ask, *"call" the interaction into being to begin with*? If the ecology spans what Grant-Davie calls *compound rhetorical situations*, there will be multiple exigencies. For Maria and Ian, for example, one exigence is *that* the USDE has created this grant to begin with, and a proposal is required to secure funding from it. But another exigence is *why* the grant was created in the first place: a difficulty in providing literacy education in poor, rural areas. We know that each grant writer has their own motivations for participating in this grant writing; we could think of *exigence* as the ecology's own "motivations" for creating a rhetorical interaction to begin with.

We must also consider *events* in the ecology, for which we have an ancient 29 (Greek) rhetorical term, *kairos*, which translates to something like "timely good fortune" or simply "lucky timing." *Kairos* is the principle that rhetors have far-from-complete control of their texts and discourses, because circumstances beyond their control can intervene to change the moment and *what it makes sense to say* in that moment. As I wrote the first draft of this paper, Michigan Governor Rick Snyder was set to deliver his annual "State of the State" address. Rather than solely trumpeting his successes as governor, circumstances forced him to focus extensively on the poisoned water supply of Flint, Michigan, which became contaminated with lead due to a decision he supported to attempt to save a small amount of money on the water supply. Snyder was supposed to be the rhetor "in control" of his own speech, but *kairos* dictated much of what the speech would be about and what Snyder could say in it.

The same power of circumstances and "being in the right place at the right 30 time" (or not) will shape the work of our grant writers at Reading Rivers.

If while they're working on their grant proposal, news is released of a significant drop in reading test scores in the area their after-school program will serve, they would suddenly have an additional reason in support of the need for funding their program. *Kairos* reminds us that many aspects of a rhetorical ecology to which we must respond are well outside our control as rhetors.

Not only does the notion of a rhetorical ecology help us know to look for 31 all the influences and factors shaping a text or discourse we can find (either as its writers or its readers), but it reminds us that *writers neither write alone nor have perfect control of their texts*. Though writing is usually portrayed as a solo activity in the movies, it is not. Recognizing rhetorical ecologies helps make clear the *interconnectedness* and blurred boundaries among various rhetorical agents, showing us how an interaction is shaped not by a single rhetor but by many, and the shape of the resulting text or discourse depends on (is contingent on) the exact interplay among those agents. Rhetorical interaction is therefore inevitably collaborative and shared.

Knowledge-Making

Much of what rhetorical theory attends to is the many ways people have of 32 making a point. This is the place Ian, Maria, and Jayla find themselves, if they have thoughtfully taken account of the rhetorical ecology in which they find themselves on this grant proposal project, and if they're well aware of their own motives as rhetors. *What are they actually going to say* to explain their program, show the need for and value of it, and make the best possible case for getting grant funds for their project? It may initially seem strange to see this question characterized by the heading *knowledge-making*, but that is quite literally what these rhetors need to do. They need to make their readers' knowledge of what they're proposing and why it's a good idea. To do this, they don't simply "transmit" existing ideas to other rhetors. Instead, their interaction with other rhetors actually makes new knowledge for those other rhetors, knowledge that hadn't existed before. Rhetorical interaction always makes new knowledge.

Narrative

The first important rhetorical principle here is that of narrative. One line of 33 thought in rhetorical theory is that humans know by storytelling — that we are, in the words of communication scholar Walter Fisher, *homo narrans*, storytelling people. Fisher, and others such as Jim W. Corder in "Argument as Emergence, Rhetoric as Love," argue that we know ourselves and the world around us through story, and that when people argue against each other, what we are actually hearing is *contending narratives*, different storylines that conflict with each other. For Corder, people *themselves* are narratives. Certainly, we know that even the most scientific knowledge-making (rhetoric) proceeds by storytelling.

Every science journal article narrates a story:[4] "We wanted to find out X so we took steps A, B, and C, and then looked at the results and saw that L, M, and N. From that, we didn't learn X but we do know Y and Z. What we don't know yet is T and U." From a rhetorical perspective, then, it behooves writers and readers to recognize just about any text or discourse as a narrative or a story, and to frame the work of rhetors as storytelling—creating an account of some knowledge to be shared between writing and reading rhetors.

So is Jayla and Maria's grant proposal an act of storytelling? Absolutely. The proposal reviewers in Washington, DC, need to understand the story of the rural children who will benefit from these grant funds, and they need to read the stories of how the grant will actually work and how it will make a difference. 34

Not only do the reviewers need to encounter this narrative, but the grant writers need to find a way to use their writing to turn their program from a mental abstraction into a flesh-and-blood event shaping real people's lives. One powerful possibility of narratives—recognized by rhetorical theorists from Aristotle to Chaim Perelman in the mid-twentieth century—is the ability of stories to make abstract concepts *present*, to "bring them before the eyes" of rhetors encountering the narrative. One powerful example of such presence is the widely seen 2016 image of a drowned Syrian refugee boy lying on a beach. The effect of this narrated image (the photo always appears with a caption or news story explaining what it portrays) is *precisely* that "making present" of an abstract idea. It is easier not to care about "refugees" when you've never been forced to *look* at one. (Just as it is easier, for example, to mock and fear gay people if you believe none of your family or neighbors are gay—which is to say, if none are *present* to you.) Jayla and Maria would be wise, therefore, to try writing a narrative that brings the children their program will affect "before the eyes" of the grant reviewers. 35

Rhetorical Appeals

Narrative and presence are just two of many tools rhetors have for making knowledge. Several others are kinds of *appeals*, in the typical sense of "things I can do to get you to see things my way." Aristotle observed that people usually make three overall kinds of appeals (*pisteis*, in Greek): to logic (*logos*), to 36

---

[4]If you associate storytelling with *fiction* ("made up"), this idea might initially be hard. But remember that factual accounts in everything from courtroom narratives ("Let me tell you the story of the attack on this victim") to news reports ("Did you see the story on that oil train derailment?!") are normally referred to as stories. "Stories" need not be fiction. (Or, reaching the same place from the opposite direction, because we cannot recognize or create objective stories, perhaps even the most factually accurate stories are nonetheless a kind of fiction.)

emotion (*pathos*), and to a rhetor's credibility (*ethos*). We still use these categories, although the ensuing 2,500 years of rhetorical theory have given us more to say about them.

Most decision-making ultimately appeals to *values*, deeply held (sometimes 37 entirely unconscious) beliefs about what is desirable, necessary, important, pleasurable, and valuable, as well as what is dangerous, destructive, contrary to self-interest, painful, unpleasant, or worthless. Maslow's hierarchy of needs (see Figure 1) is a good set of categories of human values (physiological, safety, love and belonging, self-esteem, and self-actualization). If we like or desire a thing, we have a value for it, or for what it represents; if we dislike or reject a thing, we have a value against it or what it represents. Human interaction is relentlessly based on and driven by values. Something as simple as asking your roommate to turn on a light relies on a range of values: the security value of preferring light to darkness, the esteem value of assuming you're worthy of asking other people for help, the altruism value of knowing that your roommate will be happy to offer such assistance. If the light you desire, or the light your roommate chooses to turn on, goes beyond the pure utility of lighting a dark space and is a decorative or artful light, then your request also engages aesthetic values and a desire for beautiful pleasures.

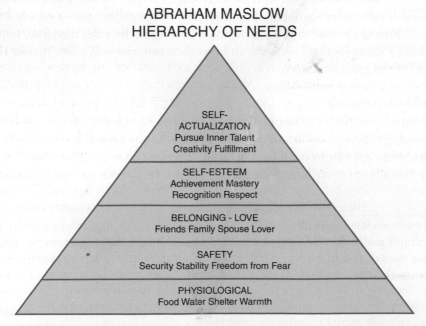

ABRAHAM MASLOW
HIERARCHY OF NEEDS

SELF-
ACTUALIZATION
Pursue Inner Talent
Creativity Fulfillment

SELF-ESTEEM
Achievement Mastery
Recognition Respect

BELONGING - LOVE
Friends Family Spouse Lover

SAFETY
Security Stability Freedom from Fear

PHYSIOLOGICAL
Food Water Shelter Warmth

Figure 1 Maslow's Hierarchy of Needs

Social-issues discussions are hugely value-driven, as George Lakoff has demon- 38 strated in his book *Moral Politics*. He argues that much of politics on the left and right in the United States can be attributed to two value sets: a conservative "strong father" set that values self-reliance, "tough love," "rugged individualism," and (therefore) private solutions to problems; and a liberal "nurturing parent" set that values inter-reliance, taking care of others, communality, and (therefore) public solutions to problems. What seem to us the best ways to address child poverty, apportion public lands for multiple uses, develop energy to power our lifestyles, maintain public safety, and explore outer space—all depend on our value sets. We will be attracted to solutions and policies that accord with our values, and we'll think that solutions and policies that contradict our values—our deepest beliefs about how the world does, can, and should work—are bad ideas.

Values are not always in conflict, of course. Most human interaction and 39 society is actually based on values held in common. Culture itself is the sum of a community's shared values. Together, these values, and the common knowledge they're based on, fuse into stories that ancient Greek rhetors referred to as *mythos*, accounts of how the world works that are shared by entire peoples. Unlike today's derivate English word *myth*, which in everyday speech means a fantasy or fiction, *mythos* spoke to the deepest foundational beliefs a people could share. According to philosopher Robert Pirsig in *Zen and the Art of Motorcycle Maintenance*, mythos is the sum of a culture's shared knowledge, "the huge body of common knowledge that unites our minds as cells are united in the body" (350). Today our mythos includes a heliocentric solar system in which planets revolve around the sun, which is one member of one galaxy among billions speeding through an expanding universe. Our mythos includes the notion that lifeforms are comprised of cells whose shapes and functions are determined by DNA and constant adaptation and mutation. Part of our mythos, in other words, is physical information and our interpretations of it. Another part is "common sense": Take an umbrella when you're going out on a rainy day. Avoid sick people to help keep from getting sick yourself. Eat a balanced diet. And one kind of common sense is our deepest foundational values. Killing puppies is bad. Treasure innocence. Protect the weak. How deep does mythos run? Pirsig argues that it is our rock-bottom definition of *sanity*: to believe something other than your culture's mythos is to appear insane to your fellow humans. Or from a different direction, if you want to map our mythos, look at what counts as sanity by seeing what counts as its opposite, insanity.

This feels, maybe, a long way from Ian, Jayla, and Maria's grant writing for 40 Reading Rivers, but it's not. Look at the roles mythos and values play in their grant proposal:

Mythos: Literacy, as reading and writing ability, is one of the most important kinds of knowledge a person can have.

Value: Using tax revenue to provide for needy people in difficult economic circumstances is a good thing.

Mythos: Directing shared resources to people in need demonstrates caring and facilitates problem-solving.

Mythos: Extraordinary resources should be devoted to the care of children.

Mythos: Every American is supposed to have an equal opportunity to live a "good life" of economic success.

Value: Public funds should be used to support arts-related experiences.

The difference between *mythos* and *values* is largely what proportion of the public believes, and how deeply they believe, the particular story being told. But in all these cases, our grant writers' *reasons* for arguing for a grant come down to shared cultural *beliefs*—their *mythos* and *values*—about what is good and valuable for members of society.

Traditional rhetorical theory talked about appeals not to values but to *emotion*, via the *pisti* of *pathos*. What's the connection? Emotional appeals—usually portrayed as tear-jerking or emotionally manipulative claims—are in essence direct appeals to *mythos*, because emotions are the body's way of expressing our most deeply held underlying values and desires. The bodily sensations we construct as emotions arise from the intersection of signals and values. Anger, fear, joy, shame, love—you literally feel these in your guts, and you might also choke up, break out in a sweat, blush, have your mouth go dry, cry, or tingle. Emotions unite our deepest feelings and the ideas that invoke them, and express these through bodily means. You feel rage when powerful people take advantage of helpless people. You feel terror when you encounter a threat to your life. You feel joy when something *so right* happens—it is "so right" because it aligns with your deepest values for the best of life. Emotions therefore are evidence of the immediate and visceral interpretation of experience (sensory signals) through underlying values,[5] and they are some of our most powerful motivators. Nineteenth-century rhetorician George Campbell recognized this when he distinguished between *convincing* and *persuasion*. It's very easy, he said, to get people to *believe* things with their *minds*—say, in our own times, that it's really very sad that children in some nations of the world die of starvation simply because the rich nations won't help them. But to *move* people to *action*, Campbell said, they can't just *think*—they have to *feel*, literally in their guts, the problem. Persuasion, he argued, goes beyond convincing by actually

[5]Donna Strickland considers the relationship between body knowledge, felt sense, emotion, knowledge, and belief in her article "Before Belief: Embodiment and the 'Trying Game.'"

moving people to action through feelings. We can't just convince your mind that children are dying of starvation; we are most likely to move you to spend money on the problem by making you feel sadness about it. (This is why TV ads about this problem include pictures of starving children.)

It's a question that Maria and Jayla need to keep in mind as they write their 42 grant: What will their proposal do to get reviewers not just to *think* about the problem they're trying to solve—which does not make the problem sufficiently present to move the reviewers to action—but how to *feel* the problem? Because reviewers that both think and feel the problem will better understand it and therefore be more likely to want to try to find solutions to the problem. The knowledge that Maria and Jayla have to make for their reviewers isn't just informational, it's emotional—they need to find a way to associate the problem and solution they're advocating with their reviewers' existing knowledge of values, their *mythos*.[6]

One major set of values the reviewers have is for *reasoning*—careful, logical 43 analysis, what Aristotle called *logos*.[7] Reasoning is a culture's set of rules for how to draw conclusions based on inference. Formal logic is one set of rules for doing so, but in most western cultures, we actually use more informal kinds of reasoning because they are quicker and in many ways more reliable. The statement "It's raining, I'd better take my umbrella" isn't actually logical, but it makes perfect sense to anyone who understands what "rain" and "umbrella" mean. (It's not logical because it leaves out too many premises to permit the leap the statement makes. Formal logic has to state *all* of its premises. Which is why so few people use it; it feels inhuman.) We start with a *claim*, "I'd better take my umbrella," and we're given one *reason*, because "it's raining." The *warrants*, or unstated premises, that connect the reason to the claim are numerous. Rain happens outside, where you're going. Rain makes you wet. Being wet is unpleasant and thus undesirable. Umbrellas can help keep you dry because they can keep rain from hitting you. As soon as we write out all these warrants, they turn into reasons if the audience already agrees with them, or into claims if the audience doesn't automatically agree. But most listeners *would* automatically agree with all these premises, so why state them to begin with? By treating them as warrants which can go unstated, we save time by relying on listeners' "common sense."

---

[6]Those readers raised in or familiar with western cultures may object; rhetoric's insistence that emotions not only *do* matter but *should* matter to our decision-making is certainly a minority viewpoint. Most of us are taught that arguments should *not* rely on emotional appeals for their power, and that those which do are suspect. This objection would be more convincing if those who most often raise it didn't get so emotional about it.

[7]In Greek, *logos* means both "words" and "reasoning," a fascinating association, when you think about it.

In western rationality, the vast majority of our reasoning is of this informal 44 sort, in which we rely on the shared prior knowledge of other rhetors to "complete" most of our arguments. When we say "Don't drink and drive, because it raises your chances of getting in an accident!" we don't *also* have to say "And car accidents are bad and they might even hurt or kill you and others!" — we all already know that. In most arguments, we're actually just disputing what one rhetor treats as a warrant but other rhetors want to treat as a claim requiring support. There is actually a Flat Earth Society, for example, that argues against the notion that Earth is round-ish. Most of us treat "the earth is round" as *mythos* and use it as a warrant — we simply take it for granted, as having been incontrovertibly proven long ago. But as Margaret Kantz demonstrates, a *fact* is simply a claim that a community has agreed is true. Flat Earth Society adherents change the warrant to a claim and contest the evidence that most people already think *proves* the earth is round.[8]

What kind of reasoning will Maria and Jayla use in their Reading Rivers 45 grant proposal? Their claims will likely include that the children their grant will support are disadvantaged in ways that the grant could help, and that helping these disadvantaged kids with after-school programs to boost reading and literacy is a good investment. To support those claims, they'll need evidence both of the problem they're claiming exists and for the assertion that the after-school program they propose will help solve that problem. They might also need to demonstrate how necessary *these* grant funds really are — that they can't just get the money from someplace else. And, of course, they'll need to be aware of their warrants — relying on them heavily when they believe the grant reviewers will share them, and exposing and converting warrants to supported claims when the grant writers think that the reviewers may not share their warrants. They also need to understand that warrants are how *values* (including *mythos*) connect into *reasoning*. In fact, a great proportion of warrants *are* values. In their grant proposal, Jayla and Maria will probably rely on the warrant that taxpayer funds are an optimal source of money for educational work. They can assume that their reviewers, who are employed for the very purpose of designating taxpayer funds for education, will share this underlying value, so much that the writers won't even need to make this point. Everyone will just assume it.

---

[8]Aristotle divided discourse into arguments which could be proved with certainty and those which could only be supported to a *probability* of truth. The latter, he said, were the purview of rhetoric. Today, most rhetorical theorists claim that *no* argument can be proved to certainty independent of the rhetors' own beliefs, so *all* discourse is in rhetoric's purview. This article has treated this claim as a warrant (taking it for granted and thus leaving it unstated) until now.

At the beginning of my discussion of reasoning, I asserted that reasoning is 46
actually a *value* for most people in western cultures. By using modes of reasoning they anticipate their reviewers will respect, Maria and Jayla can actually turn
their reasoning appeals into value appeals, which are more powerful. They can
expect their reviewers to value, for instance, specific examples of general statements they make. Example is one of the main ways we have of offering evidence
for our claims. Similarly, Maria and Jayla can predict that their reviewers will
value evidence which is well documented and generally agreed as factual. It is
important that their grant proposal engage both reasoning and values that the
reviewers will recognize and respect.

We are moving *very* quickly through some rhetorical principles that help 47
rhetors predict the most successful ways of interacting with other rhetors, and
that help them interpret what other rhetors are offering in the interaction.
There remains one significant principle to finish the explanation of how Jayla
and Maria might write the best possible grant proposal, and it returns again to
having their values recognized by their reviewers.

Identification

If we were to ask Jayla and Maria, "What are you trying to achieve in writing 48
this document?" one response might be "We're trying to gain funding for this
after-school program." But there's a much more powerful answer than that.
What the grant writers are trying to achieve is *identification* with their proposal
reviewers. They're trying to get their reviewers to see, feel, believe, and think
what the writers themselves do. They want their reviewers to identify with them
and their argument so completely that the only thing that makes sense to the
reviewers is to fund the proposal. But what is identification, and how do rhetors
achieve it with one another?

Aristotle recognized the basic truth that whether people listen to rhetors 49
depends on whether they find them credible, and he classified appeals to credibility as related to *ethos*, Greek for something like "one's accustomed place or
habit of being"—the idea that you know someone by where they dwell, by
their "haunts."[9] He suggested that rhetors get a sense of each other's ethos in
three ways: by assessing their expertise, their moral character, and their goodwill
toward other rhetors—their willingness to put others' interests first. We are
likely to find a rhetor who shows us authority, character, and goodwill, trust-
worthy. *Ethos* ultimately addresses the question, how does *who you are* influence
what you're saying and *how others should respond*?

---

[9]Many have discussed this concept, but my main encounter with it is through
Nedra Reynolds's *Rhetoric Review* article "Ethos as Location."

But how do we gauge a rhetor's expertise, morality, and goodwill? We have to 50 compare them to our *own sense of* what is authoritative, in good character, and in our best interests. We are holding the image that the rhetor presents up to the mirror of *our own values,* and what we want to see is *ourselves* looking back. When we trust a rhetor deeply, it is because we see some important aspect of ourselves in them. This is what rhetorical theorists mean by the term *identification.* As Kenneth Burke put it, "*A* is not identical with his colleague, *B.* But insofar as their interests are joined, A is *identified with* B. Or he may *identify himself* with B even when their interests are not joined, if he assumes that they are, or is persuaded to believe so" (544). Rhetoric, Burke says, is "the speaker's attempt to identify himself favorably with his audience" (561).

How, though, do we know "who" a rhetor "is"? *Identification* relies first 51 on *identity*, both of speakers and listeners. Jayla and Maria want to use their grant application to attempt to build identification with their reviewers, which requires them to have some sense of who those reviewers are. The work of John Ramage, a contemporary rhetoric theorist, suggests that Jayla and Maria have three ways of understanding their reviewers' identities. The first, Ramage calls *given*: identity that derives from the physical and social characteristics we're born with, such as sex, shape, ableness, ethnicity, place of birth, and status of parents. The second, Ramage says, are *readymades*—cultural identity "containers" which others apply to us. If you've seen *The Breakfast Club*, you know the student readymades in it were jock, geek, beauty queen, basket case, and criminal. Readymades are sometimes stereotypes, but often reasonably fair generalizations. Jayla and Maria will apply some readymades to their reviewers, who will be "academics" or professor-types (who the Department of Education asks to review grants), and their areas of expertise will be literacy and education. These readymades tell Maria and Jayla *a lot* about their reviewers' needs, values, and expectations—what kinds of evidence they are likely to find convincing, what situations the reviewers are likely to be in as they review, what the reviewers are likely to have read and be familiar with—what they already know, and what the grant writers will need to "teach" them in their application. Ramage's third identity category, *constructed* identities, are those that people build for themselves by blending givens, readymades, and their own interests and unique ways of being. (I, for example, am a professor of rhetoric and writing who is also a techie-gearhead and grooves on motorsports racing and building loud stereo systems, which makes me both a very predictable professor in some ways and a fairly unusual one in others.)

Maria and Jayla's grant reviewers will similarly be trying to build a sense of 52 the writers' identities, in part because the reviewers are trying to decide whether approving the Reading Rivers proposal will be a *safe investment*: Do the people who are writing the grant actually seem qualified and able to do what they're promising to do with the grant funds? This depends in part on who the writers are. So the grant proposal rules will require applicants to include their professional resumes to demonstrate their records of accomplishment with similar projects, and the reviewers will be trying to build a sense of Jayla and Maria's professional identities.[10]

If Maria and Jayla's grant proposal is successful, it will be because reviewers 53 "identify with" them as credible grant writers, with their project as sharing the interests that the grant is meant to support, and with the people whom the grant will benefit. That is, the reviewers will see in the grant proposal, its subjects, and its writers, the reviewers' own needs, values, and expectations for the grant reflected back at them. Jayla and Maria will have *made knowledge* for the reviewers of how their proposal does these things.

A final point about rhetoric as knowledge making. While "persuasion" is cer- 54 tainly one popular term for what rhetorical interaction is often attempting to achieve, philosopher Chaim Perelman gave us a better term back in the 1970s: *adherence*. (Like the adhesive on a Post-It note.) Perelman said, in everyday reality, we don't so much experience identification as all-or-nothing, or absolute. Rather, we experience it as other people more-or-less going along with us, to varying degrees.[11] It is more reasonable to seek adherence than conversion. Of course, Jayla and Maria want their grant reviewers' *complete* adherence to their ideas; but what might actually happen could be a judgment by the reviewers that "we really like your idea but this isn't the right grant to fund it; apply to that other one instead and see what happens," or "we really like your idea but we only have enough funds to give you some of what you asked for." The notion of *adherence* helps us understand responses like these. It more accurately reflects what human knowledge is actually like: provisional, evolving, partial, and variable.

RHETORICAL COMPOSITION AND INSCRIPTION: FIVE CANONS

What remains to explore in this paper is rhetoric's explanation of the various 55 aspects of creating discourses and texts. Aristotle identified five rhetorical arts or *canons*[12] involved in the making of any text or discourse:

---

[10]Some grant proposals — and most reputable scholarly publications — are reviewed "blind," with reviewers not knowing who the writers are. This prevents bias for or against a writer based on reputation, which can be necessary; but it also limits the quality of information reviewers have about who is doing the work, which has its own cost.

[11]Lorraine Code describes one aspect of rhetorical identity as a rhetor's *affectivity*, their "commitments, enthusiasms, desires, and interests" (46). This aspect of identity is what interfaces with a given set of ideas (or another rhetor as a whole) to create adherence.

[12]"Canon" in the sense of "a body of rules or principles which are agreed upon as fundamental to an art."

- **Invention**: coming up with what to say, developing the material for your piece. The grant writing team has to come up with the arguments and examples they'll use in their proposal. They "invent" the material in the piece.

- **Arrangement**: deciding what order that material should go in and what parts your piece needs. It's not enough for the grant writers to know *what* to say; they also have to know what parts their proposal will have, and what order the parts will go in, and what of their invented material will go in each part. (The instructions for the grant proposal will usually tell them much of this, because again, the text fills specific, known needs of proposal reviewers.)

- **Style**: crafting the particular expressions of your material to make it best suit the ecology. Our grant writers need to know what grant proposals of the kind they're writing *sound like*, and create that sound style. Within that sound, they have to decide the best words and sentence patterns to use to express their ideas and voices.

- **Memory**: recording your arranged, styled material in biological, technological, or cultural forms. The grant proposal will have specific "memory" requirements, such as what file formats to save the proposal in.

- **Delivery**: publishing your composition for other rhetors to encounter via specific modalities. The grant writers have to know how to send their proposal to reviewers, and in what form reviewers will need to work with the proposal.

Aristotle was thinking primarily of oratory when he named these activities, but they continue to work well centuries later in describing writing on paper, writing electronically for screens and audio, and writing in networked digital spaces of instant sharing and collaboration. The main distinction we would add to the canons is that invention, arrangement, and style deal primarily with *composing*, while memory and delivery deal with *inscribing* the composition, making a more or less permanent and portable "recording" of the ideas in the composition.[13] It is via inscription, whether by voice, writing, or other visual means, that rhetoric gains its *interactional* character by rendering private thought as a shareable, *material* experience.

Because the canons cover the main functions of composing a text or discourse, they may appear to present a firm process leading from one canon to the next and then on to the next. Remember, however, that because rhetoric is *interaction*, composing a text is itself a rhetorical interchange, at least with

56

---

[13]This is a distinction best made by Paul Prior in his book chapter "Tracing Process: How Texts Come into Being."

yourself as a rhetor but also usually with other rhetors—people you talk to along the way, bounce ideas off of, ask for help from, get directions from, ask to read a draft of your piece, etc. Because it's an interaction, both in your own mind and with others, it won't go "in order." Imagine our grant writers handling invention and arrangement: Part of their deciding what to say is deciding what order to put it in. But there is more: Style is invented, and how they say a thing will change what they say. In our current technological state, where you have to care about what modalities you present your discourse in (face-to-face? paper? screen? verbal? visual? aural?), delivery influences invention—what you want to create partially shapes what you find important to say, and vice versa. Our grant writers will say different things in a Word document than they would say in a spreadsheet or a graphical presentation. Each canon interweaves and interlocks with the others. Rhetors need to be comfortable with (or find ways to tolerate) this inevitable flux.

Current technology also requires comfort with a wide range of ways of working on each canon. Take invention: The Greeks understood invention as looking in various *places* in one's memory, and in cultural knowledge, for existing wisdom in *topics* that applied to what one wanted to say.[14] The nineteenth-century Romantics believed invention was essentially the opposite: unique inspiration that let a speaker say something that had never been heard before. At the beginning of the twenty-first century, we have a sprawling network of inscribed compositions, the Internet, which makes much of our invention an act of *curation*: managing existing ideas and remixing them into new expressions.[15] Or consider arrangement: Our word-processing technologies make it easy to move pieces around in our documents, and even to keep track of separate versions of our document and compare changes among them. Yet it is comparatively difficult to see two widely separated places in a document at the same time when it's on screen. That kind of vision of a work requires printed pages. (Or multiple monitors and copies of documents.) And delivery: Technology can make rhetorical interaction *immediate* rather than sequential. Aristotle imagined rhetors composing speeches and *then* delivering them. Today, multiple writers can simultaneously edit a document, and speeches can be composed on social media in the very act of delivering them to a world of readers. That speech can instantly be responded to in hashtagged Twitter streams

---

[14]The word *topic* shares its root with *topography*, "the lay of the land"; in Greek, *topos* means "place." Aristotle created a list of "common topics," the *Topoi*, which was essentially a list of the *mythos* of his day that related to reasoning. It included definition, comparison, relationship, and other categories of reasoning one could use to understand a subject they were arguing about. Today we would call them a special set of *warrants*.

[15]For example, by memes or by sampling (in music). Thanks to my MSU student Andy Meyer for calling my attention to curation as it relates to rhetorical invention.

that speakers can read and respond to even before finishing their speech. Making knowledge through rhetorical interaction is indeed a shared, collaborative, and in-the-moment activity.

SUMMING UP

At the beginning of this article, I said that rhetoric offers principles of human 58 interaction—it shows us how we make up our minds, how we change them, how we make meaning, how we know what we know, and how to help people identify with us. I also said this set of principles, when set in motion, is incredibly entangled—every rhetorical principle seems to link to every other rhetorical principle. It's a lot to keep track of. By following the explanations and the example of the grant writers, you've gotten at least a glimpse of how these things could actually be—what some of these rhetorical principles are, and how they actually come into play when we try to make decisions, decide who and what to believe, consider how to present ourselves to others, and try to understand where other people are coming from and why our interactions with them take the shape that they do.

If it hasn't happened already, you'll probably eventually get tired of hearing 59 the term *rhetorical* applied to everything—and the more you think about it, the more you'll probably also start applying it to everything yourself. So let me finish by trying to say more about what that term actually implies and requires. When we say that something is *rhetorical*, we're saying that it has the qualities of rhetoric, which are these: This "rhetorical" thing is **situated**, meaning that it happens in a particular place, time, and moment, and therefore that it cannot be universalized. It is *motivated*, meaning that there is some motive behind it, that therefore it is subjective rather than objective, and that our interpretation of it will depend in part on our understanding what motivates it, its exigence. It is *contingent*, meaning that its shape depends on the situation, exigence, and motivations that call it into being, and that it must be unique to its situation, not purely determined by pre-existing, universal rules. It is *interactional*, meaning that it can only exist in the interaction between itself and the rhetors who shape its meaning. It is *epistemic*, meaning that it creates knowledge for the rhetors interacting with it, rather than merely transmitting pre-existing knowledge unaltered from one rhetor to another. And it is *embodied*, meaning that it takes material form and that its material form shapes the interaction and rhetors' interpretations of it; it cannot be "just ideas."

As one who is still learning to understand rhetoric after twenty years of 60 study, and who needed more than ten years of that study just to come to the description in the previous paragraph (and all twenty to come to the totality of this paper), I don't expect everything in that last paragraph to make sense to you right now. I offer it instead as a jumping off point for things you should be trying to understand as you continue to study rhetoric.

Works Cited

Aristotle. *Rhetoric.* Translated by George Kennedy, Oxford UP, 1991.

Bitzer, Lloyd. "The Rhetorical Situation." *Philosophy and Rhetoric,* vol. 1, no. 1, Jan. 1968, pp. 1–14.

Burke, Kenneth. *A Grammar of Motives and A Rhetoric of Motives.* Meridian Books, The World Publishing Company, 1962.

Campbell, George. *The Philosophy of Rhetoric.* Harper & Brothers, New York, 1841. Facsimile ed., *Scholars' Facsimiles and Reprints,* 1992.

Code, Lorraine. *What Can She Know? Feminist Theory and the Construction of Knowledge.* Cornell UP, 1991.

Cooper, Marilyn. "Rhetorical Agency as Emergent and Enacted." *College Composition and Communication,* vol. 62, no. 3, Feb. 2001, pp. 420–49.

Corder, Jim W. "Argument as Emergence, Rhetoric as Love." *Rhetoric Review,* vol. 4, no. 1, Sept. 1985, pp. 16–32.

Edbauer, Jenny. "Unframing Models of Public Distribution: From Rhetorical Situation to Rhetorical Ecologies." *Rhetoric Society Quarterly,* vol. 35, no. 4, Fall 2005, pp. 5–24.

Fisher, Walter R. "Narration as a Human Communication Paradigm: The Case of Public Moral Argument." *Communication Monographs,* vol. 51, no. 1, Mar. 1984, pp. 1–22.

Grant-Davie, Keith. "Rhetorical Situations and Their Constituents." *Rhetoric Review,* vol. 15, no. 2, Spring 1997, pp. 264–79.

Kennedy, George. "A Hoot in the Dark: The Evolution of General Rhetoric." *Philosophy and Rhetoric,* vol. 25, no. 1, 1992, pp. 1–21.

Kirsch, Gesa E., and Jacqueline J. Royster. "Feminist Rhetorical Practices: In Search of Excellence." *College Composition and Communication,* vol. 61, no. 4, June 2010, pp. 640–72.

Lakoff, George. *Moral Politics: How Liberals and Conservatives Think.* U of Chicago P, 2002.

Lakoff, George, and Mark Johnson. *Metaphors We Live By.* 2nd ed., U of Chicago P, 2003.

Micciche, Laura R. "Writing Material." *College English,* vol. 76, no. 6, July 2014, pp. 488–505.

Perelman, Chaim. *The Realm of Rhetoric.* U of Notre Dame P, 1990.

Perl, Sondra. *Felt Sense.* Boynton/Cook Publishers, 2004.

Pirsig, Robert. *Zen and the Art of Motorcycle Maintenance: An Inquiry into Values.* Harper Perennial Modern Classics edition, HarperCollins Publishers, 1999.

Prior, Paul. "Tracing Process: How Texts Come into Being." *What Writing Does and How It Does It: An Introduction to Analyzing Texts and Textual Practices,* edited by Charles Bazerman and Paul Prior, Routledge, 2003, pp. 167–200.

Ramage, John. *Rhetoric: A User's Guide.* Pearson/Longman, 2006.

Reynolds, Nedra. "Ethos as Location: New Sites for Understanding Discursive Authority." *Rhetoric Review,* vol. 11, no. 3, Spring 1993, pp. 325–38.

Rickert, Thomas. *Ambient Rhetoric: The Attunements of Rhetorical Being.* U of Pittsburgh P, 2013.

Seegart, Natasha. "Play as Sniffication: Coyotes Sing in the Margins." *Philosophy and Rhetoric,* vol. 47, no. 2, 2014, pp. 158–78.

Strickland, Donna. "Before Belief: Embodiment and the 'Trying Game.'" *The Journal for the Assembly for Expanded Perspectives,* vol. 15, no. 1, Winter 2009–2010, pp. 78–86.

Wenger, Christy. *Yoga Minds, Writing Bodies: Contemplative Writing Pedagogy.* Parlor Press, 2015.

Questions for Discussion and Journaling

1. Compare how you've thought of rhetoric in the past to how it appears to you after this reading. Have you shared one of the conceptions listed in the beginning of the article? What differences between your previous thinking and what you think now are most obvious? Are there similarities?

2. Using your own words, explain what the term *epistemic* means. What is the difference if rhetoric is epistemic versus if it is not?

3. What difference does it make to think about rhetorical interaction in terms of an ecological network rather than in terms of isolated writers creating texts on their own for isolated readers, everyone independent of their surroundings?

4. What are at least three reasons why bodies, not just minds, matter to rhetorical interaction?

5. Are you surprised to see this guide explain emotions and feelings as central to making knowledge rather than as contrary to it? How does this guide's explanation of the role of emotion and feeling in rhetorical interaction line up with what your culture says their role should be?

6. What are *warrants* and why are they important to rhetorical interaction?

7. Given how Downs describes rhetoric, do you think music and artistic works are rhetorical? Why or why not?

8. Try explaining the concept of *adherence* in your own words. Is it a different way for you to think about human interaction and persuasion?

9. When Aristotle laid out five canons of rhetoric, public speaking was more common than public writing (because writing was expensive and time-consuming). If you were coming up with a list of "canons of rhetoric" today, when writing shared electronically is normal, what do you think the canons would be?

Applying and Exploring Ideas

1. Take an aspect of rhetorical theory discussed in this guide, like ecology or embodiment or one of the canons, and apply it to the hottest topic of discussion in your world this particular day. Does the rhetorical principle help you better understand why the discussion is happening as it is?

2. Rhetorical theory and its implications are usually very hard for people to describe to each other as they first start learning about it. The best way to learn is to give it a try. Suppose a friend or family member who you enjoy talking to asked "What are you studying?" and you said "rhetoric" and they said "What's that?" Write a two- to three-paragraph response that describes rhetoric as best you can right now and helps your friend know what's important about it.

3. Rhetoric is *situated* and *contingent* (para. 58), meaning that its use, what works best, or what it looks like, will vary depending on the situation. Make a list of implications of that principle: What does it mean for human communication to be *contingent on the situation*? For example, what does it mean for teaching and learning rhetoric if rhetoric varies according to the situation?

4. Returning to the extended example used throughout this reading of the grant writers working on a grant proposal, create an overall map of this example's rhetorical ecology. What does the network of rhetorical actors and interactions include? Who are all the "players" in this ecology? What does it look like if you draw it? What elements can you think of that would be in the ecology even if the article doesn't mention them?

5. Gather a group of three to four fellow students and have this discussion: Of the three *pisteis* (*logos, ethos, pathos*), which seems most important? Keep lists of the reasons each might be argued to be most important; then make a separate list of which reasons allow all of you to reach a consensus.

META MOMENT What is one principle you learned from this overview of rhetoric that you can see yourself using a lot in the future? What makes it so important to you?

Rhetorical Situations and Their Constituents

KEITH GRANT-DAVIE

Framing the Reading

Keith Grant-Davie is an associate professor of English at Utah State University in Logan, the "rural community in the Rocky Mountains" referenced in this selection. He has studied how readers and writers interact from a number of angles: what readers say writers are trying to do, how writers repeat themselves to make themselves clearer to readers, and how writing and speech are shaped by the context in which they take place and the context(s) to which they respond.

We've referenced the term *rhetorical situation* in earlier chapters, and it appears in this chapter's introduction as well as in the previous selection by Downs. You'll encounter it frequently throughout the rest of this chapter. The term is not an easy one to pin down, however, so you may still be wondering exactly what a rhetorical situation is. Composition theorists like Grant-Davie call an activity, an event, or a situation "rhetorical" when it's shaped by language or communication — also called **discourse** — that tries to get people to do something. In order to understand rhetoric, it's necessary to understand the motivations — the purposes, needs, values, and expectations — of the **rhetors** — that is, the people who generate it.

Advertisements are obvious examples of rhetorical communication. In advertising, a business communicates with its **audience** — potential customers — in order to persuade them to buy a product: For example, the Coca-Cola corporation hires basketball star LeBron James to command us, "Obey your thirst — drink Sprite!" But rhetorical situations don't have to be strategically planned and constructed as rhetoric: In fact, we encounter them every day, in ordinary, unplanned, un-self-conscious interactions. Imagine, for example, sitting in your kitchen with a friend who says, "Boy, I'm really

cold." In both the advertisement and your friend's declaration, language does things: It convinces us to buy something or to turn up the heat. Such communication is therefore rhetorical — that is, it's persuasive or motivated communication — and the situations in which it happens would be rhetorical situations.

Grant-Davie's article examines the elements of rhetorical situations and may help you better understand and respond to

Grant-Davie, Keith. "Rhetorical Situations and Their Constituents." *Rhetoric Review*, vol. 15, Spring 1997, pp. 264–79.

their rhetoric. Why, for example, didn't the Coca-Cola corporation simply bypass the celebrity and the ad agency and issue a statement telling us they'd like us to drink Sprite? Why didn't your chilly friend ask directly, "Can you please turn up the heat?" We need to explore the rhetorical situations of both examples in order to respond intelligently. To use an everyday example: If your little sister walks into your room yelling at the top of her lungs, you won't know how to respond until you understand what's happened and why she's yelling — is she angry, hurt, or excited? Understanding the rhetorical situation of her outburst will help you understand what's at stake and guide you in making an appropriate response.

The idea of a rhetorical situation might not be completely clear to you right away — most people need to encounter the idea in several different ways before they really start to get a handle on it. In fact, for most students, rhetorical situation — particularly the aspect of **exigence** — is itself a threshold concept. It takes some time to understand and completely changes your understanding of writing once you do. Grant-Davie explains exigence a few different ways, but the simplest explanation for it is a problem or need that can be addressed by communication. In the case of the Sprite ad, the exigence of the communication is complex: It includes the corporation's desire to sell and the consumer's desire for a product that will fill one or more needs (thirst quenching but also identification with a popular celebrity). In the case of your chilly friend, the exigence is more straightforward: Your friend wants to be warmer, but doesn't want to appear pushy or offend you by directly stating her desire for a thermostat adjustment.

You'll also encounter the term **stases**, which is a pattern or set of questions that helps explain what's at issue in a given rhetorical situation — a problem of fact, of value, or of policy. (The classic journalist's questions — Who? What? Where? When? How? Why? — are actually stases that attempt to establish fact.) Finally, you'll encounter the concept of **constraints**, which are factors that limit or focus the response to the exigence (problem or need) in a given situation. (In the case of your chilly friend, her desire to be perceived as friendly, not pushy, is a primary constraint.) These and other concepts in Grant-Davie's article will become clearer as you see them used in other readings.

Remember, when we identify language or communication as rhetorical, we're saying that it is doing something. So we could ask of Grant-Davie's article, what does it do? Keep that question in mind as you read.

Getting Ready to Read

Before you read, do at least one of the following activities:

- Ask one or more roommates or friends to describe the last serious argument or debate they had. Get them to describe the situations in which the debates took place in as much detail as they can. Make a list of what was "in the situation," following the reporter's "five Ws": Who was there? What was it about? When and where did it happen? Why did it happen (that is, what were the motivations of the arguers)?

- Watch a television commercial and look for how it "sets the scene" — how it very quickly puts viewers in the middle of one situation or another (like a family riding in a car or people eating in a restaurant or a sick person talking with a doctor). Make some notes about how the commercial uses scenery, particular language, or text to help explain "where you are" as a viewer, and ask yourself how important understanding that "scene" or situation is to understanding what's being advertised.

As you read, consider the following questions:

- What rhetorical situation gave rise to Grant-Davie's article — that is, why did he write it in the first place? Who is his intended audience? Who else has been talking about this problem/question? What text(s) is he responding to?
- Can you use the examples Grant-Davie gives to help you find examples of rhetorical situations and their components (exigence, rhetors, audience, and constraints) in your own life?

KEN BURNS'S DOCUMENTARY FILM, *The Civil War*, has mesmerized 1 viewers since it first aired on PBS in 1990. Among its more appealing features are the interviews with writers and historians like Shelby Foote and Barbara Fields, who provide the background information and interpretation necessary to transform battles, speeches, and letters from dry historical data into a human drama of characters, intentions, and limitations. In effect, their commentaries explain the rhetorical situations of the events, pointing out influential factors within the broader contexts that help explain why decisions were made and why things turned out as they did. Their analyses of these rhetorical situations show us that some events might easily have turned out otherwise, while the outcomes of other events seem all but inevitable when seen in light of the situations in which they occurred. When we study history, our first question may be "what happened?" but the more important question, the question whose answer offers hope of learning for the future as well as understanding the past, is "why did it happen?" At a fundamental level, then, understanding the rhetorical situations of historical events helps satisfy our demand for causality — helps us discover the extent to which the world is not chaotic but ordered, a place where actions follow patterns and things happen for good reasons. Teaching our writing students to examine rhetorical situations as sets of interacting influences from which rhetoric arises, and which rhetoric in turn influences, is therefore one of the more important things we can do. Writers who know how to analyze these situations have a better method of examining causality. They have a stronger basis for making composing decisions and are better able, as readers, to understand the decisions other writers have made.

Scholars and teachers of rhetoric have used the term *rhetorical situation* since 2 Lloyd Bitzer defined it in 1968. However, the concept has remained largely underexamined since Bitzer's seminal article and the responses to it by Richard Vatz and Scott Consigny in the 1970s. We all use the term, but what exactly do we mean by it and do we all mean the same thing? My purpose in this essay is to review the original definitions of the term and its constituents, and to offer a more thoroughly developed scheme for analyzing rhetorical situations. I will apply the concept of a rhetorical situation to reading or listening situations as well as to writing or speaking situations, and to what I call "compound" rhetorical situations—discussions of a single subject by multiple rhetors and audiences.[1]

Bitzer defines a rhetorical situation generally as "the context in which speak- 3 ers or writers create rhetorical discourse" (382).[2] More specifically he defines it as "a complex of persons, events, objects, and relations presenting an actual or potential exigence which can be completely or partially removed if discourse, introduced into the situation, can so constrain human decision or action as to bring about the significant modification of the exigence" (386).[3] In other words, a rhetorical situation is a situation where a speaker or writer sees a need to change reality and sees that the change may be effected through rhetorical discourse. Bitzer argues that understanding the situation is important because the situation invites and largely determines the form of the rhetorical work that responds to it. He adds that "rhetorical discourse comes into existence as a response to situation, in the same sense that an answer comes into existence in response to a question, or a solution in response to a problem" (385–86). Richard Vatz challenges Bitzer's assumption that the rhetor's response is controlled by the situation. He contends that situations do not exist without rhetors, and that rhetors create rather than discover rhetorical situations (154). In effect, Vatz argues that rhetors not only answer the question, they also ask it.[4]

Scott Consigny's reply to Bitzer and Vatz suggests that each of them is both 4 right and wrong, that a rhetorical situation is partly, but not wholly, created by the rhetor. Supporting Vatz, Consigny argues that the art of rhetoric should involve "integrity"—the ability to apply a standard set of strategies effectively to any situation the rhetor may face. On the other hand, supporting Bitzer, he argues that rhetoric should also involve "receptivity"—the ability to respond to the conditions and demands of individual situations. To draw an analogy, we could say that carpentry has integrity inasmuch as carpenters tackle most projects with a limited set of common tools. They do not have to build new tools for every new task (although the evolution of traditional tools and the development of new ones suggest that integrity is not a static property). Conversely, carpentry might also be said to have receptivity if the limited set of tools does not limit the carpenter's perception of the task. A good carpenter does not reach for the hammer every time.

Looking at these articles by Bitzer, Vatz, and Consigny together, we might 5 define a rhetorical situation as a set of related factors whose interaction creates and controls a discourse. However, such a general definition is better understood if we examine the constituents of situation. Bitzer identifies three: exigence, audience, and constraints. Exigence is "an imperfection marked by urgency; it is a defect, an obstacle, something waiting to be done, a thing which is other than it should be" (386). A rhetorical exigence is some kind of need or problem that can be addressed and solved through rhetorical discourse. Eugene White has pointed out that exigence need not arise from a problem but may instead be cause for celebration (291). Happy events may create exigence, calling for epideictic rhetoric. Bitzer defines the audience as those who can help resolve the exigence: "those persons who are capable of being influenced by discourse and of being mediators of change" (387), while constraints are "persons, events, objects, and relations which are parts of the situation because they have the power to constrain decision and action needed to modify the exigence" (388).

Bitzer's three-way division of rhetorical situations has been valuable, but to 6 reveal the full complexity of rhetorical situations, I think we need to develop his scheme further. I propose three amendments. First, I believe exigence, as the motivating force behind a discourse, demands a more comprehensive analysis. Second, I think we need to recognize that rhetors are as much a part of a rhetorical situation as the audience is. Bitzer mentions in passing that when a speech is made, both it and the rhetor become additional constituents of the situation (388), but he does not appear to include the rhetor in the situation that exists *before* the speech is made. And third, we need to recognize that any of the constituents may be plural. Bitzer includes the possibility of multiple exigences and constraints, but he seems to assume a solitary rhetor and a single audience. In many rhetorical situations, there may be several rhetors, including groups of people or institutions, and the discourse may address or encounter several audiences with various purposes for reading. The often complex interaction of these multiple rhetors and audiences should be considered. What follows, then, are definitions and discussions of the four constituents I see in rhetorical situations: exigence, rhetors, audiences, and constraints.

EXIGENCE — THE MATTER AND MOTIVATION OF THE DISCOURSE

Bitzer defines rhetorical exigence as the rhetor's sense that a situation both calls 7 for discourse and might be resolved by discourse. According to this definition, the essential question addressing the exigence of a situation would be "Why is the discourse needed?" However, in my scheme I propose that this question be the second of three that ask, respectively, what the discourse is about, why it is needed, and what it should accomplish. I derive the logic for this order of questions from the version of stasis theory explained by Jeanne Fahnestock and Marie Secor, who argue that the stases provide a natural sequence of steps for interrogating a subject. This sequence proceeds from questions of fact and definition (establishing that the subject exists and characterizing it) through questions of cause and effect (identifying the source of the subject and its consequences) and questions of value (examining its importance or quality) to questions of policy or procedure (considering what should be done about it) ("The Stases in Scientific and Literary Argument" 428–31; "The Rhetoric of Literary Criticism" 78–80). Sharon Crowley, too, has suggested stasis theory as a good tool for analyzing rhetorical situations (33).

What Is the Discourse About?

This question addresses the first two stases, fact and definition, by asking what 8 the discourse concerns. The question may be answered at quite a concrete level by identifying the most apparent topic. A speech by a politician during an election year may be about mandatory school uniforms, Medicare, an antipollution bill, the fight against terrorism, or any of a host of other topics. However, what the discourse is about becomes a more interesting and important question, and a source of exigence, if asked at more abstract levels — in other words, if the question becomes "What fundamental issues are represented by the topic of the discourse?" or "What values are at stake?" Political speeches often use specific topics to represent larger, more enduring issues such as questions of civil rights, public safety, free enterprise, constitutionality, separation of church and state, morality, family values, progress, equality, fairness, and so forth. These larger issues, values, or principles motivate people and can be invoked to lead audiences in certain directions on more specific topics. A speech on the topic of requiring school uniforms in public schools may engage the larger issue of how much states should be free from federal intervention — an issue that underlies many other topics besides school uniforms. In the first episode of *The Civil War,* historian Barbara Fields draws a distinction between the superficial matter of the war and what she sees as the more important, underlying issues that gave it meaning:

> For me, the picture of the Civil War as a historic phenomenon is not on the battlefield. It's not about weapons, it's not about soldiers, except to the extent that weapons and soldiers at that crucial moment joined a discussion about something higher, about humanity, about human dignity, about human freedom.

On the battlefield, one side's ability to select the ground to be contested has often been critical to the outcome of the engagement. In the same way, rhetors who can define the fundamental issues represented by a superficial subject matter—and persuade audiences to engage in those issues—are in a position to maintain decisive control over the field of debate. A presidential candidate may be able to convince the electorate that the more important issues in a debate about a rival's actions are not the legality of those specific actions but questions they raise about the rival's credibility as leader of the nation ("He may have been exonerated in a court of law, but what does the scandal suggest about his character?"). Attorneys do the same kind of thing in a courtroom, trying to induce the jury to see the case in terms of issues that favor their client. Granted, these examples all represent traditional, manipulative rhetoric—the verbal equivalent of a physical contest—but I believe the same principle is critical to the success of the kind of ethical argument Theresa Enos describes, where the aim is not victory over the opponent but a state of identification, where writer and reader are able to meet in the audience identity the writer has created within the discourse (106–8). In these kinds of argument, establishing acceptable issues would seem to be an essential stage, creating an agenda that readers can agree to discuss.

I am proposing stasis theory be used as an analytic tool, an organizing prin-   9
ciple in the sequence of questions that explore the exigence of a situation, but defining the issues of a discourse also involves determining the stases that will be contested in the discourse itself. The presidential candidate in the example mentioned above is abandoning the stasis of definition and choosing instead to take a stand at the stasis of value. Asking what the discourse is about, then, involves identifying the subject matter or topic at the most obvious level, but also determining issues that underlie it and the stases that should be addressed—in short, asking "what questions need to be resolved by this discourse?"

Why Is the Discourse Needed?

The second question about exigence addresses both the third and fourth stases   10
(cause and value). It addresses cause by asking what has prompted the discourse, and why *now* is the right time for it to be delivered. This aspect of exigence is related, as William Covino and David Jolliffe have observed, to the concept of *kairos*—"the right or opportune time to speak or write" (11, 62). Exigence may have been created by events that precede the discourse and act as a catalyst for it; and the timing of the discourse may also have been triggered by an occasion, such as an invitation to speak. A presidential speech on terrorism may be prompted both by a recent act of terrorism but also by a timely opportunity to make a speech. In the case of letters to the editor of a newspaper, the forum is always there—a standing invitation to address the newspaper's readership. However, letter writers are usually prompted by a recent event or by the need to reply to someone else's letter.

While addressing the stasis of cause, the question "why is the discourse   11
needed?" also addresses the value stasis in the sense that it asks why the discourse matters—why the issues are important and why the questions it raises

really need to be resolved. The answer to this question may be that the issues are intrinsically important, perhaps for moral reasons. Alternatively, the answer may lie in the situation's implications. Exigence may result not from what has already happened but from something that is about to happen, or from something that might happen if action is not taken—as in the case of many speeches about the environment.

What Is the Discourse Trying to Accomplish?

Finally, exigence can be revealed by asking questions at the stasis of policy or procedure. What are the goals of the discourse? How is the audience supposed to react to the discourse? I include objectives as part of the exigence for a discourse because resolving the exigence provides powerful motivation for the rhetor. The rhetor's agenda may also include primary and secondary objectives, some of which might not be stated in the discourse. The immediate objective of a presidential campaign speech might be to rebut accusations made by a rival, while a secondary objective might be to clarify the candidate's stance on one of the issues or help shape his image, and the broader objective would always be to persuade the audience to vote for the candidate when the time comes. 12

RHETOR(S) — THOSE PEOPLE, REAL OR IMAGINED, RESPONSIBLE FOR THE DISCOURSE AND ITS AUTHORIAL VOICE

Bitzer does not include the rhetor as a constituent of the rhetorical situation before the discourse is produced, although he includes aspects of the rhetor under the category of constraints. Vatz only points out the rhetor's role in defining the situation, yet it seems to me that rhetors are as much constituents of their rhetorical situations as are their audiences. Their roles, like those of audiences, are partly predetermined but usually open to some definition or redefinition. Rhetors need to consider who they are in a particular situation and be aware that their identity may vary from situation to situation. Neither Bitzer nor Vatz explores the role of rhetor in much depth, and an exhaustive analysis of possible roles would be beyond the scope of this essay, too; but in the following paragraphs, I will touch on some possible variations. 13

First, although for syntactic convenience I often refer to the rhetor as singular in this essay, situations often involve multiple rhetors. An advertisement may be sponsored by a corporation, written and designed by an advertising agency, and delivered by an actor playing the role of corporate spokesperson. Well-known actors or athletes may lend the ethos they have established through their work, while unknown actors may play the roles of corporate representatives or even audience members offering testimony in support of the product. We can distinguish those who originated the discourse, and who might be held legally responsible for the truth of its content, from those who are hired to shape and 14 deliver the message, but arguably all of them involved in the sales pitch share the role of rhetor, as a rhetorical team.

Second, even when a rhetor addresses a situation alone, the answer to the question "Who is the rhetor?" may not be simple. As rhetors we may speak in some professional capacity, in a volunteer role, as a parent, or in some other role that may be less readily identifiable—something, perhaps, like Wayne Booth's "implied author" or "second self"—the authorial identity that readers can infer from an author's writing (70–71). Roger Cherry makes a contrast between the ethos of the historical author and any persona created by that author (260–68). Cherry's distinction might be illustrated by the speech of a presidential candidate who brings to it the ethos he has established through his political career and uses the speech to create a persona for himself as president in the future. Then again, a rhetor's ethos will not be the same for all audiences. It will depend on what they know and think of the rhetor's past actions, so the "real" or "historical" author is not a stable "foundation" identity but depends partly on the audience in a particular rhetorical situation. Like exigence, then, audience can influence the identity of the rhetor.

Rhetors may play several roles at once, and even when they try to play just one role, their audience may be aware of their other roles. A Little League baseball umpire might, depending on his relationship with local residents, receive fewer challenges from parents at the game if he happens also to be the local police chief. The range of roles we can play at any given moment is certainly constrained by the other constituents of the rhetorical situation and by the identities we bring to the situation. However, new rhetorical situations change us and can lead us to add new roles to our repertoire. To use Consigny's terms, rhetors create ethos partly through integrity—a measure of consistency they take from situation to situation instead of putting on a completely new mask to suit the needs of every new audience and situation; and they also need receptivity—the ability to adapt to new situations and not rigidly play the same role in every one.

AUDIENCE—THOSE PEOPLE, REAL OR IMAGINED, WITH WHOM RHETORS NEGOTIATE THROUGH DISCOURSE TO ACHIEVE THE RHETORICAL OBJECTIVES

Audience as a rhetorical concept has transcended the idea of a homogenous body of people who have stable characteristics and are assembled in the rhetor's presence. A discourse may have primary and secondary audiences, audiences that are present and those that have yet to form, audiences that act collaboratively or as individuals, audiences about whom the rhetor knows little, or audiences that exist only in the rhetor's mind. Chaïm Perelman and Lucie Olbrechts-Tyteca point out that unlike speakers, writers cannot be certain who their audiences are, and that rhetors often face "composite" audiences consisting either of several factions or of individuals who each represent several different groups (214–17).

In Bitzer's scheme audience exists fairly simply as a group of real people   18
within a situation external to both the rhetor and the discourse. Douglas Park
has broadened this perspective by offering four specific meanings of audience:
(1) any people who happen to hear or read a discourse, (2) a set of readers or
listeners who form part of an external rhetorical situation (equivalent to Bitzer's
interpretation of audience), (3) the audience that the writer seems to have in
mind, and (4) the audience roles suggested by the discourse itself. The first two
meanings assume that the audience consists of actual people and correspond
to what Lisa Ede and Andrea Lunsford have called "audience addressed" (Ede
and Lunsford 156–65). Park's third and fourth meanings are more abstract,
corresponding to Ede and Lunsford's "audience invoked." Park locates both
those meanings of audience within the text, but I would suggest that the third
resides not so much in the text as in the writer before and during composing,
while the fourth is derived from the text by readers. Since writers are also readers of their own texts, they can alternate between the third and fourth meanings
of audience while composing and rereading; so they might draft with a sense of
audience in mind, then reread to see what sense of audience is reflected in the
text they have created. In some instances writers may be their own intended
audiences. One example would be personal journals, which writers may write
for themselves as readers in the future, or for themselves in the present with no
more awareness of audience as separate from self than they have when engaging
in internal dialogue.

Instead of asking "Who is the audience?," Park recommends we ask how   19
a discourse "defines and creates contexts for readers" (250). As an example of
such a context, he offers Chaïm Perelman's notion of the universal audience,
which Perelman defines in *The New Rhetoric* as an audience "encompassing all
reasonable and competent men" (157). Appealing to the universal audience creates a forum in which debate can be conducted. Likewise, Park argues, a particular publication can create a context that partly determines the nature of the
audience for a discourse that appears in it.

Like the other constituents of rhetorical situations, the roles of rhetor and   20
audience are dynamic and interdependent. As a number of theorists have
observed, readers can play a variety of roles during the act of reading a discourse, roles that are not necessarily played either before or after reading. These
roles are negotiated with the rhetor through the discourse, and they may change
during the process of reading (Ede and Lunsford 166–67; Long 73, 80; Park
249; Perelman and Olbrechts-Tyteca 216; Phelps 156–57; Roth 182–83).
Negotiation is the key term here. Rhetors' conceptions of audiences may lead
them to create new roles for themselves—or adapt existing roles—to address
those audiences. Rhetors may invite audiences to accept new identities for
themselves, offering readers a vision not of who they are but of who they could
be. Readers who begin the discourse in one role may find themselves persuaded

to adopt a new role, or they may refuse the roles suggested by the discourse. I may open a letter from a charity and read it not as a potential donor but as a rhetorician, analyzing the rhetorical strategies used by the letter writer. In that case I would see my exigence for reading the letter, and my role in the negotiation, as quite different from what the writer appeared to have had in mind for me.[5]

Rhetorical situations, then, are not phenomena experienced only by rhetors. 21 As Stephen Kucer and Martin Nystrand have argued, reading and writing may be seen as parallel activities involving negotiation of meaning between readers and writers. If reading is a rhetorical activity too, then it has its own rhetorical situations. So, if we prefer to use *writing situation* as a more accessible term than *rhetorical situation* when we teach (as some textbooks have—e.g., Pattow and Wresch 18–22; Reep 12–13), we should not neglect to teach students also about "reading situations," which may have their own exigencies, roles, and constraints.

CONSTRAINTS—FACTORS IN THE SITUATION'S CONTEXT THAT MAY AFFECT THE ACHIEVEMENT OF THE RHETORICAL OBJECTIVES

Constraints are the hardest of the rhetorical situation components to define neatly 22 because they can include so many different things. Bitzer devotes just one paragraph to them, defining them as "persons, events, objects, and relations which are parts of the situation because they have the power to constrain decision and action needed to modify the exigence." Since he assumes that rhetors are largely controlled by situations and since he observes "the power of situation to constrain a fitting response" (390), his use of the term *constraints* has usually been interpreted to mean limitations on the rhetor—prescriptions or proscriptions controlling what can be said, or how it can be said, in a given situation. A rhetor is said to work within the constraints of the situation. However, this commonly held view of constraints as obstacles or restrictions has obscured the fact that Bitzer defines constraints more as aids to the rhetor than as handicaps. The rhetor "harnesses" them so as to constrain the audience to take the desired action or point of view. This view of constraints seems useful, so I see them as working either for or against the rhetor's objectives. I refer to the kind that support a rhetor's case as positive constraints, or assets, and those that might hinder it as negative constraints, or liabilities.

Bitzer goes on to divide constraints along another axis. Some, which he 23 equates with Aristotle's inartistic proofs, are "given by the situation." These might be "beliefs, attitudes, documents, facts, traditions, images, interests, motives and the like"—presumably including beliefs and attitudes held by the audience. Other constraints, equivalent to Aristotle's artistic proofs, are developed by the rhetor: "his personal character, his logical proofs, and his style" (388).

To paraphrase, Bitzer defines constraints very broadly as all factors that may move the audience (or disincline the audience to be moved), including factors in the audience, the rhetor, and the rhetoric. Such an all-inclusive definition would seem to threaten the usefulness of constraints as a distinct constituent of rhetorical situations, so I propose excluding the rhetor and the audience as separate constituents and making explicit the possibility of both positive and negative constraints. I would define constraints, then, as all factors in the situation, aside from the rhetor and the audience, that may lead the audience to be either more or less sympathetic to the discourse, and that may therefore influence the rhetor's response to the situation—still a loose definition, but constraints defy anything tighter.

With the rhetor and the audience excluded from the category of constraints, 24 it is tempting to exclude the other artistic proofs too, thereby simplifying the category further by drawing a distinction between the rhetorical situation and the discourse that arises from it. However, clearly the situation continues after the point at which the discourse begins to address it. A rhetor continues to define, shape, reconsider, and respond to the rhetorical situation throughout the composing process, and at any given point during that process, the rhetor may be highly constrained by the emerging discourse. If we are to be coherent, what we have already written must constrain what we write next.

If constraints are those other factors in rhetorical situations, besides rhetors 25 and audiences, that could help or hinder the discourse, what might they be? I have already included the emerging text of the discourse as a constraint on what a rhetor can add to it. To this we can add linguistic constraints imposed by the genre of the text or by the conventions of language use dictated by the situation. Other constraints could arise from the immediate and broader contexts of the discourse, perhaps including its geographical and historical background. Such constraints could include recent or imminent events that the discourse might call to readers' minds, other discourses that relate to it, other people, or factors in the cultural, moral, religious, political, or economic climate—both local and global—that might make readers more or less receptive to the discourse. Foreign trade negotiations, a domestic recession, a hard winter, civil disturbances, a sensational crime or accident—events like these might act as constraints on the rhetorical situation of an election campaign speech, suggesting appeals to make or avoid making. Every situation arises within a context—a background of time, place, people, events, and so forth. Not all of the context is directly relevant to the situation, but rhetors and audiences may be aware of certain events, people, or conditions within the context that *are* relevant and should be considered part of the situation because they have the potential to act as positive or negative constraints on the discourse. The challenge for the rhetor is to decide which parts of the context bear on the situation enough to be considered constraints, and what to do about them—for instance, whether the best rhetorical strategy for a negative constraint would be to address it directly and try to dis-arm it — or even try to turn it into a positive constraint — or to say nothing about it and hope that the audience overlooks it too.

Some of my examples have complicated the roles of rhetor and audience, 26 but all so far have looked at discourses in isolation and assumed that situations are finite. It seems clear that a situation begins with the rhetor's perception of exigence, but when can it be said to have ended? Does it end when the exigence has been resolved or simply when the discourse has been delivered? I favor the latter because it establishes a simpler boundary to mark and it limits rhetorical situations to the preparation and delivery of discourses, rather than extending them to their reception, which I consider to be part of the audience's rhetorical situation. Also, as I have tried to show, exigence can be quite complex and the point at which it can be said to have been resolved may be hard to identify. The same exigence may motivate discourses in many quite different situations with-out ever being fully resolved. Major sources of exigence, like civil rights, can continue to motivate generations of rhetors.

> *Dialogue challenges the idea of rhetorical situations having neat boundaries.*

To say that a rhetorical situation ends 27 when the discourse has been delivered still leaves us with the question of how to describe discourse in a discussion. Dialogue challenges the idea of rhetorical situations having neat boundaries. When participants meet around a table and take turns playing the roles of rhetor and audience, are there as many rhetorical sit-uations as there are rhetors — or turns? Or should we look at the whole meet-ing as a single rhetorical situation? And what happens when the participants in a discussion are not gathered together at one place and time, engaged in the quick give and take of oral discussion, but instead debate a topic with each other over a period of weeks — for example, by sending and replying to letters to the editor of a newspaper? To look at a meeting as a single rhetorical situation recognizes that many of the constituents of the situation were common to all participants, and it emphasizes Bitzer's view that situations are external to the rhetor; whereas to look at each person involved in the discussion as having his or her own rhetorical situation — or each contribution to the discussion having its own situation — would seem to lean toward Vatz's view that rhetorical situ-ations are constructed by rhetors. Both views, of course, are right. Each rhetor has a different perspective and enters the debate at a different time (especially in the case of a debate carried on through a newspaper's editorial pages), so each addresses a slightly different rhetorical situation; but the situations may interlace or overlap extensively with those addressed by other rhetors in the dis-cussion. It may be useful, then, to think of an entire discussion as a compound rhetorical situation, made up of a group of closely related individual situations.

Analyzing a compound situation involves examining which constituents were common to all participants and which were specific to one or two. For example, some sources of exigence may have motivated all participants, and in these common factors may lie the hope of resolution, agreement, or compromise. On the other hand, the divisive heat of a debate may be traced to a fundamental conflict of values—and thus of exigence—among the participants.

Examples of this kind of compound rhetorical situation can be found when- 28 ever public debate arises, as it did recently in the editorial pages of a local newspaper in a rural community in the Rocky Mountains. The debate was sparked when the newspaper printed a front-page story about a nearby resort hotel, Sherwood Hills, that had erected a 46-foot, illuminated Best Western sign at the entrance to its property. Such a sign on a four-lane highway would not normally be remarkable, but the setting made this one controversial. Sherwood Hills lies hidden in trees at the end of a long driveway, off a particularly scenic stretch of the highway. There are no other residences or businesses nearby, and the area is officially designated a forest-recreation zone, which usually prohibits businesses and their signs. Several months earlier, the resort owners had applied to the county council for a permit and been told that some kind of sign on the road might be allowed, but the application had not been resolved when the sign went up.

The newspaper ran several stories reporting the resort owners' rationale (they 29 felt they had applied in good faith and waited long enough) and the council members' reaction (they felt indignant that the owners had flouted the law and were now seeking forgiveness rather than permission). The newspaper also berated the resort owners' actions in an editorial. What might have been a minor bureaucratic matter resolved behind closed doors turned into a town debate, with at least 15 letters to the editor printed in the weeks that followed. From a rhetorical perspective, I think the interesting question is why the incident sparked such a brushfire of public opinion, since not all controversial incidents covered by the newspaper elicit so many letters to the editor. Looking at the debate as a compound rhetorical situation and examining its constituents helps answer that question.

The rhetors and audiences included the resort owners, the county council, 30 the county planning commission, the Zoning Administrator, the newspaper staff, and assorted local citizens. Their debate was nominally about the sign—whether it was illegal (a question at the stasis of definition) and what should be done about it (a question at the policy stasis). These questions were sources of exigence shared by all participants in the debate. However, even greater exigence seems to have come from questions at the stasis of cause / effect—what precedent might the sign create for other businesses to ignore local ordinances?—and at the stasis of value—were the sign and the act of erecting it without a permit (and the ordinance that made that act illegal) good or bad? For most of the letter writers, the debate revolved around the issue of land use, one of the more frequently and hotly contested issues in the western United States, where the appropriate use of both public and private land is very much open to argument.

Critics of the sign generally placed a high value on unspoiled wilderness. For them the sign symbolized the commercial development of natural beauty and challenged laws protecting the appearance of other forest-recreation zones in the area. Those in favor of the sign, on the other hand, saw it not as an eyesore but as a welcome symbol of prosperity erected in a bold and justified challenge to slow-moving bureaucracy and unfair laws, and as a blow struck for private property rights. Underlying the issue of land use in this debate, then, and providing powerful exigence, was the issue of individual or local freedom versus government interference—another issue with a strong tradition in the western U.S. (as in the case of the "sagebrush rebellions"—unsuccessful attempts to establish local control over public lands). The tradition of justified—or at least rationalized—rebellion against an oppressive establishment can of course be traced back to the American Revolution, and in the 1990s we have seen it appear as a fundamental source of exigence in a number of antigovernment disputes in various parts of the nation.

Exigence and constraints can be closely related. For the critics of Sherwood Hills, the breaking of the law was a source of exigence, motivating them to protest, but the law itself was also a positive constraint in the situation, giving them a reason to argue for the removal of the sign. Certainly the law constrained the council's response to the situation. On the other hand, the law was apparently a less powerful constraint for the owners of Sherwood Hills and for many of their supporters who felt that the law, not the sign, should be changed. For many on that side of the debate, the tradition of rebelling against what are perceived to be unfair government restrictions provided both exigence and a positive constraint. The feeling that private property owners' rights had been violated was what motivated them to join the discussion, but it also gave them an appeal to make in their argument. The rhetor's sense of exigence, when communicated successfully to the audience, can become a positive constraint, a factor that helps move the audience toward the rhetor's position.

Precedents always create constraints. In the Sherwood Hills debate, several participants mentioned comparable business signs, including one recently erected at another local resort, also in a forest-recreation area. The existence of that sign was a positive constraint for supporters of the Sherwood Hills sign. However, it was also a negative constraint since the other resort had followed the correct procedure and received a permit for its sign, and since the sign was smaller and lower than the Sherwood Hills sign, had no illumination, and had been designed to harmonize with the landscape.

Other constraints emerged from local history. The highway past Sherwood Hills had recently been widened, and the dust had not yet settled from the

31

32

33

34

dispute between developers and environmentalists over that three-year project. Even before the road construction, which had disrupted traffic and limited access to Sherwood Hills, the resort had struggled to stay in business, changing hands several times before the present owners acquired it. The sign, some supporters suggested, was needed to ensure the new owners' success, on which the prosperity of others in the community depended too. The owners were also praised as upstanding members of the community, having employed local people and contributed to local charities. Two letter writers argued from this constraint that the community should not bite the hand that feeds it.

This analysis of the Sherwood Hills sign debate as a compound situation only scratches the surface, but understanding even this much about the situation goes a long way toward explaining why the incident generated such an unusual wave of public opinion. The conclusion of a compound rhetorical situation may be harder to determine than the end of a single-discourse situation, particularly if the subject of discussion is perennial. This particular dispute ended when the exchange of letters stopped and the Sherwood Hills owners reached a compromise with the county council: Both the sign and the ordinance remained in place, but the sign was lowered by ten feet.

As my discussion and examples have shown, exigence, rhetor, audience, and constraints can interlace with each other, and the further one delves into a situation the more connections between them are likely to appear. However, while the boundaries between the constituents will seldom be clear and stable, I do think that pursuing them initially as if they were discrete constituents helps a rhetor or a rhetorician look at a situation from a variety of perspectives. My efforts in the preceding pages have been to discuss the possible complexities of rhetorical situations. Teaching student writers and readers to ask the same questions, and to understand why they are asking them, will help them realize their options, choose rhetorical strategies and stances for good reasons, and begin to understand each other's roles.[6]

Notes

1. I thank *Rhetoric Review* readers John Gage and Robert L. Scott, whose careful reviews of earlier drafts of this essay helped me improve it greatly.

2. Bitzer's definition does not distinguish *situation* from *context*. The two terms may be used interchangeably, but I prefer to use *context* to describe the broader background against which a rhetorical situation develops and from which it gathers some of its parts. I see situation, then, as a subset of context.

3. In "The Rhetorical Situation" and "Rhetoric and Public Knowledge," Bitzer uses the terms *exigence* and *exigency* synonymously. I have used *exigence* in this essay mostly for reasons of habit and consistency with the original Bitzer / Vatz / Consigny discussion. I consider it an abstract noun like *diligence*, *influence*, or *coherence*. While cohesion can be located in textual

features, coherence is a perception in the reader. In the same way, exigence seems to me to describe not so much an external circumstance as a sense of urgency or motivation within rhetors or audiences. It is they who recognize (or fail to recognize) exigence in a situation and so the exigence, like the meaning in literary works, must reside in the rhetor or audience as the result of interaction with external circumstances. Although Bitzer calls those circumstances exigences, I prefer to think of them as *sources* of exigence.

4. This fundamental disagreement between Bitzer and Vatz parallels the debate within literary theory over the location of meaning: whether meaning exists in the text, independent of the reader, or whether it is largely or entirely brought by the reader to the text. Bitzer's view looks toward formalism, Vatz's toward reader-response theories, and mine toward the position that meaning is a perception that occurs in the reader but is (or should be) quite highly constrained by the text.

5. Taking poststructuralist approaches to the roles of rhetor and audience, Louise Wetherbee Phelps and Robert Roth further challenge any assumption of a static, divided relationship between the two. Phelps uses Mikhail Bakhtin's idea of heteroglossia to deconstruct the idea of a boundary between author and audience. She argues that the other voices an author engages through reading and conversation while composing are inevitably present in the text, inextricably woven with the author's voice, and that this intertextuality of the text and the author makes a simple separation of text and author from audience impossible (158–59). Roth suggests that the relationship between writers and readers is often cooperative, not adversarial (175), and that a writer's sense of audience takes the form of a shifting set of possible reading roles that the writer may try on (180–82). Neither Phelps nor Roth argue that we should abandon the terms *rhetor* and *audience*. Phelps acknowledges that although author and audience may not be divisible, we routinely act as if they were (163), and she concludes that we should retain the concept of audience for its heuristic value "as a usefully loose correlate for an authorial orientation—whoever or whatever an utterance turns toward" (171). Like Phelps, Roth recognizes that the free play of roles needs to be grounded. "What we really need," he concludes, "is a continual balancing of opposites, both openness to a wide range of potential readers and a monitoring in terms of a particular sense of audience at any one moment or phase in the composing process" (186).

6. I have summarized my analysis in a list of questions that might be used by writers (or adapted for use by audiences) to guide them as they examine a rhetorical situation. Space does not allow this list to be included here, but I will send a copy to anyone who mails me a request.

Works Cited

Bitzer, Lloyd F. "The Rhetorical Situation." *Philosophy and Rhetoric* 1 (1968): 1–14. Rpt. *Contemporary Theories of Rhetoric: Selected Readings*. Ed. Richard L. Johannesen. New York: Harper, 1971. 381–93.

———. "Rhetoric and Public Knowledge." *Rhetoric, Philosophy, and Literature: An Exploration*. Ed. Don M. Burks. West Lafayette, IN: Purdue UP, 1978. 67–93.

Booth, Wayne C. *The Rhetoric of Fiction*. 2nd ed. Chicago: U of Chicago P, 1983.

Cherry, Roger D. "Ethos Versus Persona: Self-Representation in Written Discourse." *Written Communication* 5 (1988): 251–76.

Consigny, Scott. "Rhetoric and Its Situations." *Philosophy and Rhetoric* 7 (1974): 175–86.

Covino, William A., and David A. Jolliffe. *Rhetoric: Concepts, Definitions, Boundaries*. Boston: Allyn, 1995.

Crowley, Sharon. *Ancient Rhetorics for Contemporary Students*. New York: Macmillan, 1994.

Ede, Lisa, and Andrea Lunsford. "Audience Addressed / Audience Invoked: The Role of Audience in Composition Theory and Pedagogy." *College Composition and Communication* 35 (1984): 155–71.

Enos, Theresa. "An Eternal Golden Braid: Rhetor as Audience, Audience as Rhetor." Kirsch and Roen 99–114.

Fahnestock, Jeanne, and Marie Secor. "The Rhetoric of Literary Criticism." *Textual Dynamics of the Professions*. Ed. Charles Bazerman and James Paradis. Madison: U of Wisconsin P, 1991. 76–96.

———. "The Stases in Scientific and Literary Argument." *Written Communication* 5 (1988): 427–43.

Fields, Barbara. Interview. *The Civil War*. Dir. Ken Burns. Florentine Films, 1990.

Kirsch, Gesa, and Duane H. Roen, eds. *A Sense of Audience in Written Communication*. Newbury Park, CA: Sage, 1990.

Kucer, Stephen L. "The Making of Meaning: Reading and Writing as Parallel Processes." *Written Communication* 2 (1985): 317–36.

Long, Russell C. "The Writer's Audience: Fact or Fiction?" Kirsch and Roen 73–84.

Moore, Patrick. "When Politeness Is Fatal: Technical Communication and the Challenger Accident." *Journal of Business and Technical Communication* 6 (1992): 269–92.

Nystrand, Martin. "A Social-Interactive Model of Writing." *Written Communication* 6 (1988): 66–85.

Park, Douglas. "The Meanings of 'Audience.'" *College English* 44 (1982): 247–57.

Pattow, Donald, and William Wresch. *Communicating Technical Information: A Guide for the Electronic Age*. Englewood Cliffs, NJ: Prentice, 1993.

Perelman, Chaïm. *The New Rhetoric: A Theory of Practical Reasoning*. Trans. E. Griffin-Collart and O. Bird. *The Great Ideas Today*. Chicago: Encyclopedia Britannica, Inc., 1970. Rpt. *Professing the New Rhetorics: A Sourcebook*. Ed. Theresa Enos and Stuart C. Brown. Englewood Cliffs, NJ: Prentice, 1994. 145–77.

Perelman, Chaïm, and L. Olbrechts-Tyteca. *The New Rhetoric*. Trans. John Wilkinson and Purcell Weaver. U. of Notre Dame P, 1969: 1–26. Rpt. *Contemporary Theories of Rhetoric: Selected Readings*. Ed. Richard L. Johannesen. New York: Harper, 1971. 199–221.

Phelps, Louise Wetherbee. *Audience and Authorship: The Disappearing Boundary*. Kirsch and Roen 153–74.

Reep, Diana C. *Technical Writing: Principles, Strategies, and Readings*. 2nd ed. Boston: Allyn, 1994.

Roth, Robert G. *Deconstructing Audience: A Post-Structuralist Rereading*. Kirsch and Roen 175–87.

Vatz, Richard. "The Myth of the Rhetorical Situation." *Philosophy and Rhetoric* 6 (1973): 154–61.

White, Eugene E. *The Context of Human Discourse: A Configurational Criticism of Rhetoric*. Columbia: U of South Carolina P, 1992.

Questions for Discussion and Journaling

1. Have you ever thought of writers as negotiating with their audiences? As a writer, what is the difference between imagining yourself talking to and negotiating with your audience? What would you do differently if you were doing the latter?

2. How would you define *exigence*? Why does exigence matter in rhetorical situations? (What difference does it make?)

3. Grant-Davie opens with a discussion of historical documentaries and the difference between asking "What happened?" and asking "Why did it happen?" Which question, in your view, does analyzing rhetorical situations answer? What makes you think so?

4. What are constraints? To help you work this out, consider what Grant-Davie's constraints might have been in drafting this piece. Bitzer, you learned in this piece, argues that we should think of constraints as aids rather than restrictions. How can that be?

5. As a writer, how would it help you to be aware of your rhetorical situation and the constraints it creates?

6. Grant-Davie seems to want us to use the idea of rhetorical situation mostly in an analytical way, to understand why existing discourses have taken the shape they have. In other words, he seems to be talking to us as readers. In what ways is the idea also useful for writers? That is, how is it useful to understand the rhetorical situation you're "writing into"?

7. Grant-Davie suggests that we have to ask three questions to understand the exigence of a rhetorical situation: what a discourse is about, why it's needed, and what it's trying to accomplish. What's the difference between the second question and the third question?

8. What happens if we imagine everyone in a rhetorical situation to be simultaneously a rhetor and an audience? How does imagining a writer as simultaneously rhetor and audience make you think differently about writing?

9. Based on the rhetorical situation for which Grant-Davie was writing, would you say you are part of the audience he imagined, or not? Why?

10. Other writers (Bitzer, Vatz, Consigny) have tried to explain the concept of the rhetorical situation before. Why does Grant-Davie think more work is needed?

Applying and Exploring Ideas

1. (a) Write a brief (one- to two-page) working definition of *rhetorical situation*. Be sure to give some examples of rhetorical situations to illustrate your definition.

(b) Complicate your working definition by examining how Grant-Davie, Bitzer, Vatz, and Consigny see the rhetorical situation similarly or differently from one another. You may write this as a straightforward compare-and-contrast discussion if you would like, or, to spice things up a little, write it as a dialogue and create the situation in which it occurs. (Is it an argument? A dinner-table discussion? A drunken brawl?) Where does it happen, how does it go, and what do the participants say?

2. Write a two- to three-page analysis of the rhetorical situation of Grant-Davie's own article, using the elements the article explains.

3. Identify an argument that's currently going on at your school. (Check your school newspaper or website if nothing springs to mind.) In a short (two- to three-page) analysis, briefly describe the argument. After describing the argument, analyze the rhetorical situation. Then conclude by noting whether or how your understanding of the argument changed after you analyzed the rhetorical situation.

4. Look at three course syllabi and/or three academic handouts you've received this semester or in previous semesters. What rhetorical situation does each instructor seem to be imagining? Why do you think so? Do the instructors seem to imagine their rhetorical situations differently? If so, why do you think they do this?

5. Watch a few TV commercials and notice how quickly they establish a rhetorical situation within the ad. (Not, that is, the rhetorical situation of you as audience and the company as rhetor, but the rhetorical situation inside the commercial, where actors or characters play the roles of rhetors and audiences.) Write a two- to three-page analysis that describes three commercials, the rhetorical situations they create, and whether or not you consider them to be persuasive.

META MOMENT Why do you think that your teacher assigned this article? How might this article help you achieve the goals of this chapter? How can understanding the concept of rhetorical situation potentially be useful to you in school and in your life?

Intertextuality and the Discourse Community

Photo by Kathryn King Leacock

JAMES E. PORTER

Framing the Reading

Two of the deepest conceptions of writing that our culture holds are (1) that writing must be original and (2) that if a writer "borrows" ideas from other writing without acknowledging that borrowing, the writer is plagiarizing. In the following study, James Porter argues that these common ideas about **authorship**, **originality**, and **plagiarism** don't account for how texts actually work and how writers actually write. Porter calls into question how original writers can actually be in constructing texts and, following from that question, also wonders how we should define plagiarism if true originality is so difficult to find.

The principle Porter explores in asking these questions is **intertextuality** — that is, the idea that all texts contain "traces" of other texts and that there can be no text that does not draw on some ideas from some other texts. You may rightly be skeptical of such a broad claim, so follow along carefully as Porter explains why he thinks this is true. You may be particularly interested in the section in which Porter demonstrates his argument by looking at how the Declaration of Independence was written, as he claims, collaboratively, by a number of different authors. Porter helps us understand how even writers who aren't thinking about intertextuality, or using it strategically, are always already being intertextual.

The implications of Porter's study are significant for how you understand writing and how you understand yourself as a writer. Most of us have been taught that writers are *autonomous* — that is, that they're free to do whatever they want with their texts, and also that they're solely responsible for what's in those texts. Porter's research on actual writing and writers challenges this construct. If Porter is correct, then we need a different construct of the author, one that acknowledges the extent to which commu-

nities shape what a writer chooses to say; the extent to which writers say things that have already been said (even when they believe they're being original); and the extent to which texts are constructed by many different people along the way, as readers feed ideas back to the writer. In this way, Porter actually takes up more than one threshold concept: context determines whether

Porter, James E. "Intertextuality and the Discourse Community." *Rhetoric Review*, vol. 5, no. 1, Autumn 1986, pp. 34–47.

texts are effective and seem "original," and constraints in rhetorical situations often make composing a text more complicated than it may first appear. And of course, all of this means that whether a particular piece of writing is understood to be "good" or not depends on a host of factors, many of which are outside the writer's direct control.

Getting Ready to Read

Before you read, do at least one of the following activities:

- Write a paragraph on what, in your mind, is the difference between an *author* and a *writer*. When would you choose the first term to describe the person/people behind a text, and when would you choose the second?
- Make a list of all the ways you get "help," of any kind, in your writing. Where do you get ideas, advice, feedback, and assistance?
- Find one or two friends or family members who write a great deal, either for a living, as a major part of their jobs, or as a hobby. Interview them about who or what they see contributing to their writing. To what extent do they see themselves doing their writing "on their own"?

As you read, consider the following questions:

- After reading the first page of the article, how would you define *intertextuality*? We will ask you to define it again after you have read the entire article.
- Watch for how Porter poses questions about writers' autonomy and originality. Does he finally decide that autonomy and originality are impossible?
- Do you think Porter is criticizing the Declaration of Independence? Thomas Jefferson? Explain your answer.
- If you haven't seen the Pepsi commercial that Porter discusses, try to find a version of it to watch online. Does Porter's reading of the commercial match yours, or do you understand it differently?

AT THE CONCLUSION OF Eco's *The Name of the Rose*, the monk Adso of 1
Melk returns to the burned abbey, where he finds in the ruins scraps of parchment, the only remnants from one of the great libraries in all Christendom. He spends a day collecting the charred fragments, hoping to discover some meaning in the scattered pieces of books. He assembles his own "lesser library . . . of fragments, quotations, unfinished sentences, amputated stumps of books" (500). To Adso, these random shards are "an immense acrostic that says and repeats nothing" (501). Yet they are significant to him as an attempt to order experience.

> All texts are interdependent: We understand a text only insofar as we understand its precursors.

We might well derive our own order from this scene. We might see Adso as representing the writer, and his desperate activity at the burned abbey as a model for the writing process. The writer in this image is a collector of fragments, an archaeologist creating an order, building a framework, from remnants of the past. Insofar as the collected fragments help Adso recall other, lost texts, his experience affirms a principle he learned from his master, William of Baskerville: "Not infrequently books speak of books" (286). Not infrequently, and perhaps ever and always, texts refer to other texts and in fact rely on them for their meaning. All texts are interdependent: We understand a text only insofar as we understand its precursors.

This is the principle we know as intertextuality, the principle that all writing and speech—indeed, all signs—arise from a single network: what Vygotsky called "the web of meaning"; what poststructuralists label Text or Writing (Barthes, *écriture*); and what a more distant age perhaps knew as *logos*. Examining texts "intertextually" means looking for "traces," the bits and pieces of Text which writers or speakers borrow and sew together to create new discourse.[1] The most mundane manifestation of intertextuality is explicit citation, but intertextuality animates all discourse and goes beyond mere citation. For the intertextual critics, Intertext is Text—a great seamless textual fabric. And, as they like to intone solemnly, no text escapes intertext.

Intertextuality provides rhetoric with an important perspective, one currently neglected, I believe. The prevailing composition pedagogies by and large cultivate the romantic image of writer as free, uninhibited spirit, as independent, creative genius. By identifying and stressing the intertextual nature of discourse, however, we shift our attention away from the writer as individual and focus more on the sources and social contexts from which the writer's discourse arises. According to this view, authorial intention is less significant than social context; the writer is simply a part of a discourse tradition, a member of a team, and a participant in a community of discourse that creates its own collective meaning. Thus the intertext *constrains* writing.

My aim here is to demonstrate the significance of this theory to rhetoric, by explaining intertextuality, its connection to the notion of "discourse community," and its pedagogical implications for composition.

THE PRESENCE OF INTERTEXT

Intertextuality has been associated with both structuralism and poststructuralism, with theorists like Roland Barthes, Julia Kristeva, Jacques Derrida, Hayden White, Harold Bloom, Michel Foucault, and Michael Riffaterre. (Of course, the theory is most often applied in literary analysis.) The central assumption of these critics has been described by Vincent Leitch: "The text is not an autonomous or unified object, but a set of relations with other texts. Its system of language, its grammar, its lexicon, drag along numerous bits and pieces — traces — of history so that the text resembles a Cultural Salvation Army Outlet with unaccountable collections of incompatible ideas, beliefs, and sources" (59). It is these "unaccountable collections" that intertextual critics focus on, not the text as autonomous entity. In fact, these critics have redefined the notion of "text": Text *is* intertext, or simply Text. The traditional notion of the text as the single work of a given author, and even the very notions of author and reader, are regarded as simply convenient fictions for domesticating discourse. The old borders that we used to rope off discourse, proclaim these critics, are no longer useful.

We can distinguish between two types of intertextuality: iterability and presupposition. Iterability refers to the "repeatability" of certain textual fragments, to citation in its broadest sense to include not only explicit allusions, references, and quotations within a discourse, but also unannounced sources and influences, clichés, phrases in the air, and traditions. That is to say, every discourse is composed of "traces," pieces of other texts that help constitute its meaning. (I will discuss this aspect of intertextuality in my analysis of the Declaration of Independence.) Presupposition refers to assumptions a text makes about its referent, its readers, and its context — to portions of the text which are read, but which are not explicitly "there." For example, as Jonathan Culler discusses, the phrase "John married Fred's sister" is an assertion that logically presupposes that John exists, that Fred exists, and that Fred has a sister. "Open the door" contains a practical presupposition, assuming the presence of a decoder who is capable of being addressed and who is better able to open the door than the encoder. "Once upon a time" is a trace rich in rhetorical presupposition, signaling to even the youngest reader the opening of a fictional narrative. Texts not only refer to but in fact *contain* other texts.[2] 7

An examination of three sample texts will illustrate the various facets of intertextuality. The first, the Declaration of Independence, is popularly viewed as the work of Thomas Jefferson. Yet if we examine the text closely in its rhetorical milieu, we see that Jefferson was author only in the very loosest of senses. A number of historians and at least two composition researchers (Kinneavy, *Theory* 393–49; Maimon, *Readings* 6–32) have analyzed the Declaration, with interesting results. Their work suggests that Jefferson was by no means an original framer or a creative genius, as some like to suppose. Jefferson was a skilled writer, to be sure, but chiefly because he was an effective borrower of traces. 8

To produce his original draft of the Declaration, Jefferson seems to have borrowed, either consciously or unconsciously, from his culture's Text. Much has been made of Jefferson's reliance on Locke's social contract theory (Becker). Locke's theory influenced colonial political philosophy, emerging in various 9 pamphlets and newspaper articles of the times, and served as the foundation for the opening section of the Declaration. The Declaration contains many traces that can be found in other, earlier documents. There are traces from a First Continental Congress resolution, a Massachusetts Council declaration, George Mason's "Declaration of Rights for Virginia," a political pamphlet of James Otis, and a variety of other sources, including a colonial play. The overall form of the Declaration (theoretical argument followed by list of grievances) strongly resembles, ironically, the English Bill of Rights of 1689, in which Parliament lists the abuses of James II and declares new powers for itself. Several of the abuses in the Declaration seem to have been taken, more or less verbatim, from a *Pennsylvania Evening Post* article. And the most memorable phrases in the Declaration seem to be least Jefferson's: "That all men are created equal" is a sentiment from Euripides which Jefferson copied in his literary commonplace book as a boy; "Life, Liberty, and the pursuit of Happiness" was a cliché of the times, appearing in numerous political documents (Dumbauld).

Though Jefferson's draft of the Declaration can hardly be considered his in any exclusive sense of authorship, the document underwent still more expropriation at the hands of Congress, who made eighty-six changes (Kinneavy, *Theory* 438). They cut the draft from 211 lines to 147. They did considerable editing to temper what they saw as Jefferson's emotional style: For example, Jefferson's phrase "sacred & undeniable" was changed to the more restrained "self-evident." Congress excised controversial passages, such as Jefferson's condemnation of slavery. Thus, we should find it instructive to note, Jefferson's few attempts at original expression were those least acceptable to Congress.

If Jefferson submitted the Declaration for a college writing class as his own writing, he might well be charged with plagiarism.[3] The idea of Jefferson as author is but convenient shorthand. Actually, the Declaration arose out of a cultural and rhetorical milieu, was composed of traces—and was, in effect, team written. Jefferson deserves credit for bringing disparate traces together, for helping to mold and articulate the milieu, for creating the all-important draft. Jefferson's skill as a writer was his ability to borrow traces effectively and to find appropriate contexts for them. As Michael Halliday says, "[C]reativeness does not consist in producing new sentences. The newness of a sentence is a quite unimportant—and unascertainable—property and 'creativity' in language lies in the speaker's ability to create new meanings: to realize the potentiality of language for the indefinite extension of its resources to new contexts of situation. . . . Our most 'creative' acts may be precisely among those that are realized through highly repetitive forms of behaviour" (*Explorations* 42). The creative writer is the creative borrower, in other words.

Intertextuality can be seen working similarly in contemporary forums. Recall this scene from a recent Pepsi commercial: A young boy in jeans jacket, accompanied by dog, stands in some desolate plains crossroads next to a gas station,

10

11

12

next to which is a soft drink machine. An alien spacecraft, resembling the one in Spielberg's *Close Encounters of the Third Kind*, appears overhead. To the boy's joyful amazement, the spaceship hovers over the vending machine and begins sucking Pepsi cans into the ship. It takes *only* Pepsis, then eventually takes the entire machine. The ad closes with a graphic: "Pepsi. The Choice of a New Generation."

Clearly, the commercial presupposes familiarity with Spielberg's movie or, at least, with his pacific vision of alien spacecraft. We see several American clichés, well-worn signs from the Depression era: the desolate plains, the general store, the pop machine, the country boy with dog. These distinctively American traces are juxtaposed against images from science fiction and the sixties catch-phrase "new generation" in the coda. In this array of signs, we have tradition and counter-tradition harmonized. Pepsi squeezes itself in the middle, and thus becomes the great American conciliator. The ad's use of irony may serve to distract viewers momentarily from noticing how Pepsi achieves its purpose by assigning itself an exalted role through use of the intertext. 13

We find an interesting example of practical presupposition in John Kifner's *New York Times* headline article reporting on the Kent State incident of 1970: 14

> Four students at Kent State University, two of them women, were shot to death this afternoon by a volley of National Guard gunfire. At least 8 other students were wounded.
>
> The burst of gunfire came about 20 minutes after the guardsmen broke up a noon rally on the Commons, a grassy campus gathering spot, by lobbing tear gas at a crowd of about 1,000 young people.

From one perspective, the phrase "two of them women" is a simple state-ment of fact; however, it presupposes a certain attitude—that the event, horri-ble enough as it was, is more significant because two of the persons killed were women. It might be going too far to say that the phrase presupposes a sexist attitude ("women aren't supposed to be killed in battles"), but can we imag-ine the phrase "two of them men" in this context? Though equally factual, this wording would have been considered odd in 1970 (and probably today as well) because it presupposes a cultural mindset alien from the one dominant at the time. "Two of them women" is shocking (and hence it was reported) because it upsets the sense of order of the readers, in this case the American public. 15

Additionally (and more than a little ironically), the text contains a number of traces which have the effect of blunting the shock of the event. Notice that the students were not shot by National Guardsmen, but were shot "by a volley of . . . gunfire"; the tear gas was "lobbed"; and the event occurred at a "grassy campus gathering spot." "Volley" and "lobbed" are military terms, but with connections to sport as well; "grassy campus gathering spot" suggests a picnic; "burst" can recall the glorious sight of bombs "bursting" in "The Star-Spangled Banner." 16

421

This pastiche of signs casts the text into a certain context, making it distinctively American. We might say that the turbulent milieu of the sixties provided a distinctive array of signs from which John Kifner borrowed to produce his article.

Each of the three texts examined contains phrases or images familiar to its 17 audience or presupposes certain audience attitudes. Thus the intertext exerts its influence partly in the form of audience expectation. We might then say that the audience of each of these texts is as responsible for its production as the writer. That, in essence, readers, not writers, create discourse.

THE POWER OF DISCOURSE COMMUNITY

And, indeed, this is what some poststructuralist critics suggest, those who prefer 18 a broader conception of intertext or who look beyond the intertext to the social framework regulating textual production: to what Michel Foucault calls "the discursive formation," what Stanley Fish calls "the interpretive community," and what Patricia Bizzell calls "the discourse community."

A "discourse community" is a group of individuals bound by a common 19 interest who communicate through approved channels and whose discourse is regulated. An individual may belong to several professional, public, or personal discourse communities. Examples would include the community of engineers whose research area is fluid mechanics; alumni of the University of Michigan; Magnavox employees; the members of the Porter family; and members of the Indiana Teachers of Writing. The approved channels we can call "forums." Each forum has a distinct history and rules governing appropriateness to which members are obliged to adhere. These rules may be more or less apparent, more or less institutionalized, more or less specific to each community. Examples of forums include professional publications like *Rhetoric Review, English Journal*, and *Creative Computing*; public media like *Newsweek* and *Runner's World*; professional conferences (the annual meeting of fluid power engineers, the 4C's); company board meetings; family dinner tables; and the monthly meeting of the Indiana chapter of the Izaak Walton League.

A discourse community shares assumptions about what objects are appro- 20 priate for examination and discussion, what operating functions are performed on those objects, what constitutes "evidence" and "validity," and what formal conventions are followed. A discourse community may have a well-established *ethos*; or it may have competing factions and indefinite boundaries. It may be in a "pre-paradigm" state (Kuhn), that is, having an ill-defined regulating system and no clear leadership. Some discourse communities are firmly established, such as the scientific community, the medical profession, and the justice system, to cite a few from Foucault's list. In these discourse communities, as Leitch says, "a speaker must be 'qualified' to talk; he has to belong to a community of scholarship; and he is required to possess a prescribed body of knowledge (doctrine). . . . [This system] operates to constrain discourse; it establishes limits and regularities. . . . who may speak, what may be spoken, and how it is to be said; in addition [rules] prescribe what is true and false, what is reasonable and what foolish, and what is meant and what not. Finally, they work to deny the material existence of discourse itself" (145).

A text is "acceptable" within a forum only insofar as it reflects the commu-   21
nity episteme (to use Foucault's term). On a simple level, this means that for a manuscript to be accepted for publication in the *Journal of Applied Psychology*, it must follow certain formatting conventions: It must have the expected social science sections (i.e., review of literature, methods, results, discussion), and it must use the journal's version of APA documentation. However, these are only superficial features of the forum. On a more essential level, the manuscript must reveal certain characteristics, have an *ethos* (in the broadest possible sense) conforming to the standards of the discourse community: It must demonstrate (or at least claim) that it contributes knowledge to the field, it must demonstrate familiarity with the work of previous researchers in the field, it must use a scientific method in analyzing its results (showing acceptance of the truth-value of statistical demonstration), it must meet standards for test design and analysis of results, it must adhere to standards determining degree of accuracy. The expectations, conventions, and attitudes of this discourse community — the readers, writers, and publishers of *Journal of Applied Psychology* — will influence aspiring psychology researchers, shaping not only how they write but also their character within that discourse community.

The poststructuralist view challenges the classical assumption that writing is a simple linear, one-way movement: The writer creates a text which produces some change in an audience. A poststructuralist rhetoric examines how audience (in the form of community expectations and standards) influences textual production and, in so doing, guides the development of the writer.   22

> *A poststructuralist rhetoric examines how audience . . . influences textual production and, in so doing, guides the development of the writer.*

This view is of course open to criticism for its apparent determinism, for   23
devaluing the contribution of individual writers and making them appear merely tools of the discourse community (charges which Foucault answers in "Discourse on Language"). If these regulating systems are so constraining, how can an individual emerge? What happens to the idea of the lone inspired writer and the sacred autonomous text?

Both notions take a pretty hard knock. Genuine originality is difficult   24
within the confines of a well-regulated system. Genius is possible, but it may

be constrained. Foucault cites the example of Gregor Mendel, whose work in the nineteenth century was excluded from the prevailing community of biologists because he "spoke of objects, employed methods and placed himself within a theoretical perspective totally alien to the biology of his time. . . . Mendel spoke the truth, but he was not *dans le vrai* (within the true)" (224). Frank Lentricchia cites a similar example from the literary community: Robert Frost "achieved magazine publication only five times between 1895 and 1912, a period during which he wrote a number of poems later acclaimed . . . [because] in order to write within the dominant sense of the poetic in the United States in the last decade of the nineteenth century and the first decade of the twentieth, one had to employ a diction, syntax, and prosody heavily favoring Shelley and Tennyson. One also had to assume a certain stance, a certain world-weary idealism which took care not to refer too concretely to the world of which one was weary" (197, 199).

Both examples point to the exclusionary power of discourse communities 25 and raise serious questions about the freedom of the writer: chiefly, does the writer have any? Is any writer doomed to plagiarism? Can any text be said to be new? Are creativity and genius actually possible? Was Jefferson a creative genius or a blatant plagiarist?

Certainly we want to avoid both extremes. Even if the writer is locked into a 26 cultural matrix and is constrained by the intertext of the discourse community, the writer has freedom within the immediate rhetorical context.[4] Furthermore, successful writing helps to redefine the matrix—and in that way becomes creative. (Jefferson's Declaration contributed to defining the notion of America for its discourse community.) Every new text has the potential to alter the text in some way; in fact, every text admitted into a discourse community changes the constitution of the community—and discourse communities can revise their discursive practices, as the Mendel and Frost examples suggest.

Writing is an attempt to exercise the will, to identify the self within the con- 27 straints of some discourse community. We are constrained insofar as we must inevitably borrow the traces, codes, and signs which we inherit and which our discourse community imposes. We are free insofar as we do what we can to encounter and learn new codes, to intertwine codes in new ways, and to expand our semiotic potential—with our goal being to effect change and establish our identities within the discourse communities we choose to enter.

THE PEDAGOGY OF INTERTEXTUALITY

Intertextuality is not new. It may remind some of Eliot's notion of tradition, 28 though the parameters are certainly broader. It is an important concept, though. It counters what I see as one prevailing composition pedagogy, one favoring a romantic image of the writer, offering as role models the creative essayists, the Sunday Supplement freelancers, the Joan Didions, E. B. Whites, Calvin Trillins, and Russell Bakers. This dashing image appeals to our need for intellectual heroes; but underlying it may be an anti-rhetorical view: that writers are born, not made; that writing is individual, isolated, and internal; not social but eccentric.

This view is firmly set in the intertext of our discipline. Our anthologies 29 glorify the individual essayists, whose work is valued for its timelessness and creativity. Freshman rhetorics announce as the writer's proper goals personal insight, originality, and personal voice, or tell students that motivations for writing come from "within." Generally, this pedagogy assumes that such a thing as the writer actually exists — an autonomous writer exercising a free, creative will through the writing act — and that the writing process proceeds linearly from writer to text to reader. This partial picture of the process can all too readily become *the* picture, and our students can all too readily learn to overlook vital facets of discourse production.

When we romanticize composition by overemphasizing the autonomy of the 30 writer, important questions are overlooked, the same questions an intertextual view of writing would provoke: To what extent is the writer's product itself a part of a larger community writing process? How does the discourse community influence writers and readers within it? These are essential questions, but are perhaps outside the prevailing episteme of composition pedagogy, which presupposes the autonomous status of the writer as independent *cogito*. Talking about writing in terms of "social forces influencing the writer" raises the specter of determinism, and so is anathema.

David Bartholomae summarizes this issue very nicely: "The struggle of the 31 student writer is not the struggle to bring out that which is within; it is the struggle to carry out those ritual activities that grant our entrance into a closed society" (300). When we teach writing only as the act of "bringing out what is within," we risk undermining our own efforts. Intertextuality reminds us that "carrying out ritual activities" is also part of the writing process. Barthes reminds us that "the 'I' which approaches the text is already itself a plurality of other texts, of codes which are infinite" (10).

Intertextuality suggests that our goal should be to help students learn to write 32 for the discourse communities they choose to join. Students need help developing out of what Joseph Williams calls their "pre-socialized cognitive states." According to Williams, pre-socialized writers are not sufficiently immersed in their discourse community to produce competent discourse: They do not know what can be presupposed, are not conscious of the distinctive intertextuality of the community, may be only superficially acquainted with explicit conventions. (Williams cites the example of the freshman whose paper for the English teacher begins "Shakespeare is a famous Elizabethan dramatist.") Our immediate goal is to produce "socialized writers," who are full-fledged members of their discourse community, producing competent, useful discourse within that community. Our long-range goal might be "post-socialized writers," those who have achieved such a degree of confidence, authority, power, or achievement in the discourse community so as to become part of the regulating body. They are able to vary conventions and question assumptions — i.e., effect change in communities — without fear of exclusion.

Intertextuality has the potential to affect all facets of our composition ped- 33 agogy. Certainly it supports writing across the curriculum as a mechanism for introducing students to the regulating systems of discourse communities. It raises questions about heuristics: Do different discourse communities apply different heuristics? It asserts the value of critical reading in the composition classroom. It requires that we rethink our ideas about plagiarism: Certainly *imitatio* is an important stage in the linguistic development of the writer.

The most significant application might be in the area of audience analysis. 34 Current pedagogies assume that when writers analyze audiences they should focus on the expected flesh-and-blood readers. Intertextuality suggests that the proper focus of audience analysis is not the audience as receivers per se, but the intertext of the discourse community. Instead of collecting demographic data about age, educational level, and social status, the writer might instead ask questions about the intertext: What are the conventional presuppositions of this community? In what forums do they assemble? What are the methodological assumptions? What is considered "evidence," "valid argument," and "proof"? A sample heuristic for such an analysis — what I term "forum analysis" — is included as an appendix.

A critical reading of the discourse of a community may be the best way to 35 understand it. (We see a version of this message in the advice to examine a journal before submitting articles for publication.) Traditionally, anthologies have provided students with reading material. However, the typical anthologies have two serious problems: (1) limited range — generally they overemphasize literary or expressive discourse; (2) unclear context — they frequently remove readings from their original contexts, thus disguising their intertextual nature. Several recently published readers have attempted to provide a broader selection of readings in various forums, and actually discuss intertextuality. Maimon's *Readings in the Arts and Sciences*, Kinneavy's *Writing in the Liberal Arts Tradition*, and Bazerman's *The Informed Writer* are especially noteworthy.

Writing assignments should be explicitly intertextual. If we regard each writ- 36 ten product as a stage in a larger process — the dialectic process within a discourse community — then the individual writer's work is part of a web, part of a community search for truth and meaning. Writing assignments might take the form of dialogue with other writers: Writing letters in response to articles is one kind of dialectic (e.g., letters responding to *Atlantic Monthly* or *Science* articles). Research assignments might be more community oriented rather than topic oriented; students might be asked to become involved in communities of researchers (e.g., the sociologists examining changing religious attitudes in American college students). The assignments in Maimon's *Writing in the Arts and Sciences* are excellent in this regard.

Intertextual theory suggests that the key criteria for evaluating writing should 37 be "acceptability" within some discourse community. "Acceptability" includes, but goes well beyond, adherence to formal conventions. It includes choosing the "right" topic, applying the appropriate critical methodology, adhering to standards for evidence and validity, and in general adopting the community's discourse values—and of course borrowing the appropriate traces. Success is measured by the writer's ability to know what can be presupposed and to borrow that community's traces effectively to create a text that contributes to the maintenance or, possibly, the definition of the community. The writer is constrained by the community, and by its intertextual preferences and prejudices, but the effective writer works to assert the will against those community constraints to effect change.

The Pepsi commercial and the Kent State news article show effective uses of 38 the intertext. In the Kent State piece, John Kifner mixes picnic imagery ("grassy campus gathering spot," "young people") with violent imagery ("burst of gunfire") to dramatize the event. The Pepsi ad writers combine two unlikely sets of traces, linking folksy Depression-era American imagery with sci-fi imagery "stolen" from Spielberg. For this creative intertwining of traces, both discourses can probably be measured successful in their respective forums.

CODA

Clearly much of what intertextuality supports is already institutionalized (e.g., 39 writing-across-the-curriculum programs). And yet, in freshman comp texts and anthologies especially, there is this tendency to see writing as individual, as isolated, as heroic. Even after demonstrating quite convincingly that the Declaration was written by a team freely borrowing from a cultural intertext, Elaine Maimon insists, against all the evidence she herself has collected, that "Despite the additions, deletions, and changes in wording that it went through, the Declaration is still Jefferson's writing" (*Readings* 26). Her saying this presupposes that the reader has just concluded the opposite.

When we give our students romantic role models like E. B. White, Joan Didion, 40 and Lewis Thomas, we create unrealistic expectations. This type of writer has often achieved post-socialized status within some discourse community (Thomas in the scientific community, for instance). Can we realistically expect our students to achieve this state without first becoming socialized, without learning first what it means to write within a social context? Their role models ought not be only romantic heroes but also community writers like Jefferson, the anonymous writers of the Pepsi commercial—the Adsos of the world, not just the Aristotles.

427

They need to see writers whose products are more evidently part of a larger process and whose work more clearly produces meaning in social contexts.

Notes

1. The dangers of defining intertextuality too simplistically are discussed by Owen Miller in "Intertextual Identity," *Identity of the Literary Text*, ed. Mario J. Valdés and Owen Miller (Toronto: U of Toronto P, 1985), 19–40. Miller points out that intertextuality "addresses itself to a plurality of concepts" (19).

2. For fuller discussion see Jonathan Culler, *The Pursuit of Signs* (Ithaca: Cornell UP, 1981), 100–16. Michael Halliday elaborates on the theory of presupposition somewhat, too, differentiating between exophoric and endophoric presupposition. The meaning of any text at least partly relies on exophoric references, i.e., external presuppositions. Endophoric references in the form of cohesive devices and connections within a text also affect meaning, but cohesion in a text depends ultimately on the audience making exophoric connections to prior texts, connections that may not be cued by explicit cohesive devices. See M. A. K. Halliday and Ruqaiya Hasan, *Cohesion in English* (London: Longman, 1976).

3. Miller cautions us about intertextuality and *post hoc ergo propter hoc* reasoning. All we can safely note is that phrases in the Declaration also appear in other, earlier documents. Whether or not the borrowing was intentional on Jefferson's part or whether the prior documents "caused" the Declaration (in any sense of the word) is not ascertainable.

4. Robert Scholes puts it this way: "If you play chess, you can only do certain things with the pieces, otherwise you are not playing chess. But those constraints do not in themselves tell you what moves to make." See *Textual Power* (New Haven: Yale UP, 1985), 153.

Works Cited

Barthes, Roland. *S/Z*. Trans. Richard Miller. New York: Hill and Wang, 1974.

Bartholomae, David. "Writing Assignments: Where Writing Begins." *fforum*. Ed. Patricia L. Stock. Upper Montclair, NJ: Boynton/Cook, 1983.

Bazerman, Charles. *The Informed Writer*. 2nd ed. Boston: Houghton Mifflin, 1985.

Becker, Carl. *The Declaration of Independence*. 2nd ed. New York: Random, Vintage, 1942.

Bizzell, Patricia. "Cognition, Convention, and Certainty: What We Need to Know about Writing." *PRE/TEXT* 3 (1982): 213–43.

Culler, Jonathan. *The Pursuit of Signs*. Ithaca: Cornell UP, 1981.

Dumbauld, Edward. *The Declaration of Independence*. 2nd ed. Norman: U of Oklahoma P, 1968.

Eco, Umberto. *The Name of the Rose*. Trans. William Weaver. San Diego: Harcourt Brace Jovanovich, 1983.

Fish, Stanley. *Is There a Text in This Class?* Cambridge: Harvard UP, 1980.

Foucault, Michel. *The Archaeology of Knowledge and the Discourse on Language*. Trans. A. M. Sheridan Smith. New York: Harper & Row, 1972.

Halliday, M. A. K. *Explorations in the Functions of Language*. New York: Elsevier, 1973.

Halliday, M. A. K., and Ruqaiya Hasan. *Cohesion in English*. London: Longman, 1976.

Kifner, John. "4 Kent State Students Killed by Troops." *New York Times* (5 May 1970): 1.

Kinneavy, James L. *A Theory of Discourse.* Englewood Cliffs: Prentice-Hall, 1971.

——, et al. *Writing in the Liberal Arts Tradition.* New York: Harper & Row, 1985.

Kuhn, Thomas S. *The Structure of Scientific Revolutions.* 2nd ed. Chicago: U of Chicago P, 1970.

Leitch, Vincent B. *Deconstructive Criticism.* New York: Cornell UP, 1983.

Lentricchia, Frank. *After the New Criticism.* Chicago: U of Chicago P, 1980.

Maimon, Elaine P., et al. *Readings in the Arts and Sciences.* Boston: Little, Brown, 1984.

——, *Writing in the Arts and Sciences.* Cambridge: Winthrop, 1981.

Miller, Owen. "Intertextual Identity." *Identity of the Literary Text.* Ed. Mario J. Valdés and Owen Miller. Toronto: U of Toronto P, 1985, 19–40.

Scholes, Robert. *Textual Power.* New Haven: Yale UP, 1985.

Williams, Joseph. "Cognitive Development, Critical Thinking, and the Teaching of Writing." Conference on Writing, Meaning, and Higher Order Reasoning, University of Chicago, 15 May 1984.

Appendix

Forum Analysis

Background

— Identify the forum by name and organizational affiliation.

— Is there an expressed editorial policy, philosophy, or expression of belief? What purpose does the forum serve? Why does it exist?

— What is the disciplinary orientation?

— How large is the forum? Who are its members? Its leaders? Its readership?

— In what manner does the forum assemble (e.g., newsletter, journal, conference, weekly meeting)? How frequently?

— What is the origin of the forum? Why did it come into existence? What is its history? Its political background? Its traditions?

— What reputation does the forum have among its own members? How is it regarded by others?

Discourse Conventions

Who Speaks/Writes?

— Who is granted status as speaker/writer? Who decides who speaks/writes in the forum? By what criteria are speakers/writers selected?

— What kind of people speak/write in this forum? Credentials? Disciplinary orientation? Academic or professional background?

— Who are the important figures in this forum? Whose work or experience is most frequently cited?

— What are the important sources cited in the forum? What are the key works, events, experiences that it is assumed members of the forum know?

To Whom Do They Speak / Write?

— Who is addressed in the forum? What are the characteristics of the assumed audience?

— What are the audience's needs assumed to be? To what use(s) is the audience expected to put the information?

— What is the audience's background assumed to be? Level of proficiency, experience, and knowledge of subject matter? Credentials?

— What are the beliefs, attitudes, values, prejudices of the addressed audience?

What Do They Speak / Write About?

— What topics or issues does the forum consider? What are allowable subjects? What topics are valued?

— What methodology or methodologies are accepted? Which theoretical approach is preferred: deduction (theoretical argumentation) or induction (evidence)?

— What constitutes "validity," "evidence," and "proof" in the forum (e.g., personal experience / observation, testing and measurement, theoretical or statistical analysis)?

How Do They Say / Write It?

Form

— What types of discourse does the forum admit (e.g., articles, reviews, speeches, poems)? How long are the discourses?

— What are the dominant modes of organization?

— What formatting conventions are present: headings, tables and graphs, illustrations, abstracts?

Style

— What documentation form(s) is used?

— Syntactic characteristics?

— Technical or specialized jargon? Abbreviations?

— Tone? What stance do writers / speakers take relative to audience?

— Manuscript mechanics?

Other Considerations?

Questions for Discussion and Journaling

1. After you read the first page of the article, we asked you to define *intertextuality*. Now that you are finished reading the entire article, define it again. How, if at all, do your two definitions differ?

2. Do you agree with Porter that intertext — the great web of texts built on and referring to each other — makes individual writers less important? Why or why not?

3. Why does Porter call the idea of an autonomous writer "romantic" (para. 4)?

4. Porter argues that the key criterion for evaluating writing should be its "acceptability" within the reader's community. How is this different from the way you might have assumed writing should be evaluated prior to reading his article? How is it different from the way(s) your own writing has been evaluated in the past?

5. If Porter is right about intertextuality and its effects on originality, then his article must not be "original," and he must not be writing as an "autonomous individual." How does his own work reflect — or fail to reflect — the principles he's writing about?

6. What harm is there, according to Porter, in imagining writing "as individual, as isolated, as heroic" (para. 39)? What problems does it cause?

Applying and Exploring Ideas

1. Choose a commercial or advertisement you've seen recently and search for traces of intertextuality in it. How many texts can you find represented in it? How do you find *cultural* intertext represented in it?

2. If we accept Porter's argument, then the typical school definition of plagiarism seems oversimplified or inaccurate. Rewrite the plagiarism policy for the course you're in now so that it accounts for Porter's notion of plagiarism but still keeps students from cheating. When you're finished, compare the original and your revised version. How much and in what ways do they differ?

3. Downs's reading earlier in this chapter describes the concept of rhetorical ecology. Briefly summarize what he meant by this term. Then, explain how Porter's description of intertextuality aligns with, relates to, or helps you better understand the idea of rhetorical ecology.

- -

META MOMENT Many of us have been taught to imagine "writers" as people who work more or less alone to get their ideas down in print. Has Porter's study changed the way you imagine writers and writing? Would adopting his notion of writers and writing change the way you write?

- -

Rhetorical Reading Strategies and the Construction of Meaning

CHRISTINA HAAS

LINDA FLOWER

Framing the Reading

In the late 1980s and early 1990s, Christina Haas and Linda Flower were doing research on how reading contributes to writing at Carnegie Mellon University's Center for the Study of Writing. Specifically, they were trying to understand what experienced readers do differently from less-experienced ones. What they found was that more-experienced readers used what they called **rhetorical** reading strategies to more efficiently come to an understanding of difficult texts.

Haas and Flower's research makes use of a somewhat imperfect method of investigation called a *think-aloud protocol* (also used by Berkenkotter and Murray and Perl in Chapter 4). Because we can't see what people think, we can at least try to hear some of what they're thinking by asking them to "think out loud." So research participants are asked first to read aloud and then to describe what they're thinking while they try to understand what the text means. The researchers make tapes of this talk, which are later transcribed for further study. The method is a good way of capturing some of what's going on in people's heads, but you may be able to see potential drawbacks to it as well.

If you read Keith Grant-Davie's article on rhetorical situations, you'll remember our discussion of the term *rhetoric* as descriptive of texts that accomplish or do things (like get you to buy a car or get you married or get you into war). Haas and Flower help us think about another angle of rhetoric: the motivation of the rhetors (speakers and writers) and the context in which the texts they create are written and read.

It may help you to know, in reading this piece, that Carnegie Mellon has been the scene of a lot of research on artificial

Haas, Christina, and Linda Flower. "Rhetorical Reading Strategies and the Construction of Meaning." *College Composition and Communication*, vol. 39, no. 2, May 1988, pp. 167–83.

intelligence — how to make machines able to think like humans. In research conducted around the time the article was written, human brains were often thought of as "information processors" much like computers — working with memory, central processors, inputs and outputs, and sensory data. Because this way of understanding the human mind was "in the air" (everyone was talking more or less this way) at that time, Haas and Flower's article carries some of that sense, too, and, for better or worse, they tend to talk about minds as quite machine-like. Knowing that, you understand a little more of the context of this article, and (Haas and Flower would say) that means you're a little better equipped to make sense of it.

This article is about reading, so you might wonder how it relates to the underlying threshold concept of this chapter, that "good" writing depends on context. But as we laid out in the introduction to the chapter, readers and writers are always working (imperfectly) to construct meaning. It is easy to misunderstand or misinterpret a piece of writing, and even when readers understand fairly well what a writer means to say, they are always making their own meanings in light of their own prior experiences, recent events, local context, and knowledge. Readers' individuality is thus part of what "good" or "effective" or "clear" writing depends on.

Getting Ready to Read

Before you read, do at least one of the following activities:

- Ask a couple of friends how they read: When do they pay attention to the writer of the text they are reading? When do they look up information like definitions or background on the subject? What strategies do they use to keep track of what they're reading (highlighting, notes in the margins, etc.)? When they encounter material they don't understand, what do they do to try to understand it? Make a list of your friends' answers and compare them with your own practices as a reader.
- Make a quick self-assessment of your reading abilities by answering the following questions: What are you good at, as a reader? What do you think you're not good at when it comes to reading? Is there anything you wish you had been taught better or differently?

As you read, consider the following questions:

- How does the reading style that Haas and Flower recommend compare with your own habits of reading and understanding texts?
- What does it mean to *construct* the meaning of a text rather than to "extract" it or find it "in" the text?
- What, according to Haas and Flower, are more-experienced readers doing that less-experienced readers aren't?

THERE IS A GROWING consensus in our field that reading should be 1 thought of as a constructive rather than as a receptive process: that "meaning" does not exist in a text but in readers and the representations they build. This constructive view of reading is being vigorously put forth, in different ways, by both literary theory and cognitive research. It is complemented by work in rhetoric which argues that reading is also a discourse act. That is, when readers construct meaning, they do so in the context of a discourse situation, which includes the writer of the original text, other readers, the rhetorical context for reading, and the history of the discourse. If reading really is this constructive, rhetorical process, it may both demand that we rethink how we teach college students to read texts and suggest useful parallels between the act of reading and the more intensively studied process of writing. However, our knowledge of how readers actually carry out this interpretive process with college-level expository texts is rather limited. And a process we can't describe may be hard to teach.

> There is a growing consensus in our field that reading should be thought of as a constructive rather than as a receptive process: that "meaning" does not exist in a text but in readers and the representations they build.

We would like to help extend this constructive, rhetorical view of reading, 2 which we share with others in the field, by raising two questions. The first is, how does this constructive process play itself out in the actual, thinking process of reading? And the second is, are all readers really aware of or in control of the discourse act which current theories describe? In the study we describe below, we looked at readers trying to understand a complex college-level text and observed a process that was constructive in a quite literal sense of the term. Using a think-aloud procedure, we watched as readers used not only the text but their own knowledge of the world, of the topic, and of discourse conventions, to infer, set and discard hypotheses, predict, and question in order to construct meaning for texts. One of the ways readers tried to make meaning of the text was a strategy we called "rhetorical reading," an active attempt at constructing a rhetorical context for the text as a way of making sense of it. However, this valuable move was a special strategy used only by more experienced readers. We observed a sharp distinction between the rhetorical process these experienced readers demonstrated and the processes of freshman readers. It may be that these student readers, who relied primarily on text-based strategies to construct their meanings, do not have the same full sense of reading as the rhetorical or social discourse act we envision.

Some of the recent work on reading and cognition gives us a good starting 3 point for our discussion since it helps describe what makes the reading process so complex and helps explain how people can construct vastly different inter-pretations of the same text. Although a thinking-aloud protocol can show us a great deal, we must keep in mind that it reveals only part of what goes on as a reader is building a representation of a text. And lest the "constructive" met-aphor makes this process sound tidy, rational, and fully conscious, we should emphasize that it may in fact be rapid, unexamined, and even inexpressible. The private mental representation that a reader constructs has many facets: it is likely to include a representation of propositional or content information, a representation of the structure—either conventional or unique—of that infor-mation, and a representation of how the parts of the text function. In addition, the reader's representation may include beliefs about the subject matter, about the author and his or her credibility, and about the reader's own intentions in reading. In short, readers construct meaning by building multi-faceted interwo-ven representations of knowledge. The current text, prior texts, and the read-ing context can exert varying degrees of influence on this process, but it is the reader who must integrate information into meaning.

We can begin to piece together the way this constructive, cognitive process 4 operates based on recent research on reading and comprehension, and on read-ing and writing. Various syntheses of this work have been provided by Baker and Brown; Bransford; Flower ("Interpretive Acts"); and Spivey. To begin with, it is helpful to imagine the representations readers build as complex networks, like dense roadmaps, made up of many nodes of information, each related to others in multiple ways. The nodes created during a few minutes of reading would probably include certain content propositions from the text. The net-work might also contain nodes for the author's name, for a key point in the text, for a personal experience evoked by the text, for a striking word or phrase, and for an inference the reader made about the value of the text, or its social or personal significance. The links between a group of nodes might reflect causal-ity, or subordination, or simple association, or a strong emotional connection.

The process of constructing this representation is carried out by both highly 5 automated processes of recognition and inference *and* by the more active problem-solving processes on which our work focuses. For instance, trying to construct a well-articulated statement of the "point" of a text may require active searching, inferencing, and transforming of one's own knowledge. The reason such transformations are constantly required can be explained by the "multiple-representation thesis" proposed by Flower and Hayes ("Images" 120). It suggests that readers' and writers' mental representations are not limited to verbally well-formed ideas and plans, but may include information coded as visual images, or as emotions, or as linguistic propositions that exist just above the level of specific words. These representations may also reflect more abstract schema, such as the schema most people have for narrative or for establishing credibility in a conversation. Turning information coded in any of these forms into a fully verbal articulation of the "point," replete with well-specified connections between ideas and presented according to the standard conventions of a given discourse, is constructive; it can involve not only translating one kind of representation into another, but reorganizing knowledge and creating new knowledge, new conceptual nodes and connections. In essence, it makes sense to take the metaphor of "construction" seriously.

It should be clear that this image of "meaning" as a rich network of disparate 6 kinds of information is in sharp contrast to the narrow, highly selective and fully verbal statement of a text's gist or "meaning" that students may be asked to construct for an exam or a book review. Statements of that sort do, of course, serve useful functions, but we should not confuse them with the multi-dimensional, mental structures of meaning created by the cognitive and affective process of reading.

If reading, then, is a process of responding to cues in the text and in the 7 reader's context to build a complex, multi-faceted representation of meaning, it should be no surprise that different readers might construct radically different representations of the same text and might use very different strategies to do so. This makes the goals of teacher and researcher look very much alike: both the teacher and the researcher are interested in the means by which readers (especially students) construct multi-faceted representations, or "meaning." The study we are about to describe looks at a practical and theoretical question that this constructive view of reading raises: namely, what strategies, other than those based on knowing the topic, do readers bring to the process of understanding difficult texts—and how does this translate into pedagogy?

Seeing reading as a constructive act encourages us as teachers to move from 8 merely *teaching texts* to *teaching readers*. The teacher as co-reader can both model a sophisticated reading process and help students draw out the rich possibilities of texts and readers, rather than trying to insure that all students interpret texts in a single, "correct" way—and in the same way. Yet this goal—drawing out the rich possibilities of texts and of readers—is easier to describe than to reach.

WHAT IS "GOOD READING"?

The notion of multiple, constructed representations also helps us understand 9 a recurring frustration for college teachers: the problem of "good" readers who appear to miss the point or who seem unable or unwilling to read critically. Many of our students are "good" readers in the traditional sense: they have large vocabularies, read quickly, are able to do well at comprehension tasks involving recall of content. They can identify topic sentences, introductions and conclusions, generalizations and supporting details. Yet these same students often frustrate us, as they paraphrase rather than analyze, summarize rather than criticize texts. Why are these students doing less than we hope for?

To interpret any sophisticated text seems to require not only careful reading 10 and prior knowledge, but the ability to read the text on several levels, to build multi-faceted representations. A text is understood not only as content and information, but also as the result of someone's intentions, as part of a larger discourse world, and as having real effects on real readers. In an earlier study, we say that experienced readers made active use of the strategy of rhetorical reading not only to predict and interpret texts but to solve problems in comprehension (Flower, "Construction of Purpose"). Vipond and Hunt have observed a related strategy of "point-driven" (vs. "story-driven") reading which people bring to literary texts.

If we view reading as the act of constructing multi-faceted yet integrated rep- 11 resentations, we might hypothesize that the problem students have with critical reading of difficult texts is less the representations they *are* constructing than those they *fail to construct.* Their representations of text are closely tied to content: they read for information. Our students may believe that if they understand all the words and can paraphrase the propositional content of a text, then they have successfully "read" it.

While a content representation is often satisfactory—it certainly meets the 12 needs of many pre-college read-to-take-a-test assignments—it falls short with tasks or texts which require analysis and criticism. What many of our students *can* do is to construct representations of content, of structure, and of conventional features. What they often *fail to do* is to move beyond content and convention and construct representations of texts as purposeful actions, arising from contexts, and with intended effects. "Critical reading" involves more than careful reading for content, more than identification of conventional features of discourse, such as introductions or examples, and more than simple evaluation based on agreeing or disagreeing. Sophisticated, difficult texts often require the reader to build an equally sophisticated, complex representation of meaning. But how does this goal translate into the process of reading?

As intriguing as this notion of the active construction of meaning is, we 13 really have no direct access to the meanings / representations that readers build. We cannot enter the reader's head and watch as the construction of meaning proceeds. Nor can we get anything but an indirect measure of the nature, content, and structure of that representation. What we can do, however, is to watch the way that readers go about building representations: we can observe their use of *reading strategies* and so infer something about the representations they build.

In order to learn something about the construction of meaning by readers, 14 we observed and analyzed the strategies of ten readers. Four were experienced college readers, graduate students (aged 26 to 31 years), three in engineering and one in rhetoric; six were student readers, college freshmen aged 18 and 19, three classified "average" and three classified "above average" by their freshman composition teachers.

We were interested in how readers go about "constructing" meaning and 15
the constructive strategies they use to do so. However, we suspected that many
academic topics would give an unfair advantage to the more experienced readers, who would be able to read automatically by invoking their knowledge of
academic topics and discourse conventions. This automaticity would, however,
make their constructive reading harder for us to see. We wanted a text that would
require equally active problem solving by both groups. So, in order to control for
such knowledge, we designed a task in which meaning was under question for all
readers, and in which prior topic knowledge would function as only one of many
possible tools used to build an interpretation. Therefore, the text began *in medias
res*, without orienting information about author, source, topic, or purpose. We
felt that in this way we could elicit the full range of constructive strategies these
readers could call upon when the situation demanded it.

The text, part of the preface to Sylvia Farnham-Diggory's *Cognitive Processes* 16
in Education, was like many texts students read, easy to decode but difficult to
interpret, with a high density of information and a number of semi-technical
expressions which had to be defined from context. The readers read and
thought aloud as they read. In addition, they answered the question "how do
you interpret the text now?" at frequent intervals. The question was asked of
readers eight times, thus creating nine reading "episodes." The slash marks indicate where the question appeared, and also mark episode boundaries, which
we discuss later. To see the effect of this manipulation on eliciting interpretive
strategies, you might wish to read the experimental text before going further.
(Sentence numbers have been added.)

> But somehow the social muddle persists.[s1] Some wonderful children
> come from appalling homes; some terrible children come from splendid
> homes.[s2] Practice may have a limited relationship to perfection—at least it
> cannot substitute for talent.[s3] Women are not happy when they are required
> to pretend that a physical function is equivalent to a mental one.[s4] Many
> children teach themselves to read years before they are supposed to be
> "ready."[s5] / Many men would not dream of basing their self-esteem on "cave
> man" prowess.[s6] And despite their verbal glibness, teenagers seem to be in a
> worse mess than ever.[s7] /
>
> What has gone wrong?[s8] Are the psychological principles invalid?[s9] Are
> they too simple for a complex world?[s10] /
>
> Like the modern world, modern scientific psychology is extremely
> technical and complex.[s11] The application of any particular set of
> psychological principles to any particular real problem requires a double
> specialist: a specialist in the scientific area, and a specialist in the real area.[s12] /
>
> Not many such double specialists exist.[s13] The relationship of a child's
> current behavior to his early home life, for example, is not a simple

problem—Sunday Supplement psychology notwithstanding.[s14] / Many variables must be understood and integrated: special ("critical") periods of brain sensitivity, nutrition, genetic factors, the development of attention and perception, language, time factors (for example, the amount of time that elapses between a baby's action and a mother's smile), and so on.[s15] Mastery of these principles is a full-time professional occupation.[s16] / The professional application of these principles—in, say a day-care center—is also a full-time occupation, and one that is foreign to many laboratory psychologists.[s17] Indeed, a laboratory psychologist may not even recognize his pet principles when they are realized in a day care setting.[s18] /

What is needed is a coming together of real-world and laboratory specialists that will require both better communication and more complete experience.[s19] / The laboratory specialists must spend some time in a real setting; the real-world specialists must spend some time in a theoretical laboratory.[s20] Each specialist needs to practice thinking like his counterpart.[s21] Each needs to practice translating theory into reality, and reality into theory.[s22]

The technique of in-process probing tries to combine the immediacy of con- 17 current reporting with the depth of information obtained through frequent questioning. It can of course give us only an indirect and partial indication of the actual representation. What it does reveal are gist-making strategies used at a sequence of points during reading, and it offers a cumulative picture of a text-under-construction.

Aside from our manipulation of the presentation, the text was a typical col- 18 lege reading task. Part of the author's introduction to an educational psychology textbook, it presented an array of facts about the social reality of learning, problems of education, and the aims of research. *Our* reading of the text, obviously also a constructed one, but one constructed with the benefit of a full knowledge of the source and context, included two main facts and two central claims. In a later analysis, we used these facts and claims to describe some of the transactions of readers and text.

Fact: Social problems exist and psychological principles exist, but there's a mismatch between them.

Fact: There are two kinds of educational specialists—real-world and laboratory.

Claim (explicit in text): The two kinds of specialists should interact.

Claim (implicit): Interaction of the two specialists is necessary to solve social problems.

The differences in "readings" subjects constructed of the text were striking 19 and were evidenced immediately. For instance, the following descriptions of three readers' readings of the text suggest the range of readers' concerns and begin to offer hints about the nature of their constructed representations of the text. These descriptions were what we called "early transactions" with the text—an analysis based on readers' comments during reading of the first two paragraphs, or ten sentences, of the text.

Seth, a 27-year-old graduate student in Engineering, by his own account a 20 voracious reader of literature in his own field, of travel books, history, and contemporary novels, is initially confused with the concepts "physical function and mental one" (sentence 4). He then explains his confusion by noting the nature of the materials: "Well, that's got some relationship with something that came before this business."

Kara, a freshman who does average college work, also thinks the text is con- 21 fusing; specifically, she says "I don't know what glibness means" (sentence 7). But whereas Seth sets up a hypothesis about both the content of the text and its source—"I think it's part of an article on the fact that the way you turn out is not a function of your environment"—and reads on to confirm his hypothesis, Kara's reading proceeds as a series of content paraphrases—"It's talking about children coming from different homes . . . and women not being happy." She continues to interpret the text a chunk at a time, paraphrasing linearly with little attempt to integrate or connect the parts. She reacts positively to the text—"I love the expression 'what has gone wrong'" (sentence 8)—and, despite her initial confusion with "glibness," she seems satisfied with her simple reading: "I just feel like you're talking about people—what's wrong with them and the world."

Not all the freshman student readers' transactions with the text were as 22 superficial and oversimplified as Kara's—nor were they all as contented with their readings of the text. Bob—an above-average freshman with a pre-med major—paraphrases content linearly like Kara, but he also sets up a hypothetical structure for the text: "It seems that different points are being brought out and each one has a kind of a contradiction in it, and it seems like an introduction. . . ." Unlike Kara, however, he becomes frustrated, unable to reconcile his own beliefs with what he's reading: "Well, I don't think they're too simple for a complex world. I don't think these are very simple things that are being said here. I think the situations—women, children, and men—I think they're pretty complex . . . so I don't understand why it said 'too simple for a complex world'" (sentence 10).

Our more experienced reader, Seth, also sets up a hypothesis about the text's 23 structure: "Maybe he's [the author] contrasting the verbal glibness with caveman instinct." But Seth goes further: "I think the author is trying to say that it's some balance between your natural instinct and your surroundings but he's not sure what that balance is." These hypotheses try to account for not only the propositional content of the text, but also the function of parts ("contrasting"), the author's intent, and even the author's own uncertainty.

Seth continues to read the text, noting his own inexperience with the area of psychology—"I'm thinking about Freud and I really don't know much about psychology"—and trying to tie what he has just read to the previous paragraph: "I guess the psychological principles have something to do with the way children turn out. But I don't know if they are the physical, environmental things or if they're a function of your surroundings and education." 24

In these "early transactions" with the text, we see a range of readings and vast differences in the information contained in the readers' representations: Kara is uncertain of the meaning of a word and somewhat confused generally; she paraphrases content and is satisfied with the text and her reading of it. If we have a hint about the representations of text that Kara is building it is that they are focused primarily on content and her own affective responses and that they are somewhat more limited than those of the other readers. Bob's comments suggest that he may be building representations of structure as well as content, and that he is trying to bring his own beliefs and his reading of the text into line. 25

Seth is concerned with the content, with possible functions—both for parts of the text and for the text as a whole—with the author's intentions, with the experimental situation and with missing text; he also attends to his own knowledge (or lack of it) and to his prior reading experiences. What this suggests is that Seth is creating a multi-dimensional representation of the text that includes representations of its content, representations of the structure and function of the text, representations of author's intention and his own experience and knowledge as a reader of the text. 26

The "texts" or representations of meaning that the readers created as they were wrestling with the text and thinking aloud were dramatically different in both quantity—the amount of information they contained—and quality—the kinds of information they contained and the amount of the original text they accounted for. However, with no direct access to the internal representations that readers were building, we looked instead at the overt strategies they seemed to be using. 27

STRATEGIES FOR CONSTRUCTING MEANING

The initial transactions with text suggested some differences among readers. Our next move was to more systematically analyze these differences. Each protocol contained two kinds of verbalizations: actual reading of the text aloud and comments in which the readers were thinking aloud. About half of these comments were in response to the question, "How do you interpret the text now?" and the rest were unprompted responses. Each comment was sorted into one of three categories, based on what the readers seemed to be "attending to." This simple, three-part coding scheme distinguished between Content, Function / Feature, and Rhetorical reading strategies. These strategies are readily identifiable with some practice; our inter-rater reliability, determined by simple 28 pair-wise comparisons, averaged 82%. Later, after about 20 minutes' instruction in the context of a college reading classroom, students could identify the strategies in the reading of others with close to 70% reliability.

Comments coded as *content strategies* are concerned with content or topic 29 information, "what the text is about." The reader may be questioning, interpreting, or summing content, paraphrasing what the text "is about" or "is saying." The reader's goal in using content strategies seems to be getting information from the text. Some examples of comments coded as content strategies:

"So we're talking about psychological principles here."

"I think it's about changing social conditions, like families in which both parents work, and changing roles of women."

"I don't know what glibness is, so it's still confusing."

As Table 1 shows, both student and more experienced readers spent a large proportion of their effort using content strategies. On the average, 77% of the reading protocol was devoted to content strategies for students, 67% for the older readers. Building a representation of content seems to be very important for all of the readers we studied.

Function/feature strategies were used to refer to conventional, generic func- 30 tions of texts, or conventional features of discourse. These strategies seemed closely tied to the text: readers frequently named text parts, pointing to specific words, sentences, or larger sections of text—"This is the main point." "This must be an example," "I think this is the introduction." While content strategies seemed to be used to explain what the text was "saying," function/feature strategies were often used to name what the text was "doing": "Here he's contrasting," "This part seems to be explaining. . . ." In short, the use of these strategies suggests that readers are constructing spatial, functional, or relational structures for the text. Some examples of comments coded as function/feature strategies:

"I guess these are just examples."

"Is this the introduction?"

"This seems to be the final point."

TABLE 1 MEAN PROPORTION OF STRATEGIES USED

	STUDENTS	EXPERIENCED READERS
Content Strategies	77% (58.1)	67% (58.0)
Feature Strategies	22% (15.8)	20% (18.0)
Rhetorical Strategies	1%* (.3)	13%* (9.3)

*Difference significant at .05 level. Numbers in parentheses indicate the mean number of protocol statements in each category.

Predictably, these strategies accounted for less of the protocol than did the content strategies: 22% for students, 20% for more experienced readers (see Table 1). And the groups of readers looked similar in their use of this strategy. This, too, may be expected: Identifying features such as introductions, examples, and conclusions is standard fare in many junior high and high school curricula. In addition, these students are of at least average ability within a competitive private university. We might ask if more basic readers — without the skills or reading experiences of these students — might demonstrate less use of the function / feature strategies. Further, these readers were all reading from paper; people reading from computer screens — a number which is rapidly increasing — may have difficulty creating and recalling spatial and relational structures in texts they read and write on-line (Haas and Hayes 34–35).

Rhetorical strategies take a step beyond the text itself. They are concerned with 31 constructing a rhetorical situation for the text, trying to account for author's purpose, context, and effect on the audience. In rhetorical reading strategies readers use cues in the text, and their own knowledge of discourse situations, to re-create or infer the rhetorical situation of the text they are reading. There is some indication that these strategies were used to help readers uncover the actual "event" of the text, a unique event with a particular author and actual effects. One reader likened the author of the text to a contemporary rhetorician: "This sounds a little like Richard Young to me." Readers seem to be constructing a rhetorical situation for the text and relating *this* text to a larger world of discourse. These examples demonstrate some of the range of rhetorical strategies: comments concerned with author's purpose, context or source, intended audience, and actual effect. Some examples of rhetorical reading strategies:

"So the author is trying to make the argument that you need scientific specialists in psychology."

"I wonder if it [the article] is from *Ms.*"

"I don't think this would work for the man-in-the-street."

"I wonder, though, if this is a magazine article, and I wonder if they expected it to be so confusing."

While the groups of readers employed content and function / feature strategies 32 similarly, there is a dramatic difference in their use of the rhetorical strategy category. Less than 1% (in fact, one statement by one reader) of the students' protocols contained rhetorical strategies, while 13% of the experienced readers' effort went into rhetorical strategies. This is particularly striking when we consider the richness and wealth of information contained in these kinds of comments. For instance, setting this article into the context of *Ms.* magazine brings with it a wealth of unstated information about the kind of article that appears in that source, the kind of writers that contribute to it, and the kind of people who read it.

Rhetorical reading appears to be an "extra" strategy which some readers used 33 and others did not. Mann-Whitney analyses show no significant differences in the use of content or function / feature strategies, and an interesting — $p >$ 0.5 — difference between the two groups in use of rhetorical strategies. The small numbers in parentheses indicate the mean number of protocol statements in each category for each group of readers; the significance tests, however, were performed on the proportions of strategies used by each reader.

An example of two readers responding to a particularly difficult section of 34 text reveals the differences in the use of strategies even more clearly than do the numbers.

> *Student Reader*: Well, basically, what I said previously is that there seems to be a problem between the real-world and the laboratory, or ideal situation versus real situation, whatever way you want to put it — that seems to be it.

> *Experienced Reader*: Ok, again, real world is a person familiar with the social influences on a person's personality — things they read or hear on the radio. . . . And laboratory specialists are more trained in clinical psychology. And now I think this article is trying to propose a new field of study for producing people who have a better understanding of human behavior. This person is crying out for a new type of scientist or something. (Ph.D. Student in Engineering)

While the student reader is mainly creating a gist and paraphrasing content, the experienced reader does this and more — he then tries to infer the author's purpose and even creates a sort of strident persona for the writer. If readers can only build representations for which they have constructive tools or strategies, then it is clear that this student reader — and in fact all of the student readers we studied — are not building rhetorical representations of this text. In fact, these student readers seem to be focused almost exclusively on content. The student reader above is a case in point: her goal seems to be to extract information from the text, and once that is done — via a simple paraphrase — she is satisfied with her reading of the text. We called this type of content reading "knowledge-getting," to underscore the similarity to the knowledge-telling strategy identified by Bereiter and Scardamalia (72) in immature writers. In both knowledge-getting and knowledge-telling, the focus is on content; larger rhetorical purposes seem to play no role.

It is useful to see rhetorical reading not as a separate and different strategy but 35 as a progressive enlargement of the constructed meaning of a text. These student readers seldom "progressed" to that enlarged view. Reading for content is usually dominant and crucial — other kinds of strategies build upon content representations. Functions and features strategies are generic and conventional — easily identified in texts and often explicitly taught. Rhetorical strategies include not only a representation of discourse as discourse but as *unique* discourse with a real author, a specific purpose, and actual effects. This possible relationship between strategies may point to a building of skills, a progression which makes intuitive sense and is supported by what we know about how reading is typically taught and by teachers' reports of typical student reading problems.

The difference in the use that experienced and student readers make of these strategies does not in itself make a convincing case for their value. Rhetorical reading strategies certainly *look* more sophisticated and elaborate, but an important question remains: What does rhetorical reading *do* for readers? We might predict that constructing the additional rhetorical representation—requiring more depth of processing—would be an asset in particularly problematic reading tasks: texts in a subject area about which the reader knows little, or texts complex in structure. It might also be important in those reading tasks in which recognizing author's intention is crucial: propaganda, satire, even the interpretation of assignments in school.

However, let us consider a rival hypothesis for a moment: maybe rhetorical strategies are simply "frosting on the cake." Maybe good readers use these strategies because reading for information is easier for them, and they have extra cognitive resources to devote to what might be largely peripheral concerns of the rhetorical situation.

We suspect that this was not the case, that rhetorical reading is not merely "frosting on the cake" for several reasons: first, in the absence of a rhetorical situation for the text, *all* experienced readers constructed one. Second, the more experienced readers seemed to be using all the strategies in tandem; i.e., they used the rhetorical strategies to help construct content, and vice versa. They did not "figure out" the content, and then do rhetorical reading as an "embellishment." Rhetorical reading strategies were interwoven with other strategies as the readers constructed their reading of the texts.

And third, in the "tug of war" between text and reader which characterizes constructive reading (Tierney and Pearson 34), we found that the rhetorical readers seemed to recognize and assimilate more facts and claims into their reading of the text. Recall that there were two facts and two claims which we felt constituted a successful reading of this text. We used readers' recognition of these facts and claims to gauge and to describe the kind of representation they had constructed.

Fact: Social problems exist and psychological principles exist, but there's a mismatch between them.

Fact: There are two kinds of educational specialists—real-world and laboratory.

Claim (explicit in text): The two kinds of specialists should interact.

Claim (implicit): Interaction of the two specialists is necessary to solve social problems.

In recognizing facts in the text, both groups of readers did well. But there 40 were very interesting differences in the patterns of recognition of claims in the text. Readers who used the rhetorical strategies, first, recognized more claims, and second, identified claims sooner than other readers. As we described earlier, our presentation of the text to the readers created nine reading episodes; each asked for the readers' interpretation of "the text so far" at the end of the episode. This allowed us some measure of constructed meaning by plotting the points at which readers recognized each fact or claim. We said that readers recognized a claim when they mentioned it as a possibility. This "recognition" was often tentative; readers made comments such as "So maybe this section is saying the two kinds of scientists should communicate," or "I guess this could solve the stuff at the beginning about social muddle."

The "episode line" in Figure 1 shows the points at which two readers (a stu- 41 dent and a more-experienced reader) recognized Claim 1, plotted in relation to the point at which the text would reasonably permit such recognition. Figure 2 shows this information for the same readers recognizing Claim 2. Claim 2 is never explicitly stated, it only becomes easy to infer in the final episode. Of all the implicit meanings the text *could* convey, we saw this second claim as central to the coherence of the argument.

As Figure 3 illustrates, all student readers got Claim 1, but only at episode 9, 42 where it was explicitly stated—for the second time—in the text. (Claim 1 is first stated in episode 8.) More experienced readers, on the other hand, had all inferred Claim 1 much earlier—by episode 7. In addition, student readers did not recognize the unstated second claim at all, although all experienced readers inferred it, some as early as episode 8.

At episode 4 (the first point at which it would be possible to infer Claim 1), 43 25% of the experienced readers had inferred and mentioned this idea.

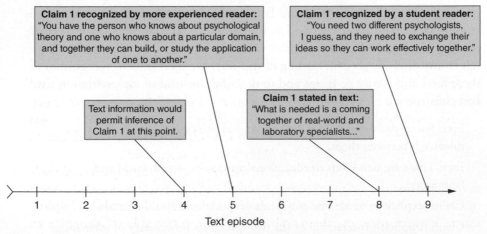

Figure 1 When did a reader recognize Claim 1? "The two kinds of specialists should interact."

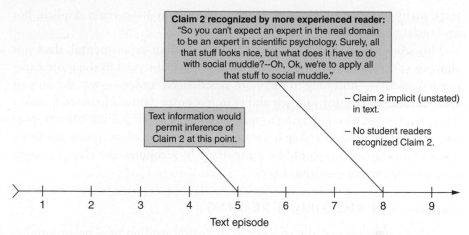

Figure 2 When did a reader recognize Claim 2? "Interaction of two kinds of specialists is necessary to solve social problems."

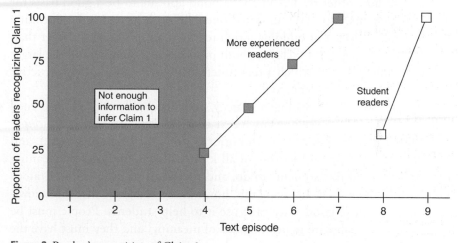

Figure 3 Readers' recognition of Claim 1

At episode 5, 50% of these readers recognized it, at episode 6, 75% saw it, and by episode 7, all of the experienced readers had inferred Claim 1. In contrast, none of the student readers recognized this claim until episode 8, when it was cued in the text. At that point, 33% of the students noted it. At episode 9, when Claim 1 was restated, the rest of the students recognized it.

Claim 2 was never explicitly stated in the text, but half the experienced read- 44 ers had inferred this claim at episode 8 and all had inferred it at episode 9. None of the student readers offered any hints that they had recognized this implicit claim. It seems that the rhetorical readers were better able to recognize an important claim that was *never explicitly spelled out in the text*. In sophisticated texts, many important high-level claims—like Claim 2—remain implicit, but are crucial nonetheless.

This study, because it is observational rather than experimental, does not 45 allow us to conclude that the rhetorical reading we observed in the more experienced readers—and only in the more experienced readers—was the only or even the dominant cause for their ability to recognize claims. However, it makes sense that readers who are trying to make inferences about author, context, purpose, and effect, who are trying to create a representation of the text as the result of a purposeful action, would be more likely to recognize the claims—both implicit and explicit—within a text.

THE ROLE OF RHETORICAL READING

This study suggests that the strategy of rhetorical reading may be an import- 46 ant element in the larger process of critical reading. The constructive process we observed in readers actively trying to understand the author's intent, the context, and how other readers might respond appears to be a good basis for recognizing claims, especially unstated ones the reader must infer. Speaking more generally, this act of building a rich representation of text—larger than the words on the page and including both propositional content and the larger discourse context within which a text functions—is the kind of constructive reading we desire our students to do.

However, is rhetorical reading a strategy students could easily adopt if cued 47 to do so? Being able to see one's own text and the texts of others as *discourse acts*—rather than bodies of facts and information—is desirable, useful, and important for reading and writing of all kinds. This is the kind of meaning building we would like students to do, and rhetorical reading is one strategy that may help them do it. In saying this, however, we recognize that this knowledge will do us little good if we can't use it to help students. People must be *able* to construct elaborate representations of meaning, and they must have the strategies to do so. How this is to come about is not clear.

Our first attempt at "suggestive" teaching—introducing the students to 48 the concept of rhetorical reading and encouraging them to use it—found that while students could identify the rhetorical reading strategy in the reading of others, they were less successful at using it. Can we expect merely to hand students tools for building rich representations of text and set them to work? Or will rhetorical reading require active teaching—teaching by direct instruction, by modelling, and by encouraging students to become contributing and committed members of rhetorical communities?

Although the answers to these questions are not yet clear, we offer here our 49 own reading of these results: first, some readers are actively concerned with the situations from which texts arise. These readers seemed to expend some effort in representing the rhetorical situation of a text they are reading. However, reading is a complex cognitive activity. It involves constructing representations on several levels, and student readers, even good students, seem to be bogged down in content: they focus on knowledge-getting while reading.

We believe that teaching students to read rhetorically is genuinely difficult. It 50 is difficult in the way that teaching students to *write* rhetorically is difficult. In fact, this work with student and experienced *readers* provides a potential parallel to research results with student and expert *writers*. While expert writers, like those Flower, Hayes, Schriver, Carey, and Haas have studied, work within a rhetorical framework — imagining audience response, acknowledging context, and setting their own purposeful goals — student writers often concentrate on content and information — they "knowledge tell," in Bereiter and Scardamalia's terms. Similarly, these student readers seem to concentrate on knowledge, content, what the text is about — not taking into account that the text is the product of a writer's intentions and is designed to produce an effect on a specific audience.

While experienced readers may understand that both reading and writing are 51 context-rich, situational, constructive acts, many students may see reading and writing as merely an information exchange: knowledge-telling when they write, and "knowledge-getting" when they read. Helping students move beyond this simple, information-exchange view to a more complex rhetorical model — in both their reading and their writing — is one of the very real tasks which faces us as teachers. And research with real readers and writers continues to offer insights into the equally complex ways all of us construct meaning.

Works Cited

Baker, Linda, and Ann L. Brown. "Metacognitive Skills and Reading." *Handbook of Reading Research*. Ed. R. Barr, Michael L. Kamil, and Peter Mosenthal. New York: Longman, 1984. 353–94.

Bereiter, Carl, and Marlene Scardamalia. "Cognitive Coping Strategies and the Problem of Inert Knowledge." *Learning and Thinking Skills: Research and Open Questions*. Ed. Susan Chipman, J. Segal, and Robert Glaser. Hillsdale, NJ: Lawrence Erlbaum Associates, 1985. 65–80.

Bransford, John. *Cognition: Learning, Understanding and Remembering*. Belmont, CA: Wadsworth Publishing Company, 1979.

Farnham-Diggory, Sylvia. *Cognitive Processes in Education: A Psychological Preparation for Teaching and Curriculum Development*. New York: Harper and Row, 1972.

Flower, Linda. "The Construction of Purpose in Writing and Reading." *College English* 50 (1988): 528–50.

Flower, Linda. "Interpretive Acts: Cognition and the Construction of Discourse." *Poetics* 16 (April 1987): 109–30.

Flower, Linda, and John R. Hayes. "Images, Plans, and Prose: The Representation of Meaning in Writing." *Written Communication* 1 (January 1984): 120–60.

Flower, Linda, John R. Hayes, Karen Schriver, Linda Carey, and Christina Haas. *Planning in Writing: A Theory of the Cognitive Process.* ONR Technical Report # 1. Pittsburgh: Carnegie Mellon, 1987.

Haas, Christina, and John R. Hayes. "What Did I Just Say? Reading Problems in Writing with the Machine." *Research in the Teaching of English* 20 (February 1986): 22–35.

Scardamalia, Marlene. "How Children Cope with the Cognitive Demands of Writing." *Writing: The Nature, Development, and Teaching of Written Communication (Vol. 2).* Ed. Carl Frederiksen, M. F. Whiteman, and J. F. Dominic. Hillsdale, NJ: Lawrence Erlbaum Associates, 1981. 81–103.

Spivey, Nancy N. "Construing Constructivism: Reading Research in the United States." *Poetics* 16 (April 1987): 169–93.

Tierney, Robert, and P. David Pearson. "Toward a Composing Model of Reading." *Composing and Comprehending.* Ed. Julie M. Jensen. Urbana, IL: NCTE, 1984. 33–45.

Vipond, Douglas, and Russell Hunt. "Point-driven Understanding: Pragmatic and Cognitive Dimensions of Literary Reading." *Poetics* 13 (June 1984): 261–77.

- -

Questions for Discussion and Journaling

1. Haas and Flower spend a lot of time pointing out that readers "construct" "representations" of a text's content and what it means. Why is this particular language of construction and representation so important to them? How is it different from the ways in which we usually talk about what happens when readers read?

2. One claim this article makes is that when readers try to understand texts, they bring their own knowledge to them. What kinds of knowledge did you bring to this article that helped you make sense of it (or not)?

3. Haas and Flower seem to criticize reading that's merely for "information exchange." Why? What do they consider inadequate about using readings simply to convey information?

4. What does it mean to see texts "as purposeful actions" (para. 12)? What are some examples you've seen of texts that serve as actions?

5. Consider how Haas and Flower went about answering their research questions. What were some advantages and some drawbacks to their methods? What do you think might be the biggest weakness of their approach? How would you have done it?

6. Think back to the last time someone gave you some instruction in how to read. When was it? What were you taught? What differences are there between what you were taught and what Haas and Flower say is important to teach about reading?

7. Can you identify instances in the past where you've been a rhetorical reader? If so, what were you reading? How was it similar to and different from your usual reading practice?

8. The chapter introduction argues that rhetoric shows us how texts and discourse are meaning-making. What parts of Haas and Flower's explanations of how readers *construct meaning* rather than *receive information* from a text help you better understand what it means for textual rhetorical interaction to be meaning-making rather than simply transcription and absorption?

Applying and Exploring Ideas

1. Use a text your teacher gives you to conduct your own read-aloud/think-aloud experiment. After recording yourself reading the text and stopping at predetermined points to talk about how you understand the text at that moment, listen to your recording and try to find patterns that describe how you read and understand while reading. Then write up a few pages discussing what you've learned that you can share with classmates.

2. Write a summary of Haas and Flower's article that discusses the following: Why was it written? Who was meant to read it (and how can you tell)? What do Haas and Flower seem to be trying to do with the article? How can your understanding of the text be improved by identifying the rhetorical situation?

3. Make a list of the rhetorical reading strategies that Haas and Flower discuss, trying to include even those they only imply without explicitly stating. Use this list to help you write a set of instructions on reading rhetorically for the next group of students who will take the class you're in now. What should they look for in texts? What questions should they ask about texts to ensure they're reading rhetorically?

4. Locate a text that seems to be purely informational (like an instruction manual or directions for taking the SAT). Reading it rhetorically — that is, trying to understand the motivation of the writer and the audience's needs — can you find aspects of the text that go beyond information to claims, opinion, and argument?

- -

META MOMENT   How can you benefit from knowing the results of Haas and Flower's study? How does reading and understanding this article help you achieve the goals of this chapter listed on page 368? How do you see it relating to the threshold concept discussed in the chapter introduction?

- -

Helping Students Use Textual Sources Persuasively

MARGARET KANTZ

Framing the Reading

Given this chapter's focus on rhetoric, several of its pieces suggest that writing and reading are not just about transmitting and receiving information. Texts don't mean the same thing to every reader because, as rhetorical theory shows (and the previous reading by Haas and Flower explored), readers construct meaning by interacting with texts, putting something of themselves into the text and drawing meaning from the text's context.

Margaret Kantz's work takes us to the next logical step, discussing how it is that we write a new text from other existing texts. In Kantz's article we follow the learning experiences of a particular student, Shirley. Whereas Shirley had been taught in high school that "research" meant compiling facts and transmitting them to a teacher, she must now learn to use a variety of conflicting sources to make an original **argument** on the subject she's researching. Kantz analyzes how Shirley has moved from the realm of reporting "just the facts" to the more sophisticated world of arguing about what the facts might be, and she shows readers how many new ideas are involved in that change.

A key concept in this change is learning to recognize that facts aren't so much inherently true statements as they are **claims** — that is, assertions that most of a given audience has agreed are true because for that audience sufficient proof has already been given. You, like most people, would probably classify the statement "the Earth is round" as a "fact." Its status as a fact, however, depends on our mutual agreement that "round" is an adequate description of the Earth's actual, imperfectly spherical shape. What Kantz wants us to see is that what makes the statement a fact is not how "true" the statement is but that most people have agreed that it's true and treat it as true. Statements about which we haven't reached this consensus remain claims, statements that people argue about. Kantz's work here demonstrates why it's so important to read texts — even "factual" works like textbooks and encyclopedias — as consisting of claims, not facts.

This idea that textbooks and other "factual" texts aren't inherently true but instead simply represent a consensus of opinion is

Kantz, Margaret. "Helping Students Use Textual Sources Persuasively."
College English, vol. 52, no. 1, Jan. 1990, pp. 74–91.

a major conceptual change from the way most students are taught in school before college. It is also a major implication of rhetorical theory. You will encounter the idea that writing is always personal (not purely factual and objective) if you read Murray's article in this chapter. You will encounter the idea that different readers construct their own meanings from texts and that truth is built through consensus if you read Haas and Flower's article in this chapter. Rhetorical theory suggests that people are limited to subjective, partial knowledge formed through consensus because we are embedded in particular moments — we can never see an issue from every angle or perspective simultaneously, leaving our knowledge incomplete and provisional. It is this idea that Kantz is working on while exploring the difference between facts and claims.

While Kantz wrote this piece as a professor at Central Missouri State University, she conducted the research for it as a graduate student at Carnegie Mellon University. One of her professors there was Linda Flower and one of her classmates was Christina Haas, whose names you might have noticed earlier in this chapter (and, if you pay close attention, in Kantz's works-cited list). We make this point to remind you that texts are authored by real people, and these people are often connected both inside and outside of their texts — another example of the concept of rhetorical ecology and its idea of networks of rhetors.

Getting Ready to Read

Before you read, do at least one of the following activities:

- Think about an argument you've had recently in which people disagreed about the facts of an issue. How did you resolve the factual dispute? Did the arguers ever agree on what the facts were? If not, how was the argument resolved?
- Write down, in a few quick sentences, how you define these terms: *fact, claim, opinion*, and *argument*.
- Watch three commercials and count the number of facts and the number of claims in each. Then think about what's most persuasive in the ads: the facts, the claims, or a combination of the two.

As you read, consider the following questions:

- How does Kantz know what she knows? What is the basis for her claims?
- What is Kantz's research question or problem? What does she want to know, or what is she trying to solve?
- What challenges do the students about whom Kantz writes face in making sense of conflicting sources?

ALTHOUGH THE RESEARCHED ESSAY as a topic has been much written 1 about, it has been little studied. In the introduction to their bibliography, Ford, Rees, and Ward point out that most of the over 200 articles about researched essays published in professional journals in the last half century describe classroom methods. "Few," they say, "are of a theoretical nature or based on research, and almost none cites even one other work on the subject" (2). Given Ford and Perry's finding that 84% of freshman composition programs and 40% of advanced composition programs included instruction in writing research papers, more theoretical work seems needed. We need a theory-based explanation, one grounded in the findings of the published research on the nature and reasons for our students' problems with writing persuasive researched papers. To understand how to teach students to write such papers, we also need a better understanding of the demands of synthesis tasks.

As an example for discussing this complex topic, I have used a typical col- 2 lege sophomore. This student is a composite derived from published research, from my own memories of being a student, and from students whom I have taught at an open admissions community college and at both public and private universities. I have also used a few examples taken from my own students, all of whom share many of Shirley's traits. Shirley, first of all, is intelligent and well-motivated. She is a native speaker of English. She has no extraordinary knowledge deficits or emotional problems. She comes from a home where education is valued, and her parents do reading and writing tasks at home and at their jobs. Shirley has certain skills. When she entered first grade, she knew how to listen to and tell stories, and she soon became proficient at reading stories and at writing narratives. During her academic life, Shirley has learned such studying skills as finding the main idea and remembering facts. In terms of the relevant research, Shirley can read and summarize source texts accurately (cf. Spivey; Winograd). She can select material that is relevant for her purpose in writing (Hayes, Waterman, and Robinson; Langer). She can make connections between the available information and her purpose for writing, including the needs of her readers when the audience is specified (Atlas). She can make original connections among ideas (Brown and Day; Langer). She can create an appropriate, audience-based structure for her paper (Spivey), take notes and use them effectively while composing her paper (Kennedy), and she can present information clearly and smoothly (Spivey), without relying on the phrasing of the original sources (Atlas; Winograd). Shirley is, in my experience, a typical college student with an average academic preparation.

Although Shirley seems to have everything going for her, she experiences 3 difficulty with assignments that require her to write original papers based on textual sources. In particular, Shirley is having difficulty in her sophomore-level writing class. Shirley, who likes English history, decided to write about the

Battle of Agincourt (this part of Shirley's story is biographical). She found half a dozen histories that described the circumstances of the battle in a few pages each. Although the topic was unfamiliar, the sources agreed on many of the facts. Shirley collated these facts into her own version, noting but not discussing discrepant details, borrowing what she assumed to be her sources' purpose of retelling the story, and modelling the narrative structure of her paper on that of her sources. Since the only comments Shirley could think of would be to agree or disagree with her sources, who had told her everything she knew about the Battle of Agincourt, she did not comment on the material; instead, she concentrated on telling the story clearly and more completely than her sources had done. She was surprised when her paper received a grade of C–. (Page 1 of Shirley's paper is given as Appendix A.)

Although Shirley is a hypothetical student whose case is based on a real 4 event, her difficulties are typical of undergraduates at both private and public colleges and universities. In a recent class of Intermediate Composition in which the students were instructed to create an argument using at least four textual sources that took differing points of view, one student, who analyzed the coverage of a recent championship football game, ranked her source articles in order from those whose approach she most approved to those she least approved. Another student analyzed various approaches taken by the media to the Kent State shootings in 1970, and was surprised and disappointed to find that all of the sources seemed slanted, either by the perspective of the reporter or by that of the people interviewed. Both students did not understand why their instructor said that their papers lacked a genuine argument.

The task of writing researched papers that express original arguments pres- 5 ents many difficulties. Besides the obvious problems of citation format and coordination of source materials with the emerging written product, writing a synthesis can vary in difficulty according to the number and length of the sources, the abstractness or familiarity of the topic, the uses that the writer must make of the material, the degree and quality of original thought required, and the extent to which the sources will supply the structure and purpose of the new paper. It is usually easier to write a paper that uses all of only one short source on a familiar topic than to write a paper that selects material from many long sources on a topic that one must learn as one reads and writes. It is easier to quote than to paraphrase, and it is easier to build the paraphrases, without comment or with random comments, into a description of what one found than it is to use them as evidence in an original argument. It is easier to use whatever one likes, or everything one finds, than to formally select, evaluate, and interpret material. It is easier to use the structure and purpose of a source as the basis for one's paper than it is to create a structure or an original purpose. A writing-from-sources task can be as simple as collating a body of facts from a few short texts on a familiar topic into a new text that reproduces the structure, tone, and purpose of the originals, but it can also involve applying abstract concepts from one area to an original problem in a different area, a task that involves learning the relationships among materials as a paper is created that may refer to its sources without resembling them.

Moreover, a given task can be interpreted as requiring an easy method, a diffi- 6 cult method, or any of a hundred intermediate methods. In this context, Flower has observed, "The different ways in which students [represent] a 'standard' reading-to-write task to themselves lead to markedly different goals and strategies as well as different organizing plans" (*Role* iii). To write a synthesis, Shirley may or may not need to quote, summarize, or select material from her sources; to evaluate the sources for bias, accuracy, or completeness; to develop original ideas; or to persuade a reader. How well she performs any of these tasks—and whether she thinks to perform these tasks—depends on how she reads the texts and on how she interprets the assignment. Shirley's representation of the task, which in this case was easier than her teacher had in mind, depends on the goals that she sets for herself. The goals that she sets depend on her awareness of the possibilities and her confidence in her writing skills.

Feeling unhappy about her grade, Shirley consulted her friend Alice. Alice, 7 who is an expert, looked at the task in a completely different way and used strategies for thinking about it that were quite different from Shirley's.

"Who were your sources?" asked Alice. "Winston Churchill, right? A French 8 couple and a few others. And they didn't agree about the details, such as the sizes of the armies. Didn't you wonder why?"

"No," said Shirley. "I thought the history books would know the truth. 9 When they disagreed, I figured that they were wrong on those points. I didn't want to have anything in my paper that was wrong."

"But Shirley," said Alice, "you could have thought about why a book entitled 10 *A History of France* might present a different view of the battle than a book subtitled *A History of British Progress.* You could have asked if the English and French writers wanted to make a point about the history of their countries and looked to see if the factual differences suggested anything. You could even have talked about Shakespeare's *Henry V*, which I know you've read—about how he presents the battle, or about how the King Henry in the play differs from the Henrys in your other books. You would have had an angle, a problem. Dr. Boyer would have loved it."

Alice's representation of the task would have required Shirley to formally 11 select and evaluate her material and to use it as proof in an original argument. Alice was suggesting that Shirley invent an original problem and purpose for her paper and create an original structure for her argument. Alice's task is much more sophisticated than Shirley's. Shirley replied, "That would take me a year to do! Besides, Henry was a real person. I don't want to make up things about him."

"Well," said Alice, "You're dealing with facts, so there aren't too many choices. 12
If you want to say something original you either have to talk about the sources
or talk about the material. What could you say about the material? Your paper
told about all the reasons King Henry wasn't expected to win the battle. Could
you have argued that he should have lost because he took too many chances?"

"Gee," said Shirley, "That's awesome. I wish I'd thought of it." 13

This version of the task would allow Shirley to keep the narrative structure 14
of her paper but would give her an original argument and purpose. To write the
argument, Shirley would have only to rephrase the events of the story to take an
opposite approach from that of her English sources, emphasizing what she perceived as Henry's mistakes and inserting comments to explain why his decisions
were mistakes—an easy argument to write. She could also, if she wished, write
a conclusion that criticized the cheerleading tone of her British sources.

As this anecdote makes clear, a given topic can be treated in more or less 15
sophisticated ways—and sophisticated goals, such as inventing an original purpose and evaluating sources, can be achieved in relatively simple versions of a
task. Students have many options as to how they can fulfill even a specific task
(cf. Jeffery). Even children can decide whether to process a text deeply or not,
and purpose in reading affects processing and monitoring of comprehension
(Brown). Pichert has shown that reading purpose affects judgments about what
is important or unimportant in a narrative text, and other research tells us that
attitudes toward the author and content of a text affect comprehension (Asch;
Hinze; Shedd; Goldman).

One implication of this story is that the instructor gave a weak assignment 16
and an ineffective critique of the draft (her only comment referred to Shirley's
footnoting technique; cf. Appendix A). The available research suggests that
if Dr. Boyer had set Shirley a specific rhetorical problem such as having her
report on her material to the class and then testing them on it, and if she had
commented on the content of Shirley's paper during the drafts, Shirley might
well have come up with a paper that did more than repeat its source material
(Nelson and Hayes). My teaching experience supports this research finding. If
Dr. Boyer had told Shirley from the outset that she was expected to say something original and that she should examine her sources as she read them for
discrepant facts, conflicts, or other interesting material, Shirley might have tried
to write an original argument (Kantz, "Originality"). And if Dr. Boyer had suggested that Shirley use her notes to comment on her sources and make plans for
using the notes, Shirley might have written a better paper than she did (Kantz,
Relationship).

Even if given specific directions to create an original argument, Shirley might 17
have had difficulty with the task. Her difficulty could come from any of three
causes: (1) Many students like Shirley misunderstand sources because they read
them as stories. (2) Many students expect their sources to tell the truth; hence,

they equate persuasive writing in this context with making things up. (3) Many students do not understand that facts are a kind of claim and are often used persuasively in so-called objective writing to create an impression. Students need to read source texts as arguments and to think about the rhetorical contexts in which they were written rather than to read them merely as a set of facts to be learned. Writing an original persuasive argument based on sources requires students to apply material to a problem or to use it to answer a question, rather than simply to repeat it or evaluate it. These three problems deserve a separate discussion.

Because historical texts often have a chronological structure, students believe 18 that historians tell stories, and that renarrating the battle casts them as a historian. Because her sources emphasized the completeness of the victory / defeat and its decisive importance in the history of warfare, Shirley thought that making these same points in her paper completed her job. Her job as a reader was thus to learn the story, i.e., so that she could pass a test on it (cf. Vipond and Hunt's argument that generic expectations affect reading behavior. Vipond and Hunt would describe Shirley's reading as story-driven rather than point-driven.) Students commonly misread texts as narratives. When students refer to a textbook as "the story," they are telling us that they read for plot and character, regardless of whether their texts are organized as narratives. One reason Shirley loves history is that when she reads it she can combine her story-reading strategies with her studying strategies. Students like Shirley may need to learn to apply basic organizing patterns, such as cause-effect and general-to-specific, to their texts. If, however, Dr. Boyer asks Shirley to respond to her sources in a way that is not compatible with Shirley's understanding of what such sources do, Shirley will have trouble doing the assignment. Professors may have to do some preparatory teaching about why certain kinds of texts have certain characteristics and what kinds of problems writers must solve as they design text for a particular audience. They may even have to teach a model for the kind of writing they expect.

The writing version of Shirley's problem, which Flower calls "writer-based 19 prose," occurs when Shirley organizes what should be an expository analysis as a narrative, especially when she writes a narrative about how she did her research. Students frequently use time-based organizing patterns, regardless of the task, even when such patterns conflict with what they are trying to say and even when they know how to use more sophisticated strategies. Apparently such common narrative transitional devices such as "the first point" and "the next point" offer a reassuringly familiar pattern for organizing unfamiliar material. The common strategy of beginning paragraphs with such phrases as "my first source," meaning that it was the first source that the writer found in the library or the first one read, appears to combine a story-of-my-research structure with a knowledge-telling strategy (Bereiter and Scardamalia, *Psychology*). Even when students understand that the assignment asks for more than the fill-in-the-blanks, show-me-you've-read-the-material approach described by Schwegler and Shamoon, they cling to narrative structuring devices. A rank ordering of sources, as with Mary's analysis of the football game coverage with the sources listed in an order of ascending disapproval, represents a step away from storytelling and toward synthesizing because it embodies a persuasive evaluation.

In addition to reading texts as stories, students expect factual texts to tell 20 them "the truth" because they have learned to see texts statically, as descriptions of truths, instead of as arguments. Shirley did not understand that non-fiction texts exist as arguments in rhetorical contexts. "After all," she reasoned, "how can one argue about the date of a battle or the sizes of armies?" Churchill, however, described the battle in much more detail than Shirley's other sources, apparently because he wished to persuade his readers to take pride in England's tradition of military achievement. Guizot and Guizot de Witt, on the other hand, said very little about the battle (beyond describing it as "a monotonous and lamentable repetition of the disasters of Crecy and Poitiers" [397]) because they saw the British invasion as a sneaky way to take advantage of a feud among the various branches of the French royal family. Shirley's story / study skills might not have allowed her to recognize such arguments, especially because Dr. Boyer did not teach her to look for them.

When I have asked students to choose a topic and find three or more sources 21 on it that disagree, I am repeatedly asked, "How can sources disagree in different ways? After all, there's only pro and con." Students expect textbooks and other authoritative sources either to tell them the truth (i.e., facts) or to express an opinion with which they may agree or disagree. Mary's treatment of the football coverage reflects this belief, as does Charlie's surprise when he found that even his most comprehensive sources on the Kent State killings omitted certain facts, such as interviews with National Guardsmen. Students' desire for truth leads them to use a collating approach whenever possible, as Shirley did (cf. Appendix A), because students believe that the truth will include all of the facts and will reconcile all conflicts. (This belief may be another manifestation of the knowledge-telling strategy [Bereiter and Scardamalia, *Psychology*] in which students write down everything they can think of about a topic.) When conflicts cannot be reconciled and the topic does not admit a pro or con stance, students may not know what to say. They may omit the material altogether, include it without comment, as Shirley did, or jumble it together without any plan for building an argument.

The skills that Shirley has practiced for most of her academic career — finding 22 the main idea and learning content — allow her to agree or disagree. She needs a technique for reading texts in ways that give her something more to say, a technique for constructing more complex representations of texts that allow room for more sophisticated writing goals. She also needs strategies for analyzing her reading that allow her to build original arguments.

> The skills that Shirley has practiced for most of her academic career—finding the main idea and learning content—allow her to agree or disagree. She needs a technique for reading texts in ways that give her something more to say.

One way to help students like Shirley 23 is to teach the concept of rhetorical situation. A convenient tool for thinking about this concept is Kinneavy's triangular diagram of the rhetorical situation. Kinneavy, analyzing Aristotle's description of rhetoric, posits that every communicative situation has three parts: a speaker/writer (the Encoder), an audience (the Decoder), and a topic (Reality) (19). Although all discourse involves all three aspects of communication, a given type of discourse may pertain more to a particular point of the triangle than to the others, e.g., a diary entry may exist primarily to express the thoughts of the writer (the Encoder); an advertisement may exist primarily to persuade a reader (the Decoder). Following Kinneavy, I posit particular goals for each corner of the triangle. Thus, the primary goal of a writer doing writer-based discourse such as a diary might be originality and self-expression; primary goals for reader-based discourse such as advertising might be persuasion; primary goals for topic-based discourse such as a researched essay might be accuracy, completeness, and mastery of subject matter. Since all three aspects of the rhetorical situation are present and active in any communicative situation, a primarily referential text such as Churchill's *The Birth of Britain* may have a persuasive purpose and may depend for some of its credibility on readers' familiarity with the author. The term "rhetorical reading," then (cf. Haas and Flower), means teaching students to read a text as a message sent by someone to somebody for a reason. Shirley, Mary, and Charlie are probably practiced users of rhetorical persuasion in non-academic contexts. They may never have learned to apply this thinking in a conscious and deliberate way to academic tasks (cf. Kroll).

The concept of rhetorical situation offers insight into the nature of students' 24 representations of a writing task. The operative goals in Shirley's and Alice's approaches to the term paper look quite different when mapped onto the points on the triangle. If we think of Shirley and Alice as Encoders, the topic as Reality, and Dr. Boyer as the Decoder, we can see that for Shirley, being an Encoder means trying to be credible; her relationship to the topic (Reality) involves a goal of using all of the subject matter; and her relationship to the Decoder involves an implied goal of telling a complete story to a reader whom Shirley thinks of as an examiner—to use the classic phrase from the famous book by Britton et al.—i.e., a reader who wants to know if Shirley can pass an exam on the subject of the Battle of Agincourt. For Alice, however, being an Encoder means having a goal of saying something new; the topic (Reality) is a resource to be used; and the Decoder is someone who must be persuaded that Alice's ideas have merit. Varying task representations do not change the dimensions of the rhetorical situation: the Encoder, Decoder, and Reality are always present. But the way a writer represents the task to herself does affect the ways that she thinks about those dimensions—and whether she thinks about them at all.

In the context of a research assignment, rhetorical skills can be used to read 25 the sources as well as to design the paper. Although teachers have probably always known that expert readers use such strategies, the concept of rhetorical reading is new to the literature. Haas and Flower have shown that expert readers use rhetorical strategies "to account for author's purpose, context, and effect on the audience . . . to recreate or infer the rhetorical situation of the text" (176; cf. also Bazerman). These strategies, used in addition to formulating main points and paraphrasing content, helped the readers to understand a text more completely and more quickly than did readers who concentrated exclusively on content. As Haas and Flower point out, teaching students to read rhetorically is difficult. They suggest that appropriate pedagogy might include "direct instruction . . . modeling, and . . . encouraging students to become contributing and committed members of rhetorical communities" (182). One early step might be to teach students a set of heuristics based on the three aspects of the communicative triangle. Using such questions could help students set goals for their reading.

In this version of Kinneavy's triangle, the Encoder is the writer of the source 26 text, the Decoder is the student reader, and Reality is the subject matter. Readers may consider only one point of the triangle at a time, asking such questions as "Who are you (i.e., the author / Encoder)?" or "What are the important features of this text?" They may consider two aspects of the rhetorical situation in a single question, e.g., "Am I in your intended (primary) audience?"; "What do I think about this topic?"; "What context affected your ideas and presentation?" Other questions would involve all three points of the triangle, e.g., "What are you saying to help me with the problem you assume I have?" or "What textual devices have you used to manipulate my response?" Asking such questions gives students a way of formulating goals relating to purpose as well as content.

If Shirley, for example, had asked a Decoder-to-Encoder question—such as 27 "Am I in your intended audience?"—she might have realized that Churchill and the Guizots were writing for specific audiences. If she had asked a Decoder-to-Reality question—such as "What context affected your ideas and presentation?"—she might not have ignored Churchill's remark, "All these names [Amiens, Boves, Bethencourt] are well known to our generation" (403). As it was, she missed Churchill's signal that he was writing to survivors of the First World War, who had vainly hoped that it would be a war to end all wars. If Shirley had used an Encoder-Decoder-Reality question—such as "What are you saying to help me with the problem you assume I have?"—she might have understood that the authors of her sources were writing to different readers for different reasons. This understanding might have given her something to say. When I gave Shirley's source texts to freshmen students, asked them to use the material in an original argument, and taught them this heuristic for rhetorical reading, I received, for example, papers that warned undergraduates about national pride as a source of authorial bias in history texts.

A factual topic such as the Battle of Agincourt presents special problems 28 because of the seemingly intransigent nature of facts. Like many people, Shirley believes that you can either agree or disagree with issues and opinions, but you can only accept the so-called facts. She believes that facts are what you learn from textbooks, opinions are what you have about clothes, and arguments are what you have with your mother when you want to stay out late at night. Shirley is not in a position to disagree with the facts about the battle (e.g., "No, I think the French won"), and a rhetorical analysis may seem at first to offer minimal rewards (e.g., "According to the Arab, Jewish, and Chinese calendars the date was really . . .").

Alice, who thinks rhetorically, understands that both facts and opinions 29 are essentially the same kind of statement: they are claims. Alice understands that the only essential difference between a fact and an opinion is how they are received by an audience. (This discussion is derived from Toulmin's model of an argument as consisting of claims proved with data and backed by ethical claims called warrants. According to Toulmin, any aspect of an argument may be questioned by the audience and must then be supported with further argument.) In a rhetorical argument, a fact is a claim that an audience will accept as being true without requiring proof, although they may ask for an explanation. An opinion is a claim that an audience will not accept as true without proof, and which, after the proof is given, the audience may well decide has only a limited truth, i.e., it's true in this case but not in other cases. An audience may also decide that even though a fact is unassailable, the interpretation or use of the fact is open to debate.

For example, Shirley's sources gave different numbers for the size of the 30 British army at Agincourt; these numbers, which must have been estimates, were claims masquerading as facts. Shirley did not understand this. She thought that disagreement signified error, whereas it probably signified rhetorical purpose. The probable reason that the Guizots give a relatively large estimate for the English army and do not mention the size of the French army is so that their French readers would find the British victory easier to accept. Likewise, Churchill's relatively small estimate for the size of the English army and his high estimate for the French army magnify the brilliance of the English victory. Before Shirley could create an argument about the Battle of Agincourt, she needed to understand that, even in her history textbooks, the so-called facts are claims that may or may not be supported, claims made by writers who work in a certain political climate for a particular audience. She may, of course, never learn this truth unless Dr. Boyer teaches her rhetorical theory and uses the research paper as a chance for Shirley to practice rhetorical problem-solving.

For most of her academic life, Shirley has done school tasks that require her 31 to find main ideas and important facts; success in these tasks usually hinges on agreeing with the teacher about what the text says. Such study skills form an essential basis for doing reading-to-write tasks. Obviously a student can only use sources to build an argument if she can first read the sources accurately (cf. Brown and Palincsar; Luftig; Short and Ryan). However, synthesizing tasks often require that readers not accept the authors' ideas. Baker and Brown have pointed out that people misread texts when they blindly accept an author's ideas instead of considering a divergent interpretation. Yet if we want students to learn to build original arguments from texts, we must teach them the skills needed to create divergent interpretations. We must teach them to think about facts and opinions as claims that are made by writers to particular readers for particular reasons in particular historical contexts.

Reading sources rhetorically gives students a powerful tool for creating a 32 persuasive analysis. Although no research exists as yet to suggest that teaching students to read rhetorically will improve their writing, I have seen its effect in successive drafts of students' papers. As mentioned earlier, rhetorical reading allowed a student to move from simply summarizing and evaluating her sources on local coverage of the championship football game to constructing a ratio-nale for articles that covered the fans rather than the game. Rhetorical analysis enabled another student to move from summarizing his sources to understanding why each report about the Kent State shootings necessarily expressed a bias of some kind.

As these examples suggest, however, rhetorical reading is not a magical 33 technique for producing sophisticated arguments. Even when students read their sources rhetorically, they tend merely to report the results of this analysis in their essays. Such writing appears to be a college-level version of the knowledge-telling strategy described by Bereiter and Scardamalia (*Psychology*) and may be, as they suggest, the product of years of exposure to pedagogical practices that enshrine the acquisition and expression of information without a context or purpose.

To move students beyond merely reporting the content and rhetorical ori-34 entation of their source texts, I have taught them the concept of the rhetorical gap and some simple heuristic questions for thinking about gaps. Gaps were first described by Iser as unsaid material that a reader must supply to infer from a text. McCormick expanded the concept to include gaps between the text and the reader; such gaps could involve discrepancies of values, social conven-tions, language, or any other matter that readers must consider. If we apply the concept of gaps to Kinneavy's triangle, we see that in reading, for exam-ple, a gap may occur between the Encoder-Decoder corners when the reader is not a member of the author's intended audience. Shirley fell into such a gap. Another gap can occur between the Decoder-Reality corners when a reader disagrees with or does not understand the text. A third gap can occur between the Encoder-Reality points of the triangle if the writer has misrepresented or misunderstood the material. The benefit of teaching this concept is that when a student thinks about a writer's rhetorical stance, she may ask "Why does he think that way?" When a student encounters a gap, she may ask, "What effect does it have on the success of this communication?" The answers to both questions give students original material for their papers.

Shirley, for example, did not know that Churchill began writing *The Birth* 35 *of Britain* during the 1930s, when Hitler was rearming Germany and when the British government and most of Churchill's readers ardently favored disarmament. Had she understood the rhetorical orientation of the book, which was published eleven years after the end of World War II, she might have argued that Churchill's evocation of past military glories would have been inflammatory in the 1930s but was highly acceptable twenty years later. A gap between the reader and the text (Decoder-Reality) might stimulate a reader to investigate whether or not she is the only person having this problem; a gap between other readers and the sources may motivate an adaptation or explanation of the material to a particular audience. Shirley might have adapted the Guizots' perspective on the French civil war for American readers. A gap between the author and the material (Encoder-Reality) might motivate a refutation.

To discover gaps, students may need to learn heuristics for setting rhetorical 36 writing goals. That is, they may need to learn to think of the paper, not as a rehash of the available material, but as an opportunity to teach someone, to solve someone's problem, or to answer someone's question. The most salient questions for reading source texts may be "Who are you (the original audience of Decoders)?"; "What is your question or problem with this topic?"; and "How have I (the Encoder) used these materials to answer your question or solve your problem?" More simply, these questions may be learned as "Why," "How," and "So what?" When Shirley learns to read sources as telling not the eternal truth but a truth to a particular audience and when she learns to think of texts as existing to solve problems, she will find it easier to think of things to say.

For example, a sophomore at a private university was struggling with an 37 assignment that required her to analyze an issue and express an opinion on it, using two conflicting source texts, an interview, and personal material as sources. Using rhetorical reading strategies, this girl discovered a gap between Alfred Marbaise, a high school principal who advocates mandatory drug testing of all high school students, and students like those he would be testing:

> Marbaise, who was a lieutenant in the U.S. Marines over thirty years ago
> . . . makes it very obvious that he cannot and will not tolerate any form of

drug abuse in his school. For example, in paragraph seven he claims, "When students become involved in illegal activity, whether they realize it or not, they are violating other students . . . then I become very, very concerned . . . and I will not tolerate that."

Because Marbaise has not been in school for nearly forty years himself, he does not take into consideration the reasons why kids actually use drugs. Today the social environment is so drastically different that Marbaise cannot understand a kid's morality, and that is why he writes from such a fatherly but distant point of view.

The second paragraph answers the So what? question, i.e., "Why does it matter that Marbaise seems by his age and background to be fatherly and distant?" Unless the writer / reader thinks to ask this question, she will have difficulty writing a coherent evaluation of Marbaise's argument.

The relative success of some students in finding original things to say about 38 their topics can help us to understand the perennial problem of plagiarism. Some plagiarism derives, I think, from a weak, nonrhetorical task representation. If students believe they are supposed to reproduce source material in their papers, or if they know they are supposed to say something original but have no rhetorical problem to solve and no knowledge of how to find problems that they can discuss in their sources, it becomes difficult for them to avoid plagiarizing. The common student decision to buy a paper when writing the assignment seems a meaningless fill-in-the-blanks activity (cf. Schwegler and Shamoon) becomes easily understandable. Because rhetorical reading leads to discoveries about the text, students who use it may take more interest in their research papers.

Let us now assume that Shirley understands the importance of creating an 39 original argument, knows how to read analytically, and has found things to say about the Battle of Agincourt. Are her troubles over? Will she now create that A paper that she yearns to write? Probably not. Despite her best intentions, Shirley will probably write another narrative / paraphrase of her sources. Why? Because by now, the assignment asks her to do far more than she can handle in a single draft. Shirley's task representation is now so rich, her set of goals so many, that she may be unable to juggle them all simultaneously. Moreover, the rhetorical reading technique requires students to discover content worth writing about and a rhetorical purpose for writing; the uncertainty of managing such a discovery task when a grade is at stake may be too much for Shirley.

Difficult tasks may be difficult in either (or both of) two ways. First, they 40 may require students to do a familiar subtask, such as reading sources, at a higher level of difficulty, e.g., longer sources, more sources, a more difficult topic. Second, they may require students to do new subtasks, such as building notes into an original argument. Such tasks may require task management skills, especially planning, that students have never developed and do not know how to attempt. The insecurity that results from trying a complex new task in a high-stakes situation is increased when students are asked to discover a problem worth writing about because such tasks send students out on a treasure hunt with no guarantee that the treasure exists, that they will recognize it when they find it, or that when they find it they will be able to build it into a coherent argument. The paper on Marbaise quoted above earned a grade of D because the writer could not use her rhetorical insights to build an argument presented in a logical order. Although she asked the logical question about the implications of Marbaise's persona, she did not follow through by evaluating the gaps in his perspective that might affect the probable success of his program.

A skillful student using the summarize-the-main-ideas approach can set her 41 writing goals and even plan (i.e., outline) a paper before she reads the sources. The rhetorical reading strategy, by contrast, requires writers to discover what is worth writing about and to decide how to say it as or after they read their sources. The strategy requires writers to change their content goals and to adjust their writing plans as their understanding of the topic develops. It requires writers, in Flower's term, to "construct" their purposes for writing as well as the content for their paper (for a description of constructive planning, see Flower, Schriver, Carey, Haas, and Hayes). In Flower's words, writers who construct a purpose, as opposed to writers who bring a predetermined purpose to a task, "create a web of purposes . . . set goals, toss up possibilities . . . create a multidimensional network of information . . . a web of purpose . . . a bubbling stew of various mental representations" (531–32). The complex indeterminacy of such a task may pose an intimidating challenge to students who have spent their lives summarizing main ideas and reporting facts.

Shirley may respond to the challenge by concentrating her energies on a 42 familiar subtask, e.g., repeating material about the Battle of Agincourt, at the expense of struggling with an unfamiliar subtask such as creating an original argument. She may even deliberately simplify the task by representing it to herself as calling only for something that she knows how to do, expecting that Dr. Boyer will accept the paper as close enough to the original instructions. My students do this frequently. When students decide to write a report of their reading, they can at least be certain that they will find material to write about.

Because of the limits of attentional memory, not to mention those caused by 43 inexperience, writers can handle only so many task demands at a time. Thus, papers produced by seemingly inadequate task representations may well be essentially rough drafts. What looks like a bad paper may well be a preliminary step, a way of meeting certain task demands in order to create a basis for thinking about new ones. My students consistently report that they need to marshal all of their ideas and text knowledge and get that material down on the page (i.e., tell their knowledge) before they can think about developing an argument (i.e., transform their knowledge). If Shirley's problem is that she has shelved certain task demands in favor of others, Dr. Boyer needs only to point out what Shirley should do to bring the paper into conformity with the assignment and offer Shirley a chance to revise.

The problems of cognitive overload and inexperience in handling complex 44 writing tasks can create a tremendous hurdle for students because so many of them believe that they should be able to write their paper in a single draft. Some students think that if they can't do the paper in one draft that means that something is wrong with them as writers, or with the assignment, or with us for giving the assignment. Often, such students will react to their drafts with anger and despair, throwing away perfectly usable rough drafts and then coming to us and saying that they can't do the assignment.

The student's first draft about drug testing told her knowledge about her 45 sources' opinions on mandatory drug testing. Her second draft contained the rhetorical analysis quoted above, but presented the material in a scrambled order and did not build the analysis into an argument. Only in a third draft was this student able to make her point:

> Not once does Marbaise consider any of the psychological reasons why kids
> turn away from reality. He fails to realize that drug testing will not answer their
> questions, ease their frustrations, or respond to their cries for attention, but will
> merely further alienate himself and other authorities from helping kids deal with
> their real problems.

This comment represents Terri's answer to the heuristic "So what? Why does the source's position matter?" If we pace our assignments to allow for our students' thoughts to develop, we can do a great deal to build their confidence in their writing (Terri raised her D+ to an A). If we treat the researched essay as a sequence of assignments instead of as a one-shot paper with a single due date, we can teach our students to build on their drafts, to use what they can do easily as a bridge to what we want them to learn to do. In this way, we can improve our students' writing habits. More importantly, however, we can help our students to see themselves as capable writers and as active, able, problem-solvers. Most importantly, we can use the sequence of drafts to demand that our students demonstrate increasingly sophisticated kinds of analytic and rhetorical proficiency.

Rhetorical reading and writing heuristics can help students to represent 46 tasks in rich and interesting ways. They can help students to set up complex goal structures (Bereiter and Scardamalia, "Conversation"). They offer students many ways to think about their reading and writing texts. These tools, in other words, encourage students to work creatively.

And after all, creativity is what research should be about. If Shirley writes 47 a creative paper, she has found a constructive solution that is new to her and which other people can use, a solution to a problem that she and other people share. Creativity is an inherently rhetorical quality. If we think of it as thought leading to solutions to problems and of problems as embodied in questions that people ask about situations, the researched essay offers infinite possibilities. Viewed in this way, a creative idea answers a question that the audience or any single reader wants answered. The question could be, "Why did Henry V win the Battle of Agincourt?" or, "How can student readers protect themselves against nationalistic bias when they study history?" or any of a thousand other questions. If we teach our Shirleys to see themselves as scholars who work to find answers to problem questions, and if we teach them to set reading and writing goals for themselves that will allow them to think constructively, we will be doing the most exciting work that teachers can do, nurturing creativity.

Appendix A: Page 1 of Shirley's paper

The battle of Agincourt ranks as one of England's greatest military triumphs. It was the most brilliant victory of the Middle Ages, bar none. It was fought on October 25, 1414, against the French near the French village of Agincourt.

Henry V had claimed the crown of France and had invaded France with an army estimated at anywhere ~~between~~ *from* 10,000[1] ~~and~~ *to* 45,000 men[2]. During the seige of Marfleur dysentery had taken (1/3) of them[3], his food supplies had been depleted[4], and the fall rains had begun. In addition the French had assembled a huge army and were marching toward him. Henry decided to march to Calais, where his ships were to await him[5]. He intended to cross the River Somme at the ford of Blanchetaque[6], but, falsely informed that the ford was guarded[7], he was forced to follow the flooded Somme up toward its source. The French army was shadowing him on his right. Remembering the slaughters of Crecy and <u>Poictiers</u>, the French constable, Charles d'Albret, hesitated to fight[8], but when Henry forded the Somme just above Amiens[9] and was just

---

1. Carl Stephinson, <u>Medieval History,</u> p. 529.
2. (Guizot, Monsieur and Guizot, Madame,) <u>World's Best Histories-France, Volume II</u>, p. 211.
3. Cyrid E. Robinson, <u>England-A History of British Progress,</u> p. 145.

Appendix A: Page 1 of Shirley's paper (*continued*)

4. Ibid.

5. Winston Churchill, <u>A History of the English-Speaking Peoples, Volume I:</u>
<u>The Birth of Britain</u>, p. 403.

6. Ibid.

7. Ibid.

You footnote material that does not need to be footnoted.

8. Robinson, p. 145.

9. Churchill, p. 403.

Works Cited

Asch, Solomon. *Social Psychology.* New York: Prentice, 1952.

Atlas, Marshall. *Expert-Novice Differences in the Writing Process.* Paper presented at the American Educational Research Association, 1979. ERIC ED 107 769.

Baker, Louise, and Ann L. Brown. "Metacognitive Skills and Reading." *Handbook of Reading Research.* Eds. P. David Person, Rebecca Barr, Michael L. Kamil, and Peter Mosenthal. New York: Longman, 1984.

Bazerman, Charles. "Physicists Reading Physics: Schema-Laden Purposes and Purpose Laden Schema." *Written Communication* 2.1 (1985): 3–24.

Bereiter, Carl, and Marlene Scardamalia. "From Conversation to Composition: The Role of Instruction in a Developmental Process." *Advances in Instructional Psychology.* Ed. R. Glaser. Vol. 2. Hillsdale, NJ: Lawrence Erlbaum Associates, 1982. 1–64.

——. *The Psychology of Written Composition.* Hillsdale, NJ: Lawrence Erlbaum Associates, 1987.

Briscoe, Terri. "To test or not to test." Unpublished essay. Texas Christian University, 1989.

Britton, James, Tony Burgess, Nancy Martin, Alex McLeod, and Harold Rosen. *The Development of Writing Abilities (11–18).* Houndmills Basingstoke Hampshire: Macmillan Education Ltd., 1975.

Brown, Ann L. "Theories of Memory and the Problem of Development: Activity, Growth, and Knowledge." *Levels of Processing in Memory.* Eds. Laird S. Cermak and Fergus I. M. Craik. Hillsdale, NJ: Laurence Erlbaum Associates, 1979. 225–58.

——, Joseph C. Campione, and L. R. Barclay. *Training Self-Checking Routines for Estimating Test Readiness: Generalizations from List Learning to Prose Recall.* Unpublished manuscript. University of Illinois, 1978.

—— and Jeanne Day. "Macrorules for Summarizing Texts: The Development of Expertise." *Journal of Verbal Learning and Verbal Behavior* 22.1(1983): 1–14.

—— and Annmarie S. Palincsar. *Reciprocal Teaching of Comprehension Strategies: A Natural History of One Program for Enhancing Learning.* Technical Report #334. Urbana, IL: Center for the Study of Reading, 1985.

Churchill, Winston S. *The Birth of Britain*, New York: Dodd, 1956. Vol. 1 of *A History of the English-Speaking Peoples.* 4 vols. 1956–58.

Flower, Linda. "The Construction of Purpose in Writing and Reading." *College English* 50.5 (1988): 528–50.

——. *The Role of Task Representation in Reading to Write.* Berkeley, CA: Center for the Study of Writing, U of California at Berkeley and Carnegie Mellon. Technical Report, 1987.

——. "Writer-Based Prose: A Cognitive Basis for Problems in Writing." *College English* 41 (1979): 19–37.

Flower, Linda, Karen Schriver, Linda Carey, Christina Haas, and John R. Hayes. *Planning in Writing: A Theory of the Cognitive Process.* Berkeley, CA: Center for the Study of Writing, U of California at Berkeley and Carnegie Mellon. Technical Report, 1988.

Ford, James E., and Dennis R. Perry. "Research Paper Instruction in the Undergraduate Writing Program." *College English* 44 (1982): 825–31.

Ford, James E., Sharla Rees, and David L. Ward. *Teaching the Research Paper: Comprehensive Bibliography of Periodical Sources*, 1980. ERIC ED 197 363.

Goldman, Susan R. "Knowledge Systems for Realistic Goals." *Discourse Processes* 5 (1982): 279–303.

Guizot and Guizot de Witt. *The History of France from Earliest Times to 1848.* Trans. R. Black. Vol. 2. Philadelphia: John Wanamaker (n.d.).

Haas, Christina, and Linda Flower. "Rhetorical Reading Strategies and the Construction of Meaning." *College Composition and Communication* 39 (1988): 167–84.

Hayes, John R., D. A. Waterman, and C. S. Robinson. "Identifying the Relevant Aspects of a Problem Text." *Cognitive Science* 1 (1977): 297–313.

Hinze, Helen K. "The Individual's Word Associations and His Interpretation of Prose Paragraphs." *Journal of General Psychology* 64 (1961): 193–203.

Iser, Wolfgang. *The Act of Reading: A Theory of Aesthetic Response.* Baltimore: The Johns Hopkins UP, 1978.

Jeffery, Christopher. "Teachers' and Students' Perceptions of the Writing Process." *Research in the Teaching of English* 15 (1981): 215–28.

Kantz, Margaret. "Originality and Completeness: What Do We Value in Papers Written from Sources?" Conference on College Composition and Communication. St. Louis, MO, 1988.

——. *The Relationship Between Reading and Planning Strategies and Success in Synthesizing: It's What You Do with Them that Counts.* Technical report in preparation. Pittsburgh: Center for the Study of Writing, 1988.

Kennedy, Mary Louise. "The Composing Process of College Students Writing from Sources," *Written Communication* 2.4 (1985): 434–56.

Kinneavy, James L. *A Theory of Discourse.* New York: Norton, 1971.

Kroll, Barry M. "Audience Adaptation in Children's Persuasive Letters." *Written Communication* 1.4 (1984): 407–28.

Langer, Judith. "Where Problems Start: The Effects of Available Information on Responses to School Writing Tasks." *Contexts for Learning to Write: Studies of Secondary School Instruction.* Ed. Arthur Applebee. Norwood, NJ: ABLEX Publishing Corporation, 1984. 135–48.

Luftig, Richard L. "Abstractive Memory, the Central-Incidental Hypothesis, and the Use of Structural Importance in Text: Control Processes or Structural Features?" *Reading Research Quarterly* 14.1 (1983): 28–37.

Marbaise, Alfred. "Treating a Disease." *Current Issues and Enduring Questions.* Eds. Sylvan Barnet and Hugo Bedau. New York: St. Martin's, 1987. 126–27.

McCormick, Kathleen. "Theory in the Reader: Bleich, Holland, and Beyond." *College English* 47.8 (1985): 836–50.

McGarry, Daniel D. *Medieval History and Civilization.* New York: Macmillan, 1976.

Nelson, Jennie, and John R. Hayes. *The Effects of Classroom Contexts on Students' Responses to Writing from Sources: Regurgitating Information or Triggering Insights.* Berkeley, CA: Center for the Study of Writing, U of California at Berkeley and Carnegie Mellon. Technical Report, 1988.

Pichert, James W. "Sensitivity to Importance as a Predictor of Reading Comprehension." *Perspectives on Reading Research and Instruction.* Eds. Michael A. Kamil and Alden J. Moe. Washington, D.C.: National Reading Conference, 1980. 42–46.

Robinson, Cyril E. *England: A History of British Progress from the Early Ages to the Present Day.* New York: Thomas Y. Crowell Company, 1928.

Schwegler, Robert A., and Linda K. Shamoon. "The Aims and Process of the Research Paper." *College English* 44 (1982): 817–24.

Shedd, Patricia T. "The Relationship between Attitude of the Reader Towards Women's Changing Role and Response to Literature Which Illuminates Women's Role." Diss. Syracuse U, 1975. ERIC ED 142 956.

Short, Elizabeth Jane, and Ellen Bouchard Ryan. "Metacognitive Differences between Skilled and Less Skilled Readers: Remediating Deficits through Story Grammar and Attribution Training." *Journal of Education Psychology* 76 (1984): 225–35.

Spivey, Nancy Nelson. *Discourse Synthesis: Constructing Texts in Reading and Writing.* Diss. U Texas, 1983. Newark, DE: International Reading Association, 1984.

Toulmin, Steven E. *The Uses of Argument.* Cambridge: Cambridge UP, 1969.

Vipond, Douglas, and Russell Hunt. "Point-Driven Understanding: Pragmatic and Cognitive Dimensions of Literary Reading." *Poetics* 13, (1984): 261–77.

Winograd, Peter. "Strategic Difficulties in Summarizing Texts." *Reading Research Quarterly* 19 (1984): 404–25.

- -

Questions for Discussion and Journaling

1. Kantz writes that Shirley "believes that facts are what you learn from textbooks, opinions are what you have about clothes, and arguments are what you have with your mother when you want to stay out late at night" (para. 28). What does Kantz contend that facts, opinions, and arguments actually are?

2. Make a list of the things Kantz says students don't know, misunderstand, or don't comprehend about how texts work. Judging from your own experience, do you think she's correct about student understanding? How many of the things she lists do you feel you understand better now?

3. As its title indicates, Kantz's article has to do with using sources *persuasively*. Did her article teach you anything new about the persuasive use of sources to support an argument? If so, what?

4. Do you think Kantz contradicts herself when she says that we should think of sources neither as stories nor as repositories of truth? Explain why or why not.

5. Kantz offers a number of critiques of students thinking of all texts as narratives and using narrative arrangements very frequently in their own writing (see para. 19). How do you think she might respond to the argument in Downs's piece earlier in this chapter that narrative and storytelling are principle modes of human knowing and knowledge-making? Are the two in conflict, and if so, how would you resolve this situation?

6. Which of the students in Kantz's article do you most identify with, and why?

7. Do you think Kantz's ideas will change your own approach to doing research and writing with sources? If so, how?

Applying and Exploring Ideas

1. Kantz places some blame for students' writing difficulties on poorly written assignments that don't clearly explain what teachers want. Conduct your own mini review of college writing assignments you've received. How many do you think gave sufficient explanation of what the professor was looking for? As you look at assignments that did give good directions, what do they have in common? That is, based on those assignments, what did you need to be told in order to have a good understanding of what you were being asked to write? Write one to two pages about what you find, and share what you write in class.

2. Write a short reflection on the relationship between creativity and research as you've learned to understand it prior to this class and as Kantz talks about it. Where do your ideas overlap with hers? Where does her thinking influence yours? And where does it not seem to work for you?

- -

META MOMENT   One of our goals for this book is to have you consider constructs or conceptions of writing that don't hold up under close scrutiny. How would you name the constructs that Kantz is calling into question? Why would it be useful for you as a writer in college or in professional settings to understand her findings and claims?

- -

All Writing Is Autobiography

DONALD M. MURRAY

Framing the Reading

By the time you've gotten to college, it's very likely that at least one teacher has told you not to use "I" in your school papers. Push the question, and you might be told that academic writing (especially if it uses research) isn't supposed to be "personal" — rather, you should strive to be as objective as possible, and objectivity demands being impersonal. If the paper isn't about you, you can't be in it. But this chapter, along with others in this book, should be making you question these claims. Principles of rhetorical ecology assert that people make meaning through networks of interaction — meaning is not objective but arises through the interaction of subjective people. Meaning *is* personal, depending (*contingent*) on your particular *position in* your ecology, and on your *prior knowledge* (see Chapter 5).

Donald M. Murray probably had the same erroneous voices in mind when he decided to write this article for the writing teachers who read *College Composition and Communication* — and he did not accept what they had to say. Having made his living as a writer (including winning a Pulitzer Prize as a newspaper columnist, writing textbooks, and publishing a range of poetry and fiction), Murray knew that personal positionality within a rhetorical ecology should and must impact writing. Writing, he thought, is *always* personal, whatever else it is. So he sat down to catalog the various ways that writing of any sort — and the ecology from which it emerges — does *include the writer* as an individual being — the ways that, in a sense, all writing is **autobiography**. One impact of this principle is on this chapter's threshold concept, "good" writing depends on context: The sound of writing depends in part on who's talking and what they want to sound like, and writers will shape their voice to the context.

Some readers object to Murray's argument because they misunderstand his use of the term *autobiography*, assuming he's referring to all writing as books in which

people tell the stories of their lives. Murray makes it clear, though, that he's not thinking that research papers and workplace memos are autobiographies. Rather, Murray is referring to the autobiographical *nature* of texts, all of which necessarily contain traces of their creators. If you understand autobiography in this sense, it will be easier to fairly weigh Murray's arguments.

Murray, Donald M. "All Writing Is Autobiography." *College Composition and Communication*, vol. 42, no. 1, Feb. 1991, pp. 66–74.

Murray's arguments are explicitly about writing, but his broader focus is *all* rhetorical activities. We exist in any rhetorical ecology as distinct entities or selves. While these selves, as Murray argues, take much of their shape from the communities in which they take form, they present as distinctive individuals. While Murray was writing at a time when understandings of rhetorical ecology were just beginning to emerge, and thus he doesn't reference that particular construct in his thinking here, his ideas about writing as autobiography are important to understanding the nature of agents, and agency, in rhetorical ecologies.

As we discussed in Chapters 1–3, this book is also about how actual research about writing challenges many of the commonsense "rules" or ideas or conceptions we're taught about writing as young people. In this case, Murray is challenging the ideas that you can keep yourself out of your writing and (again as demonstrated earlier in this chapter, in Downs) that research writing is purely factual and objective. Murray is sharing a more complicated conception about writing that does a better job explaining the actual writing we do and see around us.

Getting Ready to Read

Before you read, try at least one of the following activities:

- Think back to what you've been taught about how "personal" your school or work writing (that is, not your diary, journal, poetry, songwriting, or other "expressive" writing) can be. What kinds of rules or guidance did you get? If you have friends or classmates around, compare notes with them.
- How "personal" is your favorite writing — that is, how clear is the writer's voice or opinions in it?

As you read this article, consider the following questions:

- What reasons does Murray give for his contention that all writing is autobiography?
- What genres of writing does Murray discuss? Why these?
- Why did Murray choose to write *as* he did (for example, by using poetry), *where* he did (in the scholarly journal *College Composition and Communication*), and *for whom* he did? (You may need to do some research to answer this question.) What did he hope to accomplish?

I PUBLISH IN MANY FORMS — poetry, fiction, academic article, essay, 1
newspaper column, newsletter, textbook, juvenile nonfiction and I have even
been a ghost writer for corporate and government leaders — yet when I am at
my writing desk I am the same person. As I look back, I suspect that no matter

how I tuned the lyre, I played the same tune. All my writing—and yours—is autobiographical.

To explore this possibility, I want to share a poem that appeared in the March 2 1990 issue of *Poetry.*

AT 64, TALKING WITHOUT WORDS

The present comes clear when rubbed
with memory. I relive a childhood
of texture; oatmeal, the afternoon rug,
spears of lawn, winter finger tracing
frost on window glass, August nose
squenched against window screen. My history
of smell: bicycle oil, leather catcher's
mitt, the sweet sickening perfume of soldiers
long dead, ink fresh on the first edition.
Now I am most alone with others, companioned
by silence and the long road at my back,
mirrored by daughters. I mount the evening
stairs with mother's heavy, wearied
step, sigh my father's long complaint.
My beard grows to the sepia photograph
of a grandfather I never knew. I forget
if I turned at the bridge, but arrive
where I intended. My wife and I talk
without the bother of words. We know Lee
is 32 today. She did not stay twenty
but stands at each room's doorway. I place
my hand on the telephone. It rings.

What is autobiographical in this poem? I was 64 when I wrote it. The child- 3 hood memories were real once I remembered them by writing. I realized I was mirrored by daughters when the line arrived on the page. My other daughter would have been 32 on the day the poem was written. Haven't you all had the experience of reaching for the phone and hearing it ring?

There may even be the question of autobiographical language. We talk about 4 our own language, allowing our students their own language. In going over this draft my spellcheck hiccuped at "squenched" and "companioned." As an academic I gulped; as a writer I said, "Well they are now."

Then Brock Dethier, one of the most perceptive of the test readers with 5 whom I share drafts, pointed out the obvious—where all the most significant information is often hidden. He answered my question, "What is autobiographical in this poem?" by saying, "Your thinking style, your voice." Of course.

We are autobiographical in the way we write; my autobiography exists in the examples of writing I use in this piece and in the text I weave around them. I have my own peculiar way of looking at the world and my own way of using language to communicate what I see. My voice is the product of Scottish genes and a Yankee environment, of Baptist sermons and the newspaper city room, of all the language I have heard and spoken.

> We are autobiographical in the way we write; my autobiography exists in the examples of writing I use in this piece and in the text I weave around them.

In writing this paper I have begun to understand, better than I ever have before, that all writing, in many different ways, is autobiographical, and that our autobiography grows from a few deep taproots that are set down into our past in childhood.

Willa Cather declared, "Most of the basic material a writer works with is acquired before the age of fifteen." Graham Greene gave the writer five more years, no more: "For writers it is always said that the first 20 years of life contain the whole of experience — the rest is observation."

Those of us who write have only a few topics. My poems, the novel I'm writing, and some of my newspaper columns keep returning to my family and my childhood, where I seek understanding and hope for a compassion that has not yet arrived. John Hawkes has said, "Fiction is an act of revenge." I hope not, but I can not yet deny the importance of that element in my writing. Revenge against family, revenge against the Army and war, revenge against school.

Another topic I return to is death and illness, religion and war, a great tangle of themes. During my childhood I began the day by going to see if my grandmother had made it through the night; I ended my day with, "Now I lay me down to sleep, I pray the Lord my soul to keep. If I should die before I wake, I pray the Lord my soul to take."

I learned to sing "Onward Christian Soldiers Marching as to War," and still remember my first dead German soldier and my shock as I read that his belt buckle proclaimed God was on *his* side. My pages reveal my obsession with war, with the death of our daughter, with that territory I explored in the hours between the bypass operation that did not work and the one that did.

Recently, Boynton / Cook / Heinemann published *Shoptalk*, a book I began in Junior High School that documents my almost lifelong fascination with how writing is made. I assume that many people in this audience are aware of my obsession with writing and my concern with teaching that began with my early discomfort in school that led to my dropping out and flunking out. My academic writing is clearly autobiographical.

Let's look now at a Freshman English sort of personal essay, what I like to call a reflective narrative. I consider such pieces of writing essays, but I suppose others think of them in a less inflated way as newspaper columns. I write a column, *Over Sixty*, for the *Boston Globe*, and the following one was published October 10th of 1989. It was based on an experience I had the previous August.

Over sixty brings new freedoms, a deeper appreciation of life and the time to celebrate it, but it also brings, with increasing frequency, such terrible responsibilities as sitting with the dying.

Recently it was my turn to sit with my brother-in-law as he slowly left us, the victim of a consuming cancer.

When I was a little boy, I wanted—hungered—to be a grown-up. Well, now I am a grown-up. And when someone had to sit with the dying on a recent Saturday, I could not look over my shoulder. I was the one. My oldest daughter will take her turn. She is a grown-up as well, but those of us over sixty have our quota of grown-upness increase. Time and again we have to confront crisis: accident, sickness, death. There is no one else to turn to. It is our lonely duty.

Obligation has tested and tempered us. No one always measures up all the time. We each do what we can do, what we must do. We learn not to judge if we are wise, for our judgments boomerang. They return. At top speed and on target.

Most of us, sadly and necessarily, have learned to pace ourselves. We have seen friends and relatives destroyed by obligation, who have lost themselves in serving others. There is no end to duty for those who accept it.

And we have seen others who diminish by shirking responsibility. When we call them for help the door is shut. We hear silence.

We grow through the responsible acceptance of duty, obligation balanced by self-protection. We teeter along a high wire trying to avoid guilt or sanctimoniousness as we choose between duty and avoidance.

And so my mind wanders as Harry sleeps, blessedly without pain for the moment, moving steadily toward a destination he seems no longer to fear.

He would understand that as we mourn for him, we mourn for ourselves. Of course. We are learning from his dying how to live. We inevitably think of what he did that we can emulate and what we should try to avoid.

And we learn, from his courage and his example, not to fear death. I remember how horrified I was years ago when a mother of a friend of mine, in her late eighties, feeling poorly in the middle of the night, would get up, change into her best nightgown, the one saved for dying, and go back to sleep.

Now I understand. During my last heart attack I had a volcanic desire to live but no fear of dying. It was not at all like my earlier trips to the edge.

Harry continues my education. He did not want trouble while he lived and now he is dying the same way, causing no trouble, trying to smile when he wakes, trying to entertain me.

He needs the comfort of sleep and I leave the room, turning outside his door to see how quickly his eyes close. He wants nothing from us now. Not food, not drink, not, we think, much companionship. He accepts that his road is lonely and he does not even show much impatience at its length.

It is not a happy time, alone in the house with a dying man, but it is not a dreadful time either. I pat the cat who roams the house but will not go to the room where Harry lies; I read, write in my daybook, watch Harry, and take time to celebrate my living.

This house, strange to me, in an unfamiliar city, is filled with silence. No music, no TV, just the quiet in which I can hear his call. But he does not call. I cannot hear his light breathing. Every few minutes I go to the door to see if the covers still rise and fall.

He would understand as I turn from him to watch the tree branch brush the roof of the house next door, as I spend long moments appreciating the dance of shadows from the leaves on the roof, then the patterns of sunlight reflected up on the ceiling of the room where I sit, as I celebrate my remaining life.

Again I stand at the edge of the door watching, waiting, and take instruction from his dying. We should live the hours we have in our own way, appreciating their passing. And we should each die in our own way. I will remember his way, his acceptance, his not giving trouble, his lonely, quiet passing.

14 This is simple narrative with the facts all true, but it is really not that simple; few things are in writing or in life. The details are selective. A great deal of family history is left out. A great many details about the day, the illness, where it was taking place and why were left out. In fact, I wrote it in part for therapy, and it began as a note to myself several weeks after the experience to help me cut through a jungle of thoughts and emotions, to try to recover for myself what was happening that day. Later I saw that it might speak to others, give comfort or form to their own autobiographies. I did not write the whole truth of that day, although the facts in the piece are accurate; I wrote a limited truth seeking a limited understanding, what Robert Frost called "a momentary stay of confusion."

15 Yes, I confess it, I wrote, and write, for therapy. Writing autobiography is my way of making meaning of the life I have led and am leading and may lead.

16 Let's look at another autobiographical poem, one of my favorites, which, I suppose, means that it was one I especially needed to write for no autobiographical reason I can identify. It has not yet been published, although a great many of the best poetry editors in the country have failed in their obligation to Western culture by rejecting it.

BLACK ICE

On the first Saturday of winter, the boy
skated alone on Sailor's Home Pond, circling
from white ice to black, further each time
he rode the thin ice, rising, dipping, bending
the skin of the water until the crack raced
from shore to trick him but he heard, bent
his weight to the turn, made it back in time.

That winter he saw the fish frozen in ice,
its great unblinking eye examining him
each time he circled by. He dreamt that eye
all summer, wondered if Alex had seen
the fish eye before he rode the black ice,
did not hear the crack sneak out from shore,
imagined he learned to skate on water.

At night, after loving you, I fall back
to see that fish eye staring down, watch
Alex in shoe skates and knickers from below
as he skates overhead, circling faster, faster,
scissor legs carrying him from white ice

to black. His skates sing their cutting song,
etching larger, larger circles in my icy sky.

It is true that the boy, myself, skated on thin ice and that he skated at Sailor's   17
Home Pond in Quincy, Massachusetts, although the thin ice may not have
been on that pond. He did not, however, see a fish in the ice until he wrote
the poem, although he was obsessed with the eyes of the fish, haddock and
cod, that followed him when he went to Titus's fish store in Wollaston. Readers
believe that Alex is my brother, although I was an only child. There was no
Alex; no one I knew had drowned by falling through the ice until I received the
poem; I did not, after loving, stare up to see him skating above me until after I
wrote the poem. I do now. The poem that was for a few seconds imaginary has
become autobiographical by being written.

Ledo Ivo, the Latin American writer, said, "I increasingly feel that my writ-   18
ing creates me. I am the invention of my own words" (*Lives on the Line,* Ed.
Doris Meyer, U of California P, 1988). Don DeLillo explains, "Working at sentences and rhythms is probably the most satisfying thing I do as a writer. I think
after a while a writer can begin to know himself through his language. He sees
someone or something reflected back at him from these constructions. Over
the years it's possible for a writer to shape himself as a human being through

the language he uses. I think written language, fiction, goes that deep. He not only sees himself but begins to make himself or remake himself" (*Anything Can Happen,* Ed. Tom LeClair and Larry McCaffery, U of Illinois P, 1988).

We become what we write. That is one of the great magics of writing. I am 19 best known as a nonfiction writer, but I write fiction and poetry to free myself of small truths in the hope of achieving large ones. Here are the first pages from a novel I am writing.

> Notebook in his lap, pen uncapped, Ian Fraser sat in the dark green Adirondack chair studying the New Hampshire scene that had so often comforted him as he put in his last years in his Washington office. The green meadow sloping unevenly over granite ledge to the lake and the point of land with its sentinel pine that marked the edge of his possession, and across the lake the hills rising into mountains touched with the reds, oranges, yellows that would flame into autumn this week or next. He was settled in at last and ready to begin the book he had so long delayed, but he could not write until he scanned this quiet scene with his infantryman's eyes for it still was, as were all his landscapes, a field of fire.
>
> He had to know where to dig in, where the enemy would attack, what was at his back. He supposed it was what had attracted him to this old farmhouse, he could hold this position, he had a good field of fire. First he scanned the lake. Left to right, far edge to near, not one boat or canoe, nothing breaking the surface, no wind trail or wake. Now right to left to see what might be missed. Nothing.
>
> The point of land, his furthest outpost. Scraggly pines, hulking ledge, ideal cover. He studied it close up, knew the pattern of shadows, where the ledge caught the light, where crevice was always dark. This is ridiculous, he thought, an old man whose wars are all over, but he could not stop the search for the enemies that had been there at the edge of other fields so long ago, so recent in memory.
>
> The woods left, on the other side from sentinel point. Sweep his eyes at the woods a half a field away, open ground any enemy would have to cross. He made himself still; anyone watching would not know his eyes were on patrol. He could have hidden a platoon in these woods, tree and bush, ledge and rock wall, but there was no shadow that moved, no unexpected sound, no leaves that danced without wind.
>
> And yet, Ian felt a presence as if he, the watcher, were being watched. He scanned the woods on the left again, moving from lake edge up. Nothing.
>
> Now the woods on the right, he had cut back from the house when he bought it, saying he needed sun for vegetables. He needed open field. More hardwoods here, more openness, the road unseen beyond. It was where someone would come in. His flood lights targeted these woods, but it was

not night. He examined these familiar woods, suddenly looking high in the old oak where a pileated woodpecker started his machine gun attack. Ian studied squirrel and crow, the pattern of light and dark, followed the trail of the quiet lake breeze that rose through the woods and was gone.

Now the field of fire itself, where a civilian would think no-one could hide. He smiled at the memory of a young paratrooper, himself, home on leave, telling Claire, who would become his first wife, to stand at the top of the field and spot him if she could as he crept up the slope, taking cover where there seemed no cover. She was patient with his soldiering—then. She knew her quarry and did not laugh as this lean young man crawled up the slope moving quickly from ledge to slight hollow to the cover of low bush blueberries that July in 1943.

He never knew if she saw him or not.

Do I have a green lawn that reaches down to a New Hampshire lake? No. Do 20 I still see when I visit a new place, forty-six years after I have been in combat, a good field of fire? Yes. Did I have another wife than Minnie Mae? Yes. Was her name Claire? No. Did I play that silly game in the field when I was home on leave? Yes. Is the setting real? Let Herman Melville answer, "It is not down on any map: true places never are."

What is true, what is documentally autobiographical, in the novel will not 21 be clear to me when I finish the last draft. I confess that at my age I am not sure about the source of most of my autobiography. I have written poems that describe what happened when I left the operating table, looked back and decided to return. My war stories are constructed of what I experienced, what I heard later, what the history books say, what I needed to believe to survive and recover—two radically different processes.

I dream every night and remember my dreams. Waking is often a release 22 from a greater reality. I read and wear the lives of the characters I inhabit. I do not know where what I know comes from. Was it dreamt, read, overheard, imagined, experienced in life or at the writing desk? I have spun a web more coherent than experience.

But of course I've been talking about fiction, a liar's profession, so let us turn 23 to the realistic world of nonfiction. That novel from which I have quoted is being written, more days than not, by a technique I call layering that I describe in the third edition of *Write to Learn:*

One technique, I've been using, especially in writing the novel, is to layer my writing. Once I did quite a bit of oil painting and my pictures were built up, layer after layer of paint until the scene was revealed to me and a viewer. I've been writing each chapter of the novel the same way, starting each day at the beginning of the chapter, reading and writing until the timer bings and my daily stint is finished. Each day I lay down a new layer of text and when I read it the next day, the new layer reveals more possibility.

There is no one way the chapters develop. Each makes its own demands, struggles towards birth in its own way. Sometimes it starts with a sketch, other times the first writing feels complete [next day's reading usually shows it is not]; sometimes I race ahead through the chapter, other times each paragraph is honed before I go on to the next one. I try to allow the text to tell me what it needs.

I start reading and when I see—or, more likely, hear—something that needs doing, I do it. One day I'll read through all the written text and move it forward from the last day's writing; another time I'll find myself working on dialogue; the next day I may begin to construct a new scene [the basic element of fiction]; one time I'll stumble into a new discovery, later have to set it up or weave references to it through the text; I may build up background description, develop the conflict, make the reader see a character more clearly; I may present more documentation, evidence, or exposition, or hide it in a character's dialogue or action.

Well, that is academic writing, writing to instruct, textbook writing. It is 24 clearly nonfiction, and to me it is clearly autobiography. And so, I might add, is the research and scholarship that instructs our profession. We make up our own history, our own legends, our own knowledge by writing our autobiography.

This has enormous implications for our students, or should have. In *Note-* 25 *books of the Mind* (U of New Mexico P, 1985), a seminal book for our discipline, Vera John-Steiner documents the importance of obsession. "Creativity requires a *continuity of concern*, an intense awareness of one's active inner life combined with sensitivity to the external world." Again and again she documents the importance of allowing and even cultivating the obsessive interest of a student in a limited area of study. I read that as the importance of encouraging and supporting the exploration of the autobiographical themes of individual students—and the importance of allowing ourselves to explore the questions that itch our lives.

I do not think we should move away from personal or reflective narrative in 26 composition courses, but closer to it; I do not think we should limit reflective narrative to a single genre; I do not think we should make sure our students write on many different subjects, but that they write and rewrite in pursuit of those few subjects which obsess them.

But then, of course, I am writing autobiographically, telling other people to 27 do what is important to me.

And so all I can do is just rest my case on my own personal experience. I 28 want to read my most recent poem in which the facts are all true. I had not seen as clearly before I wrote the poem the pattern of those facts, the way I—and a generation of children in the United States and Germany and Britain and Japan and China and Spain and France and Italy and Russia and so many other countries—was prepared for war. This piece of writing is factually true but watch out as you hear it. Writing is subversive and something dangerous may happen as you hear my autobiography.

A woman hearing this poem may write, in her mind, a poem of how she was ²⁹ made into a docile helpmate by a society that had its own goals for her. A black may write another autobiography as mine is heard but translated by personal history. A person who has been mistreated in childhood, a person who is a Jew, a person whose courage was tested at the urging of jeering peers on a railroad bridge in Missouri, will all hear other poems, write other poems in their mind as they hear mine.

WINTHROP 1936, SEVENTH GRADE

December and we comb our hair wet,
pocket our stocking caps and run,
uniformed in ice helmets,

to read frost etched windows:
castle, moat, battlements, knight,
lady, dragon, feel our sword

plunge in. At recess we fence
with icicles, hide coal in
snow balls, lie freezing

inside snow fort, make ice balls
to arc against the enemy; Hitler.
I lived in a town of Jews,

relatives hidden in silences,
letters returned, doors shut,
curtains drawn. Our soldier

lessons were not in books taught
by old women. In East Boston,
city of Mussolinis, we dance

combat, attack and retreat, sneak,
hide, escape, the companionship
of blood. No school, and side

staggered by icy wind we run
to the sea wall, wait
for the giant seventh wave

to draw back, curl mittens
round iron railing, brace
rubber boots, watch

the entire Atlantic rise
until there is no sky. Keep
mittens tight round iron rail,

prepare for the return of ocean,
that slow, even sucking back,
the next rising wave.

I suspect that when you read my poem, you wrote your own autobiography. 30
That is the terrible, wonderful power of reading: the texts we create in our own
minds while we read—or just after we read—become part of the life we believe
we lived. Another thesis: all reading is autobiographical.

- -

Questions for Discussion and Journaling

1. Remember that one of the goals of this book is to help you consider threshold
   concepts about writing that help you rethink how writing actually works. Write
   a paragraph that explains how Murray shapes your thinking about this chapter's
   threshold concept, *"good" writing depends on context.*

2. Murray argues that "all writing, in many different ways, is autobiographical, and
   that our autobiography grows from a few deep taproots that are set down into
   our past childhood" (para. 7). He lists a variety of ways that writing is autobiographical. What are they?

3. A central concern in Murray's piece is the writer's voice. Have other pieces you've
   read in this chapter concerned themselves with how writers sound in their writing or with where this sound emerges from? If so, in what readings and in what
   ways?

4. Murray's article was published in a peer-reviewed, scholarly journal, yet it does
   not share the typical features of that genre. Murray's writing is more informal,
   more "literary," and easier to read in some ways. Make a list of the ways that
   Murray's article is different from the other scholarly articles in this chapter. Then
   consider some reasons why Murray would have wanted to break out of the usual
   "rules" for writing in the scholarly article genre.

5. What features, in contrast to the previous question, mark Murray's article as
   belonging to the genre of "scholarly article"?

6. Consider the implications of Murray's arguments: If he's right, how do his ideas
   change the way you think about writing? Would they encourage you to write any
   differently than you currently do?

7. Consider the last few texts that you have written, whether for school, work, or
   personal reasons. Consider the ways that these texts are — or are not — autobiography in the sense that Murray describes.

Applying and Exploring Ideas

1. Write a one- to two-page response to Murray that explains your reaction to his piece and gives reasons for your thinking. You could write your piece a number of different ways: as a letter to Murray or to a friend; as an article in the same style as Murray's; or as a review of the article (like a review of a new album or movie).

2. If you've heard before that writing — especially academic writing — should be impersonal and keep the writer out, Murray's article might inspire you to argue against that point of view. Take one to two pages and free-write comments you might make to a teacher or other authority figure who told you in the past to write "objectively" and keep yourself out of the text.

3. At the end of this piece, Murray offers a second thesis, that along with writing, all *reading* is autobiographical. In order to test this claim, talk with a classmate about how they responded to another piece that you've read in this book. As they share their reactions with you, ask them some probing questions, such as:

   • Why do you think you read it that way instead of this way?

   • What experiences have you had in the past that helped you read this or made it harder for you to understand?

   • When you struggled with a particular idea, can you point to a reason in your own experience that would explain why that was hard for you?

   Once you've heard their responses, compare them with your own. Now write one to two pages explaining Murray's claim that all reading is autobiography, and then arguing for or against that claim.

- -

META MOMENT Name two or three ways that understanding Murray's claims here can have a positive impact on you as a writer and / or on your attitude about writing.

- -

The Value of Rhetorical Analysis Outside Academia

Winston Zhou, Courtesy of Julia Arbutus

JULIA ARBUTUS

Framing the Reading

Julia Arbutus is double majoring in Financial Economics and English at the University of Maryland, Baltimore County (UMBC). She wrote this essay in Spring 2017 for a class called "Texts and Contexts." She is the editor-in-chief of the student-run newspaper, *The Retriever*, and treasurer of UMBC's Musical Theatre Club. She hopes to pursue a career as a journalist in Baltimore after she graduates.

Arbutus wrote this piece in response to one of the assignments at the end of this chapter, which asked her to consider a set of texts that disagree. She chose articles that focused on a topic in popular culture that was being hotly debated at the time, but which you might not even remember now (or ever have known about): a semi-topless photo shoot of *Harry Potter* actress Emma Watson in 2017. Arbutus chose a topic from popular culture to illustrate that all of us benefit from being able to use rhetorical theory to analyze daily arguments and rhetorical choices. Her primary argument is that rhetorical analysis isn't just something for scholars to do or for students to do in school.

Getting Ready to Read

Before you read, do at least one of the following activities:

- Google Emma Watson, who is the subject of the analysis Arbutus conducts here, to learn more about her involvement with feminist causes and the photo shoot Arbutus studies.
- Review the main claims of Grant-Davie, Kantz, and Porter in this chapter, whom you will see that Arbutus cites.

As you read, consider the following questions:

- Does Arbutus emphasize points from other readings in this chapter that also stood out to you? If she brings up ideas that you missed, you might want to review those readings.
- How does Arbutus put her essay together? How does she organize it? How does she provide evidence for her claims?

Several studies have suggested that a rhetorical focus, one that emphasizes the 1
social and literacy context of a piece, has often been influential in "[guiding] the
development of the writer" (Porter 401) to "effect change and establish [their]
identities" (Porter 402). As an increased number of academic scholars share their
work, the academic community gains new research outlooks, while the scholars
gain communication experience within their field—they learn what works rhetorically and what does not. On the readers' side, Kantz emphasizes that those looking to assemble new information should care about "why . . . the source's position
matter[s]" (Kantz 442), a sentiment that Grant-Davie further reiterates when, as
he is analyzing events, he focuses on the question "why did it happen?" as opposed
to "what happened?" (349). These deeper, contemplative questions ultimately help
the reader analyze academic texts more effectively and completely.

While these studies have primarily addressed the importance of including 2
rhetorical analysis in classrooms and wider intellectual circles throughout the
country, they have not given any attention to the usefulness of rhetorical analysis in daily life. Rhetoric, however, can be used to determine the legitimacy or
credibility of any form of media or to shape one's own narrative identity. Where
Grant-Davie, Porter, and Kantz suggest a reader take a more active role in communication analysis within academia, I analyze three sources that disagree to
demonstrate the significance of rhetoric in the daily evaluation of sources from
an analytical perspective and in the formation of creative, original discussions.

UNDERSTANDING THE RHETORICAL SITUATION

To understand rhetoric in a more common, daily context, however, we must 3
first understand its role within academia. Keith Grant-Davie, James E. Porter,
and Margaret Kantz each provide insight into smaller subsets of rhetoric,
explaining its components, the discourse communities that surround it, and the
facets of facts and opinions, respectively.

Within his essay "Rhetorical Situations and Their Constituents," Grant- 4
Davie defines rhetorical situations and explains how writers who understand
their composition are better equipped to determine causality. Grant-Davie
classifies a rhetorical situation as a "[set] of interacting influences from which
rhetoric arises" that consists of four major elements: the rhetor, the exigency,
the audience, and the constraints (349). The rhetor is the force responsible for
the rhetorical discourse, using ethos to instill a unique identity and integrity
in the writing. Depending on the rhetorical situation, Grant-Davie argues that
a rhetor "[needs] to consider who they are . . . and be aware that their identity may vary" (354). While uniformity in voice is suggested, versatility is also
valued—a rhetor should be able to respond to different rhetorical situations
and the exigencies that accompany them in a number of ways.

The exigency drives the rhetorical discourse, motivating the rhetor to 5 respond. It can be anything from a major political decision to the importance of community gardens, but its importance can always be described in terms of the larger values an issue represents. A major political decision could represent principles of freedom or safety, while the importance of community gardens can be traced back to human health. In considering the exigency, the rhetor must also pay attention to the questions "Why is the discourse needed?" and "What is the discourse trying to accomplish?" which allow the rhetor to determine "why the issues are important" and the "goals of the discourse," respectively (353). These questions provide a focus for the rhetor throughout their writing and context for the audience as they find meaning within the text.

It is through the rhetor's construction of the exigency that the audience 6 of a particular discourse experiences the rhetorical situation as they read. Grant-Davie asserts "The roles of the rhetor and audience are dynamic and interdependent" (356). Just as the rhetor should be prepared to adapt his role for different situations, so should the audience; both parties are encouraged to see the exigency from different perspectives, as they both extract meaning from the discourse and exigency.

Constraints, according to Grant-Davie, "[work] either for or against the 7 rhetor's objectives," enabling them to "take the desired action or point of view" (357). The rhetor's job is to identify these constraints, both positive and negative, and determine their importance. Since constraints can add and detract from the rhetor's argument, the rhetor must be prepared to either challenge negative constraints, turning them into positive constraints that help an argument, or ignore them entirely. Constraints can include relevant historical, religious, geographical, and economic backgrounds, precedents, and linguistics, among others. Grant-Davie does not believe that constraints can be imposed by both the rhetor and the audience; rather, he contends that this definition is too "all-inclusive" and would "threaten the usefulness" (357) of constraints, even if it does further demonstrate the interlocking relationship between the rhetor and the audience. In streamlining this definition to only include constraints imposed by the rhetor, Grant-Davie ensures that connections to the discourse do not encompass all aspects of the exigency—in that case, constraints would be synonymous to the rhetorical situation.

Throughout his article, Grant-Davie ultimately emphasizes the initiative 8 we must take to look at rhetorical discourse in terms of rhetor, exigency, audience, and constraints and to try to identify why the discourse was written and what it is trying to accomplish. Where "Rhetorical Situations and Their Constituents" looks at the relationship between all of the elements of a rhetorical situation, Porter's "Intertextuality and the Discourse Community" explores the subtleties of the rhetoric involved in the rhetorical discourse, specifically within the confines of constraints. Porter explains the concept of intertextuality, or "the principle that all writing and speech . . . arise from a single network" (396). Intertextuality, which can constrain the rhetorical freedom of the rhetor, allows for the greater social context of the discourse to shine through, rather than the rhetor's intent. The two types of intertextuality are iterability and presupposition. Where iterability "refers to the 'repeatability' of certain textual fragments . . . [like] allusions, references, and quotations within a discourse" (397), presupposition "refers to assumptions a text makes about its referent, its readers, and its context" (398). Texts are never written in isolation; there is always at least one other text that it directly borrows from or references. This interconnection between texts makes us what Porter calls the "discourse community," a group of similarly-minded people "bound by a common interest who communicate through approved channels" (400). The community may communicate through journals, conferences, or meetings, and often have conversations about the type of rhetoric accompanying their discourse — which can include anything from the format of the discourse to the characteristics of valid evidence. Porter further stresses our need to produce "'socialized writers'" (404). We must be knowledgeable of the presuppositions, iterability, and the conversations about discourse happening within specific fields of thought and communities of people with the same common goal. Only then will we begin to see our own work as a product of not only ourselves, but also those around us, a larger community of individuals working intertextually.

Kantz ties both Grant-Davies's and Porter's technical arguments about the components of rhetorical situations together in her more theoretical essay "Helping Students Use Textual Sources Persuasively." She argues primarily for the restructuring of the synthesis paper assignment, wherein students are expected to construct original opinions of their sources. Kantz uses an anecdote to illustrate her point, utilizing a fictitious college sophomore, Shirley, who is asked to write a research paper, but only summarizes the information set forth in her sources instead of collating them as evidence for an original argument. If she had looked for the discrepancies within her sources — the points of disconnect — she could have written a much more creative essay that explored a new idea or concept. Kantz believes that many students misunderstand texts because they "read them as stories," "expect them to tell the truth," and "do not understand that facts are a kind of claim . . . used persuasively in so-called objective writing to create an impression" (433). Kantz elaborates on this final statement by saying that facts and opinions are both just claims, differing only in how they are received by an audience. Facts are those which an audience will accept as the truth without requiring proof, while opinions are treated more skeptically. Only by delving deeper into the "So what?" of a text does Kantz believe students can "improve [their] writing habits" (442).

Grant-Davie, Porter, and Kantz all express the importance of examining rhe- 10
torical discourse more closely and with greater attention to the many different
interlocking parts. Only by recognizing these parts will we be able to construct
more innovative work and address discourse communities more effectively.

A RHETORICAL READING OF EMMA WATSON'S
PHOTOSHOOT CONTROVERSY

Though we might not always realize it, rhetorical strategies are at play within 11
the media we encounter in our everyday life. Rhetors of blog posts, newspaper
articles, and even Facebook statuses navigate constraints and presuppositions
to convince their audience that their
particular argument—a response to the
exigency—is the most important and
correct one. Once we recognize these
rhetorical strategies, we can ascertain
which argument we believe is the most
truthful and we can subsequently use these
strategies in our own writing.

> Though we might not always
> realize it, rhetorical strategies
> are at play within the
> media we encounter in our
> everyday life.

Recently, Emma Watson posed semi-topless for a photoshoot with *Vanity* 12
Fair. Even though a bolero-style shrug kept her from being fully topless,
this photoshoot divided many people, specifically within the feminist
community. Many were outraged with Watson's semi-topless display, like Julia
Hartley-Brewer. She took to Twitter to ridicule Watson, saying "Emma Watson:
'Feminism, feminism . . . gender wage gap . . . why oh why am I not taken
seriously . . . feminism . . . oh, and here are my tits!'" (@JuliaHB1). Others still
were outraged by the overwhelming critical response to Watson's semi-topless
display and began sharing personal pictures in support of Watson on Twitter
accompanied by the hashtag, "#WhatFeministsWear" (Weiner).

Various articles were written in response to this event, but the three I will be 13
exploring in further detail are from *The Huffington Post*, *The Spectator*, and *The
Independent*, respectively. In *The Huffington Post* article, "Emma Watson's Boobs
Prove Why We Still Need Feminism," Hannah Cranston speaks out in support
of Watson's photoshoot, arguing for a greater inclusion of free choice within
feminist ideology. Charlotte Gill wrote the article "Emma Watson's 'have your
cake and eat it' feminism is hard to swallow" for *The Spectator*, and she asserts
that Watson's photoshoot was not a feminist act in the slightest; rather, Watson
turned her back on the more modest feminism she once preached and thus can
no longer be a strong female role model for young girls. Finally, in *The Independent*, Biba Kang explains that the argument over feminism must be examined
intersectionally within her article "Did Emma Watson pose 'topless' because
of the patriarchy or despite of it? I doubt she knows herself." She explores the

privilege Watson has as a white, western woman within the beauty industry and uses this controversy to expose the non-western diversity imbalance.

Though Cranston, Gill, and Kang all respond to the controversy surrounding 14 Watson's photoshoot with *Vanity Fair*, they each respond to a different underlying issue. Cranston focuses on solidifying what feminism actually means—"women having a CHOICE" (Cranston)—and redefining what it means to be a woman—"women can be smart and sexual and sassy and sophisticated and still want to make the same amount of money as their male counterparts, ALL AT THE SAME TIME" (Cranston). In targeting this aspect of feminism, Cranston concentrates on the most basic level of what it means to truly be a feminist and thus responds in support of women having free choice to wear and do what they want. Gill also concentrates on this basic definitional level, but takes a different direction. She denounces the "superficiality of third-wave feminism" and instead focuses on the underlying question of whether or not nudity—or semi-nudity—really empowers women or if it only "confirms what a trivial, shallow industry feminism has become" (Gill). Gill's article centers on what constitutes feminism, how people have come to perceive it, and what it really should mean: empowering women to go "saving the world" (Gill). In this regard, she is responding to Cranston's statement, "Women have a choice," by essentially saying "Women need to be held accountable for misplaced feminism," or, even "Women should not dress immodestly." Where Cranston and Gill both look to define feminism, Kang looks at the causes of feminism, the reasons behind why women do the things they do and how those reasons relate to intersectionality. The driving question behind her article is "'Am I doing this *because* of the patriarchy or *in spite* of the patriarchy?'" (Kang) which allows Kang to explore the complex relationship between feminism and sexual expression in a society that does not always accept non-western women. She is responding directly to the underlying issue of white feminism in society, and specifically within the beauty industry, that perpetuates a cycle of racism and colorism. These respective schools of thought drive Cranston's, Gill's, and Kang's discourse and showcase what they believe is important within the context of Watson's photoshoot controversy. Cranston and Gill see the definition of feminism as important and seek to reevaluate how society views feminism, while Kang views intersectionality as the most important aspect of feminist discourse, which guides her argument in a completely different direction than Cranston's and Gill's.

Each argument varies in construction due to its rhetor, who argues from 15 a specific feminist identity, as she appeals to her desired audience. In *The Huffington Post* article, Cranston writes from a very liberal, pro-woman's choice perspective, calling out society for not being able to "handle a woman who is both 'sexual AND serious'" (Cranston). She states the most "egregious" comment made against Watson was that she is a "'bad feminist'" (Cranston), implying that even amidst the slut-shaming and bullying Watson faced as a result of her photoshoot, the slight against feminism was still the greatest offender. Based on the political alignment of *The Huffington Post*, Cranston's audience immediately includes liberals, a point emphasized with an anti-Trump comment stating that the news surrounding Watson's photoshoot had "seemingly overtaken the discussion of Trump's latest tweet (a welcome tangent, might I add)" (Cranston). This tangential comment has nothing to do with Watson or feminism—besides the fact that it references Trump—so it really has nothing to do within this article, except to further point out where Cranston lies on the political spectrum. Her audience is even narrower than liberals, however. She is primarily speaking to liberal feminists who believe "the fight towards gender equality is contingent on women having a CHOICE" (Cranston). Many conservative feminists—or even conservatives in general—would not read beyond the first few sentences, or even the title. Cranston's complete support of Watson would not attract much support from those who believe in a more structured, reserved feminism.

In *The Spectator* article, Gill writes from a conservative feminist perspective. 16 Her article is riddled with sarcasm, contributing to Gill's air of moral authority; she calls Watson's complaints about the female princess stereotype "laughable," considering Watson played Belle in a recent adaptation of *Beauty and the Beast*, and states how she thinks, "frankly," a "UN ambassador has better things to worry about than frocks and fairytales" (Gill). Gill's mocking tone strengthens her criticism of Watson, implying Watson is being frivolous with her responsibilities as a feminist and a figurehead of gender equality. Gill additionally calls "third-wave feminism" a "trivial, shallow industry," reducing it to a commercialized movement, while exalting what she sees as feminism to a higher state of legitimacy. She looks down on the feminism Watson practices and does not even believe it is worthy of the title of feminism at all. *The Spectator* publishes for a conservative audience, so it makes sense that Gill's article appeals to a conservative feminist audience. Where Cranston believes in free choice for all, Gill believes in a toned-down version of choice, a choice that still holds women accountable for how they act. Belittling Watson's photoshoot decision, Gill speaks to anyone who believes that ideas are more important than the liberation that some women see comes with taking back their bodies. In labeling Watson's feminism as being of the "'have your cake and eat it'" sort, Gill suggests that those who have not swallowed this brand of feminism have seen past something that everyone else has fallen for—and those in her audience who have seen past Watson's feminist contradictions belong to an elite level of feminists because of it.

In *The Independent* article, Kang writes from a largely liberal feminist per- 17 spective, but also includes her identity as a non-western woman to criticize yet another aspect of Watson's photoshoot. Though Kang believes Watson had every right to "present her adult sexuality" in such a way, she believes calling Watson's shoot a "'feminist act' ignores that it is only certain body types that magazines such as *Vanity Fair* choose to show in a sexual light in the first place" (Kang). Kang proceeds to attack the normalized notions of western beauty standards; her moral authority stems from this non-western identity and her view that westernized ideals are less than inclusive. She urges all feminists to ask themselves "'Am I doing this *because* of the patriarchy or *in spite* of the patriarchy?'" effectively helping them to determine what is driving their actions and how best to approach certain aspects of their lives (Kang). Like *The Huffington Post, The Independent* publishes for a largely liberal audience, but instead of writing for a specifically feminist audience, Kang writes for a western feminist audience to educate them about the perils of white feminism and privilege. Kang's title — "Did Emma Watson pose 'topless' because of the patriarchy or despite of it? I doubt she knows herself" — reads like it would be more suitable for conservative feminists, but once one begins to read her article, it is clear she does not believe Watson should be "held to unfair standards for the crime of expressing that she thinks women should be equal to men" (Kang) and is thus writing to those Gill would call "third-wave feminists" (Gill). Kang further specializes her audience when she addresses body image ideals that are prevalent in western society, but even as she narrows her audience, she also broadens it. She has a message she wants to bring to western society, and she talks both to supporters and non-supporters of Watson, trying to help them to understand the underlying issues present — "Watson is profiting from standards which favor her, and contributing to a culture which keeps other women from attaining her levels of success" (Kang). Kang's article is educational to everyone, and as she speaks from a non-western perspective, she can provide insights about privilege to her primarily western audience.

Each of these articles engages in a unique discourse community. Where Cranston's article speaks primarily to liberal feminists, Gill counteracts this by speaking to conservative feminists who believe in modest boundaries. Kang's conversation, however, extends into feminist intersectionality, exploring how both western beauty ideals and privilege contribute to a society in which non-western women are not typically represented. 18

These articles also exhibit constraints, some in the form of presuppositions, that both add and detract from their arguments. Cranston's credibility as a reliable rhetor falls under question when one reads her short biography, which states she is a "Millennial Internet Personality and TV Host" (Cranston). Though Cranston is the host and executive producer of YouTube's Think Tank and a regular guest host on The Young Turks, both popular online news networks, many people view the word "millennial" as degrading. The choice of "Internet Personality" further alienates her; many people associate the term with lazy teenagers who make videos for a living and do not do any sort of legitimate work. Cranston's most prominent constraint, however, which ends up being both positive and negative, is her breakdown of what feminism actually stands for, which, to her, is free choice. Cranston presupposes that those reading her 19 article value free choice and view the reclamation of the female body as liberating. Everyone seems to have their own definition of what feminism is or what feminism should be, so even though Cranston—and many others—may celebrate the intersection between "flaunting one's figure and a feminist agenda," some people may regard those two ideas as "mutually exclusive" (Cranston). Feminists who believe there should still be some degree of modesty in female action would not appreciate Cranston's argument as much as feminists who view choice as the driving force behind equality.

Gill's most prominent constraint is positive: Not many people will be writing 20 in an anti-Watson, conservative feminist vein, so simply by having an unpopular opinion—there is a "real whiff of hypocrisy" (Gill) surrounding Watson's *Vanity Fair* photoshoot—she will receive more viewership. While this viewership does not guarantee people will agree with her argument, it draws more people in who will be willing to read it. Throughout her article, Gill uses Watson's own words against her, making it seem strange that Watson is giving in to ideals that were not a part of her feminist ideology beforehand and calling out Watson's ability to "contradict [the] very platitudes" (Gill) she is so vocal about supporting. Gill presupposes that the majority of her audience value empowerment in the form of breaking traditional gender roles, not reclaiming female sexuality or femininity, and because of this negative constraint, she could alienate her audience members who believe that one can be traditionally "girly" and still be a feminist.

Though Kang takes such a distinct look at the implications of Watson's pho- 21 toshoot, the majority of the constraints surrounding her argument are positive. Her unique argument is even a positive constraint; as it is a new take on the controversy, more people may read it because it is written from a perspective no one has thought about yet. Additionally, she manages to appeal to all feminists—both conservative and liberal—in defining feminism in terms of "women [being] equal to men" (Kang). She turns the entire argument about Watson's feminism around to unite *all* feminists under a shared hatred for the patriarchy, acknowledging the prevalent "influence" (Kang) sexism has on many worldviews and presupposing the consensus that can be reached in a denouncement of the patriarchy. The biggest negative constraint Kang faces is her discussion of western beauty ideals and the privilege Watson profits from. Some people may not believe this article is the place to discuss feminism in an intersectional sense; this topic change could be seen as almost a derailment from the original controversy. Others, however, could see this issue as being about more than just defining feminism, which would turn the negative constraint into a positive one and add to Kang's argument.

Cranston, Gill, and Kang explore diverse aspects of what each believes is 22 the most important part of feminism and therefore construct their arguments according to their identities within the feminist community. Though each responds to a slightly different underlying exigency, each article finds its roots in the facets of feminist thought as its rhetor seeks to minimize or challenge the constraints that confine her argument and thus better reach her audience.

A CALL FOR RHETORICAL LITERACY

In these three articles, Cranston, Gill, and Kang construct their original dis- 23 course in a creative and analytical way, using their own identities as rhetors within their respective discourse communities to respond to the issues they believe are most significant and convince their audience that their opinion is the correct one. After investigating the rhetorical situations surrounding each article, we, as the audience, can probably determine which one is the most credible or least biased—and which one we believe. Without the ability to perform rhetorical analyses, however, we would not even know where to begin to break down the rhetoric of the articles and understand them on a deeper level. Rhetorical analysis drives us to "find answers to problem questions" (Kantz 442), allowing for original thought and change within communities. When we have the tools to recognize rhetorical strategies at play in our daily lives, we can develop educated and informed opinions by questioning the credibility of a rhetor or examining how the rhetor deals with constraints. Rhetorical literacy is especially important now that we live in a time when news sources might not even be reporting truthfully. We cannot live within the spheres of thought specific articles or media sources might produce; rather, we must all realize how the rhetorical strategies present in the media work to shift our thinking. Because without effective analysis, we will not be able to construct original opinions, and instead of thinking for ourselves, we will remain beholden to the will of the media.

Works Cited

@JuliaHB1. "Emma Watson: 'Feminism, feminism . . . gender wage gap . . . why oh why am I not taken seriously . . . feminism . . . oh, and here are my tits!'" *Twitter*, 1 Mar. 2017, 1:40 a.m., twitter.com/juliahb1/status/836873834414366720?lang=en.

Cranston, Hannah. "Emma Watson's Boobs Prove Why We Still Need Feminism." *The Huffington Post*, 2 Mar. 2017, huffingtonpost.com/entry/emma-watsons-boobs-prove-why-we-still-need-feminism_us_58b8bd55e4b02b8b584df9f4. Accessed 3 Mar. 2017.

Gill, Charlotte. "Emma Watson's 'have your cake and eat it' feminism is hard to swallow." *The Spectator*, 2 Mar. 2017, blogs.spectator.co.uk/2017/03/emma-watsons-cake-eat-feminism-hard-swallow/. Accessed 3 Mar. 2017.

Grant-Davie, Keith. "Rhetorical Situations and Their Constituents." Wardle and Downs, pp. 347–64.

Kang, Biba. "Did Emma Watson pose 'topless' because of the patriarchy or despite of it? I doubt she knows herself." *The Independent*, 3 Mar. 2017, independent.co.uk/voices/emma-watson-topless-shot-vanity-fair-photo-feminism-patriarchy-what-you-want-a7609236.html. Accessed 3 Mar. 2017.

Kantz, Margaret. "Helping Students Use Textual Sources Persuasively." Wardle and Downs, pp. 428–45.

Porter, James E. "Intertextuality and the Discourse Community." Wardle and Downs, pp. 395–409.

Wardle, Elizabeth, and Doug Downs, editors. *Writing about Writing*. 3rd ed., Bedford/St. Martin's, 2014.

Weiner, Zoe. "#WhatFeministsWear: Tweets in Support of Emma Watson Prove Feminists Can Wear Whatever They Want." *Allure*, 6 Mar. 2017, allure.com/story/emma-watson-hashtag-what-feminists-wear. Accessed 3 Apr. 2017.

- -

Questions for Discussion and Journaling

1. Arbutus relies on and cites several of the readings from this chapter to frame her essay. How does she do this? What is her purpose in citing these scholars?

2. What elements of the articles that disagree about Watson's choices does Arbutus analyze?

3. What is Arbutus's primary claim about why rhetoric is important in our daily lives?

4. Why does Arbutus believe that it is more important than ever for citizens to be able to engage in rhetorical analysis?

Applying and Exploring Ideas

1. Arbutus looks at different texts on the same topic that disagree and works to understand why and how they disagree, and how readers should navigate these differences. What is your own experience navigating sources that disagree? For example, when you have been conducting research for a paper and find sources that contradict one another, have you been taught how to handle this? If you are watching news stories where people disagree with one another, how do you work to understand the differences?

2. Look for an example in your daily life of sources that disagree (on TV, in the newspaper, etc.). What are these sources? What do they disagree about? What's your initial inclination about which to agree and disagree with?

3. Look again at the sources that disagree from the previous question, applying some of the lenses that Arbutus uses. You can ask, for example, who are the rhetors? What is the exigence? What assumptions are the rhetors making about their audiences? Once you have considered these questions, do your views about the believability of the sources change?

- -

META MOMENT   What are a few questions you can ask yourself when you encounter arguments in your daily life in order to help you better establish whether the rhetor is credible and should be believed?

- -

Writing about Rhetoric

Assignment Option 1

RHETORICAL ANALYSIS OF A PREVIOUS WRITING EXPERIENCE

Think back: What's the most memorable piece of writing you've ever done? What was the situation? And how did that situation help shape the writing? In this four-to five-page rhetorical analysis of a memorable writing experience, your task as a writer is to reflect on how that particular writing experience was a result of the particular situation it was related to — how the situation helped determine what you wrote and why.

Writers are always responding to the situations they're writing in, from, and for, more or less consciously. But even when you're not aware of it, you're responding to rhetorical situations (and were even before you knew that term or concept). This assignment can show you how you've already been doing that and spur your thinking about what possibilities writing holds if you do it more consciously.

Analysis Description and Object of Study. Your rhetorical analysis will be based on some significant piece of writing or writing experience that you've had in the last several years. That writing could have been for school, work, family, or your personal life. It could have been completely private (like a journaling experience) or all-the-way public, like a blog or other online post. It could have been a single short document, like a poem or song lyrics, or it could have been an extended project or experience that involved multiple pieces of writing. The key requirement here is that it has to have been a memorable or important enough experience that you can clearly remember the circumstances surrounding the writing.

Once you know what experience and writing you want to focus on, you need to reflect on and analyze that experience and writing from a rhetorical perspective. What does that mean? Remember that your overall research question — what you're trying to find out that you don't already know — is how did your rhetorical situation help shape that piece of writing. Based on the principles Grant-Davie demonstrates as well as work you do in class, consider the following questions about the experience you had and the circumstances surrounding it:

- Why did you need to write to begin with (exigence)? Since it's easier not to write than it is to write, there had to be some reason or purpose behind your writing, some problem to be solved or addressed. What was that?

- Where did that need come from (context)? What gave rise to it? This is a historical question: To understand the circumstances that demanded writing, you need to know what led to those circumstances.

- What constraints did you face as a writer? What were the givens in your situation — the aspects of it you could not change that controlled what you could do with your writing?

- Who was meant to read and use your writing and what did you want them to do with it (audience)? How was your writing supposed to do something for, to, or with the readers you imagined it for?

The answers to all of these questions, and others, will help you talk about why this piece of writing took the shape that it did.

Planning, Drafting, and Revising. In order to make your analysis most meaningful and clear both to you and to other readers, it will need to include at least the following features:

- An introduction explaining what inquiry your research question poses

- Some description of the writing you're focusing on and the experience itself. You might even include an electronic copy of the writing you're talking about, if one is still available, but in many cases that may not be possible. Whether you can do that or not, take whatever space is necessary in your analysis to describe as clearly as possible what this writing and experience were.

- An extended discussion of the questions above in order to describe and analyze the rhetorical situation in which the writing or experience occurred

- A conclusion including implications of your reflection: What did you learn from this? What principles can you draw to help you in future writing situations?

What Makes It Good? While your rhetorical analysis of a writing experience may take a number of different shapes, it will tend to include these traits:

- Meaningful and accurate use of rhetorical terms such as exigence, constraints, audience (or readers), purpose, motivation, and context

- A focus on and clear account of how the writing you're analyzing was shaped by the situation and circumstances in which you were writing it

- A main point about the writing, the situation, or rhetorical principles more broadly

- Readable and usable flow through the main parts of the piece (such as a description of the writing itself and the experience of writing it, to the aspects of the rhetorical situation that shaped it)

- Evidence that you understand how rhetorical situations constrain writing (in the broad sense of *constrain* that Grant-Davie offers)

Assignment Option 2

NAVIGATING SOURCES THAT DISAGREE

In this chapter you have considered how writers and readers play an active role in constructing texts and making meaning. Grant-Davie, Kantz, and Haas and Flower have demonstrated that understanding the rhetorical situation is central to actively engaging and creating texts. In order to explore this idea further, you will examine texts that appear to disagree and analyze them rhetorically in order to understand how and why their authors disagree.

Brainstorming.   Find an issue that is currently being debated publicly, either in your local campus community or in a larger state or national arena. Make sure that this is a complex issue rather than a simple black-and-white problem. The more nuanced or more difficult the debate is, the more useful your analysis will be — to you as well as others.

Research and Analysis.   Carefully choose three different sources within your debate that do not agree. Look for texts that demonstrate nuanced kinds of disagreement rather than just settling for obvious "pro" and "con" sources. Remember that the point of this assignment is to help you learn something about how texts are constructed and how meaning is made. If you choose obvious texts to analyze, you won't learn nearly as much as you could have — and your paper will be much harder to write.

Once you have chosen your three sources, decide how to analyze them. Go back to the readings in this chapter and use them to create a list of questions that you could ask of each artifact. Creating this list of questions is something that your entire class could do together. For example, you could list questions about the rhetorical situations for each text, as well as for the larger context of the debate in which they exist. You might also ask who the authors (or rhetors) are and what their values, motivations, and constraints might be. You could ask questions about the arguments that the authors are making. What are their points? Do they disagree on everything or just some points? What kinds of evidence do they use? Do they seem to believe that the same things even count as evidence?

Once you have created a list of questions to ask in your rhetorical analysis, ask them of each text in turn. Take notes as you analyze your text.

Once you have answered the same questions about each text, organize your notes. You might make a chart for yourself so that you can see answers to the questions for each side by side.

Planning.   Now that you have conducted the research and analyzed the texts, look at your organized notes and then take a step back and ask yourself what you found. Go back to your original question and try to answer it: How and why do the authors of these texts disagree? You might have one clear answer to this question, and you might have several potential ideas regarding why they can't agree.

Make a list of your main findings. These can serve as primary claims in the analysis essay you will draft. Under each claim/finding, list some examples/evidence from your analysis notes to support and illustrate your claims.

Drafting.   Write an analytical, research-based essay in which you provide an answer to the question: Why do authors of texts in the debate on X disagree? And how?

Provide background information on the debate and the three texts you chose to analyze. Also explain how you conducted your analysis, pointing to the authors in this chapter who helped you figure out what questions to ask about the artifacts. Then make your claim(s) in answer to the question, and provide the textual evidence from your analysis to support your claims. End your essay with some sort of "so what?" Tell your readers, who are most likely your teacher and classmates, why it would be useful to have this analysis and why it is important to understand how texts are constructed and how meaning is made — or not.

Revising.   Good, thoughtful work usually takes time, planning, and reconsideration. What you've been asked to do in this activity is not easy, and you are more likely to write an effective text if you take the time to get feedback from some other writers you trust. Work with a classmate or a writing center tutor, and ask these writers if they think that you have effectively completed the assignment. Ask them to help you in specific ways. For example, ask them if you have given thoughtful reasons for why the sources disagree. Do they think you need more evidence? Do they believe your claims? Are they persuaded by the evidence that you provide? As readers, are they helped by the organization you chose for your paper? If not, what changes would help them? Consider your peers' feedback and make appropriate revisions. Note that at this point in the drafting process, you would do well to focus your revisions on global issues rather than fixating on eliminating "errors" or finding a bigger word. This assignment asks you to conduct a careful analysis, and that is what your revision should focus on strengthening.

What Makes It Good?   Your essay will be evaluated in terms of how well it accomplished the goals set out. Remember that your essay should answer the following questions: Why do authors of texts in the debate on X disagree? And how? A strong essay will orient the reader by initially providing enough background information on the debate and the three texts you chose to analyze. A strong essay will make clear claim(s) in answer to the questions and provide the textual evidence that is convincing and clear to the reader. An effective essay will be organized such that the reader can follow along without having to work to figure out where you are going. It will also be polished and edited so that the reader understands what you are arguing and is not distracted from your claims.

Assignment Option 3

RHETORICAL READING ANALYSIS: RECONSTRUCTING A TEXT'S CONTEXT, EXIGENCE, MOTIVATIONS, AND AIMS

This assignment asks you to practice the rhetorical reading strategies that Haas and Flower describe in "Rhetorical Reading Strategies and the Construction of Meaning" (p. 432). As a college writer, you need to make rhetorical reading a normal habit. To read texts rhetorically is to read them as if they're people talking to you, people with motivations that may not always be explicit but are always present. It means talking about not only what a text says or what it means, but what it does. (Start a war? Make a friend smile? Throw shade? Refocus everyone's attention? Woo a lover?) When you read a text trying to figure out what it does or why a person would go to the trouble of writing it, you're reading rhetorically.

For this rhetorical reading project, the object of your analysis will be a scholarly journal article or book chapter. Working in this genre will give you important additional practice for reading scholarly work rhetorically in your later classes, and you'll probably have a lot to learn about how scholarly communities work in order to do the assignment well. Your task is to rhetorically read a text and compose a four- to five-page piece that explains your interpretation of what the writer meant the text to accomplish, and why.

Select a Text. Your instructor might simply have you use any of the scholarly articles in this book (or choose from a smaller group of them). Or, you might find a scholarly article of your own, either in writing and rhetoric studies or in your major. You'll probably be more engaged in the project if the subject is of interest to you, so be sure to pick an article about something you care about. Whatever text you choose, you must be able to trace where it was published, when, and by whom.

Summarize the Text. The first rule of rhetorical reading is: read in order to first be able to write a summary of about one page. As you read, take notes about these aspects of the text in order to be able to write an effective summary:

- The territory the text covers and the niche it occupies, which may be its research questions or its thesis, if you can identify one. (Return to the Swales CARS model in Chapter 3 for help with this)
- The text's main parts or sections
- The author's underlying theoretical framework (underlying theories or principles it uses to study or interpret whatever it's focused on) if the author shares this
- Research methods, if the author shares these (for help with this you might return to Chapter 3)

501

- The author's findings, main claims, main discoveries
- The implications of the piece (which will be mostly in the conclusion and potentially in the introduction as well if they are stated directly)

Now that you know basically what the author is saying and how, you can move on to consider rhetorical elements.

Historicize the Text.   Along with summarizing what the text says, you'll need to collect some basic information on the text's origins. Most of this information is contextual, meaning that it lies outside of the text itself and you can't just read the text to find what you want to know. As you look for origins, try to answer these questions:

- *Who wrote it*? This might be in the article itself, although sometimes biographies are not provided. You can use a web search to learn more about the author.
- *Who published it*? What journal or book did it originally appear in, and who publishes that journal or book? What can you learn about that publisher? What kinds of work do they usually publish, and what is the purpose of the journal or book it appeared in? Search for the journal's or publisher's web page to answer these questions.
- *Who reads this*? Most journals or publishers have an "About" page that will describe their intended readership. You could also use Google Scholar and look at citations for this book or journal to find out who is citing it.
- *When was the text written*? This information tells you two things: (1) What the writer could and could not have known at that point in time, and (2) where on a historical "timeline" the text fits — whether it was written before, during, or after a particular conversation the field or a society was having, for example.

By asking these questions you are building your sense of the text's history — how it fit in a particular rhetorical ecology, that web of rhetors, circumstances, events, and material objects that would have originally given rise to the text to begin with. Effective rhetorical reading is impossible without such historicizing.

Write Your Interpretation of the Text's Context, Exigence, Motivations, and Aims.   Now you are ready to write your answers to the central questions: What does this text do (or did it do when it was written) and why did the author want it to do that? In your rhetorical analysis you will provide your interpretation of the text's history and contents in order to make some claims about its exigence and the writer's motivations and aims, given the context in which the text was written.

There is no set format for your rhetorical analysis, but you want to be sure you do the following:

- Discuss the text's *context*: where and when it appeared, what the historical moment was, and pertinent information about the writer and publisher.

- Discuss the *conversation* in which the article participates: It may be helpful to use Swales's CARS terms of *territory* and *niche* to assist this discussion.

- Summarize what the article *says*: Incorporate the short (approximately one-page) summary that you created after reading the article.

- Describe the writer's main *argument*: their central claim, the support for that claim, and any major warrants that readers must agree with in order to build adherence with the argument. (If any of this language is confusing to you, read or reread Downs, p. 369.)

- Draw conclusions about the *exigence*, *motivations*, and *aims* of the text: What was writer trying to accomplish in this text, and why?

- Offer evidence for your interpretations: When you make a claim about the text or its context, what evidence do you have to support that claim? It could be quotations from the text or information from external sources that you've found in your research to historicize the text.

An analysis that accomplishes each of these functions should be both an interesting rhetorical reading of your article and highly informative for the reader of your analysis. Most importantly, it will be an excellent example of rhetorical reading.

What Makes It Good?   Your analysis should demonstrate that you understood the text you read, that you were able to find and interpret evidence about its history and context, and that you can clearly explain these things to readers and provide evidence to support your claims.

CHAPTER 7

COMMUNITIES

Threshold Concept: People Collaborate to Get Things Done with Writing

Start your drive

$10 can provide up to $90 worth of food!

The Second Harvest Food Bank virtual food drive is a representational web-based tool that allows individuals and organizations to hold an online food drive. While we love donations in any form, our virtual food drive allows us to serve more clients, more efficiently. It's fast, easy and fun!

Second Harvest Food Bank of Orlando.

How do groups and communities influence readers, writers, and texts? How do *people collaborate to get things done with writing*? That is the threshold concept this chapter addresses. People don't write in a vacuum. Their literate histories influence their current writing practices (as demonstrated in Chapter 5), but their purposes for writing texts, and the people to and with whom they write, also influence how they write, what they write, how their texts are used, and how users make meaning of their texts. People use texts and discourse in order to *do something*, to *make meaning*. And those texts and language then *mediate meaningful activities*. (**Mediate** here means "intervene in order to shape" — see the Glossary entry for more.) People construct meaning through texts and language, and texts construct meaning as people use them.

In the photo shown here, the Second Harvest Food Bank of Central Florida is using their website to encourage possible donors to host a "virtual" food drive. To explain how a virtual food drive works, the writers use visuals, alphabetic text, numbers, and colors. They create these materials for the possible food drive hosts to use so that they don't have to create anything themselves. This page thus serves multiple purposes: to encourage people to host virtual food drives, to convince them that doing so is easy, and to provide the needed materials for doing so. These materials can also be "recomposed" and reused in another setting to encourage others to sponsor food drives for the hungry. The text here, therefore, is all about getting things done — helping readers make meaning about hunger and helping them take action to feed the hungry.

Writing intended to be used to accomplish things is extremely *social* and *relational* — it is created amidst and shaped by complex webs of people and other texts. Consider, for example, another way that food banks might raise money to feed the hungry: "appeal letters" they send out to past volunteers and donors during the November and December holiday season. The staff member who writes such a letter is influenced by her understanding of the ideas and interests of the people reading it — what they need, want, and value — as well as by her own training as a fundraiser, all of her past writing experiences, her supervisor's expectations, and her own and other staff members' experiences with past fundraising letters. The letter she writes mediates the activities of fundraising and feeding the hungry.

Readers' responses to this letter will in turn shape the work of the food bank, and the food bank and its donors, volunteers, and clients will all influence how future fundraising letters are written. The letter thus mediates the work of the food bank — how it is understood or whether it can be done at all. If the letter is not effective, the food bank might have to cut back services, and it will revise how future fundraising letters are written or distributed. At the same time, the letter might make some readers think differently about hunger and poverty — through the letter, meaning is constructed about hunger, poverty, and fundraising, and activities around them are mediated. For example, the writer might want potential donors to think about hungry children, and thus include a photo of a child in the letter — not the stereotypical "homeless person" that might first come to people's minds — and emphasize the number of hungry children in the area. In doing so, she is shaping meaning for the readers.

As Writing Studies and related fields began to understand writing as social and relational, a number of theories emerged to explain writing as a sociocultural activity, that is, an activity in which individuals in a given culture socially collaborate toward a shared end. (Remember that a **theory** is not a guess or speculation but a systematic explanation for some aspect of people's lived experience.) In this chapter, we introduce you to three sociocultural theories of writing: James Paul Gee's theory of **Discourses** (p. 507), the theory of **discourse communities** in John Swales's work (p. 544), and **activity theory** in Elizabeth Wardle's work (p. 636). Each seeks to explain how texts are constructed as a result of the needs and activities of various groups, and how groups of people use communication to achieve their shared goals and purposes. You could be wondering why, if a theory is supposed to be a good explanation for a given phenomenon, there are so many — why not just one *right* one? The answer is simply that complex phenomena, like writing, have many different aspects that are best explained by specific theories — so a complete explanation requires multiple theories. Gee's Discourse theory is good at explaining how language itself creates community. (Gee's piece is followed by Tony Mirabelli's article demonstrating the theory in action.) Both John Swales and Ann Johns describe evolving theories of discourse communities (and are followed by Peri Klass's, Lucille McCarthy's, Sean Branick's, and Arielle Feldman's studies demonstrating discourse communities in action). Swales and Johns describe how communities built around shared discourse accomplish their ends. And activity theory, as Wardle introduces it, provides the perspective of writing as a tool used by participants in **activity systems** that organize people around shared activities and goals.

Each of these theories, and the researchers working with them, help you consider how texts construct meaning for the people who read, write, and otherwise use them. You'll consider the expectations, norms, histories, and people who influence, construct, and interpret texts, and you'll consider how texts help groups get work done and achieve shared goals — or impede work when they are not successful. You'll also think carefully about the discourse (language *in use*) that helps or hinders people in their efforts to make meaning, get work done, accomplish goals, and become part of new groups (or not).

The authors whose work appears in this chapter are describing something you do every day: When you go to your dorm and interact with your roommates, for example, you are in one discourse community; when you go to biology class, you are in another. And most of us are quite efficient at navigating multiple discourse communities: What you learn in biology about evolution might conflict with what you are taught in your Bible study course, for example, but most of you learn to manage that tension and figure out how to talk and interact differently in different settings. The language and texts you use in each discourse community help you accomplish your collective purposes there.

CHAPTER GOALS

- Understand the threshold concept, *people collaborate to get things done with writing.*
- Improve as a reader of complex, research-based texts.
- Acquire vocabulary for talking about discourse, discourse communities, and your experiences as a writer.
- Understand that language and texts (genres) mediate group activities.
- Gain tools for examining the discourse and texts used by various communities.

Literacy, Discourse, and Linguistics

Introduction

JAMES PAUL GEE

Framing the Reading

James Paul Gee (his last name is pronounced like the "gee" in "gee whiz") is a Regents' Professor and Mary Lou Fulton Presidential Chair in Literacy Studies at Arizona State University. Gee has taught linguistics at the University of Wisconsin at Madison, Stanford University, Northeastern University, Boston University, and the University of Southern California. His book *Sociolinguistics and Literacies* (1990) was important in the formation of the interdisciplinary field known as "New Literacy Studies," and he's published a number of other works on literacy as well, including *Why Video Games Are Good for Your Soul* (2005). His most recent book is *Teaching, Learning, Literacy in Our High-Risk High-Tech World: A Framework for Becoming Human* (2017). Based on his research, he's a widely respected voice on literacy among his peers.

In this article, Gee introduces his term ***Discourses***, which he explains as "saying (writing)-doing-being-valuing-believing combinations" that are "ways of being in the world." (The capital D is important for Gee, to make a *Discourse* distinct from *discourse*, or "connected stretches of language" that we use every day to communicate with each other.)

As you read this article for the first time, try to (1) define terms and (2) apply what Gee is saying to your own experience by trying to think of related examples from your own life. Think back to the underlying threshold concepts of this chapter: *people collaborate to get things done with writing.* They use texts and discourse in order to *do something*, to *make meaning*; the texts and language they create *mediate meaningful activities*; and people construct meaning through texts and language, and texts

construct meaning as people use them. Ask yourself how the Discourses that Gee talks about help people make meaning or not, get things done or not.

You'll find one particularly controversial argument in the article. Gee insists that you can't "more or less" embody a

Gee, James Paul. "Literacy, Discourse, and Linguistics: Introduction." *Journal of Education*, vol. 171, no.1, 1989, pp. 5–17.

Discourse — you're either recognized by others as a full member of it or you're not. Many readers can't make this argument line up with their perceptions of their own experiences in acquiring new Discourses; they haven't experienced this "all-or-nothing" effect. When you encounter that subargument, or others you might have trouble accepting, your job as a reader is to stay engaged in the *overall* argument while "setting aside" the particular argument you're not sure about.

We do expect that readers will typically be able to see how their own experiences fit within Gee's arguments on the whole, and that beginning to understand your own Discourses — "identity kits" built around language, and ways-of-being-in-the-world — will help you recognize the ways that your writing fits into broader social groups and patterns.

Getting Ready to Read

Before you read, do at least one of the following activities:

- Google the term *mushfake*. What comes up?
- Consider two or three activities you take part in that are very different from each other, having different languages and purposes (for example, college, volunteering, and a hobby like gaming). Does one influence the way you do the others, or do they remain distinctly separate in your life? Explain.

As you read, consider the following questions:

- Why is Gee so concerned with how people learn Discourses? What does it have to do with education?
- Does Gee's discussion of Discourses sound similar to ideas you've encountered in other chapters in this book? If so, which ones?

WHAT I PROPOSE in the following papers, in the main, is a way of talking 1 about literacy and linguistics. I believe that a new field of study, integrating "psycho" and "socio" approaches to language from a variety of disciplines, is emerging, a field which we might call literacy studies. Much of this work, I think (and hope), shares at least some of the assumptions of the following papers. These papers, though written at different times, and for different purposes, are, nonetheless, based on the claim that the focus of literacy studies or applied linguistics should not be language, or literacy, but social practices. This claim, I believe, has a number of socially important and cognitively interesting consequences.

"Language" is a misleading term; it too often suggests "grammar." It is a tru- 2 ism that a person can know perfectly the grammar of a language and not know how to use that language. It is not just *what* you say, but *how* you say it. If I enter my neighborhood bar and say to my tattooed drinking buddy, as I sit down, "May I have a match please?" my grammar is perfect, but what I have said is wrong nonetheless. It is less often remarked that a person could be able to use a language perfectly and *still* not make sense. It is not just *how* you say it, but what you *are* and *do* when you say it. If I enter my neighborhood bar and say to my drinking buddy, as I sit down, "Gime a match, wouldya?," while placing a napkin on the bar stool to avoid getting my newly pressed designer jeans dirty, I have said the right thing, but my "saying-doing" combination is nonetheless all wrong.

F. Niyi Akinnaso and Cheryl Ajirotutu (1982) present "simulated job inter- 3 views" from two welfare mothers in a CETA job training program. The first woman, asked whether she has ever shown initiative in a previous job, responds: "Well, yes, there's this Walgreen's Agency, I worked as a microfilm operator, OK. And it was a snow storm, OK. And it was usually six people workin' in a group . . ." and so forth (p. 34). This woman is simply using the wrong grammar (the wrong "dialect") for this type of (middle-class) interview. It's a perfectly good grammar (dialect), it just won't get you this type of job in this type of society.

The second woman (the authors' "success" case) responds to a similar ques- 4 tion by saying " . . . I was left alone to handle the office. I didn't really have a lot of experience. But I had enough experience to deal with any situations that came up . . . and those that I couldn't handle at the time, if there was someone who had more experience than myself, I asked questions to find out what procedure I would use. If something came up and if I didn't know who to really go to, I would jot it down . . . on a piece of paper, so that I wouldn't forget that if anyone that was more qualified than myself, I could ask them about it and how I would go about solving it. So I feel I'm capable of handling just about any situation, whether it's on my own or under supervision" (p. 34). This woman hasn't got a real problem with her grammar (remember this is *speech*, not *writing*), nor is there any real problem with the *use* to which she puts that grammar, but she is expressing the *wrong values*. She views being left in charge as just another form of supervision, namely, supervision by "other people's" knowledge and expertise. And she fails to characterize her own expertise in the overly optimistic form called for by such interviews. Using this response as an example of "successful training" is only possible because the authors, aware that language is more than grammar (namely, "use"), are unaware that communication is more than language use.

At any moment we are using language we must say or write the right thing 5 in the right way while playing the right social role and (appearing) to hold the right values, beliefs, and attitudes. Thus, what is important is not language, and surely not grammar, but *saying (writing)-doing-being-valuing-believing combinations*. These combinations I call "Discourses," with a capital "D" ("discourse" with a little "d," to me, means connected stretches of language that make sense, so "discourse" is part of "Discourse"). Discourses are ways of being in the world; they are forms of life which integrate words, acts, values, beliefs, attitudes, and social identities as well as gestures, glances, body positions, and clothes.

A Discourse is a sort of "identity kit" which comes complete with the appro- 6
priate costume and instructions on how to act, talk, and often write, so as to take on a particular role that others will recognize. Being "trained" as a linguist meant that I learned to speak, think, and act like a linguist, and to recognize others when they do so. Some other examples of Discourses: (enacting) being an American or a Russian, a man or a woman, a member of a certain socioeconomic class, a factory worker or a boardroom executive, a doctor or a hospital patient, a teacher, an administrator, or a student, a student of physics or a student of literature, a member of a sewing circle, a club, a street gang, a lunchtime social gathering, or a regular at a local bar. We all have many Discourses.

How does one acquire a Discourse? It turns out that much that is claimed, 7
controversially, to be true of second language acquisition or socially situated cognition (Beebe, 1988; Dulay, Burt, & Krashen, 1982; Grosjean, 1982; Krashen, 1982, 1985a, 1985b; Krashen & Terrell, 1983; Lave, 1988; Rogoff & Lave, 1984) is, in fact, more obviously true of the acquisition of Discourses. Discourses are not mastered by overt instruction (even less so than languages, and hardly anyone ever fluently acquired a second language sitting in a classroom), but by enculturation ("apprenticeship") into social practices through scaffolded and supported interaction with people who have already mastered the Discourse (Cazden, 1988; Heath, 1983). This is how we all acquired our native language and our home-based Discourse. It is how we acquire all later, more public-oriented Discourses. If you have no access to the social practice, you don't get in the Discourse, you don't have it. You cannot overtly teach anyone a Discourse, in a classroom or anywhere else. Discourses are not bodies of knowledge like physics or archeology or linguistics. Therefore, ironically, while you can overtly teach someone *linguistics*, a body of knowledge, you can't teach them *to be a linguist*, that is, to use a Discourse. The most you can do is to let them practice being a linguist with you.

The various Discourses which constitute each of us as persons are chang- 8
ing and often are not fully consistent with each other; there is often conflict and tension between the values, beliefs, attitudes, interactional styles, uses of language, and ways of being in the world which two or more Discourses represent. Thus, there is no real sense in which we humans are consistent or well integrated creatures from a cognitive or social viewpoint, though, in fact, most Discourses assume that we are (and thus we do too, while we are in them).

All of us, through our *primary socialization* early in life in the home and peer 9
group, acquire (at least) one initial Discourse. This initial Discourse, which I call our *primary Discourse*, is the one we first use to make sense of the world and

interact with others. Our primary Discourse constitutes our original and home-based sense of identity, and, I believe, it can be seen whenever we are interacting with "intimates" in totally casual (unmonitored) social interaction. We acquire this primary Discourse, not by overt instruction, but by being a member of a primary socializing group (family, clan, peer group). Further, aspects and pieces of the primary Discourse become a "carrier" or "foundation" for Discourses acquired later in life. Primary Discourses differ significantly across various social (cultural, ethnic, regional, and economic) groups in the United States.

After our initial socialization in our home community, each of us interacts 10 with various non-home-based social institutions—institutions in the public sphere, beyond the family and immediate kin and peer group. These may be local stores and churches, schools, community groups, state and national businesses, agencies and organizations, and so forth. Each of these social institutions commands and demands one or more Discourses and we acquire these fluently to the extent that we are given access to these institutions and are allowed apprenticeships within them. Such Discourses I call *secondary Discourses*.

We can also make an important distinction between *dominant Discourses* and 11 *nondominant Discourses*. Dominant Discourses are secondary Discourses the mastery of which, at a particular place and time, brings with it the (potential) acquisition of social "goods" (money, prestige, status, etc.). Nondominant Discourses are secondary Discourses the mastery of which often brings solidarity with a particular social network, but not wider status and social goods in the society at large.

Finally, and yet more importantly, we can always ask about how much *tension* 12 *or conflict* is present between any two of a person's Discourses (Rosaldo, 1989). We have argued above that some degree of conflict and tension (if only because of the discrete historical origins of particular Discourses) will almost always be present. However, some people experience more overt and direct conflicts between two or more of their Discourses than do others (for example, many women academics feel conflict between certain feminist Discourses and certain standard academic Discourses such as traditional literary criticism). I argue that when such conflict or tension exists, it can deter acquisition of one or the other or both of the conflicting Discourses, or, at least, affect the fluency of a mastered Discourse on certain occasions of use (e.g., in stressful situations such as interviews).

Very often dominant groups in a society apply rather constant "tests" of the 13 fluency of the dominant Discourses in which their power is symbolized. These tests take on two functions: they are tests of "natives" or, at least, "fluent users" of the Discourse, and they are *gates* to exclude "non-natives" (people whose very conflicts with dominant Discourses show they were not, in fact, "born" to them). The sorts of tension and conflict we have mentioned here are particularly acute when they involve tension and conflict between one's primary Discourse and a dominant secondary Discourse.

Discourses, primary and secondary, can be studied, in some ways, like lan- 14 guages. And, in fact, some of what we know about second language acquisition is relevant to them, if only in a metaphorical way. Two Discourses can *interfere* with one another, like two languages; aspects of one Discourse can be *transferred* to another Discourse, as one can transfer a grammatical feature from one language to another. For instance, the primary Discourse of many middle-class homes has been influenced by secondary Discourses like those used in schools and business. This is much less true of the primary Discourse in many lower socioeconomic black homes, though this primary Discourse has influenced the secondary Discourse used in black churches.

Furthermore, if one has not mastered a particular secondary Discourse which 15 nonetheless one must try to use, several things can happen, things which rather resemble what can happen when one has failed to fluently master a second language. One can fall back on one's primary Discourse, adjusting it in various ways to try to fit it to the needed functions; this response is very common, but almost always socially disastrous. Or one can use another, perhaps related, secondary Discourse. Or one can use a simplified, or stereotyped version of the required secondary Discourse. These processes are similar to those linguists study under the rubrics of *language contact*, *pidginization*, and *creolization*.

I believe that any socially useful definition of "literacy" must be couched in 16 terms of the notion of Discourse. Thus, I define "*literacy*" as *the mastery of or fluent control over a secondary Discourse*. Therefore, literacy is always plural: *literacies* (there are many of them, since there are many secondary Discourses, and we all have some and fail to have others). If we wanted to be rather pedantic and literalistic, then we could define "literacy" as "mastery of or fluent control over secondary Discourses *involving print*" (which is almost all of them in a modern society). But I see no gain from the addition of the phrase "involving print," other than to assuage the feelings of people committed (as I am not) to reading and writing as decontextualized and isolable skills. We can talk about *dominant literacies* and *nondominant literacies* in terms of whether they involve mastery of dominant or nondominant secondary Discourses. We can also talk about a literacy being *liberating* ("powerful") if it can be used as a "meta-language" (a set of meta-words, meta-values, meta-beliefs) for the critique of other literacies and the way they constitute us as persons and situate us in society. Liberating literacies can reconstitute and resituate us.

My definition of "literacy" may seem innocuous, at least to someone already 17 convinced that decontextualized views of print are meaningless. Nonetheless, several "theorems" follow from it, theorems that have rather direct and unsettling consequences.

First theorem: Discourses (and therefore literacies) are not like languages in 18 one very important regard. Someone can speak English, but not fluently. However, someone cannot engage in a Discourse in a less than fully fluent manner.

You are either in it or you're not. Discourses are connected with displays of an identity; failing to fully display an identity is tantamount to announcing you don't have that identity, that at best you're a pretender or a beginner. Very often, learners of second languages "fossilize" at a stage of development significantly short of fluency. This can't happen with Discourses. If you've fossilized in the acquisition of a Discourse prior to full "fluency" (and are no longer in the process of apprenticeship), then your very lack of fluency marks you as a non-member of the group that controls this Discourse. That is, you don't have the identity or social role which is the basis for the existence of the Discourse in the first place. In fact, the lack of fluency may very well mark you as a *pretender* to the social role instantiated in the Discourse (an *outsider* with pretensions to being an *insider*).

There is, thus, no workable "affirmative action" for Discourses: you can't 19 be let into the game after missing the apprenticeship and be expected to have a fair shot at playing It. Social groups will not, usually, give their social goods — whether these are status or solidarity or both — to those who are not "natives" or "fluent users" (though "mushfake," discussed below, may sometimes provide a way for non-initiates to gain access). While this is an *empirical* claim, I believe it is one vastly supported by the sociolinguistic literature (Milroy, 1980, 1987; Milroy & Milroy, 1985).

This theorem (that there are no people who are partially literate or semilit- 20 erate, or, in any other way, literate but not fluently so) has one practical consequence: notions like "functional literacy" and "competency-based literacy" are simply incoherent. As far as literacy goes, there are only "fluent speakers" and "apprentices" (metaphorically speaking, because remember, Discourses are not just ways of talking, but ways of talking, acting, thinking, valuing, etc.).

Second theorem: Primary Discourses, no matter whose they are, can never 21 really be liberating literacies. For a literacy to be liberating it must contain both the Discourse it is going to critique and a set of meta-elements (language, words, attitudes, values) in terms of which an analysis and criticism can be carried out. Primary Discourses are initial and contain only themselves. They can be embedded in later Discourses and critiqued, but they can never serve as a meta-language in terms of which a critique of secondary Discourses can be carried out. Our second theorem is not likely to be very popular. Theorem 2 says that all primary Discourses are limited. "Liberation" ("power"), in the sense I am using the term here, resides in acquiring at least one more Discourse in terms of which our own primary Discourse can be analyzed and critiqued.

This is not to say that primary Discourses do not contain critical attitudes 22 and critical language (indeed, many of them contain implicit and explicit racism and classism). It is to say that they cannot carry out an *authentic* criticism, because they cannot verbalize the words, acts, values, and attitudes they use, and they cannot mobilize explicit meta-knowledge. Theorem 2 is quite traditional and conservative — it is the analogue of Socrates's theorem that the unexamined life is not worth living. Interestingly enough, Vygotsky (1987, chapter 6) comes very closely to stating this theorem explicitly.

Other theorems can be deduced from the theory of literacy here developed, 23 but these two should make clear what sorts of consequences the theory has. It should also make it quite clear that the theory is *not* a neutral meta-language in terms of which one can argue for *just any* conclusions about literacy.

Not all Discourses involve writing or reading, though many do. However, all 24 writing and reading is embedded in some Discourse, and that Discourse always involves more than writing and reading (e.g., ways of talking, acting, valuing, and so forth). You cannot teach anyone to write or read outside any Discourse (there is no such thing, unless it is called "moving a pen" or "typing" in the case of writing, or "moving one's lips" or "mouthing words" in the case of reading). Within a Discourse you are always teaching more than writing or reading. When I say "teach" here, I mean "apprentice someone in a master-apprentice relationship in a social practice (Discourse) wherein you scaffold their growing ability to say, do, value, believe, and so forth, within that Discourse, through demonstrating your mastery and supporting theirs even when it barely exists (i.e., you make it look as if they can do what they really can't do)." That is, you do much the same thing middle-class, "super baby" producing parents do when they "do books" with their children.

> [A]ll writing and reading is embedded in some Discourse, and that Discourse always involves more than writing and reading (e.g., ways of talking, acting, valuing, and so forth).

Now, there are many Discourses connected to schools (different ones for 25 different types of school activities and different parts of the curriculum) and other public institutions. These "middle-class mainstream" sorts of Discourses often carry with them power and prestige. It is often felt that good listeners and good readers ought to pay attention to *meaning* and not focus on the petty details of mechanics, "correctness," the superficial features of language. Unfortunately, many middle-class mainstream status-giving Discourses often *do* stress superficial features of language. Why? Precisely because such superficial features are the *best* test as to whether one was apprenticed in the "right" place, at the "right" time, with the "right" people. Such superficial features are exactly the parts of Discourses most impervious to overt instruction and are only fully mastered when everything else in the Discourse is mastered. Since these Discourses are used as "gates" to ensure that the "right" people get to the "right" places in our society, such superficial features are ideal. A person who writes in a petition or office memo: "If you cancel the show, all the performers would have did all that hard work for nothing" has signaled that he or she isn't the "right sort of person" (was not fully acculturated to the Discourse that supports this identity). That signal stays meaningful long after the content of the memo is forgotten, or even when the content was of no interest in the first place.

Now, one can certainly encourage students to simply "resist" such "superfi- 26 cial features of language." And, indeed, they will get to do so from the bottom of society, where their lack of mastery of such superficialities was meant to place them anyway. But, of course, the problem is that such "superficialities" cannot be taught in a regular classroom in any case; they can't be "picked up" later, outside the full context of an early apprenticeship (at home and at school) in "middle-class-like" school-based ways of doing and being. That is precisely why they work so well as "gates." This is also precisely the tragedy of E. D. Hirsch, Jr.'s much-talked-about book *Cultural Literacy* (1987), which points out that without having mastered an extensive list of trivialities people can be (and often are) excluded from "goods" controlled by dominant groups in the society. Hirsch is wrong in thinking that this can be taught (in a classroom of all places!) apart from the socially situated practices that these groups have incorporated into their homes and daily lives. There is a real contradiction here, and we ignore it at the peril of our students and our own "good faith" (no middle-class "super baby" producing parents ignore it).

Beyond changing the social structure, is there much hope? No, there is not. 27 So we better get on about the process of changing the social structure. Now, whose job is that? I would say, people who have been allotted the job of teaching Discourses, for example, English teachers, language teachers, composition teachers, TESOL teachers, studies-skills teachers. We can pause, also, to remark on the paradox that even though Discourses cannot be overtly taught, and cannot readily be mastered late in the game, the University wants teachers to overtly teach and wants students to demonstrate mastery. Teachers of Discourses take on an impossible job, allow themselves to be evaluated on how well they do it, and accept fairly low status all the while for doing it.

So what can teachers of Discourses do? Well, there happens to be an advan- 28 tage to failing to master mainstream Discourses, that is, there is an advantage to being socially "maladapted." When we have really mastered anything (e.g., a Discourse), we have little or no conscious awareness of it (indeed, like dancing, Discourses wouldn't work if people were consciously aware of what they were doing while doing it). However, when we come across a situation where we are unable to accommodate or adapt (as many minority students do on being faced, late in the game, with having to acquire mainstream Discourses), we become consciously aware of what we are trying to do or are being called upon to do. Let me give an example that works similarly, that is, the case of classroom second language learning. Almost no one really acquires a second language in a classroom. However, it can happen that exposure to another language, having to translate it into and otherwise relate it to your own language, can cause you to become consciously aware of how your first language works (how it means). This "metaknowledge" can actually make you better able to manipulate your first language.

Vygotsky (1987) says that learning a foreign language "allows the child 29 to understand his native language as a single instantiation of a linguistic system" (p. 222). And here we have a clue. Classroom instruction (in language, composition, study skills, writing, critical thinking, content-based literacy, or whatever) can lead to metaknowledge, to seeing how the Discourses you have already got relate to those you are attempting to acquire, and how the ones you are trying to acquire relate to self and society. Metaknowledge is liberation and power, because it leads to the ability to manipulate, to analyze, to resist while advancing. Such metaknowledge can make "maladapted" students smarter than "adapted" ones. Thus, the liberal classroom that avoids overt talk of form and superficialities, of how things work, as well as of their sociocultural-political basis, is no help. Such talk can be powerful so long as one never thinks that in talking about grammar, form, or superficialities one is getting people to actually acquire Discourses (or languages, for that matter). Such talk is always political talk.

But, the big question: If one cannot acquire Discourses save through active 30 social practice, and it is difficult to compete with the mastery of those admitted early to the game when one has entered it as late as high school or college, what can be done to see to it that metaknowledge and resistance are coupled with Discourse development? The problem is deepened by the fact that true acquisition of many mainstream Discourses involves, at least while being in them, active complicity with values that conflict with one's home- and community-based Discourses, especially for many women and minorities.

The question is too big for me, but I have two views to push nonetheless. 31 First, true acquisition (which is always full fluency) will rarely if ever happen. Even for anything close to acquisition to occur, classrooms must be active apprenticeships in "academic" social practices, and, in most cases, must connect with these social practices as they are also carried on outside the "composition" or "language" class, elsewhere in the University.

Second, though true acquisition is probably not possible, "mushfake" Dis- 32 course is possible. Mack (1989) defines "mushfake," a term from prison culture, as making "do with something less when the real thing is not available. So when prison inmates make hats from underwear to protect their hair from lice, the hats are mushfake. Elaborate craft items made from used wooden match sticks are another example of mushfake." "Mushfake Discourse" means partial acquisition coupled with metaknowledge and strategies to "make do" (strategies ranging from always having a memo edited to ensure no plural, possessive, and third-person "s" agreement errors to active use of black culture skills at "psyching out" interviewers, or to strategies of "rising to the meta-level" in an interview so the interviewer is thrown off stride by having the rules of the game implicitly referred to in the act of carrying them out).

"Mushfake," resistance, and metaknowledge: this seems to me like a good 33 combination for successful students and successful social change. So I propose that we ought to produce "mushfaking," resisting students, full of metaknowledge. But isn't that to politicize teaching? A Discourse is an integration of saying, doing, and *valuing*, and all socially based valuing is political. All successful teaching, that is, teaching that inculcates Discourse and not just content, is political. That too is a truism.

As a linguist I am primarily interested in the functioning of language in Dis- 34 courses and literacies. And a key question in this sort of linguistics is how language-within-Discourses is acquired (in socially situated apprenticeships) and how the languages from different Discourses transfer into, interfere with, and otherwise influence each other to form the linguistic texture of whole societies and to interrelate various groups in society. To see what is at stake here, I will briefly discuss one text, one which clearly brings out a host of important issues in this domain. The text, with an explanation of its context, is printed below. The text is demarcated in terms of "lines" and "stanzas," units which I believe are the basis of speech:

> CONTEXT OF TEXT A young middle-class mother regularly reads storybooks to both her 5- and 7-year-old daughters. Her 5-year-old had had a birthday party, which had had some problems. In the next few days the 5-year-old has told several relatives about the birthday party, reporting the events in the language of her primary Discourse system. A few days later, when the mother was reading a storybook to her 7-year-old, the 5-year-old said she wanted to "read" (she could not decode), and *pretended* to be reading a book, while telling what had happened at her birthday party. Her original attempt at this was not very good, but eventually after a few tries, interspersed with the mother reading to the other girl, the 5 year-old produced the following story, which is not (just) in the language of her primary Discourse system:

STANZA ONE (Introduction)

1. This is a story
2. About some kids who were once friends
3. But got into a big fight
4. And were not

STANZA TWO (Frame: Signalling of Genre)

5. You can read along in your storybook
6. I'm gonna read aloud

[story-reading prosody from now on]

STANZA THREE (Title)

7. "How the Friends Got Unfriend"

STANZA FOUR (Setting: Introduction of Characters)

8. Once upon a time there was three boys 'n three girls
9. They were named Betty Lou, Pallis, and Parshin, were the girls
10. And Michael, Jason, and Aaron were the boys
11. They were friends

STANZA FIVE (Problem: Sex Differences)

12. The boys would play Transformers
13. And the girls would play Cabbage Patches

STANZA SIX (Crisis: Fight)

14. But then one day they got into a fight on who would be which team
15. It was a very bad fight
16. They were punching
17. And they were pulling
18. And they were banging

STANZA SEVEN (Resolution 1: Storm)

19. Then all of a sudden the sky turned dark
20. The rain began to fall
21. There was lightning going on
22. And they were not friends

STANZA EIGHT (Resolution 2: Mothers punish)

23. Then um the mothers came shooting out 'n saying
24. "What are you punching for?
25. You are going to be punished for a whole year"

STANZA NINE (Frame)

26. The end
27. Wasn't it fun reading together?
28. Let's do it again
29. Real soon!

This text and context display an event, which I call *filtering*, "in the act" 35 of actually taking place. "Filtering" is a process whereby aspects of the language, attitudes, values, and other elements of certain types of secondary Discourses (e.g., dominant ones represented in the world of school and trans-local government and business institutions) are *filtered* into primary Discourse (and, thus, the process whereby a literacy can influence home-based practices). Filtering represents *transfer* of features from secondary Discourses into primary Discourses. This transfer process allows the child to practice aspects of dominant secondary Discourses in the very act of acquiring a primary Discourse. It is a key device in the creation of a group of elites who appear to demonstrate quick and effortless mastery of dominant secondary Discourses, by "talent" or "native ability," when, in fact, they have simply *practiced* aspects of them longer.

The books that are part of the storybook reading episodes surrounding this 36 child's oral text encode language that is part of several specific secondary Discourses. These include, of course, "children's literature," but also "literature" proper. Such books use linguistic devices that are simplified analogues of "literary" devices used in traditional, canonical "high literature." These devices are often thought to be natural and universal to literary art, though they are not. Many of them have quite specific origins in quite specific historical circumstances (though, indeed, some of them are rooted in universals of sense making and are devices that occur in nonliterary talk and writing).

One device with a specific historical reference is the so-called "sympathetic 37 fallacy." This is where a poem or story treats natural events (e.g., sunshine or storms) as if they reflected or were "in harmony" or "in step" with (sympathetic with) human events and emotions. This device was a hallmark of 19th-century Romantic poetry, though it is common in more recent poetry as well.

Notice how in the 5-year-old's story the sympathetic fallacy is not only used, 38 but is, in fact, the central organizing device in the construction of the story. The fight between the girls and boys in stanza 6 is immediately followed in stanza 7 by the sky turning dark, with lightning flashing, and thence in line 22: "and they were not friends." Finally, in stanza 8, the mothers come on the scene to punish the children for their transgression. The sky is "in tune" or "step" with human happenings.

The function of the sympathetic fallacy in "high literature" is to equate the 39 world of nature (the macrocosm) with the world of human affairs (the microcosm) as it is depicted in a particular work of art. It also suggests that these human affairs, as they are depicted in the work of literary art, are "natural," part of the logic of the universe, rather than conventional, historical, cultural, or class-based.

In the 5-year-old's story, the sympathetic fallacy functions in much the same 40 way as it does in "high literature." In particular, the story suggests that gender differences (stanza 4: boy versus girl) are associated with different interests (stanza 5: Transformers versus Cabbage Patches), and that these different interests inevitably lead to conflict when male and female try to be "equal" or "one" or sort themselves on other grounds than gender (stanza 6: "a fight on who would be which team").

The children are punished for transgressing gender lines (stanza 8), but *only* 41 *after* the use of the sympathetic fallacy (in stanza 7) has suggested that *division by gender*, and the conflicts which transgressing this division lead to, are sanctioned by nature — are "natural" and "inevitable" not merely conventional or constructed in the very act of play itself.

Notice, then, how the very form and structure of the language, and the lin- 42 guistic devices used, carry an *ideological message*. In mastering this aspect of this Discourse, the little girl has unconsciously "swallowed whole," ingested, a whole system of thought, embedded in the very linguistic devices she uses. This, by the way, is another example of how linguistic aspects of Discourses can never be isolated from nonlinguistic aspects like values, assumptions, and beliefs.

Let's consider how this text relates to our theory of Discourse and literacy. 43 The child had started by telling a story about her birthday to various relatives, over a couple of days, presumably in her primary Discourse. Then, on a given day, in the course of repeated book reading episodes, she reshapes this story into another genre. She incorporates aspects of the book reading episode into her story. Note, for example, the introduction in stanza 1, the frame in stanza 2, the title in stanza 3, and then the start of the story proper in stanza 4. She closes the frame in stanza 9. This overall structure shapes the text into "storybook reading," though, in fact, there is no book and the child can't read. I cannot help but put in an aside here: note that this girl is engaged in an apprenticeship in the Discourse of "storybook reading," a mastery of which I count as a literacy, though in this case there is no book and no reading. Traditional accounts of literacy are going to have deep conceptual problems here, because they trouble themselves too much over things like books and reading.

Supported by her mother and older sister, our 5-year-old is mastering the 44 secondary Discourse of "storybook reading." But this Discourse is itself an aspect of apprenticeship in another, more mature Discourse, namely "literature" (as well as, in other respects, "essayist Discourse," but that is *another* story). This child, when she goes to school to begin her more public apprenticeship into the Discourse of literature, will look like a "quick study" indeed. It will appear that her success was inevitable given her native intelligence and verbal abilities. Her success was inevitable, indeed, but because of her earlier apprenticeship. Note too how her mastery of this "storybook reading" Discourse leads to the incorporation of a set of values and attitudes (about gender and the naturalness of middle-class ways of behaving) that are shared by many other dominant Discourses in our society. This will facilitate the acquisition of other dominant Discourses, ones that may, at first, appear quite disparate from "literature" or "storybook reading."

It is also clear that the way in which this girl's home experience interpolates 45 primary Discourse (the original tellings of the story to various relatives) and secondary Discourses will cause *transfer* of features from the secondary Discourse to the primary one (thanks to the fact, for instance, that this is all going on at home in the midst of primary socialization). Indeed, it is *just such* episodes that are the *locus* of the process by which dominant secondary Discourses filter from public life into private life.

The 5-year-old's story exemplifies two other points as well. First, it is rather 46 pointless to ask, "Did she really intend, or does she really know about such meanings?" The Discourses to which she is apprenticed "speak" *through her* (to other Discourses, in fact). So, she can, in fact, "speak" quite beyond herself (much like "speaking in tongues," I suppose). Second, the little girl ingests an ideology whole here, so to speak, and not in any way in which she could analyze it, verbalize it, or critique it. This is why this is not an experience of learning a liberating literacy.

To speak to the educational implications of the view of Discourse and liter- 47 acy herein, and to close these introductory remarks, I will leave you to meditate on the words of Oscar Wilde's Lady Bracknell in *The Importance of Being Earnest*. "Fortunately, in England, at any rate, education produces no effect whatsoever. If it did, it would prove a serious danger to the upper classes, and probably lead to acts of violence in Grosvenor Square" (quoted in Ellman, 1988, p. 561).

References

Akinnaso, F. N., & Ajirotutu, C. S. (1982). Performance and ethnic style in job interviews. In J. J. Gumperz (Ed.), *Language and social identity* (pp. 119–144). Cambridge: Cambridge University Press.

Beebe, L. M. (Ed.) (1988). *Issues in second language acquisition: Multiple perspectives.* New York: Newbury House.

Cazden, C. (1988). *Classroom discourse: The language of teaching and learning.* Portsmouth, NH: Heinemann.

Dulay, H., Burt, M., & Krashen, S. (1982). *Language two.* New York: Oxford University Press.

Ellman, R. (1988). *Oscar Wilde.* New York: Vintage Books.

Grosjean, F. (1986). *Life with two languages.* Cambridge: Harvard University Press.

Heath, S. B. (1983). *Ways with words: Language, life, and work in communities and classrooms.* Cambridge: Cambridge University Press.

Hirsch, E. D. (1987). *Cultural literacy: What every American needs to know.* Boston: Houghton Mifflin.

Krashen, S. (1982). *Principles and practice in second language acquisition.* Hayward, CA: Alemany Press.

Krashen, S. (1985a). *The input hypothesis: Issues and implications.* Harlow, U.K.: Longman.

Krashen, S. (1985b). *Inquiries and insights.* Hayward, CA: Alemany Press.

Krashen, S., &. Terrell, T. (1983). *The natural approach: Language acquisition in the classroom.* Hayward, CA: Alemany Press.

Lave, J. (1988). *Cognition in practice.* Cambridge: Cambridge University Press.

Mack, N. (1989). The social nature of words: Voices, dialogues, quarrels. *The Writing Instructor,* 8, 157–165.

Milroy, J., & Milroy, L. (1985). *Authority in language: Investigating language prescription and standardisation*. London: Routledge & Kegan Paul.

Milroy, L. (1980). *Language and social networks*. Oxford: Basil Blackwell.

Milroy, L. (1987). *Observing and analysing natural language*. Oxford: Basil Blackwell.

Rogoff, B., & Lave, J. (Eds.). (1984). *Everyday cognition: Its development in a social context*. Cambridge: Harvard University Press.

Rosaldo, R. (1989). *Culture and truth: The remaking of social analysis*. Boston: Beacon Press.

Vygotsky, L. S. (1987). *The collected works of L. S. Vygotsky, Volume 1: Problems of general psychology. Including the volume thinking and speech* (R. W. Rieber & A. S. Carton, Eds.). New York: Plenum.

- -

Questions for Discussion and Journaling

1. What does Gee mean when he says that you can speak with perfect grammar and yet be "wrong nonetheless" (para. 2)? Does this conflict with what you've been taught in school about grammar?

2. Gee argues that you can say something in the right way but do the wrong thing, which he calls the "'saying-doing' combination" (para. 2). What does this mean? How does this impact people's ability to make meaning together?

3. Explain Gee's distinction between *Discourse* with a capital *D* and *discourse* with a lowercase *d*. Does it make sense to you? Why or why not?

4. What does Gee mean by the terms *primary Discourse, secondary Discourse, dominant Discourse*, and *nondominant Discourse*?

5. What does it mean to say that "Discourses are connected with displays of an identity" (para. 18)? What are the implications of this claim, if it is true?

6. Gee argues that members of dominant Discourses apply "constant 'tests'" (para. 13) to people whose primary Discourse is not the dominant one. Why do you think these dominant Discourse "tests" happen? What is the benefit to members of the dominant Discourse? What goals (and whose goals) are being *mediated* through such Discourse tests?

7. What is **metaknowledge** and what is its value, according to Gee?

8. Consider a Discourse that you believe you are already a part of. How do you *know* you are a part of it? How did you become a part of it?

9. Consider a Discourse to which you do not belong but want to belong — a group in which you are or would like to be what Gee calls an *apprentice*. What is hardest about learning to belong to that Discourse? Who or what aids you the most in becoming a part? Do you ever feel like a "pretender"? If so, what marks you as a pretender?

Applying and Exploring Ideas

1. Write a description of the "saying (writing)-doing-being-valuing-believing" of your own primary Discourse (the one you were enculturated into at birth). Be sure to note things like grammatical usage, common phrases, tone of voice, formality of speech, and values related to that Discourse. Once you have done this, write a description of the "saying (writing)-doing-being-valuing-believing" of *academic* Discourse as you have encountered it so far. Finally, discuss sources of transfer (overlap) and sources of conflict between these two Discourses.

2. Gee argues that English teachers are the ones who have to do something about the fact that people from nondominant Discourses can't join dominant Discourses late in life. Write a letter to one of your high school or college English teachers in which you explain what Discourses are, describe the difference between dominant and nondominant Discourses, and ask the teacher to take some specific action of your choosing to better help students from nondominant Discourses.

3. Gee notes that there are often conflicts and tensions between Discourses. Consider different Discourses you belong to that have different values, beliefs, attitudes, language use, etc. How do you navigate between or among these Discourses?

4. How does Gee help you better understand (or give evidence for) the threshold concept of this chapter, that people collaborate to get things done with writing?

META MOMENT   What have you learned from Gee that you can usefully apply elsewhere in your life? How does Gee help you understand your experiences (or those of other people) better?

Learning to Serve

The Language and Literacy of Food Service Workers

TONY MIRABELLI

Tony Mirabelli

Framing the Reading

Tony Mirabelli earned a Ph.D. in Education in Language, Literacy, and Culture from the University of California, Berkeley, in 2001 and was a lecturer in the Graduate School of Education there from 2004 to 2018. As an Assistant Director of Berkeley's Athletic Study Center, he now manages its Academic Support program.

Mirabelli's article focuses on theories about language use in communities to examine how workers in a diner use language and texts to interact. He is interested in the language and literacy practices of blue-collar service workers. In fact, he introduces the concept of **multiliteracies** to argue that these workers do not just read texts — they also read people and situations.

If you read James Gee earlier in this chapter, this argument should be familiar to you. Gee argues that we give too much focus to print-based literacies and that they cannot be separated from what he called the "saying (writing)-doing-being-valuing-believing" within Discourses. The connection between Gee and Mirabelli is not accidental. Mirabelli relies on assumptions from an academic area called New Literacy Studies, which Gee was instrumental in establishing. As you might expect, therefore, Mirabelli cites Gee when defining his theoretical terms. (And if you look at the publication information for the book in which Mirabelli's article appears, you'll find that Gee reviewed that book for the publisher.) Remember that in Chapter 2 we challenged you to see written academic texts as conversations between people. Mirabelli's article provides a good place for you to test this way of seeing texts.

Mirabelli's focus on the everyday literacies of a diner should illustrate the underlying threshold concepts of this chapter in very clear ways. The people in the diner use texts and discourse in order to *do something* and to *make meaning*. The texts (for example, the menu) and specialized language they create and use together *mediate the activities* they are trying to accomplish in the diner. Ultimately, people in a restaurant use writing to collaborate on getting dining done.

WHAT THEY DON'T LEARN in SCHOOL

Literacy in the Lives of Urban Youth

edited by JABARI MAHIRI

Mirabelli, Tony. "The Language and Literacy of Food Service Workers." *What They Don't Learn in School*, edited by Jabari Mahiri, Peter Lang, 2004, pp. 143–62.

Getting Ready to Read

Before you read, do at least one of the following activities:

- Think back to your first job. What was it like learning to do it? What did you have to learn? In particular, what terms, language, and vocabulary did you have to learn? What texts helped you do the work of that job (remember to consider even mundane texts like notes, menus, and so on)? How difficult did you find it? Why?
- Find some friends who have worked in food service, and have them compare notes: Are there different Discourses for different kinds of food service?

As you read, consider the following questions:

- How many kinds of literacies do you imagine there are? Is there a literacy for *every* kind of reading? How many kinds of reading are there?
- How do Discourses avoid stereotyping people? Is that possible? What are the consequences of this kind of stereotyping?

BITTERWAITRESS.COM IS ONE of the newest among a burgeoning num- 1 ber of worker-produced websites associated with the service industry.[1] The menu on the first page of this website offers links to gossip about celebrity behavior in restaurants, gossip about chefs and restaurant owners, accounts from famous people who were once waitresses,[2] and customer-related horror stories. There is also a forum that includes a "hate mail" page that posts email criticisms of the website itself, as well as general criticisms of waitressing, but the criticisms are followed by rebuttals usually from past or present waitresses. Predictably, most of the criticisms either implicitly or explicitly portray waitresses as ignorant and stupid. One email respondent didn't like what he read on the customer horror story page and sent in this response:

> If you find your job [as a waitress] so despicable, then go get an education and get a REAL job. You are whining about something that you can fix. Stop being such a weakling, go out and learn something, anything, and go make a real contribution to society. . . . Wait, let me guess: you do not have any marketable skills or useful knowledge, so you do what any bumbling fool can do, wait on tables. This is your own fault.

This response inspired a number of rebuttals of which the following two best 2 summarize the overall sentiment expressed in response to the rant above. The first is from the webmaster of bitterwaitress.com:

> Is it possible that I have an education, maybe I went to, oh say, Duke, and I just waitressed for some free time? Or that there are very many people in the

525

industry who do this so that they CAN get an education? Not all of us were born with a trust fund.—There is, I might add, considerably more or less to a job than a "clear cut" salary. If you . . . live in New York, . . . you'll know that empty stores and un-crowded subways are half the reason to work at night. By the way, what are the three Leovilles? What are the two kinds of tripe? Who was Cesar Ritz' partner? What is the JavaScript for a rollover? I guess I would have to ask a bumbling fool those questions. So, tell me then.

The second is from a mother of four: 3

I might not have a college education, but I would love to see those so called intelligent people get a big tip out of a bad meal, or from a person who is rude and cocky just because that's the way they are—that takes talent and it's not a talent you can learn at any university. So, think about it before you say, "poor girl—too dumb to get a real job. . . ?"

Assumptions that waitresses (and waiters) are ignorant and stupid and that 4
waiting on tables contributes little to society are not new. The rebuttals to commonplace, pejorative understandings of the food service industry suggest, however, that there is complexity and skill that may go unrecognized by the general
public or institutions such as universities. Indeed institutions, particularly government and corporate entities in the United States, like the Bureau of Labor
Statistics or the National Skills Labor Board, define waiting on tables as a low
skilled profession. By defining this kind of work as low skilled, there is a con-
comitant implication that the more than one-third of America's workforce who
do it are low skilled.

Service occupations, otherwise known as "in-person" services (Reich, 1992) 5
or "interactive services" (Leidner, 1993; MacDonald and Sirianni, 1996),
include any kind of work which fundamentally involves face-to-face or voice-
to-voice interactions and conscious manipulation of self-presentation. As distinguished from white-collar service work, this category of "emotional proletariat"
(MacDonald and Sirianni, 1996) is comprised primarily of retail sales workers,
hotel workers, cashiers, house cleaners, flight attendants, taxi drivers, package
delivery drivers, and waiters, among others. According to the U.S. Bureau of
Labor Statistics (1996), one-fifth of the jobs in eating, drinking, and grocery
store establishments are held by youth workers between the ages of 16 and 24.
While this kind of work is traditionally assumed to be primarily a stop-gap for
young workers who will later move up and on to other careers, it also involves
youths who will later end up in both middle- and working-class careers. It
should not be forgotten that more than two thirds of the workers involved in
food service are mature adults—many or most who began their careers in the
same or similar industries. Interactive service work is a significant part of the
economy in the U.S. today, and the Bureau of Labor Statistics predicts that jobs
will be "abundant" in this category through 2006.

Economists such as Peter Drucker (1993) suggest that interactive service 6
workers lack the necessary education to be "knowledge" workers. These economists support general conceptions that service work is "mindless," involving
routine and repetitive tasks that require little education. This orientation further
suggests that these supposedly low skilled workers lack the problem identifying,
problem solving, and other high level abilities needed to work in other occupations. However, relatively little specific attention and analysis have been given
to the literacy skills and language abilities needed to do this work. My research
investigates these issues with a focus on waiters and waitresses who work in
diners. Diner restaurants are somewhat distinct from fast food or fine-dining
restaurants, and they also epitomize many of the assumptions held about low
skilled workplaces that require interactive services. The National Skills Standard
Board, for instance, has determined that a ninth-grade level of spoken and written language use is needed to be a waiter or a waitress. Yet, how language is spoken, read, or written in a restaurant may be vastly different from how it is used
in a classroom. A seemingly simple event such as taking a customer's food order
can become significantly more complex, for example, when a customer has a
special request. How the waitress or waiter understands and uses texts such as
the menu and how she or he "reads" and verbally interacts with the customer
reflect carefully constructed uses of language and literacy.

This chapter explores these constructed ways of "reading" texts (and cus- 7
tomers) along with the verbal "performances" and other manipulations of self-
presentation that characterize interactive service work. In line with MacDonald
and Sirianni (1996), I hope this work will contribute to the development of
understandings and policies that build more respect and recognition for service
work to help ensure it does not become equated with servitude.

LITERACY AND CONTEMPORARY THEORY

In contrast to institutional assessments such as the National Skills Standards 8
Board (1995), current thinking in key areas of education, sociology, anthropology and linguistics views language, literacy, and learning as embedded in
social practice rather than entirely in the minds of individuals (Street, 1984;
Gee, 1991; Lave and Wenger, 1991; Kress, 1993; Mahiri and Sablo, 1996;
New London Group, 1996; Gee, Hull, and Lankshear, 1996). As earlier chapters in this book have noted, Gee (1991: 6) — a key proponent of this conception of literacy — explains that to be literate means to have control of "a
socially accepted association among ways of using language, of thinking, and of
acting that can be used to identify oneself as a member of a socially meaningful
group or 'social network.'" In a similar fashion, research work located explicitly
within workplace studies proposes that literacy is "a range of practices specific
to groups and individuals of different cultures, races, classes and genders" (Hull
et al., 1996: 5).

In most societal institutions, however, literacy continues to be defined by 9 considerations of achievement and by abstract, standardized tests of individual students. Also, there is a decided focus on printed texts over other mediums of communication like visual and audio. Such a focus limits our understanding of literacy in terms of its use in specific situations in multiple modes of communication. The New Literacy Studies orientation that shapes the work reported in this book argues that literacy extends beyond individual experiences of reading and writing to include the various modes of communication and situations of any socially meaningful group or network where language is used in multiple ways. The New London Group (1996), for example, claims that due to changes in the social and economic environment, schools too must begin to consider language and literacy education in terms of "multiliteracies." The concept of multiliteracies supplements traditional literacy pedagogy by addressing the multiplicity of communications channels and the increasing saliency of cultural and linguistic diversity in the world today. Central to this study is the understanding that literate acts are embedded in specific situations and that they also extend beyond the printed text involving other modes of communication including both verbal and nonverbal. In this chapter, I illustrate something of the character of literacies specific to the "social network" of waiting on tables and show how they are distinct from the conceptions of literacy commonly associated with formal education. This is not simply to suggest that there is a jargon specific to the work, which of course there is, but that there is something unique and complex about the ways waiters and waitresses in diners use language and literacy in doing their work.

METHODOLOGY

Taken together, extant New Literacies Studies research makes a formidable 10 argument for the need to re-evaluate how we understand literacy in the workplace — particularly from the perspective of interactive service workers. The research reported here is modeled after Hull and her colleagues' groundbreaking ethnographic study of skill requirements in the factories of two different Silicon Valley computer manufacturing plants (1996). Instead of studying manufacturing plants, the larger research study I conducted and that underpins the study reported here involves two diner restaurants — one that is corporately owned and one that is privately owned. In this chapter, however, I focus only on the one that is privately owned to begin addressing the specific ways that language use and literacy practices function in this kind of workplace.

To analyze the data, I relied on some of the methodological tools from 11 the work of Hull and her colleagues (1996). In short, I looked at patterns of thought and behavior in the setting; I identified key events taking place; I did conversational analysis of verbal interactions; and I conducted sociocultural analyses of key work events.

The data used in this chapter came from direct participation, observation, 12 field notes, documents, interviews, tape recordings, and transcriptions, as well as from historical and bibliographic literature. I myself have been a waiter (both part-time and full-time over a ten-year period), and I was actually employed at the privately owned restaurant during my data collection period. In addition to providing important insights into worker skills, attitudes, and behaviors, my experience and positioning in this setting also enabled access to unique aspects of the work that might have otherwise gone unnoticed. The primary data considered in this chapter were collected during eight-hour periods of participant observation on Friday and / or Saturday nights in the restaurant. I chose weekend nights because they were usually the busiest times in the diner and were therefore the most challenging for the workers. Weekend shifts are also the most lucrative for the restaurant and the workers.

LOU'S RESTAURANT

Lou's Restaurant[3] is a modest, privately owned diner restaurant patterned in 13 a style that is popular in the local region. It has an open kitchen layout with a counter where individual customers can come and sit directly in front of the cooks' line and watch the "drama" of food service unfold while enjoying their meals. The food served at Lou's is Italian-American and it includes pastas, seafood, and a variety of sautéed or broiled poultry, beef, and veal. As is often the case with diner restaurants, Lou's has over ninety main course items, including several kinds of appetizers and salads, as well as a number of side dishes. The primary participants focused on in this chapter are three waiters at Lou's: John, Harvey, and myself.

After finishing my master's degree in English literature and deciding to move 14 out of the state where I taught English as a Second Language at a community college, I ended up working as a waiter for two years at Lou's. This work allowed me to survive financially while further advancing my academic career. At the time I began my study at this site, the only waiter to have worked longer than two years at Lou's was John. Like myself, John began working in the restaurant business to earn extra money while in school after he had been discharged from the Marines, where he had been trained as a radio operator, telephone wireman, and Arabic translator. Two days after his honorable discharge, he started working in the restaurant that four years later would become Lou's. He subsequently has worked there for ten years. John also is the most experienced waiter at Lou's, and although the restaurant does not have an official "head" waiter, John is considered by his peers to be the expert. In an interview, he noted that it took almost ten years before he felt that he had really begun to master his craft.

Harvey might also be considered a master waiter, having been in the pro- 15 fession for over thirty years. However, at the beginning of the study he had been with Lou's for only two weeks. He was initially reticent to participate in the study because he said he lacked experience at this restaurant, and "didn't know the menu." Having left home when he was 14 years old to come "out West," over the years he had done a stint in the Air Force, held a position as a postal clerk, worked as a bellhop and bartender, and even had the opportunity to manage a local cafe. He decided that he did not like managerial work because he missed the freedom, autonomy, and customer interaction he had as a waiter and took a position at Lou's.

THE MENU

Harvey's concern over not knowing the menu was not surprising. The menu is the most important printed text used by waiters and waitresses, and not knowing it can dramatically affect how they are able to do their work. The menu is the key text used for most interactions with the customer, and, of course, the contents of menus vary greatly from restaurant to restaurant. But, what is a menu and what does it mean to have a literate understanding of one? 16

The restaurant menu is a genre unto itself. There is regularity and predictability in the conventions used such as the listing, categorizing, and pricing of individual, ready-made food items. The menu at Lou's contains ninety main course items, as well as a variety of soups, salads, appetizers, and side dishes. In addition, there are numerous selections where, for example, many main course items offer customers a choice of their own starch item from a selection of four: spaghetti, ravioli, french fries, or a baked potato. Some of the main course items, such as sandwiches, however, only come with french fries — but if the customer prefers something such as spaghetti, or vegetables instead of fries, they can substitute another item for a small charge, although this service is not listed in the menu. In addition to the food menu, there is also a wine menu and a full service bar meaning that hard liquor is sold in this restaurant. There are twenty different kinds of wine sold by the glass and a selection of thirty-eight different kinds of wine sold by the bottle, and customers can order most other kinds of alcoholic beverages. 17

In one context, waitresses and waiters' knowing the meaning of the words in the menus means knowing the process of food production in the restaurant. But this meaning is generally only used when a customer has a question or special request. In such situations the meaning of the words on the page are defined more by the questions and the waiters or waitresses' understanding of specific food preparation than by any standard cookbook or dictionary. For example, the *Better Homes and Gardens New Cook Book* (1996) presents a recipe for marinara sauce calling for a thick sauce all sautéed and simmered for over thirty minutes. At Lou's, a marinara sauce is cooked in less than ten minutes and is a light tomato sauce consisting of fresh tomatoes, garlic, and parsley sautéed in 18 olive oil. At a similar restaurant nearby—Joe's Italian Diner—marinara sauce is a seafood sauce, albeit tomato based. Someone who is familiar with Italian cooking will know that marinara sauce will have ingredients like tomatoes, olive oil, and garlic, but, in a restaurant, to have a more complete understanding of a word like *marinara* requires knowing how the kitchen prepares the dish. Clearly, the meanings of the language used in menus are socially and culturally embedded in the context of the specific situation or restaurant. To be literate here requires something other than a ninth-grade level of literacy. More than just a factual, or literal interpretation of the words on the page, it requires knowledge of specific practices—such as methods of food preparation—that take place in a particular restaurant.

On one occasion Harvey, the new but experienced waiter, asked me what 19 "pesto" sauce was. He said that he had never come across the term before, and explained that he had never worked in an Italian restaurant and rarely eaten in one. Pesto is one of the standard sauces on the menu, and like marinara, is commonly found on the menus of many Italian-American restaurants. I explained that it comprised primarily olive oil and basil, as well as garlic, pine nuts, Parmesan cheese, and a little cream. Harvey then told me that a customer had asked him about the sauce, and since he could not explain what it was, the customer did not order it.

On another occasion a mother asked Harvey if her child could have only car- 20 rots instead of the mixed vegetables as it said in the menu. Although he initially told her this was not possible, explaining that the vegetables were premixed and that the cooks would have to pick the carrots out one by one, the mother persisted. After a few trips from the table to the cooks' line, Harvey managed to get the carrots, but the customer then declined them because everyone had finished eating. Later, I explained to Harvey that it would have been possible to go to the back of the restaurant where he could find the vegetables in various stages of preparation. While the cooks only have supplies of premixed vegetables on the line, Harvey could have gone to the walk-in refrigerator and picked up an order of carrots himself to give to the cooks.

Harvey's interactions with his customers highlight how much of what he 21 needs to know to be a good waiter is learned within the specific situations and social networks in which that knowledge is used. The instantiation of the meaning of words like *pesto* and *marinara* often occurs in the interaction between co-workers as well as with customers. Conversation becomes a necessary element in achieving an appropriately literate understanding of the menu.

Harvey's understanding and use of the menu and special requests also 22 involves more than his knowledge of food preparation. It involves the manipulation of power and control. Sociocultural theories of literacy consider the role of power and authority in the construction of meaning (Kress, 1993). From his perspective, the order of carrots was not simply an order of carrots, but a way of positioning one's self in the interaction. The customer saw her desire for the carrots as greater than what was advertised in the menu and thus exercised authority as a customer by requesting them despite Harvey's attempt to not make the carrots an option. While such a request might seem fairly innocuous in isolation, when considered in the specific situation of Lou's at that time — that is, peak dinner hour — it becomes more complex.

Special requests and questions can extend the meaning of the menu beyond 23 the printed page and into the conversation and interaction between the waiter or waitress and the customer. Furthermore, special requests and questions can be as varied as the individual customers themselves. The general public shares a diner restaurant menu, but it is used by each individual patron to satisfy a private appetite. How to describe something to an individual customer and satisfy their private appetite requires not only the ability to *read* the menu, but also the ability to *read* the customer. This is achieved during the process of the dinner interaction, and it includes linguistic events such as greeting the customer or taking food orders and involves both verbal and non-verbal communication. In such events the meaning of the menu is continually reconstructed in the interaction between the waitress or waiter and the individual customer, and as a text functions as a "boundary object" that coordinates the perspectives of various constituencies for a similar purpose (Star and Griesmer, 1989); in this case the satisfaction of the individual patron's appetite. The degree to which private appetite is truly satisfied is open to debate, however. Virtually everyone who has eaten at a restaurant has his or her favorite horror story about the food and / or the service, and more often than not these stories in some way involve the menu and an unfulfilled private appetite.

In addition to being a text that is shared by the general public and used 24 by the individual patron to satisfy a private appetite, the menu is also a text whose production of meaning results in ready-made consumable goods sold for profit. The authors of a printed menu, usually the chefs and owners of the restaurant, have their own intentions when producing the hard copy. For example, it is common practice to write long extensively itemized menus in diner restaurants like Lou's. As was pointed out earlier, Lou's menu has over ninety selections from which to choose, and many of these can be combined with a range of additional possible choices. Printing a large selection of food items gives the appearance that the customer will be able to make a personal — and *personalized* — selection from the extensive menu. In fact, it is not uncommon for patrons at Lou's to request extra time to read the menu, or ask for recommendations before making a choice. The authors of the printed menu at Lou's constructed a text that appears to be able to satisfy private appetites, but they ultimately have little control over how the patron will interpret and use the menu.

The waiters and waitresses, however, do have some control. While customers 25 certainly have their own intentions when asking questions, waitresses and waiters have their own intentions when responding. When customers ask questions about the menu, in addition to exercising their own authority, they also introduce the opportunity for waiters and waitresses to gain control of the interaction. A good example of how this control could be manipulated by a waiter or waitress comes from Chris Fehlinger, the web-master of bitterwaitress.com, in an interview with *New Yorker* magazine:

> "A lot of times when people asked about the menu, I would make it sound so elaborate that they would just leave it up to me," he said, "I'd describe, like, three dishes in excruciating detail, and they would just stutter, 'I, I, I can't decide, you decide for me.' So in that case, if the kitchen wants to sell fish, you're gonna have fish." He also employed what might be called a "magic words" strategy: "All you have to do is throw out certain terms, like guanciale, and then you throw in something like saba, a reduction of the unfermented must of the Trebbiano grape. If you mention things like that, people are just, like, 'O.K.!'" (Teicholz, 1999)

The use of linguistic devices like obfuscating descriptions and "magic words" 26 is not unusual — particularly for waiters in fine dining restaurants. In *The World of the Waiters* (1983), Mars and Nicod examined how English waiters use devices to "get the jump" and gain control of selecting items from the menu. Their position of authority is further substantiated in fine dining restaurants by the common practice of printing menus in foreign languages, such as French, because it shifts the responsibility of food ordering from the customer, who often will not understand the language, to the waiter.

While diner restaurants generally do not print their menus in incomprehen- 27 sible terms, they do, as at Lou's, tend to produce unusually long ones that can have a similar effect. But, diner menus like Lou's which offer Italian-American cuisine do use some language that is potentially unfamiliar to the clientele (e.g., *pesto*). The combination of menu length and potentially confusing language creates frequent opportunities for waiters and waitresses to get a jump on the customer. Customers at Lou's tend to ask questions about the meaning of almost every word and phrase in the menu. Not being able to provide at least a basic description of a menu item, as shown by Harvey's unfamiliarity with pesto, usually results in that item not being ordered.

Knowing what a customer wants often goes beyond simply being able to 28 describe the food. It also involves knowing which descriptions will more likely sell and requires being able to apply the menu to the specific situation. For instance, in the following transcription I approach a table to take a food order while one customer is still reading the menu (Customer 3b). She asks me to explain the difference between veal scaloppini and veal scaloppini sec.

TONY: (to Customer 3a and Customer 3b) hi

CUSTOMER 3B: what's the difference between scaloppini and scaloppini sec?

TONY: veal scaloppini is a tomato based sauce with green onions and mushrooms / veal scaloppini sec is with marsala wine green onions and mushrooms

CUSTOMER 3B: I'll have the veal scaloppini sec.

TONY: ok / would you like it with spaghetti / ravioli / french fries

CUSTOMER 3B: ravioli

CUSTOMER 3A: and / I'll get the tomato one / the veal scaloppini with mushrooms

TONY: with spaghetti / ravioli / french fries

CUSTOMER 3A: can I get steamed vegetables

TONY: you want vegetables and no starch? / it already comes with vegetables / (.) (Customer 3a nods yes) ok / great / thank you

CUSTOMER 3A: thanks

The word *sec* functions not unlike one of Fehlinger's "magic" words. Custom- 29 ers who are interested in ordering veal frequently ask questions about the distinctions between the two kinds of scaloppini. I discovered over time that my description of the veal scaloppini sec almost always resulted in the customer ordering the dish. It seemed that mentioning marsala wine piqued customer interest more than tomato sauce did. One customer once quipped that marsala is a sweet wine and wanted to know why the word *sec*—meaning *dry*—was used. I replied that since no fat was used in the cooking process, it was considered "dry" cooking. In situations like this the menu is situated more in a conversational mode than a printed one. The transition from print to spoken word occurs due to the customer's inability to understand the menu, and / or satisfy his or her private appetite which results in a request for assistance. As a result the waiter or waitress can become the authority in relation to not only the printed text, but within the interaction as well. Eventually, I began to recommend this dish when customers asked for one, and the customers more often than not purchased it.

This particular food-ordering event also is interesting with regard to the cus- 30 tomer's request for steamed vegetables. When I asked what kind of pasta she would like with her meal, she asked for steamed vegetables. The menu clearly states that vegetables are included with the meal along with the customer's choice of spaghetti, ravioli, or french fries. When she requested steamed vegetables, I simply could have arranged for her to have them and persisted in asking her which pasta she would like, but instead I anticipated that she might not want any pasta at all. I knew that, while it was not printed on the menu, the kitchen could serve her a double portion of steamed vegetables with no pasta. Most importantly, this customer's ability to order food that would satisfy her private appetite depended almost entirely upon my suggestions and understanding of the menu. Mars and Nicod (1984: 82), discussing a situation in a similar restaurant, noted a waiter who would say, "You don't really need a menu . . . I'm a 'walking menu' and I'm much better than the ordinary kind . . . I can tell you things you won't find on the menu." Examples like this illustrate not only how waitresses and waiters gain control of their interactions with customers, but also how other modes of communication—such as conversations—are used to construct complex forms of meaning around printed texts like menus. Thus, the meaning of words in a menu are embedded in the situation, its participants, and the balance of power and authority, and this meaning manifests itself in more than one mode of communication.

Reading menus and reading customers also involves a myriad of cultural distinctions. Although there is not the space to discuss them here, age, gender, race, and class are all relevant to interactions between customers and waiter or waitress. The argument can be made that diner restaurants like Lou's promote a friendly, family-like atmosphere. Historically diners in the U.S. have been recognized as being places where customers can find a familial environment. Popular media today support this characteristic—particularly via television—where restaurant chains explicitly advertise that their customers are treated like family, and a number of television situation comedies have long used restaurants, diners, bars, and cafés as settings where customers and employees interact in very personal and intimate ways. This cultural atmosphere can have a tremendous impact on interactions with the customers. There is sometimes miscommunication or resistance where a customer may or may not want to be treated like family, or the waitress or waiter may or may not want to treat a customer like family. At Lou's, in addition to having an intimate understanding of food production and being able to describe it to a customer in an appealing fashion, reading a menu and taking a customer's food order also requires the ability to perform these tasks in a friendly, familial manner. 31

The following example reveals the complexity of meanings involved in taking a customer's food order and the expression of "family." Al is a regular customer who almost always comes in by himself and sits at the counter in front of the cooks' line. He also always has the same thing to eat, a side order of spaghetti marinara, and never looks at the menu. Perhaps more important to Al than the food he eats are the people he interacts with at Lou's. He will sit at the counter and enjoy the badinage he shares with the other customers who sit down next to him at the counter, the waitresses and waiters as they pass by his seat, and the cooks working just across the counter. On this particular evening, however, 32 he was joined by his son, daughter-in-law, and young adult granddaughter, and rather than sitting at the counter, he sat in a large booth. Although I immediately recognized Al, I had never waited on him and his family before, and I was not sure how informal he would like the interaction to be. So I began with a fairly formal greeting saying "hello" instead of "hi" and avoided opportunities to make small talk with Al and his family:

TONY: hello::=

CUSTOMER 2D: =hello

AL: hey(.) what they put in the water?/I don't know/is it the ice or what is it?

CUSTOMER 2S: (chuckles from Customer 2d, Customer 2s, and Customer 2c)

TONY: does the water taste strange?

CUSTOMER 2S: no

TONY: do you want me to get you another water?

AL: no/I don't want any water

TONY: ok

AL: I had a couple of drinks before I came

CUSTOMER 2S: (chuckles)=

TONY: (in reference to the water tasting strange) =it could be/it could be/I don't know

CUSTOMER 2D: (to Customer 2s) are you having anything to drink?

CUSTOMER 2S: I'll have a beer/American beer/you have Miller draft?

TONY: (while writing down the order) Miller Genuine

CUSTOMER 2D: and I'll have a tequila sunrise

AL: (to Customer 2d) what are you having?

CUSTOMER 2D: tequila sunrise

AL: oh/you should fly/you should fly

TONY: (to Customer 2a) Al/you want anything?

CUSTOMER 2S: (to Customer 2a) a beer?/or anything?

AL: no/I've had too much already

CUSTOMER 2S: are you sure

CUSTOMER 2D: we'll get you a coffee later

TONY: (nod of affirmation to daughter-in-law)

AL: I've been home alone drinking

TONY: ugh ogh::/(chuckles along with Customer 2s)

Al's comment about the water tasting funny and his drinking at home alone 33
both provided opportunities for me to interact more intimately with Al and his
family, but instead I concerned myself solely with taking their drink orders. Al's
desire for me to interact in a more familial manner became more apparent when
I returned to take their food order.

CUSTOMER 2D: (as the drinks are delivered) ah / great / thank you

TONY: (placing drinks in front of customers) there you go / you're welcome

AL: (to Customer 2s) so we're flying to Vegas (mumbles)

TONY: all right / you need a few minutes here?

CUSTOMER 2S: no / (to Customer 2a) are you ready or do you want to wait?

CUSTOMER 2D: you made up your mind yet?

AL: (mumble) made up my mind yet

CUSTOMER 2D: oh / ok

TONY: al / what can I get for you?

AL: I said I haven't made up my mind yet

TONY: oh / ok (everyone at the table chuckles except Al)

AL: I always have pasta you know / I would walk out there (points to the
counter) the guy says / I know what you want

TONY: ok / I'll be back in a few minutes

CUSTOMER 2D: come back in a few minutes / thanks

While I misunderstood Al when I asked if he was ready to order, for him the 34
greater transgression was simply asking if he was ready to order. Al expected
me to know what he was going to eat because he's a regular; he's like family.
He wanted a side order of spaghetti marinara and didn't want to have to speak
regarding his food order. To be successful in fulfilling Al's private appetite
required more than the ability to describe food according to individual customer preferences. A side order of spaghetti marinara represents not merely a
food item on a menu, nor a satisfying mix of pasta and tomatoes, but also,
depending on the way it is ordered and served, a gesture of friendliness: "I
always have pasta you know / I would walk out there (points to the counter) the
guy says / I know what you want." To be literate with a menu also means knowing when and how to express emotion (or not express emotion) to a customer
through its use.

Being able to take a customer's order without him or her reading the menu 35
are important ways of expressing friendliness and family at Lou's. John, the
most experienced waiter on staff, often can be found running to get an order of

homemade gnocchi from the back freezer and delivering them to the cooks when they are too busy to get back there themselves. Or, he might step in behind the bar to make his own cappuccino when the bartender is busy serving other customers. On one occasion, like many others, John had a customer request a special order called *prawns romano*, a pasta dish consisting of fettuccine with prawns in a white sauce with green onions, tomatoes, and garlic. This is not listed on any menu in the restaurant, but it is something that the cooks occasionally offer as an evening special. John politely asked whether or not the cooks could accommodate his customer's request, and they complied. One can frequently hear John greeting many of his customers with some variation of, "Can I get you the usual?" Alternatively, in the case of special requests, some variant of, "That's no problem" is an often used phrase. Just like a friend for whom it would be no problem, John attempts to satisfy his customer's special requests in a similar fashion.

Yet, friendliness is often a feigned performance. Being friendly is an experi- 36 ential phenomenon that is learned through participation. To be a good waitress or waiter generally requires being able to perform friendliness under any number of circumstances. To be successful at the practice of being friendly requires performing certain techniques over and over until they can be performed on an unconscious level. Referred to as *emotional labor* (Hochschild, 1983: 6–7), this kind of work "requires one to induce or suppress feeling in order to sustain the outward countenance that produces the proper state of mind in others." Emotional labor also is an integral part to how a waitress constructs meaning in a menu. While emotional labor may not yield the same monetary results in restaurants like Lou's, it is still essential to the work. For example, John is masterful in the way he utilizes emotional labor. On one particularly busy evening John was trapped in a line at the bar waiting to place his drink order. He was clearly anxious, and was looking at his food order tickets to see what he needed to do next. The crowd of customers waiting to be seated spilled out of the foyer and into the aisle near where the waitresses and waiters were waiting to place their drink orders. One customer, who recognized John, caught his attention:

JOHN: hi=

CUSTOMER: =hi can I get a glass of wine

JOHN: sure (.) what do you want

CUSTOMER: are you busy

JOHN: NO (.) I got it (.) what do you want

John's friendly "hi" and overemphatic "no" were intended to suggest to the cus- 37 tomer that he was not busy, when he clearly was. As he later explained, he knew that the customer knew he was really busy, but he also knew that if he was friendly and accommodating, the customer probably would give him a nice tip for his trouble, which the customer did. His feigned amiability in agreeing to get the customer a drink was more or less a monetary performance. John had learned to use language for financial gain. One should not be fooled by the apparent simplicity in the preceding interaction. While it may be brief, being able to be friendly and accommodating under extreme circumstances like the "dinner rush" requires years of practice in a real work setting learning to be able to say, "hi—sure—NO, I got it."

Although interactions with customers have been presented individually, the reality of how these events occur is quite different. Unlike fine-dining restaurants where the dinner experience can extend over a few hours, diners operate on high volume, serving to a great number of patrons in a short amount of time. George Orwell, reflecting on the difficulty involved in this work, wrote, "I calculated that [a waiter] had to walk and run about 15 miles during the day and yet the strain of the work was more mental than physical. . . . One has to leap to and fro between a multitude of jobs—it is like sorting a pack of cards against the clock" (Orwell, 1933). Because one person may be serving as many as ten tables or more at one time, the process of serving each individual table will overlap with the others. Food orders are taken numerous times in a half-hour period during busy dinner hours at Lou's. The preceding transcriptions were taken from tape-recorded data collected on Friday evenings around 7 o'clock. My own interactions were recorded during a period when I had what is referred to as a *full station,* meaning that all of the tables under my supervision were filled with customers. By this point in the evening I had two customers at the counter, a party of four and six parties of two, for a total of eighteen customers—all of whom were in the process of ordering their meals within the same half-hour to forty-five minute period.

Literacy practices in this environment are nothing like those found in traditional classrooms, but they might be more comparable to those found in the emergency ward of a hospital or an air-traffic controller's tower. Interaction with texts and participants takes place in a rapid succession of small chunks. During the dinner hours, there are no long drawn out monologues. Time is of the essence during the busiest dinner hours for all participants involved: from the waiters and waitresses to the cooks, bartenders, and busboys. In two hundred lines of transcribed dialogue during a busy dinner period, for example, I never paused longer than thirty-nine seconds, and no participant spoke more than forty-one words in one turn. Even these pauses were usually the result of other work being completed, such as preparing a salad or waiting to order a drink. During this period, virtually all the conversation, reading, and writing were related to the immediate situational context. As this research has shown, language use was far more complex than one might assume in situations and events that involve taking a customer's food order. In addition to knowing how food is prepared, what will appeal to specific customers, and how to present this information in a friendly manner, the waiter or waitress must also remain

38

39

conscious of the number of other tables waiting to have their orders taken and the amount of time that will take. Reading menus and reading customers requires the ability to think and react quickly to a multitude of almost simultaneously occurring literate events.

CONCLUSION

Menus at Lou's are texts that are catalysts for interaction between staff and cus- 40 tomers, and their meaning is firmly embedded in this interaction. Meaning is constructed from the menu through more than one mode of communication and between a variety of participants. This process involves knowledge of food preparation, use of specific linguistic devices like magic words and other ways of describing food, the ability to read individual customers' tastes and preferences, the general expectation to perform in a friendly manner, and all during numerous virtually simultaneous and similar events. Yet, there is much left unconsidered in this chapter, particularly regarding the nature of power and control. While waitresses and waiters are frequently able to manipulate control over customer decisions while taking a food order, this control is often tenuous and insignificant beyond the immediate interaction.

> Menus at Lou's are texts that are catalysts for interaction between staff and customers, and their meaning is firmly embedded in this interaction.

Little also has been said in this chapter about the role of management. Extensive 41 research has already been done in the area of management control, literacy, and worker skills (Braverman, 1974; Hochschild, 1983; Kress, 1993; Leidner, 1993; Hall, 1993; Hull et al., 1996; MacDonald and Sirianni, 1996; Gee, Hull, and Lankshear, 1996). These researchers consider how literacy practices are manipulated by management to maintain control over the worker. Whether it be scientific management where workers are deskilled and routinized, or Fast Capitalism where forms of control are more insidious and shrouded in the guise of "empowering" the worker, there is little research on interactive service work beyond the fast food industry that explores how this rhetoric plays itself out in a real world situation. This leaves open to debate questions regarding the effectiveness of Fast Capitalism as a form of control over the worker. While my research has shown that waiters and waitresses can exercise some level of authority, skill, and wit through their use of language with customers, they must also interact with management and other staff where authority and control play out in different ways.

In the end, however, the customer has ultimate authority over the waiter or 42 waitress. Diner waitressing has a long history of prejudice dating back to the beginning of the industrial revolution and involves issues of gender regarding our general perceptions and ways of interacting (Cobble, 1991; Hall, 1993). Waitressing is integrally tied to domesticated housework and likewise has historically been treated as requiring little skill or ability. In fact, the stigma of servitude that plagues waitressing and other similar kinds of work are not only the result of less than respectable treatment from management, but from customers as well. In her sociological study of diner waitresses in New Jersey, Greta Paules sums it up best:

> That customers embrace the service-as-servitude metaphor is evidenced by the way they speak to and about service workers. Virtually every rule of etiquette is violated by customers in their interactions with the waitress: the waitress can be interrupted; she can be addressed with the mouth full; she can be ignored and stared at; and she can be subjected to unrestrained anger. Lacking status as a person, she, like the servant, is refused the most basic considerations of polite interaction. She is, in addition, the subject of chronic criticism. Just as in the nineteenth century servants were perceived as ignorant, slow, lazy, indifferent, and immoral (Sutherland 1981), so in the twentieth century service workers are condemned for their stupidity, apathy, slowness, incompetence, and questionable moral character. (1991:138–39)

The low status of waitressing and waitering belies the complex nature of this 43 kind of work and the innovative and creative ways in which such workers use language.

Notes

1. Some of the more than 20 websites I have found so far like waitersrevenge.com are award winning. They include sites for taxi drivers, hotel workers, and the like.

2. How to appropriately refer to waitresses and waiters is not a simple decision. Terms like *server* and *food server* are alternatives, but all are problematic. I personally do not like *server* or *food server* because they are too closely related to the word *servitude*. The waiter / waitress distinction is problematic not simply because it differentiates genders, but also because it is associated with a kind / class of service. Often in fine-dining restaurants today both men and women are referred to as waiters, but it is more commonly the practice in the "diner" style restaurant to maintain the distinctive terms. This is historically connected to the diner waitressing being regarded as inferior to fine-dining waitering because it was merely an extension of the domesticated duties of the household.

3. Pseudonyms have been used throughout this chapter.

Works Cited

Better homes and gardens new cook book. (1996). New York: Better Homes and Gardens.

Braverman, H. (1974). *Labor and monopoly capital: The degradation of work in the twentieth century.* New York: Monthly Review Press.

Bureau of Labor Statistics. (1996). Washington, D.C.: U.S. Department of Labor.

Cobble, S. (1991). *Dishing it out: Waitresses and their unions in the 20th century.* Urbana: University of Illinois Press.

Drucker, P. (1993). *Innovation and entrepreneurship: Practice and principles.* New York: Harper-business.

Gee, J. (1991). *Sociolinguistics and literacies: Ideology in discourses.* New York: Falmer.

Gee, J., Hull, G., and Lankshear, C. (1996). *The new work order: Behind the language of the new capitalism.* Sydney: Allen & Unwin.

Gowen, S. (1992). *The politics of workplace literacy.* New York: Teachers College Press.

Hall, E. (1993). Smiling, deferring, and good service. *Work and occupations,* 20 (4), 452–471.

Hochschild, A. (1983). *The managed heart.* Berkeley: University of California Press.

Hull, G. (Ed.). (1997). *Changing work, changing workers: Critical perspectives on language, literacy, and skills.* New York: State University of New York Press.

Hull, G. et al. (1996). *Changing work, changing literacy? A study of skills requirements and development in a traditional and restructured workplace. Final Report.* Unpublished manuscript. University of California at Berkeley.

Kress, G. (1993). Genre as social process. In B. Cope and M. Kalantzis (Eds.), *The powers of literacy: A genre approach to teaching writing* (pp. 22–37). London: Falmer.

Kress, G. (1995). *Writing the future: English and the making of a cultural innovation.* London: NATE.

Lave, J. and Wenger, E. (1991). *Situated learning: Legitimate peripheral participation.* New York: Cambridge University Press.

Leidner, R. (1993). *Fast food, fast talk: Service work and the routinization of everyday life.* Berkeley: University of California Press.

MacDonald, C. and, Sirianni, C. (Eds.). (1996). *Working in the service society.* Philadelphia: Temple University.

Mahiri, J. and Sablo, S. (1996). Writing for their lives: The non-school literacy of California's urban African American youth. *Journal of Negro Education,* 65 (2), 164–180.

Mars, G. and Nicod, M. (1984). *The world of waiters.* London: Unwin Hyman.

New London Group. (1996). A pedagogy of multiliteracies: Designing social futures. *Harvard Educational Review,* 66 (1), 60–92.

NSSB (National Skills Standards Board). (1995). *Server skill standards: National performance criteria in the foodservice industry.* Washington, D.C.: U.S. Council on Hotel, Restaurant and Institutional Education.

Orwell, G. (1933). *Down and out in Paris and London.* New York: Harcourt Brace.

Paules, G. (1991). *Dishing it out: Power and resistance among waitresses in a New Jersey restaurant.* Philadelphia: Temple University Press.

Reich, R. (1992). *The work of nations.* New York: Vintage.

Star, L. and Griesmer, J. (1989). Institutional ecology, translations and boundary objects: Amateurs and professionals in Berkeley's Museum of Vertebrate Zoology, 1907–1939. *Social Studies of Science,* 19.

Street, B. (1984 April 5). *Literacy in theory and practice.* London: Cambridge University Press.

- -

Questions for Discussion and Journaling

1. How does Mirabelli begin his article? What can you infer about his intended audience(s) and purpose(s) from the way he begins? What are the effects for his audience of the way he begins?

2. Mirabelli chooses to focus on participation in a restaurant Discourse. Why? What is he contributing to the conversation on Discourses by doing so?

3. What is the "traditional" view of literacy, according to Mirabelli, and what is the view of literacy that New Literacy Studies takes? What are *multiliteracies*?

4. What seems to be Mirabelli's research question, and where does he state it? What kind of data did Mirabelli collect to analyze the diner discourse community? What seem to be his primary findings in answer to his research question?

5. Mirabelli spends a good deal of his analysis focusing on the genre of the menu, and in doing so, he also discusses the diner's specialized vocabulary (**lexis**,) and methods of intercommunication. Why does Mirabelli focus on the genre of the menu? Is this an effective focus for him as he attempts to answer the research question you identified above? Why or why not?

6. Mirabelli argues that literacy in the diner includes not only reading the menu but also reading the customers. Do you agree that reading customers is a form of literacy? Why or why not?

7. Have you ever participated in a discourse community that is strongly stereotyped like restaurant work is? What are the stereotypes? Using Mirabelli, consider the various "multiliteracies" of this discourse community.

Applying and Exploring Ideas

1. Writing, according to this chapter's threshold concept, can be used to help people collaborate to get things done. The chapter introduction uses the term *mediate* to explain how writing does this: Written texts mediate the experiences of people who are collaborating on an activity. How does Mirabelli's study help you better understand this idea of mediation?

2. Select a Discourse you're interested in and develop a research question about it. What would you want to know, for example, about how the Discourse works, what it takes to enculturate or gain membership in it, and how it differs from other Discourses?

3. How has Mirabelli helped you better understand the threshold concepts of this chapter: that people use texts and discourse in order to *do something*, to *make meaning*, and that the texts and language they create *mediate meaningful activities*?

- -

META MOMENT What did you learn from Mirabelli that can help you make sense of situations in your own life, both seemingly mundane situations like your part-time job, as well as more complex situations like learning to write in your major?

- -

Reflections on the Concept of Discourse Community

JOHN SWALES

Framing the Reading

John Swales is a linguist specializing in discourse analysis and "English for Academic Purposes" (EAP), the study of international uses of English in scholarly fields. He is one of the leading researchers of genre analysis, particularly as applied to EAP. As this article describes, he was the first linguist to attempt a systematic description and definition of the concept of a **discourse community**. While he has taught around the world, he did the work you'll read about as a professor at the University of Michigan, where he worked from 1985 until retiring in 2007. He remains an active scholar, continuing to research and publish in his field.

As Swales describes in the introduction to this article, it was originally given as a conference presentation, published in a French journal, and then reprinted in English in the American journal *Composition Forum*, which has a feature called "Retrospectives," where authors can reflect on something they wrote earlier. This article reflects on work he originally developed in the late 1980s, and ultimately published as part of his 1990 book *Genre Analysis: English in Academic and Research Settings*. In this article you will see Swales refine his original concept of discourse community, asking what else he would say about it twenty-five years after publishing his first work on it. You will also see him talk about the progress of knowledge and the ways that conversants in a field need to continually build ideas by testing and critiquing what a given conversation initially offers. Swales lays out his original theory about discourse communities *and* updates it simultaneously. Swales also talks about student work on discourse communities produced in classes very much like the one you are in now, which is an unusual feature in academic articles like this one.

If you've read Chapter 2, you are likely to experience Swales's discussion here as a strong demonstration of the ideas of *conversational inquiry* and *genre analysis* discussed there. In part, this is because many ideas about academic genres were developed by Swales himself. It is also because Swales, like other scholars, is participating in a scholarly conversation across time.

Swales, John M. "The Concept of Discourse Community: Some Recent Personal History." *Composition Forum*, vol. 37, Fall 2017. http://compositionforum.com/issue/37/swales-retrospective.php

Getting Ready to Read

Before you read, do at least one of the following activities:

- Look up *discourse community* on Wikipedia and read the introduction to the entry. Swales discusses this entry in his article.
- Look up Swales's own Wikipedia entry and note his areas of expertise.

As you read, consider the following questions:

- Where are moments in the piece where Swales moves between the functions of (1) theorizing "discourse community" and (2) reflecting on how the scholarly conversation around discourse community has taken shape?
- What terms do you have to look up as you read, and is there any pattern to the kind of terms they are?

I FIRST HEARD THE TERM "DISCOURSE COMMUNITY" early in 1986, fairly soon after I had moved to the United States; it was used in a talk at the University of Michigan given by Lillian Bridwell-Bowles. I cannot remember much of the talk at today's distance, but I do remember how I immediately recognized that the concept of discourse community was precisely the concept I had been looking for since it would provide socio-rhetorical context for my ongoing exploration of (mainly) academic genres. By the time *Genre Analysis* was eventually published in 1990, discourse community (DC) had become a member of a trio of interlocking concepts, the other two being genre and language-learning task (Swales 1990; Flowerdew 2015). For most of the next few years, I did not pay much attention to the concept, but I did keep mentioning to my doctoral students that the strange configuration of units in the small building where I had my office would make a splendid dissertation research site. This was because the North University Building (now demolished) had the university's Computer Center on the first floor, the university's Herbarium (its large collection of dried plants) on the second floor, while above it was the English Language Institute (ELI), divided into a teaching section and a testing section, and missioned to provide courses and services for international students on the large Ann Arbor campus. However, I was unable to persuade any of the students to take it on, so around 1995 I decided I would do the study myself. The basic idea was to see whether we had three different coherent and cohering discourse communities, each on its own floor in the same building. The book appeared in 1998 with the title of *Other Floors, Other Voices: A Textography of a Small University Building* (Swales 1998). I described the study as a "textography" to indicate that it was something more than a discourse analysis but something less than a full-blown ethnography.

One of the many things that I did learn in the investigative process was that university clocks move at different speeds in different parts of a university. The clock goes very slowly in the Herbarium. If a botanist wants to borrow some specimens from Michigan, he or she needs to agree to keep them for at least two years, and may actually keep them for decades. The reference books that the systematic botanists employ for keying out the plants they are studying have a shelf-life for decades. One major project, to describe all the plants of western Mexico, began in 1946 and was still continuing up to a few years ago. In the ELI, the shelf-life of its products, typically textbooks and tests, runs some 5–10 years or so before they are revised or replaced. While in the Computer Center, the shelf-life of computer manuals, etc., is often just a matter of months before an update appears or some patch is incorporated. Another discovery was that the botanists utilized a very different set of scholarly genres from those to which I had become accustomed; they were, in increasing order of importance or status, a "treatment" (a description of a selected group of plants), a "flora" (the description of all the plants in some region), and a "monograph" (a study of all the plants in one family, wherever they are found). Toward the end of the volume, I concluded that the denizens of the Herbarium formed a very distinct discourse community, while the ELI had many of the elements of a DC, even though there was a rather different ethos in the teaching and testing divisions (over such matters as to what "counts" as a publication), which remained a source of strain. On the other hand, in the Computer Center, the part-time employment of ever-changing streams of short-stay students meant that any sense of community, a sense that "we are all more or less on the same page", never really developed.

From then on, my thoughts about discourse communities lay largely dormant until in 2013 I was asked to give a talk at a well-known university in North Carolina. The professor who invited me suggested I speak about "the concept of discourse community", which I agreed to do. So I started to look around in order to bring myself up to date. My first surprise was that the old material in Genre Analysis seemed to be very much alive and well. The Wikipedia entry, for example, opens with this two-sentence paragraph:

> A **discourse community** is a group of people who share a set of discourses, understood as basic values and assumptions, and ways of communicating about their goals. Linguist John Swales defined discourse communities as "groups that have goals and purposes, and use communication to achieve their goals."[1]

Further, in the middle of this first page, we find: 4

Swales presents six defining characteristics:

A discourse community:
1. has a broadly agreed set of common public goals;
2. has mechanisms of intercommunication among its members;
3. uses its participatory mechanisms to provide information and feedback;
4. utilizes and possesses one or more genres in the communicative furtherance of its aims;
5. In addition to owning genres, it has acquired some specific lexis;
6. has a threshold level of members with a suitable degree of relevant content and discoursal expertise[2]

If one scrolls down the Google entries for discourse community, it seems 5
about a quarter consists of extracts from published or presented work, such as
Beaufort (1998), Borg (2003), and Johns (1997). Another quarter consists of
entries from encyclopedia-type websites such as *Researchomatic* and the *NCTE
briefs*. Most of the rest are either posts from instructors expounding the concept
for their composition students, or blogs from those students, summarizing and
applying the six criteria to their own experiences. One surprising aspect of these
posts and blogs was that there were very few criticisms of or objections to the six
criteria, one of the very few coming from a student named Jordan Rosa: "Questions I still have: Are these the only characteristics of a discourse community, or
are there more? How many more?" Good for you, Jordan!

I soon discovered that the main reason for this flurry of activity in using the 6
six old criteria derived from an extensive DC extract from *Genre Analysis* in
Wardle and Downs' highly successful composition textbook *Writing about writing: A college reader* (Wardle & Downs 2011). Here is a PowerPoint slide from
one of the more interesting instructor uptakes by Heather Wayne, at that time a
teaching assistant in English at the University of Central Florida. (I have added
some explanatory notes in parentheses):

Using the 6 criteria, are these discourse communities?   7
1. A soccer team
2. A sorority / fraternity
3. UCF (University of Central Florida)
4. Publix employees (Publix is a supermarket chain in southeastern USA)
5. The Hong Kong Study Circle (a postal history group examined in Genre Analysis)
6. Republican voters
7. College Democrats at UCF

8. Composition scholars
9. Occupants of Nike dorms (a student resident hall)
10. Our class[3]

Not unexpectedly, I have been in somewhat of two minds about all this 8
attention to the six defining criteria for a discourse community. (And I
notice in passing that Wikipedia uses the present tense ("Swales presents")
for something written twenty-five years ago.) On the one hand, there has
been a sense of (doubtless vainglorious) gratification that something I had
dreamed up in the late 1980s was still alive and well, while, on the other,
there has been a feeling of dismay at the inertia—at the unthinking acceptance of something that was written before most of today's undergraduates
were born and at a time before globalization, before all of those advances in
computers and computer-based communications, and particularly before the
emergence of social media.

25 YEARS LATER—A CHANGED WORLD

The basic idea of a rhetorical discourse community arose in contrast to the 9
longer-standing sociolinguistic concept of speech community. The latter was
premised on a homogeneous assemblage of people who share place, background, language variety and who largely share social, religious, and cultural
values. Such communities tend to be small and isolated, such as those existing
in mountain villages, or on small islands, or in desert oases. In some contrast,
the former is a largely heterogeneous, socio-rhetorical assemblage of people
who broadly share occupational or recreational experiences, goals, and interests. Thus, members of a DC may have different first languages, different reli-
gions, and belong to diverse ethnicities. Examples might include members of
GERAS or of TESOL, all those who work in an animal clinic, or those who
are members of a local choir.

However, it is unclear whether, in this era of cell-phones, family disper- 10
sion, a fluid and uncertain job market for the young, the rise of international
trade, and the decline of local crafts and industries, traditional speech communities continue to exist in meaningful numbers. In addition, discourse
communities both influence and are influenced by the larger communities
within which they are situated. In consequence, when a university becomes
established in a town, the presence of this constellation of discourse communities influences the wider urban environment; as a result, the urban environment provides services that are helpful to the university, such as cheap
student housing, cheap restaurants, museums, and more bookshops, which in
turn further consolidates our sense of a university town like Cambridge,
Heidelberg, or Uppsala. And the same shaping forces create other kinds of

town: religious ones like Lourdes, Assisi, or Mecca; sporting towns like Le Mans, St. Andrews, or Saratoga; or government towns like Washington, Ottawa, or Canberra. In other words, both concepts have developed fuzzier boundaries as the world has changed.

A second set of problems is that the concept of discourse community as orig- 11 inally conceived was overly static. While this perhaps did not matter so much in 1990, in today's more unsettled and uncertain world, it looms larger as a problem; in particular, the concept did not firmly or directly address how people either join or leave DCs. For this, it is helpful to turn to Lave and Wenger's "Community of practice" concept (Lave & Wenger 1991), in which they explain the processes of entry, apprenticeship, membership, seniority, and exit through retirement, death, translocation, etc. A third problematic area is that both the discourse community concept and that of communities of practice tend to view their objects of study through an overly idealistic lens, especially in terms of assumptions about shared beliefs, values, motives, and allegiances among its members (Harris 1989). For instance, when we visit a department in the university that is new to us, our immediate impression is typically one of a homogeneous and sedate disciplinary world with wide agreements about such matters as methodology and epistemology. However, the more we get to know it, the more it seems to be fragmented and compartmentalized, and per- haps even fractious and adversarial (Tannen 1998). To an outsider, a linguistics department, for instance, might seem to represent a collectivity of folks with a like-minded interest in language. However, to an insider, there are clear differ- ences between a phonetician and a phonologist, or between those who pursue the relationship between language and mind, and those who pursue the rela- tionship between language and society. Sometimes, of course, difference leads to fracture. As in a number of universities, the biology department at Michigan has split into two, one dealing with micro- and molecular biology and the other dealing with ecology and evolution. As a senior biologist said to me at the time of the split, "We biologists are either skin-in or skin-out". Finally, like many in major U.S. universities, I used to have a split appointment: 50% of effort in the Department of Linguistics and 50% in the English Language Institute. I suspect I was always a little too practical and pragmatic for my mostly theoret- ical linguistics colleagues, while a little too research-minded for my fellow EAP instructors in the ELI.

THREE TYPES OF DISCOURSE COMMUNITY IN ACADEMIA

The term *discourse community* is now more than thirty years old since it was 12 apparently first coined by Martin Nystrand, a professor of English at the University of Wisconsin–Madison (Nystrand 1982). Since then, it has been

> [W]e have come to see that these communities are, in fact, differentiated by various factors, such as how localized they are, what origins they have had, and what types of activity are central to their existence.

widely used and discussed (sometimes critically) by scholars in applied language studies as a way of recognizing that communications largely operate within conventions and expectations established by communities of various kinds. As this interest in the concept has proliferated, we have come to see that these communities are, in fact, differentiated by various factors, such as how localized they are, what origins they have had, and what types of activity are central to their existence. So, it is the main purpose of this section to offer a categorization of different types of discourse community; if you will, to draw an outline map of the discourse community territory.

Local discourse communities

There are essentially three sub-types of these: residential, vocational, and occu- 13 pational, but only the last of these really applies to the university context. These are groupings of people who all work at the same place (as in a factory or a university department), or at the same occupation in the same area (all the bakers in a town). These DCs have acquired many abbreviations and acronyms as well as some special words and phrases that are needed in order to get their jobs done more quickly and more efficiently—terminologies that are not used, nor even often understood, by the general public. For example, when I worked in Aston University, one of the main eating places on campus was the Vauxhall Dining Centre. So, when we had visitors, if I were not careful, I would say some form of "Let's go to the VD Centre for lunch". When I saw consternation on their faces, I would hurriedly have to explain that I was not suggesting eating at the clinic for venereal diseases!

I am, of course, familiar with my local discourse community in Michigan's 14 ELI. I know when the building is unlocked and how to gain access when it is locked, where the toilets are, and who to ask for technical help. I know which codes to use for the photocopier, and where to find certain office supplies, and so on. However, when I travel to another university for a conference, I do not know any of these things and, unless the signage is excellent, I will probably soon get lost. Lower-level university staff typically belong to just their local departmental discourse community, while mid-level staff may belong in addition to the communities of, for instance, departmental budget officers, who get together for regular meetings and discussions. High-level administrators probably belong to some professional association and travel to that association's national convention. Members of these DCs also have acquired expectations and conventions of behavior that orchestrate their working days. One further consequence is that implicit value systems emerge which determine what is seen as good and less good work. Further, members of these DCs may get together socially outside of work, which further reinforces the community. Often, in these communities, there are apprentice arrangements (such as probationary periods) whereby new members are scrutinized as they attempt to acculturate into accepted occupational behaviors.

Focal discourse communities

Focal communities are the opposite in many ways of local ones. They are typ- 15 ically associations of some kind that reach across a region, a nation, and internationally. They may be informal groupings or more formal ones with rules, elections and paid memberships. One informal group that I belong to is Southeast Michigan Birders, and this is part of an email message I received recently:

> At about 3 p.m. yesterday three owls flew over Wisner Hwy. As they flew closer to the road they swooped lower and disappeared into the woods. Because of the open fields and time of day I suspected SEO, but thought probably not because I have never associated SEO with an affinity for landing in woods.

I suspect that I may be the only person reading this journal who would know 16 that SEO is the standard U.S. acronym for Short-eared Owl. Indeed, many types of discourse communities develop shorthand expressions, such as abbreviations and acronyms, to aid speed of communication. Members of such groups can be of different nationalities, ages, and occupations, and can differ quite considerably in their economic circumstances and educational backgrounds. They come together because of a focus on their hobby or recreational preference. Today, these kinds of DC are much aided by modern conveniences such as email and the cell phone. In some cases, they may produce a newsletter or have some other kind of publication that is distributed among the members.

The other major kind of focal discourse community is *professional* rather than 17 *recreational*. In many professions, there has emerged over the years a national association that is designed to bind the members together and advance the profession in terms of protecting its rights and using its specialized expertise to lobby against what it views as ill-considered policies and in favor of those that it believes to be more soundly based. GERAS and BAAL (the British Association of Applied Linguists) would be typical examples. Many of these associations have a national conference, whereby individuals from far-flung places gather together to learn of latest developments, review the latest products in exhibition areas, and listen to luminaries in their field. These days, they typically have very active websites, wherein members can receive updates and express their opinions and preferences. If they are academically inclined, these associations often also support one or more journals for their members, such as *ASp* or *TESOL Quarterly*.

"Folocal" discourse communities

The third and final main type of discourse community has characteristics of 18 both local and focal DCs, which is why I have coined the fused term "folocal" as a neologistic amalgam of the "local" and "focal". These are hybrid communities whose members have a double—and sometimes split—allegiance, as they are confronted by internal and external challenges and pressures. Consider the situation of the local branch of your bank, or a car dealership in your area. The people who work in such places have both their own ways of going about their tasks, and their own conventionalized ways of talking about those tasks and with their customers. However, they also are in contact and receive instructions from regional or national offices that in part determine how they carry out their duties. In effect, they are subjected to both centripetal and centrifugal forces.

Perhaps a clearer instance is that of a university department in a research- 19 active university. Members of such departments are members of both a local DC and a focal one. They understand how things operate in their own institution as they go about their teaching and administrative activities. Unlike outsiders, they know when rooms and buildings are locked, and where and to whom to make an application for some small amount of money. But they are also specialized scholars whose closest colleagues are likely to be elsewhere, perhaps even in other countries, and whose activities involve presenting at conferences in other places and publishing in distant journals. As is well known, there often emerges a conflict between the local demands on their time and the focal demands on that time—a conflict that is presumably becoming exacerbated as more and more higher education institutions are pressuring their faculty to publish in recognized international journals (Bennett 2014). These, then, are some of the typical competing pressures of belonging to a "folocal" discourse community.

DISCOURSE COMMUNITY AND IDENTITY

Many people are occasional members of more than one discourse community. 20 In my own case, I am a member of the institute where I have had an office for the last thirty years, but also I am active in the wider world of English for Academic Purposes by, for instance, serving on a number of editorial boards. My current hobbies are bird-watching and butterfly-watching, and I belong to various associations that support these similar but not identical activities. In the past, I was a member of a focal DC that brought together a very disparate group of people who were interested in the postal history of Hong Kong, about a hundred philatelists from some twenty countries. Our student services secretary is a dedicated "Whovian" (i.e., a fan of the Dr Who TV program), and last year he flew to London to attend the *Dr Who 50th Anniversary Celebration*. As we move from one DC to another, our verbal and social behavior adapts to the new environment, but I do not believe that this necessarily implies that we adopt new identities, or that we are somehow merely an aggregation of different personae. (Unless, of course, we are spies or under-cover agents.) My beliefs about this were brilliantly exemplified (and with an astonishing economy of words, including but a single opening verb) by Alexander Pope:

> See the same man, in vigour, in the gout;
> Alone, in company; in place, or out;
> Early at business, and at hazard late;
> Mad at a fox-chase, wise at a debate;
> Drunk at a borough, civil at a ball,
> Friendly at Hackney, faithless at Whitehall.
> Epistle 1: To Cobham, 1734 (Williams 1969: 162–163)

As Pope avers, it is "*the same man*" (or woman), healthy or ill, employed or not, at work or gambling, wild at sport or sensible in discussion, drunk at an election, good-mannered at a dance, reliable and amiable in the East End of London, but not to be trusted at the seat of the central government.

RECONSIDERING DC CRITERIA

Given the foregoing—ossified criteria for DCs, problems with the concept, 21 and three contrasting types of discourse community—it is certainly time to re-imagine the concept itself, first by reflecting on the original six criteria and then more generally. In each case, I will give the Wikipedia summaries followed by updates.

1. A DC has a broadly agreed set of goals

A DC has a potentially discoverable set of goals. These may be publicly and 22 explicitly formulated (as in "mission" or "vision" statements); they may be generally or partially recognized by its members; they may be broadly consensual; or they may be separate but contiguous (as when older and younger members have different ideas about the best future direction of the DC, or when there is a clash between academic researchers and practitioners, as in the just-holding-together American Psychological Association). This expansion then is designed to recognize that a DC is not necessarily utopian in flavor; it also acknowledges that DCs can flourish in darker worlds, such as those represented by Al-Q'aida, price-fixing cabals, or industry pressure groups.

2. A DC has mechanisms of intercommunication among its members

Fine, but we now need to emphasize the roles of new digital channels, such as emails, 23 blogs, tweets, etc., and we also need to stress that without any means of intercommunication of any kind, there is no real community. Subscribers to *Le Monde* may share certain characteristics, but they do not form a discourse community.

3. A DC uses its participatory mechanisms to provide information and feedback

This third criterion was always sadly incomplete. A DC uses its participatory 24 mechanisms to manage the operations of the DC and to promote (usually) recruitment, change, growth, and development, and to orchestrate (rarely) retrenchment and demise. In other words, these mechanisms are used to initiate actions and activities, rather than simply providing information. For instance, the employer and employees in a small shop may get together to discuss relocating; a London club may vote to admit women; or a university department, in a series of faculty meetings, may decide to drop a degree option because of low enrollment.

4. A DC utilizes and hence possesses one or more genres in the communicative furtherance of its aims

The use of "possesses" is rather strange as it soon becomes clear that there are 25 not enough genres in the world for them to be "possessed" by individual DCs. A DC utilizes an evolving selection of genres in the furtherance of its sets of goals and as a means of instantiating its participatory mechanisms. These sets of genres are often particularized, as the genres are performed, re-performed, and refined, but they are rarely owned (i.e., uniquely the property of a particular DC). For instance, most university departments have regular staff meetings, but these evolve differently, with emerging differences about speaking and voting roles, about ancillary genres, such as agendas and minutes, and about allowable topics and interventions.

5. In addition to owning genres, it has acquired some specific lexis

A DC has acquired and continues to refine DC-specific terminology. Classi- 26 cally, this consists of abbreviations and shorthands of all kinds, not including various kinds of codes. For example, hospitals in the U.S. have a rich menu of codes that the staff employ, especially in emergencies, partly for efficiency and partly to keep information from patients and the general public. So, "code 236 on floor six" might indicate a heart attack on that floor. In the older ELI, when we still had a placement test, we might have said among ourselves of a new international student, "She looks like a 73 across the board". More widely, at the University of Michigan and indeed elsewhere, unofficial labels are common.

Our football stadium is often referred to as "The Big House"; the central administration building is known as "the Mondrian cube" because of its architecture; and the Shapiro Library more often than not goes by its discarded old name "the UGLI" (the old name being "The Undergraduate Library"). Further, disciplinary terminology can be *sui generis*: recall that the classic genre set for systematic botany consists of *treatment*, *flora*, and *monograph*.

6. A DC has a threshold of members with a suitable degree of relevant content and discoursal expertise

A DC has an explicit or implicit hierarchy and / or structure which, inter alia, 27 manages the processes of entry into and advancement within the discourse community. The stress here on managing DC affairs reduces the somewhat static impression that the 1990 formulation produces.

We can now add two new criteria.

7. A DC develops a sense of "silential relations" (Becker 1995)

A DC develops a sense of "silential relations" (Becker 1995), whereby there is a 28 sense of things that do not need to be said or to be spelt out in detail in either words or writing. Bridge players invariably say "four clubs" rather than "I bid four clubs". Or consider the case of discoveries in the world of nature. If the discovery is of a large mammal, it will make the front pages of the world's major newspapers. If it is of a bird, it will merit an article, including pictures or perhaps a video, in a specialized journal (Gross 1990). But suppose we have a new plant; here is a typical write-up:

> **Bunchosia itacarensis** W R Anderson, sp. nov.–Type: Brazil. Bahia: Mun.
> Itacaré, 3 km S of Itacaré, forest at edge of ocean, Dec fl, *Mori et al.* 13081
> (Holotype: MICH! CEPEC, NY, not seen).

We only know that this is a discovery because of the laconic abbreviated Latin 29 phrase *sp. nov.*; also note the interesting shorthand convention in "MICH!" The exclamation mark indicates that the author has actually examined the University of Michigan specimen.

8. A DC develops horizons of expectation

A DC develops horizons of expectation, defined rhythms of activity, a sense of its 30 history, and value systems for what is good and less good work. Consider again the concept of the university clocks moving at different speeds that was discussed in the opening section. Or reflect on how DCs evolve rotas and rosters. Thus, in the ELI, every other Friday, somebody is responsible for clearing out the communal fridge; every so often, the administrative staff carry out a stock-taking; there is a fire-drill once a year, as well as a Christmas party; the first staff meeting of the year includes the director's review of the previous year, and so on.

Generally speaking, and with some flexibility, all eight criteria can usually be 31 applied to all three types of community.

SO, WHERE DO WE STAND?

It would seem that we can set up operable criteria for looking at groups in order 32 to examine whether those groups qualify for DC status. On the other hand, actually defining discourse communities, or sub-types of them, has proved rather intractable; twenty years ago Bazerman observed that "most definitions of discourse community get ragged around the edges rapidly" (Bazerman 1994: 128), and today that situation has not greatly changed. And yet, it remains seductive, as Paul Prior explains:

> Why does DC theory have such strange features: instant adoptability, resilience in the face of critique, resistance to calls for theoretical specification, the protean character of its fundamental assumptions as it migrates across theoretical and empirical traditions? (Prior 2003: 1)

It is doubtful, then, in present formulations that the concept is a robust social 33 construct. A historian might argue that it does not account for economic and political forces; a sociologist might say that it fails to acknowledge the effects of broader social structures; an educationist might claim that it downplays acquisitional trajectories, as well as the roles of individual agency; and an anthropologist could argue that it ignores powerful aspects of cultural history. But I would counter-argue that this probably does not matter as long as our focus is on rhetorical principles of organization, on discoursal expectations, on significative linguistic tokens, and on intriguing textual extracts. Such attention on these more surface features provides insight into what at first sight might seem standard, ordinary and predictable. On this topic, I will give the last word to James Porter, whose important book is unfortunately little known outside the United States:

> The term "discourse community" is useful for describing a space that was unacknowledged before because we did not have a term for it. The term realigns the traditional unities—writer, audience, text—into a new configuration. What was before largely scene, unnoticed background, becomes foreground. (Porter 1992: 84)

It is precisely this foregrounding realignment that makes the DC concept useful 34 for languages for specific and academic purposes, and for EAP and other practitioners as they work to give students the oracy and literacy skills to survive and flourish in their diverse educational environments.

Notes

1. http://en.wikipedia.org/wiki/Discourse_community.
2. Idem.
3. Idem.

Works Cited

Bazerman, Charles. 1994. *Constructing Experience*. Carbondale, IL: Southern Illinois University Press.

Beaufort, Anne. 1998. *Writing in the Real World: Making the transition from school to work*. New York: Teachers College Press.

Becker, Alton L. 1995. *Beyond Translation: Essays toward a modern philology*. Ann Arbor, MI: University of Michigan Press.

Bennett, Karen (Ed.). 2014. *The Semiperiphery of Academic Writing: Discourses, communities and practices*. London: Palgrave MacMillan.

Borg, Eric. 2003. "Key concepts in ELT. Discourse communities." *ELT Journal* 57/4, 398–400.

Flowerdew, John. 2015. "John Swales's approach to pedagogy in Genre Analysis: A perspective from 25 years on." *Journal of English for Academic Purposes* 19, 102–112.

Gross, Alan G. 1990. *The Rhetoric of Science*. Cambridge, MA: Harvard University Press.

Harris, Joseph. 1989. "The idea of community in the study of writing." *College Composition and Communication* 40, 11–22.

Johns, Ann M. 1997. *Text, Role and Context*. Cambridge: Cambridge University Press.

Lave, Jean & Etienne Wenger. 1991. *Situated Learning: Legitimate peripheral participation*. Cambridge: Cambridge University Press.

Nystrand, Martin. 1982. *What Writers Know: The language, process, and structure of written discourse*. New York: Academic Press.

Porter, James E. 1992. *Audience and Rhetoric: An archaeological composition of the discourse community*. Englewood Cliffs, NJ: Prentice Hall.

Prior, Paul. 2003. "Are communities of practice really an alternative to discourse communities?" Presentation at the American Association of Applied Linguistics Conference, Arlington, Virginia.

Swales, John M. 1990. *Genre Analysis: English in academic and research settings*. Cambridge: Cambridge University Press.

Swales, John M. 1998. *Other Floors, Other Voices: A textography of a small university building*. Mahwah, NJ: Lawrence Erlbaum.

Tannen, Deborah. 1998. *The Argument Culture*. New York: Random House.

Wardle, Elizabeth & Douglas Downs. 2011. *Writing about Writing: A college reader*. Boston: Bedford/St. Martins.

Williams, Aubrey (Ed.) 1969. *Poetry and Prose of Alexander Pope*. Boston: Houghton Mifflin.

Questions for Discussion and Journaling

1. In para. 11, Swales states the central concept of discourse-community theory in just a few lines. In your own words, what is it?

2. Swales seems both surprised and disappointed that "there were very few criticisms of or objections to the six criteria" for identifying discourse communities (para. 5). What does his dismay suggest about the purpose of doing scholarly research?

3. As he returns after twenty-five years to his original notions of discourse communities, Swales identifies three problem areas with his original theory. How would you summarize them?

4. Based on Swales's discussion of types of discourse communities and what make a community, consider the role of *allegiance* in determining community membership. To what extent is identifying with and feeling some loyalty to a discourse community essential for being a part of it?

5. Swales suggests that "many people are occasional members of more than one discourse community" (para. 20). If you've read Gee, how does Swales's statement square with Gee's assertion that virtually all individuals embody multiple Discourses?

6. If a group of people share interest in a given text or object — Swales uses the example of "subscribers to *Le Monde*" (because this article was originally published in a French journal, remember) (para. 23) — but don't interact with each other or communicate about their shared interest, Swales says they do not form a discourse community. Why is interaction so essential to being a discourse community?

Applying and Exploring Ideas

1. The concept of discourse community has "developed fuzzier boundaries as the world has changed" (para. 10). Do you prefer this "fuzzier" sense of what might count as a discourse community, or is the concept less helpful if the definition is not entirely clear or precise?

2. Swales seems to take for granted that in his first work on discourse communities, twenty-five years ago, he discussed incomplete or perhaps inaccurate ideas about it. This is true of all research. We learn more and gain more complete understandings over time. Identify some other older ideas you've encountered in readings in this book that seem to need updating in light of how the world has changed. Then, consider what this means about the nature of inquiry or research. How might students engage differently in inquiry if they expect that ideas are always incomplete and will change?

3. Using the taxonomy of "types of discourse community in academia" that Swales offers starting in paragraph 12, identify some of the discourse communities you occupy as a university student. Explain why you identify a given community as a

particular type suggested by Swales. Do you occupy any communities that seem to be of a different type than any he outlines?

4. If you've also read Gee's or Wardle's pieces in this chapter, write a one- to two-page comparison of the sociocultural theories of writing they use — Discourse theory and activity theory, respectively — with Swales's theory of discourse communities. Focus on what each is particularly good at explaining and what each might overlook or attend less closely to.

5. As Swales "reconsiders DC criteria," he wants to shift his first criterion from "A DC has a broadly agreed set of goals" to "*a potentially discoverable set of goals*" (para. 22, emphasis added). What is the difference, and why would Swales be more comfortable with the latter version?

6. Choose a discourse community you are a well-established member of, and write as thorough a description as you can, in one single-spaced page, of its *silential relations* (para. 28). What does the discourse community treat as "goes without saying," taken for granted, or needing no description for experienced members of the community?

- -

META MOMENT   Have you ever been *aware of* becoming a member of a discourse community, consciously learning how to fit in? How was this process different from a discourse community you joined unconsciously and easily over time?

- -

Discourse Communities and Communities of Practice

Membership, Conflict, and Diversity

ANN M. JOHNS

Ann M. Johns

Framing the Reading

Ann M. Johns, like Gee, is a well-known linguist. While she was at San Diego State University, Johns directed the American Language Institute, the Writing Across the Curriculum Program, the Freshman Success Program, and the Center for Teaching and Learning, and she still found time to research and write twenty-three articles, twenty-two book chapters, and four books (including *Genre in the Classroom* [2001] and *Text, Role, and Context*, from which the following reading is taken). Since retiring from San Diego State, Johns continues to write articles and consult around the world.

Like Gee, Johns gives you some things to look for and consider when trying to figure out what is happening in any situation where language and texts play a part: What are people doing here? Do they have shared goals? How do they communicate with one another? How do newcomers learn what to do here?

While building on Swales's earlier theorizing of discourse communities, Johns's work shows us another important set of considerations relating to this chapter's threshold concept that people collaborate to get things done with writing. Johns doesn't simply explain discourse communities, but focuses on how and why conflicts occur in them. In doing so, she focuses primarily on *academic* discourse communities. She talks about some of the "expected" **conventions** of discourse in the academy (what she calls "uniting forces"), and then describes sources of contention. Johns brings up issues of rebellion against discourse community conventions, change within conventions of communities, the relationship of **identity** to discourse community membership, and

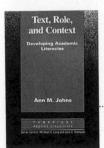

the problems of **authority** and control over acceptable community discourse. Johns's exploration of conflicts within discourse communities should remind you that such communities are always changing and are not static. Thus, even though newcomers may

Johns, Ann M. "Discourse Communities and Communities of Practice: Membership, Conflict, and Diversity." *Text, Role, and Context: Developing Academic Literacies*, Cambridge UP, 1997, pp. 51–70.

be expected to **enculturate**, they can also make change within communities — and change the way that people get work done and make meaning together. As always, this reading will be easier for you if you can try to relate what Johns describes to your own experiences or to things you have witnessed or read about elsewhere.

Getting Ready to Read

Before you read, do at least one of the following activities:

- If you've read other articles in this chapter already, make a list of the difficulties or problems you've had with concepts related to discourses so far. What have you not understood? What has not made sense? What questions have you been left with?
- Write a quick note to yourself about *membership:* What does the idea of *membership* mean to you? When you hear that word, what do you associate it with? What memories of it do you have? Do you often use it or hear it?

As you read, consider the following questions:

- What does it mean to have *authority* in relation to texts and discourse communities?
- How does trying to become a member of a discourse community impact your sense of self? Do you feel your "self" being compressed or pressured, or expanding?
- How are discourse communities related to *identity?*

If there is one thing that most of [the discourse community definitions] have in common, it is an idea of language [and genres] as a basis for sharing and holding in common: shared expectations, shared participation, commonly (or communicably) held ways of expressing. Like audience, discourse community entails assumptions about conformity and convention (Rafoth, 1990, p. 140).

What is needed for descriptive adequacy may not be so much a search for the conventions of language use in a particular group, but a search for the varieties of language use that work both with and against conformity, and accurately reflect the interplay of identity and power relationships (Rafoth, 1990, p. 144).

A SECOND IMPORTANT CONCEPT in the discussion of socioliteracies is 1 *discourse community.* Because this term is abstract, complex, and contested,[1] I will approach it by attempting to answer a few of the questions that are raised in the literature, those that seem most appropriate to teaching and learning in academic contexts.

1. Why do individuals join social and professional communities? What appear to be the relationships between communities and their genres?

2. Are there levels of community? In particular, can we hypothesize a general academic community or language?

3. What are some of the forces that make communities complex and varied? What forces work against "shared participation and shared ways of expressing?" (Rafoth, 1990, p. 140).

I have used the term discourse communities because this appears to be the ⟨2 most common term in the literature. However, *communities of practice*, a related concept, is becoming increasingly popular, particularly for academic contexts (see Brown & Duguid, 1995; Lave & Wenger, 1991). In the term *discourse communities*, the focus is on texts and language, the genres and lexis that enable members throughout the world to maintain their goals, regulate their membership, and communicate efficiently with one another. Swales (1990, pp. 24–27) lists six defining characteristics of a discourse community:

1. [It has] a broadly agreed set of common public goals.

2. [It has] mechanisms of intercommunication among its members (such as newsletters or journals).

3. [It] utilizes and hence possesses one or more genres in the communicative furtherance of its aims.

4. [It] uses its participatory mechanisms primarily to provide information and feedback.

5. In addition to owning genres, [it] has acquired some specific lexis.

6. [It has] a threshold level of members with a suitable degree of relevant content and discoursal expertise.

The term communities of practice refers to genres and lexis, but especially 3 to many practices and values that hold communities together or separate them from one another. Lave and Wenger, in discussing students' enculturation into academic communities, have this to say about communities of practice:

> As students begin to engage with the discipline, as they move from exposure to experience, they begin to understand that the different communities on campus are quite distinct, that apparently common terms have different meanings, apparently shared tools have different uses, apparently related objects have different interpretations. . . . As they work in a particular community, they start to understand both its particularities and what joining takes, how these involve language, practice, culture and a conceptual universe, not just mountains of facts (1991, p. 13).

Thus, communities of practice are seen as complex collections of individuals who share genres, language, values, concepts, and "ways of being" (Geertz, 1983), often distinct from those held by other communities.

In order to introduce students to these visions of community, it is useful to 4 take them outside the academic realm to something more familiar, the recreational and avocational communities to which they, or their families, belong. Thus I begin with a discussion of nonacademic communities before proceeding to issues of academic communities and membership.

COMMUNITIES AND MEMBERSHIP

Social, Political, and Recreational Communities

People are born, or taken involuntarily by their families and cultures, into some 5 communities of practice. These first culture communities may be religious, tribal, social, or economic, and they may be central to an individual's daily life experiences. Academic communities, on the other hand, are selected and voluntary, at least after compulsory education. Therefore, this chapter will concentrate on communities that are chosen, the groups with which people maintain ties because of their interests, their politics, or their professions. Individuals are often members of a variety of communities outside academic life: social and interest groups with which they have chosen to affiliate. These community affiliations vary in terms of individual depth of interest, belief, and commitment. Individual involvement may become stronger or weaker over time as circumstances and interests change.

Nonacademic communities of interest, like "homely" genres, can provide a 6 useful starting point for student discussion. In presenting communities of this type, Swales uses the example of the Hong Kong Study Circle (HKSC),[2] of which he is a paying member, whose purposes are to "foster interest in and knowledge of the stamps of Hong Kong" (1990, p. 27). He was once quite active in this community, dialoging frequently with other members through HKSC publications.[3] However, at this point in his life, he has other interests (birds and butterflies), and so he is now an inactive member of HKSC. His commitments of time and energy have been diverted elsewhere.

Members of my family are also affiliated with several types of communities. 7 We are members of cultural organizations, such as the local art museum and the theater companies. We receive these communities' publications, and we attend some of their functions, but we do not consider ourselves to be active. We also belong to a variety of communities with political aims. My mother, for example, is a member of the powerful lobbying group, the American Association of Retired Persons (AARP). The several million members pay their dues because of their interests in maintaining government-sponsored retirement (Social Security) and health benefits (Medicare), both of which are promoted by AARP lobbyists in the U.S. Congress. The AARP magazine, *Modern Maturity,* is a powerful organ of the association, carefully crafted to forward the group's aims. Through this publication, members are urged to write to their elected representatives about legislation, and they are also informed about which members of Congress are "friends of the retired." However, members are offered more than politics: Articles in the magazine discuss keeping healthy while aging, remaining beautiful, traveling cheaply, and using the Internet. AARP members also receive discounts on prescription drugs, tours, and other benefits.[4]

Recently, my husband has become very active in a recreational discourse 8 community, the international community of cyclists.[5] He reads publications such as *Bicycling* ("World's No. 1 Road and Mountain Bike Magazine") each month for advice about better cyclist health ("Instead of Pasta, Eat This!"),[6] equipment to buy, and international cycling tours. Like most other communities, cycling has experts, some of whom write articles for the magazines to which he subscribes, using a register that is mysterious to the uninitiated: "unified gear triangle"; "metal matrix composite." Cyclists share values (good health, travel interests), special knowledge, vocabulary, and genres, but they do not necessarily share political or social views, as my husband discovered when conversing with other cyclists on a group trip. In publications for cyclists, we can find genres that we recognize by name but with community-related content: editorials, letters to the editor, short articles on new products, articles of interest to readers (on health and safety, for example), advertisements appealing to readers, and essay/commentaries. If we examine magazines published for other interest groups, we can find texts from many of the same genres.

As this discussion indicates, individuals often affiliate with several communities at the same time, with varying levels of involvement and interest. People may join a group because they agree politically, because they want to socialize, or because they are interested in a particular sport or pastime. The depth of an individual's commitment can, and often does, change over time. As members come and go, the genres and practices continue to evolve, reflecting and promoting the active members' aims, interests, and controversies.

Studying the genres of nonacademic communities, particularly those with 10 which students are familiar, helps them to grasp the complexity of text production and processing and the importance of understanding the group practices, lexis, values, and controversies that influence the construction of texts.

Professional Communities

Discourse communities can also be professional; every major profession has its 11 organizations, its practices, its textual conventions, and its genres. Active community members also carry on informal exchanges: at conferences, through e-mail interest groups, in memos, in hallway discussions at the office, in laboratories and elsewhere, the results of which may be woven intertextually into public, published texts. However, it is the written genres of communities that are accessible to outsiders for analysis. We need only to ask professionals about their texts in order to collect an array of interesting examples. One of the most thoroughly studied professional communities is the law. In his *Analysing Genre: Language Use in Professional Settings* (1993), Bhatia discusses at some length his continuing research into legal communities that use English and other languages (pp. 101–143). He identifies the various genres of the legal profession: their purposes, contexts, and the form and content that appear to be conventional. He also contrasts these genres as they are realized in texts from various cultures.

However, there are many other professional discourse communities whose 12 genres can be investigated, particularly when students are interested in enculturation. For example, students might study musicians who devote their lives to pursuing their art but who also use written texts to dialogue with others in their profession. To learn more about these communities, I interviewed a bassoonist in our city orchestra.[7] Along with those who play oboe, English horn, and contrabassoon, this musician subscribes to the major publication of the double-reed community, *The International Double Reed Society Journal.* Though he has specialized, double-reed interests, he reports that he and many other musicians also have general professional aims and values that link them to musicians in a much broader community. He argues that all practicing musicians within the Western tradition[8] share knowledge; there is a common core of language and values within this larger community. Whether they are guitarists, pianists, rock musicians, or bassoonists, musicians in the West seem to agree, for example, that the strongest and most basic musical intervals are 5–1 and 4–1, and that other chord intervals are weaker. They share a basic linguistic register and an understanding of chords and notation. Without this sharing, considerable negotiation would have to take place before they could play music together. As in other professions, these musicians have a base of expertise, values, and expectations that they use to facilitate communication. Thus, though a musician's first allegiance may be to his or her own musical tradition (jazz) or instrument (the bassoon), he or she will still share a great deal with other expert musicians — and much of this sharing is accomplished through specialized texts.

What can we conclude from this section about individual affiliations with 13 discourse communities? First, many people have chosen to be members of one or a variety of communities, groups with whom they share social, political, professional, or recreational interests. These communities use written discourses that enable members to keep in touch with each other, carry on discussions, explore controversies, and advance their aims; the genres are their vehicles for communication. These genres are not, in all cases, sophisticated or intellectual, literary or high-browed. They are, instead, representative of the values, needs, and practices of the community that produces them. Community membership may be concentrated or diluted; it may be central to a person's life or peripheral. Important for the discussion that follows is the juxtaposition of generalized and specialized languages and practices among these groups. Musicians, lawyers, athletes, and physicians, for example, may share certain values, language, and texts with others within their larger community, though their first allegiance is to their specializations. Figure 1 illustrates this general/specific relationship in communities.

In the case of physicians, for example, there is a general community and a set of values and concepts with which most may identify because they have all had a shared basic education before beginning their specializations. There are publications, documents, concepts, language, and values that all physicians can, and often do, share. The same can be said of academics, as is shown in the figure. There may be some general academic discourses,[9] language, values, and concepts that most academics share. Thus faculty often identify themselves with a college or university and its language and values, as well as with the more specialized areas of interest for which they have been prepared.

This broad academic identification presents major problems for scholars and literacy practitioners, for although it is argued that disciplines are different (see Bartholomae, 1985; Belcher & Braine, 1995; Berkenkotter & Huckin, 1995;

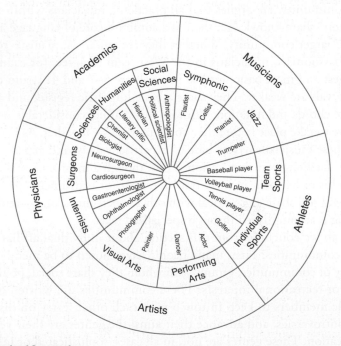

Figure 1 Levels of Community

Carson et al., 1992; Lave & Wenger, 1991, among others), many faculty believe that there is a general academic English as well as a general set of critical thinking skills and strategies for approaching texts.

Because this belief in a general, shared academic language is strong and 16 universal, the next section of this chapter is devoted to this topic.

Academic Communities

What motivates this section more than anything else is its usefulness as a start- 17 ing point in the exploration of academic literacies and its accessibility to students at various levels of instruction who need to become more aware of the interaction of roles, texts, and contexts in academic communities. Many literacy faculty have mixed classes of students from a number of disciplines or students just beginning to consider what it means to be an academic reader and writer. For these students, and even for some of the more advanced, a discussion of what are considered to be general academic languages and textual practices is a good place to start their analyses—although not a good place to finish.

In the previous section it was noted that professionals may affiliate at various 18 levels of specificity within their discourse communities. They often share language, knowledge, and values with a large, fairly heterogeneous group, though their first allegiances may be with a specialized group within this broader "club." This comment can apply to individuals in academic communities as well. Faculty have their own discipline-specific allegiances (to biology, chemistry, sociology, engineering); nonetheless, many believe that there are basic, generalizable linguistic, textual, and rhetorical rules for the entire academic community that can apply.

Discipline-specific faculty who teach novices at the undergraduate level, and 19 some who teach graduate students as well, sometimes complain that their students "do not write like academics" or "cannot comprehend" academic prose, arguing that these are general abilities that we should be teaching. The discussion that follows acknowledges their complaints and sets the stage for discussions of more specific academic issues and pedagogies in later chapters.

Language, Texts, and Values

This section on academic textual practices draws principally from three sources: 20 "Reflections on Academic Discourse" (Elbow, 1991); *Words and Lives: The Anthropologist as Author* (Geertz, 1988); and *The Scribal Society: An Essay on Literacy and Schooling in the Information Age* (Purves, 1990) (see also Dudley-Evans, 1995). Elbow and Purves are well-known composition theorists from different theoretical camps who were cited in Chapter I. Geertz, an anthropologist, has studied academic communities and their genres for many years. All three of these experts live in the United States, and this may affect their views; however, in many universities in the world in which English is employed, these beliefs about general text features are also shared, except perhaps in literature and some of the humanities disciplines. Following is a composite of the arguments made by the three academics about the nature, values, and practices in general expository academic prose, including some commentary on each topic.

1. *Texts must be explicit.* Writers should select their vocabulary carefully and 21 use it wisely. In some cases, such as with certain noun compounds, paraphrase is impossible because specialized academic vocabulary must be used. Citation must be constructed carefully. Data analysis should be described and discussed explicitly. The methodology should be stated so clearly that it is replicable. Ambiguity in argumentation should be avoided.

Comment. Faculty often complain that students are "careless" in their use of 22 vocabulary, in their citation practices, and in their argumentation and use of data. Because many literacy classes value the personal essay and because many readings in literacy classes are in story form or are adapted or specially written for these classes, students are not exposed to the exactness of some academic prose. One of our responsibilities in developing socioliterate practices is to expose students to authentic academic texts and to analyze these texts for their specificity.

2. *Topic and argument should be prerevealed in the introduction.* Purves says 23 that experienced academics, particularly when writing certain kinds of texts, should "select a single aspect of [a] subject and announce [their] theses and purposes as soon as possible" (1990, p. 12).

Comment. Finding the argument in a reading and noticing how data, exam- 24 ples, or narration are used to support this argument are essential academic abilities that are praised by faculty from many disciplines. In like manner, understanding and presenting a clear argument that is appropriate to a genre are writing skills that appear high on faculty wish lists for students, particularly for those who come from diverse rhetorical traditions (see Connor, 1987). Most faculty require that arguments and purposes appear early, generally in an introduction. One of the discipline-specific faculty with whom I work tells her students not to "spend much time clearing their throats." She wants them to "get right down to the argument."

We must be aware, however, that the pressure to reveal topic, purposes, and 25 argumentation early in a written text may be a culture-specific value and apply only to certain kinds of texts within specific communities. There is considerable discussion in the contrastive rhetoric and World Englishes literature about the motivations for text organization and content and the necessity (or lack thereof) for prerevealing information. Local cultures and first languages, as well as academic disciplines, can influence how and where arguments appear.

3. *Writers should provide "maps" or "signposts" for the readers throughout the* 26 *texts, telling the readers where they have been in the text and where they are going.*

By using a variety of tactics, writers can assist readers in predicting and summarizing texts and in understanding the relationships among topics and arguments. Most of these tactics fall under the metadiscourse rubric.

Comment. Metadiscourse is defined in the following way: 27

> It is writing about reading and writing. When we communicate, we use metadiscourse to name rhetorical actions: *explain, show, argue, claim, deny, suggest, add, expand, summarize;* to name the part of our discourse, *first, second . . . in conclusion;* to reveal logical connections, *therefore . . . if so . . .* to guide our readers, *Consider the matter of* (Williams, 1989, p. 28).

Literacy textbooks for both reading and writing often emphasize the understanding and use of metadiscourse in texts. However, it is important to note that language and culture can have considerable influence on the ways in which metadiscourse is used. For example, in countries with homogeneous cultures, academic written English may have fewer metadiscoursal features (Mauranen, 1993) than in heterogeneous, "writer-responsible" cultures (see Hinds, 1987) such as the United States, Great Britain, or Australia. As in the case of all texts, academic discourses are influenced by the cultures and communities in which they are found, often in very complicated ways.

4. *The language of texts should create a distance between the writer and the text* 28 *to give the appearance of objectivity.* Geertz (1988) speaks of academic, expository prose as "author-evacuated"; the author's personal voice is not clearly in evidence, because the first person pronoun is absent and arguments are muted. He compares author-evacuated prose with the "author-saturated" prose of many literary works, in which individual voice pervades. As mentioned earlier, this "author-evacuation" is particularly evident in pedagogical genres, such as the textbook. One way to create the evacuated style is to use the passive, a common rhetorical choice for the sciences, but there are other ways as well.

Comment. Discipline-specific faculty sometimes tell us that students are 29 unable to write "objectively" or to comprehend "objective" prose.[10] These students have not mastered the ability to clothe their argumentation in a particular register, to give it the kind of objective overlay that is valued in academic circles. When I asked one of my first-year university students to tell the class what he had learned about academic English, he said: "We can't use 'I' anymore. We have to pretend that we're not there in the text." In many cases, he is right. Literacy teachers need to help students to analyze texts for their author-evacuated style, and to discuss the particular grammatical and lexical choices that are made to achieve the appearance of objectivity and distance.

5. *Texts should maintain a "rubber-gloved" quality of voice and register.* They 30 must show a kind of reluctance to touch one's meanings with one's naked fingers (Elbow, 1991, p. 145).

569

Comment. For some academic contexts, writers appear to remove themselves 31 emotionally and personally from the texts, to hold their texts at arms' length (metaphorically). The examination of texts in which this "rubber-gloved quality" is evident will provide for students some of the language to achieve these ends. What can students discover? Many academic writers abjure the use of emotional words, such as *wonderful* and *disgusting;* they hide behind syntax and "objective" academic vocabulary.

6. *Writers should take a guarded stance, especially when presenting argumen-* 32 *tation and results.* Hedging through the use of modals (*may, might*) and other forms (*It is possible that . . .*) is perhaps the most common way to be guarded.

Comment. Hedging appears to be central to some academic discourses, par- 33 ticularly those that report research. In a study of two science articles on the same topic published for two different audiences, Fahenstock (1986) found that the article written for experts in the field was replete with hedges ("*appear to* hydrolyze," "*suggesting* that animal food"), as scientists carefully reported their findings to their peers. However, the article written for laypersons was filled with "facts," much like those in the textbooks described in Chapter 3. For these and other reasons, we need to introduce students to expert and nonexpert texts; we need to expose them at every level to the ways in which genre, context, readers, writers, and communities affect linguistic choices.

7. *Texts should display a vision of reality shared by members of the particular dis-* 34 *course community to which the text is addressed (or the particular faculty member who made the assignment).*

Comment. This may be the most difficult of the general academic requirements, 35 for views of reality are often implicit, unacknowledged by the faculty themselves and are not revealed to students. Perhaps I can show how this "reality vision" is so difficult to uncover by discussing my research on course syllabi. I have been interviewing faculty for several years about the goals for their classes, goals that are generally stated in what is called a syllabus in the United States, but might be called a class framework or schedule of assignments in other countries. These studies indicated that most faculty tend to list as goals for the course the various topics that will be studied. The focus is exclusively on content. They do not list the particular views of the world that they want students to embrace, or the understandings that they want to encourage. In a class on "Women in the Humanities," for example, the instructor listed topics to be covered in her syllabus, but she did not tell the students that she wanted them to analyze images of women in cultures in order to see how these images shape various cultural contexts. In a geography class, the instructor listed topics to be covered, but he did not tell his students about his goals for analysis and synthesis of texts. Why are the critical-thinking goals and disciplinary values hidden by most faculty? I don't know. Perhaps instructors believe that students should intuit the values, practices, and genres required in the course; or the faculty have difficulty explicitly stating goals that are not related to content. Certainly content is the most commonly discussed issue at discipline-specific (DS) curriculum meetings, and this may influence faculty choices. In a later chapter I will discuss one of the questionnaires that I use to elicit from faculty the "views of reality" or "ways of being" that my students and I would like to see stated explicitly in the syllabi.

In contrast to DS faculty, we literacy faculty are often most interested in pro- 36 cesses and understandings, in developing students' metacognition and metalanguages — and these interests are often reflected in our syllabi. [Following,] for example, are the student goals for a first-year University writing class developed by a committee from my university's Department of Rhetoric and Writing Studies:[11]

a. To use writing to clarify and improve your understanding of issues and texts

b. To respond in writing to the thinking of others and to explore and account for your own responses

c. To read analytically and critically, making active use of what you read in your writing

d. To understand the relationships between discourse structure and the question at issue in a piece of writing, and to select appropriate structures at the sentence and discourse levels

e. To monitor your writing for the grammar and usage conventions appropriate to each writing situation

f. To use textual material as a framework for understanding and writing about other texts, data or experiences

No matter what kind of class is being taught, faculty need to discuss critical- 37 thinking and reading and writing goals frequently with students. They need to review why students are given assignments, showing how these tasks relate to course concepts and student literacy growth.

8. *Academic texts should display a set of social and authority relations; they should* 38 *show the writer's understanding of the roles they play within the text or context.*[12]

Comment. Most students have had very little practice in recognizing the lan- 39 guage of social roles within academic contexts, although their experience with language and social roles outside the classroom is often quite rich. Some students cannot recognize when they are being talked down to in textbooks, and they cannot write in a language that shows their roles vis-à-vis the topics studied or the faculty they are addressing. These difficulties are particularly evident among ESL/EFL students; however, they are also found among many other students whose exposure to academic language has been minimal. One reason for discussing social roles as they relate to texts from a genre, whether they be "homely" discourses or professional texts, is to heighten students' awareness of the interaction of language, roles, and contexts so that they can read and write with more sophistication.

9. *Academic texts should acknowledge the complex and important nature of inter-* 40 *textuality, the exploitation of other texts without resorting to plagiarism.* Students

> *One reason for discussing social roles as they relate to texts from a genre . . . is to heighten students' awareness of the interaction of language, roles, and contexts so that they can read and write with more sophistication.*

need to practice reformulation and reconstruction of information so that they do not just repeat other texts by "knowledge telling" (Bereiter & Scardamalia, 1989) but rather use these texts inventively for their purposes (called "knowledge transforming"; Bereiter & Scardamalia, 1989).

Comment. Carson (1993), in a large 41 study of the intellectual demands on undergraduate students, found that drawing from and integrating textual sources were two of the major challenges students face in attaining academic literacy. And no wonder. Widdowson (1993, p. 27) notes that

> When people make excessive and unacknowledged use of [another's text], and are found out, we call it plagiarism. When people are astute in their stitching of textual patchwork, we call it creativity. It is not easy to tell the difference. . . . If a text is always in some degree a conglomerate of others, how independent can its meaning be?

Drawing from sources and citing them appropriately is the most obvious 42 and most commonly discussed aspect of intertextuality. As a result, Swales and Feak (1994) claim that citation may be the defining feature of academic discourses. However, there are other, more subtle and varied borrowings from past discourses, for, as Widdowson notes, "Any particular text is produced or interpreted in reference to a previous knowledge of other texts" (1993, p. 27).

10. *Texts should comply with the genre requirements of the community or* 43 *classroom.*

Comment. This, of course, is another difficult challenge for students. As men- 44 tioned earlier, pedagogical genres are often loosely named and casually described by DS faculty. It is difficult to identify the conventions of a student research paper, an essay examination response, or other pedagogical genres because, in fact, these vary considerably from class to class. Yet DS faculty expect students to understand these distinctions and to read and write appropriately for their own classes. My students and I often ask faculty: "What is a good critique for your class?" or "What is a good term paper?" We request several student-written models and, if possible, interview the faculty member about their assigned texts and tasks.

This section has outlined what may be some general rules for academic liter- 45 acy, most of which are refined within each discipline and classroom. Although it would be difficult to defend several of these beliefs because of the wide range of academic discourses and practices, listing and discussing these factors can prepare students for an examination of how texts are socially constructed and whether some of the points made here are applicable to specific texts.

Of course, we also need to expose students to texts that contradict these rules for academic discourse. We should examine literary genres, which break most of the rules listed. We should look at specialized texts that have alternative requirements for register. In any of our pedagogical conversations, the objective should not be to discover truths but to explore how social and cultural forces may influence texts in various contexts. 46

COMMUNITY CONFLICTS AND DIVERSITY

So far, the discussion of communities and their genres has focused on the unit-ing forces, particularly the language, practices, values, and genres that groups may share. It has been suggested that people can join communities at will and remain affiliated at levels of their own choosing. For a number of reasons, this is not entirely accurate. In some cases people are excluded from communities because they lack social standing, talent, or money, or because they live in the wrong part of town. In other cases, community membership requires a long initiatory process, and even then there is no guarantee of success. Many stu-dents work for years toward their doctoral degrees, for example, only to find that there are no faculty positions available to them or that their approach to research will not lead to advancement. 47

Even after individuals are fully initiated, many factors can separate them. Mem-bers of communities rebel, opposing community leaders or attempting to change the rules of the game and, by extension, the content and argumentation in the texts from shared genres. If the rebellion is successful, the rules may be changed or a new group may be formed with a different set of values and aims. There may even be a theoretical paradigm shift in the discipline. In academic communities, rebellion may result in the creation of a new unit or department, separate from the old community, as has been the case recently in my own university.[13] Even without open rebellion, there is constant dialogue and argument within communities as members thrash out their differences and juggle for power and identity, promoting their own content, argumentation, and approaches to research. 48

Although much could be said about factors that affect communities outside the academic realm, the following discussion will focus on a few of the rich and complex factors that give academic communities their character. 49

The Cost of Affiliation

If students want to become affiliated with academic discourse communities, or even if they want to succeed in school, they may have to make considerable sacrifices. To become active academic participants, they sometimes must make 50 major trade-offs that can create personal and social distance between them and their families and communities. Students are asked to modify their language to fit that of the academic classroom or discipline. They often must drop, or at least diminish in importance, their affiliations to their home cultures in order to take on the values, language, and genres of their disciplinary culture. The literature is full of stories of the students who must make choices between their communities and academic lives (see, for example, Rose's *Lives on the Boundary,* 1989). In an account of his experiences, Richard Rodriguez (1982, p. 56), a child of Mexican immigrant parents, wrote the following:

> What I am about to say to you has taken me more than twenty years to admit:
> a primary reason for my success in the classroom was that I couldn't forget
> that schooling was changing me and separating me from the life I had enjoyed
> before becoming a student. . . . If because of my schooling, I had grown
> culturally separated from my parents, my education has finally given me ways of
> speaking and caring about that fact.

Here Rodriguez is discussing his entire schooling experience; however, as stu- 51 dents advance in schools and universities, they may be confronted with even more wrenching conflicts between their home and academic cultures and languages. In her story of a Hispanic graduate student in a Ph.D. sociology program in the United States, Casanave (1992) tells how the tension between this student's personal values and language and her chosen department's insistence on its own scientific language and genres finally drove her from her new academic community. When she could no longer explain her work in sociology in everyday language to the people of her primary communities (her family and her clients), the student decided to leave the graduate program. The faculty viewed her stance as rebellious, an open refusal to take on academic community values. By the time she left, it had become obvious to all concerned that the faculty were unable, or unwilling, to bend or to adapt some of their disciplinary rules to accommodate this student's interests, vocation, and language.

A graduate student from Japan faced other kinds of affiliation conflicts when 52 attempting to become a successful student in a North American linguistics program (Benson, 1996). This student brought from her home university certain social expectations: about faculty roles, about her role as a student, and about what is involved in the production of texts. She believed, for example, that the faculty should provide her with models of what was expected in her papers; she felt that they should determine her research topics and hypotheses. This had been the case in her university in Japan, and she had considerable difficulty understanding why the American faculty did not conform to the practices of her home country. She tried to follow her professors' instructions with great care, but they chastised her for "lacking ideas." In her view, the faculty were being irresponsible; however, some faculty viewed her as passive, unimaginative, and dependent. What she and many other students have found is that gaining affiliation in graduate education means much more than understanding the registers of academic language.

These examples are intended to show that full involvement or affiliation in academic discourse communities requires major cultural and linguistic tradeoffs from many students. Faculty expect them to accept the texts, roles, and contexts of the discipline, but acceptance requires much more sacrifice and change than the faculty may imagine. In our literacy classes, we can assist academic students in discussing the kinds of problems they encounter when attempting to resolve these conflicts. However, we can also assist our faculty colleagues, who often are unaware of their students' plight, through workshops, student presentations, and suggestions for reading. 53

Issues of Authority

What happens after a person has become an academic initiate, after he or she has completed the degree, published, and been advanced? There are still community issues to contend with, one of which relates to authority. Bakhtin (1986, p. 88) noted that "in each epoch, in each social circle, in each small world of family, friends, acquaintances and comrades in which a human being grows and lives, there are always authoritative utterances that set the tone." 54

In academic circles, these "authoritative utterances" are made by journal or e-mail interest-group editors, by conference program planners, and by others. At the local level, this authority can be held by department chairs or by chairs of important committees. Prior (1994, p. 522) speaks of these academically powerful people as "an elite group that imposes its language, beliefs and values on others through control of journals, academic appointments, curricula, student examinations, research findings and so on." It is important to note that Prior extends his discussion beyond authority over colleagues to broad authority over students through curricula and examinations. This type of pedagogical authority is very important, as all students know, so it will be discussed further. 55

In many countries, provincial and national examinations drive the curricula, and theoretical and practical control over these examinations means authority over what students are taught. In the People's Republic of China, for example, important general English language examinations have been based for years on word frequency counts developed in several language centers throughout the country. Each "band," or proficiency level on the examination, is determined by "the most common 1,000 words," "the most common 2,000 words," and so on.[14] Although features of language such as grammar are tested in these examinations, it is a theory about vocabulary, based on word frequency, that is 56 central. It is not surprising, then, that most Chinese students believe that vocabulary is the key to literacy, particularly the understanding of "exact" meanings of words. When I have worked with teachers in China, I have frequently been asked questions such as "What is the exact meaning of the term 'discourse'? What does 'theory' mean?" These teachers requested a single definition, something I was often unable to provide.

The centralized power over important examinations in China, over the 57 TOEFL and graduate entrance examinations in the United States, and over the British Council Examinations in other parts of the world gives considerable authority within communities to certain test developers and examiners. This authority permits little pedagogical latitude to teachers preparing students for these "gate-keeping" examinations. As practitioners, we can use test preparation pedagogies, or we can critique these examinations (Raimes, 1990), as we should; but we cannot institute large-scale change until we gain control and authority over the examination system.

With students at all academic levels, we practitioners should raise the issues 58 of authority, status, and control over community utterances in literacy classes. About their own social groups, we can ask: "Who has status in your clubs and why? Who has status in your ethnic or geographical communities and why? How do they exert control over people, over utterances, and over publications?" When referring to academic situations and authority, we can ask: "Who wrote this textbook? What are the authors' affiliations? Are they prestigious? How does the language of the textbook demonstrate the author's authority over the material and over the students who read the volume?" We can also ask: "Who writes your important examinations? What are their values?" Or we can ask: "Who has status in your academic classrooms? Which students have authority and why?" And finally, we might ask: "How can you gain authority in the classroom or over texts?"

Throughout a discussion of authority relationships, we need to talk about 59 communities, language, and genres: how texts and spoken discourses are used to gain and perpetuate authority. We can assist students to analyze authoritative texts, including those of other students, and to critique authority relationships. Our students need to become more aware of these factors affecting their academic lives before they can hope to produce and comprehend texts that command authority within academic contexts.

Conventions and Anticonventionalism

There are many other push and pull factors in academic communities, factors 60 that create dialogue, conflict, and change. Communities evolve constantly, though established community members may attempt to maintain their power and keep the new initiates in line through control over language and genres.

A student or a young faculty member can be punished for major transgressions from the norm, for attempting to move away from what the more established, initiated members expect. In order to receive a good grade (or be published), writers often must work within the rules. Understanding these rules, even if they are to be broken, appears to be essential.

As individuals within an academic community become more established 61 and famous, they can become more anticonventional, in both their texts and their lives. Three famous rule breakers come to mind, though there are others. Stephen J. Gould, a biologist, has written a series of literate essays for the general public, principally about evolution, that look considerably different from the scientific journal article. Gould has broken his generic traditions to "go public" because he already has tenure at Harvard, he likes to write essays, and he enjoys addressing a public audience (see Gould, 1985). Deborah Tannen, an applied linguist, has also "gone public," publishing "pop books" about communication between men and women that are best-sellers in the United States (see Tannen, 1986, 1994). She continues to write relatively conventional articles in journals, but she also writes often for the layperson. Clifford Geertz, the anthropologist, refuses to be pigeon-holed in terms of topic, argumentation, or genre. Using his own disciplinary approaches, he writes texts on academic cultures as well as the "exotic" ones that are typical to anthropologists (see Geertz, 1988). Gould, Tannen, and Geertz have established themselves within their disciplines. Now famous, they can afford to defy community conventions as they write in their individual ways.

Rule breaking is a minefield for many students, however. They first need to 62 understand some of the basic conventions, concepts, and values of a community's genres. Learning and using academic conventions is not easy, for many students receive little or no instruction. To compound the problems, students need constantly to revise their theories of genres and genre conventions (see Bartholomae, 1985). Some graduate students, for example, often express confusion about conventions, anticonventions, and the breaking of rules, for faculty advice appears to be idiosyncratic, based not on community conventions but on personal taste. Some faculty thesis advisers, particularly in the humanities, require a careful review of the literature and accept nothing else; others may insist on "original"[15] work without a literature review. For some advisers there is a "cookie cutter" macrostructure that all papers must follow; others may prefer a more free-flowing, experimental text. Graduate students complain that discovering or breaking these implicit rules requires much research and many visits to faculty offices, as well as many drafts of their thesis chapters (see Schneider & Fujishima, 1995).

It should be clear from this discussion that we cannot tell students "truths" 63 about texts or community practices. However, we can heighten student awareness of generic conventions, and we can assist students in formulating questions that can be addressed to faculty. In our literacy classes, we are developing researchers, not dogmatists, students who explore ideas and literacies rather than seek simple answers.

Dialogue and Critique

In any thriving academic community, there is constant dialogue: disagreements 64 among members about approaches to research, about argumentation, about topics for study, and about theory. The journal *Science* acknowledges this and accepts two types of letters to the editor to enable writers to carry out informal dialogues. In other journals, sections are set aside for short interchanges between two writers who hold opposing views (see the *Journal of Second Language Writing*, for example). Most journals carry critiques of new volumes in book review sections, and many published articles are in dialogue with other texts. Academic communities encourage variety and critique (within limits), because that is how they evolve and grow.

Most professional academics know the rules for dialogue: what topics are 65 currently "hot," how to discuss these topics in ways appropriate for the readers of their genres, how far they can go from the current norms, and what they can use (data, narratives, nonlinear texts) to support their arguments. Some professionals who understand the rules can also break them with impunity. They can push the boundaries because they know where the discipline has been and where it may be going, and how to use their authority, and the authority of others, to make their arguments. In a volume on academic expertise, Geisler (1994) comments that there are three "worlds" with which expert academics must be familiar before they can join, or contravene, a disciplinary dialogue: the "domain content world" of logically related concepts and content; the "narrated world" of everyday experience; and the "abstract world" of authorial conversation. Academic experts must manipulate these worlds in order to produce texts that can be in dialogue or conflict with, yet appropriate to, the communities they are addressing.

This discussion has suggested that communities and their genres are use- 66 ful to study not only because they can share conventions, values, and histories but because they are evolving: through affiliation of new, different members; through changes in authority; through anticonventionalism, dialogue, and critique. Students know these things about their own communities; we need to draw from this knowledge to begin to explore unfamiliar academic communities and their genres.

This chapter has addressed some of the social and cultural factors that influ- 67 ence texts, factors that are closely related to community membership. Although there is much debate in the literature about the nature of discourse communities and communities of practice, it can be said with some certainty that community affiliations are very real to individual academic faculty. Faculty refer to themselves as "chemists," "engineers," "historians," or "applied linguists"; they read texts from community genres with great interest or join in heated debates with their peers over the Internet. They sometimes recognize that the language, values, and genres of their communities (or specializations) may differ from those of another academic community, though this is not always the case. At a promotions committee made up of faculty from sixteen departments in which I took part, a member of the quantitative group in the Geography Department said of a humanities text, "We shouldn't accept an article for promotion without statistics." And we all laughed, nervously.

Academics, and others, may belong to several communities and have in common certain interests within each. Thus, faculty may have nothing in common with other faculty in their disciplines but the discipline itself; their social, political, and other interests can, and often do, vary widely. In one department, for example, musical interests can be diverse. There may be country-western fans, opera fans, jazz enthusiasts, and those whose only musical experiences consist of listening to the national anthem at baseball games. Recreational interests may also differ. Among faculty, there are motorcyclists and bicyclists, hikers and "couch potatoes," football fans and those who actually play the sport. 68

A complex of social, community-related factors influences the socioliteracies of faculty and the students who are in their classes. As literacy practitioners, we need to help our students examine these factors by bringing other faculty and students, and their genres, into our classrooms, as well as drawing from our own students' rich resources. 69

Notes

1. Some of the contested issues and questions are: "How are communities defined?" (Rafoth, 1990); "Do discourse communities even exist?" (Prior, 1994); "Are they global or local? Or both?" (Killingsworth, 1992); "What is the relationship between discourse communities and genres?" (Swales, 1988b, 1990).

2. Note that most communities use abbreviations for their names and often for their publications. All community members recognize these abbreviations, of course.

3. These written interactions are impossible for the noninitiated to understand, I might point out.

4. When I asked my mother to drop her AARP membership because of a political stand the organization took, she said, "I can't, Ann. I get too good a deal on my medicines through my membership."

5. Those of us who are outsiders call them "gearheads." Often, terms are applied to insiders by community outsiders.

6. Brill, D. (1994, November). What's free of fat and cholesterol, costs 4 cents per serving, and has more carbo than pasta? Rice! *Bicycling*, pp. 86–87.

7. I would like to thank Arlan Fast of the San Diego Symphony for these community insights.

8. Knowledge is also shared with musicians from other parts of the world, of course. However, some of the specific examples used here apply to the Western musical tradition.

9. For example, *The Chronicle of Higher Education* and several pedagogical publications are directed to a general academic audience.

10. "Objective" appears in quotation marks because, though academic writing may have the appearance of being objective, all texts are biased.

11. Quandahl, E. (1995). Rhetoric and writing studies 100: A list of goals. Unpublished paper, San Diego State University, San Diego, CA.

12. When I showed this point to Virginia Guleff, a graduate student, she said, "So students have to know their place!" Perhaps we should put it this way: They need to know different registers in order to play different roles. The more people use these registers, the more effective they can become and, not incidentally, the more power they can have over the situation in which they are reading or writing.

13. San Diego State's new Department of Rhetoric and Writing Studies is composed of composition instructors who asked to leave the Department of English, as well as of faculty from the previously independent Academic Skills Center.

14. "Most common" appears in quotation marks because what is most common (other than function words) is very difficult to determine. These lists are influenced by the type of language data that is entered into the computer for the word count: whether it is written or spoken, its register, etc. If data are varied, other vocabulary become common.

    At one point in my career, I attempted to develop low-proficiency English for Business textbooks for adults using a famous publisher's list of most common words. I failed because the data used to establish the frequency lists were taken from children's books. The common words in children's language and those most common in business language are considerably different (Johns, 1985).

15. Since I am arguing here that all texts rely on other texts, I put "original" in quotation marks.

References

Bakhtin, M. M. (1986). *Speech genres and other late essays.* (V. W. Mc Gee, Trans.). C. Emerson & M. Holquist (Eds.). Austin: University of Texas Press.

Bartholomae, D. (1985). Inventing the university. In M. Rose (Ed.), *When a writer can't write: Studies in writer's block and other composing process problems* (pp. 134–165). New York: Guilford Press.

Belcher, D., & Braine, G. (Eds.). (1995). *Academic writing in a second language: Essays on research and pedagogy.* Norwood, NJ: Ablex.

Benson, K. (1996). *How do students and faculty perceive graduate writing tasks? A case study of a Japanese student in a graduate program in linguistics.* Unpublished manuscript, San Diego State University.

Bereiter, C., & Scardamalia, M. (1989). Intentional learning as a goal of instruction. In J. Resnick (Ed.), *Knowing, learning* (pp. 361–392). Hillsdale, NJ: Lawrence Erlbaum.

Berkenkotter, C., & Huckin, T. (1995). *Genre knowledge in disciplinary communities.* Hillsdale, NJ: Lawrence Erlbaum.

Bhatia, V. J. (1993). *Analyzing genre: Language use in professional settings.* London & New York: Longman.

Brill, D. (1994, November). What's free of fat and cholesterol, costs 4 cents per serving, and has more carbo than pasta? Rice! *Bicycling,* 86–87.

Brown, J. S., & Duguid, P. (1995, July 26). Universities in the digital age. *Xerox Palo Alto Paper.* Palo Alto, CA: Xerox Corporation.

Carson, J. G. (1993, April). *Academic literacy demands of the undergraduate curriculum: Literacy activities integrating skills.* Paper presented at the International TESOL Conference, Atlanta, GA.

Carson, J. G., Chase, N., Gibson, S., & Hargrove, M. (1992). Literacy demands of the undergraduate curriculum. *Reading Research and Instruction, 31,* 25–50.

Casanave, C. P. (1992). Cultural diversity and socialization: A case study of a Hispanic woman in a doctoral program in Sociology. In D. Murray (Ed.), *Diversity as a resource: Redefining cultural literacy* (pp. 148–182). Arlington, VA: TESOL.

Connor, U. (1987). Argumentative patterns in student essays: Cross-cultural differences. In U. Connor & R. B. Kaplan (Eds.), *Writing across languages: Analysis of L2 text* (pp. 57–71). Reading, MA: Addison-Wesley.

Dudley-Evans, T. (1995). Common-core and specific approaches to teaching academic writing. In D. Belcher & G. Braine (Eds.), *Academic writing in a second language: Essays on research and pedagogy* (pp. 293–312). Norwood, NJ: Ablex.

Elbow, P. (1991). Reflections on academic discourse. *College English, 53(2),* 135–115.

Fahenstock, J. (1986). Accommodating science. *Written Communication, 3,* 275–296.

Geertz, C. (1983). *Local knowledge: Further essays in interpretive anthropology.* New York: Basic Books.

Geertz, C. (1988). *Words and lives: The anthropologist as author.* Palo Alto, CA: Stanford University Press.

Geisler, C. (1994). Literacy and expertise in the academy. *Language and Learning Across the Disciplines, 1,* 35–57.

Gould, S. J. (1985). *The flamingo's smile.* New York: Norton.

Hinds, J. (1987). Reader versus writer responsibility: A new typology. In U. Connor & R. B. Kaplan (Eds.), *Writing across languages: An analysis of L2 texts* (pp. 141–152). Reading, MA: Addison-Wesley.

Johns, A. M. (1985). The new authenticity and the preparation of commercial reading texts for lower-level ESP students. *CATESOL Occasional Papers, 11,* 103–107.

Killingsworth, M. J. (1992). Discourse communities—local and global. *Rhetoric Review, 11,* 110–122.

Lave, J., & Wenger, E. (1991). *Situated learning: Legitimate peripheral participation.* New York: Cambridge University Press.

Mauranen, A. (1993). Contrastive ESP rhetoric Metatext in Finnish-English economic texts. *English for Specific Purposes, 12,* 3–22.

Prior, P. (1994). Response, revision and disciplinarity: A microhistory of a dissertation prospectus in sociology. *Written Communication, 11,* 483–533.

Purves, A. C. (1990). *The scribal society: An essay on literacy and schooling in the information age.* New York: Longman.

Rafoth, B. A. (1990). The concept of discourse community: Descriptive and explanatory adequacy. In G. Kirsch & D. H. Roen (Eds.), *A sense of audience in written communication* (pp. 140–152). *Written Communication Annual, Vol. 5.* Newbury Park, CA: Sage.

Raimes, A. (1990). The TOEFL Test of Written English: Some causes for concern. *TESOL Quarterly, 24,* 427–442.

Rodriguez, R. (1982). *Hunger of memory: The education of Richard Rodriguez.* New York: Bantam Books.

Rose, M. (1989). *Lives on the boundary: The struggles and achievements of America's underprepared.* New York: Free Press.

Schneider, M., & Fujishima, N. K. (1995). When practice doesn't make perfect: The case of a graduate ESL student. In D. Belcher & G. Braine (Eds.), *Academic writing in a second language: Essays on research & pedagogy* (pp. 3–22). Norwood, NJ: Ablex.

Swales, J. M. (1988b). Discourse communities, genres and English as an international language. *World Englishes, 7,* 211–220.

Swales, J. M. (1990). *Genre analysis: English in academic and research settings.* New York: Cambridge University Press.

Swales, J. M., & Feak, C. B. (1994). *Academic writing for graduate students: Essential tasks and skills.* Ann Arbor: University of Michigan Press.

Tannen, D. (1986). *That's not what I meant: How conversational style makes or breaks your relations with others.* New York: W. Morrow.

Tannen, D. (1994). *Talking from 9–5: How women's and men's conversational styles affect who gets heard, who gets credit, and what gets done at work.* New York: W. Morrow.

Widdowson, H. G. (1993). The relevant conditions of language use and learning. In M. Krueger & F. Ryan (Eds.), *Language and content: Discipline- and content-based approaches to language study* (pp. 27–36). Lexington, MA: D. C. Heath.

Williams, J. (1989). *Style: Ten lessons in clarity and grace.* (3rd ed.). Glenview, IL: Scott Foresman.

- -

Questions for Discussion and Journaling

1. What are some of the complications Johns outlines related to joining a discourse community?

2. Johns notes that people joining a new discourse community can rebel against some of its conventions and in so doing actually change the discourse community. Explain what this means and try to think of some historical examples where this has happened. If you read Gee (p. 507), compare Johns's view of *change* in discourse communities with Gee's view.

3. Have you ever felt that learning to write or speak in a new discourse community conflicted with your sense of self, your values, your beliefs? If so, what happened? If not, why do you think you have been exempt from this sort of conflict?

4. Johns cites a number of examples to argue that learning to write and speak in new ways is not just a cognitive matter, but also impacts values and identity. She says, "full involvement or affiliation . . . requires major cultural and linguistic

tradeoffs" (para. 53). Draw on some examples of your own to explain what you think this means. Do you agree or disagree with her claim here? Why?

5. How do you feel about your *authority* over the kinds of texts you have been asked to write so far in college?

6. Why is rule breaking a "minefield" for students, but not for the more "famous" or established academic writers Johns cites? Have you ever been punished or rewarded for rule breaking related to texts? What happened?

Applying and Exploring Ideas

1. In paragraph 58, Johns outlines a number of questions that teachers should discuss with their students regarding authority and control of language in their classrooms. Go through and answer her list of questions in as much detail as you can. When you are finished, reread your answers and use them to help you write a letter to an incoming student in which you explain the concepts of *discourse communities*, *authority*, and *control*, and explain the relationships among them. Then, explain why having an explicit understanding of these concepts is useful and give specific examples from your own experiences to illustrate what you are saying.

2. Plan an insurrection in your writing classroom. What are some writing rules you'd like to break? Do these rules represent the values or authority of a particular discourse community? How would breaking these rules impact your membership in the discourse community and your own identity? Try writing a Declaration of Independence from the particular rule or rules in question, and then see if your classmates are persuaded by it to vote in favor of revolution.

3. Explain some ways in which Johns helps you better understand the underlying threshold concepts of this chapter, that people collaborate to get things done with writing.

- -
META MOMENT How would understanding what Johns is writing about help you in becoming a member of new discourse communities? In other words, how can you apply what you learned from her to situations outside your writing class?
- -

Learning the Language

PERRI KLASS

Adrian Mihai

Framing the Reading

Perri Klass holds an M.D. from Harvard and is currently professor of journalism and pediatrics at New York University,
where she has also served as the Director of the Arthur L. Carter Journalism Institute.
She is also the National Medical Director for Reach Out and Read, work for which
she received the 2007 American Academy of Pediatrics Education Award. The Reach
Out and Read organization incorporates books in pediatric care and encourages families to read aloud together. Dr. Klass wrote a monthly column for the *New York Times*
called "18 and Under," and another column for that newspaper called "Hers," which
chronicled her life as a mother going through medical school. She has also written
several novels and nonfiction books. The following excerpt is taken from her book of
essays recording her life as a medical student.

We have included this short essay because it illustrates many of the concepts
described theoretically elsewhere in this chapter — namely, that groups of people
(discourse communities) use language and texts in specialized ways as they
collaborate to accomplish their goals. Their specialized **lexis** helps to mediate
their activities (in this case, it not only helps doctors treat patients, but also helps
doctors be more detached about the life and death situations they face on a daily
basis). Klass's piece also illustrates Ann Johns's claim that belonging to a discourse
community is not just a matter of **cognition** (of knowing about something), but also
impacts values and identity, that "full involvement or affiliation . . . requires major
cultural and linguistic tradeoffs."

Getting Ready to Read

Before you read, do at least one of the following activities:

- If you or someone close to you has ever been in the hospital,
  try to remember some of the language or special phrasing
  that you heard the doctors and nurses use. How did that
  language make you feel?

Klass, Perri. *A Not Entirely Benign Procedure: Four Years as a Medical Student.*
Putnam Books, 1987.

- Think of a club, group, or workplace you are a part of and write down as many specialized words and phrases used there as you can think of. What purpose do these specialized words serve?

As you read, do the following:

- Highlight or underline every place where Klass explains the purposes, benefits, or consequences of using specialized language.
- Star or circle every place where Klass's examples help you understand Gee's or Johns's theories a little better — or at least places where you think the examples relate to Gee or Johns.

"MRS. TOLSTOY IS YOUR BASIC LOL in NAD, admitted for a soft rule- 1 out MI," the intern announces. I scribble that on my patient list. In other words, Mrs. Tolstoy is a Little Old Lady in No Apparent Distress who is in the hospital to make sure she hasn't had a heart attack (rule out a Myocardial Infarction). And we think it's unlikely that she has had a heart attack (a *soft* rule-out).

If I learned nothing else during my first three months of working in the 2 hospital as a medical student, I learned endless jargon and abbreviations. I started out in a state of primeval innocence, in which I didn't even know that "s̄CP, SOB, N/V" meant "without chest pain, shortness of breath, or nausea and vomiting." By the end I took the abbreviations so much for granted that I would complain to my mother the English professor, "And can you believe I had to put down *three* NG tubes last night?"

"You'll have to tell me what an NG tube is if you want me to sympathize 3 properly," my mother said. NG, nasogastric — isn't it obvious?

I picked up not only the specific expressions but also the patterns of speech 4 and the grammatical conventions; for example, you never say that a patient's blood pressure fell or that his cardiac enzymes rose. Instead, the patient is always the subject of the verb: "He dropped his pressure." "He bumped his enzymes." This sort of construction probably reflects the profound irritation of the intern when the nurses come in the middle of the night to say that Mr. Dickinson has disturbingly low blood pressure. "Oh, he's gonna hurt me bad tonight," the intern might say, inevitably angry at Mr. Dickinson for dropping his pressure and creating a problem.

When chemotherapy fails to cure Mrs. Bacon's cancer, what we say is, "Mrs. 5 Bacon failed chemotherapy."

"Well, we've already had one hit today, and we're up next, but at least we've 6 got mostly stable players on our team." This means that our team (group of doctors and medical students) has already gotten one new admission today, and it is our turn again, so we'll get whoever is admitted next in emergency, but at least most of the patients we already have are fairly stable, that is, unlikely to drop their pressures or in any other way get suddenly sicker and hurt us bad. Baseball metaphor is pervasive. A no-hitter is a night without any new admissions. A player is always a patient—a nitrate player is a patient on nitrates, a unit player is a patient in the intensive care unit, and so on, until you reach the terminal player.

It is interesting to consider what it means to be winning, or doing well, 7 in this perennial baseball game. When the intern hangs up the phone and announces, "I got a hit," that is not cause for congratulations. The team is not scoring points; rather, it is getting hit, being bombarded with new patients. The object of the game from the point of view of the doctors, considering the players for whom they are already responsible, is to get as few new hits as possible.

This special language contributes to a sense of closeness and professional 8 spirit among people who are under a great deal of stress. As a medical student, I found it exciting to discover that I'd finally cracked the code, that I could understand what doctors said and wrote, and could use the same formulations myself. Some people seem to become enamored of the jargon for its own sake, perhaps because they are so deeply thrilled with the idea of medicine, with the idea of themselves as doctors.

I knew a medical student who was referred to by the interns on the team as 9 Mr. Eponym because he was so infatuated with eponymous terminology, the more obscure the better. He never said "capillary pulsations" if he could say "Quincke's pulses." He would lovingly tell over the multinamed syndromes—Wolff-Parkinson-White, Lown-Ganong-Levine, Schönlein-Henoch—until the temptation to suggest Schleswig-Holstein or Stevenson-Kefauver or Baskin-Robbins became irresistible to his less reverent colleagues.

And there is the jargon that you don't ever want to hear yourself using. You 10 know that your training is changing you, but there are certain changes you think would be going a little too far.

The resident was describing a man with devastating terminal pancreatic can- 11 cer. "Basically he's CTD," the resident concluded. I reminded myself that I had resolved not to be shy about asking when I didn't understand things. "CTD?" I asked timidly.

The resident smirked at me. "Circling The Drain." 12

The images are vivid and terrible. "What happened to Mrs. Melville?" 13

"Oh, she boxed last night." To box is to die, of course. 14

Then there are the more pompous locutions that can make the beginning 15 medical student nervous about the effects of medical training. A friend of mine was told by his resident, "A pregnant woman with sickle-cell represents a failure of genetic counseling."

Mr. Eponym, who tried hard to talk like the doctors, once explained to me, 16 "An infant is basically a brainstem preparation." The term "brainstem preparation," as used in neurological research, refers to an animal whose higher brain functions have been destroyed so that only the most primitive reflexes remain, like the sucking reflex, the startle reflex, and the rooting reflex.

And yet at other times the harshness dissipates into a strangely elusive euphe- 17 mism. "As you know, this is a not entirely benign procedure," some doctor will say, and that will be understood to imply agony, risk of complications, and maybe even a significant mortality rate.

The more extreme forms aside, one most important function of medical jargon is to help doctors maintain some distance from their patients. By reformulating a patient's pain and problems into a language that the patient doesn't even speak, I suppose we are in some sense taking those pains and problems under our jurisdiction and also reducing their emotional impact. This lin- 18

> The more extreme forms aside, one most important function of medical jargon is to help doctors maintain some distance from their patients.

guistic separation between doctors and patients allows conversations to go on at the bedside that are unintelligible to the patient. "Naturally, we're worried about adeno-CA," the intern can say to the medical student, and lung cancer need never be mentioned.

I learned a new language this past summer. At times it thrills me to hear 19 myself using it. It enables me to understand my colleagues, to communicate effectively in the hospital. Yet I am uncomfortably aware that I will never again notice the peculiarities and even atrocities of medical language as keenly as I did this summer. There may be specific expressions I manage to avoid, but even as I remark them, promising myself I will never use them, I find that this language is becoming my professional speech. It no longer sounds strange in my ears — or coming from my mouth. And I am afraid that as with any new language, to use it properly you must absorb not only the vocabulary but also the structure, the logic, the attitudes. At first you may notice the new and alien assumptions every time you put together a sentence, but with time and increased fluency you stop being aware of them at all. And as you lose that awareness, for better or for worse, you move closer and closer to being a doctor instead of just talking like one.

Questions for Discussion and Journaling

1. Klass describes entering the hospital as a medical student "in a state of primeval innocence" but quickly learning all the "endless jargon and abbreviations" (para. 2). What she is describing is the process of enculturating into a discourse community. How does this kind of enculturation happen in general?

2. Klass explains that doctors always make patients the subject of the verb: "He dropped his pressure" or "Mrs. Bacon failed chemotherapy" (paras. 4–5). What is the difference between talking about patients in that way, versus saying "His blood pressure fell" or "chemotherapy did not help her"? What role does the phrasing give to the patient? What role does the phrasing give the doctor? What purpose does this kind of phrasing serve for doctors working every day in a hospital setting?

3. Klass alludes to the title of her book, *A Not Entirely Benign Procedure*, explaining how that phrase is used to describe a procedure that is painful and perhaps life-threatening. Why would doctors use phrases like this? And why do you think that Klass chose this phrase as the title for her book?

Applying and Exploring Ideas

1. Make a list of all the reasons that Klass provides for why doctors use what she calls "medical jargon."

2. Using the list of reasons for using medical jargon that you compiled in answering question 1 above, write a page or two in which you draw on these examples to explain and illustrate the threshold concepts of this chapter: people collaborate to get things done with writing, texts and language *mediate meaningful activities*, and people construct meaning through texts and language.

3. Klass and Johns both talk about how joining and participating in new discourse communities requires a change in identity. In particular, Klass explains that to use any new language properly, "you must absorb not only the vocabulary but also the structure, the logic, the attitudes." As this happens, she says, "you move closer and closer to being a doctor instead of just talking like one" (para. 19). Before you read Klass, you were asked to think of a club, group, or workplace you are a part of and write down as many specialized words and phrases used there as you can think of. Go back to that list, and then draw on it to write a short essay modeled after Klass's in which you describe the process of learning to talk in that setting, and how learning the language helped you take on the identity of that club/group/workplace. Before you conclude, be sure to talk about the trade-offs involved in that enculturation.

- -
META MOMENT   What is one thing you learned from Klass that you can use/apply elsewhere in your experience?
- -

A Stranger in Strange Lands

A College Student Writing across the Curriculum

LUCILLE P. McCARTHY

Lucille McCarthy

Lucille McCarthy earned her Ph.D. from the University of Pennsylvania, and she is currently a professor of English and Director of the M.A. Program at the University of Maryland, Baltimore County, where she has taught since 1988. Her many articles and books demonstrate her interest in pedagogies that help promote student learning and writing. Five of her six books and many of her articles focus on student classroom experiences and have won awards such as the James N. Britton Award for Research in the English Language Arts and a National Council of Teachers of English award for Research Excellence in Technical and Scientific Communication. Her books include *Thinking and Writing in College: A Naturalistic Study of Students in Four Disciplines* (1991; with Barbara Walvoord).

McCarthy published the article reprinted here in 1987. At that time, researchers in other fields had used **case studies** and **ethnographic research** extensively, but researchers in the field of Writing Studies had only begun to consider what we could learn about writing by using those methods. In writing this article, McCarthy notes that researchers know that writing is strongly influenced by **social context** — that some people write well in one setting (e.g., at home alone) and not very well in another (e.g., on a timed exam), or that some people write well in one genre (e.g., poetry) but not very well in another (e.g., a literary criticism essay). But McCarthy wanted to know more about *how* writing is influenced by social settings; in particular, she wanted to know how college writers and their writing are influenced by their different classroom settings.

At the time that McCarthy conducted her study, no one else had followed individual students as they wrote across the university. Since McCarthy published her study, a number of such **longitudinal studies** have been published. While no single case study can produce results that are **generalizable**, a number of case studies taken together can do so. Thus, if you are interested

McCarthy, Lucille P. "A Stranger in Strange Lands: A College Student Writing across the Curriculum." *Research in the Teaching of English*, vol. 21, no. 3, 1987, pp. 233–65.

in making claims about how writers write in college, you should read the longitudinal studies that followed McCarthy.

McCarthy followed a student named "Dave" as he wrote in three different classes (or discourse communities) — composition, biology, and poetry. Dave got good grades in the first two classes but struggled in poetry. McCarthy tried to find out why Dave was so unsuccessful in poetry and ultimately concluded that even though the writing tasks across all the classes had some similarities, Dave *thought* they were very different, and he had very different kinds of support for the writing in each of the classes.

We have included McCarthy's study here because she demonstrates one way to understand the threshold concept that individuals participate in community activities (like college courses) through the use of texts and language. In particular, she demonstrates what can happen when newcomers do or don't understand and share the values and conventions of a new discourse community in which they are participating. She also demonstrates what happens when the "old-timers" in a community (like teachers) aren't able to successfully share conventions, strategies, and values with "newcomers" (like students). If you've read Swales or Johns on discourse communities, you can consider how Dave's experiences across various classes is like visiting a variety of discourse communities, some of which use texts in ways that seem very strange to him.

Getting Ready to Read

Before you read, try the following activity:

- Consider a class where you have an easy time writing and a class where the writing is hard for you. Think about why you might have different levels of success with these writing tasks.

As you read, consider the following questions:

- What research question(s) does McCarthy set out to answer?
- What major findings does McCarthy discover in answer to her research question(s)?

DAVE GARRISON, A COLLEGE JUNIOR and the focus of the present 1 study, was asked how he would advise incoming freshmen about writing for their college courses. His answer was both homely and familiar.

"I'd tell them," he said, "first you've got to figure out what your teachers 2 want. And then you've got to give it to them if you're gonna get the grade." He paused a moment and added, "And that's not always so easy."

No matter how we teachers may feel about Dave's response, it does reflect 3
his sensitivity to school writing as a social affair. Successful students are those
who can, in their interactions with teachers during the semester, determine
what constitutes appropriate texts in each classroom: the content, structures,
language, ways of thinking, and types of evidence required in that discipline
and by that teacher. They can then produce such a text. Students who cannot
do this, for whatever reason — cultural, intellectual, motivational — are those
who fail, deemed incompetent communicators in that particular setting. They
are unable to follow what Britton calls the "rules of the game" in each class
(1975, p. 76). As students go from one classroom to another they must play a
wide range of games, the rules for which, Britton points out, include many conventions and presuppositions that are not explicitly articulated.

In this article, writing in college is viewed as a process of assessing and 4
adapting to the requirements in unfamiliar academic settings. Specifically, the
study examined how students figured out what constituted appropriate texts
in their various courses and how they went about producing them. And, further, it examined what characterized the classroom contexts which enhanced
or denied students' success in this process. This study was a 21-month project
which focused on the writing experiences of one college student, Dave, in three
of his courses, Freshman Composition in the spring of his freshman year, and,
in his sophomore year, Introduction to Poetry in the fall and Cell Biology in the
spring. Dave, a biology / pre-med major, was typical of students at his college in
terms of his SAT scores (502 verbal; 515 math), his high school grades, and his
white, middle-class family background.

As I followed Dave from one classroom writing situation to another, I came 5
to see him, as he made his journey from one discipline to another, as a stranger
in strange lands. In each new class Dave believed that the writing he was doing
was totally unlike anything he had ever done before. This metaphor of a newcomer in a foreign country proved to be a powerful way of looking at Dave's
behaviors as he worked to use the new languages in unfamiliar academic territories. Robert Heinlein's (1961) science fiction novel suggested this metaphor
originally. But Heinlein's title is slightly different; his stranger is in a *single*
strange land. Dave perceived himself to be in one strange land after another.

BACKGROUND TO THE STUDY

The theoretical underpinnings of this study are to be found in the work of 6
sociolinguists (Hymes, 1972a, 1972b; Gumperz, 1971) and ethnographers of
communication (Basso, 1974; Heath, 1982; Szwed, 1981) who assume that
language processes must be understood in terms of the contexts in which they
occur. All language use in this view takes place within speech communities and
accomplishes meaningful social functions for people. Community members

share characteristic "ways of speaking," that is, accepted linguistic, intellectual, and social conventions which have developed over time and govern spoken interaction. And "communicatively competent" speakers in every community recognize and successfully employ these "rules of use," largely without conscious attention (Hymes, 1972a, pp. xxiv–xxxvi).

A key assumption underlying this study is that writing, like speaking, is a 7 social activity. Writers, like speakers, must use the communication means considered appropriate by members of particular speech or discourse communities. And the writer's work, at the same time, may affect the norms of the community. As students go from one class to another, they must define and master the rules of use for written discourse in one classroom speech community after another. And their writing can only be evaluated in terms of that particular community's standards.

Some recent practical and theoretical work in writing studies has emphasized 8 that writers' processes and products must be understood in terms of their contexts, contexts which are created as participants and settings interact (Bazerman, 1981; Bizzell, 1982; Cooper, 1986; Faigley, 1985; Whiteman, 1981). Studies of writing in non-academic settings have shown just how complex these writing environments are and how sophisticated the knowledge—both explicit and tacit—is that writers need in order to operate successfully in them (Odell & Goswami, 1985). And classrooms offer no less complex environments for writing. As Ericson (1982) points out, the classroom learning environment includes not only the teacher and the student, but also the subject matter structure, the social task structure, the actual enacted task, and the sequence of actions involved in the task. In addition, in many classrooms students may be provided with too few instructional supports to help them as they write (Applebee, 1984). Specifically, college classroom contexts for writing, Herrington (1985) argues, must be thought of in terms of several speech communities, viewed "in relation not only to a school community, but also to the intellectual and social conventions of professional forums within a given discipline" (p. 333). These overlapping communities influence the ways students think and write and interact in college classrooms, and will shape their notions of what it means to be, for example, an engineer or a biologist or a literary critic.

Research which has directly examined particular classroom contexts for writing 9 has provided insight into their diversity (Applebee, 1984; Calkins, 1980; Florio & Clark, 1982; Freedman, 1985; Herrington, 1985; Kantor, 1984). Though these studies suggest that an individual student is likely to encounter a number of quite different classroom writing situations, there is also evidence that individual student writers may employ consistent patterns across tasks as they interpret assignments, reason, and organize their knowledge (Dyson, 1984; Langer, 1985, 1986).

What has not yet been done, however, is to follow individual college students 10 as they progress across academic disciplines. In this study I offer information about how one college student fares in such a journey across the curriculum. That is, I detail how this student's behavior changed or remained constant across tasks in three classroom contexts and how those contexts influenced his success. Though this study is limited in scope to the experiences of a single student as he wrote for three college courses, it addresses questions central to much writing across the curriculum scholarship:

1. What are the tasks students encounter as they move from one course to another?

2. How do successful students interpret these tasks? Further, how do students determine what constitutes appropriate texts in that discipline and for that teacher, and how do they produce them?

3. What are the social factors in classrooms that foster particular writing behaviors and students' achievement of competence in that setting?

The ultimate aim of this study is to contribute to our understanding of how students learn to write in school. Findings from this study corroborate the notion that learning to write should be seen not only as a developmental process occurring within an individual student, but also as a social process occurring in response to particular situations.

METHODS

The research approach was naturalistic. I entered the study with no hypotheses to test and no specially devised writing tasks. Rather, I studied the writing that was actually being assigned in these classrooms, working to understand and describe that writing, how it functioned in each classroom, and what it meant to people there. My purpose was to get as rich a portrait as possible of Dave's writing and his classroom writing contexts. To this end I combined four research tools: observation, interviews, composing-aloud protocols, and text analysis. The data provided by the protocols and text analysis served to add to, crosscheck, and refine the data generated by observation and interviews. Using this triangulated approach (Denzin, 1978), I could view Dave's writing experiences through several windows, with the strengths of one method compensating for the limitations of another. 11

The Courses

The college is a private, co-educational, liberal arts institution located in a large, northeastern city. Of its 2,600 students nearly half are business, accounting, and computer science majors. Yet over half of students' courses are required liberal arts courses, part of the core curriculum. Two of Dave's courses in this study 12

593

are core courses: Freshman Composition and Introduction to Poetry. The third, Cell Biology, is a course taken by biology majors; it was Dave's third semester of college biology. All three were one-semester courses. In the descriptions of these courses that follow, I use pseudonyms for the teachers.

In Freshman Composition, which met twice a week for 90 minutes, students 13 were required to write a series of five similarly structured essays on topics of their choice. These two- or four-page essays were due at regular intervals and were graded by the professor, Dr. Jean Carter. Classes were generally teacher-led discussions and exercises, with some days allotted for students to work together in small groups, planning their essays or sharing drafts. Dr. Carter held one individual writing conference with each student at mid semester.

Introduction to Poetry is generally taken by students during their sophomore 14 year, and it, like Freshman Composition, met for 90 minutes twice a week. In this class students were also required to write a series of similar papers. These were three-to-six page critical essays on poems that students chose from a list given them by their professor, Dr. Charles Forson. These essays, like those in Freshman Composition, were due at regular intervals and were graded by the professor. The Poetry classes were all lectures in which Dr. Forson explicated poems. However, one lecture early in the semester was devoted entirely to writing instruction.

Cell Biology, which Dave took in the spring of his sophomore year, met 15 three times a week, twice for 90-minute lectures and once for a three-hour lab. In this course, like the other two, students were required to write a series of similar short papers, three in this course. These were three-to-five page reviews of journal articles which reported current research in cell biology. Students were to summarize these articles, following the five-part scientific format in which the experiment was reported. They were then to relate the experiment to what they were doing in class. These reviews were graded by the professor, Dr. Tom Kelly.

The Participants

The participants in this study included these three professors, Drs. Carter, 16 Forson, and Kelly. All were experienced college teachers who had taught these courses before. All talked willingly and with interest about the writing their students were doing, and both Dr. Carter and Dr. Forson invited me to observe their classes. Dr. Kelly said that it would not be productive for me to observe in his Cell Biology course because he spent almost no time talking directly about writing, so pressed was he to cover the necessary course material.

The student participants in this study were Dave and two of his friends. I first 17 met these three young men in Dr. Carter's Freshman Composition class where I was observing regularly in order to learn how she taught the course, the same one I teach at the college. As I attended that course week after week, I got to know the students who sat by me, Dave and his friends, and I realized I was no longer as interested in understanding what my colleague was teaching as I was in understanding what these students were learning. As the study progressed, my focus narrowed to Dave's experiences, although none of the three students knew this. The contribution of Dave's friends to this study was to facilitate my understanding of Dave. At first, in their Freshman Composition class, these students saw my role as a curious combination of teacher and fellow student. As the study progressed, my role became, in their eyes, that of teacher / inquirer, a person genuinely interested in understanding their writing. In fact, my increasing interest and ability to remember details of his writing experiences seemed at times to mystify and amuse Dave.

At the beginning of this study Dave Garrison was an 18-year-old freshman, 18 a biology pre-med major who had graduated the year before from a parochial boys' high school near the college. He described himself as a "hands-on" person who preferred practical application in the lab to reading theory in books. Beginning in his sophomore year, Dave worked 13 hours a week as a technician in a local hospital, drawing blood from patients, in addition to taking a full course load. He "loved" his hospital work, he said, because of the people and the work, and also because difficulties with chemistry has made him worry about being accepted in medical school. In the hospital he was getting an idea of a range of possible careers in health care. The oldest of four children, Dave lived at home and commuted 30 minutes to campus. He is the first person in his family to go to college, though both of his parents enjoy reading, he said, and his father writes in his work as an insurance salesman. When Dave and I first met, he told me that he did not really like to write and that he was not very good, but he knew that writing was a tool he needed, one that he hoped to learn to use better.

Instrumentation and Analytic Procedures

I collected data from February 1983 through November 1985. A detailed, 19 semester by semester summary is presented in Table 1.

Observation

I observed in all three classes in order to help me understand the contexts for 20 writing in which Dave was working. During the observation I recorded field notes about the classroom activities and interactions I was seeing, and as soon as possible after the observation I read my notes and fleshed them out where possible. Returning to fill out the notes was particularly important when I had participated in the classroom activities as I did in Freshman Composition. In that class I participated in Dave's small group discussions of drafts and did the in-class writing exercises along with the students. I wrote my field notes on the right-side pages of a spiral notebook, leaving the pages opposite free for later notes.

TABLE 1 DATA COLLECTION RECORD

OBSERVATION
Freshman Composition (Freshman year. Spring, 1983) • Participant observation in 1 class per week for 9 weeks. • All class documents were collected and analyzed.
Introduction to Poetry (Sophomore year. Fall, 1983) • Observation of the 90-minute lecture devoted to writing instruction. • All class documents were collected and analyzed.
Cell Biology (Sophomore year. Spring, 1984) • Observation of a lab session for 15 minutes.
INTERVIEWS
Freshman Composition • Frequent conversations and 2 hour-long interviews with the professor, Dr. Carter. • Frequent conversations with the students before and after class.
Poetry • 1 hour-long interview with the professor, Dr. Forson. • 4 hour-long interviews with the students at one-month intervals.
Cell Biology • 2 hour-long interviews with the professor, Dr. Kelly. • 4 hour-long interviews with the students at one-month intervals.
Junior Year Follow-up (Fall, 1984) • 2 hour-long interviews with the students.
PROTOCOLS WITH RETROSPECTIVE INTERVIEWS
Freshman Composition • 1 protocol and interview audiotaped as Dave composed the first draft of his fourth (next to last) essay.
Poetry • 1 protocol and interview audiotaped as Dave composed the first draft of his third (last) paper.
Cell Biology • 1 protocol and interview audiotaped as Dave composed the first draft of his third (last) review.

(Continued)

TABLE 1 DATA COLLECTION RECORD (*continued*)

TEXT ANALYSIS
Freshman Composition   • Dave's fourth essay with the teacher's responses was analyzed. All drafts of all essays were collected.
Poetry   • Dave's third paper with the teacher's responses was analyzed. All drafts of all essays were collected.
Cell Biology   • Dave's third review with the teacher's responses was analyzed. All drafts of all essays were collected.

Interviews

I interviewed Dave, his two friends, and the three professors in order to elicit 21 their interpretations of the writing in each class. Questions were often suggested by the participants' earlier comments or by emerging patterns in the data that I wanted to pursue. Interviews with professors generally took place in their offices and centered on their assignments, their purposes for having students write, and the instructional techniques they used to accomplish their purposes.

The interviews with the students took place in my office on campus and 22 lasted one hour. I chose to interview Dave and his friends together in a series of monthly interviews because I believed I could learn more from Dave in this way. The students often talked to and questioned each other, producing more from Dave than I believe I ever could have gotten from one-on-one sessions with him. I did on two occasions, however, interview Dave alone for one hour when I wanted to question him in a particularly intensive way.

During all interviews I either took notes or made audiotapes which I later 23 transcribed and analyzed. All hour-long interviews with the students were taped.

Analysis of the Observation and Interviews

I read and reread my field notes and the interview transcripts looking for pat- 24 terns and themes. These organized the data and suggested the salient features of writing in each context, its nature and meaning, and of Dave's experiences there. These patterns and themes then focused subsequent inquiry. I was guided in this process by the work of Gilmore and Glatthorn (1982) and Spradley (1979, 1980).

Composing-Aloud Protocols and Retrospective Interviews

Late in each of the three semesters, I audiotaped Dave as he composed aloud   25
the first draft of a paper for the course we had focused on that semester. Dave
wrote at the desk in my office, his pre-writing notes and his books spread out
around him, and I sat nearby in a position where I could observe and make
notes on his behaviors. The protocols lasted 30 minutes and were followed by a
30-minute retrospective interview in which I asked Dave to tell me more about
the process he had just been through. I reasoned that in the retrospective interviews Dave's major concerns would be reemphasized, whereas the smaller issues
that may have occupied him during composing would be forgotten. Because I
followed Dave across time and collected all his written work for each assignment, I could examine what preceded and what followed the composed-aloud
draft. I could thus see how the protocol draft related to Dave's entire composing
process for a task.

The information provided by the protocols generally corroborated what he   26
had said in the interviews. Of particular interest, however, were the points at
which the protocol data contradicted the interview data. These points spurred
further inquiry. Though composing-aloud was never easy for Dave, who characterized himself as a shy person, he became more and more comfortable with it
as the semesters progressed. He did produce, in each of the protocol sessions, a
useful first draft for his final paper in each course.

Analysis and Scoring of the Protocols and Retrospective Interviews

I analyzed the transcripts of the protocols and interviews, classifying and count-   27
ing what I called the *writer's conscious concerns*. These concerns were identified as anything the writer paid attention to during composing as expressed
by (1) remarks about a thought or behavior or (2) observed behaviors. I chose
to focus on Dave's conscious concerns because I expected that they would
include a broad range of writing issues and that they would reflect the nature
and emphases of the classrooms for which he was writing. The protocols would
thus provide the supporting information I needed for this study. In identifying
and classifying the writer's conscious concerns, I was guided by the work of
Berkenkotter (1983), Bridwell (1980), Flower and Hayes (1981), Perl (1979),
and Pianko (1979).

The analysis of the transcripts was carried out in a two-part process. First I   28
read them several times and drew from them four general categories of writer's
concerns, along with a number of subcategories. Then, using this scheme, I classified and counted the writer's remarks and behaviors. The first protocol was, of
course, made during Dave's writing for Freshman Composition. The categories from that composing session were used again in analyzing the protocols
from Poetry and Cell Biology. To these original categories were added new ones
to describe the concerns Dave expressed as he composed for the later courses.

In this way I could identify both concerns that were constant across courses as well as those that were specific to particular classroom writing situations.

I carried out the analyses of the protocols alone because of the understanding 29
of the writing context that I brought to the task. I viewed this knowledge as an asset in identifying and classifying Dave's writing concerns. Thus, instead of agreement between raters, I worked for "confirmability" in the sense of agreement among a variety of information sources (Guba, 1978, p. 17).

Text Analysis

The final window through which I looked 30
at Dave's writing experiences was text analysis. I analyzed the completed papers, with
the professors' comments on them, of the
assignments Dave had begun during the
protocol sessions. If Dave is understood to
be a stranger trying to learn the language
in these classroom communities, then his
teachers are the native-speaker guides who
are training him. In this view, students and
teachers in their written interactions share

> If Dave is understood to be a stranger trying to learn the language in these classroom communities, then his teachers are the native-speaker guides who are training him.

a common aim and are engaged in a cooperative endeavor. Their relationship is like that of people conversing together, the newcomer making trial efforts to communicate appropriately and the native speaker responding to them.

Thus, in order to examine the conventions of discourse in each classroom 31
and get further insight into the interaction between Dave and his professors, I drew upon the model of conversation proposed by Grice (1975). Grice says that conversants assume, unless there are indications to the contrary, that they have a shared purpose and thus make conversational contributions "such as are required . . . by the accepted purpose or direction of the talk exchange in which they are engaged" (p. 45). He terms this the "Cooperative Principle." From the Cooperative Principle Grice derives four categories or conditions which must be fulfilled if people are to converse successfully: Quality, Quantity, Relation, and Manner. When conversation breaks down, it is because one or more of these conditions for successful conversation have been violated, either accidentally or intentionally. On the other hand, people conversing successfully fulfill these conditions, for the most part without conscious attention. Grice's four conditions for conversational cooperation provided my text analysis scheme. They are

1. *Quality.* Conversants must speak what they believe to be the truth and that for which they have adequate evidence.

2. *Quantity.* Conversants must give the appropriate amount of information, neither too much nor too little.

3. *Relation.* The information that conversants give must be relevant to the aims of the conversation.

4. *Manner.* The conversants must make themselves clear, using appropriate forms of expression.

In my examination of Dave's last paper for each course, I considered both 32 his work and his professor's response as conversational turns in which the speakers were doing what they believed would keep the Cooperative Principle in force. Dave's written turns were taken to display the discourse he believed was required in each setting so he would be deemed cooperative. I identified which of Grice's four conditions for successful conversation Dave paid special attention to fulfilling in each context. In this process I drew from the interview and protocol data as well as from the texts. I then counted and categorized Dave's teachers' written responses to his papers according to these same four conditions. A response was identified as an idea the teacher wanted to convey to Dave and could be as short as a single mark or as long as several sentences. Of particular interest were, first, the extent to which Dave and each teacher agreed upon what constituted cooperation, and, second, what the teacher pointed out as violations of the conditions of cooperation, errors that jeopardized the Cooperative Principle in that setting. Further, the form and language of each teacher's response provided insight into the ways of speaking in that particular discipline and classroom.

The text analysis data added to and refined my understanding of Dave's 33 classroom writing situations. And, conversely, my analyses of Dave's texts were informed by what I knew of the classroom writing situations. For this reason, I again elected to work alone with the texts.

Validity of the findings and interpretations in this study were ensured by 34 employing the following techniques. (1) Different types of data were compared. (2) The perspectives of various informants were compared. (3) Engagement with the subject was carried on over a long period of time during which salient factors were identified for more detailed inquiry. (4) External checks on the inquiry process were made by three established researchers who knew neither Dave nor the professors. These researchers read the emerging study at numerous points and questioned researcher biases and the bases for interpretations. (5) Interpretations were checked throughout with the informants themselves. (See Lincoln & Guba, 1985, for a discussion of validity and reliability in naturalistic inquiry.)

RESULTS AND DISCUSSION

Information from all data sources supports three general conclusions, two con- 35 cerning Dave's interpretation and production of the required writing tasks and one concerning social factors in the classrooms that influenced him as he wrote.

First, although the writing tasks in the three classes were in many ways similar, Dave interpreted them as being totally different from each other and totally different from anything he had ever done before. This was evidenced in the interview, protocol, and text analysis data.

Second, certain social factors in Freshman Composition and Cell Biology 36 appeared to foster Dave's writing success in them. Observation and interview data indicated that two unarticulated aspects of the classroom writing contexts influenced his achievement. These social factors were (1) the functions that writing served for Dave in each setting, and (2) the roles that participants and students' texts played there. These social factors were bound up with what Dave ultimately learned from and about writing in each class.

Third, Dave exhibited consistent ways of figuring out what constituted 37 appropriate texts in each setting, in his terms, of "figuring out what the teacher wanted." Evidence from the interviews and protocols shows that he typically drew upon six information sources, in a process that was in large part tacit. These information sources included teacher-provided instructional supports, sources Dave found on his own, and his prior knowledge.

The Writing Assignments: Similar Tasks, Audiences, and Purposes

My analysis of the assignments, combined with the observation and interview 38 data, showed that the writing in the three classes was similar in many ways. It was, in all cases, informational writing for the teacher-as-examiner, the type of writing that Applebee found comprised most secondary school writing (1984). More specifically, the task in Cell Biology was a summary, and in Freshman Composition and Poetry it was analysis, closely related informational uses of writing. Dave's audiences were identified as teacher-as-examiner by the fact that all assignments were graded and that Dave, as he wrote, repeatedly wondered how his teacher would "like" his work.

Further similarities among the writing in the three courses included the pur- 39 pose that the professors stated for having their students write. All three said that the purpose was not so much for students to display specific information, but rather for students to become competent in using the thinking and language of their disciplines. Dr. Kelly, the biologist, stated this most directly when he explained to me why he had his students write reviews of journal articles: "I want students to be at ease with the vocabulary of Cell Biology and how experiments are being done. . . . Students need to get a feeling for the journals, the questions people are asking, the answers they're getting, and the procedures they're using. It will give them a feeling for the excitement, the dynamic part of this field. And they need to see that what they're doing in class and lab is actually *used* out there." Students' summaries of journal articles in Cell Biology were, in other words, to get them started speaking the language of that discourse community.

Learning the conventions of academic discourse was also the purpose of students' writing in Freshman Composition. Dr. Carter was less concerned with the content of the students' five essays than she was with their cohesiveness. She repeatedly stated that what would serve these students in their subsequent academic writing was the ability to write coherent prose with a thesis and subpoints, unified paragraphs, and explicitly connected sentences. In an interview she said, "Ideas aren't going to do people much good if they can't find the means with which to communicate them. . . . When these students are more advanced, and the ability to produce coherent prose is internalized, then they can concentrate on ideas. That's why I'm teaching the analytic paper with a certain way of developing the thesis that's generalizable to their future writing." Dr. Carter's goal was, thus, to help students master conventions of prose which she believed were central to all academic discourse. 40

And likewise in Poetry the purpose of students' writing was to teach them how people in literary studies think and write. In his lecture on writing, early in the semester, Dr. Forson stated this purpose and alluded to some of the conventions for thinking and writing in that setting. He told students, "The three critical essays you will write will make you say something quite specific about the meaning of a poem (your thesis) and demonstrate how far you've progressed in recognizing and dealing with the devices a poet uses to express his insights. You'll find the poem's meaning in the poem itself, and you'll use quotes to prove your thesis. Our concern here is for the *poem,* not the poet's life or era. Nor are your own opinions of the poet's ideas germane." 41

Dr. Forson then spent 20 minutes explaining the mechanical forms for quoting poetry, using a model essay that he had written on a poem by Robert Herrick. He ended by telling students that they should think of their peers as the audience for their essays and asking them not to use secondary critical sources from the library. "You'll just deal with what you now know and with the poetic devices that we discuss in class. Each group of poems will feature one such device: imagery, symbolism, and so forth. These will be the tools in your tool box." 42

Thus in all three courses Dave's tasks were informational writing for the teacher-as-examiner. All were for the purpose of displaying competence in using the ways of thinking and writing appropriate to that setting. And in all three courses Dave wrote a series of similar short papers, due at about three-week intervals, the assumption being that students' early attempts would inform their subsequent ones, in the sort of trial-and-error process that characterizes much language learning. Further, the reading required in Poetry and Cell Biology, the poems and the journal articles, were equally unfamiliar to Dave. We might expect, then, that Dave would view the writing for these three courses as quite similar, and, given an equal amount of work, he would achieve similar levels of success. This, however, is not what happened. 43

Dave's Interpretation of the Writing Tasks

The Writer's Concerns While Composing

In spite of the similarities among the writing tasks for the three courses, evi- 44
dence from several sources shows that Dave interpreted them as being totally
different from each other and totally different from anything he had ever done
before. Dave's characteristic approach across courses was to focus so fully on the
particular new ways of thinking and writing in each setting that commonalities
with previous writing were obscured for him. And interwoven with Dave's conviction that the writing for these courses was totally dissimilar was his differing
success in them. Though he worked hard in all three courses, he made B's in
Freshman Composition, D's and C's in Poetry, and A's in Cell Biology.

The protocol data explain in part why the writing for these classes seemed so 45
different to Dave. Dave's chief concerns while composing for each course were
very different. His focus in Freshman Composition was on textual coherence.
Fifty-four percent of his expressed concerns were for coherence of thesis and
subpoints, coherence within paragraphs, and sentence cohesion. By contrast, in
Poetry, though Dave did mention thesis and subpoints, his chief concerns were
not with coherence, but with the new ways of thinking and writing in that setting. Forty-four percent of his concerns focused on accurately interpreting the
poem and properly using quotes. In Cell Biology, yet a new focus of concerns is
evident. Seventy-two percent of Dave's concerns deal with the new rules of use
in that academic discipline. His chief concerns in Biology were to accurately
understand the scientific terms and concepts in the journal article and then to
accurately rephrase and connect these in his own text, following the same five-
part structure in which the published experiment was reported. It is no wonder
that the writing for these classes seemed very different to Dave. As a newcomer
in each academic territory, Dave's attention was occupied by the new conventions of interpretation and language use in each community. (See Table 2.)

The same preoccupations controlled his subsequent work on the papers. In 46
each course Dave wrote a second draft, which he then typed. In none of these
second drafts did Dave see the task differently or make major changes. He is,
in this regard, like the secondary students Applebee (1984) studied who were
unable, without teacher assistance, to revise their writing in more than minor
ways. And Dave revised none of these papers after the teachers had responded.

We can further fill out the pictures of Dave's composing for the three classes by 47
combining the protocol findings with the observation and interview data. In his
first protocol session, in April of his freshman year, Dave composed the first draft
of his fourth paper for Freshman Composition, an essay in which he chose to analyze the wrongs of abortion. To this session Dave brought an outline of this thesis
and subpoints. He told me that he had spent only 30 minutes writing it the night
before, but that the topic was one he had thought a lot about. As he composed,

TABLE 2 CONCERNS EXPRESSED DURING COMPOSING-ALOUD PROTOCOLS AND
RETROSPECTIVE INTERVIEWS

	PERCENT OF COMMENTS		
	Freshman Composition	*Poetry*	*Cell Biology*
Concerns Expressed in All Three Courses			
Features of Written Text			
Coherent thesis / subpoint structure	22	18	0
Coherent paragraph structure	15	13	3
Cohesive sentences	17	8	3
Editing for mechanical correctness	9	3	3
Communication Situation (assignment, reader-writer roles, purpose)	8	6	5
On-Going Process	18	6	12
Emerging Text	11	2	2
Concerns Specific to Poetry			
Appropriately using quotes from poem	0	32	0
Making a correct interpretation of the poem	0	12	0
Concerns Specific to Cell Biology			
Following the 5-part scientific guidelines	0	0	20
Correctly understanding the content of the article being summarized Rephrasing &	0	0	37
connecting appropriate parts of the article	0	0	15
Total	100	100	100
Number of comments	64	62	60

Dave was most concerned with and apparently very dependent upon, his outline, commenting on it, glancing at it, or pausing to study it 14 times during the
30 minutes of composing. Dave's next most frequently expressed concerns were
for coherence at paragraph and sentence levels, what Dr. Carter referred to as
coherence of mid-sized and small parts. These were the new "rules of use" in this

setting. Dave told me that in high school he had done some "bits and pieces" of writing and some outlines for history, but that he had never before written essays like this. The total time Dave spent on his abortion essay was five hours.

In Dave's Poetry protocol session seven months later, in November of his 48 sophomore year, he composed part of the first draft of his third and last paper for that class, a six-page analysis of a poem called "Marriage" by contemporary poet Gregory Corso. To this session he brought two pages of notes and his *Norton Anthology of Poetry* in which he had underlined and written notes in the margins beside the poem. He told me that he had spent four hours (of an eventual total of 11) preparing to write: reading the poem many times and finding a critical essay on it in the library. During his pre-writing and composing, Dave's primary concern was to get the right interpretation of the poem, "the true meaning" as he phrased it. And as Dave wrote, he assumed that his professor knew the true meaning, a meaning, Dave said, that "was there, but not there, not just what it says on the surface." Further, Dave knew that he must argue his interpretation, using not his own but the poet's words; this was his second most frequently expressed concern.

As Dave composed, he appeared to be as tied to the poem as he had been 49 to his outline in Freshman Composition the semester before. He seemed to be almost *physically* attached to the *Norton Anthology* by his left forefinger as he progressed down the numbers he had marked in the margins. He was, we might say, tied to the concrete material, the "facts" of the poem before him. Dave never got his own essay structure; rather, he worked down the poem, explicating from beginning to end. In the retrospective interview he said, "I didn't really have to think much about my thesis and subs because they just come naturally now. . . . But anyway it's not like in Comp last year. Here my first paragraph is the introduction with the thesis, and the stanzas are the subpoints." Dave's preoccupation with the poem and the new conventions of interpreting and quoting poetry resulted in a paper that was not an analysis but a summary with some interpretation along the way. His focus on these new rules of use appeared to limit his ability to apply previously learned skills, the thesis-subpoint analytical structure, and kept him working at the more concrete summary level.

This domination by the concrete may often characterize newcomers' first 50 steps as they attempt to use language in unfamiliar disciplines (Williams, 1985). Dave's professor, Dr. Forson, seemed to be familiar with this phenomenon when he warned students in his lecture on writing: "You must remember that the poet ordered the poem. *You* order your essay with your own thesis and subtheses. Get away from 'Next. . . . Next'." But if Dave heard this in September, he had forgotten it by November. Dave's experience is consonant with Langer's (1984) finding that students who know more about a subject as they begin to write are likely to choose analysis rather than summary. And these students receive higher scores for writing quality as well.

In his writing for Cell Biology the following semester, Dave's concerns were 51 again focused on the new and unfamiliar conventions in this setting. Before writing his last paper, a four-page review of an experiment on glycoprotein reported in *The Journal of Cell Biology,* Dave spent three hours preparing. (He eventually spent a total of eight hours on the review.) He had chosen the article in the library from a list the professor had given to students and had then read the article twice, underlining it, making notes, and looking up the definitions of unfamiliar terms. To the protocol session Dave brought these notes, the article, and a sheet on which he had written what he called "Dr. Kelly's guidelines," the five-part scientific experiment format that Dr. Kelly wanted students to follow: Background, Objectives, Procedures, Results, and Discussion.

In his composing aloud, Dave's chief concerns in Biology were, as in Poetry 52 the semester before, with the reading, in this case the journal article. But here, unlike Poetry, Dave said the meaning was "all out on the table." In Poetry he had had to interpret meaning from the poem's connotative language; in Biology, by contrast, he could look up meanings, a situation with which Dave was far more comfortable. But as he composed for Biology, he was just as tied to the journal article as he had been to the poem or to his outline in previous semesters. Dave paused frequently to consult the article, partially covering it at times so that his own paper was physically closer to what he was summarizing at that moment.

Dave's first and second most commonly expressed concerns during the Biol- 53 ogy protocol session were for rephrasing and connecting parts of the article and for following Dr. Kelly's guidelines. These were, in essence, concerns for coherence and organization, what Dave was most concerned with in Freshman Composition. But the writing for Biology bore little relation in Dave's mind to what he had done in Freshman Composition. In Biology he was indeed concerned about his organization, but here it was the five-part scientific format he had been given, very different, it seemed to him, than the thesis / subpoint organization he had had to create for his freshman essays. In fact, until I questioned him about it at the end of the semester, Dave never mentioned the freshman thesis / subpoint structure. And the concerns for coherence at paragraph and sentence levels that had been so prominent as he wrote for Freshman Composition were replaced in Biology by his concern for rephrasing the article's already coherent text. In Freshman Composition Dave had talked about trying to get his sentences and paragraphs to "fit" or "flow" together. In Biology, however, he talked about trying to get the article into his own words, about "cutting," "simplifying," and "combining two sentences." Again, it is no wonder that Dave believed that this writing was totally new. It took one of Dave's friend's and my prodding during an interview to make Dave see that he had indeed written summaries before. Lots of them.

The Nature of Cooperation in the Three Courses

The text analysis data provide further insight into why Dave perceived the 54 writing in these courses as so dissimilar. The data provide information about what was, in Grice's terms, essential to maintaining the Cooperative Principle in these written exchanges. Analyses of the teachers' responses to Dave's papers show that his concerns in each class generally did match theirs. Put differently, Dave had figured out, though not equally well in all classes, what counted as "cooperation" in each context, and what he had to do to be deemed a competent communicator there. (See Table 3.)

Analysis of Dave's finished essay for Freshman Composition suggests that 55 his concerns for textual coherence were appropriate. Dave knew that to keep the Cooperative Principle in force in Dr. Carter's class, he had to pay special attention to fulfilling the condition of *Manner,* to making himself clear, using appropriate forms of expression. He succeeded and was deemed cooperative by Dr. Carter when she responded to his contribution with a telegraphic reply on the first page: "18/20." Apart from editing two words in Dave's text, she made no further comments, assuming that Dave and she shared an understanding of what constituted cooperation in her class and of what her numbers meant. (She had explained to students that she was marking with numbers that semester in an attempt to be more "scientific," and she had defined for them the "objective linguistic features of text" to which her numbers referred.) Dave did understand the grade and was, of course, very pleased with it.

In an interview, Dr. Carter explained her grade to me. "Though his content 56 isn't great," she said, "his paper is coherent, not badly off at any place. . . . He gave a fair number of reasons to develop his paragraphs, he restated his point at the end, and there is no wasted language. It's not perfectly woven together, but it's good." Though Dr. Carter mentioned the "reasons" Dave gave as evidence for his contentions, she was concerned not so much with their meaning as with their cohesiveness. Cooperation in this setting thus depended upon fulfilling

TABLE 3 TEACHERS' RESPONSES TO DAVE'S PAPERS

NUMBER OF RESPONSES INDICATING VIOLATIONS OF CONDITIONS FOR COOPERATION				
	Quality	*Quantity*	*Relevance*	*Manner*	*Grade*
Composition	0	0	0	2	18/20
Poetry	8	0	0	11	C+
Cell Biology	0	0	0	14	96

the condition of *Manner*. Dave knew this and expected only a response to how well he had achieved the required form, not to the content of his essay.

In his writing for Poetry the following semester, Dave was attempting to keep 57 the Cooperative Principle in force by paying special attention to two conditions, *Quality* and *Manner*. That is, first he was attempting to say what was true and give adequate evidence, and, second, he was attempting to use proper forms of expression. This is evidenced in the interview and protocol as well as the text data. Analysis of Dr. Forson's 19 responses to Dave's paper shows that Dave's concerns matched those of his teacher, that Dave had figured out, though only in part, what counted as cooperation in that setting. Dr. Forson's responses all referred to violations of the same conditions Dave had been concerned with fulfilling, *Quality* and *Manner*. In seven of his eight marginal notes and in an endnote, Dr. Forson disagreed with Dave's interpretation and questioned his evidence, violations of the *Quality* condition. Mina Shaughnessy (1977) says that such failure to properly coordinate claims and evidence is perhaps the most common source of misunderstanding in academic prose. The ten mechanical errors that Dr. Forson pointed out were violations of the condition of *Manner*, violations which may jeopardize the Cooperative Principle in many academic settings. Dave's unintentional violations in Poetry of the *Quality* and *Manner* conditions jeopardized the Cooperative Principle in that exchange, resulting in the C+ grade.

Dr. Kelly's responses to Dave's writing in Biology were, like those in Fresh- 58 man Composition, much briefer than Dr. Forson's. Dr. Kelly's 14 marks or phrases all pointed out errors in form, unintentional violations of the Gricean condition of *Manner*. But these were apparently not serious enough to jeopardize the aims of the written conversation in Biology; Dave's grade on the review was 96.

This application of Grice's rubric for spoken conversation to student-teacher 59 written interaction gives further insight into the differences in these classroom contexts for writing. It is evident that successfully maintaining the Cooperative Principle was a more complicated business in Poetry than in Freshman Composition or Biology. In Biology, Dave was unlikely to violate the condition of *Quality*, as he did in Poetry, because he was only summarizing the published experiment and thus only had to pay attention to the condition of *Manner*. In Poetry, by contrast, he was called upon to take an interpretive position. This assumed that he had already summarized the poem. He had not. Thus his analytical essay took the form of a summary, as we have seen. In Biology, on the other hand, the writing was supposed to be a summary that then moved to a comparison of the summarized experiment to what was going on in class.

For Dave, the latter assignment was more appropriate. Novices in a field may 60 need the simpler summary assignment that helps them understand the new reading, the new language that they are being asked to learn. They may then be ready to move to analysis or critique. One wonders if Dave's success in Poetry would have been enhanced if he had been asked to write out a summary of the poem first. He could then have worked from that summary as he structured his own critical essay.

Similarly, in Freshman Composition, Dave was unlikely to violate the con- 61 dition of *Quality*, to say something untrue or provide inadequate evidence for his claim. Though Dave did have to provide evidence for his subpoints, he was not evaluated for his content, and thus he concentrated on the condition of *Manner*. Further, the writing in Freshman Composition did not require Dave to master unfamiliar texts as it did in both Poetry and Biology. And for Dave the task of integrating new knowledge from his reading into his writing in those courses was his salient concern, as we have seen.

The apparent absence of attention paid in any of these classes to fulfilling 62 the conditions of *Quantity* or *Relation* is puzzling. Perhaps Dave's prior school writing experience had trained him to include the right amount of information (*Quantity*) and stay on topic (*Relation*).

The text analysis data, then, show that what counted as cooperation in these 63 three classes was indeed quite different. Dr. Forson, in his extensive responses, apparently felt it necessary to reteach Dave how people think and write in his community. This is understandable in light of Dave's numerous unintentional violations of the Cooperative Principle. Further, though Dr. Forson told students that he was being objective, finding the meaning of the poem in the text, he told me that his responses to students' papers were to argue his interpretation of the poem and, thus, to justify his grade.

The differing language and forms of these professors' responses probably also 64 added to Dave's sense that in each classroom he was in a new foreign land. Response style may well be discipline-specific as well as teacher-specific, with responses in literary studies generally more discursive than in the sciences. Further, Dr. Forson's responses were in the informal register typically used by an authority speaking to a subordinate (Freedman, 1984). His responses to Dave's paper included the following: "You misfire here." "I get this one. Hurrah for me!" "Pardon my writing. I corrected this in an automobile." The informality, and the word "corrected" in particular, leave little doubt about the authority differential between Dr. Forson and Dave. By contrast, Dave seemed to interpret the numerical grade in Biology as more characteristic of a conversation between equals. In a comment that may say more about their classroom interaction than their written interaction, Dave spoke of Dr. Kelly's brief responses to his review: "Yeah. He's like that. He treats us like adults. When we ask him questions, he answers us." Dave's apparent mixing of his spoken and written interaction with Dr. Kelly emphasizes the point that students' and teachers' writing for each other in classrooms is as fully contextualized as any other activity that goes on there.

Before Dave turned in his last papers in Poetry and Biology, I asked him 65 to speculate about the grade he would get. When he handed in his six-page paper on the Corso poem, "Marriage," on which he had spent eleven hours, he told me that he hoped for an A or B: "I'll be really frustrated on this one if the grade's not good after I've put in the time on it." A week later, however, he told me in a resigned tone and with a short laugh that he'd gotten a C+. By contrast, when he turned in his last review in Biology, he told me he knew he would get an A. When I questioned him, he replied, "I don't know how I know. I just do." And he was right: his grade was 96. Dave obviously understood far better what constituted cooperation in Biology than he did in Poetry.

Social Aspects of the Classrooms That Influenced Dave's Writing

Why was Dave's success in writing in these classrooms so different? The answers to 66 this question will illuminate some of the dimensions along which school writing situations differ and thus influence student achievement. It would be a mistake to think that the differing task structure was the only reason that Dave was more successful in Biology and Freshman Composition than he was in Poetry. Assignments are, as I have suggested, only a small part of the classroom interaction, limited written exchanges that reflect the nature of the communication situation created by participants in that setting. Two unarticulated qualities in the contexts for writing in Freshman Composition and Biology appeared to foster Dave's success in those classes. These were (1) the social functions Dave's writing served for him in those classes, and (2) the roles played by participants and by students' texts there.

The Functions Dave Saw His Writing as Accomplishing

It has been argued that the social functions served by writing must be seen 67 as an intrinsic part of the writing experience (Clark & Florio, 1983; Hymes, 1972a, 1972b; Scribner & Cole, 1981). Evidence from interviews and observations indicate that the writing in Freshman Composition and Biology was for Dave a meaningful social activity, meaningful beyond just getting him through the course. Further, Dave and his teachers in Freshman Composition and Biology mutually understood and valued those functions. This was not the case in Poetry. The data show a correlation not only between meaningful social functions served by the writing and Dave's success with it, but also between the writing's social meaning and Dave's ability to remember and draw upon it in subsequent semesters.

In Freshman Composition Dave's writing served four valuable functions for 68 him. He articulated all of these.

1. Writing to prepare him for future writing in school and career
2. Writing to explore topics of his choice

3. Writing to participate with other students in the classroom

4. Writing to demonstrate academic competence

In Biology Dave also saw his writing as serving four valuable functions:

1. Writing to learn the language of Cell Biology, which he saw as necessary to his career

2. Writing to prepare him for his next semester's writing in Immunology

3. Writing to make connections between his classwork and actual work being done by professionals in the field

4. Writing to demonstrate academic competence

Evidence from interviews and observation shows that Dr. Carter and Dr. Kelly saw writing in their classes as serving the same four functions that Dave did.

On the other hand, in Poetry, though Dave's professor stated four functions 69 of student writing, Dave saw his writing as serving only one function for him: writing to demonstrate academic competence. Dave, always the compliant student, did say after he had received his disappointing grade in Poetry that the writing in Poetry was probably good for him: "Probably any kind of writing helps you." Though he may well be right, Dave actually saw his writing for Poetry as serving such a limited function — evaluation of his skills in writing poetry criticism for Dr. Forson — that he was not really convinced (and little motivated by the notion) that this writing would serve him in any general way.

Dave contended that any writing task was easy or difficult for him according to 70 his interest in it. When I asked him what he meant by interesting, he said, "If it has something to do with my life. Like it could explain something to me or give me an answer that I could use now." Writing must have, in other words, meaningful personal and social functions for Dave if it is to be manageable, "easy," for him. These functions existed for Dave in Freshman Composition and Biology, providing the applications and personal transaction with the material that may be generally required for learning and forging personal knowledge (Dewey, 1949; Polanyi, 1958).

Dave's Poetry class, however, served no such personally meaningful func- 71 tions. Six weeks after the Poetry course was finished, I asked Dave some further questions about his last paper for that course, the discussion of the Corso poem on which he had worked 11 hours. He could remember almost nothing about it. When I asked him to speculate why this was, he said, "I guess it's because I have no need to remember it." By contrast, when I asked Dave in the fall of his junior year if his Cell Biology writing was serving him in his Immunology course as he had expected, he said, "Yes. The teacher went over how to write up our labs, but most of us had the idea anyway from last semester because we'd read those journal articles. We were already exposed to it."

Of course the functions of his writing in Biology served Dave better than 72 those in Poetry in part because he was a biology major. The writing for Cell Biology fit into a larger whole: his growing body of knowledge about this field and his professional future. The material in Cell Biology was for Dave a comprehensible part of the discipline of Biology which was in turn a comprehensible part of the sciences. Dave was, with experience, gradually acquiring a coherent sense of the language of the discipline, how biologists think and speak and what it is they talk about. And his understanding of the language of biology was accompanied by an increasing confidence in his own ability to use it. Both of these are probably necessary foundations for later, more abstract and complex uses of the language (Piaget, 1952; Perry, 1970; Williams, 1985).

In the required one-semester Poetry class, however, the poems seemed to 73 Dave to be unrelated to each other except for commonly used poetic devices, and his writing about them was unrelated to his own life by anything at all beyond his need to find the "true meaning" and get an acceptable grade. Dave's different relationship to the languages of these disciplines was shown when he said, "In Biology I'm using what I've *learned*. It's just putting what I've learned on paper. But in Poetry, more or less each poem is different, so it's not *taught* to you. You just have to figure it out from that poem itself and hope Dr. Forson likes it." Nor, in Poetry, was Dave ever invited to make personally meaningful connections with the poems. And he never did it on his own, no doubt in part because he was so preoccupied with the new ways of thinking and speaking that he was trying to use.

In Freshman Composition the social function of writing that was perhaps 74 most powerful for Dave was writing to participate with other students in the classroom. In his peer writing group Dave, for the first time ever, discussed his writing with others. Here he communicated personal positions and insights to his friends, an influential audience for him. That an important social function was served by these students' work with each other is suggested by their clear memory, a year and a half later, both of their essays and of each others' reactions to them.

The four social functions that Dave's writing in Freshman Composition 75 accomplished for him enhanced his engagement with and attitude toward the writing he did in that class. This engagement is reflected in Dave's memory not only of his essays and his friends' reactions to them, but also in his memory and use of the ideas and terms from that course. When Dave talked about his writing during his sophomore and junior years, he used the process terms he had learned in Freshman Composition: prewriting, revision, and drafts. He also used other language he had learned as a freshman, speaking at times about his audience's needs, about narrowing his topic, about connecting his sentences, providing more details, and choosing his organizational structure. This is not to say that Dave had mastered these skills in every writing situation nor that he always accurately diagnosed problems in his own work. In fact, we know that he did not. It is to say, however, that Dave did recognize and could talk about some of the things that writing does involve in many situations. Thus, the value of this course for Dave lay not so much in the thesis/subpoint essay structure. Rather, Dave had, as a result of his experiences in Freshman Composition, learned that writing is a process that can be talked about, managed, and controlled.

Thus the social functions that writing served for Dave in each class were 76 viewed as an intrinsic part of his writing experiences there. Where these functions were numerous and mutually understood and valued by Dave and his teacher, Dave was more successful in figuring out and producing the required discourse. And then he remembered it longer. In Poetry, where his writing served few personally valued ends, Dave did less well, making a C on the first paper, a D on the second, and a C+ on the third. It should be noted, in addition, that grades themselves serve a social function in classrooms: defining attitudes and roles. Dave's low grades in Poetry probably further alienated him from the social communication processes in that classroom community and helped define his role there.

The Roles Played by the Participants and by Students' Texts

Other social aspects of these classroom contexts for writing which affected 77 Dave's experiences were the roles played by the people and texts in them. Such roles are tacitly assigned in classroom interaction and create the context in which the student stranger attempts to determine the rules of language use in that territory. Here we will examine (1) Dave's role in relation to the teacher, (2) Dave's role in relation to other students in the class, and (3) the role played by students' texts there.

Dave's Role in Relation to the Teacher

This is a particularly important role relationship in any classroom because it 78 tacitly shapes the writer-audience relation that students use as they attempt to communicate appropriately. In all three classes Dave was writing for his teachers as pupil to examiner. However, data from several sources show that there were important variations in the actual "enactments" (Goffman, 1961) of this role-relationship.

In Composition, both Dave and his professor played the role of writer. 79 Throughout the semester Dr. Carter talked about what and how she wrote, the long time she spent in prewriting activities, the eight times she typically revised her work, and the strategies she used to understand her audience in various situations. She spoke to students as if she and they were all writers working together, saying such things as "I see some of you write like I do," or "Let's work together to shape this language." And, as we have seen, she structured the course to provide opportunities for students to play the role of writer in their peer groups. She also asked them to describe their writing processes for several of their essays. Dave told me in an interview during his junior year, "In high school I couldn't stand writing, but in Comp I started to change because I knew more what I was doing. I learned that there are steps you can go through, and I learned how to organize a paper." As a freshman, Dave understood for the first time something of what it feels like to be a writer.

In Biology both Dave and his teacher, Dr. Kelly, saw Dave as playing the 80 role of newcomer, learning the language needed for initiation into the profession. Dr. Kelly played the complementary role of experienced professional who was training Dave in the ways of speaking in that discipline, ways they both assumed Dave would learn in time.

In Poetry, on the other hand, Dave played the role of outsider in relation- 81 ship to his teacher, the insider who knew the true meanings of poetry. And Dave stayed the outsider, unable ever to fully get the teacher's "true meaning." This outsider / insider relationship between Dave and Dr. Forson was created by a number of factors: (1) Their spoken and written interaction, (2) the few meaningful social functions served for Dave by the writing in that class, (3) the demanding nature of the analytic task, combined with (4) the limited knowledge Dave commanded in that setting, (5) the limited number of effective instructional supports, and (6) the low grades Dave got, which further alienated him from the communication processes in that class. (To the instructional supports provided in Poetry we will return below.) Because Dave's outsider role was not a pleasant one for him, he seemed increasingly to separate his thinking from his writing in Poetry, saying several times that he had the right ideas, the teacher just did not like the way he wrote them.

Dave's Role in Relationship to Other Students

Students' relationships with each other, like those between students and teach- 82 ers, are created as students interact within the classroom structures the teacher has set up. These classroom structures grow out of teachers' explicit and tacit notions about writing and learning. What specifically were the relationships among students in Freshman Composition, Biology, and Poetry?

In Composition, as we have seen, students shared their writing and responded 83 to each other's work. The classroom structure reflected Dr. Carter's perhaps tacit notion that writing is a social as well as intellectual affair. However, in neither Poetry nor Biology was time built into the class for students to talk with each other about their writing. Dave lamented this as he wrote for Poetry early in his sophomore year, because, he said, he now realized how valuable the small group sessions had been in Freshman Composition the semester before.

In Biology, Dave told me students did talk informally about the journal 84 articles they had selected and how they were progressing on their summaries.

Dr. Kelly, who circulated during lab, was at times included in these informal talks about writing. And it is no surprise that students discussed their writing in this way in Biology in light of Dr. Kelly's notions about writing. It is, he believes, an essential part of what scientists do. He told me that it often comes as a rude shock to students that the way biologists survive in the field is by writing. He said, "These students are bright, and they can memorize piles of facts, but they're not yet good at writing. They know what science *is*," he told me, "but they don't know what scientists *do*." Thus, writing up research results is seen by Dr. Kelly as an integral part of a biologist's lab work. No wonder his students talked about it.

In Poetry, however, there was little talk of any kind among students. Classes 85 were primarily lectures where Dr. Forson explicated poems and explained poetic devices. Only occasionally did he call on one of the 22 students for an opinion. This lack of student interaction in Poetry was in line with the image of the writer that Dr. Forson described for students, an image that may be widely shared in literary studies: A person alone with his or her books and thoughts. Dr. Forson did, however, tell students that he himself often got his ideas for writing from listening to himself talk about poems in class. Yet, in conversation with me, he said that he did not want students discussing the poems and their writing with each other because he feared they would not think for themselves. Dave picked up on this idea very clearly. It was not until the fall of his junior year that he admitted to me that he and his girlfriend had worked together on their papers. They had discussed the interpretations of the poems and how they might best write them, but, he told me, they had been careful to choose different poems to write about so that Dr. Forson wouldn't know they had worked together. This absence of student interaction in Poetry may have contributed to the outsider role that Dave played in that class.

Throughout this study I was amazed at the amount of talk that goes on all 86 the time outside class among students as they work to figure out the writing requirements in various courses. What Dave's experience in Poetry may suggest is that where student collaboration in writing is not openly accepted, it goes on clandestinely.

The Roles Played by Students' Texts

What were students' texts called and how were they handled? Interview and 87 observation data show that students' texts were treated quite differently in these three courses, and this affected how Dave saw the assignments, and, perhaps more important, how he saw himself as writer.

In Freshman Composition Dave wrote what he referred to as "essays"; in 88 Biology, "reviews"; in Poetry, "papers." This latter term is commonly used, of course, but it is one that Emig (1983, p. 173) says suggests a low status text: "Paper"—as if there were no words on the sheet at all. In Poetry the high status

615

texts, the ones that were discussed and interpreted, were the poems. Students' works were just more or less successful explications of those. Furthermore, in Poetry the one model essay the students read was written by the teacher. Though students were told they should think of their peers as their audience, in fact they never read each other's essays at all. Students' texts were, rather, passed only between student and teacher as in a private conversation.

In Biology, student texts enjoyed a higher status. Excellent student reviews 89 were posted and students were encouraged to read them; they were to serve as models. Some student writers were thus defined as competent speakers in this territory, and the message was clear to Dave: This was a language that he too could learn given time and proper training.

And in Freshman Composition, of course, student texts were the *objects* of 90 study. The class read good and flawed student texts from former semesters and from their own. This not only helped Dave with his writing, it also dignified student writing and elevated his estimation of his own work. Student texts were not, in short, private affairs between teacher and student; they were the subject matter of this college course.

Thus the roles that were enacted by teachers, students, and students' texts 91 were quite different in each classroom and were an integral part of Dave's writing experiences there. The participants' interaction and the social functions that writing serves are important factors working to create the communication situation. And this communication situation, it has been suggested, is the fundamental factor shaping the success of writing instruction (Langer & Applebee, 1984, p. 171).

The Information Sources Dave Drew Upon

In a process that was in large part tacit, Dave drew upon six sources for infor- 92 mation about what constituted successful writing in Freshman Composition, Poetry, and Biology. These included teacher-provided instructional supports, sources Dave found on his own, and his prior experience. Many of these have been mentioned above. They are summarized in Table 4.

Of particular interest are the information sources Dave drew upon (or failed 93 to draw upon) in Poetry, the course in which the writing assignment was the most demanding and in which Dave did least well in assessing and producing the required discourse. The information source that Dr. Forson intended to be most helpful to students, the instructional support on which he spent a great deal of time, was his response to their papers. However, his extensive comments did not help Dave a great deal in learning how to communicate in that setting. Dave said that the comments on his first paper did help him some with his second, but he really did not refer to Dr. Forson's responses on the second paper as he wrote the third. Nor did Dave use the comments on the

TABLE 4 INFORMATION SOURCES DAVE DREW UPON IN ASSESSING REQUIRED DISCOURSE

INFORMATION SOURCES	FRESHMAN COMPOSITION	POETRY	CELL BIOLOGY
What teachers said in class about writing	Constant lectures & exercises about process & products	• One lecture • General statements to the class about their papers when returning them	• Ten minutes giving "guidelines" when returning 1st set of reviews of reviews • Informal comments in lab
Model texts	Many, including flawed models	• One, written by teacher • One, written by professional (from library)	• The articles being summarized served as models. • Posted student reviews
Talk with other students	Frequent groups in class	With friend outside class	Informal, in class
Teachers' written responses to writing	Read responses & revised early essays accordingly	Read. No revision required	Read. No revision required
Dave's prior experience	The extent to which Dave drew upon prior experience is difficult to say. In each class he believed he had no prior experience to draw from. However, we know he had had related prior experience.		
Personal talk with teacher	One conference with teacher	None	None

third paper when preparing for the essay question on the final exam. Dr. Forson required no revision in direct response to his comments, and the expected carry-over of his responses from one paper to the next did not occur. Rather, Dave repeated similar mistakes again and again. The assumption that trial and error will improve students' writing across a series of similar tasks did not hold true for Dave's work in Poetry.

Neither was the model text in Poetry, Dr. Forson's analysis of the Herrick poem that he went over in lecture, as useful an information source for Dave as Dr. Forson had hoped it would be. Dave told me that though he had looked at

94

Dr. Forson's model critical essay as he wrote his first paper, it had not helped him a great deal. "Seeing how someone else did it," he said, "is a lot different than doing it yourself." In Freshman Composition and Biology, however, the model texts, both excellent and flawed ones, were more numerous. And in Biology, the model provided by the article Dave was summarizing was virtually inescapable. Model texts are, it seems reasonable, particularly important to newcomers learning the conventions of discourse in a new academic territory.

An information source which Dave was not adept at using in any course was 95 direct questioning of the professor, the native-speaker expert in each setting. Dave never voluntarily questioned a teacher, though in October of his sophomore year, when he was doing poorly in Poetry, he did make an attempt to speak with Dr. Forson at his office. But when Dr. Forson was not there, Dave waited only a short time and then left — relieved, he said. He did not return. In Freshman Composition, however, Dave was required to interact with Dr. Carter individually in his mid-semester conference. That interview provided an additional information source upon which Dave could draw as he assessed and adapted to the writing requirements in that class.

DISCUSSION

What, then, can we learn from Dave's experiences? First, this study adds to 96 existing research which suggests that school writing is not a monolithic activity or global skill. Rather, the contexts for writing may be so different from one classroom to another, the ways of speaking in them so diverse, the social meanings of writing and the interaction patterns so different, that the courses may be for the student writer like so many foreign countries. These differences were apparent in this study not only in Dave's perceptions of the courses but in his concerns while writing and in his written products.

Second, the findings of this study have several implications for our under- 97 standing of writing development. This study suggests that writing development is, in part, context-dependent. In each new classroom community, Dave in many ways resembled a beginning language user. He focused on a limited number of new concerns, and he was unable to move beyond concrete ways of thinking and writing, the facts of the matter at hand. Moreover, skills mastered in one situation, such as the thesis-subpoint organization in Freshman Composition, did not, as Dave insisted, automatically transfer to new contexts with differing problems and language and differing amounts of knowledge that he controlled. To better understand the stages that students progress through in achieving competence in academic speech communities, we need further research.

Dave's development across his freshman and sophomore years, where he 98 was repeatedly a newcomer, may also be viewed in terms of his attitude toward writing. Evidence over 21 months shows that his notion of the purpose of school writing changed very little. Though there were, as we have seen, other functions accomplished for Dave by his writing in Freshman Composition and Biology, he always understood the purpose of his school writing as being primarily to satisfy a teacher-examiner's requirements. A change that did occur, however, was Dave's increased understanding of some of the activities that writers actually engage in and an increased confidence in his writing ability. As a freshman, he had told me that he did not like to write and was not very good, but by the fall of his junior year he sounded quite different. Because of a number of successful classroom experiences with writing, and an ability to forget the less successful ones, Dave told me, "Writing is no problem for me. At work, in school, I just do it."

Whether Dave will eventually be a mature writer, one who, according to 99 Britton's (1975) definition, is able to satisfy his own purposes with a wide range of audiences, lies beyond the scope of this study to determine. We do know, however, that Dave did not, during the period of this study, write for a wide range of audiences. Nor did he, in these classes, define his own audiences, purposes, or formats, though he did in Freshman Composition choose his topics and in Poetry and Biology the particular poems and articles he wrote about. What this study suggests is that college undergraduates in beginning-level courses may have even less opportunity to orchestrate their own writing occasions than do younger students. Balancing teachers' and students' purposes is indeed difficult in these classrooms where students must, in 14 weeks, learn unfamiliar discourse conventions as well as a large body of new knowledge.

The findings of this study have several implications for the teaching of writ- 100 ing. They suggest that when we ask what students learn from and about writing in classrooms, we must look not only at particular assignments or at students' written products. We must also look at what they learn from the social contexts those classrooms provide for writing. In Freshman Composition, Dave learned that writer was a role he could play. In Biology, writing was for Dave an important part of a socialization process; he was the newcomer being initiated into a profession in which, he learned, writing counts for a great deal. From his writing in Poetry, Dave learned that reading poetry was not for him and that he could get through any writing task, no matter how difficult or foreign. This latter is a lesson not without its value, of course, but it is not one that teachers hope to teach with their writing assignments.

This study also raises questions about how teachers can best help student 101 "strangers" to become competent users of the new language in their academic territory. Because all writing is context-dependent, and because successful writing requires the accurate assessment of and adaptation to the demands of particular writing situations, perhaps writing teachers should be explicitly training students in this assessment process. As Dave researched the writing requirements

619

in his classroom, he drew upon six information sources in a process that was for him largely tacit and unarticulated. But Dave was actually in a privileged position in terms of his potential for success in this "figuring out" process. He had, after all, had years of practice writing in classrooms. Furthermore, he shared not only ethnic and class backgrounds with his teachers, but also many assumptions about education. Students from diverse communities may need, even more than Dave, explicit training in the ways in which one figures out and then adapts to the writing demands in academic contexts.

For teachers in the disciplines, "native-speakers" who may have used the lan- 102 guage in their discipline for so long that it is partially invisible to them, the first challenge will be to appreciate just how foreign and difficult their language is for student newcomers. They must make explicit the interpretive and linguistic conventions in their community, stressing that theirs is one way of looking at reality and not reality itself. As Fish (1980) points out, "The choice is never between objectivity and interpretation, but between an interpretation that is unacknowledged as such and an interpretation that is at least aware of itself" (p. 179). Teachers in the disciplines must then provide student newcomers with assignments and instructional supports which are appropriate for first steps in using the language of their community. Designing appropriate assignments and supports may well be more difficult when the student stranger is only on a brief visit in an academic territory, as Dave was in Poetry, or when the student comes from a community at a distance farther from academe than Dave did.

Naturalistic studies like the present one, Geertz says, are only "another 103 country heard from . . . nothing more or less." Yet, "small facts speak to large issues" (1973, p. 23). From Dave's story, and others like it which describe actual writers at work in local settings, we will learn more about writers' processes and texts and how these are constrained by specific social dynamics. Our generalizations and theories about writing and about how people learn to write must, in the final analysis, be closely tied to such concrete social situations.

References

Applebee, A. (1984). *Contexts for learning to write: Studies of secondary school instruction.* Norwood, NJ: Ablex.

Basso, K. (1974). The ethnography of writing. In R. Bauman and J. Sherzer (Eds.), *Explorations in the ethnography of speaking* (pp. 425–432). New York: Cambridge University Press.

Bazerman, C. (1981). What written knowledge does: Three examples of academic discourse. *Philosophy of the Social Sciences, 11,* 361–387.

Berkenkotter, C. (1983). Decisions and revisions: The planning strategies of a publishing writer. *College Composition and Communication, 34,* 156–169.

Bizzell, P. (1982). Cognition, convention, and certainty: What we need to know about writing. *PRE/TEXT, 3,* 213–243.

Bridwell, L. (1980). Revising strategies in twelfth grade students' transactional writing. *Research in the Teaching of English, 14,* 197–222.

Britton, J., Burgess, T., Martin, N., McLeod, A., & Rosen, H. (1975). *The development of writing abilities 11–18.* London: Macmillan.

Calkins, L. (1980). Research update: When children want to punctuate: Basic skills belong in context. *Language Arts, 57,* 567–573.

Clark, C., & Florio, S., with Elmore, J., Martin, J., & Maxwell, R. (1983). Understanding writing instruction: Issues of theory and method. In P. Mosenthal, L. Tamor, & S. Walmsley (Eds.), *Research on writing: Principles and methods* (pp. 236–264). New York: Longman.

Cooper, M. (1986). The ecology of writing. *College English, 48,* 364–375.

Denzin, N. (1978). *Sociological methods.* New York: McGraw-Hill.

Dewey, J. (1949). *The child and the curriculum and the school and society.* Chicago: University of Chicago Press.

Dyson, A. (1984). Learning to write / learning to do school: Emergent writers' interpretations of school literacy tasks. *Research in the Teaching of English, 18,* 233–264.

Emig, J. (1983). *The web of meaning: Essays on writing, teaching, learning, and thinking.* Upper Montclair, NJ: Boynton/Cook.

Ericson, F. (1982). Taught cognitive learning in its immediate environments: A neglected topic in the anthropology of education. *Anthropology & Education Quarterly, 13(2),* 148–180.

Faigley, L. (1985). Nonacademic writing: The social perspective. In L. Odell & D. Goswami (Eds.), *Writing in nonacademic settings* (pp. 231–248). New York: Guilford Press.

Fish, S. (1980). Interpreting the Variorium. In J. Tompkins (Ed.), *Reader response criticism: From formalism to post-structuralism.* Baltimore: Johns Hopkins University Press.

Florio, S., & Clark, C. (1982). The functions of writing in an elementary classroom. *Research in the Teaching of English, 16,* 115–130.

Flower, L., & Hayes, J. (1981). The pregnant pause: An inquiry into the nature of planning. *Research in the Teaching of English, 15,* 229–244.

Freedman, S. (1984). The registers of student and professional expository writing: Influences on teachers' responses. In R. Beach & L. Bridwell (Eds.), *New directions in composition research* (pp. 334–347). New York: Guilford Press.

Freedman, S. (1985). *The acquisition of written language: Response and revision.* New York: Ablex.

Geertz, C. (1973). *The interpretation of cultures.* New York: Basic Books.

Gilmore, P., & Glatthorn, A. (1982). *Children in and out of school: Ethnography and education.* Washington, DC: Center for Applied Linguistics.

Goffman, E. (1961). *Encounters: Two studies in the sociology of interaction.* New York: Bobbs-Merrill.

Grice, H. (1975). *Logic and conversation.* 1967 William James Lectures, Harvard University. Unpublished manuscript, 1967. Excerpt in Cole and Morgan (Eds.), *Syntax and semantics, Vol. III: Speech acts* (pp. 41–58). New York: Academic Press.

Guba, E. (1978). *Toward a method of naturalistic inquiry in educational evaluation.* Los Angeles: Center for the Study of Evaluation, University of California at Los Angeles.

Gumperz, J. (1971). *Language in social groups.* Stanford, CA: Stanford University Press.

Heath, S. B. (1982). Ethnography in education: Defining the essentials. In P. Gilmore & A. Glatthorn (Eds.), *Children in and out of school: Ethnography and education* (pp. 33–55). Washington, DC: Center for Applied Linguistics.

Heinlein, R. (1961). *Stranger in a strange land*. New York: Putnam.

Herrington, A. (1985). Writing in academic settings: A study of the contexts for writing in two college chemical engineering courses. *Research in the Teaching of English, 19*, 331–359.

Hymes, D. (1972a). Introduction. In C. Cazden, V. P. John, & D. Hymes (Eds.), *Functions of language in the classroom* (pp. xi–lxii). New York: Teachers College Press.

Hymes, D. (1972b). Models of the interaction of language and social life. In J. Gumperz & D. Hymes (Eds.), *Directions in sociolinguistics* (pp. 35–71). New York: Holt, Rinehart, & Winston.

Kantor, K. (1984). Classroom contexts and the development of writing intuitions: An ethnographic case study. In R. Beach & L. Bridwell (Eds.), *New directions in composition research* (pp. 72–94). New York: Guilford.

Langer, J. (1984). The effects of available information on responses to school writing tasks. *Research in the Teaching of English, 18*, 27–44.

Langer, J. (1985). Children's sense of genre: A study of performance on parallel reading and writing tasks. *Written Communication, 2*, 157–188.

Langer, J. (1986). Reading, writing, and understanding: An analysis of the construction of meaning. *Written Communication, 3*, 219–267.

Langer, J., & Applebee, A. (1984). Language, learning, and interaction: A framework for improving the teaching of writing. In A. Applebee (Ed.), *Contexts for learning to write: Studies of secondary school instruction* (pp. 169–182). Norwood, NJ: Ablex.

Lincoln, Y., & Guba, E. (1985). *Naturalistic inquiry*. Beverly Hills, CA: Sage Publications.

Odell, L., & Goswami, D. (1985). *Writing in nonacademic settings*. New York: Guilford Press.

Perl, S. (1979). The composing process of unskilled college writers. *Research in the Teaching of English, 13*, 317–336.

Perry, W. G. (1970). *Forms of intellectual and ethical development in the college years*. New York: Holt, Rinehart, and Winston.

Piaget, J. (1952). *The origins of intelligence in children*. New York: International Universities Press.

Pianko, S. (1979). A description of the composing processes of college freshman writers. *Research in the Teaching of English, 13*, 5–22.

Polanyi, M. (1958). *Personal knowledge: Towards a post-critical philosophy*. Chicago: University of Chicago Press.

Scribner, S. & Cole, M. (1981). Unpackaging literacy. In M. F. Whiteman (Ed.), *Variation in writing: Functional and linguistic-cultural differences* (pp. 71–88). Hillsdale, NJ: Lawrence Erlbaum.

Shaughnessy, M. (1977). *Errors and expectations*. New York: Oxford University Press.

Spradley, J. (1979). *The ethnographic interview*. New York: Holt, Rinehart and Winston.

Spradley, J. (1980). *Participant observation*. New York: Holt, Rinehart and Winston.

Szwed, J. (1981). The ethnography of literacy. In M. F. Whiteman (Ed.), *Variation in writing: Functional and linguistic-cultural differences* (pp. 13–23). Hillsdale, NJ: Lawrence Erlbaum.

Whiteman, M. F. (1981). *Variation in writing: Functional and linguistic-cultural differences*. Hillsdale, NJ: Lawrence Erlbaum.

Williams, J. (1985, March). *Encouraging higher order reasoning through writing in all disciplines*. Paper presented at the Delaware Valley Writing Council-PATHS Conference, Philadelphia.

Questions for Discussion and Journaling

1. What are McCarthy's research questions, and what methods did she use to research answers to these questions? What other methods might she have used, and how might they have altered her findings?

2. McCarthy analyzed Dave's experiences using Grice's "Cooperative Principle." Explain what this principle is and how it helped McCarthy understand Dave's struggles and successes.

3. Why did Dave struggle in his poetry class? What might Dave and his teacher have done to improve Dave's chances of success in that class?

4. Earlier in this chapter, Ann M. Johns described the importance of discourse communities for the ways that people do — and don't — use language, and the difficulties that can occur when students attempt to use academic language. How does the concept of discourse community shed light on Dave's experiences?

5. How do you see McCarthy's work related to the threshold concept emphasized in this chapter that texts and the language discourse communities they create *mediate meaningful activities*? Can you connect this research to the broader threshold concept that people collaborate to get things done with writing?

6. How does Dave's experience writing in college compare with your own? What aspects of writing in college frustrate or puzzle you? What has been hardest for you about writing in college? Why?

7. Do you find the same variance in expectations of your writing from class to class that Dave experiences, or are the expectations you encounter more consistent? What have been your strategies so far for handling any differing expectations you're finding? Does McCarthy's work give you any ideas for different strategies?

Applying and Exploring Ideas

1. For several weeks, keep a writer's journal about your experiences writing in different classrooms. What are you asked to write? What instructions are you given? What feedback are you given? Do you talk with others about the assignments? What genres are you asked to write? How well do you do? Do you understand the grades and comments your teachers give you? At the end of the weeks of journaling, write about your findings and share them with the class.

2. Write a plan for setting up a study like McCarthy's that examines your own experiences across classrooms. Draw on Johns to help you think about designing the study. What do you want to know, and why? What data will you collect and analyze? Write a two-page paper in which you outline the answers to these questions. Note that you aren't *conducting* a study, just imagining how you would *plan* to do so.

META MOMENT What have you learned from McCarthy that can help you in your own college classroom experiences?

Coaches Can Read, Too

An Ethnographic Study of a Football Coaching Discourse Community

SEAN BRANICK

University of Dayton Athletics

Framing the Reading

Sean Branick was a first-year student in Elizabeth Wardle's composition class at the University of Dayton when he wrote this paper. He was enrolled in a special pilot two-semester composition sequence that allowed him to work on this ethnography for a full academic year. His paper was chosen as one of the best from two such courses and printed in a university publication called *Looking for Literacy: Reporting the Research.* Branick's interest in the discourse community of football coaches arose from his own experience as a high school football player and as a student coach in college. He later served as a student football coach at the University of Hawaii at Mānoa and a defensive line intern at Ohio State University, and now he teaches social studies in Gahanna, Ohio.

Branick applies Swales's and Johns's concept of discourse community to a community that many people do not immediately think of as including literacy: football. In this way, his view of literacy is as expansive as Gee's and Mirabelli's. He begins by explaining the characteristics of effective football coaches, and then explains in detail why he believes that coaches constitute a discourse community. But he doesn't stop there. He goes on to identify some special "literacies" that he believes effective coaches possess. Like Mirabelli, Branick's interest in "mundane" sports texts and literacies should help you better understand the underlying threshold concepts of this chapter: football players and coaches use texts and discourse to *make meaning* in order to *do something.* Their texts and the language they create and use together *mediate activities* that are meaningful to them and their fans. Coaches and athletes, too, collaborate to get things done with writing.

Getting Ready to Read

Before you read, do the following activity:

- Ask yourself whether you agree that football coaches constitute a *discourse community* according to Swales's and Johns's definition.

As you read, consider the following question:

- In his introduction, Branick includes the three "moves" that Swales identifies in his CARS model of research introductions, described in Chapter 3 (pp. 61–63) — establishing the territory, establishing a niche, and explaining how he will fill that niche. See if you can identify where each move happens in the text.

THE PROFESSION OF COACHING football is one of the most influential 1 professions that exists in today's world. It is a profession essential to the game whether it is a third-grade team or a pro team. Coaches may range from parents volunteering with a child's youth program to people who dedicate every waking hour to the game. Coaches are made up of both everyday Joes and legends that will live in memory as long as the game is played. It is a profession that requires putting the athletes first: "The main responsibility of the coach is to enable their athletes to attain levels of performance not otherwise achievable" (Short "Role," S29). It is a profession very visible to the public yet it has many behind-the-scenes factors that may be often overlooked that directly relate to success. Among these are the idea of goal-focused coaching, coaching with confidence, and the characteristics of effective coaches.

GOAL-FOCUSED COACHING

Whether on the football field or off the football field, people have always used 2 the process of setting and chasing goals to achieve a desired outcome. A goal is often the universal starting point in many things, including football. Anthony Grant, a sport psychologist, takes an in-depth look at the process of effectively setting a goal in order to achieve a desired result. He talks about how the coach should help facilitate the entire process of using goals, which consists of the following: "an individual sets a goal, develops a plan of action, begins action, monitors his or her performance (through observation and self-reflection), evaluates his or her performance (thus gaining insight) and, based on this evaluation, changes his or her actions to further enhance performance, and thus reach his or her goal" (751).

Grant explains that there are five important parts to this goal-focused coach- 3 ing concept. The first part is setting good goals. The coach must help the player set goals that coincide with his values, are well defined, and are realistically achievable. The second part is developing a strong working relationship between the coach and player. This means that a coach must work to develop an honest relationship to help create an environment conducive to growth where the player will feel comfortable being open and honest with the coach. The third

625

aspect is developing a solution focus, which means helping the athlete develop solutions to help him achieve his goals. The fourth part is managing process. This includes developing action steps and holding the athlete accountable for completing the agreed steps. The fifth and final aspect is achieving the desired outcome.

CHARACTERISTICS OF AN EFFECTIVE COACH

While successful coaches have been exposed to the spotlight throughout history, 4 certain personal qualities of these coaches have emerged as essential to success in the coaching business. Sports psychologist Sandra Short explores five specific qualities of effective coaches. The first of these qualities is being a teacher. This is important because coaches must be able to teach their players about the game and what to do during competition.

The second quality is being organized. Being organized is typically a behind- 5 the-scenes job but it is important because a coach must be organized to keep track of players, competitions, and practice schedules. It is important to organize a plan for success and be able to stick to it. Coaches in team sports must be organized before stepping onto the playing field so that they will know how to handle specific situations such as substitutions and timeout management.

The third quality is being competitive. Coaches must have an inner desire to 6 compete and work to instill that desire to compete in their athletes. Being competitive must be a foundational quality in athletes. It doesn't matter how gifted an athlete is or how much he knows, if he does not have the desire to compete then he will not be successful.

The fourth quality is being a learner. Coaches must continue to learn every 7 day they are on the job. They must learn about their players' personality and they must learn about the newest trends, philosophies, and strategies in the sport that they coach.

The fifth and final quality mentioned is being a friend and mentor. It is 8 important to be a positive role model for their players to look up to. A coach should also offer support and counseling when a player may need it. Fulfilling this role can bring about a deeper level of satisfaction for both the coach and the athlete.

CONFIDENCE IN COACHING

Another aspect of coaching that has been studied is coaching confidence and its 9 relationship with imagery. Sports psychologist Sandra Short argues that imagining being confident helps increase real confidence and the feeling of effectiveness. During pregame preparations, if a coach pictures himself as a confident, successful coach, he is more likely to exude real confidence.

Another point Short made is that coaches who use imagery to put together 10 game plans feel more comfortable with the plans that they come up with. Coaches who make their plans and play out the game using their imaginations are more likely to see strengths and weaknesses in their plans and adjust their plans accordingly.

A third point made is that coaches who imagine in a "cognitive specific way," 11 that is through clear specific examples, will have more confidence in their teaching abilities. In other words, coaches who specifically imagine teaching skills and techniques will acquire confidence in teaching these attributes and therefore be more effective teachers: "The confidence a coach portrays affects the confidence athletes feel. . . . The coach acting confident is one of the most effective strategies coaches can use to increase athletes' 'feelings of efficacy'" (Short, "Relationship" 392).

There have been many articles written on the X's and the O's (specific strategies) of the game. Seminars have been held on the newest strategies. Books have been written on the characteristics of good coaches. Studies have been done on confidence in coaching, the method of setting goals, and the role of the coach in coach-athlete relationships; however scholars have yet to study a coach's ability to read his players and the game as a form of literacy. Many people may think that literacy is not part of the responsibilities that go with coaching. However, they couldn't be farther from the truth. Tony Mirabelli gives an unorthodox definition of literacy, arguing that "Literacy extends beyond individual experiences of reading and writing to include the various modes of communication and situations of any socially meaningful group" (146). He talks about reading people and knowing when to do something to help them as forms of literacy.

> *Many people may think that literacy is not part of the responsibilities that go with coaching. However, they couldn't be farther from the truth.* 12

This idea of multiple literacies can be applied to football coaching staff as 13 well. Coaches need to be able to do so much more than just read. They need to know how to read people. They need to know how to read their players so that they can find out how to get the most out of them. They must also know how to read and teach the plays. The coaches must know their plays because many plays have certain "reads" or "progressions" that the coach must be able to teach the players. Coaches also must be able to read the game so that they can call the best plays that suit certain situations properly.

Coaching as a complex literacy practice has not been examined. How do 14 football coaches, as members of a specific discourse community, go about reading their players and the game in order to get optimal performance and a

627

positive end result? To figure this out, I conducted an ethnographic study on how the coaches at the University of Dayton go about reading people and reading the game.

METHODS

I recorded football coaches at the University of Dayton during their pregame 15 speeches and interviewed those coaches afterwards; I also interviewed a coaching graduate assistant at the University of Cincinnati via email. The recording of the pregame speeches took place before a home game on a Saturday afternoon. In the pregame speeches, Coach Kelly and Coach Whilding attempted to bring out the best in their players. I conducted an interview with Coach Whilding, the offensive coordinator, the following week, and with Coach Kelly, the head coach at the time, during the winter of the following season. Each interview took place in the coaches' offices. The email interview with Coach Painter, the graduate assistant at the University of Cincinnati, took place in the winter as well. In it, I asked similar questions to those used for the University of Dayton coaches. (Interview questions are attached as Appendix A.) I asked questions about how coaches go about reading their players and the game and also about the coach's personal history and motivation for coaching.

I used these methods because they allowed me to take a direct look at what 16 the coaches were saying and then get a look at the thought process behind it. The interviews involved open-ended questions that helped bring out coaching philosophies on many different issues, including the issue of reading their players and the game. This idea of reading players and the game is directly reflective of Tony Mirabelli's idea of multiple literacies.

I analyzed the data collected by applying John Swales's six characteristics of 17 a discourse community. The characteristics I focused on are the set of common goals, the genres, and the specific lexis used.

RESULTS

Because we are studying the multiple literacies of football coaches by looking at 18 coaching as a discourse community, it will be clearest to separate the results for the characteristics of a discourse community and the results for multiple literacies.

Characteristics of a Discourse Community

A football coaching staff is an excellent example of a discourse community. The 19 characteristics are clearly defined and easy to recognize. The clearest characteristics to pick up on are the goals, lexis, and genres.

Goals. Coach Kelly and Coach Whilding helped make up one of the most 20 successful coaching staffs in the history of division 1 college football. This is mainly due to their ability to set and achieve goals, both team and personal goals. There is always the goal of winning the game. The University of Dayton had goal charts with a list of about 10 goals for every game, for offense, defense, and special teams. They use these charts with stickers to help monitor how well they achieve these goals and figure out the goals they need to work on.

Coaches also have many individual goals. Many of these goals include get- 21 ting the most out of their players physically and mentally. Coaches always strive to make their players push themselves to heights that they never thought they could reach. Coaches also have the goal of seeing their players develop as people. Coach Whilding talked about how he enjoyed seeing his players succeed in real-life situations after football: "It's good to see those guys mature and go on and get good jobs and raise families and be very responsible people in their communities."

Along with these goals, there are many rewards. While many big time college 22 coaches may receive a hefty paycheck, Coach Whilding explained that some of the rewards are not monetary: "I know guys who just hate to get up in the morning and hate to go to work, and I have just never felt that way."

Lexis. Another important characteristic of discourse communities is that 23 there is a specialized lexis, or set of terms that is unique to the community. There are many terms that are involved in football coaching communities that may not make sense to most people but, among a team, make perfect sense and help the community better do its work and achieve its goals.

Some of the more common terms might make more sense to the public, such 24 as touchdown or tackle. There are, however, terms that might not make sense to anybody outside the team. Examples of these may be passing routes such as "Y corner," "Follow," or "Green Gold." They could also be things like blocking schemes such as "Bob," "Sam," or "Combo." There are terms for everything, and it takes many repetitions during practice to learn all of this lexis. The lexis helps save time because one word may describe several actions. This lexis is also important because the lexis varies from team to team, so if the opposing team hears it, they will not know what it means. Without many hours spent preparing and practicing, the players and the coaches would not have this advantage in communication.

Genres. A genre is a text that helps facilitate communication between peo- 25 ple, and in this example all communication takes place within the discourse community. There are certain genres that help a football team and football coaching staff operate efficiently. Genres often use the unique lexis that was previously mentioned.

Perhaps the most essential genre is the playbook. The playbook is created by 26 the coaches and shows all the plays that they plan on running and the proper way that the players are supposed to run them. The players get the playbooks

629

at the beginning of the season and need to learn the plays before they are "installed" during practice. The players must guard these books and make sure that no members from opposing teams get the information. The playbook is essential to success because there are many plays and without a playbook the players would become confused and make mistakes that could be disastrous to the outcome of the football game.

Another genre is a scouting report. The scouting report is also made up by 27 the coaches for the players. It shows the other team's personnel, what plays they like to run, and when they like to run them. It helps the players know what to expect going into the game so they can prepare accordingly. The coaches will usually spend the day after a game putting together a scouting report and distribute the report to their players at the beginning of the week.

A third genre is a play-calling sheet. This is made up by the coaches and is only 28 for the coaches, mainly the offensive coordinator. The play-calling sheet helps the coach remember all the plays that they have and what situation that the plays are favorable in. Without a play-calling sheet, the coach would have to remember the names of all the plays on his own, and that is something that could be a distraction to calling the proper plays, and could effectively cost a team a game.

Now that we understand what exactly a football coaching discourse com- 29 munity is and what it is made up of, we can learn exactly how the concept of literacy applies to this group.

Multiple Literacies

Many people do not see the concept of literacy as something that would apply 30 to a football coaching staff. However, Mirabelli defines literacy as not just reading and writing but things such as reading people. He uses the example of a waiter reading his customers in his article. This same idea can be applied to a football coaching discourse community.

Interpersonal Literacies

One of the literacies for a football coach is the ability to read the players. This 31 can be described as an interpersonal literacy. There are two types of reading the coach needs to do. First, coaches must be able to read players to know when they are ready to play; second, coaches must be able to read their players to know how to motivate them properly to get the most out of them.

There are different characteristics to look for when it comes to knowing when 32 players are ready to play. Two are comfort and knowledge. Coach Painter from Cincinnati emphasized player comfort: "Knowing their personality is a big part of reading them. When a player is ready to play they will be in a comfortable mode. Whether that is listening to music, jumping around, or even reading, when a player is loose and comfortable they are ready to compete." Coach Kelly emphasized knowledge of the game: "Do they have the knowledge to perform? What we try to do is put them in as many stressful situations as possible from a mental point of view to see if they can handle that in practice. If they can handle that in practice . . . then we cut 'em loose and let 'em play." He went on to state that another way of finding out whether or not a player has that knowledge and is ready to play is by sitting down one on one with him. Coach Kelly elaborates, "I can get a good feel for a young man when I'm sitting in a room with him, watching practice or game tape, asking him questions. . . . If there is a lot of hesitation or if they are totally off then I know we're not there yet."

Coaches must be able to read their players in order to motivate them prop- 33 erly. Every coach emphasized that each player is unique and will respond to different types of motivation in different ways. This can be done by taking an emotional, fiery approach or a calm and collected approach. Coach Kelly emphasized the importance of motivation, explaining,

> That's a key element in becoming a coach. Can they motivate? Can they identify what makes this guy go? Can you hit that button and how fast can you hit that button? The sooner you find that motivational tool the better off you're going to be. You can tell immediately if it works or not.

Finding out what motivates each individual is no easy task, but Coach Whild- 34 ing explains, "You have to be able to understand 'How do I reach that player . . . that young man?' And there are a lot of ways to do that. Through the years, you figure it out." He went more in depth and explained that you have to be able to reach everybody as an individual player and that there are many types of players: "There are some that like to yell and scream and get excited. There are others who don't play well like that, who are a little quieter and keep it within themselves but are still very motivated." Coach Painter from Cincinnati points out the balance between these two opposing motivational styles: "You have to use both and know when to use them. . . . Too much fire and you will lose the team and its effectiveness. Too much calm and you will lose control over the environment."

These explanations show that reading players to know when they are ready 35 to play and reading players to know how to motivate them are two very difficult parts of the coaching profession. They require balance, patience, and perseverance. Coach Whilding sums it up, saying, sometimes "it just doesn't work and you find out you have to just use another method."

Situational Literacies

A second essential coaching literacy is being able to read a game. The coaches 36 must be able to actively read a game in order to put their players in the best possible situations to attempt to win the game. Reading a game can be broken down into two categories: pregame and in-game.

The week leading up to a game is a week filled with preparation. Preparation 37 is important because it "will allow you the ability to put players in the places they need to be at the times they need to be there to make plays. From there it's out of your hands" (Painter). Coaches study the opposing team in and out and then formulate a game plan. They consolidate this game plan along with information on the opposition into a packet, make copies of the packet, and distribute the copies to the team. This helps players stay on the same page as the coaches and prepare mentally for the game. This mental preparation will make players feel more comfortable as to what to expect during the game: "You do a lot of preparation during the week, getting ready for the week. We watch a lot of tape. You have to have an idea of what their base defense is, what their coverage is going to be, when they're going to blitz, what down they're going to blitz, what are their favorite ones" (Whilding). Coach Kelly elaborated on the importance of preparation by explaining that you have to get a good idea of what the coach likes to do in certain situations and when you feel like you know the opposing coach, it becomes a game of feel: "It's really important to me to know what's going on in that coach's mind" (Kelly).

It is also important to be able to read the game in real time. Ways of reading 38 and reacting during the game may be as simple as knowing when to call timeouts, call certain plays, or make substitutions, or may be more complicated such as knowing what type of halftime adjustments to make. Coach Whilding explains that a key aspect of making these adjustments is that "You have to get a feel on the field for what is working, and I think that's something you develop through the years . . . and it changes from week to week, from year to year sometimes, depending on your personnel. You have to know your personnel. What you're good at, what you're not good at."

Because coaches don't always have the best view and are not in a position to 39 be heard by all the players when they are on the field, sometimes they will delegate this responsibility to their players. Coach Painter explains, "Our players are allowed a small amount of freedom on the fly. We ask our quarterback to check us out of plays when necessary, but we have established what and when he can make such checks." These checks (changing the play at the line) give the team a better chance of calling a play that will be more likely to be successful.

Halftime adjustments are also very important. Sometimes a team will come 40 out in the first half and do something that was not expected or maybe a certain strategy is not working the way the coach expected it to. The coaches will come together at the end of the half and discuss possible changes that might help the team. They then use halftime to explain these changes and make sure everyone is on the same page. This can turn into a chess match because sometimes one team will adjust to something that another team does, but at the same time the other team changes up what they were doing. Coach Painter explains it best by saying, "Your opponent is going to adjust, if you do not then you will be at a disadvantage. No matter how much preparation you have put in, there are going to be things you did not expect. This is where your on the field adjustments give you the final edge."

Relationship Between Textual, Situational, and Interpersonal Literacies

Coaching functions as a discourse community that uses a variety of complex 41 literacies—textual, interpersonal, and situational. All of these literacies can be seen functioning together in a game situation.

Before the game the coach had to spend time evaluating his players and 42 deciding who was going to play. To do this he used interpersonal literacies. Now fast forward to a game situation. Let's say that the team we are looking at is on offense. While the players are playing the game, there are assistant coaches in the press box watching to see how the defense reacts to what the offense does. They are looking for any keys or tips that could give the offense an advantage. This is an example of situational literacies. The assistant coaches in the press box will then communicate what they see to the coach calling the offense. This process involves using lexis. The coach will then process what the assistant coaches told him and will look at his play-calling sheet and decide what play to run. The play-calling sheet is an example of a genre. He will then tell the quarterback what play to run. The name of the play consists of lexis as well. The quarterback will tell the team the play and then they will line up. The quarterback will then look at the defense and see if anything needs to be changed. This is an example of situational literacies. If he decides to "check" (change) the play based on what he sees in the defense, he will use lexis to do so. The quarterback will then call "hike" (lexis) and the ball will be snapped and the play will be run with the hopes of scoring a touchdown, which is the goal on any given play.

CONCLUSION

The world of coaching is more complicated than it may seem to the public 43 eye. Whether it is looking at some of the characteristics of a coaching community or looking at the tasks that coaches partake in, such as reading players and the game, there are still many characteristics and responsibilities that are unexplored to those outside of these communities. After looking in depth at some of the behind-the-scenes factors that go into coaching, I hope to have helped increase knowledge on the literacy aspects involved in coaching. I hope this helps spark interest in the connection between literacy and sports. This connection will now help people have a better sense of empathy with what the coaches are thinking when they make a specific call on the field or partake in an action off the field, and hopefully I have brought people closer to being able to answer the common question asked at any sporting event: "What was that coach thinking?!"

Works Cited

Grant, Anthony M. "The Goal-Focused Coaching Skills Questionnaire: Preliminary Findings." *Social Behavior & Personality: An International Journal* 35.6 (2007): 751–60. Print.

Hasbrouck, Jan and Carolyn Denton. "Student-Focused Coaching: A Model for Reading Coaches." *Reading Teacher* 60.7 (2007): 690–93. Print.

Mirabelli, Tony. "Learning to Serve: The Language and Literacy of Food Service Workers." *What They Don't Learn in School.* Ed. Jabari Mahiri. New York: Peter Lang, 2004: 143–62. Print.

Short, Sandra E. "Role of the Coach in the Coach-Athlete Relationship." Spec. issue of *Lancet* 366 (2005): S29–S30. Print.

——— . "The Relationship Between Efficacy Beliefs and Imagery Use in Coaches." *The Sport Psychologist* 19.4 (2005): 380–94. Print.

Swales, John. "The Concept of Discourse Community." *Genre Analysis: English in Academic and Workplace Settings.* Boston: Cambridge UP, 1990: 21–32. Print.

APPENDIX A: INTERVIEW QUESTIONS FOR COACHES

Interpersonal Literacies

1. How do you tell when a player is ready or not ready to play? Are there specific things that you look for (body language and attitude, etc.) or is it more intuitive?

2. In what ways do you go about motivating your players? Do you prefer a calm or a fiery approach? How did your coaches go about motivating you when you played? Do you feel like you have become an effective motivator?

3. Do you focus more on motivating players during the week or during a pregame speech? When do you think it is more effective? Are there any specific examples that stick out when you made an attempt to motivate a player and it was either very successful or unsuccessful? If you were unsuccessful how did you change your approach?

4. Would you consider your approach to correcting athletes more of positive reinforcement or negative reinforcement? Do you think that players respond better to one method than the other? Is it better to correct mistakes publicly or privately? How do the players react to each method?

Situational Literacies

1. What do you feel are the most important factors to reading and calling a game? Do you use any specific methods to help you mediate reading the game (scripting plays, play-calling sheet with specific situations)?

2. Do you put any of this on your players (system of checks or audibles, plays that are run differently depending on the defense's look)?

3. How much of the outcome of a game do you feel is attributed to pregame coaching preparations (game planning, watching film)?

4. How important are in-game decisions such as halftime adjustments, substitutions, and when to gamble on big plays? Do you go with the overall feel of the game or do you look for specific details when it comes to making a game-time decision?

Questions for Discussion and Journaling

1. Before you began to read, you were asked to consider whether you think football coaches are a discourse community. After reading Branick's paper, have you changed your opinion in any way? If so, what did he say that got you to think differently?

2. Branick's methods include analyzing the coaches' discourse community using John Swales's six characteristics of a discourse community. How effectively does he conduct this analysis? What, if anything, would you change or expand, and why?

3. Branick claims, "There have been many articles written on the X's and O's . . . of the game . . . however scholars have yet to study a coach's ability to read his players and the game as a form of literacy" (para. 12). Does Branick convince you that these abilities are, in fact, a form of literacy? Explain why or why not.

Applying and Exploring Ideas

1. Brainstorm some groups that you think might be discourse communities but which, like football coaches, might not immediately come to mind as such. Why do you think they wouldn't be immediately understood as discourse communities?

2. Pick one of the groups you listed in question 1 and try to sketch out quickly, with a partner or by yourself, whether they meet Swales's six characteristics of a discourse community as described by Branick.

3. Listing characteristics of a discourse community is only the first step in a project. The next step is identifying a genuine question about some aspect of the discourse community, as Branick does here. What else would you like to explore about the discourse community you identified in question 2?

META MOMENT   How does Branick help you see the relevance of your work in this class to parts of your life that you had not thought about as being related to writing and literacy? Does he share any conclusions or insights that you can apply to your own experiences?

Identity, Authority, and Learning to Write in New Workplaces

Courtesy of Nkosi Shanga

ELIZABETH WARDLE

Framing the Reading

Elizabeth Wardle is the Howe Professor and Director of the Roger & Joyce Howe Center for Writing Excellence at Miami University. She was finishing her Ph.D. at about the time that Ann M. Johns was retiring; you can thus think of her work as growing from the work of the scholars you have read so far. She is interested in how people learn to write, not as children but as adults moving among different discourse communities or **activity systems**. The following article is one that she researched as a Ph.D. student. While in graduate school, Wardle was asked to use language that did not feel "right" or "natural" to her. She struggled to find the right **register** and **lexis** for her writing, and writing in "academic" ways seemed to stifle her creative voice. You can see, then, why she would be interested in researching someone else who was struggling to enculturate in a new activity system.

This article is the result of that study. It describes a new employee, fresh out of college, trying to communicate with a new workplace community and failing — miserably. The reasons he failed included a lack of authority in the new activity system, a specific form of rebellion against the values of that activity system that Wardle calls *non-participation*, and a sense of identity that conflicts with the new activity system. Wardle applies the frame of activity theory, which has some similarities to discourse community theories. It provides a lens (which Wardle outlines) for looking at how groups of people engage in shared activities to accomplish their shared goals, relying on tools, conventions/rules, and division of labor, among other things.

Like Mirabelli, McCarthy, and Branick in this chapter, Wardle is applying theory to a common situation in order to help readers better understand how people use texts and discourse to make meaning together, and where and why they sometimes run into trouble trying to do that. In particular, Wardle uses the frame provided by **activity theory** to help explain the problems that the new employee, Alan, had when he began a new job. Activity theory is often a particularly helpful way of looking at how people collaborate to get things done with writing — this chapter's central threshold concept.

Wardle, Elizabeth. "Identity, Authority, and Learning to Write in New Workplaces." *Enculturation*, vol. 5, no. 2, 2004, www.enculturation.net/5_2/wardle.html.

This is because activity theory examines social organizations of people ("subjects") attempting to achieve shared objects or goals through collaboration (division of labor) and use of particular tools, including writing.

Getting Ready to Read

Before you read, do at least one of the following activities:

- Think over your time in college and write a few paragraphs about whether your identity has been changed by your college experiences to date, and, if it has, *how* it has changed. How can you explain the changes (or lack of change)?
- Make a list of terms or phrases you're using now that you weren't at the beginning of your college experience. Do you associate any of this new language with participation in new groups (discourse communities or activity systems)?

As you read, consider the following questions:

- How does Wardle describe being a "newcomer" to an activity system? Is there anything familiar about her description that you recognize from your own experience?
- How is the idea of an *activity system* different from *Discourse* and *discourse communities,* as discussed in previous readings in this chapter?

DESPITE THE MEDIA'S CONTINUED representation of communication as "utilitarian and objective" (Bolin), and the acceptance of this view by much of the public and even by many academics, research in rhetoric and composition over the past twenty years has moved toward a much more complex view of communication. Of particular interest to professional communication specialists is research suggesting that learning to write in and for new situations and workplaces is complex in ways that go far beyond texts and cognitive abilities. This research posits that for workers to be successfully enculturated into new communities of practice[1] (Lave and Wenger) or activity systems (Engeström; Russell, "Rethinking" and "Activity Theory"), including learning to write in ways that are appropriate to those new communities, neophytes must learn and conform to the conventions, codes, and genres of those communities (Bazerman; Berkenkotter, Huckin, and Ackerman; Berkenkotter and Huckin; Bizzell). However, *when and how much* each neophyte must conform largely depends on how much authority and cultural capital[2] the neophyte possesses or cultivates to accomplish work effectively. Additionally, issues of identity and values are

> *Learning to write in and for new situations and workplaces is complex in ways that go far beyond texts and cognitive abilities.*

important factors in neophytes' abilities and willingness to learn to write in and for new workplaces, as they must choose between ways of thinking and writing with which they are comfortable and new ways that seem foreign or at odds with their identities and values (Doheny-Farina; Doheny-Farina and Odell). Researchers who examine issues of identity and authority as important aspects of communicating in workplace settings find that workers' identities are bound up in myriad ways with the genres they are asked to appropriate (Dias et al.; Dias and Paré; Paré). According to Anis Bawarshi, "a certain genre replaces or . . . adds to the range of possible selves that writers have available to them" (105).

As composition widens its focus beyond academic writing, it is increasingly 2 important to consider what it means to write in the workplace. Not only will such knowledge help us prepare students for the writing beyond the classroom, but, as Bolin points out, those of us working in rhetoric and composition must continue to respond to complaints by the media and general public that we have not fulfilled our responsibilities and "polished" students' language use so that they can convey information "clearly." We can respond to these complaints more effectively when we better understand the ways in which writing is bound up with issues of identity and authority. While we recognize the importance of identity and authority issues in the process of enculturating new workers, we do not always fully understand how these issues influence their writing.

Here I first outline theories of identity and authority that are useful in 3 understanding how newcomers learn to write in and for new situations. The socio-historic theoretical perspective I offer draws on research from two groups: compositionists who focus on cultural-historical activity theory[3] (Russell, "Rethinking" and "Activity Theory"; Prior; Dias et al.) and sociologists who study apprenticeship (Lave and Wenger; Wenger). Combined, these lines of research expand genre theory (Bawarshi; Russell, "Rethinking") and describe the complexities of learning to write, both in school and the workplace (Dias et al.; Dias and Paré; Prior). The socio-historic view usefully illuminates the construction of subject positions and subjectivities specifically within institutions and disciplines.

Second, I illustrate some of the difficulties inherent in writing and identity 4 formation by telling the story of one new worker who struggled with written conventions and codes in his new workplace largely because of issues of identity and authority: how he saw himself versus how other members of this workplace community saw him. Most importantly, I argue that rather than assisting in the new worker's enculturation, members of the community expected a type of servitude: they perceived him not as a community member but as a tool, an identity that he fought strongly against.

IDENTITY

To tease out relationships between identity and writing in the workplace, we need theories that consider the workplace as a legitimate and important influence on subject formation. Socio-historic theories provide one such perspective and describe identity construction within institutions. Like other postmodern theories, socio-historic theories see identity—the "subject"—as a complex "construction of the various signifying practices . . . formed by the various discourses, sign systems, that surround her" (Berlin 18). However, socio-historic theories view the subject as not only *constructed* by signifying practices but also as *constructing* signifying practices: "writers' desires are [not] completely determined, as evidenced by the fact that textual instantiations of a genre are rarely if ever exactly the same" (Bawarshi 91). Socio-historic theories also provide specific tools for analyzing the "levers" within institutions, allowing for a detailed examination of power and the formation of subject positions. Activity theory (Cole; Cole and Engeström; Cole and Scribner; Engeström; Russell, "Rethinking" and "Activity Theory"), for example, which focuses on the relationships among shared activities within communities and individual participants' sometimes competing understandings of motives, conventions, and divisions of labor for carrying out the activities, provides a framework for understanding the interactions of individuals, groups, and texts that enables researchers to illustrate the complex interactions among various aspects of an activity system (see Figure 1). 5

Activity theorists such as David Russell have also argued the importance of the relationship between writing and identity: as we encounter genres mediating new activity systems, we must determine whether we can and / or must appropriate those genres, thus expanding our involvement within those systems. We must also consider whether expanding involvement in one system forces us away from other activity systems we value—away from "activity systems of family, neighborhood, and friends that construct ethnic, racial, gender, and class identit(ies)" ("Rethinking" 532). Writers can sometimes "challenge the genre positions and relations available to them," thus changing genres rather than choosing between the genres and their various activity systems (Bawarshi 97). However, socio-historic theories do not view such resistance as the result of self-will or "inherent forces within each human being that love liberty, seek to enhance their own powers or capacities, or strive for emancipation" (Rose 35), but rather suggest that "resistance arises from the contradictions individuals experience in their multiple subject positions" (Bawarshi 100). As writers shape and change genres, the power of those genres also shapes and enables writers' identities (Bawarshi 97). 6

Sociologist Etienne Wenger's theory of communities of practice (shaped, initially, with Jean Lave) is particularly useful for describing workplace 7

639

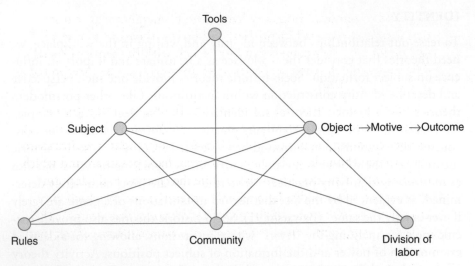

Figure 1 Activity System Triangle (*Information from Engeström: Learning by Expanding*)

enculturation as it is affected by and as it affects written practices. Wenger specifically focuses on matters of identity within *workplace* groups and activities, describing identity as a "negotiated experience . . . a layering of events of participation and reification by which our experience and its social interpretation inform each other" (149). According to Wenger, "layers build upon each other to produce our identity as a very complex interweaving of participative experience and reificative projections" (151). To "find their own unique identities" within new organizations (Wenger 156), newcomers must choose levels and types of engagement; they must find modes of belonging. Wenger describes three interrelated modes of belonging: engagement, imagination, and alignment.

- *Engagement* entails defining a "common enterprise" that newcomers and old-timers pursue together to develop "interpersonal relationships" and "a sense of interacting trajectories that shape identities in relation to one another" (184). While engagement can be positive, "a lack of mutuality in the course of engagement creates relations of marginality that can reach deeply into [newcomers'] identities" (193).

- *Imagination*, "a process of expanding . . . self by transcending . . . time and space and creating new images of the world and [self]" (176), entails newcomers "locating [their] engagement in a broader system . . . defining a trajectory that connects what [they] are doing to an extended identity . . . [and] assuming the meaning of foreign artifacts and actions" (185). While imagination can lead to a positive mode of belonging, it can also "be disconnected and ineffective . . .

it can be so removed from any lived form of membership that it detaches [newcomers'] identit[ies] and leaves [them] in a state of uprootedness." Newcomers can lose "touch with the sense of social efficacy by which [their] experience of the world can be interpreted as competence" (178).

- *Alignment* entails "negotiating perspectives, finding common ground . . . defining broad visions and aspirations . . . [and] walking boundaries . . . reconciling diverging perspectives" (186–87). Alignment "requires share- able artifacts / boundary objects able to create fixed points around which to coordinate activities. It can also require the creation and adoption of broader discourses that help reify the enterprise and by which local actions can be interpreted as fitting within a broader framework" (187). However, alignment "can be a violation of [a person's] sense of self that crushes [their] identity" (181).

To fully participate, according to Wenger, new workers must find ways to engage in the work that other community members do, including the writing they do; newcomers must be able to imagine their own work — and writing — as being an important part of a larger enterprise. And they must be comfortable that the larger enterprise and its smaller components — down to the writing conventions of that community — are compatible with the identities they envision for themselves. Joining new workplace communities, then, is not simply a matter of learning new skills but also of fielding new calls for identity construction. This understanding of identity suggests that people *enact* and *negotiate* identities in the world over time: "Identity is dynamic (Hecht, 1993), and it is something that is presented and re-presented, constructed and reconstructed in interaction (including written communication)" (Rubin 9). 8

At times, however, participation in new communities requires accepting for oneself identities that are at odds with the values of other communities to which one belongs (Lave and Wenger; Russell, "Rethinking"). One way newcomers reconcile the competing demands of various communities is to choose to participate in some aspects of a new community and not others. Such choices are a source of power in that "power derives from belonging as well as from exercising control over what we belong to" (Wenger 207). In addition, choices about participation impact newcomers' emerging identities within communities of practice. For example, the choice of non-participation can lead to marginalization within the workplace (Wenger 167). Identity formation in any new community, then, is a negotiation in which newcomers have some measure of "control over the meanings in which [they] are invested" and can "assert [their] identities as productive of meaning" (Wenger 188, 208) — even if they do so by refusing to participate in some workplace activities. 9

Achieving enculturation in workplace communities requires neophytes to 10 engage in new practices—including new *written* practices. Some new written practices may be opposed to newcomers' values and ethics; others may simply be foreign to them; still others may ask them to give up some measure of authority to which they believe they are entitled. The resultant struggles will often be visible in their written practices. If new workers fail to write in ways that a workplace community of practice recognizes as effective and appropriate, the reasons may be related to identity rather than ability: "Stylistic options 'leak' clues about writers' social identities. Rhetorical choices help writers construct the social identities they wish to project in given writing episodes" (Rubin 4). Thus, failing to write in ways communities establish as appropriate can be a form of resistance that "does not arise from ignorance of standard forms [but rather] entails considerable language awareness" (Rubin 7). On the other hand, new workers may not be consciously aware that their writing choices are matters of identification: "marking social identity in writing is . . . oftentimes quite below the focal awareness of the writer" (8). Because each individual "is heterogeneously made up of various competing discourses, conflicted and contradictory scripts . . . our consciousness [is] anything but unified" (Berlin 18).

AUTHORITY

As Wenger's theory implies, authority (like identity) is continually negotiated 11 within communities of practice. Authority is bestowed by institutions, can be just as easily withdrawn by those same institutions or its members, and must be maintained through appropriate expressions of authority (Bourdieu). Bruce Lincoln argues that authority is best understood in relational terms "as the effect of a posited, perceived, or institutionally ascribed asymmetry between speaker and audience that permits certain speakers to command not just the attention but the confidence, respect, and trust of their audience, or . . . to make audiences act *as if* this were so" (4). When speakers possess authority, exercising that authority "need not involve argumentation and may rest on the naked assertion that the identity of the speaker warrants acceptance of the speech" (5). Those listening accept the speaker's pronouncement because the speaker *is who she is*. At any given time, however, faith in a speaker's authority can be suspended (either momentarily or forever) if "an explanation is requested . . ." because "the relation of trust and acceptance characteristic of authority is suspended, at least temporarily, in that moment" (6). Authority, then, is an intangible quality granted to persons through institutions, which renders their pronouncements as accepted by those in that institution's communities of practice, but which must be maintained through individuals' speech and actions.

Conversely, a person can understand clearly how to speak in ways that are 12 acceptable in particular circumstances, but if not endowed with some recognized institutional authority, all the relevant and appropriate words in the world will not command it: "authority comes to language from outside. . . . Language at most represents this authority, manifests and symbolizes it" (Bourdieu 109). Bourdieu, while not specifically explaining enculturation, suggests that authority may be a kind of "social magic," dependent upon the "social position of the speaker," and reinforced by her ability to appropriately adjust her speech acts:

> Most of the conditions that have to be fulfilled in order for a performative utterance to succeed come down to the question of the appropriateness of the speaker—or, better still, his social function—and of the discourse he utters . . . it must be uttered by the person legitimately licensed to so do . . . it must be uttered in a legitimate situation . . . in front of legitimate receivers . . . [and] it must be enunciated according to the legitimate forms (syntactic, phonetic, etc.). (Bourdieu 111–12)

Thus, if the neophyte is granted some measure of authority by an institu- 13 tion but does not quickly learn the appropriate speech conventions of her new community of practice, she may soon lose the authority with which she began. While newcomers to a community normally experience a "grace period" for adopting community practices, it does not last forever and soon the neophyte must express her authority in her new community appropriately: "[L]earning to become a legitimate participant in a community involves learning how to talk (and be silent) in the manner of full participants" (Lave and Wenger 105).

If we understand writing as one tool among many through which knowledge, 14 identity, and authority are continually negotiated, then we must view learning to write in new ways as a complex and often messy network of tool-mediated human relationships best explored in terms of the social and cultural practices that people bring to their shared uses of tools. If we accept these assumptions, we find ourselves faced with several questions: What happens when new workers find that to "get along" in a new workplace they must accept basic assumptions about what is valuable and appropriate that are contrary to their own—or that, in fact, degrade them to the status of an object or tool? What happens when a new worker's assumptions are frequently made obvious to the community, and those assumptions fly in the face of accepted ways of doing things?

LEARNING TO WRITE IN A NEW WORKPLACE: ALAN'S STORY

My story of "Alan"—a computer support specialist who did not learn / choose 15 to write in ways his humanities department colleagues (primarily professors and graduate students) found appropriate and legitimate—illustrates answers to some of the questions about identity and authority as they intersect with writing in the workplace. For seven months, I observed and interviewed Alan, a new computer specialist in a humanities department at a large Midwestern university. I also collected 140 email messages he wrote and many others that were written to him and spent time in public computer labs listening as people discussed their computer problems with Alan. Finally, near the end of the study, I conducted a written survey with all members of the humanities department regarding their use of computers and technology and their awareness of various initiatives Alan had discussed with them via email.

Alan and the other members of the humanities department were constantly 16 at cross purposes—he did not write in ways the community members saw as appropriate, and he did not view their conventions as ones he should adopt, given his position in the community. Most importantly, the community of practice did not appear to view him as a fledging member but rather as an object—a tool enabling them to get work done. His discursive choices can be viewed as an attempt to reject the identity of tool and to appropriate authority for himself. Thus, Alan's story serves to illustrate some of the complexities associated with learning to write in new workplaces.

Who Is Alan and What Is His Place in the Humanities Department?

Alan was a 23-year-old white male who received a B.A. in art and design from 17 a large Midwestern university. He became interested in computers as an undergraduate and as his interest in computers grew, he performed two computer-related work-study jobs on campus. He decided he liked working with computers and looked for a computer job when he graduated. Alan's first professional position was as computer support specialist responsible for several thousand "users" in various locations at the same university from which he graduated. He was unhappy in this position, primarily because he felt his supervisor did not give him enough responsibility, instead assigning the most difficult tasks to student workers who had been in the department for a long time. He left this job for another in an academic humanities department within the same university, again as a computer support specialist.

In the academic department, Alan was the sole computer support special- 18 ist, surrounded by faculty members with varying computer abilities. While no one else performed a job similar to his, the department included other support staff—all women, primarily administrative assistants—and Alan supervised one student worker several hours per week. Alan's supervisor, the department chair (a white male in his early fifties with a Ph.D. and numerous publications and awards), initially left most computer-related decisions to Alan, though the chair's collaborative administrative style made the division of labor unclear to newcomers. A Computer Resources Committee also interacted regularly with Alan, but whether they had authority over him was unclear. The mentoring he received was fairly hands-off, resembling what Lave and Wenger call "benign community neglect" (93), a situation that left Alan to find his own way, which he saw as a vote of confidence.

What Was Alan's View of Himself and His Authority?

Alan's sense of what it meant to fill a support staff position was very different 19 from the faculty's sense. He left his previous position because it had not allowed him much responsibility, his supervisors "relied on students' work more than" his, and he felt he "was getting no respect." This previous experience strongly informed his understanding of his current job. Because Alan had some measure of institutional authority by way of the cultural capital associated with technical knowledge, Alan did not initially have to prove himself knowledgeable or competent in the ways many new workers do. He was immediately ascribed authority and respect due to his assumed technical expertise in a place where such expertise was rare. When I asked Alan to name and describe his position he replied: "I am basically a systems administrator, which means I am God here. Anywhere in this department. Except for with the department chair." This continued to be Alan's attitude during his tenure in the department. He often indicated that there was no one "above him" but the department chair. During his fourth week in the position, Alan told me he "couldn't believe how much authority" he had, "how high up in the computer world responsibility-wise" he was. He stressed that his title put "only one other person above" him in the university or the department.

Alan's sense of his level of authority was evident in the way he talked about 20 the faculty members in the department. He described the faculty members as "just users; nobodies [who] use the computers I set up." He indicated they were beneath him: "I put myself down on their level." To Alan, the faculty were simply "users" of his tools. He did not seem to understand—or care about—the faculty members' work or how his tools enabled them to do that work. His focus was on what *he* did: making machines work. His comments illustrate his attempt to find a mode of belonging through imagination; unfortunately, he imagined an identity for himself fairly removed from the reality of the situation.

In reality, he was hired in a support staff position, as a "tool" to fix things 21 the faculty needed. The faculty clearly viewed Alan as support personnel. They were happiest when things worked smoothly and when Alan's work hummed along invisibly and successfully behind the scenes. When his assistance was required, they expected him to appear immediately; some faculty even went so far as to copy email messages to the chair and computer resources committee to ensure that Alan knew there would be repercussions if he did not appear when called upon. Alan's view of everyone else as "just users" came across clearly in his writing (which primarily took place via email) and eventually called his competence into question such that department members often failed to respond to him, were ignorant of his initiatives to help them, and laughed at him and his emails. This misalignment between Alan's imagined role for himself and the role imagined for him by others led to a lack of the positive engagement Wenger argues may help newcomers enculturate; Alan and the other members

645

of the humanities department were not actively engaging or mutually negotiating their work together.

How Did Alan Relate to the Department in Writing?

A number of discourse conventions existed in the department that could have 22 afforded Alan further authority. Had he adopted these conventions, Alan could have achieved alignment with the department, for example using emails as "boundary objects able to create fixed points around which to coordinate activities" (Wenger 187). Alan did not adopt the conventions of the department, however. Although it is possible for writers "to enact slightly different intentions" and "resist the ideological pull of genres in certain circumstances," their resistance will only be "recognized and valued as resistance and not misinterpretation, or worse, ignorance" if it is "predicated on one's knowledge of a genre" (Bawarshi 92). Alan's written interactions with the department were seen not as resistance but as ignorance, and identified him as an outsider without authority.

One of the conventions Alan did not follow when he wrote involved the 23 department's approximately 15 or 20 listservs, each reaching a specific audience. Tailoring emails to a particular audience was an accepted writing convention in the activity system. During the beginning of each fall semester, listserv addresses were sent out and department members were encouraged to use the list that most directly reached their message's audience. Alan chose to use the list that reached all department members for nearly every email he wrote — despite the fact that he administered all the lists and knew lists more tailored to his messages existed. His email activity did not "fit within [the] broader structures," demonstrating his lack of alignment with the department (Wenger 173).

A survey of the department I conducted indicated that Alan's lack of audi- 24 ence awareness and tailoring had negative consequences for his identity in the department: most people were unaware of his efforts to better their computer system because they either did not read or did not remember reading the information he sent out via email. In other words, the members of the department did not see Alan as engaged in work with and for them. For example, much of his time was spent setting up a new departmental computer network that would benefit all department members by providing them private, disk-free storage space. He discussed this in emails many times, but usually in emails that mentioned a number of other items directed at more specialized audiences. As a result, over half the survey respondents did not know he was setting up a new network. People indicated on the survey that they stopped reading an email if the first item of business did not relate to them.

Other accepted departmental conventions governed the content and 25 style of emails. The community members were highly literate, hyper-aware language users, in the traditional sense of the terms, who valued professional, grammatically correct, Standard English in written communication. The unspoken convention that email within the department be grammatically correct was pervasive and widely practiced in the community. Abiding by this convention was difficult for Alan, who explicitly said on several occasions that he felt his writing abilities were not good. His emails show a number of grammatical errors including sentence fragments, double negatives, and misplaced punctuation. In addition, Alan's emails often contained directives about the use of computers and labs; he frequently implied that people should respect his authority and position in the department by doing what he asked. His utterances were intended to be "*signs of authority* . . . to be believed and obeyed" (Bourdieu 66). However, he sent these emails to many irrelevant audiences and his grammar, punctuation, and sentence structure often undermined his authority as understood by audience members.

Although Alan was institutionally authorized to speak about technology, and 26 recognized as a technical authority, he was not able to "speak in a way that others . . . regard[ed] as acceptable in the circumstances" (Thompson 9). Survey respondents' comments suggested that people dismissed Alan's legitimacy because of his writing choices. While he appeared to feel this dismissal, he did not change his writing behavior and his institutional authority began to erode.

What Was the Outcome?

The fact that Alan, a newcomer, used email in ways that old-timers saw as inap- 27 propriate—and that this use of email caused conflict—is not surprising; after all, newcomers are expected to make missteps. But rather than adapting and changing to communicate more effectively in his new workplace, Alan resisted and clung to his own ways of writing, causing conflict and breakdowns in the community of practice. Members of the department were similarly unwilling to change their view of what they found acceptable in email. They insisted on what Bourdieu calls "the dominant competence" and imposed their idea of linguistic competence as "the only legitimate one" (56). The community didn't negotiate or compromise its idea of linguistic competence for Alan; the only real possibility for negotiation had to come from Alan—and it did not.

Because our identities are shaped to some extent by the communities in 28 which we choose to participate—as well as by those settings we inhabit and in which we choose *not* to participate (Wenger 164)—workers such as Alan may also be demonstrating their desire to identify with communities of practice other than the primary ones in which they work by refusing to appropriate new ways of writing. By refusing to participate in communication conventions adopted by the majority of members of the community, Alan attempted to assert the identity he imagined for himself (powerful network administrator) and to resist the one imposed on him by the workplace. Pushing past resistance to work effectively with others requires people to relinquish aspects of their desired primary identities: "[L]egitimate participation entails the loss of certain identities even as it enables the construction of others" (Hodges 289). Clearly, Alan did not feel this was an acceptable proposition. The result for Alan, as Wenger might predict, was increasing marginalization. His emails were not only the butt of cruel and constant jokes in the department, but they also failed to garner support and convey necessary information. People ignored his emails or laughed at them, and neither response was conducive to getting work done. Ultimately, Alan's choice of non-participation resulted in "disturbances and breakdowns in work processes" (Hasu and Engeström 65).

Socio-historic activity theory argues that such situations can lead to positive 29 developments because breakdowns can potentially serve as catalysts for change: "Discoordination and breakdown often lead to re-mediation of the performance and perspectives, sometimes even to re-mediation of the overall activity system in order to resolve its pressing inner contradictions" (Hasu and Engeström 65). However, for a breakdown to lead to positive change, those involved must be willing to consider and negotiate various perspectives and everyone must be willing to appropriate some new ways of seeing and doing. This did not happen in Alan's case. He clung to his own ways of writing and communicating, which demonstrated that he was not engaging, aligning, and imagining a role for himself as a member of the humanities department. Other members of the humanities department no more changed to accommodate Alan than Alan did to fit in with them.

After a year and a half, Alan left and found employment elsewhere. 30

DISCUSSION

Clearly, Alan's enculturation into the humanities department was not success- 31 ful. He was an outsider, a worker unlike the other community members in age, education, occupation, linguistic abilities, and concern for conventions. Since new workers are often different in these ways and still manage to negotiate communication strategies that are effective and acceptable enough so that work can be done, what might account for Alan's resistance to writing in ways that his new community saw as legitimate and appropriate?

One reason for his resistance was that Alan and other members of his depart- 32 ment had a different understanding of the division of labor in the department and, thus, a different view of Alan's authority. Alan might have viewed changing his writing habits as an admission that he did not play the role he imagined for himself within the department. Despite his vocal assertions to the contrary, he was not "God" in the department. While he entered the department with some measure of authority by virtue of his technical expertise, he had to prove himself and create his *ethos* continually through language — perhaps even more than through action for this particular workplace. This was something he could not or would not do.

However, a socio-linguistic analysis I conducted of Alan's writing suggests 33 that he did not feel as much authority as he claimed to have, even from the beginning of his time in the department when he had the most cooperation and respect because of his technical capital. Of 150 sentences I studied for the analysis, only 39 were directives. While all of Alan's emails were usually sent to department-wide listservs, the overwhelming majority of his directives (28 of the 39) were addressed to graduate students alone. Only 3 were written to faculty or staff members, and 6 were written to the department as a whole. Alan's use of directives suggests that while he claimed to have authority and see the faculty as simply "users," he did not, in fact, feel much authority over them, so he confined most of his directives to graduate students. Even then, Alan used hedges over two-thirds of the time, suggesting that his felt sense of authority was shaky. This understanding best matched the department's understanding. He could make technical changes and monitor and limit operations; however, he could not force people to act in the ways he wanted them to or prohibit them from using equipment, as he threatened in more than one email.

Given the limitations of his actual authority — which conflicted with his 34 desired authority — Alan's refusal to change his writing might have been one way of claiming an identity he wanted, one that included the authority and autonomy to which he felt entitled. However, his refusal to write in ways seen as acceptable by the department had the opposite effect: his method of writing stripped him of the institutional authority originally invested in him. Although Alan's words could be understood, they were not "likely to be listened to [or] recognized as acceptable." He lacked "the competence necessary in order to speak the legitimate language," which could have granted him "linguistic capital . . . a profit of distinction" (Bourdieu 55). Since authoritative language is useless "without the collaboration of those it governs," Alan's initial authority was lessened with each utterance seen by the department as illegitimate (Bourdieu 113). We should keep in mind that Alan's choices are unlikely to have been conscious; quite often linguistic action is not "the outcome of conscious calculation" (Thompson 17).

A second reason for Alan's failure to adopt community writing conventions 35 might have been his resistance to being used as a tool. As a support person, Alan joined this activity system as one of its tools, not as a community member. As a technical worker with a B.A. in a university humanities department filled with people who had M.A.s and Ph.D.s, he and the other members of the workplace were not mutually engaged. Rather, the community members used him as a tool to help achieve goals Alan did not share or value. Computer system administrators (like many other workers) are used as tools to do work that others cannot. As a result of his position, Alan was not part of the community of practice; rather, his ability to maintain computer networks figured in as one of many pieces of the humanities community: the community members needed him and his activity to use their computers.

Though Alan was hired to function as a tool, he did not sit quietly like a 36 hammer or wrench until he was needed, he did not perform exactly the same way each time he was needed, and he did not remain silent when his work was complete. As a person, Alan didn't always choose to perform his tasks when and how community members wanted. In addition, he initiated and responded to dialogue, and (most frustrating for members of the humanities department) chose to do so in ways contrary to the community expectations. Alan's refusal to write in ways that the faculty felt he should was, perhaps, one means of flouting their linguistic authority, demonstrating that he was not a servant or tool to be used at will. Rather than quietly performing the tasks asked of him, and writing about them in the ways the community members saw as legitimate, Alan resisted the department by seeing *them* as *his* tools and by choosing non-participation over acquiescence to their written conventions. Alan's method of resistance did bring him to the conscious attention of department members; they quickly came to see him as a human being who did not silently serve them in response to their every need or desire. However, his method of resistance did not enable Alan to complete his own work successfully, nor did it lead the humanities department to include him as a human member of their community. Thus, Alan's method of resistance in this case was successful on one level, but detrimental to both himself and the workplace on other levels.

Alan's example illustrates that learning to write in new communities entails 37 more than learning discrete sets of skills or improving cognitive abilities. It is a process of involvement in communities, of identifying with certain groups, of choosing certain practices over others; a process strongly influenced by power relationships — a process, in effect, bound up tightly with identity, authority, and experience. Alan's case also suggests that enculturation theories have overlooked an important point: not all new workers are expected, or themselves expect, to enculturate into a community. Some, perhaps many in our service-oriented society, are present in communities of practice not as members but as tools. Given these points, those of us interested in how people learn to write in new environments, in school and beyond, and those of us struggling to teach new ways of writing to students who resist what we ask of them, must continue to study and consider the importance of factors beyond texts and cognitive ability.

Acknowledgments

Thanks to Rebecca Burnett (Iowa State University) and Charie Thralls (Utah State University) for encouraging this study and responding to early drafts; to David Russell (Iowa State University) and Donna Kain (Clarkson University) for responding to later drafts; and to Lisa Coleman and Judy Isaksen, *Encultura-tion* guest editor and board member respectively, for their helpful reviews.

Notes

1. "A community of practice is a set of relations among persons, activity, and world, over time and in relation with other tangential and overlapping communities of practice" (Lave and Wenger 98).

2. "Knowledge, skills, and other cultural acquisitions, as exemplified by educational or technical qualifications" (Thompson 14).

3. Though relatively new to many in our field, activity theory is used more and more widely within composition studies; see, for example, Bazerman and Russell; Berkenkotter and Ravotas; Dias, et al.; Dias and Paré; Grossman, Smagorinsky and Valencia; Harms; Hovde; Kain; Russell, "Rethinking" and "Activity Theory"; Smart; Spinuzzi; Wardle; Winsor. Activity theory's implications for composition instruction are outlined in Russell's "Activity Theory and Its Implications for Writing Instruction" and in Wardle's *Contradiction, Constraint, and Re-Mediation: An Activity Analysis of FYC* and "Can Cross-Disciplinary Links Help Us Teach 'Academic Discourse' in FYC?"

Works Cited

Bawarshi, Anis. *Genre and the Invention of the Writer: Reconsidering the Place of Invention in Composition.* Logan: Utah State UP, 2003. Print.

Bazerman, Charles. *Shaping Written Knowledge: The Genre and Activity of the Experimental Article in Sciences.* Madison: U of Wisconsin P, 1988. Print.

Bazerman, Charles, and David Russell. *Writing Selves/Writing Societies: Research from Activity Perspectives.* Fort Collins: The WAC Clearinghouse and *Mind, Culture, and Activity*, 2002. Print.

Berkenkotter, Carol, Thomas Huckin, and Jon Ackerman. "Conversations, Conventions, and the Writer." *Research in the Teaching of English* 22 (1988): 9–44. Print.

Berkenkotter, Carol, and Thomas Huckin. "Rethinking Genre from a Sociocognitive Perspective." *Written Communication* 10 (1993): 475–509. Print.

Berkenkotter, Carol, and Doris Ravotas. "Genre as a Tool in the Transmission of Practice and across Professional Boundaries." *Mind, Culture, and Activity* 4.4 (1997): 256–74. Print.

Berlin, James. "Poststructuralism, Cultural Studies, and the Composition Classroom: Postmodern Theory in Practice." *Rhetoric Review* 11 (1992): 16–33. Print.

Bizzell, Patricia. "Cognition, Convention, and Certainty: What We Need to Know about Writing." *PRE/TEXT* 3 (1982): 213–43. Print.

Bolin, Bill. "The Role of the Media in Distinguishing Composition from Rhetoric." *Enculturation* 5.1 (Fall 2003): n. pag. Web. 1 July 2004.

Bourdieu, Pierre. *Language and Symbolic Power.* Ed. John B. Thompson. Trans. Gino Raymond and Matthew Adamson. Cambridge: Harvard UP, 1991. Print.

Cole, Michael. *Cultural Psychology.* Cambridge: Harvard UP, 1996. Print.

Cole, Michael, and Yrgo Engeström. "A Cultural-Historical Approach to Distributed Cognition." Ed. Gavriel Salomon. *Distributed Cognitions: Psychological and Educational Considerations.* Cambridge: Cambridge UP, 1993. 1–46. Print.

Cole, Michael, and Sylvia Scribner. *The Psychology of Literacy.* Cambridge: Harvard UP, 1981. Print.

Dias, Patrick, and Anthony Paré, eds. *Transitions: Writing in Academic and Workplace Settings.* Cresskill: Hampton, 2000. Print.

Dias, Patrick, Aviva Freedman, Peter Medway, and Anthony Paré. *Worlds Apart: Acting and Writing in Academic and Workplace Contexts.* Mahwah: Lawrence Erlbaum, 1999. Print.

Doheny-Farina, Stephen. "A Case Study of an Adult Writing in Academic and Non-Academic Settings." *Worlds of Writing: Teaching and Learning in Discourse Communities at Work.* Ed. Carolyn B. Matalene. New York: Random, 1989. 17–42. Print.

Doheny-Farina, Stephen, and Lee Odell. "Ethnographic Research on Writing: Assumptions and Methodology." *Writing in Nonacademic Settings.* Eds. Lee Odell and Dixie Goswami. New York: Guilford, 1985. 503–35. Print.

Engeström, Yrgo. *Learning by Expanding: An Activity-Theoretical Approach to Developmental Research.* Helsinki: Orienta-Konsultit, 1987. Print.

Grossman, Pamela L., Peter Smagorinsky, and Sheila Valencia. "Appropriating Tools for Teaching English: A Theoretical Framework for Research on Learning to Teach." *American Journal of Education* 108 (1999): 1–29. Print.

Harms, Patricia. *Writing-across-the-Curriculum in a Linked Course Model for First-Year Students: An Activity Theory Analysis.* Ames: Iowa State UP, 2003. Print.

Hasu, Mervi, and Yrgo Engeström. "Measurement in Action: An Activity-Theoretical Perspective on Producer-User Interaction." *International Journal of Human-Computer Studies* 53 (2000): 61–89. Print.

Hodges, Diane. "Participation as Dis-Identification With/In a Community of Practice." *Mind, Culture, and Activity* 5 (1998): 272–90. Print.

Hovde, Marjorie. "Tactics for Building Images of Audience in Organizational Contexts: An Ethnographic Study of Technical Communicators." *Journal of Business and Technical Communication* 14.4 (2000): 395–444. Print.

Kain, Donna J. *Negotiated Spaces: Constructing Genre and Social Practice in a Cross-Community Writing Project.* Ames: Iowa State UP, 2003. Print.

Lave, Jean, and Etienne Wenger. *Situated Learning: Legitimate Peripheral Participation.* New York: Cambridge UP, 1991. Print.

Lincoln, Bruce. *Authority: Construction and Corrosion.* Chicago: U of Chicago P, 1994. Print.

Paré, Anthony. "Genre and Identity: Individuals, Institutions, and Ideology." *The Rhetoric and Ideology of Genre.* Eds. Richard Coe, Lorelei Lingard, and Tatiana Teslenko. Cresskill: Hampton, 2002. Print.

Prior, Paul. *Writing/Disciplinarity: A Sociohistoric Account of Literate Activity in the Academy.* Mahwah: Lawrence Erlbaum, 1998. Print.

Rose, Nikolas. *Inventing Ourselves: Psychology, Power, and Personhood.* Cambridge: Cambridge UP, 1996. Print.

Rubin, Donald L. "Introduction: Composing Social Identity." *Composing Social Identity in Written Language.* Ed. Donald Rubin. Hillsdale: Lawrence Erlbaum, 1995. 1–30. Print.

Russell, David. "Rethinking Genre in School and Society: An Activity Theory Analysis." *Written Communication* 14 (1997): 504–39. Print.

——— . "Activity Theory and Its Implications for Writing Instruction." *Reconceiving Writing, Rethinking Writing Instruction*. Ed. Joseph Petraglia. Mahwah: Lawrence Erlbaum, 1995. 51–77. Print.

Smart, Graham. "Genre as Community Invention: A Central Bank's Response to Its Executives' Expectations as Readers." *Writing in the Workplace: New Research Perspectives*. Ed. Rachel Spilka. Carbondale: Southern Illinois UP, 1993. 124–40. Print.

Spinuzzi, Clay. "Pseudotransactionality, Activity Theory, and Professional Writing Instruction." *Technical Communication Quarterly* 5.3 (1996): 295–308. Print.

Thompson, John B. "Editor's Introduction." *Language and Symbolic Power*. By Pierrie Bourdieu. Cambridge: Harvard UP, 1999. 1–31. Print.

Wardle, Elizabeth. *Contradiction, Constraint, and Re-Mediation: An Activity Analysis of FYC*. Ames: Iowa State UP, 2003. Print.

——— . "Can Cross-Disciplinary Links Help Us Teach 'Academic Discourse' in FYC?" *Across the Disciplines* 1 (2004): n. pag. Web. 1 July 2004.

Wenger, Etienne. *Communities of Practice: Learning, Meaning, and Identity*. New York: Cambridge UP, 1998. Print.

Winsor, Dorothy. "Genre and Activity Systems: The Role of Documentation in Maintaining and Changing Engineering Activity Systems." *Written Communication* 16.2 (1999): 200–24. Print.

- -

Questions for Discussion and Journaling

1. Drawing on Wardle (who cites Wenger), what are the three ways that newcomers try to belong in a new community? Give a specific example to illustrate each "mode of belonging." Then consider why a newcomer might choose *not* to participate in some aspect of a new community.

2. Wardle quotes Rubin as saying that "stylistic options 'leak' clues about writers' social identities" (para. 10). Explain what this means. Do you have examples from your own experience?

3. Wardle quotes Hasu and Engeström, well-known activity-theory scholars, as saying that conflict and breakdown can actually be positive (para. 29), helping to reshape how a community does things in ways that are more productive. However, the conflicts between Alan and his work community did not have positive results. Why do you think this is? How could his conflicts have been handled so that they *did* result in positive change?

4. Toward the end of the article, Wardle quotes Thompson as saying that the choices we make with language are very often unconscious (para. 34); that is, we might be using language in resistant ways unintentionally. Do you agree that this is possible, or do you think that people are usually making conscious choices when they use language?

5. Wardle seems to be arguing that Alan did not successfully join his new workplace community because he was resisting it: He did not want to adopt the identity that

people in that community imagined for him. James Gee (p. 507) would likely have a very different opinion; he would most likely argue that Alan could not have joined the Humanities Department activity system even if he had wanted to. Take a look at Gee's article and then consider whether you agree more with Wardle or with Gee.

6. Think of all the people you know who have some sort of institutionally ascribed authority. (Hint: One of them probably assigned this reading!) Can you think of a time when one or more of them lost their authority in your eyes or someone else's through their linguistic actions or behaviors? If so, what happened?

Applying and Exploring Ideas

1. Write a reflective essay of a few pages in which you (first) define what it means to have authority over texts and within activity systems, and (second) discuss your feelings about your own authority (or lack of it) within any activity system you would like to focus on. Consider, for example, how you know whether you have authority there and how you gained text and discourse authority there (if you did); alternatively, consider how it feels to be at the mercy of someone else's authority in an activity system.

2. Make a list of all the tools that mediate the activities of this writing class. How do they help you do the work of the class? How would the work be different if the tools were different? Do you think there are tools that could make the class more effective that are currently not used?

3. How does the concept of *authority* relate to this chapter's threshold concept that people collaborate in order to get things done with writing?

- -

META MOMENT   How might thinking about sources of authority help you as a writer on the job, in college, or in your personal writing?

- -

Galaxy-Wide Writing Strategies Used by Official *Star Wars* Bloggers

ARIELLE FELDMAN

Framing the Reading

Arielle Feldman wrote this paper as a first-year student in a composition class at the University of Central Florida (UCF) in Spring 2017. Her paper was first published in UCF's *Stylus*, a journal of research from UCF first-year composition courses. Feldman majors in public relations and communication with an emphasis on video production and social-media management, and since writing the piece has also gone to work for UCF's College of Arts and Humanities as a communication assistant who writes news stories about college faculty and students.

Feldman's paper offers one example of research into the formation of a specific discourse community, in this case the community of *Star Wars* fandom. Going beyond what has become a typical assignment of explaining how a given community fits John Swales's six (now eight) criteria for a discourse community, Feldman instead studies how one text, the *StarWars.com* blog, contributes to community formation. As she argues, from Swales, "Contributing to a discourse community is all about achieving common goals through member connectivity," so she focuses on how the Lucasfilm blog does so. But Feldman's piece is of interest not only for the "tools" she discusses blog writers using but also as an example of how to do this kind of research, and the opportunities and challenges an approach like hers creates. As you read, pay close attention to her research methods and assumptions about what we can deduce from her data.

Getting Ready to Read

Stylus: A Journal of First-Year Writing, Department of Writing and Rhetoric, University of Central Florida

stylus
a journal of first-year writing

Galaxy-Wide Writing Strategies Used by Official *Star Wars* Bloggers
ARIELLE FELDMAN

Did I Create the Process? Or Did the Process Create Me?
JADELLE CELESTINE

Changing Scenes: The Rise and Success of Diversity on Broadway
KATY GENTRY

The Language Transition Process and Its Influence on Language Use
LETICIA LINSLEY

Liking in Group Messaging: Perception versus Meaning
CHLOE LAROCHELLE

The Extent of Influence that Genre Conventions Have on TED Talks
PRISCILLA SIMOTAS

Volume 8 | Issue 2 | Fall 2017
The Journal of the First-Year Writing Program at the University of Central Florida

Before you read, do at least one of the following activities:

- Visit the *StarWars.com* "News + Blog" page that Feldman writes about in order to familiarize yourself with the scene she's studying.

Feldman, Arielle. "Galaxy-Wide Writing Strategies Used by Official Star Wars Bloggers." *Stylus*, vol. 8, no. 2, Fall 2017, pp. 1–5.

- Read either Swales's or Johns's pieces in this chapter in order to review Swales's list of criteria for what makes a discourse community a discourse community.

As you read, consider the following questions:

- What is Feldman's research question, and how does her focus throughout her article pursue that question?
- How does Feldman's article incorporate research that doesn't have to do with discourse communities but helps her draw conclusions about her data?

A LONG TIME AGO IN A GALAXY far, far away, a movie came out that 1 changed cinema forever. While it actually wasn't all too long ago (May 25, 1977, to be exact) and the galaxy far, far away was our own Milky Way, the film amazed audiences as if it were otherworldly. This fan base that has stood the test of time is a discourse community, since it is a "group of people who link up in order to pursue objectives" (Swales 220). What began as a cult-like following grew to become a worldwide network of loyal fans. The objective of this community is to show appreciation for the variety of movies, toys, books, TV shows, video games, and more that have been released under the *Star Wars* brand.

As a discourse community, this ever-expanding group of sci-fi devotees 2 achieves their objective by using several "mechanisms of intercommunication." These mechanisms are necessary in order to exchange information between members, and hence keep the community alive (Swales 221). Many communities choose "blogs" as one of their primary means of circulating material. Blogs, which are regularly updated websites that focus on one or several topics, serve as useful discourse tools. In fact, the act of "blogging" is seen as so valuable that Lucasfilm, the company who owns the movie franchise, runs an official blog where writers produce *Star Wars*-related content. The corresponding discourse these writers supply is the focus of this paper.

The bloggers of *StarWars.com* act as certified creators of *Star Wars* online 3 material and inherently have to appease thousands of readers. They are usually the first to distribute important community news, such as actor announcements for new movies or dates of conventions. Therefore, the articles must be presented in a way that is easily digestible to fans. In order to achieve this goal, the writers employ tools that enhance the effectiveness of their articles, which are usually spread across external social media. These tools are intertextuality, organization, and nostalgia. Article effectiveness can be deduced from the number of shares accumulated by each, which is presented beneath every post in a Facebook share button.

METHODS

To observe how the *StarWars.com* blog creates content for their discourse com- 4
munity, I took into consideration the last thirty articles that were posted as of
March 23, 2017. This gave me an adequate sample size to observe and record
my findings. Using all of the information that was provided publicly for me, I
documented each article's title, number of Facebook shares, category, date published, tags, author(s), and number of comments. My research uncovered strategies the bloggers utilize to achieve maximum post success.

RESULTS

Writing Strategy #1: Intertextuality

Intertext can best be summarized as "the bits and pieces of Text which writers 5
or speakers borrow and sew together to create new discourse" (Porter 397). At
the beginning of this essay, an example of *Star Wars* intertext was used: "a long
time ago in a galaxy far, far away." This displays intertextuality because it is such
a recognizable saying to *Star Wars* fans. So, by including the phrase, I set the
tone for the rest of my paper to be about the films. The importance of bloggers
borrowing *Star Wars* phrases for their articles is more than just for brand recognition (although that, too, is a benefit of their application). The use of technical
jargon is crucial to a discourse community's identity. By possessing a lexis, or a
"shared and specialized terminology," the group can establish itself and create
connectivity amongst its members (Swales 222).

While fan devotion may vary in the community, some being die-hards while 6
others casual viewers, knowledge of familiar terms from *Star Wars* is usually consistent across the board. It is the responsibility of the blogger to use the community
lexis to their advantage when attempting to attract members to their posts. Generating blog traffic greatly benefits Lucasfilm because the bloggers typically use
their posts to subliminally advertise *Star Wars* products. Intertextuality is thus one
of the many driving forces that yields views and makes the blog posts profitable.
However, the value of intertextuality goes beyond just being a marketing ploy.

For example, in the blog column "From a Certain Point of View," two 7
StarWars.com writers debate on a topic, which can range from who the best
droid[1] is to which *Star Wars* video game is the most underrated. The title serves
as intertext itself, since it is an exact line taken from *Star Wars: Episode VI—
Return of the Jedi*. There is a scene in the movie where the story's protagonist,
Luke Skywalker, demands an explanation from the ghost of his deceased Jedi[2]
mentor, Obi-Wan Kenobi. The dialogue between the two is included below:

> LUKE: Ben! Why didn't you tell me? You told me that Darth Vader betrayed
> and murdered my father.

OBI-WAN: Your father was seduced by the Dark Side of the Force. He ceased to be the Jedi Anakin Skywalker and became Darth Vader. When that happened, the good man who was your father was destroyed. So, what I told you was true, *from a certain point of view*.

The bloggers' reference to Obi-Wan looking at the fate of Luke's father "from 8 a certain point of view" not only connects back to *Star Wars*, but also describes what the format of the column is: two bloggers giving their "point of view" on a concept. The ability of writers "to borrow traces effectively and to find appropriate contexts for them" is what keeps the posts relevant to the community and qualifies the writers as fans themselves (Porter 399). This segues into the second benefit of intertextuality, which is how it can create an emotional connection between bloggers and their audience. Readers enjoy the playful *Star Wars* references because it shows how the bloggers are true fans. This creates a shared experience between readers and writers; the commonality of knowing *Star Wars* intertext forms a bond between the two parties and encourages appreciation of the bloggers' discourse.

Writing Strategy #2: Organization

While intertext helps the bloggers attract the *Star Wars* fan demographic, varying 9 organizational patterns make their posts more appropriate for social media. This is important since blogs and social media have become intertwined. Articles posted on *StarWars.com* are instantly shared on the official *Star Wars* social media account. Social media is also where blog posts get the most exposure. As of December 2016, 1.2 billion people use Facebook daily, which is much more traction than the comparatively niche *StarWars.com* gets (*Facebook Newsroom*). There are many different organizational formats that the *StarWars.com* writers put to use in their articles, but almost one-third of the thirty I studied presented their information in a list.

"Ranking *Rebels*" is another column on *StarWars.com*. New articles for 10 "Ranking *Rebels*" come out after each episode of the TV show *Star Wars Rebels*. The author, who goes by the nickname "Geek Girl Diva," uses the column to give her thoughts on the show in a numbered list. Each number dictates a "highlight," or a favorite moment of the episode (see Figure 1). Adopting these categories gives Geek Girl Diva the leeway to delve deeply into topics while keeping her commentary condensed and structured.

Articles that list out topics to be covered perform well on blogs and social 11 media platforms. In a study done by Fractl, a content marketing agency, it was discovered that lists "have the most reliable social traction, averaging around 21,000 shares per month with a variance of less than 2.5%" (Lehr). The results show how lists are an efficient way to present content, especially when covering a widely beloved topic like *Star Wars*.

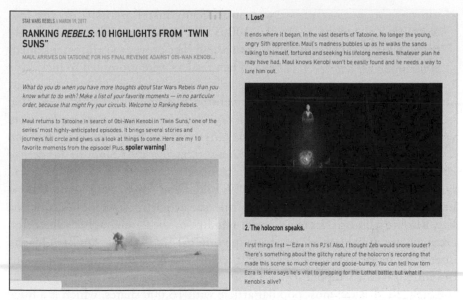

Figure 1 Excerpts from the blog post "Ranking *Rebels*: 10 Highlights from 'Twin Suns'"

Writing Strategy #3: Nostalgia

Despite the effectiveness of intertext and lists, neither of those attributes holds   12
a candle to nostalgia. The "nostalgia effect," as I like to call it, is when *Star Wars*
.com bloggers choose to create material that evokes positive memories of the
past for fans. Even the screenwriters of the new *Star Wars* films implement this
tactic. *Star Wars: Episode VII — The Force Awakens*, for example, incorporated
nostalgia by having the original *Star Wars* cast reprise their iconic roles while
also making several references to older movies in the script. The bloggers make
sure they're doing the same by focusing on subjects that are more likely to
resonate with long-term *Star Wars* fans.

The top three most shared *Star Wars.com* posts from my sample met the   13
"nostalgia requirement." With over 5,700 shares, the third most popular post
is a "From a Certain Point of View" article discussing which of the *Star Wars*
video games is the most underrated. One blogger's pick is a game that came
out in the late 90s, while the other's choice was released in 2005. Cassidee
Moser, the first author who praises an old school 90s Nintendo game, even
says so herself that she enjoys how the game is "a buffet of *Star Wars* moments
sewn together with threads of familiar elements pulled from the original
trilogy" (Moser and Gallegos). Fans are notorious for preferring the original
trilogy, the three initial movies that came out between 1977 and 1983, over the

> Nostalgia is channeled through the use of intertext, while organizational structures provide ways to properly present the information online.

more recent installments from the late 2000s and today. *StarWars.com* recently ran a poll that proves the aforementioned. When readers were prompted to pick their favorite *Star Wars* film, 69% of responders chose an original trilogy film (*A New Hope, The Empire Strikes Back,* or *Return of the Jedi*) over a prequel[3] film (*The Phantom Menace, Attack of the Clones,* or *Revenge of the Sith*).

The second most shared article, "5 Things You Might Not Know About 14 Lightsabers," is also in list format. While the article focuses more on recent *Star Wars* installments, its topic is still relevant to the demographic whose first experience with lightsabers[4] was from the original *Star Wars* movies. It holds the interest of *Star Wars* fans new *and* old, presenting new canon information about the famous movie weapon.

Lastly, there is the most popular article with 16,000 shares, which is a huge 15 jump from the previous article that topped out at 9,000 shares. The article is an interview with a comic book writer who is working on a series about Darth Vader, the *Star Wars* antagonist who is arguably the most renowned character in the franchise (Soule). The whole premise of the comic series is teeming with nostalgia. Dan Brooks, senior editor of *StarWars.com*, states in the introduction that the story "promises to shed light on some of [Darth] Vader's early acts and forays into the dark side, including how he built his red-bladed lightsaber, hunting down surviving Jedi, and more." The series would therefore answer questions hardcore *Star Wars* fans may have about the infamous villain the movies revolve around. As a longstanding fan of the films, this article grabbed my attention the most. Darth Vader is the face of *Star Wars*, so what better way to attract members and promote discourse amongst fans than to create an entire series about his untold history? The bloggers then wrote an article about this work in progress and turned it into entertaining publicity.

CONCLUSION

Contributing to a discourse community is all about achieving common goals 16 through member connectivity (Swales 220). By using the *Star Wars* lexis, following organizational techniques that fare well on the Internet, and promoting the feeling of nostalgia, bloggers have developed a system for creating valuable discourse that *Star Wars* fans share and respond to. These writing strategies build off of one another. Nostalgia is channeled through the use of intertext, while organizational structures provide ways to properly present the information online. Using these strategies fosters connections between bloggers and readers and expands the community by attracting more *Star Wars* fans to the blog. If Obi-Wan Kenobi was a writer, he might have said that discourse "surrounds us, penetrates us, and binds the galaxy together," since it is a great "Force" that unites *Star Wars* fans all over the world (Lucas).

Notes

1. A droid is a robot that possesses artificial intelligence.

2. A Jedi is a member of a group of wizard-like warriors who guard peace in the galaxy and can harness the power of "the Force."

3. The prequel films take place in a time period before that of the original films story-wise, despite being released several years after the original 70s and 80s movies.

4. Lightsabers are laser-swords used by Jedi that were introduced in the very first film.

Works Cited

Facebook Newsroom. Facebook, 2016, https://newsroom.fb.com/.

Geek Girl Diva (Shana O'Neil). "Ranking *Rebels*: 10 Highlights from 'Twin Suns.'" *StarWars.com*, Lucasfilm, 19 Mar. 2017, www.starwars.com/news/ranking-rebels-10-highlights-from-twin-suns.

Lehr, Andrea. "New Data: What Types of Content Perform Best on Social Media?" *HubSpot*, 2 Feb. 2015, www.blog.hubspot.com/marketing/content-social-media-popularity.

Moser, Cassidee, and Anthony Gallegos. "From A Certain Point of View: What is the Most Underrated *Star Wars* Video Game?" *StarWars.com*, Lucasfilm, 3 Mar. 2017, www.starwars.com/news/from-a-certain-point-of-view-what-is-the-most-underrated-star-wars-video-game.

"Poll: Which *Star Wars* Movie Is Your Favorite?" *StarWars.com*, Lucasfilm, 20 May 2015, www.starwars.com/news/poll-which-star-wars-movie-is-your-favorite.

Porter, James E. "Intertextuality and the Discourse Community." Wardle and Downs, pp. 395–409. Originally published in *Rhetoric Review* vol. 5, no. 1, 1986, pp. 34–47.

Soule, Charles. "In Marvel's New Darth Vader Series, We Will See the Sith Lord's Rise, the Construction of His Lightsaber, and More." Interview by Dan Brooks. *StarWars.com*, Lucasfilm, 10 Mar. 2017, www.starwars.com/news/in-marvels-new-darth-vader-series-we-will-see-the-sith-lords-rise-the-construction-of-his-lightsaber-and-more.

Star Wars: Episode IV—A New Hope. Screenplay by George Lucas, Lucasfilm, 1977.

Star Wars: Episode VI—Return of the Jedi. Screenplay by George Lucas and Lawrence Kasdan, Lucasfilm, 1983.

Swales, John. "The Concept of Discourse Community." Wardle and Downs, pp. 215–29. Originally published in *Genre Analysis: English in Academic and Research Settings*, Cambridge UP, 1990, pp. 21–32.

Wardle, Elizabeth, and Doug Downs, editors. *Writing about Writing: A College Reader*. 2nd ed., Bedford/St. Martin's, 2014.

Questions for Discussion and Journaling

1. In paras. 7–8, Feldman discusses the relationship between use of intertextuality and a writer's credibility. How does she explain that relationship, and what does it have to do with words like "membership" and "authenticity"?

2. One premise of Feldman's study is that "article effectiveness can be deduced from the number of shares" the article accumulates (para. 3). What would be some reasons that a text could be shared extensively yet not be "effective"? Do you think Feldman's premise is reliable?

3. Most of Feldman's explanation of *intertextuality* has to do with *lexis*. If you've read Porter's article on intertextuality (p. 416), review it briefly. What are other ways to create intertextuality besides particular instances of jargon or terms specific to a discourse community?

4. Name and explain one way that Feldman's research actually extends Swales's work on how discourse communities are formed through discourse. What is a way she goes beyond what Swales already offers us?

5. In order to study the formation of the *Star Wars* fan community, Feldman examines a text which helps form the community but is actually created by the company which owns the films, rather than by fans themselves. How does her choice of text to study influence what she might be learning about community formation?

Applying and Exploring Ideas

1. Feldman argues that members of a discourse community have a *responsibility* to use the community's lexis (para. 6). Why does she say so? Does it seem strange to you to imagine a writer having a responsibility to hold a community together with their work? Can you think of an experience you've had in creating or contributing to texts for a discourse community you belong to that gave you similar responsibility?

2. If you were to do research similar to Feldman's, what discourse community would you choose to study and what text(s) might you look at to study its formation? Write a one- to two-paragraph speculation on such a research project.

3. In Swales's article earlier in this chapter, he expands his six criteria for recognizing a discourse community (reported in his earlier chapter that Feldman cites) to eight, adding "a sense of 'silential relations'" (things that go without saying in a community) and "horizons of expectation" or "defined rhythms of activity," things the community comes to expect (para. 28–30). Looking at the data Feldman reports from her study, do you see either of these new criteria applying to *StarWars.com* and the *Star Wars* fan discourse community?

4. *Lexis* and *nostalgia* are two concepts Feldman analyzes extensively in her research, and together the two might create a sense that discourse communities are powerfully organized and driven by *what they already know*. How, if this is the case, does a discourse community make room for *new* ideas? How does it

keep from becoming merely an echo chamber of people comfortably reminding one another of what they already know? Consider a discourse community you're familiar with, as a member, and write a page-long description of how it negotiates between repeating known information (through tools like lexis, intertextuality, or nostalgia) and bringing in new ideas and approaches to what it does.

META MOMENT Consider a discourse community you're a member of. Are you aware of ways it uses intertextuality or nostalgia in its texts in order to build community identity?

Writing about Discourse Communities

Assignment Option 1

DISCOURSE COMMUNITY ETHNOGRAPHY

Choose a discourse community that has made an impact on you or one that interests you and explore its goals and characteristics. Then choose a particular point of interest within that discourse community to consider in more detail. Write a five- to eight-page report that describes the discourse community and explores the particular point of interest (or research question) that you want to focus on. Use the data you collect to make and support your claims.

Collecting Data. Choose a discourse community to study, and get permission to do so from the people involved in it. Then do the following:

- *Observe members of the discourse community* while they are engaged in a shared activity; take detailed notes. What are they doing? What kinds of things do they say? What do they write? How do you know who is "in" and who is "out"?

- *Collect anything people in that community read or write* (their genres) — even short things like forms, sketches, notes, IMs, and text messages.

- *Interview at least one member of the discourse community.* Ask permission to record each interview and then transcribe it. You might ask questions like: How long have you been here? Why are you involved? What do X, Y, and Z words mean? How did you learn to write A, B, or C? How do you communicate with other people (on your team, at your restaurant, etc.)?

Data Analysis. First, try analyzing the data you collect using the characteristics of a discourse community found in Swales (p. 544) or Johns (p. 560). This will give you an overall picture of the discourse community. Then, focus on what you've learned in order to find something that is especially interesting, confusing, or illuminating. You can use Johns, Branick, McCarthy, Wardle, or Feldman as helpful examples. In trying to determine what to focus on, you might ask yourself questions such as:

- Are there conflicts within the community? If so, what are they? Why do the conflicts occur? Do texts mediate these conflicts or make them worse in some way?

- Are any genres especially effective in helping the community work toward its goals — or keeping the community from working toward its goals? Why?

- Do some participants in the community have difficulty speaking and writing there? Why?

- Who has authority here? How is that authority demonstrated in written and oral language? Where does that authority come from?

- Are members of this community stereotyped in any way in regard to their literacy knowledge? If so, why?

Planning and Drafting.   As you develop answers to some of the above questions, start setting some priorities. Given all you have learned above, what do you want to focus on in your writing? Is there something interesting regarding goals of the community? Are there conflicts in the community? What do you see in terms of the lexis and mediating genres? Do you see verbal and written evidence of how people gain authority and/or enculturate in the community?

At this point you should stop and write a refined research question for yourself that you want to address in your writing. Now that you have observed and analyzed data, what question(s) would you like to explore in your final report? (Consult the articles by Wardle, McCarthy, Mirabelli, Feldman, and Branick in this chapter for examples of how you might do this.)

If your teacher has assigned you to write a fairly formal research report, then your final text ought to have the following parts, or you should make the following moves (unless there's a good reason not to):

- Begin with a very brief **literature review** of the existing literature (published research) on the topic: "We know X about discourse communities" (citing Johns and others as appropriate).

- Name a niche ("But we don't know Y" or "No one has looked at X").

- Explain how you will occupy the niche.

- Describe your research methods.

- Discuss your findings in detail. (Use Wardle, McCarthy, and Mirabelli as examples of how to do this — quote from your notes, your interview(s), the texts you collected, etc.)

- Include a works-cited page.

What Makes It Good?   Your assignment will be most successful if you've collected and analyzed data and explored the way that texts mediate activities within a particular discourse community. The assignment asks you to show a clear understanding of what discourse communities are and to demonstrate your ability to analyze them carefully and thoughtfully. It also asks that you not simply list the features of your discourse community but that you explore in some depth a particularly interesting aspect of that community. Since this assignment asks you to practice making the moves common to academic research articles, it should be organized, readable, fluent, and well edited.

- -

Assignment Option 2

REFLECTION ON GAINING AUTHORITY IN NEW DISCOURSE COMMUNITIES

This assignment asks you to continue the reflection you began while reading Wardle in this chapter in order to (first) define what it means to have authority over texts and within discourse communities or activity systems, and (second) analyze your own experiences gaining authority (or not) within any discourse community or activity system you would like to focus on.

Defining Terms and Explaining Ideas. First, revisit Wardle, Johns, Gee, and/or Klass in this chapter in order to write a working definition of what it means to have *authority* when it comes to reading, writing, speaking, and using texts in a new community. Once you've done this, use those same sources and any others you find helpful from this chapter to draft an explanation of how people become competent in this community, and then how they gain authority there (in other words, how they *enculturate*).

Analyzing Your Own Experiences. Drawing on the definitions and explanations you have already drafted, turn to your own experience in any discourse community or community of practice, and answer the following questions, drawing on specific examples and experiences to support your answers: Who has authority with texts and language in your chosen community? What does that look like? How do you know? Do you have authority with texts and language there? If so, how did you gain it? If not, why not?

Planning and Drafting. It may help you to begin by outlining your text and then drafting three different sections:

- Defining authority and discourse communities
- Explaining how newcomers enculturate and gain authority in new discourse communities
- Analyzing your experiences with authority in a particular discourse community

Once you have drafted each of those sections, try to write a conclusion that focuses on the "so what?" Here, you can talk about why thinking about these things matters and what others can learn from your experiences and analysis.

What Makes It Good?   Your analysis and reflection here will be good if you carefully think through the complicated ideas and terms, drawing on readings to assist you, and if you use those to help you carefully reflect on and analyze your experience. Equally important is the ending, where it is essential that you help readers (in this case, most likely your classmates) consider what they can learn from your analysis.

- -

Assignment Option 3
WRITING THAT MAKES A DIFFERENCE IN A COMMUNITY

For this assignment, you'll create a three- to four-page report or a one- to two-minute video that profiles a specific text created by a discourse community in order to solve a problem or help get things done in your college town or home town. This project asks you to look at how a text created by a discourse community (or activity system) impacts a broader public or community, and to learn from its writers what decisions they made in designing and composing the text.

Research a Text and Organization.   This project presents two research challenges: (1) finding the writing you want to study, and (2) interviewing its writers.

This assignment asks you find a text that benefits the public in some way and that is created by a member or members of some discourse community — a local organization, a government agency, a church, a hobbyist group, or some other special-interest group. You can find this kind of text by looking either in your college or home communities. You might first choose an organization and then choose one of its texts. Or, you might find an interesting text and identify the organization that created and published it.

What kind of text should you choose to study? It must be writing that is intended to make a change, serve the public, or solve a problem, rather than an internal business text: a flyer, a story, a how-to guide, assistive materials, an event advertisement, an election sign, an Internet meme, a billboard, a podcast, a public service announcement, a call for volunteers, or a poster. The writing must be for an audience "outside" the organization that created it — not member-to-member communication or texts that help members of an organization run that organization, but a text the organization creates to communicate with some larger public or constituency.

Whatever text you choose, you need to be sure you can find and speak with the writer(s) of the text; you will need to interview them to get the "story" of that text and discuss their choices in designing and composing the text. The more local your organization, the easier it will likely be to get in touch with the writers. If the organization has a phone number, calling may get you quicker results than emailing.

Conduct a Text-Based Interview with the Writer(s).   Once you've selected a text and contacted the writers to schedule an interview, you're ready to dig into the story about this writing. Before the interview you need to read and analyze the text. What is it? Who is its audience? How is it designed? Where does it circulate?

You then need to do background research on the organization prior to your interview — Google it, look at its webpages or social media presence, and get a sense of the organization's background and history in your area.

Prepare five to seven interview questions, such as: Who wrote the text? How did multiple people divide the work (if they did)? Where did the writing happen? What are the goals for the text and how do they align with the goals of the organization? What challenges or difficult choices might the authors have encountered in writing it? How have they seen it accomplish its purposes and be successful (or not)? Also write some open questions such as "what else do you want me to know about this text or how you wrote it?"

When you go to the interview, take at least one copy of the text you want to discuss. It is often easier for writers to remember what they did and why if the text they wrote can be looked at as a reminder.

You should record the interview so that you can transcribe and consult it later. You must ask for permission to do this. If you already know that you'd rather do a short video than a prose report for this project, you should video-record your interviews. If the writing is associated with a specific scene, workspace, or material resource or need, consider capturing images or video of these things (again, always with permission) as well as images of the text itself. Whether you choose the prose report or short-video option for this assignment, being able to include images of the writing itself will be extremely helpful in letting readers visualize what you're writing about.

Planning and Drafting.   Now your job is to show readers this writing, explain its origins and how it was written, and describe its impact on the community it speaks to.

Review your text analysis and interview materials (written notes and your interview recording). Draft a summary paragraph of the story of this writing: What was its exigence? How was it created? Where did it go and how was it used? Did it succeed? What main point emerges from this story: What should readers, or viewers, understand from your research? Perhaps it's something about how this kind of text works, how writing more broadly works, or what writers have to think about when they compose. Perhaps its simply a powerful story of a community being assisted or improved by writing.

When you have a sense of what, broadly, you'd like to say about this writing and its story, if you haven't already decided between a short video and a prose report, now is the time.

- Ask yourself whether the writing's story is better shown in images or told in words. (No matter which choice you make, you'll do both, but the prose report will usually rely more on telling the story, and the short video will put more weight on showing the story through images.)

- Ask yourself if you'd rather use a lot of words or fewer words. Two minutes of video is only enough time to speak about one double-spaced page of text.

- Ask yourself how much time you have available for composing. Even a short video takes much longer to compose and edit well than prose usually does to write.

Once you know what modalities you'll compose in, begin drafting your text, and be sure to cover the following ground (in any order that makes sense, given what you are trying to convey):

- The nature of this writing (what is it and who has created it)

- The exigence, motivation, and purpose for this writing (who needs it, why, and what it should accomplish)

- How the writing circulates in its community

- How the writing was created / the story of how it came to be

- How the writing has impacted the problem it was meant to address

- Any future this writing has

For either video or prose composing, you'll need to choose the elements you'll include in your text — images of the text itself and the writers (used with their permission), quotes from the interview or paraphrases you compose, parts or sections of the piece. If you're composing video, you'll need to decide which elements will be sound or voiceover, which clips from your interviews you'll use, and what information you'll convey in titles or captions on screen. You'll need to create both a storyboard that sketches a flow of piece and a script for any voiceover.

What Makes It Good? Your prose report or video will be good if it conveys the story of the text you studied: where it came from, what it was meant to work on, how it was designed to do so, and how it wound up working. It should create a good reading or viewing experience — well organized, showing the text you studied, and making an interesting point about the text, its writers, and/or its work in the community.

GLOSSARY

ACTIVITY SYSTEM   In his 1997 article "Rethinking Genre in School and Society: An Activity Theory Analysis," David Russell describes an *activity system* as "any ongoing, object-directed, historically conditioned, dialectically structured, tool-mediated human interaction." In simpler terms, an activity system consists of a group of people who act together over time as they work toward a specific goal. The people in the system use many kinds of tools, both physical (like computers or books) and symbolic (like words), to do their work together. The group's behaviors and traditions are influenced by their history, and when one aspect of the system changes, other aspects of it change in response.

ACTIVITY THEORY   *Activity theory* is a systematic explanation for how groups of people organize themselves and divide labor in order to accomplish a shared goal. The theory focuses particularly on people's social interactions and their use of tools. For any given **activity system** — one of these groups of people with a shared objective, such as nurses in a hospital emergency room — writing researchers who study it are most interested in how writing and language function as tools in accomplishing the group's shared goals.

ARGUMENT   *Argument* can describe any of the many ways by means of which people try to convince others of something.

Mathematically, arguments are the individual propositions of a proof. In a legal context, formal arguments are used to persuade a judge or jury to rule in favor of a particular position. In everyday use, or on talk radio or cable news shows, arguments tend to consist of people yelling at each other but rarely convincing or being convinced. We call all these forms of argument *agonistic,* meaning that they pit people against each other in a win / lose contest.

In an intellectual or academic context, argument is inquiry-based or conversational, and it describes the attempt to build knowledge by questioning existing knowledge and proposing alternatives. Rather than aiming simply to show who is right or wrong, inquiry-based argument aims to cooperatively find the best explanation for whatever is in question.

AUDIENCE   An *audience* is anyone who hears or reads a text — but it is also anyone a writer imagines encountering his or her text. This means that there is a difference between intended or "invoked" audience and actual or "addressed" audience. For example, when Aristotle composed *On Rhetoric* in about 350 BCE, his intended audience was his students, and for a time they were also his actual audience. (We would also call them his primary audience, the ones who first encountered his text.) Today, Aristotle's actual audience — the people who read him in coursepacks, on iPads, and on Kindles — are secondary audiences for Aristotle's work.

AUTHORITY   An *authority* is an accepted source, an expert, or a person with power or credibility. *Authority* (as an abstract noun) connotes confidence and self-assurance. In this book, the term is generally used to refer to people who understand the **conventions** or accepted practices of a **discourse community** and thus are able to speak, write, or act with credibility and confidence. A writer's **ethos** is based in part on his or her authority.

AUTHORSHIP   To "author" a text is to create or originate it; the *authorship* of a text then is a question of who created or originated it. Most traditional Western notions of authorship presume that **originality** is one key component of authorship. The term is seen by some scholars as problematic if it assumes sole authorship — **invention** by just one person — because it seems to discount the importance of social interaction and the fact that virtually every idea we can have already draws from other ideas authored by other people. The question becomes, where do we draw the line on who has authored what? For a related discussion, see **plagiarism**.

AUTOBIOGRAPHY   Literally, *autobiography* is writing about one's own life. ("Auto" = self, "bio" = life, and "graphy" = writing.) The **genre** of autobiography is a book-length text containing a retrospective account of the author's life. More broadly, *autobiographical* means simply about, or having to do with, one's own life. Donald Murray and others contend that all writing is autobiographical — that is, one's writing always has some connection to one's own life and a writer can never completely remove all traces of her life from her writing.

AUTOETHNOGRAPHY   *Autoethnography* is an **ethnography**, or cultural study, of one's own experiences and interaction with the world.

CARS ("CREATE A RESEARCH SPACE") MODEL   The *CARS model* is based on John Swales's description of the three typical "moves" made in the introductions to academic research articles. Swales conducted an analysis of research articles in many disciplines and discovered that most introductions in all disciplines do the following:

1. establish a territory (by describing the topic of study);
2. establish a niche (by explaining the problem, gap, or question that prompted the current study); and
3. occupy the niche (by describing the answer to the question or problem, and / or outlining what will be done in the article).

CASE STUDIES   *Case studies* are detailed observations and analyses of an event, situation, individual, or small group of people. Case study research, according to Mary Sue MacNealy in her book *Strategies for Empirical Research in Writing,* refers to "a carefully designed project to systematically collect information about an event, situation, or small group of persons or objects for the purpose of exploring, describing, and / or explaining aspects not previously known or considered" (197). Case studies are considered to be qualitative research.

CLAIM   A *claim* is an assertion that a writer tries to convince his or her readers of. An example might be "*Wired* magazine is great." To believe or accept a claim, readers need to know the reasons why a writer believes the claim or wants readers to accept it — saying, for example, "*Wired* includes really interesting articles about people in the technological world." Readers may also need evidence to believe the claim or its reasons, such as "Every month *Wired* has several stories that interview the people who invented netbooks, the iPhone, cloud computing, and the most cutting-edge technological innovations."

COGNITION   *Cognition* describes anything having to do with thought or mental activity. In **Writing Studies**, *cognitive* and *cognition* have to do with the internal thinking processes that writers use to write. Scholars in this field have contrasted the internal, private, personal nature of cognition with the social aspects of writing — that is, with the writer's external interactions with their surroundings, culture, and **audience**. A great deal of research about cognition in Writing Studies was conducted in the 1980s and sought to find and describe the mental processes that writers use to solve problems related to writing.

CONCEPTION   A *conception* is a belief about or understanding of something, with the same root as the term *concept*, meaning "something conceived," or an idea formed in the mind. A "conception" is the way in which you perceive or regard a thing. For example, one "conception of writing" might be that "writing typically requires revision."

CONSTRAINTS *Constraints* are factors that limit or otherwise influence the persuasive strategies available to the **rhetor**. More precisely, in "Rhetorical Situations and Their Constituents," Keith Grant-Davie defines constraints as "all factors in the situation, aside from the rhetor and the audience, that may lead the audience to be either more or less sympathetic to the discourse, and that may therefore influence the rhetor's response to the situation" (p. 397).

CONSTRUCT *Construct*, the verb (pronounced conSTRUCT), means "to build or to put together" ("con" = with, and "struct" = shape or frame). By turning the verb into a noun (pronounced CONstruct), we make the word mean, literally, "a thing that has been constructed." In everyday use, we use the noun construct only in the realm of ideas or concepts. The ideas of freedom, justice, wealth, and politics, for example, are all constructs, or ideas that we have built up over time. What is important to remember about constructs is that, while they may seem to be "natural" or "inevitable," they're actually unchallenged **claims** that can be questioned, contested, redefined, or reinvented.

CONTEXT Literally, a *context* is the substructure for a woven fabric ("con" = with / together, "text" = weaving, fabric). In **Writing Studies**, *context* typically refers to where a text comes from or where it appears. (A written work first started being called a *text* because it's "woven" from words in the same way that textiles are woven from threads.) Contexts can consist of other text(s) as well as the circumstances or setting in which a text was created — for example, various contexts for the statement "We hold these truths to be self-evident" include the Declaration of Independence, the meeting of the Continental Congress in spring and summer of 1776, and the broader socio-historical environment that describes pre–Revolutionary War America.

CONTINGENT One of the claims of this book is that meaning is *contingent*; that is, it depends. In other words, meaning is conditional. For example, "good writing" depends upon the **context**, purpose, and **audience**. Ideas about meaning as being contingent and conditional are taken up most directly in Chapter 6, where authors claim that meaning depends on context and that principles for good communication depend on the specific situation and are not universal.

CONTRIBUTE, CONTRIBUTION In academic contexts, one makes a *contribution* by adding to an ongoing conversation on a given research subject, issue, problem, or question. In **Writing Studies**, *contribution* is commonly discussed in terms of Kenneth Burke's parlor metaphor, where Burke describes scholarship as an ongoing conversation at a party: You arrive late and other guests are already in conversation; you join one conversation by listening for a while and then, once you have something to add, making a contribution to the conversation; after a time, you join another conversation, while the first one continues without you.

CONVENTIONS In **Writing Studies**, writing is understood to be governed by *conventions* — that is, agreements among people about the best ways to accomplish particular tasks (such as starting new paragraphs, or citing sources, or deciding how to punctuate sentences). That people have to come to agreements about such questions means that there is no "natural" or pre-existing way to accomplish the tasks; rather, people simply agreed to do *A* rather than *B*. Tabbing the first line of a paragraph one-half inch is a convention; ending sentences with periods is a convention; citing sources in parentheses is a convention, as are parentheses themselves. Conventions are a kind of **construct**, and like constructs, they can be questioned, challenged, and changed, if key decision makers agree to alter them or to establish another convention in their place.

CORPUS (ANALYSIS) A *corpus analysis* is a detailed examination of a collection or *corpus* of related texts, phrases, utterances, etc. (*Corpus* means "body" — the word *corpse* also derives from it.) For example, John Swales conducted a corpus analysis of academic writing to discover how people in various fields introduce their research.

CREATE A RESEARCH SPACE MODEL: see *CARS ("Create a Research Space") model*

DISCOURSE At its most basic, *discourse* is language in action, or language being used to accomplish something. Discourse can describe either an instance of language (e.g., "His discourse was terse and harsh") or a collection of instances that all demonstrate some quality (e.g., "Legal discourse tries to be very precise"). Because groups of people united by some activity tend to develop a characteristic discourse, we can talk about communities that are identified by their discourse — thus, **discourse community**. James Paul Gee uses *Discourse* with an uppercase D to differentiate his specialized meaning of the term.

DISCOURSE COMMUNITY Scholars continue to debate the meaning of *discourse community*, as the selections in this book suggest. For the sake of simplicity, we will use John Swales's definition from his 1990 book, *Genre Analysis: English in Academic and Research Settings.* According to Swales, a discourse community is made up of individuals who share common goals agreed upon by most members; further, it has "mechanisms of intercommunication among its members," "uses its participatory mechanisms primarily to provide information and feedback," has and uses "one or more genres" that help the group achieve its shared goals, "has acquired some specific lexis," and has "a reasonable ratio" of "novices and experts" (24–27). Swales also suggests that discourse communities are shaped in part by what their members know without having to tell each other and by shared rhythms of activity.

EDITING *Editing* is the correction of minor **errors** in a written text. Editing usually comes at the end of the writing process. It should not be confused with **revision**, which involves major rethinking, rewriting, and restructuring of texts.

EMBODIED, EMBODIMENT **Rhetorical** interaction happens with, to, and by beings with material bodies. The term *embodiment* reminds us that such interaction is contingent on the bodies that give it shape. It is easy to assume that rhetorical interaction is simply ideas worked on mentally apart from bodies; when we look for how rhetorical interaction is embodied, we remember that the interaction depends on material bodies as well as ideas.

ENCULTURATE A newcomer *enculturates* when he or she learns to become a part of a group or "culture" (including an **activity system**, **discourse community**, or community of practice). Becoming successfully enculturated usually requires gaining some level of competence in the activities and language practices of the group.

EPISTEMIC The term *epistemic* has to do with the making of knowledge. Research is an epistemic pursuit because it is about developing new knowledge. *Epistemology* is the branch of philosophy that deals with human knowledge: where it comes from and how people know what they know. Communication, including writing, is also an epistemic activity — it makes new knowledge — as we can see when we read a piece and come away with a new idea that we didn't know before but also that wasn't in the text we just read.

ERROR *Error* is the term for "mistakes" in grammar (e.g., subject-verb agreement, like "Dogs barks loudly"), punctuation, or usage (e.g., using *that* where some readers would prefer *which*). *Mistakes* is in quotes here because such "errors" are as often differences of opinion regarding **convention** or taste as they are actual problems that every English speaker or writer would agree are violations of rules.

ETHNOGRAPHY, ETHNOGRAPHIC RESEARCH *Ethnography* is a research **methodology** for carefully observing and describing people participating in some activity. At its broadest, ethnography can be written of entire cultures; more narrowly, ethnographies may involve writing about a class of students, a church and its members, or a video game arcade and the gamers who play there.

ETHOS In classical rhetoric, ethos is one of the three "**pisteis**" or persuasive appeals, along with **logos** and **pathos**. In a narrow sense, *ethos* describes the credibility, expertise, or competence that a writer or speaker establishes with an **audience** through his or her **discourse**. More broadly, *ethos* is a term for the sense of "personality" that **rhetors** perceive about one another. Ultimately *ethos* describes a rhetor's "way of being in" or "inhabiting" their world. As such, it has to do with a rhetor's **identity** and is a basis for **identification** among rhetors. As a persuasive appeal, ethos derives from **authority**, character (the perceived values, morals, and ethics of a writer), and good-will (the readers' sense that the writer has the readers' best interests at heart and is not purely self-interested).

EXIGENCE *Exigence* is the need or reason for a given action or communication. All commu-nication exists for a reason. For example, if you say, "Please turn on the lights," we assume the reason you say this is that there's not enough light for your needs — in other words, the exigence of the situation is that you need more light.

GENERALIZABLE, GENERALIZE *Generalizable* is a term used to refer to research findings that can apply (or *generalize*) to a larger group than the one that was studied. Generalizable research typically examines a group of statistically significant size under rigorous experimen-tal conditions. Qualitative research is not generalizable, strictly speaking, while quantitative research may be.

GENRE *Genre* comes from the French word for "kind" or "type" and in **rhetoric** studies relates to categories of texts. For example, the poem, the short story, the novel, and the mem-oir are genres of literature; memos, proposals, reports, and executive summaries are genres of business writing; hiphop, bluegrass, trance, pop, new age, and electronica are genres of music; and the romantic comedy, drama, and documentary are genres of film. Genres meet the needs of the **rhetorical situations** in which they function — for example, wedding invi-tations or newspaper advice columns — and evolve over time with the activities which they support. At their broadest, genres can be understood as "shared expectations among some group(s) of people" (Russell 513).

GENRE SYSTEM *Genre systems* are sets of genres that function together to accomplish some activity (see also **activity theory**). For example, in a college class (an **activity system**), the syllabus, assignment guides, teacher feedback on assignments, and exams combine to create a genre system because a series of different genres interrelate and depend on each other for their full use and meaning.

HEURISTICS *Heuristics* are approaches or patterns for problem solving. For example, a heu-ristic for deciding what to have for dinner tonight might be the following: (1) check the fridge; (2) check the pantry; and (3) eat whatever can be assembled most quickly and palatably from the ingredients there.

IDENTIFICATION *Identification* represents the recognition of common ground among **rhetors**. When someone says "I can identify with that statement," they are saying the statement is in some way equivalent to some part or aspect of themselves. Rhetorical theorist Kenneth Burke suggested that persuasion is actually an act of creating identification, so that one rhetor convinces other rhetors to see themselves in or aligned with the speaker's ideas.

IDENTITY *Identity* comprises your characteristics or personality, consisting of those factors that create a sense of "who you are." Recent theory suggests that individuals may have multi-ple and / or changing identities, not one "true," stable identity.

INSCRIPTION *Inscription* refers to the act of marking a medium in order to create writing. Writing Studies researcher Paul Prior divides writing into two separate acts, composition and inscription, where composing is designing a text and its ideas, and inscribing is using tools and media to set the text on some object. While inscription can happen without composition (photocopying) and composition can happen without inscription (conversation), what we describe as *writing* cannot happen without both. Prior reminds us that a medium (what gets inscribed) can be anything from a t-shirt to a plastic disc to a clay tablet to paper, while inscribing tools can be anything from knives and sticks to pencils to printers to DVD burners.

INTERTEXTUAL, INTERTEXTUALITY *Intertextuality* refers to the idea that all texts are made up of other texts — and thus, to the resulting network of texts that connect to any given text or idea. At the most basic level, texts share words: That is, every text uses words that other texts have used. Sometimes texts use words that, in their combination, are considered unique; in those cases, following Western **conventions**, those words must be formally marked as quotations. Intertextuality can go beyond just language, however, by referencing the ideas and events that other texts have focused on. If, for example, I claim that people whose governments abuse them have the right to make a better government, I haven't used a quotation from the Declaration of Independence, but most people familiar with that document could "hear it" in my statement. Intertextuality thus is an effect even more than an intention — I don't have to intend to be intertextual in order to be intertextual.

INVENTION *Invention* comprises the **processes**, strategies, or techniques writers use to come up with what to say in their writing. While the term suggests the notion of "making things up," a significant part of invention is not saying brand-new things but rather combing one's memory and written resources for things that have already been said that will work. Ancient rhetorical theorists such as Aristotle thought carefully about how stock arguments they called *common topics* could help a speaker — for instance, the idea "that which has happened frequently before is likely to happen again," which could be recalled through invention and included in many pieces of writing.

KAIROS *Kairos* represents the element of "being in the right place at the right time" that removes some agency from a **rhetor**. *Kairos* carries a sense of a moment when, by timely good fortune, circumstances beyond the rhetor's control favor an **argument** that the rhetor wishes to make. For example, a law enforcement officer in favor of heightened surveillance of U.S. citizens can use the *kairos* of a recent terrorist attack to strengthen her argument by pointing out how the attack demonstrates the need for greater surveillance. The officer is of course not responsible for the attack but can use the "fortunate" occurrence of that particular moment to her advantage.

LEXIS *Lexis* is a term used for the specific vocabulary used by a group or field of study.

LITERACY, LITERACIES *Literacy* denotes fluency in a given practice. In its original use, the term referred to *alphabetic literacy* — that is, to fluency in reading and writing "letters," or alphabetic text. This kind of literacy was contrasted with orality, which was characterized as a lack of literacy. Over time, however, in academic circles, the meaning of *literacy* and *literate* has broadened to encompass fluency in other areas; most academics therefore now use the term *literacies* (plural) and discuss digital, electronic, musical, visual, oral, mathematical, and gaming literacies, among many other kinds.

LITERACY SPONSOR *Literacy sponsor* is a term coined by Deborah Brandt to describe people, ideas, or institutions that help others become literate in specific ways. A sponsor could be a parent or sibling who taught you to read, a teacher who helped you learn to love books, or a manufacturing company that requires its employees to be able to read. The sponsors of alphabetic literacy in your life might be very different from the sponsors of visual literacy, musical literacy, or other forms of literacy in your life. (*Pandora,* for instance, can be a musical literacy sponsor for people who use it.)

LITERATURE REVIEW, REVIEW OF THE LITERATURE A *literature review* (or *review of the literature*) is a text that explains the existing conversation about a particular topic. Literature reviews are usually found at the beginning of research articles or books, but are sometimes written as separate projects. Note that *literature* in this case refers to published research in an area, not to novels or short stories.

LOGOS   Logos is one of the three major "proofs" or "appeals" (**pisteis**) identified by Aristotle as central to persuasion. (The others are **ethos** and **pathos**.) In **rhetorical theory**, Aristotle used the term *logos* to refer to persuasion by verbal reasoning. In Greek, *logos* literally means "word," referring to language, or "reason," or kinds of reasoning, including logic. Aristotle did not limit logos appeals to formal logic, but also understood a logos appeal as any appeal that an **audience** would recognize as reasoning by any kind of inference.

LONGITUDINAL STUDY   A *longitudinal study* is a research study that examines an individual, group, event, or activity over a substantial period of time. For example, rather than studying a student's writing habits for just a few days or weeks, a longitudinal study might look at his or her habits over several years.

MEDIATE   People use texts in order to get things done. They read in order to learn something (for example, they read instructions in order to figure out how to put together a new desk); they write in order to communicate something (for example, a student might write an e-mail to let her mom know she is short on money). When a text helps people accomplish an activity as in these examples, we say the text *mediates* the activity. To mediate is to help make things happen, to play a role in situations and enable communication and activities to take place. In the examples offered above, reading the instructions mediates assembly of the desk; sending Mom an e-mail mediates receiving $200 to buy much needed school supplies.

METAKNOWLEDGE   *Metaknowledge* is knowledge about knowledge — that is, what we can determine about our learning, its processes, and its products.

METHODOLOGIES   In an academic or scholarly context, *methodologies* are procedures for conducting research — the formalized, field-approved methods used to address particular kinds of **research questions**. Some examples of methodologies in **Writing Studies** are **case study**, **ethnography**, experiment, quasi-experiment, and discourse analysis. *Methodology* can also mean the particular combination of methods used in any particular study. For example, the methodologies used by Sondra Perl in "The Composing Processes of Unskilled College Writers" include **case study** and discourse analysis.

MINDFULNESS   *Mindfulness* means thinking carefully about what one is doing — that is, purposefully and carefully paying attention. This term derives from Zen Buddhism and has become a key concept in modern psychology. It is often used by researchers interested in helping writers effectively **transfer** knowledge about writing. For a writer to be mindful, for example, means not just to come up with something to say, but to pay attention to how she came up with something to say. In the future, she may be able to mindfully try that procedure again, adapting it to the new situation.

MODES, MULTIMODALITY   A *mode* (or *modality*) refers to the senses or faculties readers use to experience a text; typical modalities are linguistic (verbal), alphabetic-print, visual / image, aural, color, and kinesthetic / touch. In another sense, *modality* means mode of **inscription** of texts, with typical examples being paper, codex / book, or electronic / networked. *Multimodality* refers to texts that combine multiple modes, such as alphabetic, visual, and aural. Technically, all texts are multimodal because there are no texts that use just one mode. For example, a novel that is entirely verbal (without any images) inscribed in black alphabetic print engages verbal, print, and color modalities simultaneously.

MOTIVATED   To be *motivated* is to have particular reasons and desires for doing, saying, or thinking something. All **rhetorical** interaction is motivated — that is, there is a motive behind it. The reasons that motivate a particular interaction also give it a bias or slant: Motivation is inevitably subjective and thus works against neutrality or objectivity.

MULTILITERACIES   *Multiliteracies* is a term that reflects the recent, broader understanding of **literacy** as consisting of more than mastery of the "correct" use of alphabetic language. Multi-literacies include the ability to compose and interpret texts showing **multimodality** (including

676

oral, written, and audio components, among other possibilities), as well as the ability to make meaning in various **contexts**. A group of scholars known as the New London Group is generally credited with coining the term *multiliteracies*.

MULTIMODAL: see *modes*

MUSHFAKE *Mushfake* is a term used by James Paul Gee to describe a partially acquired **Discourse**, a Discourse that people use to "make do" when they participate in or communicate with a group to which they don't belong. Gee borrows the term from prison culture, in which *mushfake* refers to making do with something when the real thing is not available.

NARRATIVE *Narrative* is most often a synonym for *story* or *storytelling*; the word carries the sense of an accounting or retelling of events, usually in the order they occurred. In the context of **Writing Studies**, we focus on narratives as **epistemic**, a way of making knowledge and meaning through **rhetorical** interaction. Narrative is so central to how people make and convey truth that very few kinds of knowledge-making can happen without it, including scientific research (almost always explained by using narrative) and legal reasoning (which almost always uses narratives of actual events to establish the facts of a case to which the law must be applied, and also uses narrative to explain the development through time of a given law or legal principle).

ORIGINALITY *Originality* is the quality of being singular, unique, and entirely made up or invented, as opposed to imitative or derivative. American culture presumes that writers will have originality — that they will invent work never seen before — and judges the quality of **authorship** in part on its originality. This simplified view of **invention** is assumed by many scholars to be inaccurate in that it fails to describe how people develop ideas through social interaction. This can lead to difficulties in defining and identifying **plagiarism**.

PATHOS Pathos is one of the three major "proofs" or "appeals" (**pisteis**) identified by Aristotle as central to persuasion. (The others are **ethos** and **logos**.) In **rhetorical theory**, Aristotle used the term *pathos* to refer to persuasion by appeal to emotions and values, which he opposed to appeals to reasoning (logos) or to personal credibility (ethos). Aristotle recognized that even though emotions are not always "logical" or reason-driven, they are powerful motivators and thus persuasive. Western philosophy has long believed pathos to undermine logos, but current understandings of rhetorical theory recognize that appeals to reasoning are actually simultaneously appeals to values and thus act as pathos appeals in **argument**.

PEER-REVIEWED JOURNAL Journals are collections of relatively short articles (between five and thirty pages, usually) on a related topic, published periodically (monthly or quarterly, usually) — just like a magazine. Some journals are scholarly — meaning that their articles are written by scholars in a field or discipline to other scholars studying in the same field. Their purpose is to report on new research: Scholarly journals are the main sites in which scholarly conversations are carried on. Most of the articles collected in this book come from scholarly journals, such as *College Composition and Communication* or *College English*. Some of these scholarly conversations can be very specialized — the kind that perhaps only twenty-five or fifty people in the entire world would share enough background knowledge to understand. (Imagine an article on a brand-new branch of theoretical physics or a piece on a new kind of black hole — topics that not many people study.) That specialization poses two problems for a journal: First, how does the editor of a journal — who might be an expert on a few specialty areas in a field (say, on "writing process" and on "pedagogy" in composition) but can't be an expert on all of them — actually know whether a given article knows what it's talking about? Second, so many people doing research want to publish in any given journal, the journal doesn't have space for them all. In fact, it might only have space for a small percentage of what gets submitted to it. How can it choose which pieces to publish and which not to? The answer to both questions is *peer review*: the editor sends submissions to other experts in the specialty the article is reporting on — usually between two and four other readers. They report back to the journal's editor on the relative value of a submission — how significant a **contribution** it makes, how it fits in the ongoing conversation — and on its quality — how well its **argument** is made, how good its research is. They can make suggestions to the editor about how the piece needs to be improved before publication and thus guide **revisions** that most articles are required to make before finally being published. Peer review, then, is a major feature of scholarly journals, and most library databases (along with Google Scholar) let you limit searches to just peer-reviewed journals. (Almost all scholarly books are peer-reviewed as well.)

PISTEIS *Pisteis* is the Greek term for proofs that a **rhetor** can offer in support of an **argument**. Most often this term refers to what Aristotle called "artistic" proofs, meaning those that rhetors invent and embed in their **discourse**. The three such proofs Aristotle identified are **logos, ethos,** and **pathos**.

PLAGIARISM *Plagiarism* literally means *kidnapping* in Latin; in contemporary English, the word refers to the theft of a text or idea. (Authors sometimes think of their writings or ideas as their "children," thus the link to kidnapping.) Definitions of plagiarism tend to come down to taking another's ideas without giving them credit and thus pretending that you invented the ideas yourself. In cultures that highly value intellectual property — the idea that one's ideas are one's own and that use of those ideas by others deserves either credit or payment — plagiarism is an ethical violation punishable by community sanction (such as failing a class or losing one's job). Plagiarism's cousin copyright infringement is an actual crime punishable by fine or imprisonment.

A significant difficulty with the idea of plagiarism is that **originality** and **authorship** are technically quite difficult to trace in ways that new digital technologies are making impossible to miss or deny. In sampling, remixing, and mash-up cultures where ideas are freely reused and reincorporated to make new texts, authorship becomes very difficult to trace, and it becomes difficult to tell what counts as original work.

PLANNING While **invention** focuses on coming up with what to say in one's writing, *planning* focuses more broadly on how to get a piece written. Therefore, it includes not only invention but arrangement, which is the art of organizing what one has to say to present it most effectively. Planning also includes **process** considerations, such as considering what work needs to be done to complete a piece, what order to do it in, and when to do it in order to meet a deadline.

PROCESS *Process* refers to the variety of activities that go into writing / composing, including, at minimum,

- *planning* (inventing and arranging ideas),
- *drafting* (creating actual text from previously unwritten ideas),
- *revising* (developing a text or a portion of a text further after an initial draft),
- *editing* (fine-tuning, polishing, or correcting problems in a text), and
- *production* (inscribing a composition in its final, "produced" form, whether in print, online / digital, or some other material format).

Process theory is the study of the methods by which various writers compose and produce texts. The process movement, which took place within the field of Composition Studies in the 1970s, was the widespread adoption by writing teachers of instruction that focused on teaching students successful writing processes rather than focusing solely on the quality of their written products.

REGISTER In the field of linguistics, *register* refers to a type of language used in a particular setting. Changing one's register might mean changing the kinds of words used, as well as the way one says the words. For example, a person might say, "I've finished my homework" to her parents, using one register, while she might say (or text), "I'm finally dooooooooooooone!" to her friends.

RESEARCH QUESTION A *research question* is a focused statement of what a particular inquiry is trying to find out. For example, a writing researcher might ask, "What effect does natural light have on writers' processes?" To remind researchers that they're asking a specific question to which they do not have an answer — not simply offering a "topic" or subject for their research — research questions are stated as questions, sentences that end with a question mark. Researchers use research questions to keep in mind that they are not compiling information on a subject, but developing knowledge on it that doesn't exist yet.

REVIEW OF THE LITERATURE: see *literature review*

REVISION *Revision* is the act of developing a piece of writing by writing — that is, by adding additional material, shifting the order of its parts, or deleting significant portions of what has already been written. The purpose of revision is to "see again" ("re-vision"), which is necessary because what one could see in originally drafting a piece has been changed by the drafting. This might become clearer if you think of writing as driving at night. When you begin to write, you know a certain amount about where you're going in your project, just as, when you're driving at night, your headlights let you see two hundred yards (but only two hundred yards) ahead. Writing (or driving) further takes you to new places, where you continually see something different, rethink your position, and decide how to proceed.

  Because revision can go on for some time, many professional writers find that most of their writing time is actually spent revising, not creating the first draft. Also, it is important to distinguish revision from **editing,** the correction of minor mistakes in a near-final draft.

RHETOR Originally (in Greek) a *public speaker, rhetor* means one who engages in rhetorical interaction or **discourse**. *Writer* and *speaker* are common synonyms.

RHETORIC *Rhetoric* is the study or performance of human interaction and communication or the product(s) of that interaction and communication. Because most human interaction is persuasive by nature — that is, we're trying to convince each other of things, even when we say something simple like "that feels nice" — one way to think of rhetoric is as the study of persuasion. *Rhetoric* can refer to a field of knowledge on this subject, to systematic explanations for and predictions of how persuasion works, or to the performance art of human interaction and persuasion itself.

  Rhetoric always has to do with these specific principles:

1. Human communication, or **discourse**, is **situated** in a moment, a particular time and place, which is part of a larger **rhetorical ecology**. That moment and ecology are the **context** of the communication. A particular text takes it meaning in part from its context, so knowledge of the context is necessary in order to know the text's meaning. For example, "Help me!" means one thing when your mom is standing next to a van full of groceries and another when she's standing next to a van with a flat tire. Her discourse is situated in a particular context.

2. Communication is **motivated** by particular **rhetors'** purposes, needs, and values. No communication is unmotivated.

3. Communication is interactional, "back-and-forth" between rhetors. Readers actually complete the meaning of a writer's text. Successful writers therefore think carefully about who their **audience** is and what the audience values and needs.

4. Communication is **epistemic**, which means that it creates new knowledge. We often talk about "reporting" or "transmitting" information as if we can find information and pass it along unaltered. But we actually can't transmit information without altering it, so our communication makes new knowledge as it goes.

5. Communication is **embodied** and material, meaning that it exists not simply in the mental realm of ideas but takes place via material bodies that themselves shape the meaning of the communication.

6. Communication is shaped by technology. *Technology* simply refers to use of tools, and it is certainly possible to communicate without technology (through purely organic means such as by voice). Practically speaking, though, almost all communication in any culture in which you're reading this book is assisted and shaped by technology. Rhetoric teaches us to look for how technology influences even communication that doesn't directly use it.

7. Communication is contingent, meaning that what we consider good communication depends on the circumstances and context in which it happens. Because communication depends on context, we can't make universal rules about what makes good communication.

RHETORICAL   *Rhetorical* refers to a phenomenon such as human interaction that has the qualities of being **situated, motivated,** interactive, **epistemic, embodied,** and contingent. (See the definition of **rhetoric.**) *Rhetorical study*, for example, is the investigation of human communication as situated, motivated, interactive, epistemic, embodied, and contingent. *Rhetorical reading* involves reading a text as situated, motivated, etc. *Rhetorical analysis* is a way of analyzing texts to find what choices their embodied **rhetor** (speaker or writer) made based on their purpose and motivation, their situatedness and **context**, and how they interact with and make new knowledge for their **audience.**

RHETORICAL ECOLOGY   An *ecology* is, literally, the interactions among groups of living things and their environments (and the scientific study of those interactions). More broadly, *ecology* has come to refer to any network of relationships among beings and their material surroundings. In **rhetorical** terms, *ecology* refers to the web of relationships and interactions between all the rhetors and all the material in a **rhetorical situation**. Like other meanings of *ecology*, it is difficult to define the boundaries of a rhetorical ecology because elements in an ecology will also connect to elements outside the ecology.

RHETORICAL SITUATION   *Rhetorical situation* is the particular circumstance of a given instance of communication or **discourse.** The rhetorical situation includes **exigence** (the need or reason for the communication), **context** (the circumstances that give rise to the exigence, including location in time / history and space / place / position), **rhetor** (the originator of the communication — its speaker or writer), and **audience** (the auditor, listener, or reader of the rhetor's discourse). The rhetorical situation is a moment in a larger **rhetorical ecology**, the network of relationships among rhetors in the situation.

RHETORICAL THEORY   *Rhetorical theory* is a set or system of principles for and explanations of human interaction from the perspective of **rhetoric**, which emphasizes the **situated**, contingent, and **motivated** nature of communication. Rhetorical theory has historically emphasized persuasion but can be more broadly understood as explaining and predicting how we make up our minds and how we change them.

SITUATED   *Situated* means located at a particular place and time, and therefore dependent on a specific **context** and set of circumstances. In everyday language, we use *situated* to describe an object's or person's place: "The piano was situated on the left side of the great room," or "She situated herself between the two potted ferns." In a scholarly, **rhetorical** sense, we mean roughly the same thing, but use the term to call attention to the uniqueness of the moment and place of situation: "The President's speech is situated at a very tense time of diplomatic relations with Libya." Situatedness is a key element of rhetorical activities: When we say a given activity or experience is "rhetorical," we mean that it has the quality of being situated in time and space (among other qualities). That is the opposite of being universal: A universal rule is one that applies in all times and places. In contrast, most rules are situated, applying only to specific times, places, and circumstances.

SOCIAL CONTEXT   *Social context* is the environment, situation, or culture in which something is embedded. Key aspects of the social context of **discourse** might include participants, goals, setting, race, class, gender, and so on.

STASES *Stases* (we often say "the stases") are a problem-solving pattern (a **heuristic**) that helps writers develop **argument**s by asking a set of specific questions about the subject. First described in the **rhetorical theory** of Aristotle, the word *stases* shares the same root as the words *state, status*, and *stasis* (the singular of *stases*), all of which denote condition or being. Stases have to do with the state of things, so that when we consider the stases, we are taking stock, or asking, "What is the state of things?" The stases include (1) questions of fact, (2) questions of value, and (3) questions of policy:

1. What is the nature of the thing in question? How would we define or name the thing? What caused the thing? For example, if a four-legged creature with a wagging tail shows up at your back door, your first question might be "What is [the nature of] that?" Your answer might be that it's a "stray dog."

2. What is the quality or value of the thing? Is it good or bad? Desirable or undesirable? Wanted or unwanted? Happy or sad? Liked or disliked? Your answer to this will depend on a complex set of calculations, taking into account the nature of the thing and the **context** in which it is encountered. To extend our example, let's say you decide the stray dog is good because you like dogs and this one is appealing.

3. What should be done about it? What policy should we establish toward it? What is the best thing to do with respect to it? In the case of our example, you might decide that the best policy would be to take in the stray dog, at least temporarily, and feed it.

SYMBOL A *symbol* is a thing that represents or stands for something else — usually an object standing for an idea or an abstract concept. In the U.S. flag, which is itself a symbol, white stars stand for (symbolize) individual states and the blue field in which they all rest symbolizes unity. Language is a symbol (or sign) system; all words are symbols for the objects or concepts they're associated with.

THEORY A *theory* is a systematic explanation for some aspect of people's lived experience and observation. For a given experience — say, an apple falling on one's head — people propose explanations, or theories, for why the experience happens as it does, or why it doesn't happen some other way (e.g., a theory of gravity). People then test the theory against more observed experiences, seeing if those experiences are consistent with the explanation suggested by the theory, and seeing whether the theory can predict what will happen in future experiences. Theories are, for a long time, not "right" or "wrong" but "stronger / better" or "weaker / poorer" at explaining the phenomenon in question. The better or stronger a theory is, the more completely it accounts for existing phenomena (experiences, events, and objects) and the more accurately it makes testable predictions about future events. For example, a theory that tries to explain how people make up or change their minds has to be able to account for existing cases of this and predict how future cases will work. Theories — such as the theory in **Writing Studies** that "writing is a process" — become treated as essentially factual when we recognize that though they are still **constructs** (made-up explanations that can only approximate the truth), they're very good explanations widely supported by many kinds of evidence.

THRESHOLD CONCEPTS *Threshold concepts* are ideas that literally change the way you experience, think about, and understand a subject. Every specialized field of study (or discipline — history, biology, mathematics, etc.) has threshold concepts that learners in that field must become acquainted with in order to fully understand the ideas of that field of study. Threshold concepts, once learned, help the learner see the world differently. They can be hard to learn (what researchers Jan Meyer and Ray Land call "troublesome") for a variety of reasons, including the possibility that they might directly conflict with ideas you already have. Once you're aware of these new and troublesome threshold concepts and you really start to understand them, they are hard to unlearn — Meyer and Land say they are "irreversible." Very often, learning threshold concepts doesn't just change the way you think about the subject, but also the way you think about yourself. But what makes them most powerful is that they help you understand a whole set of other ideas that are hard to imagine without knowing the threshold concept — so they let you do a whole lot of learning at once by helping entire sets of ideas "fall into place."

TONE *Tone* is a reader's judgment of what a text sounds like, sometimes also termed the dominant mood of a text. It is important to note that tone is not a characteristic actually in a text but rather one constructed in the interaction among the writer, the reader, and the text. Tone emerges not just from the language (word choice and sentence structure) of a text but also from a reader's judgment of the **rhetorical situation** and the writer's **ethos** and motivation.

TRANSFER Sometimes called *generalization* or *repurposing, transfer* refers to the act of applying existing knowledge, learned in one kind of situation, to new situations. For example, a writer who learns how to write a summary in her College Writing I class in English is expected to transfer that summary-writing knowledge to her "history of the telescope" project in astronomy. Transfer, we are learning, is not automatic — people learn many things that they forget and / or don't or can't use in different circumstances. Research suggests that learning in particular ways (for example, being **mindful**) can increase the likelihood of later transfer.

VOICE *Voice* is the way a writer "sounds" in a text, or the extent to which you can "hear" a writer in his or her text. The definition of this term has changed over time. It has been used to refer to authenticity in writing, as well as to a written text that seems to be "true" to who its author is and what he or she wants to say. Author bell hooks has argued that finding a voice or "coming to voice" can be seen as an act of resistance. In *Writing about Writing* we use the term *voice* to refer to a writer's ability to speak with some **authority** and expertise deriving from his or her own experiences and knowledge. According to this view, writers have multiple voices, any one of which may find expression, depending on the precise **context** of utterance.

WRITING STUDIES *Writing Studies* is one of the terms used to describe a field or discipline that takes writing and composing as its primary objects of study. Another term commonly used to describe this field of study is *Rhetoric and Composition.* Most of the readings in this book are written by Writing Studies scholars.

Works Cited

MacNealy, Mary Sue. *Strategies for Empirical Research in Writing.* Longman, 1999.

Meyer, J. H. F., and R. Land. "Threshold Concepts and Troublesome Knowledge (2): Epistemological Considerations and a Conceptual Framework for Teaching and Learning." *Higher Education,* vol. 49, 2005, pp. 373–88.

Russell, David. "Rethinking Genre in School and Society: An Activity Theory Analysis." *Written Communication,* vol. 14, no. 4, Oct. 1997, pp. 504–54.

Swales, John. *Genre Analysis: English in Academic and Research Settings.* Cambridge UP, 1990.

ACKNOWLEDGMENTS

Arbutus, Julia. "The Value of Rhetorical Analysis Outside of Academia." Reprinted by permission of the author.

Berkenkotter, Carol. "Decisions and Revisions: The Planning Strategies of a Publishing Writer." *College Composition and Communication,* vol. 34, no. 2, May 1983, pp. 156–69. Copyright 1983 by the National Council of Teachers of English. Reprinted with permission.

Brandt, Deborah. "Sponsors of Literacy." *College Composition and Communication,* vol. 49, no. 2, May 1998, pp. 165–85. Copyright 1998 by the National Council of Teachers of English. Reprinted with permission.

Branick, Sean. "Coaches Can Read, Too: An Ethnographic Study of a Football Coaching Discourse Community." Reprinted by permission of the author.

Celestine, Jaydelle. "Did I Create the Process? Or Did the Process Create Me?" *Stylus,* vol. 8, no. 2, Fall 2017, pp. 1–12. Reprinted by permission of the author.

Cisneros, Sandra. "Only Daughter" Copyright © 1990 by Sandra Cisneros. First published in *GLAMOUR*, November 1990. By permission of Susan Bergholz Literary Services, New York, NY, and Lamy, NM. All rights reserved.

DePalma, Michael-John, and Kara Poe Alexander. "A Bag Full of Snakes: Negotiating the Challenges of Multimodal Composition." Reprinted from *Computers and Composition*, vol. 37, 2015, pp. 182–200. With permission from Elsevier.

Feldman, Arielle. "Galaxy-Wide Writing Strategies Used by Official Star Wars Bloggers." *Stylus,* vol. 8, no. 2, Fall 2017, pp. 1–5. Reprinted by permission of the author.

Gee, James Paul. "Literacy, Discourse, and Linguistics: Introduction." *Journal of Education,* vol. 171, no. 1, 1989, pp. 5–17. Reprinted by permission of James Paul Gee, Mary Lou Fulton Presidential Professor of Literacy Studies, Arizona State University.

Grant-Davie, Keith. "Rhetorical Situations and Their Constituents." *Rhetoric Review,* vol. 15, no. 2, Spring 1997, pp. 264–79. Reprinted by permission of the publisher Taylor & Francis Ltd., http://www.tandfonline.com.

Hass, Christina, and Linda Flower. "Rhetorical Reading Strategies and the Construction of Meaning." *College Composition and Communication*, vol. 39, no. 2, May 1988, pp. 167–83. Copyright 1988 by the National Council of Teachers of English. Reprinted with permission.

Johns, Ann M. "Discourse Communities and Communities of Practice: Membership, Conflict, and Diversity." In *Text, Role, and Context: Developing Academic Literacies*. Copyright © Cambridge University Press, 1997. Reproduced with permission of Cambridge University Press through PLSclear.

Swales, John M. "The Concept of Discourse Community." In *Genre Analysis: English in Academic and Research Settings*, pp. 21–32, 1990. © Cambridge University Press,1990. Reproduced with permission of Cambridge University Press through PLSclear.

Swales, John M. "Reflections on the Concept of Discourse Community." Reprint from *ASp*, the research journal of GERAS (Groupe d'étude et de recherche en anglais de spécialité). Reprinted with permission.

Tejada, Jr. Arturo, Esther Gutierrez, Brisa Galindo, DeShonna Wallace, and **Sonia Castaneda.** "Challenging Our Labels: Rejecting the Language of Remediation." *Young Scholars in Writing*, vol. 11, 2014, pp. 5–16. Department of English, Language & Literature, University of Missouri-Kansas City. Used with permission of the authors.

Villanueva, Victor. From *Bootstraps: From an Academic of Color*, pp. 66–77. Urbana, IL: National Council of Teachers of English (NCTE), 1993. Copyright 1993 by the National Council of Teachers of English. Reprinted with permission.

Wan, Julie. "Chinks in My Armor: Reclaiming One's Voice." *Stylus*, vol. 9, no. 1, Spring 2018, pp. 1–6. Reprinted by permission of the author.

Wardle, Elizabeth. "Identity, Authority, and Learning to Write in New Workplaces." *Enculturation*, vol. 5, no. 2, 2004. Reprinted by permission of the author.

Williams, Joseph M. "The Phenomenology of Error." *College Composition and Communication*, vol. 32, no. 2, May 1981, pp. 152–68. Copyright 1981 by the National Council of Teachers of English. Reprinted with permission.

Young, Vershawn Ashanti. "Should Writers Use They Own English?" *Iowa Journal of Cultural Studies*, vol. 12, 2010, pp. 110–18. Copyright © 2010 by The University of Iowa. Available at: http://dx.doi.org/10.17077/2168-569X.1095. Reprinted with permission of the author.

INDEX

academic communities. *See* discourse communities

academic performance and sponsorship, 250–53

academic reading and writing, 18–19

activity systems, 670. *See also* discourse communities
- defined, 670
- in workplaces, new, 636, 637–40, 648, 649

activity theory, 505–6
- defined 670

Alexander, Kara Poe, and Michael-John DePalma, "A Bag Full of Snakes: Negotiating the Challenges of Multimodal Composition," 174–203

"All Writing Is Autobiography" (Murray), 473–84

appeals, as element of rhetoric, 381–82

appropriation and literacy diversion, 258–62

Arbutus, Julia, "The Value of Rhetorical Analysis Outside Academia," 486–96

argument
- consensus-seeking, 33
- defined, 670
- developing, from sources, 452–71
- and *kairos*, 676
- and *stases,* 682

Aristotle
- persuasion, study of, 9
- rhetorical theory of, 682

assignments. *See* major writing assignments

audience, 396
- analyzing and adapting to, 16, 21, 71, 176, 192
- authority of writer, 642–43
- awareness of, 134, 139, 168
- conceptualizing, for multimodal composition, 179–86, 190–94
- defined, 670
- and exigence and constraints, 400–411
- "grabbing," 164–67, 169
- and rhetor, relationship with, 388, 404–6, 488–89
- and rhetorical situation, 681
- universal, 405

authority
- with audience, 642–43
- defined, 671
- in discourse communities, 575–76
- gaining, as writing assignment, 666–67

voice and, 684

authorship
- Declaration of Independence and, 420, 427
- defined, 671
- originality and plagiarism, 416

autobiography
- defined, 671
- writing as, 473–84

autoethnography
- defined, 671
- as writing assignment, 230–33

"Bag Full of Snakes: Negotiating the Challenges of Multimodal Composition, A" (DePalma and Alexander), 174–203

Bawarshi, Ani, 23

Bazerman, Charles, 38

Berkenkotter, Carol, "Decisions and Revisions: The Planning Strategies of a Publishing Writer," 123–35

body's signals, as communication, 373–76

bloggers, *Star Wars,* 655–61

Bootstraps: From an American Academic of Color, excerpt from (Villanueva), 272–83

Brandt, Deborah, "Sponsors of Literacy," 244–65

Branick, Sean, "Coaches Can Read, Too: An Ethnographic Study of a Football Coaching Discourse Community," 624–34

Burke, Kenneth, 55

"Burkean Parlor"
- collaboration, 55, 71, 72
- as writing assignment, 74–77

call for proposals (CFP), 39–40

CARS (Create a Research Space) model, 61–62
- defined, 671

case studies, 589. *See also* research studies
- defined, 671
- generalizable results in, 589
- as research method, 63, 64

Castaneda, Sonia, Arturo Tejada, Jr., Esther Gutierrez, Brisa Galindo, and Deshonna Wallace, "Challenging Our Labels: Rejecting the Language of Remediation," 286–301

CCCC Guidelines for the Ethical Conduct of Research in Composition Studies, 69

Celestine, Jaydelle, "Did I Create the Process? Or Did the Process Create Me?," 205–15